Lecture Notes in Computer Science 7793

Commenced Publication in 1973
Founding and Former Series Editors:
Gerhard Goos, Juris Hartmanis, and Jan van Leeuwen

Advanced Research in Computing and Software Science

Subline of Lectures Notes in Computer Science

T0224104

Lecture Notes in Computer Science 7916

Commenced Publication in 1973
Founding and Former Series Editors:
Gerhard Goos, Juris Hartmanis, and Jan van Leeuwen

Editorial Board

David Hutchison, UK
Takeo Kanade, USA
Josef Kittler, UK
Jon M. Kleinberg, USA
Alfred Kobsa, USA
Friedemann Mattern, Switzerland
John C. Mitchell, USA
Moni Naor, Israel
Oscar Nierstrasz, Switzerland
C. Pandu Rangan, India
Bernhard Steffen, Germany
Madhu Sudan, USA
Demetri Terzopoulos, USA
Doug Tygar, USA
Gerhard Weikum, Germany

Advanced Research in Computing and Software Science

Subline of Lecture Notes in Computer Science

Subline Series Editors

Giorgio Ausiello, University of Rome 'La Sapienza', Italy
Vladimiro Sassone, University of Southampton, UK

Subline Advisory Board

Susanne Albers, University of Freiburg, Germany
Benjamin C. Pierce, University of Pennsylvania, USA
Bernhard Steffen, University of Dortmund, Germany
Madhu Sudan, Microsoft Research, Cambridge, MA, USA
Deng Xiaotie, City University of Hong Kong
Jeannette M. Wing, Carnegie Mellon University, Pittsburgh, PA, USA

Vittorio Cortellessa   Dániel Varró (Eds.)

Fundamental Approaches to Software Engineering

16th International Conference, FASE 2013
Held as Part of the European Joint Conferences
on Theory and Practice of Software, ETAPS 2013
Rome, Italy, March 16-24, 2013
Proceedings

 Springer

Volume Editors

Vittorio Cortellessa
Università dell'Aquila
Dipartimento di Informatica
67010 Coppito - L'Aquila, Italy
E-mail: vittorio.cortellessa@univaq.it

Dániel Varró
Budapest University of Technology and Economics
Department of Measurement and Information Systems
Magyar Tudósok krt. 2, 1117 Budapest, Hungary
E-mail: varro@mit.bme.hu

ISSN 0302-9743   e-ISSN 1611-3349
ISBN 978-3-642-37056-4   e-ISBN 978-3-642-37057-1
DOI 10.1007/978-3-642-37057-1
Springer Heidelberg Dordrecht London New York

Library of Congress Control Number: 2013932562

CR Subject Classification (1998): D.2.1-5, D.3.1-4, F.3.1-3, J.1, C.3

LNCS Sublibrary: SL 1 – Theoretical Computer Science and General Issues

Typesetting: Camera-ready by author, data conversion by Scientific Publishing Services, Chennai, India

Printed on acid-free paper

Springer is part of Springer Science+Business Media (www.springer.com)

Foreword

ETAPS 2013 is the sixteenth instance of the European Joint Conferences on Theory and Practice of Software. ETAPS is an annual federated conference that was established in 1998 by combining a number of existing and new conferences. This year it comprised six sister conferences (CC, ESOP, FASE, FOSSACS, POST, TACAS), 20 satellite workshops (ACCAT, AiSOS, BX, BYTECODE, CerCo, DICE, FESCA, GRAPHITE, GT-VMT, HAS, Hot-Spot, FSS, MBT, MEALS, MLQA, PLACES, QAPL, SR, TERMGRAPH and VSSE), three invited tutorials (*e-education*, by John Mitchell; *cyber-physical systems*, by Martin Fränzle; and *e-voting* by Rolf Küsters) and eight invited lectures (excluding those specific to the satellite events).

The six main conferences received this year 627 submissions (including 18 tool demonstration papers), 153 of which were accepted (6 tool demos), giving an overall acceptance rate just above 24%. (ETAPS 2013 also received 11 submissions to the software competition, and 10 of them resulted in short papers in the TACAS proceedings). Congratulations therefore to all the authors who made it to the final programme! I hope that most of the other authors will still have found a way to participate in this exciting event, and that you will all continue to submit to ETAPS and contribute to making it the best conference on software science and engineering.

The events that comprise ETAPS address various aspects of the system development process, including specification, design, implementation, analysis, security and improvement. The languages, methodologies and tools that support these activities are all well within its scope. Different blends of theory and practice are represented, with an inclination towards theory with a practical motivation on the one hand and soundly based practice on the other. Many of the issues involved in software design apply to systems in general, including hardware systems, and the emphasis on software is not intended to be exclusive.

ETAPS is a confederation in which each event retains its own identity, with a separate Programme Committee and proceedings. Its format is open-ended, allowing it to grow and evolve as time goes by. Contributed talks and system demonstrations are in synchronised parallel sessions, with invited lectures in plenary sessions. Two of the invited lectures are reserved for 'unifying' talks on topics of interest to the whole range of ETAPS attendees. The aim of cramming all this activity into a single one-week meeting is to create a strong magnet for academic and industrial researchers working on topics within its scope, giving them the opportunity to learn about research in related areas, and thereby to foster new and existing links between work in areas that were formerly addressed in separate meetings.

ETAPS 2013 was organised by the *Department of Computer Science of 'Sapienza' University of Rome*, in cooperation with

▷ European Association for Theoretical Computer Science (EATCS)
▷ European Association for Programming Languages and Systems (EAPLS)
▷ European Association of Software Science and Technology (EASST).

The organising team comprised:

General Chair: *Daniele Gorla;*
Conferences: *Francesco Parisi Presicce;*
Satellite Events: *Paolo Bottoni* and *Pietro Cenciarelli;*
Web Master: *Igor Melatti;*
Publicity: *Ivano Salvo;*
Treasurers: *Federico Mari* and *Enrico Tronci.*

Overall planning for ETAPS conferences is the responsibility of its Steering Committee, whose current membership is:

Vladimiro Sassone (Southampton, chair), Martín Abadi (Santa Cruz), Erika Ábrahám (Aachen), Roberto Amadio (Paris 7), Gilles Barthe (IMDEA-Software), David Basin (Zürich), Saddek Bensalem (Grenoble), Michael O'Boyle (Edinburgh), Giuseppe Castagna (CNRS Paris), Albert Cohen (Paris), Vittorio Cortellessa (L'Aquila), Koen De Bosschere (Gent), Ranjit Jhala (San Diego), Matthias Felleisen (Boston), Philippa Gardner (Imperial College London), Stefania Gnesi (Pisa), Andrew D. Gordon (MSR Cambridge and Edinburgh), Daniele Gorla (Rome), Klaus Havelund (JLP NASA Pasadena), Reiko Heckel (Leicester), Holger Hermanns (Saarbrücken), Joost-Pieter Katoen (Aachen), Paul Klint (Amsterdam), Jens Knoop (Vienna), Steve Kremer (Nancy), Gerald Lüttgen (Bamberg), Tiziana Margaria (Potsdam), Fabio Martinelli (Pisa), John Mitchell (Stanford), Anca Muscholl (Bordeaux), Catuscia Palamidessi (INRIA Paris), Frank Pfenning (Pittsburgh), Nir Piterman (Leicester), Arend Rensink (Twente), Don Sannella (Edinburgh), Zhong Shao (Yale), Scott A. Smolka (Stony Brook), Gabriele Taentzer (Marburg), Tarmo Uustalu (Tallinn), Dániel Varró (Budapest) and Lenore Zuck (Chicago).

The ordinary running of ETAPS is handled by its management group comprising: Vladimiro Sassone (chair), Joost-Pieter Katoen (deputy chair and publicity chair), Gerald Lüttgen (treasurer), Giuseppe Castagna (satellite events chair), Holger Hermanns (liaison with local organiser) and Gilles Barthe (industry liaison).

I would like to express here my sincere gratitude to all the people and organisations that contributed to ETAPS 2013, the Programme Committee chairs and members of the ETAPS conferences, the organisers of the satellite events, the speakers themselves, the many reviewers, all the participants, and Springer-Verlag for agreeing to publish the ETAPS proceedings in the ARCoSS subline.

Last but not least, I would like to thank the organising chair of ETAPS 2013, Daniele Gorla, and his Organising Committee, for arranging for us to have ETAPS in the most beautiful and historic city of Rome.

———————— ■ ————————

My thoughts today are with two special people, profoundly different for style and personality, yet profoundly similar for the love and dedication to our discipline, for the way they shaped their respective research fields, and for the admiration and respect that their work commands. Both are role-model computer scientists for us all.

ETAPS in Rome celebrates *Corrado Böhm*. Corrado turns 90 this year, and we are just so lucky to have the chance to celebrate the event in Rome, where he has worked since 1974 and established a world-renowned school of computer scientists. Corrado has been a pioneer in research on programming languages and their semantics. Back in 1951, years before FORTRAN and LISP, he defined and implemented a *metacircular compiler* for a programming language of his invention. The compiler consisted of just 114 instructions, and anticipated some modern list-processing techniques.

Yet, Corrado's claim to fame is asserted through the breakthroughs expressed by the *Böhm-Jacopini Theorem* (CACM 1966) and by the invention of *Böhm-trees*. The former states that any algorithm can be implemented using only sequencing, conditionals, and while-loops over elementary instructions. Böhm trees arose as a convenient data structure in Corrado's milestone proof of the decidability inside the λ-calculus of the equivalence of terms in β-η-normal form.

Throughout his career, Corrado showed exceptional commitment to his roles of researcher and educator, fascinating his students with his creativity, passion and curiosity in research. Everybody who has worked with him or studied under his supervision agrees that he combines an outstanding technical ability and originality of thought with great personal charm, sweetness and kindness. This is an unusual combination in problem-solvers of such a high calibre, yet another reason why we are ecstatic to celebrate him. *Happy birthday from ETAPS, Corrado!*

ETAPS in Rome also celebrates the life and work of *Kohei Honda*. Kohei passed away suddenly and prematurely on December 4th, 2012, leaving the saddest gap in our community. He was a dedicated, passionate, enthusiastic scientist and –more than that!– his enthusiasm was contagious. Kohei was one of the few theoreticians I met who really succeeded in building bridges between theoreticians and practitioners. He worked with W3C on the standardisation of web services choreography description languages (WS-CDL) and with several companies on *Savara* and *Scribble*, his own language for the description of application-level protocols among communicating systems.

Among Kohei's milestone research, I would like to mention his 1991 epoch-making paper at ECOOP (with M. Tokoro) on the treatment of asynchrony in message passing calculi, which has influenced all process calculi research since. At ETAPS 1998 he introduced (with V. Vasconcelos and M. Kubo) a new concept in type theories for communicating processes: it came to be known as '*session types*,' and has since spawned an entire research area, with practical and multidisciplinary applications that Kohei was just starting to explore.

Kohei leaves behind him enormous impact, and a lasting legacy. He is irreplaceable, and I for one am proud to have been his colleague and glad for the opportunity to arrange for his commemoration at ETAPS 2013.

——————— ■ ———————

My final ETAPS 'Foreword' seems like a good place for a short reflection on ETAPS, what it has achieved in the past few years, and what the future might have in store for it.

On April 1st, 2011 in Saarbrücken, we took a significant step towards the consolidation of ETAPS: the establishment of *ETAPS e.V.* This is a *non-profit association* founded under German law with the immediate purpose of supporting the conference and the related activities. ETAPS e.V. was required for practical reasons, e.g., the conference needed (to be represented by) a legal body to better support authors, organisers and attendees by, e.g., signing contracts with service providers such as publishers and professional meeting organisers. Our ambition is however to make of '*ETAPS the association*' more than just the organisers of '*ETAPS the conference*'. We are working towards finding a voice and developing a range of activities to support our scientific community, in cooperation with the relevant existing associations, learned societies and interest groups. The process of defining the structure, scope and strategy of ETAPS e.V. is underway, as is its first ever membership campaign. For the time being, ETAPS e.V. has started to support community-driven initiatives such as open access publications (LMCS and EPTCS) and conference management systems (Easychair), and to cooperate with cognate associations (European Forum for ICT).

After two successful runs, we continue to support POST, *Principles of Security and Trust*, as a candidate to become a permanent ETAPS conference. POST was the first addition to our main programme since 1998, when the original five conferences met together in Lisbon for the first ETAPS. POST resulted from several smaller workshops and informal gatherings, supported by IFIP WG 1.7, and combines the practically important subject of security and trust with strong technical connections to traditional ETAPS areas. POST is now attracting interest and support from prominent scientists who have accepted to serve as PC chairs, invited speakers and tutorialists. I am very happy about the decision we made to create and promote POST, and to invite it to be a part of ETAPS.

Considerable attention was recently devoted to our *internal processes* in order to streamline our procedures for appointing Programme Committees, choosing invited speakers, awarding prizes and selecting papers; to strengthen each member conference's own Steering Group, and, at the same time, to strike a balance between these and the ETAPS Steering Committee. A lot was done and a lot remains to be done.

We produced a *handbook* for local organisers and one for PC chairs. The latter sets out a code of conduct that all the people involved in the selection of papers, from PC chairs to referees, are expected to adhere to. From the point of view of the authors, we adopted a *two-phase submission* protocol, with fixed deadlines in the first week of October. We published a *confidentiality policy* to set high standards for the handling of submissions, and a *republication policy* to clarify what kind of material remains eligible for submission to ETAPS after presentation at a workshop. We started an *author rebuttal phase*, adopted by most of the conferences, to improve the author experience. It is important to acknowledge that – regardless of our best intentions and efforts – the quality of reviews is not always what we would like it to be. To remain true to our commitment to the authors who elect to submit to ETAPS, we must endeavour to improve our standards of refereeing. The rebuttal phase is a step in that direction and, according to our experience, it seems to work remarkably well at little cost, provided both authors and PC members use it for what it is. ETAPS has now reached a healthy paper acceptance rate around the 25% mark, essentially uniformly across the six conferences. This seems to me to strike an excellent balance between being selective and being inclusive, and I hope it will be possible to maintain it even if the number of submissions increases.

ETAPS signed a favourable three-year publication contract with Springer for publication in the ARCoSS subline of LNCS. This was the result of lengthy negotiations, and I consider it a good achievement for ETAPS. Yet, publication of its proceedings is possibly the hardest challenge that ETAPS – and indeed most computing conferences – currently face. I was invited to represent ETAPS at a most interesting Dagstuhl Perspective Workshop on the '*Publication Culture in Computing Research*' (seminar 12452). The paper I gave there is available online from the workshop proceedings, and illustrates three of the views I formed also thanks to my experience as chair of ETAPS, respectively on open access, bibliometrics, and the roles and relative merits of conferences versus journal publications. Open access is a key issue for a conference like ETAPS. Yet, in my view it does not follow that we can altogether dispense with publishers – be they commercial, academic, or learned societies – and with their costs. A promising way forward may be based on the '*author-pays*' model, where publications fees are kept low by resorting to learned-societies as publishers. Also, I believe it is ultimately in the interest of our community to de-emphasise the perceived value of conference publications as viable – if not altogether superior – alternatives to journals. A large and ambitious conference like ETAPS ought to be able to rely on quality open-access journals to cover its entire spectrum of interests, even if that means promoting the creation of a new journal.

Due to its size and the complexity of its programme, hosting ETAPS is an increasingly challenging task. Even though excellent candidate *locations* keep being volunteered, in the longer run it seems advisable for ETAPS to provide more support to local organisers, starting e.g., by taking direct control of the organisation of satellite events. Also, after sixteen splendid years, this may be a good time to start thinking about exporting ETAPS to other continents. The US East Coast would appear to be the obvious destination for a first ETAPS outside Europe.

The strength and success of ETAPS comes also from presenting – regardless of the natural internal differences – a homogeneous interface to authors and participants, i.e., to look like one large, coherent, well-integrated conference rather than a mere co-location of events. I therefore feel it is vital for ETAPS to regulate the centrifugal forces that arise naturally in a 'union' like ours, as well as the legitimate aspiration of individual PC chairs to run things their way. In this respect, we have large and solid foundations, alongside a few relevant issues on which ETAPS has not yet found agreement. They include, e.g., submission by PC members, rotation of PC memberships, and the adoption of a rebuttal phase. More work is required on these and similar matters.

January 2013   Vladimiro Sassone
                                            ETAPS SC Chair
                                            ETAPS e.V. President

Preface

This volume contains the proceedings of FASE 2013, the 16th International Conference on Fundamental Approaches to Software Engineering, which was held in Rome, Italy, in March 2013 as part of the annual European Joint Conference on Theory and Practice of Software (ETAPS). As with previous editions of FASE, this year papers presented foundational contributions to a broad range of topics in software engineering, including verification and validation, model-driven engineering, software comprehension and testing.

This year we received 112 submissions from 32 countries, of which 25 were accepted by the Program Committee for presentation at the conference, resulting in an acceptance rate of approximately 22.3%. The submissions comprise 110 research papers and two tool demonstration papers, and the Program Committee accepted 23 of the research papers and the two tool papers. Each paper received a minimum of three reviews, and acceptance decisions were reached through online discussions among the members of the Program Committee and additional reviewers.

We were honored to host Krzysztof Czarnecki from the University of Waterloo (Canada) as the FASE keynote speaker at ETAPS 2013, who gave a talk entitled "Variability in Software: State of the Art and Future Directions." Krzysztof is an internationally recognized researcher who has contributed to a broad spectrum of research areas in the domain of software engineering. His pioneering work in the field of feature modeling, traceability management, and software variability has certainly opened new directions in these areas.

Many persons contributed to the success of FASE 2013. Authors of all submitted papers represent the core of such a conference, and we believe that the accepted papers make significant steps ahead in the software engineering area. However, this exciting program would not have been assembled without the great effort of the Program Committee members in paper reviewing and discussing under a tight schedule: thanks a lot for your active participation! We also express our full gratitude to the additional reviewers we involved in the process in the last two weeks, who were available to revise papers and produce high-quality reviews in a very short time. We thank Gabi Taentzer, the FASE Steering Committee Chair, for her timely and accurate responses to our queries about the whole process management. We also thank the ETAPS Steering and Organizing Committees for their coordination work.

We sincerely hope you enjoy these proceedings!

January 2013

Vittorio Cortellessa
Dániel Varró

Organization

Program Committee

Marco Bernardo	University of Urbino, Italy
Ruth Breu	University of Innsbruck, Austria
S.C. Cheung	The Hong Kong University of Science and Techonology, SAR China
Vittorio Cortellessa (Chair)	Università dell'Aquila, Italy
Bojan Cukic	West Virginia University, USA
Juan De Lara	Universidad Autonoma de Madrid, Spain
Ewen Denney	SGT/ NASA Ames Research Center, USA
Juergen Dingel	Queen's University, Canada
Alexander Egyed	Johannes Kepler University, Austria
Claudia Ermel	Technische Universität Berlin, Germany
Rudolf Ferenc	University of Szeged, Hungary
Holger Giese	Hasso Plattner Institute, Germany
Paul Grace	Lancaster University, UK
Reiko Heckel	University of Leicester, UK
John Hosking	University of Auckland, New Zealand
Valerie Issarny	INRIA, France
Jochen Kuester	IBM Zurich, Switzerland
Raffaela Mirandola	Politecnico di Milano, Italy
Richard Paige	University of York, UK
Dorina Petriu	Carleton University, Canada
Alfonso Pierantonio	Università dell'Aquila, Italy
Claudia Pons	Universidad Nacional de La Plata, Argentina
Abhik Roychoudhury	National University of Singapore
Andy Schürr	TU Darmstadt, Germany
Bran Selic	Malina Software Corp., Canada
Gabriele Taentzer	Philipps-Universität Marburg, Germany
Nikolai Tillmann	Microsoft Research, USA
Dániel Varró (Chair)	Budapest University of Technology and Economics, Hungary
Virginie Wiels	ONERA/DTIM, France
Andrea Zisman	City University, UK

Additional Reviewers

Aldini, Alessandro	Balogh, Gergő
Arcelli, Davide	Bapodra, Mayur
Arendt, Thorsten	Baresi, Luciano

Becker, Basil

Berardinelli, Luca

Bergmann, Gábor

Beszédes, Árpád

Bettini, Lorenzo

Bohme, Marcel

Boniol, Frédéric

Botterweck, Goetz

Brunel, Julien

Böhme, Marcel

Celebic, Boban

Chemouil, David

Cicchetti, Antonio

Cichos, Harald

Deckwerth, Frederik

Della Monica, Dario

Della Penna, Giuseppe

Di Ruscio, Davide

Dyck, Johannes

Ehrig, Hartmut

Eramo, Romina

Farwick, Matthias

Felderer, Michael

Ferreira, Ronaldo

Gabriel, Karsten

Gabrysiak, Gregor

Gallo, Francesco

Gander, Matthias

Giandini, Roxana

Guta, Gábor

Gönczy, László

Habel, Annegret

Haisjackl, Christian

Hebig, Regina

Hegedüs, Ábel

Hegedűs, Péter

Hermann, Frank

Hildebrandt, Stephan

Horváth, Ákos

Häser, Florian

Irazábal, Jerónimo

Jász, Judit

Kahsai, Temesghen

Khan, Tamim

Kiss, Ákos

Krause, Christian

Kumar, Sandeep

Küster, Jochen

Lauder, Marius

Lengyel, László

Lin, Shang-Wei

Liu, Yepang

Lluch Lafuente, Alberto

Lo, David

Lochau, Malte

Lopez-Herrejon, Roberto

Maier, Sonja

Mariani, Leonardo

Micskei, Zoltán

Milea, Narcisa Andreea

Muccini, Henry

Nagy, Csaba

Neumann, Stefan

Odell, Jim

Oliveira, Bruno

Paci, Federica

Patzina, Lars

Patzina, Sven

Pelliccione, Patrizio

Pomante, Luigi

Posse, Ernesto

Potena, Pasqualina

Reder, Alexander

Rungta, Neha

Saller, Karsten

Scandurra, Patrizia

Schrettner, Lajos

Siket, István

Soeken, Mathias

Sokolsky, Oleg

Stevens, Perdita

Strausz, György

Strüber, Daniel

Sun, Jun

Szeredi, Péter

Sánchez Cuadrado, Jesús

Tesei, Luca

Tiezzi, Francesco

Tribastone, Mirco

Ujhelyi, Zoltán

Varró, Gergely
Wang, Xinming
Wieber, Martin
Wilms, Sebastian
Wu, Rongxin
Wätzoldt, Sebastian
Ye, Chunyang

Yi, Jooyong
Zech, Philipp
Zhang, Xiangyu
Zhang, Zhenyu
Zurowska, Karolina

Table of Contents

Verification and Validation 2

Analysis Tools

Model-Driven Engineering: Applications

Model Transformations

Testing

Variability in Software:
State of the Art and Future Directions
(Extended Abstract)

Krzysztof Czarnecki

Generative Software Development Lab, University of Waterloo, Canada
kczarnec@gsd.uwaterloo.ca

Variability is a fundamental aspect of software. It is the ability to create system variants for different market segments or contexts of use. Variability has been most extensively studied in software product lines [10], but is also relevant in other areas, including software ecosystems [4] and context-aware software [15]. Virtually any successful software faces eventually the need to exist in multiple variants.

Variability introduces essential complexity into all areas of software engineering, and calls for variability-aware methods and tools that can deal with this complexity effectively. Engineering a variable system amounts to engineering a set of systems simultaneously. As a result, requirements, architecture, code and tests are inherently more complex than in single-system engineering. A developer wanting to understand a particular system variant has to identify the relevant parts of requirements and code and ignore those that pertain solely to other variants. A quality assurer verifying a variable system has to ensure that all relevant variants are correct. Variability-aware methods and tools leverage the commonalities among the system variants, while managing the differences effectively.

This talk will analyze how variability affects the software lifecycle, focusing on requirements, architecture and verification and validation, review the state of the art of variability-aware methods and tools, and identify future directions.

Variability modeling at the requirements level helps explaining a variable system and its evolution to all stakeholders, technical and nontechnical ones. A popular technique is feature models [19,11], which are hierarchically composed declarations of common and variable features and their dependencies. At the requirements level, system features represent cohesive clusters of requirements [7,8], providing convenient "mental chunks" to all stakeholders to understand the system, its variability, and its evolution. For example, changes at the code level can be explained as feature additions, removals, merges, or other kinds of modifications at the feature level [27]. As feature models provide only declarations of features, an obvious direction is to enrich them with feature specifications, such as behavioral ones (e.g., [30]). Feature models can also be enhanced with rich forms of dependencies, such as representations of feature interactions (e.g., [24]), and with quality attributes, such as performance (e.g., [2,26]). Feature-oriented software development (FOSD) aims at treating features as first-class citizens,

V. Cortellessa and D. Varró (Eds.): FASE 2013, LNCS 7793, pp. 1–5, 2013.

that is, modularizing them throughout the entire lifecycle [1]. Although promising, empirically quantifying the benefits of feature modularization is future work.

Variation points accommodate variability at the architectural level. They are locations in software artifacts where variability occurs. Variability engineering classifies variation points according to their variability type [29], such as value parameters, optional elements, element substitution or repeated instantiation, and their binding time. The Common Variability Language (CVL) [25], which is an effort by the Object Management group to standardize variability modeling, provides a comprehensive taxonomy of variation points. Many existing design and architectural patterns [16,6] can be used to implement variation points, as they are often about allowing certain system aspects to vary easily. For example, the strategy pattern is used to vary algorithms within a system. Planning and scoping variability can guide and ground architectural design: varying parts need to be localized and hidden behind common interfaces. But variability also impacts established modularity concepts. For example, variable modules need to expose configuration interfaces and their functional interfaces may need to be variable. This combination leads to the notion of variability-aware module systems [21], with implications on compositionality and type consistency. Tools and languages using such module systems also need to support staged configuration of such modules [12]. Further, variability affects other modularity topics, such as cohesion, coupling, crosscutting, and tangling. Understanding the impact of variability on modularity is a topic for future research.

Variability also affects verification and validation. Variability-aware methods leverage commonalities to reduce time and effort to check variable systems. The reduction is useful for product lines with large numbers of products, but is indispensable for ecosystem platforms, whose users may decide to instantiate any variant out of the exponential number of supported variants. Existing work includes variability-aware forms of standard analysis techniques, such as type checking (e.g., [20,13]), dataflow analyses (e.g., [5]) and model checking (e.g., [9]). In testing, variability engineering can be applied to tests in order to derive test suits along with a variant. For example, the variability model and the build system of the eCos operating system allow users to derive a system variant along with suitable tests. Researchers have also proposed the concept of shared execution of tests on multiple variants [23,22] and adapted combinatorial testing to generate sets of variants covering certain feature-combination heuristics for platform testing (e.g., [28]). However, testing variable systems offers plenty opportunities to be explored in future research, including test selection, prioritization, and generation at unit, integration, and system levels, and potentially in the context of specific changes.

Indisputably, variability has become a fundamental aspect of software engineering. Variability engineering is practiced today both in open-source (e.g., see a study of variability engineering in open-software systems software, including the Linux kernel [3]) and industry (e.g., see the experiences of Danfoss [18], GM [14], and Rolls-Royce [17]). Variability engineering also offers abundant opportunities for software researchers to explore new directions in a wide range of areas within requirements, architecture, verification and validation, and beyond, including reverse engineering, programming languages, performance, reliability, and security. Today's and future application domains pose new challenges to variability engineering to be addressed in research. They include scaling variability to systems of systems in automotive and aerospace engineering and dealing effectively with software ecosystems, cloud computing, and context-aware applications in enterprise and consumer domains.

References

1. Apel, S., Kästner, C.: An overview of feature-oriented software development. Journal of Object Technology 8(5), 49–84 (2009)
2. Benavides, D., Trinidad, P., Ruiz-Cortés, A.: Automated Reasoning on Feature Models. In: Pastor, Ó., Falcão e Cunha, J. (eds.) CAiSE 2005. LNCS, vol. 3520, pp. 491–503. Springer, Heidelberg (2005)
3. Berger, T., She, S., Lotufo, R., Wasowski, A., Czarnecki, K.: Variability modeling in the systems software domain. Technical report, gsdlab-tr. Generative Software Development Laboratory, University of Waterloo (July 06, 2012), http://gsd.uwaterloo.ca/node/465
4. Bosch, J.: From software product lines to software ecosystems. In: Proceedings of the 13th International Software Product Line Conference, SPLC 2009, Carnegie Mellon University, Pittsburgh, PA, USA, pp. 111–119 (2009)
5. Brabrand, C., Ribeiro, M., Tolêdo, T., Borba, P.: Intraprocedural dataflow analysis for software product lines. In: Proceedings of the 11th Annual International Conference on Aspect-Oriented Software Development, AOSD 2012, pp. 13–24. ACM, New York (2012)
6. Buschmann, F., Meunier, R., Rohnert, H., Sommerlad, P., Stal, M.: Pattern-oriented software architecture: a system of patterns. John Wiley & Sons, Inc., New York (1996)
7. Chen, K., Zhang, W., Zhao, H., Mei, H.: An approach to constructing feature models based on requirements clustering. In: Proceedings of the 13th IEEE International Conference on Requirements Engineering, RE 2005, pp. 31–40. IEEE Computer Society, Washington, DC (2005)
8. Classen, A., Heymans, P., Schobbens, P.-Y.: What's in a *Feature*: A Requirements Engineering Perspective. In: Fiadeiro, J.L., Inverardi, P. (eds.) FASE 2008. LNCS, vol. 4961, pp. 16–30. Springer, Heidelberg (2008)
9. Classen, A., Heymans, P., Schobbens, P.Y., Legay, A.: Symbolic model checking of software product lines. In: Proceedings of the 33rd International Conference on Software Engineering, ICSE 2011, pp. 321–330. ACM, New York (2011)
10. Clements, P., Northrop, L.: Software product lines: practices and patterns. Addison-Wesley Longman Publishing Co., Inc. (2001)
11. Czarnecki, K., Grünbacher, P., Rabiser, R., Schmid, K., Wąsowski, A.: Cool features and tough decisions: a comparison of variability modeling approaches. In: Proceedings of the Sixth International Workshop on Variability Modeling of Software-Intensive Systems, VaMoS 2012, pp. 173–182. ACM, New York (2012)
12. Czarnecki, K., Helsen, S., Eisenecker, U.: Staged Configuration Using Feature Models. In: Nord, R.L. (ed.) SPLC 2004. LNCS, vol. 3154, pp. 266–283. Springer, Heidelberg (2004)

13. Czarnecki, K., Pietroszek, K.: Verifying feature-based model templates against well-formedness OCL constraints. In: Proceedings of the 5th International Conference on Generative Programming and Component Engineering, GPCE 2006, pp. 211–220. ACM, New York (2006)

14. Flores, R., Krueger, C., Clements, P.: Mega-scale product line engineering at general motors. In: Proceedings of the 16th International Software Product Line Conference, SPLC 2012, vol. 1, pp. 259–268. ACM, New York (2012)

15. Fortier, A., Rossi, G., Gordillo, S.E., Challiol, C.: Dealing with variability in context-aware mobile software. J. Syst. Softw. 83(6), 915–936 (2010)

16. Gamma, E., Helm, R., Johnson, R., Vlissides, J.: Design patterns: elements of reusable object-oriented software. Addison-Wesley Longman Publishing Co., Inc., Boston (1995)

17. Habli, I., Kelly, T.: Challenges of establishing a software product line for an aerospace engine monitoring system. In: Proceedings of the 11th International Software Product Line Conference, SPLC 2007, pp. 193–202. IEEE Computer Society, Washington, DC (2007)

18. Jepsen, H.P., Beuche, D.: Running a software product line: standing still is going backwards. In: Proceedings of the 13th International Software Product Line Conference, SPLC 2009, Carnegie Mellon University, Pittsburgh, PA, USA, pp. 101–110 (2009)

19. Kang, K., Cohen, S., Hess, J., Nowak, W., Peterson, S.: Feature-oriented domain analysis (FODA) feasibility study. Tech. Rep. CMU/SEI-90-TR-21, CMU (1990)

20. Kästner, C., Apel, S., Thüm, T., Saake, G.: Type checking annotation-based product lines. ACM Trans. Softw. Eng. Methodol. 21(3), 14 (2012)

21. Kästner, C., Ostermann, K., Erdweg, S.: A variability-aware module system. In: Proceedings of the ACM International Conference on Object Oriented Programming Systems Languages and Applications, OOPSLA 2012, pp. 773–792. ACM, New York (2012)

22. Kästner, C., von Rhein, A., Erdweg, S., Pusch, J., Apel, S., Rendel, T., Ostermann, K.: Toward variability-aware testing. In: Proceedings of the 4th International Workshop on Feature-Oriented Software Development, FOSD 2012, pp. 1–8. ACM, New York (2012)

23. Kim, C.H.P., Khurshid, S., Batory, D.: Shared execution for efficiently testing product lines. In: IEEE International Symposium on Software Reliability Engineering (ISSRE 2012). IEEE (2012)

24. Lee, K., Kang, K.C.: Feature Dependency Analysis for Product Line Component Design. In: Bosch, J., Krueger, C. (eds.) ICSR 2004. LNCS, vol. 3107, pp. 69–85. Springer, Heidelberg (2004)

25. Object Management Group: Common variability language (CVL). OMG Revised Submission, Document (August 05, 2012), www.omgwiki.org/variability

26. Olaechea, R., Stewart, S., Czarnecki, K., Rayside, D.: Modeling and multi-objective optimization of quality attributes in variability-rich software. In: International Workshop on Non-Functional System Properties in Domain Specific Modeling Languages (NFPinDSML 2012), Innsbruck, Austria (2012)

27. Passos, L., Czarnecki, K., Sven, A., Wąsowski, A., Kästner, C., Guo, J., Hunsen, C.: Feature-oriented software evolution. In: Proceedings of the Sixth International Workshop on Variability Modeling of Software-Intensive Systems, VaMoS 2013. ACM, New York (2013)

28. Perrouin, G., Sen, S., Klein, J., Baudry, B., Traon, Y.L.: Automated and scalable t-wise test case generation strategies for software product lines. In: Proceedings of the 2010 Third International Conference on Software Testing, Verification and Validation (ICST 2010), pp. 459–468. IEEE Computer Society, Washington, DC (2010)
29. Schmid, K., John, I.: A Customizable Approach to Full-Life Cycle Variability Management. Science of Computer Programming 53(3), 259–284 (2004)
30. Shaker, P., Atlee, J.M., Wang, S.: A feature-oriented requirements modelling language. In: Proceedings of the 20th IEEE International Requirements Engineering Conference (RE 2012). ACM (2012)

Towards a Distributed Modeling Process
Based on Composite Models

Daniel Strüber, Gabriele Taentzer, Stefan Jurack, and Tim Schäfer

Philipps-Universität Marburg, Germany
{strueber,taentzer,sjurack,timschaefer}
@mathematik.uni-marburg.de

Abstract. The rising impact of software development in globally distributed teams strengthens the need for strategies that establish a clear separation of concerns in software models. Dealing with large, weakly modularized models and conflicting changes on interrelated models are typical obstacles to be witnessed. This paper proposes a structured process for distributed modeling based on the modularization technique provided by composite models with explicit interfaces. It provides a splitting activity for decomposing large models, discusses asynchronous and synchronous editing steps in relation to consistency management and provides a merge activity allowing the reuse of code generators. All main concepts of composite modeling are precisely defined based on category theory.

Keywords: distributed modeling, composite models, model transformation, EMF.

1 Introduction

Nowadays, model-driven development is a widely-spread paradigm to cope with the growing complexity of software requirements. Reliable technologies have emerged that allow specifying an application on a high level of abstraction using models. These models can then be transformed towards a running software system. Model-driven development is based on modeling languages that are usually defined using meta-modeling: a meta-model defines a language of individual models by predefining their structure. An important meta-modeling architecture has been proposed by the Object Management Group in terms of the Meta Object Facility (MOF) [18]. An essential subset of MOF has been implemented by the Eclipse Modeling Framework (EMF) [8].

When lifting concepts and tools from model-driven development to a distributed environment, a couple of challenges arise: contributors at different locations might be responsible for models that are interconnected in some sense. Thus, clear conditions and conventions for the editing of models are required to avoid the emergence of inconsistencies. Another drawback of existing tools is the sometimes monolithic nature of large models. Large models are difficult to comprehend and maintain. Thus, well-defined modularization strategies for models are required.

EMF models can be modularized using remote references between individual models. The targets of remote references are then temporarily represented by proxy elements and on demand replaced by the actual model element. In consequence, logically, all involved models constitute one big model. While this technique is sufficient for distributing a large model over a set of resources, it does not establish well-known engineering

V. Cortellessa and D. Varró (Eds.): FASE 2013, LNCS 7793, pp. 6–20, 2013.

principles such as encapsulation and information hiding. Hence, we refer to this approach as a *physical* modularization technique. In opposition, we propose *composite models* [12] as a *logical* modularization technique that establishes information hiding and allows for local consistency checks. A composite model comprises a set of components that are interconnected by export and import interfaces. Possible topologies of model components are predefined by meta-model components. We provide core tool support for composite models and their transformation.

As central contribution of this paper, we show how to utilize composite models in order to address three questions that arise when lifting model-driven development to a distributed environment: (1) How can a model be decomposed for logical modularization? (2) How can models be edited in a distributed way such that consistency between model components is preserved? (3) How can model-to-code transformation be performed when models are distributed?

Our solution to these questions is a process for distributed modeling. In order to tackle question (1), a split activity is elaborated that decomposes a given model into a set of components forming a composite model. As for question (2), we discuss how editing steps can be specified and performed in a systematic way using composite model transformation. As a tentative solution to question (3), a merge activity is introduced that allows the reuse of existing code generation components.

The remainder of this paper is structured as follows: Sect. 2 provides the model-driven development of simple web applications as a running example. Composite models are recapitulated in Sect. 3. An overview of the process forming the main contribution of this paper is given in Sect. 4. The activities constituting the process – split, edit, and merge – are elaborated in Sects. 5, 6, and 7. We present an application scenario in Sect. 8 and tool support in Sect. 9. Sect. 10 discusses related work. Sect. 11 concludes.

2   Scenario: Model-Driven Development of Web Applications

Web applications as a software domain have undergone domain analysis in visual web modeling languages such as WebML [5] or UWE [15]. A common design decision found in these modeling languages is their branching into a set of viewpoint-oriented sub-languages – such as a structural data model, a presentation model and a navigation model. When a web application is to be developed by a distributed team, it is likely that the contributors obtain responsibilities for the different viewpoints, e.g. one contributor acts as domain modeler and another one as presentation modeler. To provide a full model-driven development infrastructure, domain-specific languages such as WebML are supplemented with code generation facilities that define a language semantics.

As a running example, Fig. 1 provides the syntax for the *Simple Web Application Language (SWAL)* as a modeling language for the specification of simple web applications[1]. SWAL is specified by means of an EMF meta-model, comprising attributed model classes as nodes with directed references as edges. Classes may be abstract. References may be containment references that ensure a tree-like structure for models.

---

[1] The development of SWAL was initiated by Manuel Wimmer and Philip Langer at the Technische Universität Wien and reimplemented for its use in modeling courses at the Philipps-Universität Marburg.

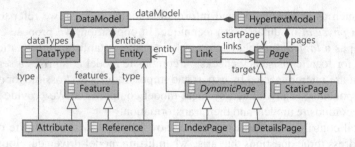

Fig. 1. SWAL meta-model

The class *HypertextModel* is used as root object of a web application to be specified. It contains a hypertext structure of interconnected pages and a *DataModel* for the specification of structural models of persistent data. Persistent data is based on distinct *Entities* which are charaterized by a number of *Features*, i.e. *Attributes* and *References*. An attribute is typed over a primitive *DataType*, a reference over an entity.

The hypertext structure is based on *Pages* being interconnected through *Links*. Depending on its content, a page can either be dynamic or static. A dynamic page refers to an entity and can either be an *index page* displaying a list of available data records or a *details page* presenting a detailed view for a specific record.

In Fig. 2, a poetry competition web application is specified. Contest, poet, and poem entities are to be displayed on interlinked index and details pages. The concrete syntax given in the presentation facilitates convenient editing by hiding

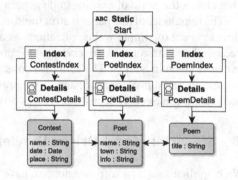

Fig. 2. Poetry contest web application model

the *DataModel* and *HypertextModel* classes: pages and entities are visualized as nodes in different layouts. Hyperlinks, references, and links between pages and entities are visualized as arrows.

3   Composite Models

This paper investigates a process for distributed modeling based on *composite models*. Composite models provide a logical modularization technique for models by declaring explicit *export and import interfaces*. Export and import interfaces identify model elements provided to and obtained from the environment, respectively. While an import is assigned to exactly one export, an export can serve an arbitrary number of imports.

The core of a component is a conventional model called the *body*. Model elements in export and import interfaces are identified with model elements in the body. Import interface elements are also identified with export elements. An interface can hide

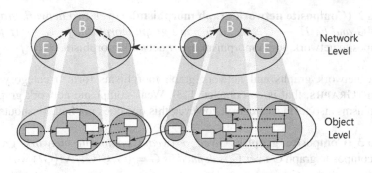

Fig. 3. Composite model with explicit export and import interfaces (taken from [11])

structural complexity of its component body, e.g. flatten its inheritance hierarchy. The interface structure of model components is predefined by meta-model components.

Consider Fig. 3 for a schematic representation of an example composite model. The network level constitutes a topology of components comprising body, export, and import nodes as well as interconnecting edges. The object level comprises a set of inter-related models, each providing a refinement for one of the network nodes, with interrelating mappings. Dashed arrows indicate how interfaces are integrated in body models, dotted arrows indicate an assignment between import and export interfaces. Mappings on object level are compatible with network level arrows in the sense that source and target nodes of mapped arrows are mapped to source and target of the image arrow.

Formalization. The internal representation of models can be well represented by graph structures. Therefore, the basis of our formalization are typed graphs and graph morphisms as defined in e.g., [6,13]. Graph morphisms are structure-preserving mappings between graphs. Typed graphs and graph morphisms form the category GRAPHS$_{TG}$. Since the following definitions of composite graphs and graph morphisms are given in a category-theoretical way, it is also possible to use other kinds of graphs and morphisms as basic ingredients of composite graphs. For example, composite graphs over typed graphs with inheritance and containment as well as inheritance and containment-preserving graph morphisms are considered in [13].

Definition 1 (Composite network graph). *A* composite network graph *is a graph G typed over graph CNG (shown on the right) by a graph morphism t : G → CNG such that the following constraints hold: (1) each* export node *is source of exactly one network edge running to a body node and (2) each* import node *is source of exactly two network edges, one edge is running to a body node and the other to an export node. If there are export nodes without outgoing edges, corresponding composite network graphs are called* weak.

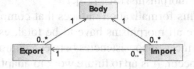

Definition 2 (Composite network graph morphism). *Given two network graphs g : $G \to CNG$ and $h\colon H \to CNG$, an injective graph morphism $f\colon G \to H$ forms a valid* composite network graph morphism, *short* network morphism, *if $h \circ f = g$.*

Composite network graphs and network graph morphisms form a category, called COMPONETGRAPHS, that is co-complete [13]. Weak composite network graphs and their morphisms also form a category; however, this one does not have pushouts.

Definition 3 (Composite graph). *Given a (weak) composite network graph G, a (weak)* composite graph $\hat{G}$ *over G is defined as $\hat{G} = (G, \mathcal{G}(G), \mathcal{M}(G))$ with*

- $\mathcal{G}(G)$ *being a set of graphs, called* local graphs, *of category* GRAPHS *with each graph uniquely refining a network node in G_N: $\mathcal{G}(G) = \{\hat{G}(n)|\ \hat{G}(n)$ is a graph and $n \in G_N\}$,*
- $\mathcal{M}(G)$ *being a set of graph morphisms, called* local (graph) morphisms, *each refining a network edge in G_E: $\mathcal{M}(G) = \{\hat{G}(e)\colon \hat{G}(i) \to \hat{G}(j)|\hat{G}(e)$ is a graph morphism and $e \in G_E$ with $s(e) = i$ and $t(e) = j\}$, and*
- *for all paths $\hat{G}(x) \circ \hat{G}(y), \hat{G}(z) : \hat{G}(A) \to \hat{G}(B)$ we have $\hat{G}(x) \circ \hat{G}(y) = \hat{G}(z)$ with $x, y, z \in G_E$.* (*commutative morphisms*)

Definition 4 (Composite graph morphism). *Given two (weak) composite graphs $\hat{G}$ and $\hat{H}$ with composite network graphs G and H, resp., a (weak)* composite (graph) morphism, *written $\hat{f}\colon \hat{G} \to \hat{H}$, is a pair $\hat{f} = (f, m)$ where*

- *$f\colon G \to H$ is a composite network graph morphism and*
- *m is a family of morphisms $\{\hat{f}(n) \mid n \in G_N\}$ such that*
  - *for all nodes $i \in G_N$: $\hat{f}(i)\colon \hat{G}(i) \to \hat{H}(f_N(i))$ is a graph morphism and*
  - *for all edges $e\colon i \to j \in G_E$: $\hat{H}(f_E(e)) \circ \hat{f}(i) = \hat{f}(j) \circ \hat{G}(e)$ (see the illustration on the right).*

$$
\begin{array}{ccc}
i & \hat{G}(i) \xrightarrow{\ \hat{f}(i)\ } \hat{H}(f_N(i)) \\
e & \hat{G}(e)\Big\downarrow \qquad\qquad \Big\downarrow \hat{H}(f_E(e)) \\
j & \hat{G}(j) \xrightarrow{\ \hat{f}(j)\ } \hat{H}(f_N(j))
\end{array}
$$

If morphism f and all morphisms in m are inclusions (injective), $\hat{f}$ is called inclusion (injective). *Given a graph $\hat{T}G$ and a composite morphism $\hat{t} : \hat{G} \to \hat{T}G$ is called* typed composite graph.

Composite graphs and graph morphisms form a category, called COMPGRAPHS, being co-complete. Weak composite graphs and weak composite morphisms form category COMPGRAPHS^{weak}. COMPGRAPHS$_{TG}$ is the category of typed composite graphs and their morphisms. (See [13].)

This formalization induces that composite graphs are consistent in a certain sense: Since all morphisms have to be total, especially the ones between import and export interfaces, inconsistencies between components in the sense of unsatisfied imports may not occur. It is up to future work to adapt composite models such that temporary inconsistencies are tolerated, i.e., partial import mappings are allowed.

4   Distributed Modeling Process: Overview

In this section, we give an overview on a modeling process that addresses three issues to facilitate distributed model-driven development: (i) How can composite models be used to structure models that lack an appropriate modularization? (ii) How can composite models be edited systematically so that inconsistencies are avoided? (iii) How can composite models be used as a blueprint for code generation? We refer to this process as a *distributed process* in terms of a collection of activities that enable a distributed team to work on a logically modularized model.

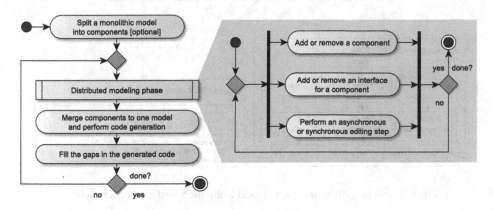

Fig. 4. Distributed modeling process

Fig. 4 gives an outline of the process: When applying composite models to an existing software development project, a monolithic model may exist that is required to be decomposed. In order to support this, we propose a splitting technique. In the distributed modeling phase following up, editing steps are performed, involving asynchronous or synchronous editing as well as changes of the network structure. Afterwards, in order to support code generation, all components may be merged together. The resulting code may have gaps to be filled in by the distributed team.

This overview refers to models on an arbitrary meta-level, e.g., models in application development or language development. However, the full potential of the process becomes evident when it is applied on two interrelated levels, e.g., application *and* language development. For instance, a legacy meta-model may be split by language developers. Conforming application models are then split according to the language decomposition by application developers. This activity is elaborated further in Sect. 5.

5   Model Splitting

This section elaborates model splitting as a migration technique for introducing logical modularization based on composite models to existing software development projects.

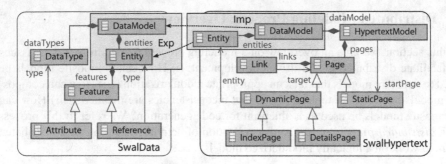

Fig. 5. Result of splitting SWAL into meta-model components

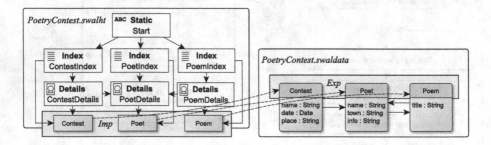

Fig. 6. Result of splitting the poetry model along the SWAL component split

It assumes a monolithic model or a set of models interconnected by remote references. It produces a composite model comprising a set of model components interconnected by export and import interfaces. Meta-models as well as their conforming models may be split. As we will prove for the special case of binary splitting, i.e., the decomposition into two components, the split of a typed model can even be uniquely derived from the split of its meta-model. Hence, our splitting strategy is especially suitable for a language-oriented split along the main view-points on the system under construction.

Example 1. In Fig. 5, SWAL has been split in two meta-model components comprising classes related to specific viewpoints: domain and hypertext modeling. Both resulting components are self-contained units in the sense that all model references run between classes within the same component. However, they are also interrelated as they are equipped with interfaces. *SwalHypertext*'s import interface contains *DataModel* and *Entity* classes mapped to the *DataModel* and *Entity* classes provided by *SwalData*'s export which allows for the exchange of data models.

Finding a proper decomposition for meta-models is challenging since it can largely benefit from automation, but on the other hand, may require some human intervention. A heuristics may be used to recommend a reasonable decomposition to the stakeholder based on some indicators of interrelation: e.g., as it is the case in the example, a high coupling of references, especially of containments, indicates classes often instantiated in combination. In turn, a stakeholder might consider it desirable to reveal more classes in interfaces than a minimal subset, e.g. he might want to provide the references running between entities to support comprehension. In any case, the benefit from finding an appropriate decomposition becomes evident considering the split of conforming models:

In Fig. 6, the poetry contest model was split towards the viewpoint meta-models introduced in Fig. 5. Both meta-model components are instantiated by conforming model components. Especially, export and import interfaces are instantiated and used for the sharing of entities between both components. As the split follows the typing of model elements and their assignment to meta-model components, it can be automatized.

Formalization. In the following, a formalization is provided for splitting a meta-model in two meta-model components with intermediate export and import interfaces and, furthermore, for splitting conforming models along that split. Any meta-model that can be represented as a plain graph can be used as input, e.g., a single self-contained model or a group of models interconnected by remote references.

Proposition 1 (Binary split of a composite graph). *Given graph G and two subgraphs G_1 and G_2 with inclusions $g_1\colon G_1 \to G$ and $g_2\colon G_2 \to G$, their interconnecting interfaces can be uniquely determined such that the resulting diagram forms a valid composite graph with two components.*

Proof idea. *The import subgraph G_I is constructed as pullback for the inclusions. The export subgraph G_E is constructed as epi-mono-factorization for the inclusion running between G_I and G_2 (see [21] for the complete proof).*

Proposition 2 (Binary split of a typed composite graph). *Given a type graph TG with a binary split and a graph G with its typing morphism t over TG. There is a unique binary split of G being type compatible with the resulting composite type graph.*

Proof idea. *Graphs G_1, G_2, G_I, G_E, inclusion and typing morphisms result from successive pullback constructions (see [21] for the complete proof).*

Considering the view-oriented splitting of large meta-models as e.g. for UML, it makes sense to iterate several binary splits. An example split scenario for UML can look like this: (1) split the structure component from the behavioral component, (2) split the structure component further into package and class structure components, (3) split the behavioral component into a basic action component and a behavior diagrams component, and (4) continue splitting this component until the well-known behavior diagrams are each separated in model components. Of course, component interfaces have to be continuously adapted during this splitting process.

6 Distributed Model Editing

A crucial challenge of collaborative editing is to preserve the consistency of models while keeping editing steps as independent as possible. Several approaches to the handling of model inconsistency, being defined as the maintenance of contradictory information within a network of models, center on the detection and resolution of inconsistencies [9,17]. The liberal strategy of allowing arbitrary operations to be applied and using a reconciliation stage relies on facilities to perform a global consistency check. However, these facilities may not always be available, e.g., for security or legal reasons. Hence, we propose a complementary strategy of *inconsistency avoidance*, giving editing steps at hand that are classified as either safe or critical to the consistency of models. We provide the notion of a *relaxed* consistency avoidance that allows performing critical steps if necessary. In contrast, a *strict* inconsistency avoidance may be an obstacle to the natural evolution of a software project and is prone to dead-lock situations.

Existing collaborative model editors such as Papyrus [19] or MagicDraw [16] implement a strategy for inconsistency avoidance by locking selected model parts for modification. These editors follow an asynchronous approach to editing single models that can be displayed and modified in multiple editors at once. As for the use of composite models, the management of consistency is facilitated by the maintenance of interfaces. It is desirable to support asynchronous and synchronous editing steps: For instance, two components with related contents might be expanded by individual contributors or in parallel by one contributor. Thus, this section discusses asynchronous as well as synchronous editing steps and their formalization based on the transformation of composite graphs. Using our basic implementation of composite model transformation comprising a rule editor and interpreter engine suite, it is possible to deploy transformation rules as editing steps, e.g. refactorings, within existing editors such as Papyrus.

Example 2. For the poetry contest application specified in the Fig. 6, new requirements might be stated, e.g., the management of books. When domain and hypertext components are developed independently, the first action done is that the domain modeler adds this new entity to the body and export of the *swaldata* component. The hypertext modeler then adds the entity to the import interface and body of the *swalht* component and creates corresponding pages for the entity resulting in the model shown in Fig. 7. In contrast, it might also be desirable to perform these changes in parallel: e.g., imagine an editing command that adds an entity and corresponding pages to both components. We distinguish these two kinds of editing as *asynchronous* and *synchronous editing*.

Formalization. Synchronous and asynchronous editing steps can be formalized a model transformations on a composite model.

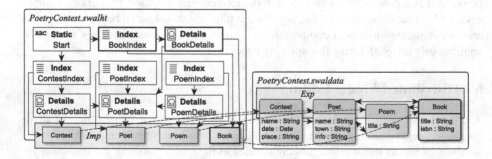

Fig. 7. Model components after editing. Thick borders indicate newly added elements.

Definition 5 (Composite graph transformation).

Given a composite graph $\hat{T}G$, a composite graph rule $\hat{p} = (\hat{L} \overset{\hat{l}}{\hookleftarrow} \hat{K} \overset{\hat{r}}{\hookrightarrow} \hat{R}, t\hat{y}pe)$ consists of composite graphs $\hat{L}$, $\hat{K}$, and $\hat{R}$ typed over $\hat{T}G$ by the triple $t\hat{y}pe = (t\hat{y}pe_{\hat{L}} : \hat{L} \rightarrow \hat{T}G, t\hat{y}pe_{\hat{K}} : \hat{K} \rightarrow \hat{T}G, t\hat{y}pe_{\hat{R}} : \hat{R} \rightarrow \hat{T}G)$ being composite morphisms and typed composite morphisms $\hat{l} : \hat{K} \hookrightarrow \hat{L}$ and $\hat{r} : \hat{K} \hookrightarrow \hat{R}$ being inclusions such that $\forall n \in K_N : \hat{p}(n) = (\hat{L}(n) \overset{\hat{l}(n)}{\hookleftarrow} \hat{K}(n) \overset{\hat{r}(n)}{\hookrightarrow} \hat{R}(n), t\hat{y}pe(n))$ is a graph rule (as defined in e.g. [6]).

A composite IC-graph transformation (step) $\hat{G} \overset{\hat{p},\hat{m}}{\Longrightarrow} \hat{H}$ of a typed composite graph $\hat{G}$ to $\hat{H}$ by a (weak) composite graph rule $\hat{p}$ and a typed injective composite morphism $\hat{m} : \hat{L} \rightarrow \hat{G}$ is given on the right, where (1) and (2) are pushouts in the category of COMPGRAPHS$_{TG}$ *(*COMPGRAPHS$_{TG}^{weak}$*).*

$$
\begin{array}{ccccc}
\hat{L} & \overset{\hat{l}}{\hookleftarrow} & \hat{K} & \overset{\hat{r}}{\hookrightarrow} & \hat{R} \\
\hat{m}\downarrow & (1) & \hat{d}\downarrow & (2) & \downarrow\hat{n} \\
\hat{G} & \overset{\hat{g}}{\hookleftarrow} & \hat{D} & \overset{\hat{h}}{\hookrightarrow} & \hat{H}
\end{array}
$$

A composite graph transformation is a sequence $\hat{G}_0 \Rightarrow \hat{G}_1 \Rightarrow ... \Rightarrow \hat{G}_n$ of direct composite graph transformations, written $\hat{G}_0 \overset{*}{\Rightarrow} \hat{G}_n$.

A composite transformation can be performed component-wise, i.e., performing the network transformation first and all local transformations for preserved network nodes afterwards if all composite morphisms are injective. Transformation step $\hat{G} \overset{\hat{p},\hat{m}}{\Longrightarrow} \hat{H}$ can be performed if $\hat{m}$ fulfills the *composite gluing condition*: the resulting structure must be a well-formed composite graph. Otherwise, it can happen that context edges dangle afterwards. The gluing condition has to be checked on the network and all local transformations. Moreover, for all network nodes that shall be deleted their local graphs have to be fully determined by the match and local graph elements may be deleted only if there are no preserved interface elements being mapped to them. Weak composite rules are not allowed to change stand-alone exports and to produce stand-alone exports by deleting their body graphs. (For more details see [11].)

Example 3. Two sample composite rules, shown in a compact representation, are provided in Fig. 8. *Del* and *New* tags indicate the containment of nodes in $\hat{L} - \hat{K}$ or $\hat{R} - \hat{K}$, respectively. Rule *a)* is a synchronous rule specifying the addition of a new entity and corresponding index and details pages to both components in parallel. Rule *b)* is an asynchronous rule removing an entity from a body and an adjacent export. Applying rule *a)* to the composite model in Fig. 6, nothing is deleted. Consequently, the composite gluing condition is obviously fulfilled. To obtain the composite model in Fig. 7, variable *name* has to be instantiated by 'book'. Additional references between book, poem, and poet entities have to be added by another editing step.

   Wrt. global consistency, a) is evidently neutral as an intact export/import relation is introduced. The editing step specified by b) is to be considered a critical one since the export interface being edited might be referred to from a remote import interface. A user performing an editing step like this may be warned and suggested to clarify the editing step to other team members. Vice versa, a) could be followed by a notification to the other contributors stating that the exported class is available for other components.

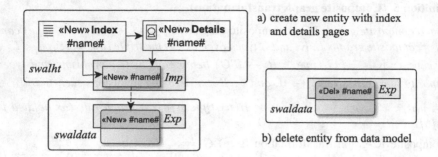

Fig. 8. Synchronous and asynchronous composite model transformation rules

7   Model Merging for Code Generation

Aiming at providing a full life-cycle of model-driven development, code generation as a semantics for composite models is to be investigated. Our long-term goal is to investigate a *distributed* code generation allowing the successive code generation for individual components. This kind of code generation is highly desirable, considering model components that may be protected by law and therefore cannot be transmitted. However, it is left to future work. As a tentative solution, we elaborate a *centralized* code generation instead. Our strategy is based the reuse of existing code generators that

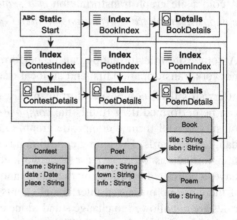

Fig. 9. Merged application model

consume a single model. Hence, a technique to support the merge of a composite model to a single model is required. We provide this technique utilizing the information provided by export and import relations.

Example 4. Fig. 9 shows the result of merging the model shown in Fig. 7: Based on their participation in export and import relations, pairs of objects are identified as related ones and glued together. The resulting model is well-typed because it conforms to the pre-split meta-model. This strategy can also be applied for the merge of meta-models.

Formalization. Composite model merging can be formalized as a colimit construction.

Proposition 3 (Graph merge). *Given a composite graph, there is a unique graph containing its merge result.*

Proof. Considering a composite graph C as a diagram in category GRAPHS$_{TG}$, its colimit consists of a simple graph G and a family of graph mophisms from all local graphs of C to G. The colimit construction is uniquely determined.

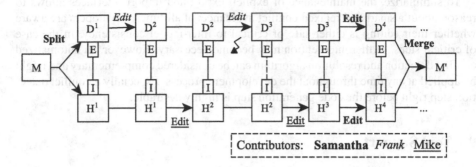

Fig. 10. Scenario for the distributed modeling process

8 Application Scenario

This section provides a simple application scenario to show how the distributed process is applied. The scenario, illustrated in Fig. 10, concerns with web application development based on the SWAL web modeling language. We assume that the language has been subject already to a split activity into domain and hypertext components that was performed by the language developers.

The starting point is monolithic model M conforming to SWAL. M is logically distributed when project manager Samantha performs a split along the given language-level decomposition. The resulting composite model comprises domain model component D and hypertext model component H being interconnected by means of export and import interfaces. Samantha now assigns team members to viewpoints: Frank receives responsibility for domain modeling. Mike becomes the hypertext modeler. The internal details of remote components are hidden to both developers respectively: Frank's scope of visibility is restricted to his assigned component being D. Mike's scope of visibility comprises his assigned component being H, and remote component D's export (cf. the notion of weak composite graphs introduced in Sect. 3). From now on, Frank and Mike perform asynchronous editing steps, reflected in increasing version numbers. Their first steps are neutral to inter-model consistency and do not require conflict handling.

Eventually, the transformation from D^2 to D^3 is a critical editing step threatening global consistency, e.g. the deletion of a model element being visible in the export. Hence, when performing this editing step, Frank receives a warning. His options are: to manually establish communication to Mike clarifying the change, to let a default message be delivered to Mike, to take back the change or to do nothing. In the two former cases, Mike can react by performing an editing step such that consistency is retained. When doing nothing, consistency might be broken. Later on, Samantha performs a synchronous editing step changing both components in parallel. Eventually, she decides that the model components have accomplished a solid state and should be merged for code generation. A global consistency check may be performed before the merge to ensure a valid result. If at some later point in time new requirements are added, further editing can be performed on the components in their state before the merge.

To summarize, the maintenance of explicit export and import interfaces allows to reason about a smart and relaxed conflict avoidance: at all times, developers are aware whether their editing is either safe or critical to inter-model consistency. In the case of critical steps, further intervention may become necessary. However, an automatized conflict detection and resolution algorithm can be considered complementary and might be applied at any time throughout the development process. Especially a conflict detection step right before the code generation step is highly desirable.

9   Tool Support

The core processing of composite models is supported by an existing editor environment based on the Eclipse Modeling Framework. For a set of individual models, wizard tools are provided allowing the derivation of export and import interfaces in order to establish model interconnection. Export and import interfaces are implemented as separate resources with special references, supported by a delegation mechanism that replaces EMF's proxy concept. Furthermore, we have implemented a model transformation language and tool set allowing the specification and execution of editing steps. The transformation language can also be used for model-to-model transformation, e.g., to support a cleanup step before code generation. The tool set is open source being provided at http://www.uni-marburg.de/fb12/swt/forschung/software along with examples and a tutorial. Automation of splitting and merging is left to future work.

10   Related Work

Basic forms of model splitting and joining are considered in [7] where a global model view is split into two local ones with a common interface. The authors show that their forms of model decomposition and integration are in bijective correspondence. In addition, they show that this result can be extended to views with a special form of constraints. While their model decomposition is a special case of our model splitting into two components with identical import and export interfaces, we do not have taken constraints into account yet.

The extraction of sub-models from large models has been considered under the heading of *model slicing*. [3] presents a tool that allows defining model slicers for domain-specific languages by determining a selection of classes and features to extract. [14] provides an elegant formalization of model slicing as it is shown that the sub-models gained from slicing along particular references constitute a lattice. A linear-time algorithm establishing this decomposition is elaborated. These approaches differ from model splitting in so far as they aim at extracting sub-models conforming to the same meta-model as the model to be sliced. In turn, model splitting is integrated into an overlying process: a meta-model is split in several components. Afterwards, models based on these meta-models are split towards these components. The splitting of a model towards components with export and import interfaces is specific to our approach. In [10], model views are constructed along query patterns. The integration of query patterns into our approach may be worthwhile in future.

As for distributed editing, an elaborated strategy for inconsistency detection is provided by Macromodeling [20]. Macromodeling allows integrating multiple models of different modeling languages on type and instance layers. A major objective of macromodeling is the check of global consistency conditions based on logical formulas. However, it does neither envision a specific modeling process nor the use of explicit interfaces. Moreover, explicit interfaces as established by composite models are orthogonal to the Connected Data Objects (CDO) [4] client-server framework for transparent distributed modeling. An integration of composite models with CDO is current work.

The merge of models can be compared to *model weaving* that is implemented by different tools, e.g., Atlas Model Weaver (AMW) [1]. AMW allows the weaving of a set of models by constructing a weave model based on a weave meta-model. It supports the manual and semi-automatic weaving of models by means of heuristic-based transformations. Model merging can also be compared to schema integration [2] where similarities between database schemes are identified in order to merge these schemes into one. Unlike model weaving or schema integration, our model merging does not determine new interrelations but assumes a set of interrelations given by import/export relations. It can be fully automatized exploiting this information. A closely related work to our kind of components and model merging are metamodel components and their composition as presented in [22].

11   Conclusion and Outlook

The global distribution of software development spawns a need for new well-defined software engineering methods. The process presented in this paper is our contribution towards model-driven distributed software development. It proposes split, edit, and merge activities based on composite models being a formally sound modularization mechanism that allows for local consistency checks and systematic transformation.

Future work is the enhancement of existing tool support towards a comprehensive tool environment supporting all parts of the presented distributed modeling process. Firstly, we aim at providing convenient editor support that allows editing components equipped with interfaces at the right level of abstraction. Secondly, splitting and merging activities are to be automatized in adequate ways. It is of our particular interest to find a heuristics that gives reasonable suggestions for splitting. Thirdly, distributed code generation deserves further research. Having a suitable tool support at hand, we are heading towards larger examples that show the scalability of this approach. We are convinced that precisely defined basic operations on composite models are a clear basis for a sound distributed modeling process.

References

1. AMW: Atlas Model Weaver, http://www.eclipse.org/gmt/amw
2. Batini, C., Lenzerini, M., Navathe, S.B.: A comparative analysis of methodologies for database schema integration. ACM Comput. Surv. 18(4), 323–364 (1986)
3. Blouin, A., Combemale, B., Baudry, B., Beaudoux, O.: Modeling Model Slicers. In: Whittle, J., Clark, T., Kühne, T. (eds.) MODELS 2011. LNCS, vol. 6981, pp. 62–76. Springer, Heidelberg (2011)

4. CDO: Eclipse Modeling Framework, http://wiki.eclipse.org/?title=CDO
5. Ceri, S., Fraternali, P., Bongio, A.: Web Modeling Language (WebML): a modeling language for designing Web sites. Computer Networks 33(1-6), 137–157 (2000)
6. Ehrig, H., Ehrig, K., Prange, U., Taentzer, G.: Fundamentals of Algebraic Graph Transformation. Monographs in Theoretical Computer Science. An EATCS Series. Springer (2006)
7. Ehrig, H., Ehrig, K., Ermel, C., Prange, U.: Consistent Integration of Models Based on Views of Visual Languages. In: Fiadeiro, J.L., Inverardi, P. (eds.) FASE 2008. LNCS, vol. 4961, pp. 62–76. Springer, Heidelberg (2008)
8. EMF: Eclipse Modeling Framework (2011), http://www.eclipse.org/emf
9. Goedicke, M., Meyer, T., Taentzer, G.: ViewPoint-oriented Software Development by Distributed Graph Transformation: Towards a Basis for Living with Inconsistencies. In: Proc. 4th IEEE Int. Symposium on Requirements Engineering (RE 1999), University of Limerick, Ireland, June 7-11. IEEE Computer Society (1999) ISBN 0-7695-0188-5
10. Guerra, E., de Lara, J.: Model View Management with Triple Graph Transformation Systems. In: Corradini, A., Ehrig, H., Montanari, U., Ribeiro, L., Rozenberg, G. (eds.) ICGT 2006. LNCS, vol. 4178, pp. 351–366. Springer, Heidelberg (2006)
11. Jurack, S.: Composite Modeling based on Distributed Graph Transformation and the Eclipse Modeling Framework. dissertation, Philipps-Universität Marburg (2012)
12. Jurack, S., Taentzer, G.: Towards Composite Model Transformations Using Distributed Graph Transformation Concepts. In: Schürr, A., Selic, B. (eds.) MODELS 2009. LNCS, vol. 5795, pp. 226–240. Springer, Heidelberg (2009)
13. Jurack, S., Taentzer, G.: Transformation of Typed Composite Graphs with Inheritance and Containment Structures. Fundamenta Informaticae 118(1-2), 97–134 (2012)
14. Kelsen, P., Ma, Q.: A Modular Model Composition Technique. In: Rosenblum, D.S., Taentzer, G. (eds.) FASE 2010. LNCS, vol. 6013, pp. 173–187. Springer, Heidelberg (2010)
15. Kraus, A., Knapp, A., Koch, N.: Model-Driven Generation of Web Applications in UWE. In: Proceedings of the 3rd International Workshop on Model-Driven Web Engineering, MDWE 2007, Como, Italy (July 17, 2007)
16. Magic Draw, http://www.magicdraw.com
17. Mougenot, A., Blanc, X., Gervais, M.-P.: D-Praxis: A Peer-to-Peer Collaborative Model Editing Framework. In: Senivongse, T., Oliveira, R. (eds.) DAIS 2009. LNCS, vol. 5523, pp. 16–29. Springer, Heidelberg (2009)
18. OMG: The Essential MOF (EMOF) Model, sec. 12 (2010), http://www.omg.org/cgi-bin/doc?formal/2006-01-01.pdf
19. Papyrus UML, http://www.papyrusuml.org
20. Salay, R., Mylopoulos, J., Easterbrook, S.M.: Managing models through macromodeling. In: 23rd IEEE/ACM International Conference on Automated Software Engineering (ASE 2008), L'Aquila, Italy, September 15-19, pp. 447–450. IEEE (2008)
21. Strüber, D., Taentzer, G., Jurack, S., Schäfer, T.: Towards a Distributed Modeling Process Based on Composite Models: Long Version. Tech. rep., Philipps-Universität Marburg (2013), http://www.uni-marburg.de/fb12/forschung/berichte/berichteinformtk
22. Weisemöller, I., Schürr, A.: Formal Definition of MOF 2.0 Metamodel Components and Composition. In: Czarnecki, K., Ober, I., Bruel, J.-M., Uhl, A., Völter, M. (eds.) MODELS 2008. LNCS, vol. 5301, pp. 386–400. Springer, Heidelberg (2008)

Change Propagation due to Uncertainty Change

Rick Salay, Jan Gorzny, and Marsha Chechik

Department of Computer Science, University of Toronto, Toronto, Canada
{rsalay,jgorzny,chechik}@cs.toronto.edu

Abstract. Uncertainty is ubiquitous in software engineering; however, it has been typically handled in adhoc and informal ways within software models. Automated change propagation is recognized as a key tool for managing the accidental complexity that comes with multiple interrelated models. In this paper, we address change propagation in the context of model uncertainty and consider the case where changes in the level of uncertainty in a model can be propagated to related models. We define such uncertainty change propagation using our earlier formalization and develop automated propagation algorithms using an SMT solver. A preliminary evaluation shows that the approach is feasible.

1 Introduction

Uncertainty is ubiquitous in software engineering. It has been studied in different contexts including requirements engineering [3], software processes [7] and adaptive systems [21]. An area that has not received much attention is the occurrence of uncertainty in software models. Model uncertainty can be the result of incomplete information about the problem domain [24], alternative design possibilities [22], stakeholder conflicts [18], etc.

Despite its importance, uncertainty is typically not treated in a first-class way in modeling languages and as a result, its treatment is adhoc, e.g., including informal notes in the model. To illustrate what we mean by model uncertainty, consider Fig. 1 which shows a UML class and sequence diagram that are part of a hypothetical automotive design model that focuses on the control of the power windows. The sequence diagram shows a scenario in which a security threat is detected and the car responds by closing the windows. However, the modelers are uncertain about various facets of the design, and their points of uncertainty are indicated using the notes attached to the model elements. The top note in the sequence diagram indicates that they are not sure whether to keep the threat detection functionality separate from the car or to put it into the car. The bottom note expresses uncertainty about whether the windows should be disabled after being closed. A corresponding note can be found for the disable() operation in the class diagram since if the message is never sent, the operation may not be needed either. Finally, the other note in the class diagram shows that other operations may be needed.

Informal approaches such as the one we have described are adequate for capturing uncertainty information as *documentation* but they do not lend themselves to automation and mechanisms such as change propagation. To help address this problem, in previous work we have proposed a language-independent approach for expressing model uncertainty using model annotations with formal semantics [20].

V. Cortellessa and D. Varró (Eds.): FASE 2013, LNCS 7793, pp. 21–36, 2013.

The *change propagation problem* [13] has been defined as follows: given a set of primary changes that have been made to software, what additional, secondary, changes are needed to maintain consistency within the system? Change propagation has been proposed as a mechanism to help manage and automate model evolution. Existing approaches to change propagation focus exclusively on model content changes (e.g., [23], [2],[15]); however, other aspects of a model may be subject to change as well: e.g., comprehensibility, completeness, etc. Model *uncertainty* is one such aspect. Changes that increase or decrease the level of uncertainty as the model evolves can force further model changes, both within the same model and across different related models – thus, uncertainty change is another context in which an automated change propagation mechanism could be used.

The key contribution of this paper is an automated approach to *uncertainty change propagation* within models. More specifically, first we identify and distinguish the problem of model uncertainty change from model content change. Second, we define the conditions for uncertainty reducing and uncertainty increasing change propagation, independently of how the uncertainty is expressed. Third, we instantiate these conditions for our formal annotation method for expressing uncertainty and define generic algorithms and tooling for computing uncertainty change propagations parameterized by a modeling language.

The remainder of the paper is organized as follows. In Sec. 2, we develop and illustrate a general approach for understanding uncertainty change and its propagation. In Sec. 3, we review the foundations of our formal annotation method for expressing model uncertainty and in Sec. 4, we apply the uncertainty change approach from Sec. 2 to this annotation method. In Sec. 5, the algorithms for uncertainty change propagation are described. In Sec. 6, they are evaluated by varying the key problem characteristics with randomly generated models. We discuss related work in Sec. 7 and make concluding remarks in Sec. 8.

2   Uncertainty Change Propagation

In this section, we develop the concept of uncertainty change propagation.

Meaning of Uncertainty. Uncertainty can be expressed as a *set of possibilities*. We can apply this approach to expressing uncertainty within a model by saying that it corresponds to the set of possible models, or *concretizations*, that are admissible given the uncertainty. A natural way to define this set is to indicate *points of uncertainty* within a model. Although we can do so using informal notes, as in the models EX1 and EX2 of Fig. 1 (this example was described in the introduction), we present a precise, formal approach in Sec. 3. A point of uncertainty can be viewed as a constraint whose satisfaction we are unsure about, so that not all of the concretizations satisfy it. For example, the note "not sure we need the operation disable()" corresponds to the constraint "class PowerWindow has the operation disable()" which may not hold in all possible models corresponding to EX1. The points of uncertainty of model EX1 in Fig. 1 suggest that the set of concretizations of EX1, denoted by [EX1], contains all class diagrams that extend EX1 by adding zero or more operations to classes Controller and/or PowerWindow and may omit the operation disable(). Similarly, the notes attached to EX2 are its

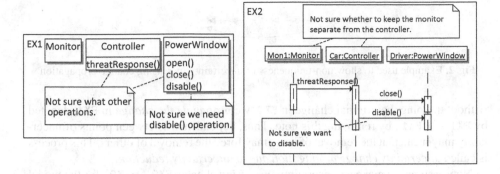

Fig. 1. A pair of related models containing uncertainty

points of uncertainty, suggesting that [EX2] contains the variants in which Mon1 and Car are merged or distinct as well as those in which the message disable() is omitted.

Uncertainty Change. A *model change* typically consists of additions, deletions and changes to the elements of the model. When we consider a model with uncertainty, an additional dimension of change becomes possible: the *level of uncertainty* may change. For example, replacing the name of the object Mon1 to MyMonitor in EX2 changes the model content but does not affect the uncertainty. However, removing the note on the message disable() reduces the uncertainty in the model, because we no longer consider concretizations that omit this message, but does not change the content of the model. Another way to change uncertainty is to increase it. For example, adding a note to say that we are not sure we need the close() message increases uncertainty without changing the content of the model.

These examples suggest that an uncertainty reducing (increasing) change to a model corresponds to reducing (increasing) the number of points of uncertainty. However, when the constraints represented by points of uncertainty depend on each other, a change at one point of uncertainty can force a corresponding change at other points of uncertainty, both *within the same model* and *in related models*. We call this process *uncertainty change propagation*. For example, suppose that EX1 and EX2 are subject to the following well-formedness constraints:

wff1 Every message in a sequence diagram must begin on a lifeline.
wff2 Every message in a sequence diagram must correspond to an operation of the message target object's class.

Assume that we perform an uncertainty reducing change in EX2, denoted by EX2 → EX2'. Specifically, we remove the note attached to the message disable() (i.e., we become sure that disable() occurs), resulting in the model EX2'. This message is contained in every concretization of EX2', and, by wff2, the only well-formed concretizations of EX1 are those containing the operation disable(), i.e., the presence of this operation is *forced* by the change to EX2 and the constraint wff2. However, now the note attached to the operation disable() no longer describes a point of uncertainty because there are no concretizations that omit this operation. To repair this violation

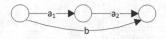

Fig. 2. Example used to show non-uniqueness of uncertainty increasing change propagation

without undoing the original change in EX2, we *propagate the change* in EX1, denoted by EX1 --→ EX1′, by removing this note. Thus, dependencies between points of uncertainty may mean that the removal of some may force the removal of others. This process is called *uncertainty change propagation due to uncertainty reduction.*

Now assume we make an uncertainty *increasing* change, EX2 → EX2′, for the model EX2 in Fig. 1. The change adds a point of uncertainty as a note saying that we are not sure whether Mon1 is needed. The well-formedness constraint wff1 implies that any concretization that omits Mon1 must also omit the message threatResponse(); however, this is not possible because there is no uncertainty indicated about the presence of this message. That is, unless the presence of this message is also made uncertain, wff1 "invalidates" our newly added point of uncertainty. In order to repair this violation and retain the new point of uncertainty, we make a further, propagated, change, EX2′ --→ EX2″, by adding a note to the message threatResponse() indicating that its presence is now uncertain. Thus, when an added point of uncertainty is invalidated by dependencies on existing constraints (e.g., well-formedness), we may need to relax these constraints by adding (a minimal set of) further points of uncertainty. This process is called *uncertainty change propagation due to uncertainty increase.*

Unlike the case of uncertainty reducing change propagation, here the required propagated change may not be unique, i.e., there may be multiple suitable minimal sets of uncertainty points that can be added and user input is required to decide among these. For example, consider the directed graph in Fig. 2 and let one of the well-formedness constraints for this graph be "if there is a path between two nodes then there is a direct link between them". Assume we add a point of uncertainty to indicate that we are unsure whether edge b exists. The well-formedness constraint forces this edge to exist due to the presence of the path $a_1 a_2$, and so this new point of uncertainty is invalidated. This can be repaired minimally in two distinct ways: saying that we are uncertain either about the existence of edge a_1 or edge a_2, requiring a user decision.

In the next two sections, we instantiate these concepts for a particular type of model with uncertainty called *MAVO*.

3   Background

In this section, we briefly review the concepts of a formal approach, introduced in [20], for defining a model with uncertainty called *MAVO*. A *MAVO* model is a conventional model whose elements are marked with special annotations representing points of uncertainty.

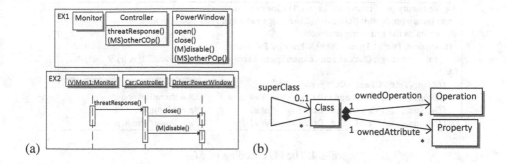

Fig. 3. (a) The models from Fig. 1 expressed using *MAVO* annotations. (b) A simplified meta-model of the UML class diagram language.

Definition 1. *A MAVO model M consists of a base model, denoted bs(M), and a set of annotations on the base model. Let T be the metamodel of bs(M). Then, [M] denotes the set of T models called the* concretizations *of M. M is called consistent iff [M] ≠ ∅.*

For example, Fig. 3(a) shows the uncertainty expressed using notes in Fig. 1 via *MAVO* annotations. The base model $bs(\texttt{EX1})$ of model EX1 is the class diagram that remains when the annotations are stripped away.

MAVO provides four types of annotations, each adding support for a different type of uncertainty in a model: Annotating an element with M indicates that we are unsure about whether it should exist in the model; otherwise, the element does exist. Thus, in EX1, the M-annotation on the operation $\texttt{disable()}$ indicates that it may or may not exist in a concretization. Annotating an element with S indicates that we are unsure whether it should actually be a collection of elements; otherwise, it is just one element. This is illustrated by the S-annotation on operation $\texttt{otherCOp()}$ in EX1. This annotation represents a set of operations in a concretization. The fact that it also has an M annotation means that this set could be empty. Annotating an element with V indicates that we are unsure about whether it should actually be merged with other elements; otherwise, it is distinct. Thus, we use the V-annotated object Mon1 to consider concretizations in which it is merged with other objects such as Car. Finally, annotating the entire model with INC indicates that we are unsure about whether it is complete. For our simple example in Fig. 3(a), both models are assumed to be complete, and so we omit this annotation.

Formalizing *MAVO* Annotations. A central benefit of using *MAVO* annotations is that they have formal semantics and thus, the set of concretizations for any *MAVO* model is precisely defined. In this section, we describe this semantics.

A metamodel represents a set of models and can be expressed as a First Order Logic (FOL) theory.

Definition 2 (Metamodel). *A metamodel is an FOL theory $T = \langle \Sigma, \Phi \rangle$, where Σ is the signature with sorts and predicates representing the element types, and Φ is a set of sentences representing the well-formedness constraints. The models that conform to*

Σ_{B1} has unary predicates Ct(Class), TR(Operation)), ...,
 and binary predicates CtOwnsTR(Class, Operation), ...
Φ_{B1} contains the following sentences:
 (Complete) $(\forall x : \text{Class} \cdot \text{Ct}(x) \lor \text{Mn}(x) \lor \text{PW}(x)) \land$
  $(\forall x : \text{Class}, y : \text{Operation} \cdot \text{ownedOperation}(x, y) \Rightarrow (\text{CtOwnsTR}(x, y) \lor ...)) \land ...$
Ct:

(Exists$_\text{Ct}$) $\exists x : \text{Class} \cdot \text{Ct}(x)$	Ct = Controller
(Unique$_\text{Ct}$) $\forall x, x' : \text{Class} \cdot \text{Ct}(x) \land \text{Ct}(x') \Rightarrow x = x'$	TR = threatResponse
(Distinct$_\text{Ct-Mn}$) $\forall x : \text{Class} \cdot \text{Ct}(x) \Rightarrow \neg \text{Mn}(x)$	Mn = Monitor
(Distinct$_\text{Ct-PW}$) $\forall x : \text{Class} \cdot \text{Ct}(x) \Rightarrow \neg \text{PW}(x)$	PW = PowerWindow

Fig. 4. The FO encoding of M_{B1}

T *are the finite FO Σ-structures that satisfy Φ according to the usual FO satisfaction relation. We denote the set of models with metamodel T by Mod(T).*

The simple class diagram metamodel in Fig. 3(b) fits this definition if we interpret boxes as sorts and edges as predicates comprising Σ_{CD} (where CD stands for "class diagram") and take the multiplicity constraints (translated to FOL) as comprising Φ_{CD}.

Like a metamodel, a *MAVO* model represents a set of models (i.e., its concretizations) and thus can also be expressed as an FOL theory. Specifically, for a *MAVO* model M, we construct a theory $FO(M)$ s.t. $Mod(FO(M)) = [M]$. We proceed as follows. (1) Let $B = bs(M)$ be the base model of a *MAVO* model M. We define a new *MAVO* model M_B which has B as its base model and its sole concretization, i.e., $bs(M_B) = B$ and $[M_B] = \{B\}$. We call M_B the *ground* model of M. (2) To construct the FOL encoding of M_B, $FO(M_B)$, we extend T to include a unary predicate for each element in B and a binary predicate for each relation instance between elements in B. Then, we add constraints to ensure that the only first order structure that satisfies the resulting theory is B itself. (3) We construct $FO(M)$ from $FO(M_B)$ by *removing* constraints corresponding to the annotations in M. This constraint relaxation allows more concretizations and thus represents increasing uncertainty. For example, if an element e in M is annotated with S then the constraint that forces e to occur at most once in every concretization is removed.

We illustrate the above construction using the *MAVO* class diagram EX1 in Fig. 3(a). (1) Let B1 = $bs($EX1$)$ be the base model of EX1 and M_{B1} be the corresponding ground *MAVO* model.

(2) We have: $FO(M_{B1}) = \langle \Sigma_{CD} \cup \Sigma_{B1}, \Phi_{CD} \cup \Phi_{B1} \rangle$ (see Definition 2), where Σ_{B1} and Φ_{B1} are model B1-specific predicates and constraints, defined in Fig. 4. They extend the signature and constraints for CD models described in Fig. 3(b). For conciseness, we abbreviate element names in Fig. 4, e.g., Controller becomes Ct, threatResponse becomes TR, etc. We refer to Σ_{B1} and Φ_{B1} as the *MAVO* predicates and constraints, respectively.

Since $FO(M_{B1})$ extends CD, the FO structures that satisfy $FO(M_{B1})$ are the class diagrams that satisfy the constraint set Φ_{B1} in Fig. 4. Assume N is such a class diagram. The *MAVO* constraint *Complete* ensures that N contains no more elements or relation instances than B1. Now consider the class Ct in B1. *Exists$_\text{Ct}$* says that N contains at least one class Ct, *Unique$_\text{Ct}$* – that it contains no more than one class Ct, and the clauses $Distinct_{Ct-*}$ – that the class Ct is different from all the other classes. Similar *MAVO* constraints are given for all other elements and relation instances in EX1. These constraints ensure that $FO(M_{B1})$ has exactly one concretization and thus $N = B1$.

(3) Relaxing the *MAVO* constraints Φ_{B1} allows additional concretizations and represents a type of uncertainty indicated by an annotation. For example, if we use the INC annotation to indicate that B1 is incomplete, we can express this by removing the *Complete* clause from Φ_{B1} and thereby allow concretizations to be class diagrams that extend B1. Similarly, expressing the effect of the M, S and V annotations for an element E correspond to relaxing Φ_{B1} by removing $Exists_E$, $Unique_E$ and $Distinct_{E-*}$ clauses, respectively. For example, removing the $Distinct_{Ct-*}$ clauses is equivalent to marking the class Ct with V (i.e., Controller may or may not be distinct from another class).

Thus, for each pair (a, e) of model M, where a is a *MAVO* annotation and e is a model element, let $\varphi_{(a,e)}$ be the corresponding *MAVO* constraint that is removed from the FO encoding of M. For the above example, $\varphi_{(V,Ct)} = Distinct_{Ct-*}$.

4   Formalizing Uncertainty Change Propagation

In this section, we formalize the notion of uncertainty change propagation between models with uncertainty expressed using *MAVO*. We then define algorithms for uncertainty reducing/increasing change propagation based on this formalization.

In Sec. 2, we argued that a point of uncertainty corresponds to a constraint which we are not sure holds. That is, there must exist a concretization for which it doesn't hold, otherwise we would be certain about the constraint and it couldn't represent a point of uncertainty. Thus, a validity requirement for a point of uncertainty is that there should be some concretization in which it does not hold.

In the FO encoding for a *MAVO* model, we attempt to guarantee this validity requirement by explicitly omitting the constraint $\varphi_{(a,e)}$ corresponding to each annotation a of an element e. However, this may not always be sufficient since the constraint may still be implied by others (e.g., well-formedness), making the annotation an invalid point of uncertainty. When all annotations satisfy the validity requirement, we say that the *MAVO* model is in *reduced normal form* (RNF).

Definition 3 (Reduced Normal Form (RNF)). *Let M be a MAVO model with $FO(M) = \langle \Sigma, \Phi \rangle$ and let Φ_A be the set of MAVO constraints corresponding to the annotations in M. M is in* reduced normal form *(RNF) iff $\forall \varphi_{(a,e)} \in \Phi_A \cdot \neg(\Phi \Rightarrow \varphi_{(a,e)})$.*

When a model is in RNF, the validity requirement holds for all of its annotations: if the *MAVO* constraint $\varphi_{(a,e)}$ for an annotation a of an element e does not follow from Φ, there must be a concretization that does not satisfy $\varphi_{(a,e)}$. We now use RNF as a way to formally define the notion of uncertainty reducing and increasing change propagation for *MAVO* models.

Definition 4. *Let M and M' be MAVO models. $M \dashrightarrow M'$ is an uncertainty reducing propagated change if $[M] = [M']$, and M' is obtained by removing annotations so that M' is in RNF.*

Definition 5. *Let M and M' be MAVO models. M --→ M' is an* uncertainty increasing propagated change *if* $[M] \subset [M']$, *and M' is obtained by adding a minimal number of annotations to M so that M' is in RNF.*

To illustrate the application of these definitions, we recast the uncertainty change propagation examples of Sec. 2 in terms of *MAVO* annotations. To be able to express *cross-model* propagation in the FO encoding, we treat both diagrams in Fig. 3(a) as part of a single bigger model. We resolve naming conflicts by appending the model name to the element name, e.g., `disable_EX1`. In the first example, we perform an uncertainty reducing change EX2 → EX2' by removing the M annotation attached to the message `disable()` and thus $\Phi_{EX2'}$ contains the additional *MAVO* constraint $Exists_{\texttt{disable\_EX2}}$. Together, $Exists_{\texttt{disable\_EX2}}$ and wff2 imply the constraint $Exists_{\texttt{disable\_EX1}}$, forcing the existence of the operation `disable()` in EX1. However, this operation has an M annotation on the operation `disable()`, so EX1 is not in RNF. We repair the problem by performing a change propagation EX1 --→ EX1' (Definition 4), removing the annotation on the operation `disable()`.

In the second example, assume that an uncertainty increasing change EX2 → EX2' is made by adding an M annotation to Mon1 to indicate that we are not sure whether it exists. However, since the message `threatResponse()` has no M annotation, $\Phi_{EX2'}$ contains the constraint $Exists_{\texttt{threatResponse}}$ and together with wff1, this implies the constraint $Exists_{\texttt{Mon1}}$. Thus, EX2' is not in RNF. Definition 5 says that to repair this, we should propagate the change, EX2' --→ EX2'', by adding a minimal set of annotations that put EX2'' into RNF. In this case, it is sufficient to add an M annotation to the message `threatResponse()` so that the above implication with wff1 does not happen. While this solution is unique and minimal, this is not the case in general (recall the example in Fig. 2).

5   Uncertainty Change Propagation Algorithms

Definitions 4 and 5 provide a specification for uncertainty change propagation. We now describe algorithms for these. Recall that *MAVO* constraints in a FO encoding of a model M correspond to *missing* annotations in M, so adding an annotation a to an element e in M is equivalent to removing the corresponding *MAVO* constraint $\varphi_{(a,e)}$ from the encoding, and vice versa.

5.1   Uncertainty Reducing Change Propagation

Fig. 5(a) shows Algorithm URCP for computing the change propagation due to an uncertainty reducing change. The objective of this algorithm is to put the input model M with $FO(M) = \langle \Sigma, \Phi \rangle$ into RNF (see Definition 3). The main loop in lines 3-16 achieves this by iterating through all annotations (a, e) of M. It then checks whether $\Phi \Rightarrow \varphi_{(a,e)}$, where $\varphi_{(a,e)}$ is the *MAVO* constraint corresponding to this annotation. If so, the annotation can be removed.

First, a satisfiability check is made in line 4 to find a satisfying instance I of $(\Phi \cup \{\neg \varphi_{(a,e)}\})$. If one is *not* found, it means that $\Phi \Rightarrow \varphi_{(a,e)}$ and so the annotation a for an element e in the output model M' can be removed (line 13). Otherwise, I is used to find other annotations that can also be removed (lines 5-11). For each annotation (a', e'), we check whether I is also a counter-example to the corresponding *MAVO* constraint $\varphi_{(a',e')}$. For example, if (a', e') is an M-annotation on some element e', the call *NotExists*(e', I) checks whether e' is missing in I. If so, then $\Phi \not\Rightarrow \varphi_{(a',e')}$, and the annotation can be removed from further consideration (line 9). Conditions for annotations S and V are checked similarly. The strategy of using a satisfying instance to more quickly eliminate annotations is inspired by a similar strategy used for computing the backbone of a propositional formula (i.e., the set of propositional variables that follow from the formula) with a SAT solver [11].

Correctness. Originally, M' is equal to M (line 1). An annotation a is removed from the element e in M' (line 13) only if the condition $\Phi \cup \{\neg\varphi_{(a,e)}\}$ is not satisfiable (line 4). Furthermore, every annotation that passes this condition is removed from consideration (set A) either on line 9 or line 15. Thus, M' is in RNF, and the algorithm correctly implements Definition 4.

For example, consider the first scenario illustrated in Sec. 4. After the first uncertainty reducing change, the annotation set A is $\{(\texttt{otherCOp\_EX1}, \text{M}), (\texttt{otherCOp\_EX1}, \text{S}), (\texttt{Mon1\_EX2}, \text{V}), (\texttt{disable\_EX1}, \text{M})\}$. Checking $(\texttt{disable\_EX1}, \text{M})$ results in UNSAT, so the M annotation is removed from the element $\texttt{disable\_EX1}$, and the tuple $(\texttt{disable\_EX1}, \text{M})$ is removed from A. Checking all other pairs in A returns SAT, so the corresponding annotations are not removed.

Complexity. A *MAVO* model restricted only to M annotations (a.k.a. a *May* model) can be seen as equivalent to a propositional formula where the M-annotated elements are the propositional variables [5]. In this case, the RNF corresponds to removing the elements in the backbone of this formula. Thus, the complexity of Algorithm URCP is at least that of computing the backbone of a propositional formula, which is NP-hard [8]. Furthermore, all other computations in the algorithm are polynomial time, so we can conclude that URCP is also NP-hard. Algorithm URCP uses a SAT solver (with that complexity). Since the outer loop is bounded by the number of annotations n_A, the SAT solver is not called more than n_A times.

5.2 Uncertainty Increasing Change Propagation

The algorithm utilizes a solver for the partial maximum satisfiability (MAXSAT) problem (e.g., see [6]). The partial MAXSAT problem takes a set of *hard* clauses Φ_H and a set of *soft* clauses Φ_S and finds a maximal subset $\Phi_{S'} \subseteq \Phi_S$ such that $\Phi_H \cup \Phi_{S'}$ is satisfiable. Thus, a solution (which may not be unique) represents a minimal relaxation of the soft constraints that with the hard constraints will allow satisfiability.

Fig. 5(b) gives an algorithm for computing the change propagation due to an uncertainty increasing change using partial MAXSAT. The input is a *MAVO* model M with $FO(M) = \langle \Sigma, \Phi_T \cup \Phi_M \rangle$ and a subset *New* of annotations of M identified as new due to an uncertainty increasing change. Φ_T are the well-formedness rules for M from its metamodel T and Φ_M are the *MAVO* constraints for the annotations missing from M. We assume that M was in RNF prior to adding annotations *New* but now may not be – this assumption is used in the discussion about correctness below.

Since M is not necessarily in RNF, it may be that $\Phi_T \cup \Phi_M \Rightarrow \varphi_{(a,e)}$ for some annotations $(a, e) \in$ *New*. Thus, according to Definition 5, we must add a minimal set

(a)

Algorithm: URCP
Input: *MAVO* model M with FO encoding
$\qquad FO(M) = \langle \Sigma, \Phi \rangle$
Output: *MAVO* model M' satisfying Def. 4
1:   $M' \leftarrow M$
2:   $A \leftarrow Annotations(M)$
3:   **for** $(a, e) \in A$ **do**
4:      **if** $SAT(\langle \Sigma, \Phi \cup \{\neg\varphi_{(e,a)}\}\rangle, I)$ **then**
       // I is a satisfying instance
5:        **for** $(a', e') \in A$ **do**
6:          **if** $(a'$ is M **and** $NotExists(e', I))$
7:          **or** $(a'$ is S **and** $NotUnique(e', I))$
8:          **or** $(a'$ is V **and** $NotDistinct(e', I))$ **then**
9:            $A \leftarrow A \setminus \{(a', e')\}$
10:          **endif**
11:        **endfor**
12:     **else**
13:        remove annotation a from e in M'
14:     **endif**
15:     $A \leftarrow A \setminus \{(a, e)\}$
16:    **endfor**
17: **return** M'

(b)

Algorithm: UICP
Input: *MAVO* model M with FO encoding
$\qquad FO(M) = \langle \Sigma, \Phi_T \cup \Phi_M \rangle$,
$\qquad$ a subset *New* of *Annotations*(M)
$\qquad$ identified as new
Output: *MAVO* model M' satisfying Def. 5
1:   $\Phi_{soft} \leftarrow \Phi_M$
2:   $\Phi_{hard} \leftarrow \Phi_T \cup \{\neg\varphi_{(a,e)} | (a, e) \in New\}$
3:   **if** $MAXSAT(\Phi_{soft}, \Phi_{hard}, \Phi_{relax})$ **then**
4:     **return** $M' \leftarrow M \cup \{(a, e) | \varphi_{(a,e) \in \Phi_{relax}}\}$
5:   **else**
6:     **return** ERROR
7:   **endif**

Fig. 5. Algorithms to compute the change propagation of *MAVO* model $M \dashrightarrow M'$: (a) due to an uncertainty reducing change; (b) due to an uncertainty increasing change

of annotations from M so that this implication no longer holds for any *New* annotation. We accomplish this by using MAXSAT to minimally relax Φ_M.

In line 1, the *MAVO* constraints Φ_M are set as the *soft* constraints since our objective is to find a minimal set of these to relax. The *hard* constraints, set in line 2, consist of the well-formedness rules and the negations of the *MAVO* constraints for the *New* annotations. Line 3 makes the MAXSAT call, and the output M' is constructed in line 4 by adding the annotations corresponding to the relaxed clauses. If no possible relaxation exists, the algorithm ends in error (line 6). This means that some of the *MAVO* constraints for new annotations are implied directly by the well-formedness constraints and so removing some new annotations is unavoidable in order for M to be in RNF.

Correctness and complexity. Since MAXSAT is guaranteed to find a relaxation (if one exists), the *MAVO* constraints for the annotations in *New* will not be implied by $FO(M')$. Furthermore since we assumed that M was already in RNF prior to adding the new annotations, none of the *MAVO* constraints for the remaining annotations (i.e., other than the new annotations) will be implied by $FO(M')$. Thus, M' is in RNF, and the UICP correctly produces the result as specified by Definition 5.

For example, consider the second scenario illustrated in Sec. 4. After the first uncertainty increasing change, Φ_{soft} is $\{Exists_{Monitor}, Unique_{Monitor}, Distinct_{Monitor}, Exists_{Controller}, \dots \}$, and Φ_{hard} is $(\neg Exists_{Mon1} \cup \Phi_T)$. MAXSAT shows that the constraint for $(Mon1, M)$ is implied, so one fix could be setting M' to M with $(\text{threatResponse}, M)$ since $Exists_{threatResponse}$ would be in Φ_{relax}.

UICP consists of single call to a partial MAXSAT algorithm and thus its complexity is equivalent to MAXSAT. For example, the implementation reported in [6] calls a SAT solver is called at most $(3n - n_A) + 1$ times, where n is the number of elements in M and n_A is the number of annotations in M.

6 Experiments

We performed a series of experiments to investigate the following research questions related to the scalability of automated uncertainty change propagation:

RQ1. How is uncertainty change propagation affected by how constrained the model is?

RQ2. How is uncertainty change propagation affected by the level of uncertainty in the model?

RQ1 helps us understand the impact of well-formedness constraints while RQ2 is related to the number of annotations.

Experimental Design. We conducted four experiments, to study each of RQ1 and RQ2 with uncertainty reducing or increasing change propagation. In our experiments, we assumed that our models are untyped randomly generated graphs. This is a reasonable simplification since typing information can be seen as a form of constraint. We discretized the space of random models into four size categories defined by the following ranges for the number of nodes: $(0, 25]$, $(25, 50]$, $(50, 75]$, $(75, 100]$ (the same categories have been used in experiments in [17]).

In the RQ1 experiments, we assumed a fixed graph density[1] of 0.11. We also assumed that a fixed percentage of model elements, 36%, are *MAVO*-annotated. Of the annotations, 48% were M, 33% were S and 43% were V (the numbers add up to greater than 100% because some elements are multiply annotated). The values of these parameters correspond to the average percentages of the corresponding annotations that we have observed in the existing case studies using *MAVO* [20,19].

To vary the degree to which the model is constrained, for each randomly generated model we computed a set of constraints that guaranteed that $k\%$ of the annotations would either be removed (for uncertainty reducing change propagation) or added (for uncertainty increasing change propagation). We considered the values of k in the set $\{0, 25, 50, 75, 100\}$.

To understand how the constraints for uncertainty reducing change propagation were generated, assume that a randomly generated *MAVO* model has n annotations. We first choose $n' = n * k/100$ of the annotations arbitrarily. Then we generate a new well-formedness constraint $\varphi_0 \Rightarrow \varphi_1 \Rightarrow \ldots \Rightarrow \varphi_{n'}$, where φ_0 is the *MAVO* constraint for an arbitrarily chosen missing annotation and the remainder are the *MAVO* constraints for the n' annotations. Since φ_0 is the *MAVO* constraint for a missing annotation, it must therefore hold, and so all the remaining sentences are implied. This causes the uncertainty reducing change propagation algorithm to remove the corresponding annotations.

---

[1] Graph density is the ratio of the number of edges to the square of the number of nodes.

For uncertainty increasing change propagation, assume that the randomly generated *MAVO* model has n missing annotations. We first choose $n' = n * k/100$ of the missing annotations arbitrarily. Then we create a new constraint $(\varphi_1 \vee \varphi_2 \vee \ldots \vee \varphi_{n'}) \Rightarrow \varphi_0$, where φ_0 is the *MAVO* constraint for an arbitrarily chosen *new* annotation and the remaining are the *MAVO* constraints for the n' annotations. Since these n' annotations are missing, all of the constraints φ_i, for $1 \leq i \leq n'$, must hold. Furthermore, each implies φ_0. Thus, the uncertainty increasing change propagation algorithm is forced to add all n' annotations in order to achieve RNF.

In the RQ2 experiments, we used the same graph density (0.11) as for RQ1 but varied the total percentage of annotations using values in the set $\{25, 50, 75, 100\}$ [2] while keeping the same relative percentages of each annotation type as for RQ1. In addition, we fixed how the model is constrained, at $k = 50\%$.

Overall, for each RQ1 experiment, we produced 20 test configurations (four sizes times five constraint levels). For each RQ2 experiment, we had 16 test configurations (four sizes times four uncertainty levels). Each test configuration was run up to 20 times – fewer if the average time of processing converged to a desired 95% confidence interval (using the Student's t-distribution).

Implementation. We used the Z3 SMT solver[3] for both algorithms. The built-in theory of uninterpreted functions and support for quantifiers made it convenient for expressing the *MAVO* FO encoding. In addition, Z3 provides an implementation of MAXSAT based on Fu and Malik [6]. Z3 v.4.1 was used for URCP while Z3 v.3.2 was used for UICP because v.4.1 had bugs in the MAXSAT implementation.

Each randomly generated model was generated in eCore[4] and then translated to SMTLib[5] using Python as input to Z3. All tests were run on a laptop with an Intel Core i7 2.8GHz processor and 8GB of RAM.

Results. Figs. 6 and 7 summarize the obtained results for the RQ1 and RQ2 experiments, respectively. The RQ1 experiment for uncertainty reduction in Fig. 6(a) shows a surprising result: the time does not seem to be significantly affected by how constrained the model is. An analysis of the URCP algorithm in Fig. 5 suggests the reason for this. Changing an annotation is much more expensive than not changing it because the former only happens when the SMT solver returns UNSAT (line 13) which requires it to consider all concretizations. Thus, on the one hand, adding more constraints should reduce the SMT solving time because it has fewer concretizations to consider. On the other hand, our constraints are designed to increase the number of changes to annotations, and so URCP is forced to perform the more expensive processing that offsets the speed gain. The results for uncertainty increase in Fig. 6(b) are similar but slightly more variable. In both uncertainty reducing and increasing cases, there seems to be consistent (but small) dip in propagation time going from 0% to 25% constrainedness. This may suggest that a small amount of constraint is optimal.

---

[2] The case of 0% annotations is omitted because no propagation occurs.

[3] http://research.microsoft.com/en-us/um/redmond/projects/z3/

[4] http://www.eclipse.org/modeling/emf/?project=emf

[5] http://www.smtlib.org/

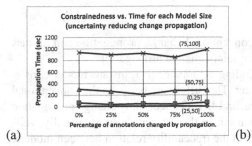
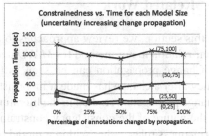

(a)   (b)

Fig. 6. RQ1 results for (a) uncertainty reducing change propagation, and (b) uncertainty increasing change propagation experiments

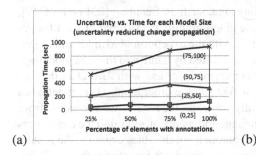
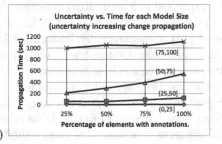

(a)   (b)

Fig. 7. RQ2 results for (a) uncertainty reducing change propagation, and (b) uncertainty increasing change propagation experiments

Both of the RQ2 experiments in Fig. 7 exhibit a similar linear increase in propagation time with increasing uncertainty. Adding annotations increases the number of concretizations so an increasing propagation time is to be expected. The linear relationship is a desirable outcome given that the number of concretizations increases exponentially relative to the number of annotations.

In summary, although in all four experiments the propagation time increased exponentially with model size, as is expected when using a SMT solver, the time was relatively unaffected by degree of constrainedness and increases linearly with the degree of uncertainty. Both of these positive results point to the feasibility of tool support for uncertainty change propagation.

Threats to Validity. The use of randomly generated models in our experiments is a threat to validity because they may not correctly reflect change propagation behaviour on real models. Another threat to validity is our approach for generating constraints. We used a method that guarantees particular levels of propagation, but such constraints may not correspond to the actual well-formedness constraints used in modeling languages.

In order to help mitigate the first threat, we tuned the parameters for generating random *MAVO* models so that the graph density and the frequencies of annotations corresponded to those we have observed with *MAVO* models created by hand for different case studies.

7   Related Work

In this section, we review approaches to conventional change propagation and discuss their relation to our method for *MAVO* uncertainty change propagation.

Change propagation can be seen as finding a "repair" to reinstate model consistency after a change has made it inconsistent. The difference between the conventional change propagation studied in the literature, and *MAVO* uncertainty change propagation is the nature of the consistency constraint used. In the former, these are usually well-formedness rules, either within a model or in the traceability relation between models. In the latter, the constraint is that the model be in RNF.

Many approaches [9,2,15,14,23] focus on attempting to formulate a model repair transformation as a set of *repair rules* representing various change scenarios where specific repair actions are performed in response to detected changes. Such rules may be expressed in a specialized constraint language, such as Beanbag [23] or EVL [9], or using logic, such as Blanc et. al [2], triple graph grammars [14], the xLinkit framework [15] or, more recently, Reder et. al. [16]. With the exception of xLinkit and Reder, these approaches require that the repair rules be created by hand, and thus are modeling-language specific. These approaches are inappropriate for use with *MAVO* as they go against the language-independent spirit of *MAVO*. On the other hand, xLinkit defines a higher order transformation that automatically generates the repair transformation from from consistency constraints and thus is language-independent, although the constraints are different from ours. [16] takes a similar approach but the rules organize the repairs into trees to simplify user selection. In the future, we intend to investigate the feasibility of automatically generating an uncertainty repair transformation for each language.

Another approach to conventional change propagation is to use a general constraint solver to find possible repairs. For example, [4] expresses the consistency constraints declaratively using Answer Set Programming (ASP) and then finds possible modifications to reinstate consistency using an ASP solver. Analysis of feature models often uses constraint solvers as well, e.g., [1]. Feature models represent a set of products in a manner similar to the *MAVO* model representation of a set of concretizations. Lopez [10] uses a SAT solver on feature models to fix inconsistencies that allow feature configurations which yield inconsistent products. Benavides [1] uses a solver for *false optional feature* detection – finding cases in which a feature is marked as optional when the constraints actually force it to occur in all products. This is similar to removing an M annotation in a *MAVO* model as part of an RNF computation. Addressing S and V annotations in addition to M , as we do in our work, extends this kind of analysis further.

Since the focus of this paper is uncertainty change propagation, we consider the work related to *expressing* model uncertainty to be out of scope; see [19] for a recent survey.

8   Conclusion

The management of uncertainty and its negative impacts in software engineering is an important problem. In this paper, we extend our earlier work on model uncertainty [20] to address the issue of change propagation due to uncertainty change. We identified two general cases of uncertainty change propagation for uncertainty reducing change and for uncertainty increasing change. We then formally specified these cases and defined algorithms for computing the propagation. Although the cases appear to be symmetric, the uncertainty reducing case produces a unique solution while the uncertainty increasing case might not, requiring user interaction. Furthermore, their solutions require different algorithms. We implemented both algorithms on top of the Z3 SMT solver and performed scalability experiments using randomly generated models. Our experiments revealed that although change propagation time increases exponentially with model size, as is expected with the use of SMT solvers, it was unaffected by how constrained the model is and only increases linearly with the degree of uncertainty in the model. These positive results suggest the feasibility of tool support for uncertainty change propagation.

Our experiences with the current work suggest some interesting future directions. The generality of SAT/SMT solving comes at a cost of potentially exponential behaviour, and we found this to be the case for our experiments involving randomly generated models. Of course, it is possible that "real" models avoid this bad behavior – this has been reported to be the case with real feature models [12]. We intend to conduct studies with real *MAVO* models to investigate this hypothesis. Another direction to improve performance is to exploit more efficient algorithms in specialized cases. For example, there may be classes of well-formedness constraints for which we can automatically generate efficient change propagation rules as a repair transformation in a manner similar to the approach used by xLinkit for conventional change propagation [15]. Finally, we intend to investigate how conventional change propagation can be combined with uncertainty change propagation to provide a more comprehensive change propagation solution. This will be an important step toward a general approach for managing model uncertainty across the software development lifecycle.

Acknowledgements. We thank Alessio Di Sandro, Vivien Suen, Michalis Famelis, Pooya SaadatPanah and Nathan Robinson for their help with developing the model generation framework used in this paper. We would also like to thank Aws Albarghouthi for his help with Z3.

References

1. Benevides, D., Segura, S., Cortes, A.: Automated Analysis of Feature Models 20 years Later: a Literature Review. Inf. Syst. 35(6), 615–636 (2010)
2. Blanc, X., Mougenot, A., Mounier, I., Mens, T.: Incremental Detection of Model Inconsistencies Based on Model Operations. In: van Eck, P., Gordijn, J., Wieringa, R. (eds.) CAiSE 2009. LNCS, vol. 5565, pp. 32–46. Springer, Heidelberg (2009)
3. Ebert, C., De Man, J.: Requirements Uncertainty: Influencing Factors and Concrete Improvements. In: Proc. of ICSE 2005, pp. 553–560 (2005)
4. Eramo, R., Pierantonio, A., Romero, J., Vallecillo, A.: Change Management in Multi-Viewpoint System Using ASP. In: Proc. Int. Wrkshp. on ODP for Enterprise Computing, pp. 433–440. IEEE (2008)
5. Famelis, M., Chechik, M., Salay, R.: Partial Models: Towards Modeling and Reasoning with Uncertainty. In: Proc. of ICSE 2012, pp. 573–583 (2012)
6. Fu, Z., Malik, S.: On Solving the Partial MAX-SAT Problem. In: Biere, A., Gomes, C.P. (eds.) SAT 2006. LNCS, vol. 4121, pp. 252–265. Springer, Heidelberg (2006)

7. Ibrahim, H., Far, B.H., Eberlein, A., Daradkeh, Y.: Uncertainty Management in Software Engineering: Past, Present, and Future. In: Proc. of CCECE 2009, pp. 7–12 (2009)
8. Kilby, P., Slaney, J., Thiébaux, S., Walsh, T.: Backbones and Backdoors in Satisfiability. In: Proc. AAAI 2005, pp. 1368–1373 (2005)
9. Kolovos, D., Paige, R., Polack, F.: Detecting and Repairing Inconsistencies across Heterogeneous Models. In: ICSTVV 2008, April 9-11, pp. 356–364 (2008)
10. Lopez-Heerejon, R., Egyed, A.: Towards Fixing Inconsistencies in Models with Variability. In: Proc. of VaMoS 2012, pp. 93–100 (2012)
11. Marques-Silva, J., Janota, M., Lynce, I.: On Computing Backbones of Propositional Theories. In: Proc. of ECAI 2010, pp. 15–20 (2010)
12. Mendonca, M., Wasowski, A., Czarnecki, K.: SAT-based Analysis of Feature Models is Easy. In: Proc. of SPLC 2009, pp. 231–240 (2009)
13. Mens, T.: Introduction and Roadmap: History and Challenges of Software Evolution. In: Software Evolution, pp. 1–11 (2008)
14. Mens, T., Van Der Straeten, R.: Incremental Resolution of Model Inconsistencies. In: Fiadeiro, J.L., Schobbens, P.-Y. (eds.) WADT 2006. LNCS, vol. 4409, pp. 111–126. Springer, Heidelberg (2007)
15. Nentwich, C., Emmerich, W., Finkelstein, A.: Consistency Management with Repair Actions. In: Proc. of ICSE 2003, pp. 455–464 (2003)
16. Reder, A., Egyed, A.: Computing Repair Trees for Resolving Inconsistencies in Design Models. In: Proc. of ASE 2012, pp. 220–229 (2012)
17. Saadatpanah, P., Famelis, M., Gorzny, J., Robinson, N., Chechik, M., Salay, R.: Comparing the Effectiveness of Reasoning Formalisms for Partial Models. In: Proc. of MoDeVVa (2012)
18. Sabetzadeh, M., Nejati, S., Chechik, M., Easterbrook, S.: Reasoning about Consistency in Model Merging. In: Proc. Workshop on Living with Inconsistency, LWI 2010 (2010)
19. Salay, R., Chechik, M., Horkoff, J.: Managing Requirements Uncertainty with Partial Models. In: Proc. of RE 2012 (2012)
20. Salay, R., Famelis, M., Chechik, M.: Language Independent Refinement Using Partial Modeling. In: de Lara, J., Zisman, A. (eds.) FASE 2012. LNCS, vol. 7212, pp. 224–239. Springer, Heidelberg (2012)
21. Sawyer, P., Bencomo, N., Whittle, J., Letier, E., Finkelstein, A.: Requirements-Aware Systems: A Research Agenda for RE for Self-adaptive Systems. In: Proc. of RE 2010, pp. 95–103 (2010)
22. van Lamsweerde, A.: Requirements Engineering - From System Goals to UML Models to Software Specifications. Wiley (2009)
23. Xiong, Y., Hu, Z., Zhao, H., Song, H., Takeichi, M., Mei, H.: Supporting Automatic Model Inconsistency Fixing. In: Proc. of ESEC/FSE 2009, pp. 315–324 (2009)
24. Ziv, H., Richardson, D., Klösch, R.: The Uncertainty Principle in Software Engineering (1996) (unpublished)

A Model-Based Synthesis Process for Choreography Realizability Enforcement

Marco Autili, Davide Di Ruscio, Amleto Di Salle, Paola Inverardi,
and Massimo Tivoli*

Università degli Studi di L'Aquila, Italy
{marco.autili,davide.diruscio,amleto.disalle,paola.inverardi,
massimo.tivoli}@univaq.it

Abstract. The near future in service-oriented system development envisions a ubiquitous world of available services that collaborate to fit users' needs. Modern service-oriented applications are often built by reusing and assembling distributed services. This can be done by considering a global specification of the interactions between the participant services, namely the choreography. In this paper, we propose a synthesis approach to automatically synthesize a choreography out of a specification of it and a set of services discovered as suitable participants. The synthesis is model-based in the sense that it works by assuming a finite state model of the services's protocol and a BPMN model for the choreography specification. The result of the synthesis is a set of distributed components, called coordination delegates, that coordinate the services' interaction in order to realize the specified choreography. The work advances the state-of-the-art in two directions: (i) we provide a solution to the problem of choreography realizability enforcement, and (ii) we provide a model-based tool chain to support the development of choreography-based systems.

Keywords: Service Choreographies, Model Driven Engineering, Service Oriented Architectures, Choreography Realizability Enforcement.

1 Introduction

The near future in service-oriented system development envisions a ubiquitous world of available services that collaborate to fit users' needs [7]. The trend is to build modern applications by reusing and assembling distributed services rather than realize standalone and monolithic programs. When building a service-based system, a possible Service Engineering (SE) approach is to compose together distributed services by considering a global specification, called *choreography*, of the interactions between the participant services. To this extent, the following two problems are usually considered: (i) *realizability check* - check whether the choreography can be realized by implementing/discovering each participant service so as it conforms to the played role; and (ii)

---

* This work is supported by the European Community's Seventh Framework Programme FP7/2007-2013 under grant agreement number 257178 (project CHOReOS - Large Scale Choreographies for the Future Internet - www.choreos.eu).

conformance check - check whether the set of services satisfies the choreography specification or not. In the literature many approaches have been proposed to address these
problems (e.g., see [2,5,11] just to mention a few). However, by moving a step forward
with respect to the state-of-the-art, a further problem worth considering concerns *realizability enforcement*. That is, given a choreography specification and a set of existing
services discovered as suitable participants, restrict the interaction among them so to
fulfill the collaboration prescribed by the choreography specification.

Contribution. In this direction, we propose a solution for realizability enforcement
in the context of the CHOReOS EU project[1]. The core objective of CHOReOS is to
leverage model-based methodologies and relevant SOA standards, while making *choreography* development a systematic process to the reuse and the assembling of services
discovered within the Internet. CHOReOS revisits the concept of choreography-based
service-oriented systems, and introduces a model-based development process and associated methods, tools, and middleware for *coordinating* services in the Internet. In
particular, we describe how to automatically synthesize a choreography out of a specification of it and a set of discovered services. Since a choreography is a network of
collaborating services, the notion of coordination protocol becomes crucial. In fact, it
might be the case that the collaborating services, although potentially suitable in isolation, when interacting together can lead to *undesired interactions*. That is interactions
that do not belong to the set of interactions modeled by the choreography specification.
To prevent undesired interactions, we automatically synthesize additional software entities, called *Coordination Delegates* (CDs), and interpose them among the participant
services. CDs coordinate the services' interaction in a way that the resulting collaboration realizes the specified choreography. This is done by exchanging suitable *coordination information* that is automatically generated out of the choreography specification.
It is worth mentioning that, dealing with black-box services, it is not always be possible to synthesize suitable CDs. That is if all the behaviours produced by composing in
parallel the participant services represent undesired interactions, then there is nothing
to do in order to enforce the specified choreography.

Progress beyond state-of-the art. As already anticipated, on the one hand, we tackle
the problem of realizability enforcement, which so far has been receiving little attention
by the SE community. On the other hand, the definition of the CHOReOS process and
its synthesis sub-process required the exploitation of state-of-the-art languages, systems, and techniques that have emerged in different contexts including SOA, model-
transformations, and distributed coordination. Their integration and interoperability
within the same technical space present the opportunity to harness the power and individual capabilities of different tools as part of a tool chain to support the systematic
development of choreography-based systems which has thus far been largely missed.

Structure of the work. The paper is structured as follows. Section 2 describes the
choreography synthesis process by means of an explanatory example, in the domain of
travel agency systems. It gives an intuition of how CDs can be generated and used to
enforce choreography realizability. In Section 3, we discuss the distributed coordination
algorithm that characterizes the coordination logic performed by a synthesized CD.
Furthermore, we provide details about the correctness of the algorithm with respect

---

[1] See at www.choreos.eu.

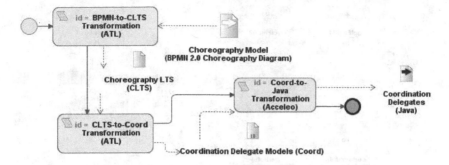

Fig. 1. The *Choreography Synthesis* process

to choreography enforcement, and we discuss the overhead due to the exchange of coordination information. Related works are discussed in Section 4. Section 5 concludes the paper and discusses future directions.

2   The Choreography Synthesis Process

The choreography synthesis process described in this section, and shown in Figure 1, is part of the overall CHOReOS development process [6]. The CHOReOS process leverages activities that range from *requirement specification* to *service discovery*, to *choreography synthesis*, to *choreography deployment and execution*, and to *design and run-time analysis*. As mentioned in Section 1, choreography synthesis is the main contribution of the work described in this paper and it aims at automatically generating CDs that correctly coordinate the discovered services in a distributed way.

For illustrative purposes we describe the synthesis process, by means of an explanatory example that concerns the development of a choreography-based *travel agency* system. Indeed, within CHOReOS, we applied our process to a real-scale case study, namely the *passenger-friendly airport scenario*. For space reasons, in this paper, we cannot show our approach at work on this scenario. However, the interested reader can refer to a demo publically available at the CHOReOS web-site[2].

Choreography Model. We use *BPMN2 Choreography Diagrams* as notation to specify choreographies. As shown in Figure 2, BPMN2 diagrams uses rounded-corner boxes to denote choreography tasks. Each of them is labeled with the roles of the two participants involved in the task, and the name of the service operation performed by the initiating participant and provided by the other one. A role contained in a light-gray filled box denotes the initiating participant. The diagram specifies that the travel agency system can be realized by choreographing four services: a `Booking Agency` service (`ba`), two `Flight Booking` services (`fb1` and (`fb2`)), and a `Hotel Booking` service (`hb`). In particular, (i) the booking of the flight has to be performed before the booking of the hotel and (ii) only the answer from one of the two flight booking services is taken into account (see the exclusive gateway represented as a rhombus in Figure 2).

---

[2] See at `http://www.choreos.eu/bin/Discover/videos`. The related development code is available at `http://www.choreos.eu/bin/Download/Software`.

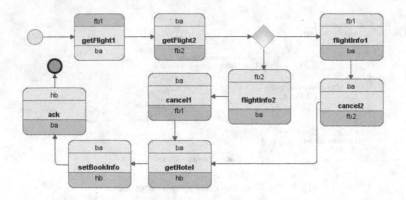

Fig. 2. BPMN2 choreography diagram for a Flight-Hotel Booking choreography

The choreography synthesis process generates the CDs required to realize a specified choreography. The generation process consists of three model transformations as discussed in the following.

BPMN-to-CLTS. By means of transformation rules implemented through the *ATLAS Transformation Language* [8] (ATL), the BPMN2 specification is transformed into an equivalent Choreography Labeled Transition System (CLTS) specification. Figure 3 shows the CLTS model for the BPMN2 choreography diagram in Figure 2. This model has been drawn by means of the developed GMF-based editor[3].

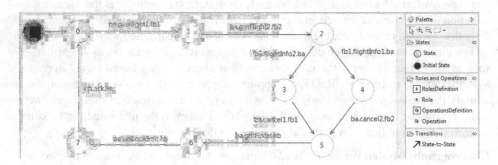

Fig. 3. CLTS model of the Flight-Hotel Booking choreography

Informally, a CLTS is a Labeled Transition System (LTS) that, for coordination purposes, is suitably extended to model choreography behavior, e.g., by considering conditional branching and multiplicities on participant instances. The transformation takes into account the main gateways found in BPMN2 Choreography Diagrams: exclusive gateways (decision, alternative paths), inclusive gateways (inclusive decision, alternative but also parallel paths), parallel gateways (creation and merging of parallel flows), and event-based gateways (choice based on events, i.e., message reception or timeout). For instance, the exclusive gateway in the BPMN2 diagram shown in Figure 2 has been

---

[3] See at http://code.google.com/p/choreos-mde/

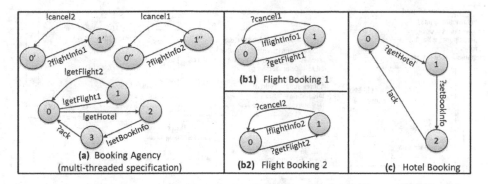

Fig. 4. LTSs for the services of the travel agency system

transformed to the exclusive branching in the CLTS diagram shown in Figure 3, hence generating two alternative paths outgoing from state 2.

Although this transformation is indispensable for the realization of the CHOReOS process, it does not represent an advance on the state-of-the-art per se. In fact, in the literature, there exist other similar attempts to transform business process models to automata-based models [3,17] (just to mention a few). For this reason, in the sequel, we do not further discuss this transformation.

Before describing the other two transformations, let us continue our example by discussing the problem underlying the notion of undesired interactions introduced in Section 1. The CLTS model in Figure 3 applies to the roles ba, fb1, fb2, and hb that, after discovery, are played by the Booking Agency, Flight Booking 1, Flight Booking 2, and Hotel Booking services, respectively. Figure 4 shows the interaction protocol of these services by using LTSs. The exclamation "!" and the question "?" marks denote required and provided operations, respectively. The Booking Agency service searches for a flight by exploiting two different flight booking services (see !getFlight1 and !getFlight2). As soon as one of the two booking services answers by sending flight information (see !flightInfo1 or !flightInfo2), the agency cancels the search on the other booking service (see !cancel1 or !cancel2).

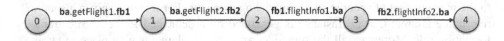

Fig. 5. A possible undesired interaction with respect to the Flight-Hotel Booking choreography

The above services have been discovered as suitable participants (i.e., each service conforms the role to be played) for the specified choreography[4]. However, this does not necessarily mean that the "uncontrolled" collaboration of the participant services is free

---

[4] Discovery issues and the problem of checking whether a service is a suitable participant for a choreography (conformance check) are out of the scope of this paper.

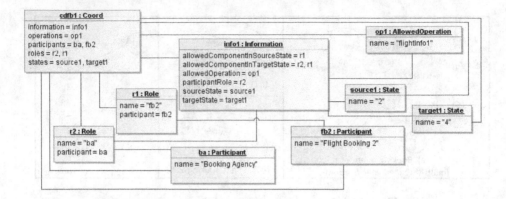

Fig. 6. Coord model for the `Flight Booking 1` service

from undesired interactions. In fact, Figure 5 shows a possible trace resulting from the parallel composition of the service protocols. This trace represents an undesired interaction, that is it is not included in the CLTS model shown in Figure 3, since both `fb1` and `fb2` proceed while only one of them should be allowed according to the exclusive branching in state 2. To prevent undesired interactions, the automatic synthesis of the CDs is carried out according to the `CLTS-to-Coord` and `Coord-to-Java` model transformations discussed below. It is worth mentioning that the kind of exclusive behaviour our running example is based on does not represent the only property that our approach is able to guarantee. In fact, in general, an undesired interaction in our approach can be represented as (the negation of) a *safety property* expressing what should not happen in the system composed by the participant services plus the CDs synthesized according to the specified CLTS.

CLTS-to-Coord. An ATL transformation is defined to automatically distribute the CLTS into a set of models, whose metamodel is denoted as `Coord` in Figure 1. A `Coord` model M_{CD_i}, for a coordination delegate CD_i, specifies the information that CD_i needs to know in order to properly cooperate with the other CDs in the system. The aim of this cooperation is to prevent undesired interactions in the global collaboration of the participant services, hence enforcing choreography realizability. Essentially, the developed ATL transformation consists of a number of rules each devoted to the managment of specific source modeling elements. For instance, given a source role name a target `Coord` instance is generated by a dedicated `Role2Cord` transformation rule. Moreover, all the source `Transition` elements give place to target `Information` elements.

Back to the example, Figure 6 shows the `Coord` model that represents the coordination information for the CD supervising `Flight Booking 1`. The `Coord` model contains the following information: when in the state 2 of the CLTS shown in Figure 3, `fb1` is allowed to perform the operation `flightInfo1` provided by `ba`, hence moving to the state 4; when in the state 2 also `fb2` is allowed to perform an operation, namely `flightInfo2`, provided by `ba`, hence moving to the state 3. However, since state 2 models an exclusive branching, only one of `fb1` and `fb2` must be allowed to proceed. Thus, concerning `fb1`, the CD supervising `Flight Booking 1` needs to know that, when in the state 2, another service, i.e., Flight Booking 2, is allowed to take a move, and hence it must be blocked in order to solve the possible concurrency problem. Symmetrically, the CD supervising Flight Booking 2 knows that Flight Booking 1 must be blocked. As detailed in Section 3, the two CDs use coordination information to "perform handshaking" and "elect a winner". This information is then exploited by the CDs to also keep track of the *global state* of the coordination protocol implied by the specified choreography, similarly to [2]. This means that each delegate can deduce the global state from the observation of the communication flow between the participant services.

Coord-to-Java. The Coord model specifies the logic that a CD has to perform independently from any target technology. To validate our approach in practical contexts, we chose Java as a possible target language of our Acceleo[5]-based model-to-code transformation. The Java code of a delegate CD_i exploits the information contained in its Coord model M_{CD_i}. Briefly, for each Coord model a Java class is generated by means of dedicated templates consisting of static and variable parts. The latter are fixed by means of the information retrieve from the source Coord model. The generated class implements an operation for each required operation of the supervised service.

Back to the example, from the cdfb1 Coord model, a *proxy* web service is generated as a *wrapper* for the operations required by Flight Booking 1. That is, the corresponding Java class implements the operation flightInfo1, which wraps the homonymous operation provided by Booking Agency and required by Flight Booking 1. Listing 1.1 shows an excerpt of the generated code for the cdfb1 class. The fb1Coord class variable is used to store the cdfb1 Coord model. Such a model is used to coordinate the wrapped operations. For instance, after that the CD for Flight Booking 1 verified that flightInfo1 is an allowed operation with respect to the choreography global state (variable globalState), it establishes, through handleRules and handleRule3, whether the request of flightInfo1 can be forwarded to Booking Agency (line 19) or not (line 28). The choreography global state is tracked by means of the asynchronous exchange of coordination information with the other CDs. Interestingly, handleRules and handleRule3 are generic and do not depend on the information contained in cdfb1.

Listing 1.1. Fragment of the generated CD for fb1

```
1  @WebService( serviceName="cdfb1", targetNamespace="http://choreos.di.univaq.it"
       ↪, portName="fb1Port" )
2  public class cdfb1 {
3
4      private static CoordinationDelegate COORDINATION_DELEGATE = new
           ↪CoordinationDelegate("cdfb1");
5      private static final String REQUEST_FLIGHTINFO1 = "flightInfo1";
6      private static Coord fb1Coord = CoordFactory.eINSTANCE.createCoord();
7      private static ChoreographyState globalState = new ChoreographyState(
           ↪ChoreographyState.INITIAL_STATE);
8
9      public void cdfb1() {
10         ...
11     }
12
13     @WebMethod( operationName="flightInfo1" )
```

---

[5] http://www.eclipse.org/acceleo/

```
14    //@Oneway
15    public void flightInfo1() throws DiscardException {
16    CoordinationDelegateFacade facade = new CoordinationDelegateFacade();
17    CoordinationResult result = facade.handleRules(REQUEST_FLIGHTINFO1,
          ↪COORDINATION_DELEGATE, fb1coord, globalState);
18
19    if (result==CoordinationResult.FORWARD) {
20
21        //Forward message to the BookingAgency Service
22        BookingAgency_Service bookingAgencyService = new BookingAgency_Service
          ↪();
23        client.BookingAgency BookingAgencyPort = BookingAgencyService.
          ↪getBookingAgencyPort();
24        BookingAgencyPort.flightInfo1();
25
26        facade.handleRule3(REQUEST_FLIGHTINFO1, COORDINATION_DELEGATE, fb1coord
          ↪, globalState);
27    }
28    if (result==CoordinationResult.DISCARD) {
29        //Discard message
30        throw new DiscardException();
31    }
32    }
33 }
```

Once the implementation code has been generated for all the required CDs, services and CDs are composed together. Figure 7 shows the architectural configuration of the composition where *ba*, *fb*1, *fb*2, and *hb* are instances of Booking Agency, Flight Booking 1, Flight Booking 2, and Hotel Booking, respectively; cdba, cdfb1, cdfb2, , and cdhb are their respective CDs.

The required/provided interface bindings between a participant service and a CD are realized by means of synchronous connectors. A CD is connected to all the other CDs by means of asynchronous connectors (see the n-ary association shown in Figure 7 as a rhombus). The latter serve to exchange coordination information. As better explained in the next section, coordination information is exchanged only when synchronization is needed, i.e., when there is more than one component that is allowed to perform some action according to the current global state of the choreography model. For instance, in our example, this happens when both fb1 and fb2 can move from the state 2. Note that, dealing with the reuse of existing (black-box) services, this is the best we can do in terms of the overhead due to the exchange of coordination information. In the next section we discuss why this is overhead is acceptable.

3   Distributed Coordination Algorithm

In this section we provide an algorithmic description of the coordination logic that a CD has to perform. The distributed coordination algorithm uses foundational notions as *happened-before* relation, *partial ordering*, *time-stamps*, and *total ordering*. The reader who is not fully familiar with such notions can refer to the work described in [9].

The standard time-stamp method is used in our approach to establish, at each CD, a total order of dependent *blocking* and *unblocking* messages, hence addressing starvation problems. Acknowledging messages are used to be sure that all the blocking messages (a CD has sent) have been actually received. In order to solve concurrency problems arising when two events associated with the same time-stamp must be compared, we

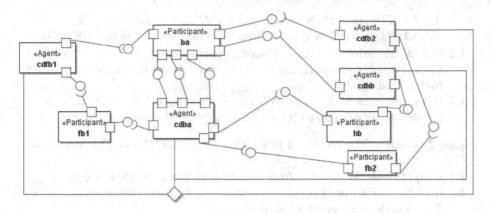

Fig. 7. Overall architecture of the choreography-based travel agency system

assume a priority order among the services to be choreographed. Since problems arising from network unreliability are out of scope, we assume that non-lossy, order-preserving and non-duplicating communications, among the CDs, are guaranteed.

In the style of [9], the distributed coordination algorithm is defined by the following rules that each delegate CD_i follows in a distributed setting, when its supervised service S_i performs a request of α, without relying on any central synchronizing entity or shared memory. These rules locally characterize the collaborative behavior of the CDs at run-time from a *one-to-many* point of view. To this end, each CD maintains its own *BLOCK queue* (i.e., the queue of blocking messages) that is unknown to the other delegates. At the beginning, each CD has its own timestamp variable set to 0 and, at each iteration of the algorithm, waits for either its supervised service to make a request or another CD to forward a request. The actions defined by each rule are assumed to form a single event (i.e., each rule has to be considered as atomic). Within the rules, we denote with TS_i the current timestamp for CD_i, and with s the current state of the CLTS model M_C of the choreography. More-over, we denote with $Coord_i[h]$ the h-th coordination information element in the Coord model of CD_i; $Coord_i[h][\texttt{sourceState}]$ (resp., $Coord_i[h][\texttt{targetState}]$) is a state of M_C that is a source (resp., target) state for the transition la-beled with $Coord_i[h][\texttt{allowedOperation}]$; $Coord_i[h][\texttt{allowedOperation}]$ is the operation that can be performed by S_i when M_C is in the state $Coord_i[h][\texttt{sourceState}]$; $Coord_i[h][\texttt{allowedServiceInSourceState}]$ (resp., $Coord_i[h][\texttt{allowedServiceInTargetState}]$) is the set of services (different from S_i) that, with respect to M_C, are allowed to move from $Coord_i[h][\texttt{sourceState}]$ (resp., $Coord_i[h][\texttt{targetState}]$). Detailed explanation of these rules is given below.

Rule 1: Upon receiving, from S_i, a request of α in the current state s of M_C,
   1.1 if there exist h *s.t.* $Coord_i[h][\texttt{sourceState}]$ $=$ s and $Coord_i[h][\texttt{allowedOperation}] = \alpha$ (i.e., α is allowed from s) **then**
     1.1.1 CD_i updates TS_i to $TS_i + 1$;
     1.1.2 for every CD_j *s.t.* $j \in Coord_i[h][\texttt{allowedServiceInSourceState}]$:

1.1.2.1 CD_i sends BLOCK(s,TS_i,from-CD_i,to-CD_j) to CD_j;

1.1.2.2 CD_i puts BLOCK(s,TS_i,from-CD_i,to-CD_j) on its BLOCK queue;

1.2 if there exist h *s.t.* $Coord_i[h][\texttt{sourceState}] \neq s$ and $Coord_i[h][\texttt{allowedOperation}] = \alpha$ (i.e., α is not allowed from s) **then** CD_i discards α;

1.3 if does not exist h *s.t.* $Coord_i[h][\texttt{allowedOperation}] = \alpha$ (i.e., α is not in the alphabet of M_C) **then** CD_i forwards α (hence synchronizing with S_i);

Rule 2: When a CD_j receives a BLOCK(s,TS_i,from-CD_i,to-CD_j) from some CD_i,

2.1 CD_j places BLOCK(s,TS_i,from-CD_i,to-CD_j) on its BLOCK queue;

2.2 if ($TS_j < TS_i$) or ($TS_i = TS_j$ and $S_i \prec S_j$) **then** CD_j updates TS_j to $TS_i + 1$; **else** CD_j updates TS_j to $TS_j + 1$;

2.3 CD_j sends ACK(s,TS_j,from-CD_j) to CD_i;

Rule 3: Once CD_i has received all the expected ACK(s,TS_j,from-CD_j) from every CD_j (see Rule 2), and it is granted the privilege (according to Rule 5) to proceed from state s,

3.1 CD_i forwards α;

3.2 CD_i updates s to $s'=Coord_i[h][\texttt{targetState}]$;

3.3 CD_i updates TS_i to $TS_i + 1$;

3.4 for every CD_j *s.t.* $j \in Coord_i[h][\texttt{allowedServiceInSourceState}]$ or $j \in Coord_i[h][\texttt{allowedServiceInTargetState}]$:

3.4.1 if $s == s'$ **then** CD_i removes any BLOCK(s,TS_i,from-CD_i,to-CD_j) from its own BLOCK queue; **else** CD_i empties its own BLOCK queue;

3.4.2 CD_i sends UNBLOCK(s',TS_i,from-CD_i) to CD_j;

Rule 4: When a CD_j receives an UNBLOCK(s',TS_i,from-CD_i) from some CD_i,

4.1 CD_j updates s to s';

4.2 if ($TS_j < TS_i$) or ($TS_i = TS_j$ and $S_i \prec S_j$) **then** CD_j updates TS_j to $TS_i + 1$; **else** CD_j updates TS_j to $TS_j + 1$;

4.3 if $s == s'$ **then** CD_j removes any BLOCK(s,TS_i,from-CD_i,to-CD_j) from its BLOCK queue; **else** CD_j empties its own BLOCK queue;

4.4 CD_j retries Rule 1 from the (updated) state s;

Rule 5: CD_i is granted the privilege to proceed from the current state s of M_C when, ranging over j, **for every** pair of messages BLOCK(s,TS_i,from-CD_i,to-CD_j) and BLOCK(s,TS_j,from-CD_j,to-CD_i) on its BLOCK queue: either (i) $TS_i < TS_j$ or (ii) $TS_i = TS_j$ and $S_i \prec S_j$;

If the conditions on Rule 1.2 hold (i.e., the conditions on Rules 1.1 and 1.3 fail), it means that S_i is trying to perform an operation that is in the alphabet of M_C but is not allowed from the current state of M_C. In this case, CD_i prevents S_i to perform that operation by discarding it. Indeed, one cannot always assume that the actual code of a (black-box) service has been developed in a way that it is possible to discard a service operation by the external environment. Actually, it can be done only if the developer had preemptively foreseen it and, for instance, an exception handling logic was aptly

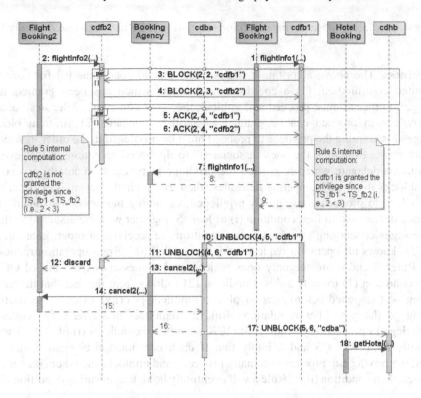

Fig. 8. An excerpt of a possible execution of the distributed coordination algorithm

coded for such an operation. However, a service client can easily detect those operations that are *controllable* by the external environment, e.g., through the declaration of *thrown* exceptions on interface operations, or of *fault messages* on WSDL operations, or simply of *error return values* for class methods. Since in this paper we focus on the automatic distribution of the choreography-based coordination logic, we avoid to address *controllability* issues and we assume that all service operations are controllable. However, the extension to account for controllability issues is straightforward.

Rule 1.3, allows CDs to be *permissive* on the operations that do not belong to the alphabet of M_C (i.e., operations "outside the scope" of the choreography). Note that one could instead choose to be *restrictive* on those operations by disabling Rule 1.3 hence preventing the service to perform those operations by discarding them (as in the case of a service trying to perform an operation that is in the alphabet of M_C but is not allowed from the current state).

Rule 4.4 resumes the execution of an unblocked CD by "restarting" from Rule 1. If this CD is still trying to handle a request α that is *pending* from the previous iteration of the algorithm (see the operation `flightInfo2` in the coordination scenario shown in Figure 8), retrying Rule 1 means to directly re-check the conditions of Rules 1.1, 1.2, and 1.3 with the new updated state and the pending α. Otherwise, it means that the CD retries Rule 1 from an updated choreography global state.

It is worthwhile to observe that conditions (i) and (ii) of Rule 5 are tested locally by a CD.

Correctness. The above algorithm satisfies three crucial conditions [9] for *correct* distributed coordination: (1) a coordination delegate which has been granted the privilege to proceed must proceed and unblock the other competing delegates before the privilege to proceed can be granted to another delegate; (2) different block messages for granting the privilege to proceed must be privileged in the order in which they are made, excluding the ones "associated" to discarded operations; (3) if every coordination delegate which is granted the privilege to proceed eventually proceeds and unblocks the other competing delegates, then every block message for granting the privilege to proceed is eventually privileged, excluding the ones "associated" to discarded operations. In fact, condition (i) of Rule 5, together with the assumption that the messages concerning coordination information are received in order, guarantees that CD_i knows all operation requests which preceded its current operation request. Since Rules 3 and 4 are the only ones which remove messages from the BLOCK queue, condition (1) trivially holds. Condition (2) follows from the fact that the total ordering $\prec$ (happened-before relation plus component priority) extends the partial ordering $\rightarrow$ (happened-before relation). Rule 2 guarantees that after CD_i requests the privilege to proceed (by sending BLOCK messages), condition (i) of Rule 5 will eventually hold. Rules 3 and 4 imply that if each coordination delegate which is granted the privilege to proceed eventually proceeds and unblocks the other competing delegates, then condition (ii) of Rule 5 will eventually hold, thus ensuring condition (3).

Analysis of the overhead due to the exchange of coordination information. The overhead due to the exchange of coordination information among the coordination delegates is acceptable. First of all, note that BLOCK messages are exchanged only when non-determinism occurs from the current state s of M_C. In the worst case[6], the non-determinism degree is asymptotically bounded by the number n of components, i.e., it is $O(n)$. For each received BLOCK message an ACK message is exchanged. UNBLOCK messages are instead exchanged at each state of M_C and for a maximum number that is $O(n)$. Thus, if m is the number of states of M_C then the maximum number of coordination information messages (BLOCK, UNBLOCK, ACK) that are exchanged is $O(3 * m * n)$, i.e., $O(m * n)$. However, very often, in the practice, $n \leq m$ holds ($m \leq n$ is less frequent). This means that the maximum number of exchanged coordination information messages can be considered as $O(m^2)$. We can, then, conclude that the introduced overhead is polynomial in the number of states of M_C and, hence, acceptable further considering that the size of coordination information messages is insignificant. Indeed, as also shown by the work described in [9], this is the minimum that one can do to ensure correct distributed coordination.

By continuing the explanatory example introduced in Section 2, we better show how CDs use, at run-time, the information in their Coord models to correctly and distributively interact with each other, hence enforcing the realizability of the choreography

---

[6] Note that, in the practice, the worst case is unusual.

specified by M_C. By referring to Figure 3, we focus on the fact that only the answer from one of the two flight booking services is taken into account. Following the rules of the distributed coordination algorithm, Figure 8 shows how Flight Booking 2 is blocked whenever Flight Booking 1 is faster in collecting the information to be provided to Booking Agency.

The shown scenario concerns an excerpt of a possible execution of the distributed coordination algorithm. It starts when the two allowed operations flightInfo1 and flightInfo2, required by Flight Booking 1 and Flight Booking 2 respectively, concurrently occur while in the current state 2 of the CLTS model of the choreography. At state 2, the timestamps for Flight Booking 1 and Flight Booking 2 are 1 and 2, respectively. Furthermore, Flight Booking 1 ≺ Flight Booking 2.

4 Related Work

The approach to the automatic generation of CDs presented in this paper is related to a number of other approaches that have been considered in the literature.

Many approaches have been proposed in the literature aiming at automatically composing services by means of BPEL, WSCI, or WS-CDL choreographers [4,5,10,13,16]. The common idea underlying these approaches is to assume a high-level specification of the requirements that the choreography has to fulfill and a behavioral specification of the services participating in the choreography. From these two assumptions, by applying data- and control-flow analysis, the BPEL, WSCI or WS-CDL description of a centralized choreographer specification is automatically derived. This description is derived in order to satisfy the specified choreography requirements.

In particular, in [16], the authors propose an approach to automatically derive service implementations from a choreography specification. In [13], the author strives towards the same goal, however assuming that some services are reused. The proposed approach exploits wrappers to make the reused services match the choreography.

Most of the previous approaches concern orchestration that is the most common approach to service composition. Conversely, our approach is one of the few in the literature that consider choreography as a means for composing services. Despite the fact that the works described in [13,16] focus on choreography, they consider the problem of automatically checking whether a choreography can be realized by a set of interacting services, each of them synthesized by simply projecting the choreography specification on the role to be played. This problem is known as *choreography realizability check*. Note that it is a fundamentally different problem with respect to the one considered in this paper, i.e., *choreography realizability enforcement*. In fact, our approach is reuse-oriented and aims at restricting, by means of the automatically synthesized CDs, the interaction behavior of the discovered (third-party) services in order to realize the specified choreography. Differently, the approaches described in [13,16] are focused on verifying whether the set of services, required to realize a given choreography, can be easily implemented by simply considering the role-based local views of the specified choreography. That is, this verification does not aim at synthesizing the coordination logic, which is needed whenever the collaboration among the services leads to global interactions that violate the choreography behavior.

In [12] a game theoretic strategy is used for checking whether incompatible component interfaces can be made compatible by inserting a converter between them. This approach is able to automatically synthesize the converter. Contrarily to what we have presented in this paper, the synthesized converter can be seen as a centralized CD.

In our previous work [1] a preliminary version of the coordination algorithm presented in Section 3 has been applied in a component-based setting, namely EJB components for J2EE component-based systems, to support automated composition and coordination of software components. In this paper, it has been completely revised to deal with service-oriented systems and solve some open issues. For instance, differently from what is done in [1], we are able to prevent undesired interactions without producing a centralized model of the coordinator.

In [14], the authors show how to monitor safety properties locally specified (to each component). They observe the system behavior simply raising a *warning message* when a violation of the specified property is detected. Our approach goes beyond simply detecting properties (e.g., a choreography specification) by also allowing their enforcement. In [14] the best thing that they can do is to reason about the global state that each component *is aware of*. Note that, differently from what is done in our approach, such a global state might not be the actual current one and, hence, the property could be considered guaranteed in an *"expired"* state. Another work in the area of the synthesis of runtime monitors from automata is described in [15]. Note that runtime monitoring is mostly focused on the detection of undesired behaviours, while runtime enforcement focuses on their prevention/solution.

5   Conclusions and Future Work

In this paper we presented a model-based synthesis process for automatically enforcing choreography realizability. The main contributions of the presented work with respect to the *choreography generation* research area are: (i) an automated solution to the problem of choreography realizability enforcement, in contrast with the fundamentally different problem of choreography realizability check; (ii) the formalization of a distributed algorithm for choreography-based coordination; (iii) the definition of model transformations capable to produce both the model and the actual implementation of a *choreographer* distributed into a set of cooperating CDs - this is done without generating any centralized model, hence addressing state-explosion problems and scalability issues; and (iv) the full automation and applicability of the approach to practical contexts, e.g., SOAP Web-Services.

In Section 4, we related our approach to existing centralized solutions. Summing up, the most relevant advantage of our approach with respect to these solutions is that the degree of parallelism of the system is maintained despite the introduction of the coordinator. Often, centralized approaches do not permit parallelism since the coordinator is usually implemented as a centralized single-threaded component and the communication with it is synchronous. For space reasons, we cannot further detail this discussion and the reader who is interested on it can refer to the CHOReOS web site.

The approach is viable and the automatically generated code allows for the correct enforcement of the specified choreography. The proposed approach has already been applied to a large-scale realistic case study, namely the passenger-friendly airport scenario and a public demo is available at the CHOReOS web-site http://www.choreos.eu/bin/Download/Software. Currently, we are applying the process at two other industrial case studies of CHOReOS in the domains of marketing and sales, and Internet of things. The results will also be publicly available by the CHOReOS web site. The current implementation of the whole approach supports the generation of Java code for coordinating SOAP-based Web-services. Considering the general-purpose nature of the approach, other languages and application domains are eligible, and other forms of wrapping can be easily realized.

An interesting future direction is the investigation of non-functional properties of the choreography, e.g., by extending the choreography specification with performance or reliability attributes and accounting for them in the CDs synthesis process.

As discussed in Section 3, our approach allows supervised services to perform an operation that is outside the scope of the specified choreography. In this sense our approach is permissive. However, it can be parameterized to be either permissive or restrictive with respect to these operations. However, simply enabling or disabling the execution of operations outside the scope of the choreography is a trivial strategy. In the future we plan to investigate, and embed into the approach implementation, more accurate strategies to suitably deal with these operations.

This paper has been mainly focused on describing the model-based and automatic synthesis of CDs at work, within a choreographic static scenario. Thus, as further future work, dynamic scenarios should be considered and our process should be revised accordingly. For instance, such scenarios are related to contexts in which services may change their behaviour according to the "global state" of the choreography.

The correctness of our coordination algorithm with respect to choreography enforcement has been informally discussed in Section 3. For a rigorous assessment of our method, as another future work, a formal proof of the algorithm is needed.

References

1. Autili, M., Mostarda, L., Navarra, A., Tivoli, M.: Synthesis of decentralized and concurrent adaptors for correctly assembling distributed component-based systems. Journal of Systems and Software 81(12), 2210–2236 (2008)
2. Basu, S., Bultan, T.: Choreography conformance via synchronizability. In: Proceedings of WWW 2011, pp. 795–804 (2011)
3. Bisztray, D., Heckel, R.: Rule-Level Verification of Business Process Transformations using CSP. In: Proceedings of GT-VMT 2007 (2007)
4. Brogi, A., Popescu, R.: Automated Generation of BPEL Adapters. In: Dan, A., Lamersdorf, W. (eds.) ICSOC 2006. LNCS, vol. 4294, pp. 27–39. Springer, Heidelberg (2006)
5. Calvanese, D., Giacomo, G.D., Lenzerini, M., Mecella, M., Patrizi, F.: Automatic service composition and synthesis: the roman model. IEEE Data Eng. Bull. 31(3), 18–22 (2008)
6. CHOReOS Consortium. CHOReOS dynamic development model definition - Public Project deliverable D2.1 (September 2011)
7. ERCIM News. Special Theme: Future Internet Technology. Number 77 (April 2009)
8. Jouault, F., Allilaire, F., Bézivin, J., Kurtev, I.: ATL: A model transformation tool. Science of Computer Programming 72(1-2), 31–39 (2008)

9. Lamport, L.: Time clocks, and the ordering of events in a distributed system. Commun. ACM 21, 558–565 (1978)
10. Marconi, A., Pistore, M., Traverso, P.: Automated Composition of Web Services: the ASTRO Approach. IEEE Data Eng. Bull. 31(3), 23–26 (2008)
11. Poizat, P., Salaün, G.: Checking the Realizability of BPMN 2.0 Choreographies. In: Proceedings of SAC 2012, pp. 1927–1934 (2012)
12. Passerone, R., De Alfaro, L., Henzinger, T.A., Sangiovanni-Vincentelli, A.L.: Convertibility Verification and Converter Synthesis: Two Faces of the Same Coin. In: ICCAD (2002)
13. Salaün, G.: Generation of service wrapper protocols from choreography specifications. In: Proceedings of SEFM (2008)
14. Sen, K., Vardhan, A., Agha, G., Rosu, G.: Efficient decentralized monitoring of safety in distributed systems. In: Proceedings of ICSE 2004 (2004)
15. Simmonds, J., Gan, Y., Chechik, M., Nejati, S., O'Farrell, B., Litani, E., Waterhouse, J.: Runtime monitoring of web service conversations. IEEE T. Services Computing 2(3) (2009)
16. Su, J., Bultan, T., Fu, X., Zhao, X.: Towards a Theory of Web Service Choreographies. In: Dumas, M., Heckel, R. (eds.) WS-FM 2007. LNCS, vol. 4937, pp. 1–16. Springer, Heidelberg (2008)
17. Van Der Aalst, W.M.P., Ter Hofstede, A.H.M., Kiepuszewski, B., Barros, A.P.: Workflow patterns. Distrib. Parallel Databases 14(1) (2003)

On Extracting Feature Models from Sets of Valid Feature Combinations

Evelyn Nicole Haslinger, Roberto Erick Lopez-Herrejon, and Alexander Egyed

Systems Engineering and Automation,
Johannes Kepler University
Linz, Austria
{evelyn.haslinger,roberto.lopez,alexander.egyed}@jku.at
http://www.jku.at/sea/

Abstract. Rather than developing individual systems, Software Product Line Engineering develops families of systems. The members of the software family are distinguished by the features they implement and Feature Models (FMs) are the de facto standard for defining which feature combinations are considered valid members. This paper presents an algorithm to automatically extract a feature model from a set of valid feature combinations, an essential development step when companies, for instance, decide to convert their existing product variations portfolio into a Software Product Line. We performed an evaluation on 168 publicly available feature models, with 9 to 38 features and up to 147456 feature combinations. From the generated feature combinations of each of these examples, we reverse engineered an equivalent feature model with a median performance in the low milliseconds.

Keywords: Feature, Feature Models, Feature Set, Reverse Engineering, Software Product Lines, Variability Modeling.

1 Introduction

Commercial software systems usually exist in different versions or variants, this can be due, for instance, to requirement changes or different customer needs. *Variability* is the capacity of software artifacts to change [1] and *Software Product Line Engineering (SPLE)* is a software development paradigm which helps to cope with the increasing variability in software products. In SPLE the engineers develop families of products rather than designing the individual products independently. SPLE practices have shown to significantly improve productivity factors such as reducing costs and time to market [2]. At the core of SPLE is a *Software Product Line (SPL)* [2], which represents a family of software systems. These systems are distinguished by the set of features they support, where a *feature* is an increment in program functionality [3]. The de facto standard to model the common and variable features of an SPL and their relationships are *Feature Models (FMs)* [4], that express which feature combinations are considered valid products (i.e. SPL members).

V. Cortellessa and D. Varró (Eds.): FASE 2013, LNCS 7793, pp. 53–67, 2013.
© Springer-Verlag Berlin Heidelberg 2013

However, companies typically do not start out building a feature model or SPL. Rather they build products and, if successful, variations of that product for different customers, environments, or other needs. A scenario, which is becoming more pervasive and frequent in industry, is to reverse engineer such product variations into an SPL. The first essential step in this process is obtaining a feature model that correctly captures the set of valid feature combinations present in the SPL. Constructing such feature model manually is time intensive and error prone. Our work is a complement to the current research in this area which assumes the existence of artifacts with variability already embedded from which an FM could extracted. In our earlier work [5], we presented an algorithm to address this problem on basic feature models. This paper extends this work by also considering feature models that can contain basic *Cross Tree Constraints (CTCs)*, that is, *requires* and *excludes* CTCs [6]. Furthermore, we also performed a more comprehensive evaluation. We used 168 publicly available feature models, with 9 to 38 features and up to 147456 feature combinations. From the generated feature combinations of each of these examples, we reverse engineered an equivalent feature model with a median performance in the low milliseconds.

2 Background and Running Example

This section provides the required background information about variability modeling with feature models and related basic technology.

2.1 Feature Models in a Nutshell

Feature models are commonly used in SPLE to define which feature combinations are valid products within an SPL. The individual features are depicted as labeled boxes and are arranged in a tree-like structure. There is always exactly one root feature that is included in every valid program configuration. Each feature, apart from root, has a single parent feature and every feature can have a set of child features. These child-parent relationships are denoted via connecting lines. Notice here that a child feature can only be included in a program configuration if its parent is included as well. There are four different kinds of relations in which a child (resp. a set of children) can interrelate with its parent:

- If a feature is *optional* (depicted with an empty circle at the child end of the relation) it may or may not be selected if its parent feature is selected.
- If a feature is *mandatory* (depicted with a filled circle at the child end of the relation) it has to be selected whenever its parent feature is selected.
- If a set of features forms an *inclusive-or* relation (depicted as filled arcs) at least one feature of the set has to be selected if their parent is selected.
- If a set of features forms an *exclusive-or* relation (depicted as empty arcs) exactly one feature of the set has to be selected if their parent is selected.

Besides the child-parent relations there are also so called *cross-tree constraints* (*CTC*), which capture arbitrary relations among features. *Basic CTCs* are the *requires* and *excludes* relation. If feature *A* *requires* feature *B*, then feature *B* has to be included whenever feature *A* is included. If two features are in an *excludes* relation then these two features cannot be selected together in any valid product configuration. The *requires* and *excludes* CTCs are the most commonly used in FMs; however, more complex CTCs can be expressed using propositional expression, for further details see [7].

Table 1. Feature Sets of Cell Phone Software Product Line

P	C	W	I	B	A	S	M	We	D	G	Mu	Si	Ar
p1	√				√	√				√	√		√	√
p2	√				√		√			√	√		√	√
p3	√				√			√	√	√		√	√
p4	√	√		√	√	√				√	√		√	√
p5	√	√		√	√	√				√	√	√		
p6	√	√		√	√	√				√	√	√	√	√
p7	√	√	√		√	√				√	√		√	√
p8	√	√	√		√	√				√	√	√		
p9	√	√	√		√	√				√	√	√	√	√
p10	√	√	√		√		√			√	√		√	√
p11	√	√	√		√		√			√	√	√		
p12	√	√	√		√		√			√	√	√	√	√
p13	√	√	√		√			√	√	√		√	√
p14	√	√	√	√	√	√				√	√		√	√
p15	√	√	√	√	√	√				√	√	√		
p16	√	√	√	√	√	√				√	√	√	√	√

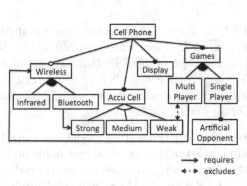

→ requires
◄·► excludes

Fig. 1. Cell Phone SPL Feature Model

Figure 1 shows the feature model of our running example, an SPL of cell phones inspired by a model of the SPLOT homepage [8]. Feature `Cell Phone` is the root feature of this feature model, hence it is selected in every program configuration. It has three mandatory child features (i.e. the features `Accu Cell`, `Display` and `Games`), which are also selected in every product configuration as their parent is always included. The children of feature `Accu Cell` form an exclusive-or relation, meaning that the programs of this SPL include exactly one of the features `Strong`, `Medium` or `Weak`. The features `Multi Player` and `Single Player` constitute an inclusive-or, which demands that at least one of these two features is selected in any valid program configuration. `Single Player` has `Artificial Opponent` as a mandatory child feature. Feature `Wireless` is an optional child feature of root, hence it may or may not be selected. Its child features `Infrared` and `Bluetooth` form an inclusive-or relation, meaning that if a program includes feature `Wireless` then at least one of its two child features has to be selected as well. The Cell Phone SPL also introduces three CTCs. While feature `Multi Player` cannot be selected together (`excludes`) with feature `Weak`, it cannot be selected without feature `Wireless`. Lastly feature `Bluetooth` requires feature `Strong`.

2.2 Basic Definitions

Definition 1. *Feature List (FL) is the list of features in a feature model.*

The FL for the Cell Phone FM is [Cell Phone, Infrared, Bluetooth, Strong, Medium, Weak, Multi Player, Single Player, Display, Games, Artificial Opponent, Accu Cell, Wireless].

Definition 2. *Feature Set (FS) is a 2-tuple [sel,$\overline{sel}$] where sel and $\overline{sel}$ are respectively the set of selected and not-selected features of a member product. Let FL be a feature list, thus sel, $\overline{sel} \subseteq FL$, sel $\cap$ $\overline{sel} = \varnothing$, and sel $\cup$ $\overline{sel} = FL$. The terms p.sel and p.$\overline{sel}$ respectively refer to the set of selected and not-selected features of product p^1.*

Definition 3. *Feature Sets Table (FST) is a set of feature sets, such that for every product p_i we have that $p_i.sel \cup p_i.\overline{sel} = FL$, where FL is a feature list of the corresponding SPL. Let $FST_{FL'}$ denote the clipping of FST that only contains features in feature list FL', i.e. $FST_{FL'} = \{FS \mid \exists\, FS' \in FST : FS'.sel \cap FL' = FS.sel \wedge FS'.\overline{sel} \cap FL' = FS.\overline{sel}\}$ and let FST_f denote the subset of FST that contains only feature sets in which feature f is selected.*

Table 1 shows the 16 valid feature sets defined by the feature model in Figure 1. Throughout the paper we use as column labels the shortest distinguishable prefix of the feature names (e.g. We for Weak). An example of a feature set is product p1 =[{C, A, S, D, G, Si, Ar}, {W, I, M, We, Mu}]. p1 is a valid product because none of the constraints imposed by the Cell Phone FM is violated.

Definition 4. *Atomic set is a group of features that always appears together in all products [6]. That is, features f_1 and f_2 belong to an atomic set if for all products p_i, $f_1 \in p_i.sel$ iff $f_2 \in p_i.sel$ and $f_1 \in p_i.\overline{sel}$ iff $f_2 \in p_i.\overline{sel}$. Let atSet be an atomic set, we denote $\overline{atSet}$ as an arbitrarily chosen representative feature of the atomic set, and $\widetilde{atSet}$ the remaining non-representative features in atSet.*

For example, in the feature sets of Table 1, features Si and Ar form an atomic set atSet. A representative can be $\overline{atSet}$ =Si and $\widetilde{atSet}$={Ar}. Both features always appear together in the products of Table 1, e.g. while product p1 includes features Si and Ar, product p15 does include neither of them.

Definition 5. *Smallest Common Product. Let S be a set of feature sets. Product $p_i \in S$ is a smallest common product of S iff $\forall\, p_j \in S : |p_i.sel| \leq |p_j.sel|$.*

Product p1 includes seven features, it is a smallest common product as there exists no product in Table 1 that includes less features.

For our reverse engineering algorithm two different kinds of graphs are constructed to represent information contained in the input FST, the implication and mutex graph, both are specializations of feature graphs.

Definition 6. *A Feature Graph FG is an ordered pair (V,E) where V is a set of features (i.e. $V \subseteq FL$) representing the vertices of the graph and E is a set of tuples of the form $(f_1, f_2) \in V \times V$, where $(a, b) \in E$ denotes that there is an edge from feature a to feature b.*

---

[1] Definition based on [6].

We say *feature f implies feature f'* in FST, whenever the proposition holds that f' is included whenever f is selected. An implication graph is used to summarize which features imply which other features in the input FST.

Definition 7. *Implication Graph IG. Let fst be an FST where all non-representative features have been removed and let fl be the feature list of fst. The IG of fst and fl is a feature graph that contains an edge from feature f_1 to feature f_2 if f_1 implies f_2 in FST, where IG does not contain any transitive connections between f_1 and f_2 i.e. $\forall f_1, f_2 \in fl : imp(f_1, f_2, fst) \wedge \neg path((f_1, f_2), IG \setminus \{(f_1, f_2)\}) \Rightarrow (f_1, f_2) \in IG$ holds for IG, where:*

- *$imp((t_1, t_2), fst) \equiv \forall fs \in fst : t_1 \notin fs.sel \vee t_1 \in fs.sel \wedge t_2 \in fs.sel$*
- *$path((x, y), G) = (x, y) \in G \vee (\exists x' : (x, x') \in G \wedge path((x', y), G))$.*

The mutex graph stores which features are not selected together in any valid product configuration of the input FST. Section 3 provides algorithms to extract the mutex and implication graph from an FST.

Definition 8. *Mutex Graph. Let fst be an FST and let fl be the FL of fst. A Mutex Graph MG of fst and fl is a feature graph that contains an edge from feature f_1 to feature f_2 iff all feature sets in fst select at most one of these features i.e. $\forall f_1, f_2 \in fl : (\forall fs \in fst : \neg f_1 \in fs.sel \vee \neg f_2 \in fs.sel) \Leftrightarrow (f_1, f_2) \in MG$ holds for MG.*

Definition 9. *A feature map $M \subseteq FL \times \mathcal{P}(FL)$ maps a single feature to a set of features, i.e. $\forall (f_1, features_1), (f_2, features_2) \in M : f_1 = f_2 \Rightarrow features_1 = features_2$ holds. Let f be a feature, M.f denotes the set of features that f maps to.*

3   Reverse Engineering Algorithm

This section describes our reverse engineering algorithm that extracts from an input FST and its FL the corresponding feature model. We start by outlining the challenges introduced by also considering CTCs then we proceed by describing the overall procedure of our algorithm and its core auxiliary function buildFM.

3.1   Challenges Created by Considering CTCs

Our previous work proposed an algorithm to reverse engineer feature models without CTCs (i.e. basic feature models) from FSTs [5]. By also considering CTCs the extraction process gets more complex, because many of the observations used for extracting basic feature models no longer hold. The reason being that CTCs do not introduce new valid feature combinations, but instead they reduce their number.

Essentially there are three core issues that need to be resolved. While the IG of an FST that corresponds to a basic feature model always yields the correct child parent relations, this is not necessarily the case for an FST that corresponds to a feature model with basic CTCs. Also the extraction of exclusive-or relations gets more complex, because two sibling features that are never selected together in any valid product configuration can either be in an exclusive-or relation or in an *excludes* CTC. The third challenge is the extraction of optional features. Previously, we used the observation that all features that are not selected in any of the smallest common products formed by features with the same parent in IG are optional. This observation is not strong enough as soon as *requires* CTCs are considered, because a feature that is not selected in any of the smallest common products might be optional but it could as well be a feature that is just in a *requires* CTC with its parent in IG.

Algorithm 1. Feature Model Extraction

1: Input: A Feature Sets Table (FST), and Feature List (FL).
2: Output: A feature model FM.
3:
4: {Start building FM from common features}
5: $splCF := splWideCommon(FST)$
6: $f \in splCF$
7: $root := [f, splCF - \{root\}, \{\}, \{\}, \{\}]$
8: $FM := [root, \{\}, \{\}]$
9:
10: {Prunes FST by removing common features}
11: $FL' := FL - splCF$
12: $FST' := FST_{FL'}$
13:
14: {Computes atomic sets}
15: $atSets := compAtomicSets(FST', FL')$
16: {Prunes FST by removing atomic sets}

17: $FL'' := FL' - \widetilde{atSets}$
18: $FST'' := FST'_{FL''}$
19:
20: {Build Mutex and Implication Graph}
21: $IG := buildImplGraph(FST'', FL'')$
22: $MG := buildMutexGraph(FST'', FL'')$
23:
24: {Build Feature Model}
25: $FL''' := FL'' - \{root\}$
26: $FST''' := FST''_{FL'''}$
27: $buildFM(FST''', FL''', atSets, root, FM, IG, MG)$
28:
29: {Extract EXCLUDES CTCs}
30: $excludes = extractExclCTC(FM, MG)$
31: $addConstraints(FM, excludes)$
32: **return** FM

3.2   Overall Procedure

Algorithm 1 shows the overall procedure to extract feature models from an input FST and its corresponding FL. The data structure used to store the extracted model is a three-tuple of the form [root, requires, excludes], where root is a feature model node, and requires and excludes are feature maps that respectively represent requires and excludes CTCs.

Definition 10. *A feature model node is a five-tuple of the form [f, mand, opt, or, xor], where f is the feature represented by the node, mand is the set of mandatory child features of f, opt is a set of feature model nodes representing* *the optional child features of f and or (resp. xor) is a set of sets of feature model nodes representing the inclusive-or (resp. exclusive-or) relations among child features of feature f.*

Auxiliary Function 1. *splWideCommon(fst) computes from a Feature Sets Table the set of features that are common to all the members of the product line, i.e. features f such that for all products $p_i \in fst$, $f \in p_i.sel$ holds.*

Line 5 calls `splWideCommon(fst)` which yields for our example the features C, D, A and G, as they are selected in every single product of Table 1. Subsequently Line 6 arbitrarily selects one of these features to be the root feature. Then Lines 7 to 8 initialize the feature model data structure.

Auxiliary Function 2. *compAtomicSets(fl, fst) computes the atomic sets in the feature sets of Feature Sets Table fst involving features in Feature List fl.*

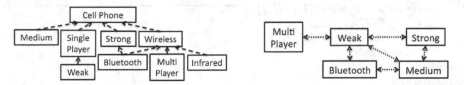

Fig. 2. Implication Graph of Cell Phone SPL   **Fig. 3.** Mutex Graph of Cell Phone SPL

For our running example $\overrightarrow{atSet}$ =Si and $\widetilde{atSet}$={Ar} is extracted as atomic set in Line 15. Lines 21 and 22 extract the implication and mutex graph as they are shown in Figure 2 and 3. To build up the implication graph the auxiliary function `buildImplGraph(fst, fl)` is used (see Algorithm 2). This function takes an FST where all non-representative features have been removed and its FL. Using these two inputs it extracts an implication graph as defined in Definition 7. The two auxiliary functions used by Algorithm 2 are defined as follows.

Auxiliary Function 3. *independent(fst,fl) returns all features in FL fl that do not imply any other feature in FST fst.*

Auxiliary Function 4. *imply(fst,fl, f) returns all features in FL fl that imply feature f in FST fst.*

The function `buildMutexGraph(fst, fl)`, that is described in Algorithm 3, extracts the mutex graph corresponding to an FST and its FL as defined in Definition 8.

Function `buildFM`, shown in Algorithm 4, traverses the implication graph IG from bottom to top and determines the types of relationships among sibling features, at the same time it also extracts the *requires* CTCs and inserts them into FM. Section 3.3 describes this function in more detail.

Auxiliary Function 5. *extractExclCTC(FM, MG) returns a feature map representing the excludes CTC. The function traverses the feature model FM to extract*

Algorithm 2. Build Implication Graph buildImplGraph(FST, FL)

1: Input: A Feature Sets Table (FST), and Feature List (FL).
2: Output: An Implication Graph IG.
3:
4: $IG := \{\}$
5: $f \in splWideCommon(FST)$
6: $FL' = FL - \{f\}$
7: $FST' = (FST_f)_{FL}$
8: $directChildren = independent(FST', FL')$
9:
10: **for** f_{in} in $directChildren$ **do**
11:    $IG = IG \cup \{[f_{in}, f]\}$
12:    $descendants = imply(FST', FL', f)$
13:    $FST'' = (FST'_f)_{descendants}$
14:    $IG = IG \cup buildImplGraph(FST'', descendants)$
15: **end for**
16: **return** IG

Algorithm 3. Build Mutex Graph buildMutexGraph(FST,FL)

1: Input: A Feature Sets Table (FST), and Feature List (FL).
2: Output: A Mutex Graph MG.
3:
4: $MG = \{\}$
5: **for** f in FL **do**
6:    $mutex = \bigcap_{fs \in FST \wedge f \in fs.sel} \overline{fs.sel}$
7:    **if** $| mutex | > 0$ **then**
8:       $MG = MG \cup (\{f\} \times mutex)$
9:    **end if**
10: **end for**
11:
12: **return** MG

a mutex graph MG'. Tuples that are elements of MG (which has been extracted from the input FST) but not element of MG' are extracted as excludes CTCs.

The last step of our reverse engineering algorithm is to extract the *excludes* CTCs (see Lines 30 to 31 in Algorithm 1). Consider Figure 7, it depicts the FM that has been extracted by buildFM and that is shown in the bottom part of Figure 7. Feature Strong is in an exclusive-or relation with Medium and Weak, hence the tuples {(Strong, Medium), (Strong, Weak)} are added to MG'. Also *requires* CTCs have to be considered while MG' is built up, i.e. *"Bluetooth requires Strong"* in FM as Strong excludes Medium and Weak, feature Bluetooth cannot be selected together with these two features either. Figure 4 shows the complete mutex graph MG' extracted by extractExclCTC(FM, MG). (Multi Player, Weak) is an element of MG (see Figure 3) but not of MG', therefore the *excludes* CTC *Multi Player excludes Weak* is added to FM. Figure 5 shows the final feature model that has been extracted by our reverse engineering algorithm. Notice that in this case the extracted FM is different from the one used as our running example in Figure 1. Nonetheless they are both equivalent in the sense that both denote the same set of feature sets.

3.3 Build Feature Model

Algorithm 4 builds up the feature model tree using the extracted graphs (i.e. the implication and mutex graph), the atomic sets and an FST. The implication

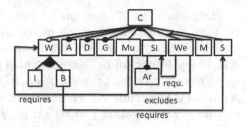

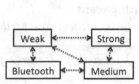

Fig. 4. Mutex Graph extracted from the FM shown in Figure 7

Fig. 5. Extracted FM

graph IG gives hints on the tree-structure of the feature model to extract, i.e. a feature is guaranteed to reach its parent in the implication graph, it is not guaranteed though that a feature is directly connected with its parent. For instance feature Multi Player has a direct connection to feature Wireless (which is not its parent feature) in IG due to the CTC *Multi Player requires Wireless*. BuildFM traverses IG from bottom to top (see Lines 5 to 11).

Algorithm 4. Build Feature Model buildFM

1: Input: A Feature Sets Table (FST), a Feature List (FL), atomic sets (at-Sets), a feature (parent), a feature model (FM) and two graphs (IG and MG).

2: Output: The modified feature model (FM).

3:

4: {Bottom to top traversal of implication graph}

5: **for** f *in* $directChildren(parent, IG)$ **do**

6:   **if** $|\ descendants(f, IG)\ | > 0$ **then**

7:     $FST' := (FST_{node.f})_{descendants(f,IG)}$

8:     $stack.push(f)$

9:     $buildFM(FST',$
      $descendants(f, IG), atSets,$
      $f, FM, IG, MG)$

10:   **end if**

11: **end for**

12:

13: {Keep only columns that are direct children of parent}

14: $FL' = directChildren(parent, IG)$

15: $FST' := FST_{FL'}$

16:

17: {Add XOR relations and compute reduced FST}

18: $xors = insertXors(FST', FL', parent,$
    $FM)$

19: $FL'' = FL' - xors$

20: $FST'' := getSmallestProduct(FST'_{FL''})$

21:

22: {Add optional relations and compute reduced FST}

23: $opts = insertOptionals(FST'', FL'',$
    $parent, FM, IG)$

24: $FL''' = FL'' - opts$

25: $FST''' := getSmallestProduct$
    $(FST_{FL'''})$

26:

27: {Add OR relations}

28: $insertOrs(FST''', FST', FL, parent,$
    $FM, IG)$

29:

30: $stack.pop()$

31: **return**

The feature list FL contains all features that are descendants of **parent** in IG, meaning that these features are either descendants of **parent** in the feature model to extract or they are in a *requires* CTC with **parent**.

Auxiliary Function 6. *descendants(f, IG) returns all features f' that can reach feature f in IG, i.e. path((f',f), IG) holds.*

Auxiliary Function 7. *directChildren(f, IG) returns all features f' that are connected to feature f in IG i.e. (f', f) ∈ IG.*

One of our core observations is that the relationships among sibling features can be extracted by only considering the valid combinations among them, these combinations are calculated in Line 15. Next the exclusive-or relations are extracted (see Line 18) using the auxiliary function **insertXors**.

Auxiliary Function 8. *insertXors(FST, FL, MG, parent, FM, IG) inserts distinct subsets $xor_i \subseteq FL$ as to be in an exclusive-or relation for which holds that all members of xor_i exclude each other and at least one of them is selected in every feature set of FST, i.e.: $\forall f_1 \in xor_i, f_2 \in xor_i : (f_1, f_2) \in MG \land \forall fs \in FST : xor_i \cap fs.sel \neq \{\}$.*

Notice here that the proposition $xor_i \cap fs.sel \neq \{\}$ in Auxiliary Function 8 ensures that two features that are only in an *excludes* CTC are not extracted as to form an exclusive-or relation.

Auxiliary Function 9. *getSmallestProducts (FST) returns an FST' that contains only the smallest common products of FST.*

An example of the use of this function is in Line 20 of Algorithm 4.

Auxiliary Function 10. *insertOptionals(FST, FL, parent, FM, IG) processes possible optional features, i.e. all features f that are not selected in any FS of FST and do not imply their sibling feature or descendant, i.e. ($\forall fs \in FST : f \in \overline{fs.sel}$) $\land$ descendants(parent, IG) $\cap$ FM.requires.f = $\varnothing$ holds, where FST contains only smallest common products. If f is a true optional feature it is inserted as such, otherwise it is pushed one level upwards in IG.*

Connections between two features exist in IG either due to *requires* CTC or child-parent relations. Features that do only have a connection in IG to the current **parent** due to a *requires* CTC are possible optional features. For a true optional feature **f** holds that each valid feature combination containing **f** is still valid if **f** is deselected not considering any features that imply **f**, i.e. $\forall fs \in fst : f \in fs.sel \Rightarrow \exists fs' \in fst : (fs.sel \setminus \{f\}) \setminus implies = fs'.sel \setminus implies$, where **implies** is the set of features that imply feature **f** in the input FST. Function **insertOptionals** checks this property and is used in Line 23, note here that this is the only auxiliary function that operates on the complete input FST of Algorithm 1. The last kind of relation that need to be extracted are inclusive-or relations. Before we do this we again change the considered clipping of the input FST (see Lines 24 to 25).

Auxiliary Function 11. *insertOrs(FST, FST', FL, parent, FM, IG) extracts disjoint subsets of FL as to form inclusive-or relations and inserts them into feature model FM.*

Let **n** be the number of included features in a smallest common product ($fs \in FST, n = |fs.sel|$), then **n** yields the number of inclusive-or relations to extract.

Features that are selected together in the products of FST have to be in different inclusive-or relations. The features in FL that are selected in the products of FST, are grouped into n disjoint subsets, where two features that are selected together in any of the products in FST are put into different subsets.[2] Each of these subsets ss_i represents a possible inclusive-or relation, but only those ss_i are inserted as to be in an inclusive-or relation for which holds: $\forall fs \in FST' : fs.sel \cap ss_i \neq \varnothing$.[3]

The remainder of this section describes how buildFM proceeds on the running example. During the first call of buildFM the variable **parent** is equal to C, Line 5 yields the set {M, Si, S, W} as direct children of C in IG. Lets choose feature W as the first direct child that is processed by the loop in Line 5 As the direct children of W (i.e. I, B and Mu) do not have descendants there are no further recursive calls for these features.

Line 15 reduces the input FST, in our example the set of descendants of W is equal to its direct children, hence FST is equal to FST'. The features I, B and Mu do not exclude each other, hence Line 18 does not extract any exclusive-or relations. Line 20 extracts the smallest common products in FST' yielding FST''= $\{[\{B\}, \{I, Mu\}], [\{I\}, \{B, Mu\}]\}$. Line 23 pushes feature Mu one level upwards in IG inserting the CTC *"Multi Player requires Wireless"*. Mu is a possible optional feature, i.e. it is not selected in any of the products in FST'' and there exists no *requires* CTC with any of its sibling features, but Mu is not a true optional feature. Consider for instance product p11 in Table 1, *p11.sel* = {C, W, I, A, Me, D, G, Mu}. If W was an optional feature then a product $p11'.sel = p11.sel \setminus \{Mu\}$ should also exist in Table 1 as this is not the case W cannot be optional.

Auxiliary function insertOrs extracts features I and B as to be in an inclusive-or relation. Figure 6 depicts the extracted Feature Model and the modified feature graph IG after the first recursive call of buildFM.

The second recursive call is performed for feature Si and its descendant feature We. Once again auxiliary function insertOptionals yields that We is not a true optional feature, hence it pushes We one level upwards in IG and inserts the *requires* CTC *"Weak requires Single Player"*.

As no further recursive calls are required, buildFM now extracts the relations among the direct children of root, i.e. features W, Si, Mu, S, M and We.

Function insertXor extracts the features S, M and We as to form an exclusive-or relation. Subsequently Line 20 calculates FST''= $\{[\{Si\}, \{W, Mu\}]\}$ that contains only the smallest common products formed by features W, Mu and Si.

Feature W is extracted as optional feature because it is neither selected in any of the products in FST'' nor does it require one of its sibling features. As feature Mu implies feature W it cannot be an optional feature. FST''' is equal to

---

[2] Please refer to [9] for an explanation how we deal with features that are not selected in any of the products in FST.

[3] If there are features that could not be inserted, this means that possibly no equivalent model is extracted. Features for which the correct place in the feature model could not be found will be pushed one level upwards in the implication graph, if the current parent is the root feature then these features are inserted as optional child features.

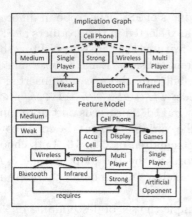

Fig. 6. IG and FM after first recursive call of buildFM

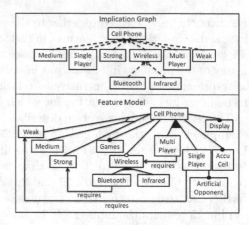

Fig. 7. IG and FM after call of buildFM

$\{[\{Si\}, \{Mu\}], [\{Mu\}, \{Ri\}]\}$, it contains the smallest common products formed by Mu and Si. Using FST''' insertOrs inserts an inclusive-or relation among these two features. Figure 7 shows the extracted feature model and the modified implication graph after the call of buildFM.

4   Evaluation

We evaluated our approach with 168 FMs publicly available from the SPLOT Homepage [8], for which the FAMA tool suite [10] was able to generate the corresponding FSTs that were then used as input to our reverse engineering algorithm[4]. The size of the FSTs described by one of these models ranges from 1 to 147456 products with an average of 1862.2 and a median of 62 products. The number of features is between 9 and 38. Of these 168 models, 69 have *requires* or *excludes* CTCs. The average number of CTCs of these 69 models is 3.12, the median is 2. The model with the most CTCs has 6 *excludes* and 11 *requires* CTCs and describes 1042 products. We executed our examples on a Windows 7 Pro system, running at 3.2Ghz, and with 8 GB of RAM. Figure 8 depicts the execution times of this evaluation. Our timing analysis shows that the average execution time is 1862.2ms and the median is 62ms, for the largest FST the execution of our reverse engineering algorithm takes only 12s. In each of these 168 cases our reverse engineering algorithm generated an equivalent model. To determine the equivalence of the input model and the reverse engineered model we used a procedure very similar to the one presented in [11].

---

[4] The code and feature models samples are available at:
http://www.jku.at/sea/content/e139529/e126342/e188736/

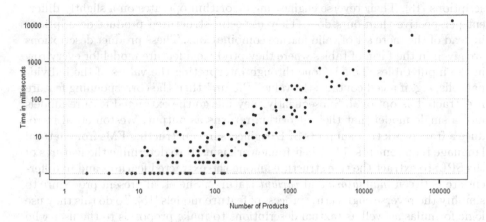

Fig. 8. Execution times of test runs

4.1 Algorithm Limitations

Each additional non-redundant CTC reduces the set of valid product configurations, however at some point it may no longer be possible to extract the hierarchy of the FM tree as too much information may be missing. Our algorithm does not cover circular *requires* CTCs, (e.g. if a feature A *requires* feature B and feature B *requires* feature A) or structural feature constructs which are equivalent to them [9]. In such case our reverse engineering algorithm produces an FM that is not equivalent to the input FST. However, we argue that such cases may indicate potential design flaws in the feature models that the software engineers should address. Our algorithm assumes that the input FST is complete, that is it contains *all* possible product configurations the FM should denote. Dealing with incomplete FSTs and incremental adaptation of existing FMs is part of our future work.

5   Related Work

This section outlines other approaches to reverse engineer feature models. Lopez-Herrejon et. al published an exploratory study on reverse engineering feature models using evolutionary algorithms [12], where *ETHOM (Evolutionary algoriTHm for Optimized feature Models)* was used for their implementation. Like our approach they also use a set of valid program configurations as an input to their algorithm. We see the advantage that they are theoretically able to reverse engineer more than one feature model that represents the input FST, which makes it possible to choose the model that contains the most meaningful feature hierarchy. Their evaluation showed though that they extracted in most cases feature models that are not equivalent to the input FST.

Acher et. al proposed a procedure to extract feature models from product descriptions [13]. Their reverse engineering algorithm operates on a slightly different perspective than ours does. They use semi-structured product descriptions instead of the mere set of valid feature combinations. These product descriptions are given in the form of tables where they produce a feature model for every row in the input tables. This is done through interpreting the values of the individual cells, e.g. if a cell contains the value "Plugin" then the corresponding feature is extracted as optional. Subsequently they merge the extracted feature models into a single model that their algorithm returns as output. Weston et. al introduce a framework that supports SPL engineers in constructing FMs from natural language requirements [14]. Their framework is used to determine the features of the SPL, to extract the tree structure among the extracted features and to differentiate between *mandatory* and *variant* features. She et. al present procedure to simplify the reverse engineering process of feature models [15]. To do this they use logic formulas as well as textual descriptions to make proposals to the user who then guides the extraction process. To extract the hierarchy of the FM tree they use an implication graph obtained from the logic formulas and similarity measures among the features of the SPL that have been extracted from the textual descriptions. Andersen et. al propose algorithms to reverse engineer feature models from propositional logic formulas, these formulas are either in disjunctive normal form (DNF) or conjunctive normal form (CNF) [16]. Note here that while an FST can be viewed as a propositional logic formula in DNF, our approach is very different from Andersen et. al's. While we use set operations to reverse engineer an FM from an FST their algorithms heavily rely on BDDs or rather SAT solvers. Moreover we want to emphasize here that Andersen et. al extracted for their evaluation feature graphs which need to be converted into feature models at a later time, either with the help of user input or an automated procedure described in their paper.

6   Conclusions and Future Work

Our evaluation shows that the proposed algorithm is able to reverse engineer feature models from input FSTs with a median execution time in the order of milliseconds. Our future work will address the following three issues. First, our current algorithm does not support circular *requires* CTCs. We plan to assess in practice if this scenario can indeed be characterized as a design error. Alternatively, we would extend the algorithm to cope with such cases. The second issue is a thorough scalability assessment. Our current evaluation is limited by FAMA's capability to generate feature sets. We expect to overcome this limitation with an approach sketched in [9]. FMs are not canonical, so there might be several non-identical FMs that represent the same FST. The third issue we plan to address is assessing the understandability of our reverse engineered models.

Acknowledgments. This research is partially funded by the Austrian Science Fund (FWF) project P21321-N15 and Lise Meitner Fellowship M1421-N15, and Marie Curie Actions - Intra-European Fellowship (IEF) project number 254965.

References

1. Svahnberg, M., van Gurp, J., Bosch, J.: A taxonomy of variability realization techniques. Softw., Pract. Exper. 35(8), 705–754 (2005)
2. Pohl, K., Bockle, G., van der Linden, F.J.: Software Product Line Engineering: Foundations, Principles and Techniques. Springer (2005)
3. Zave, P.: Faq sheet on feature interaction,
   http://www.research.att.com/pamela/faq.html
4. Kang, K., Cohen, S., Hess, J., Novak, W., Peterson, A.: Feature-Oriented Domain Analysis (FODA) Feasibility Study. Technical Report CMU/SEI-90-TR-21, Software Engineering Institute, Carnegie Mellon University (1990)
5. Haslinger, E.N., Lopez-Herrejon, R.E., Egyed, A.: Reverse engineering feature models from programs' feature sets. In: Pinzger, M., Poshyvanyk, D., Buckley, J. (eds.) WCRE, pp. 308–312. IEEE Computer Society (2011)
6. Benavides, D., Segura, S., Cortés, A.R.: Automated analysis of feature models 20 years later: A literature review. Inf. Syst. 35(6), 615–636 (2010)
7. Batory, D.: Feature Models, Grammars, and Propositional Formulas. In: Obbink, H., Pohl, K. (eds.) SPLC 2005. LNCS, vol. 3714, pp. 7–20. Springer, Heidelberg (2005)
8. Software Product Line Online Tools, SPLOT (2010),
   http://www.splot-research.org/
9. Haslinger, E.N.: Reverse engineering feature models from program configurations. Master's thesis, Johannes Kepler University (2012),
   http://www.sea.jku.at/ms/evelyn.haslinger
10. FAMA Tool Suite (2012), http://www.isa.us.es/fama/
11. Thüm, T., Batory, D.S., Kästner, C.: Reasoning about edits to feature models. In: ICSE, pp. 254–264. IEEE (2009)
12. Lopez-Herrejon, R.E., Galindo, J.A., Benavides, D., Segura, S., Egyed, A.: Reverse Engineering Feature Models with Evolutionary Algorithms: An Exploratory Study. In: Fraser, G., Teixeira de Souza, J. (eds.) SSBSE 2012. LNCS, vol. 7515, pp. 168–182. Springer, Heidelberg (2012)
13. Acher, M., Cleve, A., Perrouin, G., Heymans, P., Vanbeneden, C., Collet, P., Lahire, P.: On extracting feature models from product descriptions. In: Eisenecker, U.W., Apel, S., Gnesi, S. (eds.) VaMoS, pp. 45–54. ACM (2012)
14. Weston, N., Chitchyan, R., Rashid, A.: A framework for constructing semantically composable feature models from natural language requirements. In: Muthig, D., McGregor, J.D. (eds.) SPLC. ACM International Conference Proceeding Series, vol. 446, pp. 211–220. ACM (2009)
15. She, S., Lotufo, R., Berger, T., Wasowski, A., Czarnecki, K.: Reverse engineering feature models. In: Taylor, R.N., Gall, H., Medvidovic, N. (eds.) ICSE, pp. 461–470. ACM (2011)
16. Andersen, N., Czarnecki, K., She, S., Wasowski, A.: Efficient synthesis of feature models. In: de Almeida, E.S., Schwanninger, C., Benavides, D. (eds.) SPLC, vol. (1), pp. 106–115. ACM (2012)

On the Empirical Evaluation of Fault Localization Techniques for Spreadsheets

Birgit Hofer[1], André Riboira[2], Franz Wotawa[1],
Rui Abreu[2], and Elisabeth Getzner[1]

[1] Institute for Software Technology,
Graz University of Technology, Graz, Austria
{bhofer,wotawa}@ist.tugraz.at, elisabeth.getzner@student.tugraz.at
[2] Department of Informatics Engineering,
Faculty of Engineering of University of Porto, Porto, Portugal
andre.riboira@fe.up.pt, rui@computer.org

Abstract. Spreadsheets are by far the most prominent example of end-user programs of ample size and substantial structural complexity. In addition, spreadsheets are usually not tested very rigorously and thus comprise faults. Locating faults is a hard task due to the size and the structure, which is usually not directly visible to the user, i.e., the functions are hidden behind the cells and only the computed values are presented. Hence, there is a strong need for debugging support. In this paper, we adapt three program-debugging approaches that have been designed for more traditional procedural or object-oriented programming languages. These techniques are Spectrum-based Fault Localization, Spectrum-Enhanced Dynamic Slicing, and Constraint-based Debugging. Beside the theoretical foundations, we present a more sophisticated empirical evaluation including a comparison of these approaches. The empirical evaluation shows that SFL (Spectrum-based Fault Localization) and SENDYS (Spectrum ENhanced Dynamic Slicing) are the most promising techniques.

Keywords: End-User debugging, spreadsheets, spectrum-based fault localization, model-based debugging.

1 Introduction

Spreadsheet tools, such as Microsoft Excel, iWork's Numbers, and OpenOffice's Calc, can be viewed as programming environments for non-professional programmers [1]. In fact, these so-called "end-user" programmers vastly outnumber professional ones: the US Bureau of Labor and Statistics estimates that more than 55 million people use spreadsheets and databases at work on a daily basis [1]. Despite this trend, as a programming language, spreadsheets lack support for abstraction, testing, encapsulation, or structured programming. As a consequence, spreadsheets are error-prone. Numerous studies have shown that existing spreadsheets contain redundancy and errors at an alarmingly high rate [2].

V. Cortellessa and D. Varró (Eds.): FASE 2013, LNCS 7793, pp. 68–82, 2013.
© Springer-Verlag Berlin Heidelberg 2013

Furthermore, spreadsheets are applications created by single end-users without planning ahead of time for maintainability or scalability. Still, after their initial creation, many spreadsheets turn out to be used for storing and processing increasing amounts of data as well as supporting increasing numbers of users over long periods of time. Therefore, debugging (i.e., locating the cell(s) that are responsible for the wrong output in a given cell) can be a rather cumbersome task, requiring substantial time and effort.

In spite of having the potential to benefit from recent developments in the software engineering domain, the truth is that only a few attempts have been made to adapt software engineering techniques to the spreadsheet world. The objective of this paper is to advance the state of the art in spreadsheet debugging by applying popular, mature techniques developed to analyze software systems. Such techniques will have a positive impact in the overall quality of spreadsheets.

In this paper, we adapt three program-debugging approaches that have been designed for more traditional procedural or object-oriented programming languages. In particular, we describe how to modify traditional fault localization techniques in order to render them applicable to the spreadsheet world. We consider the following techniques in our study: Spectrum-based Fault Localization (SFL) [3], Spectrum-enhanced dynamic slicing (SENDYS) [4], and Constraint-based Debugging (CONBUG) [5]. We evaluate the efficiency of the approaches using real spreadsheets taken from the EUSES Spreadsheet Corpus [6].

The remainder of the paper is organized as follows: Section 2 deals with the related work. In addition, existing spreadsheet debugging and testing techniques are discussed. Section 3 deals with the syntax and semantics of spreadsheets. Furthermore, the Spreadsheet Debugging problem is defined. Section 4 explains the changes that have to be made in order to use the existing debugging techniques for debugging of spreadsheets. Three traditional debugging techniques are explained in detail. Section 5 deals with the setup and the results of the empirical evaluation. Finally, Section 6 concludes this paper and presents ideas for future empirical evaluations.

2 Related Work

Since spreadsheet *developers* are typically end-users without significant background in computer science, there has been considerable effort to adapt software engineering principles to form a spreadsheet engineering discipline (e.g., [7–11]).

Some of the work presented in this paper is based on model-based diagnosis [12], namely its application to (semi-)automatic debugging (e.g., [13]). In contrast to previous work, the work presented in this paper does not use logic-based models of programs but instead uses a generic model which can be automatically computed from the spreadsheet. A similar approach has been presented recently to aid debuggers in pinpointing software failures [14]. Moreover, Jannach and Engler presented a model-based approach [15] to calculate possible error causes in spreadsheets. This approach uses an extended hitting-set algorithm and user-specified or historical test cases and assertions.

GoalDebug [16, 17] is a spreadsheet debugger for end users. Whenever the computed output of a cell is incorrect, the user can supply an expected value for a cell, which is employed by the system to generate a list of change suggestions for formulas that, when applied, would result in the user-specified output. In [16] a thorough evaluation of the tool is given. GoalDebug employs an approach similar to the constraint-based approach presented in this paper.

Spreadsheet testing is closely related to debugging. In the WYSIWYT system users can indicate incorrect output values by placing a faulty token in the cell. Similarly, they can indicate that the value in a cell is correct by placing a correct token [18]. When a user indicates one or more program failures during this testing process, fault localization techniques direct the user's attention to the possible faulty cells. However, WYSIWYT does not provide any suggestions for how to change erroneous formulas.

3 Basic Definitions

A spreadsheet is a matrix comprising cells. Each cell is unique and can be accessed using its corresponding column and row number. For simplicity, we assume a function φ that maps the cell names from a set $CELLS$ to their corresponding position (x, y) in the matrix where x represents the column and y the row number. The functions φ_x and φ_y return the column and row number of a cell respectively.

Aside from a position, each cell $c \in CELLS$ has a value $\nu(c)$ and an expression $\ell(c)$. The value of a cell can be either undefined ϵ, an error $\perp$, or any number, boolean or string value. The expression of a cell $\ell(c)$ can either be empty or an expression written in the language $\mathcal{L}$. The value of a cell c is determined by its expression. If no expression is explicitly declared for a cell, the function ℓ returns the value ϵ.

Areas are another important basic element of spreadsheets. An area is a set consisting of all cells that are within the area that is spanned by the cells $c_1, c_2 \in CELLS$. Formally, we define an area as follows:

$$c_1{:}c_2 \equiv_{def} \left\{ c \in CELLS \,\middle|\, \begin{array}{l} \varphi_x(c_1) \leq \varphi_x(c) \leq \varphi_x(c_2) \ \& \\ \varphi_y(c_1) \leq \varphi_y(c) \leq \varphi_y(c_2) \end{array} \right\}$$

Obviously, every area is a subset of the set of cells ($c_1{:}c_2 \subseteq CELLS$). After defining the basic elements of spreadsheets, we introduce the language $\mathcal{L}$ for representing expressions that are used to compute values for cells. For reasons of simplicity, we do not introduce all available functions in today's spreadsheet implementations. Instead and without restricting generality, we make use of simple operators on cells and areas. Extending the used operators with new ones is straightforward.

The introduced language takes the values of cells and constants together with operators and conditionals to compute values for other cells. The language is a functional language, i.e., only one value is computed for a specific cell. Moreover, we do not allow recursive functions. First, we define the syntax of $\mathcal{L}$.

Definition 1 (Syntax of $\mathcal{L}$). *We define the syntax of $\mathcal{L}$ recursively as follows:*

- *Constants k representing ϵ, number, boolean, or string values are elements of $\mathcal{L}$ (i.e., $k \in \mathcal{L}$).*
- *All cell names are elements of $\mathcal{L}$ (i.e., CELLS $\subset \mathcal{L}$).*
- *If e_1, e_2, e_3 are elements of the language ($e_1, e_2, e_3 \in \mathcal{L}$), then the following expressions are also elements of $\mathcal{L}$:*
  - *(e_1) is an element of $\mathcal{L}$.*
  - *If o is an operator ($o \in \{+, -, *, /, <, =, >\}$), then $e_1 \ o \ e_2$ is an element of $\mathcal{L}$.*
  - *$if(e_1; e_2; e_3)$ is an element of $\mathcal{L}$.*
- *If $c_1{:}c_2$ is an area, then $sum(c_1{:}c_2)$ is an element of $\mathcal{L}$.*

Second, we define the semantics of $\mathcal{L}$ by introducing an interpretation function $[\![\cdot]\!]$ that maps an expression $e \in \mathcal{L}$ to a value. The value is ϵ if no value can be determined or $\bot$ if a type error occurs. Otherwise it is either a number, a boolean, or a string.

Definition 2 (Semantics of $\mathcal{L}$). *Let e be an expression from $\mathcal{L}$ and ν a function mapping cell names to values. We define the semantic of $\mathcal{L}$ recursively as follows:*

- *If e is a constant k, then the constant is given back as result, i.e., $[\![e]\!] = k$.*
- *If e denotes a cell name c, then its value is returned, i.e., $[\![e]\!] = \nu(c)$.*
- *If e is of the form (e_1), then $[\![e]\!] = [\![e_1]\!]$.*
- *If e is of the form $e_1 \ o \ e_2$, then its execution is defined as follows:*
  - *If either $[\![e_1]\!] = \bot$ or $[\![e_2]\!] = \bot$, then $[\![e_1 \ o \ e_2]\!] = \bot$.*
  - *else if either $[\![e_1]\!] = \epsilon$ or $[\![e_2]\!] = \epsilon$, then $[\![e_1 \ o \ e_2]\!] = \epsilon$.*
  - *else if $o \in \{+, -, *, /, <, =, >\}$, then*

$$[\![e_1 \ o \ e_2]\!] = \begin{cases} [\![e_1]\!] \ o \ [\![e_2]\!] & \text{if all sub-expressions evaluate to a number} \\ \bot & \text{otherwise} \end{cases}$$

- *If e is of the form $if(e_1; e_2; e_3)$, then*

$$[\![e]\!] = \begin{cases} [\![e_2]\!] & \text{if } [\![e_1]\!] = \textbf{true} \\ [\![e_3]\!] & \text{if } [\![e_1]\!] = \textbf{false} \\ \epsilon & \text{if } [\![e_1]\!] = \epsilon \\ \bot & \text{otherwise} \end{cases}$$

- *If e is of the form $sum(c_1{:}c_2)$, then*

$$[\![e]\!] = \begin{cases} \sum\limits_{c \in c_1{:}c_2} [\![c]\!] & \text{if all cells in } c_1{:}c_2 \text{ have a number or } \epsilon \text{ (treated as 0) as value} \\ \bot & \text{otherwise} \end{cases}$$

Frequently, we require information about cells that are used as input in an expression. We call such cells *referenced cells*.

Definition 3 (Referenced cell). *A cell c is said to be referenced by an expression $e \in \mathcal{L}$, if and only if c is used in e.*

We furthermore introduce a function $\rho : \mathcal{L} \mapsto 2^{CELLS}$ that returns the set of referenced cells. Formally, we define ρ as follows:

Definition 4 (The function ρ). *Let $e \in \mathcal{L}$ be an expression. We define the referenced cells function ρ recursively as follows:*

- *If e is a constant, then $\rho(e) = \emptyset$.*
- *If e is a cell c, then $\rho(e) = \{c\}$.*
- *If $e = (e_1)$, then $\rho(e) = \rho(e_1)$.*
- *If $e = e_1 \ o \ e_2$, then $\rho(e) = \rho(e_1) \cup \rho(e_2)$.*
- *If $e = \mathbf{if}(e_1; \ e_2; \ e_3)$, then $\rho(e) = \rho(e_1) \cup \rho(e_2) \cup \rho(e_3)$.*
- *If $e = \mathbf{sum}(c_1{:}c_2)$, then $\rho(e) = c_1{:}c_2$.*

A spreadsheet is a matrix of cells comprising values and expressions written in a language $\mathcal{L}$. In addition, we know that the values of cells are determined by their expressions. Hence, we can state that $\forall c \in CELLS : \nu(c) = [\![\ell(c)]\!]$ must hold. Unfortunately, we face two challenges: (1) In all of the previous definitions, the set of cells need not be of finite size. (2) There might be a loop in the computation of values, e.g. a cell c with $\ell(c) = c+1$. In this case, we are not able to determine a value for cell c. In order to solve the first challenge, we formally restrict spreadsheets to comprise only a finite number of cells.

Definition 5 (Spreadsheet). *A countable set of cells $\Pi \subseteq CELLS$ is a spreadsheet if all cells in Π have a non empty corresponding expression or are referenced in an expression, i.e., $\forall c \in \Pi : (\ell(c) \neq \epsilon) \vee (\exists c' \in \Pi : c \in \rho(\ell(c')))$.*

In order to solve the second challenge, we have to limit spreadsheets to loop-free spreadsheets. For this purpose, we first introduce the notation of data dependence between cells, and furthermore the data dependence graph, which represents all dependencies occurring in a spreadsheet.

Definition 6 (Direct dependence). *Let c_1, c_2 be cells of a spreadsheet Π. The cell c_2 depends directly on cell c_1 if and only if c_1 is used in c_2's corresponding expression, i.e., $dd(c_1, c_2) \leftrightarrow (c_1 \in \rho(\ell(c_2)))$.*

The direct dependence definition states the data dependence between two cells. This definition can be extended to the general case in order to specify indirect dependence. In addition, this dependence definition immediately leads to the definition of a graph that can be extracted from a spreadsheet.

Definition 7 (Data dependence graph (DDG)). *Let Π be a spreadsheet. The data dependence graph (DDG) of Π is a tuple (V, A) with:*

- *V as a set of vertices comprising exactly one vertex n_c for each cell $c \in \Pi$*
- *A as a set comprising arcs (n_{c_1}, n_{c_2}) if and only if there is a direct dependence between the corresponding cells c_1 and c_2 respectively, i.e. $A = \bigcup (n_{c_1}, n_{c_2})$ where $n_{c_1}, n_{c_2} \in V \wedge dd(c_1, c_2)$.*

From this definition, we are able to define general dependence between cells. Two cells of a spreadsheet are dependent if and only if there exists a path between the corresponding vertices in the DDG. In addition, we are able to further restrict spreadsheets to face the second challenge.

Definition 8 (Feasible spreadsheet). *A spreadsheet Π is feasible if and only if its DDG is acyclic.*

From here on, we assume that all spreadsheets of interest are feasible. Hence, we use the terms spreadsheet and feasible spreadsheet synonymously. Standard spreadsheet programs like Excel rely on loop-free computations.

In this paper, we focus on testing and debugging of spreadsheets. In ordinary sequential programs, a test case comprises input values and expected output values. If we want to rely on similar definitions, we have to clarify the terms input, output and test case. Defining the input and output of feasible spreadsheets is straightforward by means of the DDG.

Definition 9 (Input, output). *Given a feasible spreadsheet Π and its DDG (V, A), then the input cells of Π (or short: inputs) comprise all cells that have no incoming edges in the corresponding vertex of Π's DDG. The output cells of Π (or short: outputs) comprise all cells where the corresponding vertex of the DDG has no outgoing vertex.*

$$inputs(\Pi) = \{c | \nexists (n_{c'}, n_c) \in A\}$$
$$outputs(\Pi) = \{c | \nexists (n_c, n_{c'}) \in A\}$$

All cells of a spreadsheet that serve neither as input nor as output are called intermediate cells. With this definition of input and output cells we are able to define a test case for a spreadsheet and its evaluation.

Definition 10 (Test case). *Given a spreadsheet Π, then a tuple (I, O) is a test case for Π if and only if:*

- *I is a set of tuples (c, e) specifying input cells and their values. For each $c \in inputs(\Pi)$ there must be a tuple (c, e) in I where $e \in \mathcal{L}$ is a constant.*
- *O is a set of tuples (c, e) specifying expected output values. The expected output values must be constants of $\mathcal{L}$.*

In our setting, test case evaluation works as follows: First, the functions $\ell(c)$ of the input cells are set to the constant values specified in the test case. Subsequently, the spreadsheet is evaluated. Afterwards, the computed output values are compared with the expected values stated in the test case. If at least one computed output value is not equivalent to the expected value, the spreadsheet fails the test case. Otherwise, the spreadsheet passes the test case.

In traditional programming languages, test cases are separated from the source code. Usually, there are several test cases for one function under test. Each of the test cases calls the function with different parameters and checks the correctness of the returned values. However, test cases are only implicitly encoded into spreadsheets. This means, that test cases are not explicitly separated from the formulas under test. If the user wants to add an additional test case, he or she has to duplicate the spreadsheet. A duplication of a spreadsheet for testing purposes is unpractical since the duplicates have to be updated when the spreadsheet is modified or extended. Therefore, usually only one failing test case exists. Hence, we reduce the debugging problem for spreadsheets to handle only one test case.

Definition 11 (Spreadsheet debugging problem). *Given a spreadsheet Π and a failing test case (I, O), then the debugging problem is to find a root cause for the mismatch between the expected output values and the computed ones.*

We define the spreadsheet debugging problem as a fault localization problem. This definition implies that the following debugging approaches pinpoint certain cells of a spreadsheet as possible root causes of faults. However, the approaches do not make any suggestions how to change these parts. Alternatively, the debugging problem can be defined as a fault correction problem.

4   Debugging Approaches

Traditional procedural and object-oriented program-debugging techniques cannot be directly transferred to spreadsheets for the following reasons: In a spreadsheet paradigm, the concept of code coverage does not exist since there are no explicit lines of code like in traditional programming paradigms. Moreover, there is no concept of test execution.

Therefore, in order to use traditional program-debugging techniques on spreadsheets, we have to perform some modifications: the lines of code in a traditional programming paradigm are mapped to the cells of a spreadsheet. There are cells designed to receive user input, cells to process data (using spreadsheet formulas), and cells intended to display the results. As an alternative to the code coverage of traditional programming paradigms, we compute so-called *cones* (data dependencies of each cell).

Definition 12 (The function CONE). *Given a spreadsheet Π and a cell $c \in \Pi$, then we define the function CONE recursively as follows:*

$$\text{CONE}(c) = c \cup \bigcup_{c' \in \rho(c)} \text{CONE}(c')$$

The correctness of the output cells is determined either by the user, by comparing the results of the current spreadsheet Π with another spreadsheet considered correct, or by applying techniques to automatically detect "bad smells" [19].

With these modifications, we are able to apply three traditional fault localization techniques on spreadsheets. In the following subsections, we explain these debugging techniques.

4.1 Spreadsheets Spectrum-Based Fault Localization

In traditional programming paradigms, Spectrum-based fault localization (SFL) [3] uses code coverage data and the pass/fail result of each test execution of a given system under test (SUT) as input. The code coverage data [20] is collected from test cases by means of an instrumentation approach. This data is collected at runtime and is used to build a so-called hit-spectra matrix. A hit-spectra matrix A is a binary matrix where each column i represents a system component and each row j represents a test case. The content of the matrix a_{ij} represents whether component i was used (true) or not (false) during test execution j. The results of the test executions (pass/fail) are stored in an error vector E. The error vector is a binary array where each position i represents a test execution. The value of the error vector e at position i is true if the test case i failed, otherwise false.

SFL uses similarity coefficients to estimate the likelihood of a given software component being faulty. Similarity coefficients compute the relationship between each column of the matrix (representing a system component) and the error vector. This similarity coefficient and the failure probability of the corresponding system component are directly related [21]. The coefficients are used to create rankings of system components [22] or to create interactive visualizations of the SUT, revealing the most suspicious parts of the application's source code [23].

In the spreadsheet paradigm, we cannot use the coverage data of test executions. Instead, we use the cones of the output cells (see Definition 12). From the cones, the hit-spectra matrix can be generated (each row of the matrix has the dependencies of one output cell). The error vector represents the correctness of the output cells. The hit-spectra matrix and the error vector allow the use of any SFL algorithm to compute the failure probability of each spreadsheet cell. In the empirical evaluation, we use the Ochiai similarity coefficient, since Ochiai is known to be one of the most efficient similarity coefficients used in SFL techniques [21].

4.2 Spectrum-Enhanced Dynamic Slicing Approach

Spectrum-Enhanced Dynamic Slicing (SENDYS) [4] is a technique that combines SFL with a lightweight model-based software debugging (MBSD) technique [24]. In traditional programming paradigms, similar to SFL, SENDYS uses coverage data and the result of each test execution (pass/fail) of a given SUT as input. In addition, the slices of the negative test cases are required. SENDYS works as follows: the similarity coefficients computed by means of SFL act as a priori probabilities in the MBSD approach. Each statement gets assigned its similarity coefficient as the initial fault probability. The slices of the faulty variables are treated as conflict sets and the minimal hitting sets (i.e. the diagnoses) are computed. A set h is a hitting set for set of conflict sets CO if and only if for all $c \in CO$, there exists a non-empty intersection between c and h (i.e., $\forall c \in CO : c \cap h \neq \emptyset$). From the initial statement fault probabilities, the fault probabilities of the diagnoses are computed. Therefore, the probabilities of the statements contained in the diagnosis are multiplied with the counter-probabilities of the statements not contained in the diagnosis. Afterwards, the probabilities are mapped back to the statements. For each statement, the probabilities of the diagnoses containing that statement are summed up. Finally, the statements are ranked according to their probabilities. The statement with the highest probability is ranked at the first position.

In order to apply SENDYS to the spreadsheet paradigm, we propose to make the same modifications as described in the section about the SFL technique. In addition, we have to use cones instead of slices for the MBSD part. The major difference between cones and slices are the used dependencies. For slices, control- and data dependencies are used. In contrast, cones only make use of data dependencies.

4.3   Constraint-Based Debugging

There exist several model-based software debugging (MBSD) techniques which use constraints as part of their debugging strategy, e.g. [14, 25]. In these techniques, program statements are converted into their constraint representation. Each converted statement is connected with a variable representing the health status of the statement: a statement either behaves as specified or the statement has the health status 'abnormal'. A constraint solver is used to compute all possible solutions for the health states of all statements so that the constraints of the program are feasible. All statements with the health status 'abnormal' are explanations for an observed misbehavior. Some solutions of the constraint solver contain several 'abnormal' statements. In this case, all 'abnormal' statements must be changed in order to correct the faulty program. The result of applying a constraint-based debugging technique on a faulty program is a set of 'abnormal' variables representing the health status of the corresponding statements. There is no conclusion which of the statements is more likely to be faulty. Unlike SFL and SENDYS, this method can not generate a likelihood-ranking of possibly faulty statements.

In the context of spreadsheet debugging, cells are used instead of statements: for each cell, the contained formula is converted into a set of constraints. CON-BUG [5] is a technique that is based on the above described technique, but is designed for debugging spreadsheets.

5   Empirical Evaluation

In this section, we are evaluating the previously described approaches by means of the EUSES spreadsheet corpus [6]. In the first part, we are evaluating the ranking of the faulty statements for SFL and SENDYS. In the second part, we are evaluating the size of the result set of CONBUG in comparison to the union and intersection of the slices. However, first of all we are going the explain the experimental setup.

In a first filtering step, we skipped around 240 Excel 5.0 spreadsheets that are not compatible with our implementation, since our implementation is build on Apache POI (http://poi.apache.org/) and POI does not support Excel 5.0.

In a second filtering step, we removed all spreadsheets containing less than five formulas (about 2,300 files). We have performed this filtering step because automatic fault localization only makes sense for larger spreadsheets. A small spreadsheet is still manageable and thus fault localization can be easily performed manually. For small spreadsheets, a fault correction approach makes more sense than just a fault localization approach. Finally, around 1,400 spreadsheets remain for our case study.

For each spreadsheet, we automatically created up to five first-order mutants. A mutant of a spreadsheet is created by randomly choosing a formula cell of the spreadsheet and applying a mutation operator on it. According to the classification of spreadsheet mutation operators of Abraham and Erwig [26], we used the following mutation operators:

- *Continuous Range Shrinking (CRS):* We randomly choose whether to increment the index of the first column/row or decrement the index of the last column/row in area references.
- *Reference Replacement (RFR):* We randomly choose whether to increment the row or the column index of references. We do not explicitly differentiate between single references and references in non-contiguous ranges. For this, a mutation can change a single reference in a non-contiguous range, but never changes the amount of elements in the range.
- *Arithmetic Operator Replacement (AOR):* We replace '+' with '-' and vice versa and '*' with '/'.
- *Relational Operator Replacement (ROR):* We replace the operators '=', '<', '<=', '>', '>=', and '<>' with one another.
- *Constants Replacement (CRP):*
  - For integer values, we add a random number between 0 and 1000.
  - For real values, we add a random number between 0.0 and 1.0.
  - For Boolean values, we replace 'true' with 'false' and vice versa.
- *Constants for Reference Replacement (CRR):* We replace a reference within a formula through a constant.
- *Formula Replacement with Constant (FRC):* We replace a whole formula with a constant.
- *Formula Function Replacement (FFR):* We replace 'SUM' with 'AVERAGE' and 'COUNT' and vice versa. We replace 'MIN' with 'MAX' and vice versa.

For each mutant, we check whether the following two conditions are satisfied: (1) The mutant must be valid, i.e. it does not contain any circular references. (2) The inserted fault must be revealed, i.e. at least for one output cell, the computed value of the mutant must differ from the value of the original spreadsheet. If one of these conditions is violated, we discard the mutant and generate new mutants until we obtain a mutant that satisfies both conditions. We failed to create mutants for some of the spreadsheets because in many spreadsheets, input values are absent. For this reason, the spreadsheets lack values for output variables. Please note, that the creation of test cases is out of the focus of this paper. We only rely on existing input-output pairs.

We automatically created 622 mutants. Table 1 gives an overview of the characteristic of the created mutants. The number of formulas contained in the spreadsheets ranges from 6 to more than 4,000. This indicates that the evaluated approaches are able to handle large spreadsheets.

Table 1. Characteristics of the created mutants

Characteristic	Avg	Min	Max	Std.dev	Median
Number of formulas	225.0	6	4,170	384.9	104.5
Number of incorrect output cells	1.7	1	22	1.9	1
Number of correct output cells	64.9	0	2,962	162.5	24

In the first part of the empirical evaluation, we compared the fault localization capabilities of SFL and SENDYS by applying them to the generated mutants. In addition, we contrast these techniques with two primitive techniques, namely the union and intersection of the faulty cones. Table 2 summarizes the results of this comparison. The evaluation was performed on an Intel Core2 Duo processor (2.67 GHz) with 4 GB RAM with Windows 7 Enterprise (64-bit) as operating system and Java 7 as runtime environment. SENDYS performs slightly better than SFL and the intersection of the cones. Since we only created first-order mutants, the intersection of the slices always contains the faulty cell. Please note that in case of higher-order mutants, the faulty cell could be absent in the intersection of the cones. This happens when two independent faults are contained in the same spreadsheet and both faults are revealed by different output cells. Therefore, the intersection of the cones is not the best choice. Concerning the computation time, SFL has only a small overhead compared to the union and intersection of the cones. SENDYS requires nearly five times longer for the computations.

Table 2. Average ranking and computation time of union, intersection, SFL, and SENDYS. The column 'Avg. relative ranking' shows the average ranking of the faulty cell normalized to the number of formula cells per spreadsheet. This evaluation comprises 622 spreadsheets.

Technique	Avg. absolute ranking	Avg. relative ranking	Avg. comp. time (in ms)
Union (cones of faulty output)	41.1	27.3 %	15.6
Intersection (cones of faulty output)	30.8	22.0 %	15.6
SFL	26.3	20.3 %	16.9
SENDYS	24.3	19.7 %	79.6

Figure 1 graphically compares the fault localization capabilities of the approaches for the 622 investigated faulty program versions. The x-axis represents the percentage of formula cells that is investigated. The y-axis represents the percentage of faults that are localized within that amount of cells. This figure reads as follows: if you investigate the top 40 % ranked cells in all of the 622 faulty spreadsheets, SFL and SENDYS find the fault in 80 % of the Spreadsheets. It can be seen that SFL and SENDYS perform slightly better than the intersection and marginally better than the union of the cones. This means that faults can be detected earlier than when using the intersection or the union.

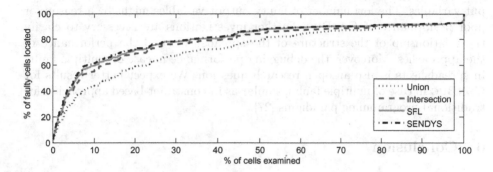

Fig. 1. Comparison of the SFL, SENDYS, the Union and Intersection of the cones in terms of the amount of formula cells that must be investigated

In the second part of the empirical evaluation, we investigate the debugging capabilities of CONBUG. We separated the evaluation of CONBUG from the evaluation of SFL and SENDYS because the prototype implementation of CON-BUG does not support all available mathematical operations available in Excel. Therefore, we filter out all spreadsheets which contain unsupported operations. Subsequently, 227 mutants remain for the evaluation of CONBUG. These mutants contain on average 219.8 formula cells. The largest mutant contains 2564 formula cells. Table 3 compares CONBUG to the union and the intersection of the cones. For completeness reasons, we add the data of SFL and SENDYS for the 227 spreadsheets. CONBUG performs better than the union, but worse than the intersection. However, CONBUG guarantees to contain the faulty cell even in the

Table 3. Average ranking and computation time of union, intersection, SFL, SENDYS, and CONBUG. The column 'Avg. relative ranking' shows the average ranking of the faulty cell normalized to the number of formula cells per spreadsheet. This evaluation comprises 227 spreadsheets.

Technique	Avg. absolute ranking	Avg. relative ranking	Avg. comp. time (in ms)
Union (cones of faulty output)	34.8	29.3 %	14.0
Intersection (cones of faulty output)	33.6	27.5 %	13.9
SFL	32.9	27.1 %	15.0
SENDYS	31.9	27.0 %	63.9
CONBUG	33.9	27.9 %	631.7

case of multiple faults. However, the faulty cell can be absent in the intersection of the cones. From Table 3 we see that the differences of the obtained results are small and might not be statistical significant.

Why are the results of Table 3 so close? One explanation might be the structure of the used spreadsheets. In particular, the 227 spreadsheets used for obtaining the results of Table 3 have 1.2 faulty output variables on average whereas the remaining 395 spreadsheets used in Table 2 have on average 2 faulty output variables. The low number of faulty output variables might be a reason for poor performance of CONBUG. Further investigations are necessary to clarify the relationship of the structure of the spreadsheets and the performance of the approaches. Moreover, the debugging performance in case of multiple faults in spreadsheets is also an open research question. We expect better results for CONBUG in case of multiple faults, similar as in constraint-based approaches for traditional programming paradigms [27].

6   Conclusion

While spreadsheets are used by a considerable number of people, there is little support for automatic spreadsheet debugging. In this paper, we addressed this gap. In particular, we adapted and applied to spreadsheets three popular debugging techniques designed for more traditional procedural or object-oriented programming languages. To this end, we formally defined the basic elements of spreadsheets and formalized fault localization in spreadsheets as spreadsheet debugging problem. In addition, we explained what modifications to the traditional debugging techniques are necessary. The main modification is to use cones instead of execution traces and slices.

We evaluated the fault localization capabilities of the proposed techniques, SFL, SENDYS, and CONBUG, using the well-known EUSES spreadsheet corpus [6]. The evaluation showed that SFL and SENDYS are the most promising techniques. However, the evaluation needs to be extended in several aspects: (1) It is necessary to evaluate higher-order mutants. (2) The discussed techniques are only a small selection of the available traditional debugging techniques. Thus, other debugging techniques should be adapted to spreadsheets. We plan to make the mutants used in this evaluation as well as higher-order mutants publicly available. This will ensure that new spreadsheet debugging techniques can be compared to the techniques discussed in this paper. Furthermore, the acceptance of such debugging techniques must be evaluated throw a user study.

SFL and SENDYS are debugging techniques which rank cells according to their likelihood of containing the fault. In contrast, CONBUG is a debugging technique that filters out cells which cannot explain the observed faulty values. Therefore, CONBUG can be used to filter out statements from the rankings of SFL and SENDYS. We plan to evaluate this filter mechanism in future work.

Acknowledgments. This work was supported by the Foundation for Science and Technology (FCT), of the Portuguese Ministry of Science, Technology, and Higher Education (MCTES), under Project PTDC/EIA-CCO/108613/2008, and the competence network Softnet Austria II (www.soft-net.at, COMET K-Projekt) funded by the Austrian Federal Ministry of Economy, Family and Youth (bmwfj), the province of Styria, the Steirische Wirtschaftsförderungsgesellschaft mbH. (SFG), and the city of Vienna in terms of the center for innovation and technology (ZIT).

References

1. Ko, A.J., Abraham, R., Beckwith, L., Blackwell, A., Burnett, M., Erwig, M., Scaffidi, C., Lawrance, J., Lieberman, H., Myers, B., Rosson, M.B., Rothermel, G., Shaw, M., Wiedenbeck, S.: The state of the art in end-user software engineering. ACM Computing Surveys (2011)
2. Chadwick, D., Knight, B., Rajalingham, K.: Quality control in spreadsheets: A visual approach using color codings to reduce errors in formulae. Software Quality Journal 9(2), 133–143 (2001)
3. Abreu, R., Zoeteweij, P., van Gemund, A.J.C.: On the accuracy of spectrum-based fault localization. In: Proceedings of the Testing: Academic and Industrial Conference Practice and Research Techniques - MUTATION, TAICPART-MUTATION 2007, pp. 89–98. IEEE Computer Society, Washington, DC (2007)
4. Hofer, B., Wotawa, F.: Spectrum enhanced dynamic slicing for better fault localization. In: Proceedings of the European Conference on Artificial Intelligence (ECAI 2012). Frontiers in Artificial Intelligence and Applications, vol. 242, pp. 420–425. IOS Press (2012)
5. Abreu, R., Riboira, A., Wotawa, F.: Constraint-based debugging of spreadsheets. In: Proceedings of the 15th Ibero-American Conference on Software Engineering (2012)
6. Fisher, M.I., Rothermel, G.: The EUSES spreadsheet corpus: A shared resource for supporting experimentation with spreadsheet dependability mechanisms. In: 1st Workshop on End-User Software Engineering, pp. 47–51 (2005)
7. Burnett, M.M., Cook, C.R., Pendse, O., Rothermel, G., Summet, J., Wallace, C.S.: End-user software engineering with assertions in the spreadsheet paradigm. In: Clarke, L.A., Dillon, L., Tichy, W.F. (eds.) ICSE, pp. 93–105. IEEE Computer Society (2003)
8. Panko, R.R.: Recommended practices for spreadsheet testing. CoRR abs/0712.0109 (2007)
9. Cunha, J., Fernandes, J.P., Mendes, J., Saraiva, J.: Mdsheet: A framework for model-driven spreadsheet engineering. In: Glinz, M., Murphy, G.C., Pezzè, M. (eds.) ICSE, pp. 1395–1398. IEEE (2012)
10. Ruthruff, J., Creswick, E., Burnett, M., Cook, C., Prabhakararao, S., Fisher II, M., Main, M.: End-user software visualizations for fault localization. In: Proceedings of the 2003 ACM Symposium on Software Visualization, SoftVis 2003, pp. 123–132. ACM, New York (2003)
11. Ayalew, Y., Mittermeir, R.: Spreadsheet debugging. Bilding Better Business Spreadsheets - from the ad-hoc to the quality-engineered. In: Proceedings of EuSpRIG 2003, Dublin, Ireland, July 24-25, pp. 67–79 (2003)
12. Reiter, R.: A theory of diagnosis from first principles. Artificial Intelligence 32(1), 57–95 (1987)

13. Abreu, R., Zoeteweij, P., van Gemund, A.J.C.: Spectrum-based multiple fault localization. In: Proc. ASE 2009. IEEE CS (2009)
14. Wotawa, F., Weber, J., Nica, M., Ceballos, R.: On the Complexity of Program Debugging Using Constraints for Modeling the Program's Syntax and Semantics. In: Meseguer, P., Mandow, L., Gasca, R.M. (eds.) CAEPIA 2009. LNCS, vol. 5988, pp. 22–31. Springer, Heidelberg (2010)
15. Jannach, D., Engler, U.: Toward model-based debugging of spreadsheet programs. In: 9th Joint Conference on Knowledge-Based Software Engineering (JCKBSE 2010), Kaunas, Lithuania, August 25-27, pp. 252–264 (2010)
16. Abraham, R., Erwig, M.: Goaldebug: A spreadsheet debugger for end users. In: 29th IEEE International Conference on Software Engineering, pp. 251–260 (2007)
17. Abraham, R., Erwig, M.: Goal-directed debugging of spreadsheets. In: Proceedings of the 2005 IEEE Symposium on Visual Languages and Human-Centric Computing, VLHCC 2005, pp. 37–44. IEEE Computer Society, Washington, DC (2005)
18. Rothermel, K.J., Cook, C.R., Burnett, M.M., Schonfeld, J., Green, T.R.G., Rothermel, G.: WYSIWYT testing in the spreadsheet paradigm: an empirical evaluation. In: Proc. ICSE 2000, pp. 230–239. ACM (2000)
19. Cunha, J., Fernandes, J.P., Ribeiro, H., Saraiva, J.: Towards a Catalog of Spreadsheet Smells. In: Murgante, B., Gervasi, O., Misra, S., Nedjah, N., Rocha, A.M.A.C., Taniar, D., Apduhan, B.O. (eds.) ICCSA 2012, Part IV. LNCS, vol. 7336, pp. 202–216. Springer, Heidelberg (2012)
20. Tikir, M.M., Hollingsworth, J.K.: Efficient instrumentation for code coverage testing. In: Proceedings of the 2002 ACM SIGSOFT International Symposium on Software Testing and Analysis, ISSTA 2002, pp. 86–96. ACM, New York (2002)
21. Abreu, R., Zoeteweij, P., van Gemund, A.: An evaluation of similarity coefficients for software fault localization. In: Proceedings of the 12th Pacific Rim International Symposium on Dependable Computing, PRDC 2006, pp. 39–46. IEEE Computer Society, Washington, DC (2006)
22. Janssen, T., Abreu, R., van Gemund, A.: Zoltar: A toolset for automatic fault localization. In: Proceedings of the 2009 IEEE/ACM International Conference on Automated Software Engineering, ASE 2009, pp. 662–664. IEEE Computer Society, Washington, DC (2009)
23. Campos, J., Riboira, A., Perez, A., Abreu, R.: Gzoltar: an eclipse plug-in for testing and debugging. In: Proceedings of the 27th IEEE/ACM International Conference on Automated Software Engineering, ASE 2012, pp. 378–381. ACM, New York (2012)
24. Wotawa, F.: Bridging the gap between slicing and model-based diagnosis. In: Proceedings of the International Conference on Software Engineering & Knowledge Engineering (SEKE 2008), pp. 836–841 (2008)
25. Wotawa, F., Nica, M.: On the compilation of programs into their equivalent constraint representation. Informatica (Slovenia) 32(4), 359–371 (2008)
26. Abraham, R., Erwig, M.: Mutation operators for spreadsheets. IEEE Transactions on Software Engineering, 94–108 (2009)
27. Hofer, B., Wotawa, F.: On the empirical evaluation of fault localization techniques for spreadsheets. In: 12th International Conference on Quality Software, pp. 41–48 (2012)

Quality of Merge-Refactorings for Product Lines

Julia Rubin[1,2] and Marsha Chechik[1]

[1] University of Toronto, Canada
[2] IBM Research in Haifa, Israel
mjulia@il.ibm.com, chechik@cs.toronto.edu

Abstract. In this paper, we consider the problem of refactoring related software products specified in UML into annotative product line representations. Our approach relies on identifying commonalities and variabilities in existing products and further merging those into product line representations which reduce duplications and facilitate reuse. Varying merge strategies can lead to producing several *semantically correct*, yet *syntactically different* refactoring results. Depending on the goal of the refactoring, one result can be preferred to another. We thus propose to capture the goal using a syntactic *quality* function and use that function to guide the merge strategy. We define and implement a *quality*-based *merge-refactoring* framework for UML models containing class and statechart diagrams and report on our experience applying it on three case-studies.

1 Introduction

A *software product line (SPL)* is a set of software-intensive products sharing a common, managed set of features that satisfy the specific needs of a particular market segment [4]. SPL engineering practices capitalize on identifying and managing *commonalities* and *variabilities* across the whole product portfolio and promote *systematic software reuse*. SPL commonalities represent artifacts that are part of each product of the product line, while SPL variabilities – those specific to some but not all products. Benefits of applying SPL engineering practices include improved time-to-market and quality, reduced portfolio size, engineering costs and more [4,9]. Numerous works, e.g., [9], promote the use of SPL practices for model-based development of complex embedded systems. Often, variants of such systems are developed for different customers and are represented and implemented using visual structural and behavioral models.

In reality, however, SPLs often emerge *ad-hoc*, when companies have to release a new product that is similar, yet not identical, to existing ones. Under tight project scheduling constraints, development teams resort to copying artifacts from one of the existing products and later modifying them independently from the original version [15,18] (the clone-and-own approach).

Cloned artifacts require synchronization: changes in one artifact might need to be repeated for all variants. In addition, it is difficult to propagate a new feature implemented in one variant into another or to define a new product by selectively "picking" some, but not all, features from the existing variants. As the result, when product variants are realized via cloning, development and maintenance efforts increase as the number of products grows. To deal with the complexity of SPL development, some approaches,

V. Cortellessa and D. Varró (Eds.): FASE 2013, LNCS 7793, pp. 83–98, 2013.

e.g., [2], advocate refactoring legacy cloned products into "single-copy" representations, eliminating duplications and explicating variabilities.

Numerous works provide guidelines and methodologies for building product line representations out of legacy systems, e.g., [14,8]. Most of such approaches, however, involve a manual review of code, design and documentation of the system aiming at identifying the set of product line features, as well as the set of components which implement these features. This manual step is time-consuming, and, in many cases, impedes adoption of SPL techniques by organizations.

Automated approaches for mining legacy product lines and refactoring them into feature-oriented product line representations have also been proposed [7,18,30,25]. In our earlier work [22,24], we focused on refactoring model-level cloned product variants and proposed a configurable *merge-refactoring* algorithm, *merge-in*, applicable to refactoring models of different types (e.g., UML, EMF and Matlab/Simulink). Our algorithm identifies similar and different elements of the input models using parameterizable *compare* and *match* operators, and then constructs a refactored model using a *merge* operator. The resulting product line model contains reusable elements representing corresponding merged elements of the original models. In [24], we formally proved that *merge-in* produces *semantically correct* refactorings for *any set* of input models and parameters: a refactored model can derive exactly the set of original products, regardless of particular parameters chosen and implementations of *compare / match / merge* used, if they satisfy well-defined correctness properties (e.g., *"each element produced by* merge *originates from an element of at least one input model"*).

Varying *merge-in* parameters allows producing different *syntactic* representations of the resulting product line due to different possible ways to match input model elements. All these representations are *semantically* equivalent and derive the same set of products. However, not all possible *syntactic* representations are desirable. Moreover, depending on the goal of the refactoring, one representation might be preferable to another. For example, a goal of the refactoring can be to highlight the variability points between the products, eliminating the "unnecessary" variability and creating a more homogeneous product portfolio. Another can be to maximize the comprehensibility of the resulting model by minimizing variability annotations for elements of a certain type. Yet another can be to reduce the size of the resulting refactoring – this might happen if the models are used for execution or code generation rather than human inspection. These different goals induce different product line representations.

Example. Consider the UML model fragments in Fig. 1(a,b) depicting two representative parts of real-life products developed by an industrial partner (since partner-specific details are confidential, we move the problem into a familiar domain of washing machines). Fig. 1(a) shows the Controller, Washer and Dryer classes of a washing machine, together with snippets of Controller's and Dryer's behaviors specified by UML statechart models. The wtrLevel attribute of Controller is used to specify the desired water level. When the water is filled to that level and heated to $30°C$, the washing machine controller notifies Washer that it can start operating and transitions from the Locking to the Washing state. After finishing washing, the controller initiates Dryer and transitions to the Drying state. Dryer operates for 45 minutes and returns the control to the Controller's statechart (by sending an appropriate signal which is

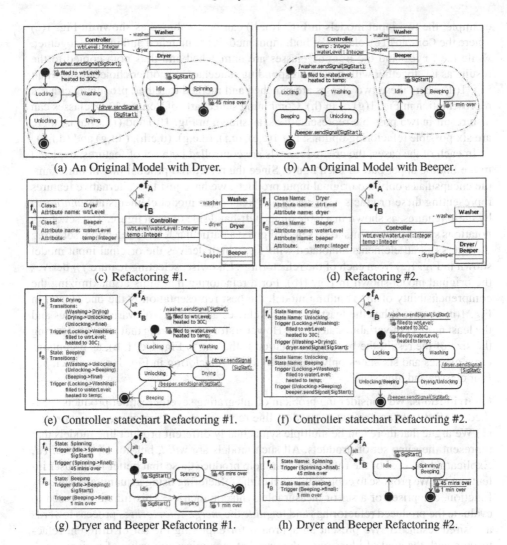

(a) An Original Model with Dryer.   (b) An Original Model with Beeper.

(c) Refactoring #1.   (d) Refactoring #2.

(e) Controller statechart Refactoring #1. (f) Controller statechart Refactoring #2.

(g) Dryer and Beeper Refactoring #1.   (h) Dryer and Beeper Refactoring #2.

Fig. 1. Fragments of Washing Machine models and some of their refactorings

omitted from the picture to save space). Then, the washing machine is unlocked, and
the wash cycle stops. Fig. 1(b) shows a similar washing machine model which lacks the
dryer but has a beeping function indicating the end of the wash cycle by signalling for
1 minute. In addition, in this model, the temp and waterLevel attributes control the
desired water temperature and water level, respectively.

These two products have a large degree of similarity and can be refactored into annotative SPL representations, where duplications are eliminated and variabilities are
explicated. We consider only those refactorings that preserve the behavior of existing
products rather than allowing novel feature combinations (e.g., a product with both
the dryer and the beeper). Even with this simplification, several choices emerge. For

example, the two input models in Fig. 1(a, b) can be combined as shown in Fig. 1(c) where the `Controller` classes of both input models are matched and merged together, while the `Dryer` and the `Beeper` classes are unmatched and thus both copied to the result "as is", together with their corresponding statecharts. Another choice is shown in Fig. 1(d) where these two classes are matched and merged together, producing either a representation in Fig. 1(g) or in (h). Combining statecharts of `Controller` classes can also result in two possible representations, as shown in Fig. 1(e) and (f). That is, there are six possible refactoring options: Fig 1(c,e), (c,f), (d,e,g), (d,e,h), (d,f,g) and (d,f,h).

In each of the cases, the created models are controlled by a set of features, depicted in the middle upper part of each figure. Since the refactored product line in our example encapsulates only the original input products, we have just two alternative features representing these products – f_A and f_B. Product line model elements are *annotated* by these features, as shown in a table on the left-hand side of each figure. The set of annotations specifies elements to be selected given a particular feature selection: selecting f_A filters out all elements annotated with f_B, which derives the original input model shown in Fig. 1(a) from each of the refactorings. Likewise, selecting feature f_B derives the original model shown in Fig. 1(b). For a refactoring that aims at maximizing the comprehensibility of the resulting model, the best representation is the one shown in Fig. 1(c, e) since it has the least number of classes and states with variable names and the least number of variable statecharts. However, for a refactoring that aims at reducing the size of the result, the best representation is the one in Fig. 1(d, f, h), as it contains three classes and six states only, compared to the refactoring in Fig. 1(c, e) which has four classes and nine states.

Contributions. We consider the problem of integrating several distinct products specified in UML into an annotative product line representation using *merge-refactorings*. (**1**) We argue that there can be multiple syntactically different product line models that represent the same set of products. All such models are *valid*, but not all are *desired*. Explicating the goal of the refactoring can help produce those that better fit the user intention. (**2**) We propose to capture the goal of the refactoring using a quantitative *quality* function, comprised of a set of measurable syntactic metrics. This function is used to evaluate the produced refactorings and to *guide* the *merge-refactorings* process towards a desired result. (**3**) We present an approach for exploring the set of different refactorings with the goal of identifying the one that maximizes the value of a given *quality* function. (**4**) We report on an implementation of a *quality*-based *merge-refactoring* framework for UML models containing class and statechart diagrams, which realizes the *merge-in* algorithm introduced in our earlier work [24]. We use the implemented framework for evaluating the effectiveness of our approach using several example product lines specified in UML, including one contributed by an industrial partner.

The remainder of this paper is organized as follows. The details on annotative product line representations and the *merge-in* refactoring algorithm are given in Sec. 2. Our *quality*-based *merge-refactoring* framework is described in Sec. 3. In Sec. 4, we present an implementation of the framework. We describe our experience applying it to three case studies in Sec. 5. A discussion and a description of related work are given in Sec. 6. Sec. 7 concludes the paper and outlines future research directions.

2   Refactoring Software Product Lines

In this section, we describe software product line models annotated by features. We also give the necessary background on *model merging*, used as a foundation of our *merge-in* product line refactoring algorithm, and summarize the *merge-in* algorithm itself.

Software Product Lines. SPL approaches can largely be divided into two types: *compositional* which implement product features as distinct fragments and allow generating specific products by composing a set of fragments, and *annotative* which assume that there is one "maximal" representation in which annotations indicate the product features that a particular fragment realizes [11,3]. A specific product is obtained by removing fragments corresponding to discarded features. Similarly to [3], our experience is that the annotative approach, which reminds code-level #ifdef statements, is easier to adopt in practice, as it does not require a paradigm shift in the way software is being commonly developed, especially in the embedded domain. We thus follow this approach here.

A *feature model* is a set of elements that describe product line features and a propositional formula defined over these features to describe relationships between them. A *feature configuration*, defining a product of a product line, is a sub-set of features from the feature model that respect the given relationships. An *annotative product line* is a triple consisting of a feature model, a domain model (e.g., a set of UML classes and statecharts), and a set of relationships that *annotate* elements of the domain model by the features of the feature model. Fig. 1(c-h) present snippets of domain models (right-hand side of each figure) whose elements are connected to features from a feature model (top-middle part of each figure) using annotation relationships (left-hand side of each figure). In this case, features f_A and f_B are alternative to each other, i.e., the propositional formula that specifies their relationship is $(f_A \vee f_B) \wedge \neg(f_A \wedge f_B)$. Thus, the only two valid feature configurations are $\{f_A\}$ and $\{f_B\}$.

A *specific product* derived from a product line *under a particular configuration* is the set of elements annotated by features from this configuration. For example, the class diagrams in Fig. 1(a) and Fig. 1(b) can be derived from the product line in Fig. 1(d) under the configurations $\{f_A\}$ and $\{f_B\}$, respectively.

Model Merging. Model merging consists of three steps: *compare*, *match* and *merge*. *Compare* is a heuristic function that calculates the similarity degree, a number between 0 and 1, for each pair of input elements. It receives models M_1, M_2 and a set of empirically assigned weights which represent the contribution of model sub-elements to the overall similarity of their owning elements. For example, a similarity degree between two classes is calculated as a weighted sum of the similarity degrees of their names, attributes, operations, etc. Comparing Washer classes in Fig. 1(a, b) to each other yields 1, as these classes are identical in the presented model fragment. Comparing Controller classes yields a lower number, e.g., 0.8, as the classes have different owned properties and behaviors.

Match is a heuristic function that receives pairs of elements together with their similarity degree and returns those pairs of model elements that are considered similar. *Match* uses empirically assigned *similarity thresholds* to decide such similarity. Consider the above example, where Washing classes had a calculated similarity degree of 1 and `Controller` classes had a similarity degree of 0.8: setting class *similarity threshold* to 0.75 results in matching both pairs of classes, while setting it to 0.85 results in matching only the `Washing` classes.

Finally, *merge* is a function that receives two models together with pairs of their matched elements and returns a merged model that contains all elements of the input, such that matched elements are unified and present in the result only once. For example, `Controller` classes in Fig. 1(a, b) can be unified as shown on the right-hand side of Fig. 1(e): matched states `Locking`, `Washing` and `Unlocking` are unified, while unmatched states `Drying` and `Beeping` are just copied to the result together with their corresponding transitions. While the *compare* and *match* functions rely on heuristically determined weights and similarity degrees, *merge* is not heuristic: its output is uniquely defined by the input set of matched elements.

***Merging-in* Product Lines.** We now describe the *merge-in* refactoring algorithm [24] that puts together input products into an annotative product-line representation. Constructing an annotative product line model consists of three steps: creating a domain model, creating a feature model, and specifying annotation relationships between the features and the domain model elements. For creation of a domain model, *merge-in* relies on *model merging*, described above. Feature models are created using an approach where features represent the original input products and are defined as alternatives to each other, *so only the original products can be derived from the constructed product line model*. Domain model elements are annotated by these features according to the product(s) that contributed them. For the example in Fig. 1(e), state `Drying` is annotated by feature f_A while state `Beeping` is annotated by f_B. State `Washing` is common (it exists in both input models) and thus is annotated by both features. Annotations of common elements are not shown in the figure to save space.

Any input product M can be seen as a "primitive" product line with only one feature f_M, one feature configuration $\{f_M\}$, and a set of annotations that relate all model elements to that feature. This representation can derive exactly one product – M. Thus, the most generic form of the *merge-in* operator obtains as input two (already constructed) product lines, each of which can be a "primitive" product line representing one input model. For example, when combining the two products in Fig. 1(a, b), we implicitly convert each of them into a product line and then *merge-in* them together. One possible outcome of that process is shown in Fig. 1(c, e), where the features representing the original models are denoted by f_A and f_B and defined as alternatives. In this case, `Dryer` and `Beeper` classes are unmatched.

Varying *compare* and *match* parameters, as well as varying the order in which input models are combined, defines the exact shape of the refactoring outcome. Two products in Fig. 1(a, b) can also be combined as shown in Fig. 1(d, f), where a lower class *similarity threshold* results in `Dryer` and `Beeper` classes being matched and merged.

All possible refactorings constructed by the algorithm are semantically "correct", each deriving the exact set of input models, regardless of the parameters chosen and regardless of the order in which input products are *merged-in*. The correctness of the *merge-in* operator relies on "reasonable" behavior of model *compare*, *match* and *merge* algorithms. Formal correctness properties of those algorithms are specified in [24].

3   Quality-Based Merge-Refactoring Framework

Even though all refactorings produced by the *merge-in* algorithm are *semantically equivalent and correct*, not all refactorings are desirable: depending on the goal of the refactoring, one representation can be preferred to another. The main objectives of our *quality*-based product line *merge-refactoring* framework are thus to (1) allow the user to explicate the goal of the refactoring process and (2) drive the refactoring process towards the result that best fits the user intention. We depict our approach in Fig. 2 and describe it below.

3.1   Explicating the Refactoring Goal

We explicitly capture the goal of the refactoring using a quantitative *quality* function. Since in our work we focus on *syntactic* properties of merge-refactorings, the *quality* function is built from a set of *metrics* – syntactically measurable indicators representing specific refactoring objectives (see Fig. 2). Typ-

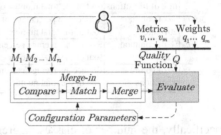

Fig. 2. Merge-Refactoring Framework

ically, such metrics can assess the size of the resulting model, determine the degree of object coupling, cohesion in methods, weighted number of methods per class and more [17]. The metrics can be reused across different organizations and domains. Each concrete *quality* function Q assigns *weights* $q_1 \ldots q_m$ to different metrics $v_1 \ldots v_m$, indicating their "importance" in the context of a specific application domain and allows the user to specify the desired outcome of the refactoring in an explicit manner.

More formally, given a product line model $\mathcal{PL}$, the *quality* function returns a number between 0 and 1, representing $\mathcal{PL}$'s "quality":

$$quality(\mathcal{PL}, \mathbb{V}, \mathbb{Q}) = \sum_{i=1 \ldots n} q_i * v_i(\mathcal{PL}),$$

where $\mathbb{V} = v_1, \ldots, v_n$ is a set of measurable metrics that, given $\mathcal{PL}$, produce a number between 0 and 1, and $\mathbb{Q} = q_1, \ldots, q_n$ is a set of metrics' weights.

Examples of Possible Quality Functions. We discuss two specific *quality* functions. The goal of the first one, Q_1, is to minimize the size of the resulting model. Since we assume that there is a large degree of similarity between input models that represent *related* products of a product line, aiming to reduce the total number of elements in the result leads to a reduction of duplications which, in turn, helps avoid repeating modifications for all variants.

We define our notion of model size using the number of classes, attributes, states and transitions. Specifically, the metrics v_1-v_4 listed in the first four rows of Table 1 measure the overall reduction of the size of the produced model when compared to the inputs. To construct Q_1, we assign these metrics equal weights, considering them equally important, as specified in the second to last column of Table 1. Q_1 prefers models that are as compact as possible, e.g., the refactoring in Fig. 1(d, f, h).

Our second goal is to produce refactorings that are the easiest for the user to comprehend. The work of [6,5] makes an argument that an increase in the size of UML models

Table 1. Quality metrics

Metric	Objective	Weight	
		Q_1	Q_2
v_1 % of reduction in # of classes	Reduce the number of classes. (out of the total number of classes in input.)	0.25	0.125
v_2 % of reduction in # of attributes	Reduce the number of class attributes. (out of the total number of attributes in input.)	0.25	0.125
v_3 % of reduction in # of states	Reduce the number of states. (out of the total number of states in input.)	0.25	0.125
v_4 % of reduction in # of transitions	Reduce the number of transitions. (out of the total number of transitions in input.)	0.25	0.125
v_5 % of common attributes	Reduce the percentage of variable class attributes (out of the total number of the class attributes.)	0.0	0.17
v_6 % of common states	Reduce an average percentage of variable states (out of the total number of states in a statechart.)	0.0	0.17
v_7 % of common transitions	Reduce an average percentage of variable transitions (out of the total number of transitions in a statechart.)	0.0	0.16

(specifically, the number of classes, aggregations, states and transitions) leads to an increase of cognitive complexity. The authors validate this claim using controlled experiments involving human subjects. However, neither these experiments nor our early work [22] considered *variability* aspects of the annotative product line representations. For example, while they minimize the size of the model, both possible merges of the Dryer and the Beeper classes in Figures 1(g) and (h) contain 66% and 50% variable states (i.e., states annotated by features), respectively. The merge of the Controller classes in Fig. 1(f) contains 50% variable states as well.

We believe that the higher is the number of common elements in a merged model, the easier it is to understand. We thus define a second *quality* function, Q_2, to combine size minimization with encouraging those refactorings which result in models with a high degree of commonalities: classes with a significant number of common attributes and statecharts with a significant number of common states and transitions. The metrics v_5-v_7 of Table 1 are designed for that purpose. They are calculated by counting the percentage of *common* sub-elements for a certain element in the model, i.e., those sub-elements that are annotated by all product line features. To achieve a reasonable degree of merging while discouraging too much variability, Q_2 gives the combination of four size-based metrics v_1-v_4 and the combination of three variability-based metrics v_5-v_7 equal importance (see the last column of Table 1). This *quality* function prefers the refactoring in Fig. 1 (c, e).

We use both Q_1 and Q_2 to evaluate refactorings of our case-study models in Sec. 5.

3.2 Constructing the Desired Refactorings

Since a *quality* function captures the criteria that are to be used when performing the *merge-refactoring* process, it could also be used to guide the process towards the desired result. As stated in Sec. 2, refactorings produced by the *merge-in* algorithm differ by the way input model elements are matched and merged, which is controlled by the *merge-in configuration parameters*. Modifying these parameters, e.g., increasing weight of state name similarities during *compare*, can result in the refactoring shown in Fig. 1(e). Instead, if we give more weight to the structural similarity of states, i.e., their distance to the initial and the final states and, recursively, the similarity of their neighbors [19], we get the result in Fig. 1(f). Likewise, lowering the class *similarity threshold* can result in a refactoring where the Dryer and the Beeper classes are matched and merged together, in addition to merging the Controller classes, as shown in Fig. 1(d).

Obviously, *merge-in* parameters cannot be decided universally because their values depend on the nature of the refactored product line and the objective of the *quality* function. It is also unreasonable to assume that the user can set and adjust these parameters manually. Moreover, generating *all* possible refactorings and evaluating them based on the given *quality* function is not a feasible approach as it does not scale well.

We thus need a systematic way for identifying those values of *merge-in* parameters that result in an optimal refactoring w.r.t. the given *quality* function Q. In our work, we propose doing so by treating parameter selection as a classical optimization problem [21], using the chosen *quality* function as an *objective function* for an optimization technique. The process (1) uses an optimization heuristic to set values of *merge-in* parameters, (2) produces the corresponding refactoring, subject to these parameters, (3) evaluates it using Q, and repeats until a result of the desired quality is reached (or a certain fixed number of iterations is performed). That is, different refactorings are generated by the *merge-in* algorithm based on the values of *compare weights* and *similarity thresholds* that are set using an optimization algorithm aimed to maximize the value of Q. Only the resulting "optimal" refactoring is returned to the user. The overall efficiency of the approach is as good as the chosen optimization algorithm because the latter selects the values of parameters for the next iteration.

4   Implementation

In this section, we describe our implementation of the *merge-in* algorithm, used as a foundation of the *merge-refactoring* framework, as well as our approach for setting the *merge-in* parameters. We focus our work on systems represented and implemented with UML models containing class and statechart diagrams – a common choice in automotive, aerospace & defense, and consumer electronics domains, where such models are often used for full behavioral code generation (e.g., using IBM Rhapsody[1]).

The core part of the *merge-in* algorithm is the *compare* function which receives two UML elements of the same type and returns their similarity degree – a number between 0 and 1. To implement *compare*, we started with existing comparison algorithms for UML classes [29,13] and statecharts [19]. These algorithms calculate the similarity degree recursively, using formulas that assign empirically defined weights to similarity degrees of appropriately chosen sub-elements.

None of the existing algorithms combined information obtained by analyzing both structural and behavior models together: comparing classes did not take into account information about similarity of their corresponding statecharts. We thus extended class comparison by considering behavior information, obtained by comparing statecharts to each other, and combining it with structural information by giving them equal weights.

---

[1] http://www-01.ibm.com/software/awdtools/rhapsody/

We also extended the statechart comparison algorithm proposed in [19] to consider state entry and exit actions, state do activities and actions on transitions, as those were used in the real-life model provided by the industrial partner.

Based on elements' similarity degrees generated by *compare*, our implementation of *match* "greedily" selects similar elements that are above a given threshold. *Merge* further combines elements deemed similar while explicating variabilities. We use the *union-merge* [26] approach to implement the *merge* function. It unifies matched elements and copies unmatched elements "as is" to the result. Our *merge* implementation is an adaptation of static union merge of TReMer+[2], extended to deal with annotations of domain model elements by features, as discussed in Sec. 2. We use IBM Rational Software Architect[3] (RSA) as our modeling environment, allowing us to reuse existing Java-based algorithms. Rhapsody models supplied by our industrial partner were first exported into UML 2.0 XMI format and then imported into RSA.

For adjusting *merge-in* parameters, we have implemented a version of the local search optimization technique [21] where the space of possible refactorings is explored by changing one parameter value at a time (hill-climbing). After evaluating the resulting refactoring and adjusting this value, we move to the next one, until all values are set. While this algorithm can miss the best result (global maximum) because it does not revisit the decisions that were already made, it is shown to be quite effective in practice for finding a "good" result (local maximum) in an efficient manner. We demonstrate the effect of adjusting the class *similarity threshold* in Sec. 5.

We *merge-in* the most similar models first: similarity degrees of all inputs – models of individual products or already constructed intermediate product lines – are evaluated, and those with the highest similarity degrees are combined first. Intuitively, merging more similar models first helps decrease the size and the number of variable elements in the result.

During our experiments, we noted that different values of *compare weights* and *similarity thresholds* can produce the same refactoring and thus the same *quality* measurements. Since our goal is to maximize a given *quality* function, any of the assignments that produce the desired result is appropriate.

5   Experience

In this section, we report on our experience applying the *quality*-based *merge-refactorings*. Our goal is to validate the feasibility of the approach for UML models in the embedded domain. In particular, we are interested in demonstrating the applicability and effectiveness of the proposed methodology for adjusting *merge-in* parameters for realistic models containing UML class and statechart diagrams, based on a given *quality* function. In what follows, we describe our subject product lines and present our results.

Subjects. We applied our refactoring approach to three sets of related products. The first is the Washing Machine example, built by us to mimic a partner's model and to highlight its characteristics. A snippet of this example is presented in Fig. 1 and the full

---

[2] http://se.cs.toronto.edu/index.php/TReMer+
[3] http://www-01.ibm.com/software/awdtools/swarchitect/

Table 2. Varying Class Similarity Threshold S_{Class}

metrics		Washing Machine							Microwave Oven				CE Product Line				
	orig.	0.7	0.75	0.78	0.8	0.85	0.9	orig.	0.7	0.75-0.85	0.9	orig.	0.6	0.65	0.7	0.75	0.8
v_1 #classes	18	6	7	8	9	11	12	8	2	3	5	45	14	15	17	20	27
v_2 #attributes	25	10	12	14	20	25	25	4	1	2	4	104	56	56	75	84	80
v_5 #var.attributes	-	3	4	5	6	4	0	-	0	2	4	-	43	43	26	32	8
v_3 #states	43	18	20	22	28	38	43	18	7	9	18	448	177	151	211	374	412
v_6 #var.states	-	6	6	5	4	0	0	-	1	0	0	-	56	64	31	13	4
v_4 #transitions	56	28	31	34	40	51	56	44	16	24	44	944	245	260	402	573	640
v_7 #var.transitions	-	19	19	18	12	0	0	-	2	4	0	-	77	85	31	19	8
Q1	-	0.587	0.528	0.469	0.333	0.148	0.083	-	0.686	0.505	0.065	-	0.646	0.635	0.496	0.351	0.284
Q2	-	0.565	0.560	0.572	0.533	0.523	0.541	-	0.797	0.561	0.372	-	0.640	0.650	0.678	0.601	0.623

version is available in [23]. The Washing Machine product line contains three different products, with a high degree of overlap in the set of classes comprising them. Specifically, each product has six classes, out of which three are identical across products (Motor, Faucet and Detergent Supplier), two are similar to each other in all three products (Controller and Washer), and one class in each product carries a unique product-specific functionality (either Dryer, Beeper or Timer). Also, statecharts of similar classes have similar structures.

The second example, Microwave Oven, has been introduced by Gomaa in [9]. It includes four different, although very similar, variants of the timer control class and their corresponding statecharts.

The final example comes from the Consumer Electronics (CE) space, contributed by an industrial partner. Here, we focus on seven behavior-intensive product components which together contain 45 classes, 104 attributes, 448 states and 944 transitions. The number of classes implementing each component ranges between 2 and 14. The number of statecharts in each component ranges between 1 and 3, with the number of states and transitions for a statechart ranging between 20 and 66 states, and 31 and 81 transitions, respectively. Of the seven components, three have a similar structure and a similar set of elements; another pair of components also contains elements that are similar to each other (but less similar to the components of the first cluster), and the remaining two components are not similar to the rest.

Space limitations and verbosity of UML models do not allow us to include pictorial illustrations of the examples. Thus, we limit the presentation to the statistical data about the case studies. The complete models for the first two examples are available in [23]. Since we cannot share details of the CE model, we built our first example, the Washing Machine, to be similar.

Results. To evaluate the effectiveness of our *quality*-based merge-refactoring approach, we analyzed different refactorings produced by varying *compare weights* and *similarity thresholds*, and evaluated them using *quality* functions Q_1 and Q_2 introduced in Sec. 3. As a starting point, we used empirically determined weights specified in [29,13,19]. We updated the weights to combine structural and behavior information when comparing classes and to take into account additional statechart elements, as described in Sec. 4. For the *similarity thresholds*, we started with the assumption that elements with the similarity degree lower than 0.5 are significantly different and should not be combined. For statecharts, we refined these estimates using the thresholds empirically determined in [19]. The values of weights and thresholds that we used are summarized in [23].

For illustration purposes, in this section we vary the class *similarity threshold* between 0.4 and 1, iteratively incrementing its value by 0.01, and evaluate the produced results using our *quality* functions. Table 2 presents the total number of elements as well as the number of *variable* elements of each type in the resulting refactoring. To save space, we show only *distinct* refactorings, omitting those that are equivalent to the presented ones. For example, in the Washing Machine case, all refactorings produced with class *similarity thresholds* between 0.4 and 0.7 are identical, and we only show the latest. In addition, the *orig* column reports the total number of input elements for each of the case studies. It is used to compare the result of the refactoring to the original models and to normalize the collected metrics during *quality* computation. A full description of the refactored product line models that were produced for each step of the first two case-studies is available in [23].

The results demonstrate that increasing the value of the class *similarity threshold* results in decreasing the value of Q_1 in all case studies because this function prefers refactorings that are as compact as possible: as the class *similarity threshold* increases, fewer classes are matched and merged, and the number of elements in the result grows. Q_2, however, does not exemplify such linear behavior because it balances the reduction in size with the goal of merging only those elements that are indeed similar. For example, when refactoring the Washing Machine, the result preferred by Q_1 is obtained by setting the class *similarity threshold* to 0.7 or lower, which causes merging of as many classes as possible, including those that are dissimilar (e.g., the one in Fig. 1(d)). This produces state machines with a large percentage of variable states and transitions. Q_2 prefers the solution produced when the *similarity threshold* is set to 0.78, which merges only elements with a high degree of commonality (e.g., see Fig. 1(c)). When the class *similarity threshold* is high (0.9), only identical classes got merged. A large number of classes, states and transition in the resulting model is captured by a low calculated value for both Q_1 and Q_2, since both of them are designed to minimize the size of the result.

For the Microwave Oven example, both Q_1 and Q_2 prefer the solution found when the class *similarity threshold* is set to 0.7 or lower (see Table 2). Since all four variants of the timer control class in this example are very similar, these classes are all merged together in the resulting refactoring. The percentage of variable states and transitions in this solution remains small, and the overall reduction in their total number is significant.

Recall that our third example had two clusters of similar components (and two other components, different from the rest). The refactoring that identifies and merges components in these clusters is produced when the class *similarity threshold* is set to 0.7. This refactoring also maximizes the value of Q_2. Similarly to the Washing Machine case, lower threshold values produce more merges resulting in a high number of variable attributes, states and transitions (and thus, lower values of Q_2), while higher thresholds result in a large number of elements in the resulting model (and thus, lower values of both Q_1 and Q_2).

In summary, we found that in all of the above cases, *quality* functions were able to distinguish between different refactorings as desired and thus were appropriate to help "drive" the refactoring process towards the preferable result. Our third case study also showed that differences in the computed *quality* values became more pronounced as models got bigger. Furthermore, the refactorings that were produced in our examples under the strategy that maximizes the value of Q_2 were identical to those constructed manually by a domain expert. This encouraging result makes us believe that our *quality-based merge-refactorings* approach is effective for the creation of annotative product line representations from a set of existing systems.

Threats to Validity. Threats to external validity are most significant for our work. These arise when the observed results cannot generalize to other case studies. Because we used a limited number of subjects and *quality* functions, our results might not generalize without an appropriate tuning. However, we attempted to mitigate this threat by using a real-life case study of considerable size as one of our examples. Thus, even though preliminary, our results show that the approach, perhaps with some additional tuning, is effective for finding good refactorings of large-scale systems.

In addition, we limit the scope of our work to physical systems in the embedded domain, where number of product variants usually does not exceed tens. The approach might not scale well to other domains, where hundreds of product variants are possible. However, we believe that the scalability issue mostly relates to the annotative product line representation itself, rather than to our attempt to distinguish between different representations.

6 Discussion and Related Work

Product Line Refactoring Approaches. Several existing approaches aim at building product lines out of legacy artifacts, e.g., [8]. These approaches mainly provide guidelines and methodologies for identifying features and their related implementation components rather than build tool-supported analysis mechanisms. Some works also report on successful experience in manual re-engineering of legacy systems into feature-oriented product lines, e.g., [14].

Koschke et al. [15] present an automated technique for comparing software variants at the architectural level and reconstructing the system's static architectural view which describes system components, interfaces and dependencies, as well their grouping into subsystems. Ryssel et al. [25] introduce an automatic approach to re-organize Matlab model variants into annotative representations while identifying variation points and their dependencies. Yoshimura et al. [30] detect variability in a software product line from its change history. None of the above approaches, however, takes into account *quality* attributes of the constructed results nor attempt to distinguish between the different refactorings based on the refactoring goal.

Product Line Quality. Oliveira et al. [20] propose a metric suite to support evaluation of product line architectures based on McCabe's *cyclomatic complexity* of their core components, which is computed using the control flow graph of the program and measures the number of linearly independent paths through a program's source code. Her et al. [10] suggest a metric to measure *reusability* of product line core assets based on their ability to provide functionality to many products of the same SPL, the number of SPL variation points that are realized by an asset, the number of replaceable components in a core asset and more. Hoek et al. [28] describe metrics for measuring *service utilization* of SPL components based on the percentage of provided and required services of a component. While these works allow measuring reusability, extensibility and implementation-level complexity of product line core assets, they do not discuss the structural complexity of annotative SPL models nor allow comparing different annotative product line models and distinguishing between them based on their representation properties. Trendowicz and Punter [27] investigate to which extend existing quality modeling approaches facilitate high quality product lines and define requirements for an appropriate quality model. They propose a goal-oriented method for modeling quality during the SPL development lifecycle, but do not propose any concrete metrics.

Numerous works, e.g., [6,5], propose software metrics for evaluating quality of UML models. While we base our approach on some of these works, they are not designed for UML models that represent software product lines and do not take variability aspects into account.

Finally, some works discuss characteristics of feature implementations in code, such as feature cohesion and coupling [1] or granularity, frequency and structure of preprocessor annotations [12,16]. However, these works are not easily generalizable to address the issue of structural complexity of models.

7   Conclusions and Future Work

Understanding and refactoring existing legacy systems can promote product line adoption by industrial organizations which have made a significant investment in building and maintaining these systems, and are not ready to abandon them for "starting from scratch". Since these systems are usually very large, automation becomes a necessity.

In this paper, we focused on integrating distinct products specified in UML into an annotative product line representation. We argued that multiple *syntactically different* yet *semantically equivalent* representations of the same product line model are possible, and *the goal of the refactoring induces which one is preferable*. We suggested an approach for guiding the refactoring process towards a result that fits best the user's intention, as captured by a syntactic *quality* function. We implemented a refactoring algorithm based on *model merging* and used it as the foundation of our *merge-refactoring* framework. We evaluated the proposed *quality*-based *merge-refactoring* approach on a set of case-studies, including a large-scale example contributed by an industrial partner. We believe that our work promotes automation of product line refactoring and reasoning about refactoring alternatives.

For future work, we are interested in enhancing our understanding of product line *quality* considerations which can help with assessing different product line model representations, produced either automatically or manually. The *quality* functions can be extended to consider additional quality attributes, allow the user to set and/or interactively choose different quality goals for different regions within the model, incorporate user feedback and more. Performing user studies for evaluating quality of annotative product line models can also be a subject of future work.

In addition, we are interested in exploring more sophisticated refactoring techniques that are able to detect fine-grained features in the combined products. This will allow creating new products in the product line by "mixing" features from different original products, e.g., the dryer and the beeper features from the models in Fig. 1. We also plan to further improve our *match* algorithms by allowing the user to affect results of this function, e.g., by setting negative matches. Exploring the use of more advanced optimization techniques, such as cross-entropy for adjusting *compare* and *match* parameters is also a subject for possible future work.

Acknowledgments. We thank Andrei Kirshin (IBM Research) for useful discussions and the anonymous reviewers for their insightful comments.

References

1. Apel, S., Beyer, D.: Feature Cohesion in Software Product Lines: an Exploratory Study. In: Proc. of ICSE 2011, pp. 421–430 (2011)
2. Beuche, D.: Transforming Legacy Systems into Software Product Lines. In: Bosch, J., Lee, J. (eds.) SPLC 2010. LNCS, vol. 6287, pp. 509–510. Springer, Heidelberg (2010)
3. Boucher, Q., Classen, A., Heymans, P., Bourdoux, A., Demonceau, L.: Tag and Prune: a Pragmatic Approach to Software Product Line Implementation. In: Proc. of ASE 2010, pp. 333–336 (2010)
4. Clements, P.C., Northrop, L.: Software Product Lines: Practices and Patterns (2001)
5. Cruz-Lemus, J.A., Genero, M., Piattini, M.: Using Controlled Experiments for Validating UML Statechart Diagrams Measures. In: Cuadrado-Gallego, J.J., Braungarten, R., Dumke, R.R., Abran, A. (eds.) IWSM-Mensura 2007. LNCS, vol. 4895, pp. 129–138. Springer, Heidelberg (2008)
6. Esperanza Manso, M., Cruz-Lemus, J.A., Genero, M., Piattini, M.: Empirical Validation of Measures for UML Class Diagrams: A Meta-Analysis Study. In: Chaudron, M.R.V. (ed.) MODELS 2008 Workshops. LNCS, vol. 5421, pp. 303–313. Springer, Heidelberg (2009)
7. Faust, D., Verhoef, C.: Software Product Line Migration and Deployment. Journal of Software Practice and Experiences 30(10), 933–955 (2003)
8. Ferber, S., Haag, J., Savolainen, J.: Feature Interaction and Dependencies: Modeling Features for Reengineering a Legacy Product Line. In: Chastek, G.J. (ed.) SPLC 2002. LNCS, vol. 2379, pp. 235–256. Springer, Heidelberg (2002)
9. Gomaa, H.: Designing Software Product Lines with UML: From Use Cases to Pattern-Based Software Architectures. Addison Wesley (2004)
10. Her, J.S., Kim, J.H., Oh, S.H., Rhew, S.Y., Kim, S.D.: A Framework for Evaluating Reusability of Core Asset in Product Line Engineering. Information and Software Technology 49(7), 740–760 (2007)
11. Kästner, C., Apel, S.: Integrating Compositional and Annotative Approaches for Product Line Engineering. In: Proc. of GPCE Workshops (McGPLE 2008), pp. 35–40 (2008)
12. Kästner, C., Apel, S., Kuhlemann, M.: Granularity in Software Product Lines. In: Proc. of ICSE 2008, pp. 311–320 (2008)
13. Kelter, U., Wehren, J., Niere, J.: A Generic Difference Algorithm for UML Models. In: Software Engineering. LNI, vol. 64, pp. 105–116 (2005)
14. Kolb, R., Muthig, D., Patzke, T., Yamauchi, K.: Refactoring a Legacy Component for Reuse in a Software Product Line: a Case Study: Practice Articles. J. of Software Maintenance and Evolution 18(2), 109–132 (2006)
15. Koschke, R., Frenzel, P., Breu, A.P., Angstmann, K.: Extending the Reflexion Method for Consolidating Software Variants into Product Lines. Software Quality Control 17(4), 331–366 (2009)
16. Liebig, J., Apel, S., Lengauer, C., Kästner, C., Schulze, M.: An Analysis of the Variability in Forty Preprocessor-Based Software Product Lines. In: Proc. of ICSE 2010, pp. 105–114 (2010)

17. McQuillan, J.A., Power, J.F.: On the Application of Software Metrics to UML Models. In: Kühne, T. (ed.) MoDELS 2006 Workshops. LNCS, vol. 4364, pp. 217–226. Springer, Heidelberg (2007)
18. Mende, T., Koschke, R., Beckwermert, F.: An Evaluation of Code Similarity Identification for the Grow-and-Prune Model. J. of Software Maintenance and Evolution 21(2), 143–169 (2009)
19. Nejati, S., Sabetzadeh, M., Chechik, M., Easterbrook, S., Zave, P.: Matching and Merging of Statecharts Specifications. In: Proc. of ICSE 2007, pp. 54–64 (2007)
20. Oliveira Junior, E., Maldonado, J., Gimenes, I.: Empirical Validation of Complexity and Extensibility Metrics for Software Product Line Architectures. In: Proc. of SBCARS 2010, pp. 31–40 (2010)
21. Pardalos, P., Resende, M.: Handbook of Applied Optimization (2002)
22. Rubin, J., Chechik, M.: From Products to Product Lines Using Model Matching and Refactoring. In: Proc. of SPLC Wrksp, MAPLE 2010, pp. 155–162 (2010)
23. Rubin, J., Chechik, M.: (2012),
    http://www.cs.toronto.edu/~mjulia/PLRefactoring/
24. Rubin, J., Chechik, M.: Combining Related Products into Product Lines. In: de Lara, J., Zisman, A. (eds.) FASE 2012. LNCS, vol. 7212, pp. 285–300. Springer, Heidelberg (2012)
25. Ryssel, U., Ploennigs, J., Kabitzsch, K.: Automatic Variation-Point Identification in Function-Block-Based Models. In: Proc. of GPCE 2010, pp. 23–32 (2010)
26. Sabetzadeh, M., Easterbrook, S.: View Merging in the Presence of Incompleteness and Inconsistency. Requirement Engineering 11, 174–193 (2006)
27. Trendowicz, A., Punter, T.: Quality Modeling for Software Product Lines. In: Proc. of ECOOP Workshops, QAOOSE 2003 (2003)
28. van der Hoek, A., Dincel, E., Medvidovic, N.: Using Service Utilization Metrics to Assess the Structure of Product Line Architectures. In: Proc. METRICS 2003, pp. 298–308 (2003)
29. Xing, Z., Stroulia, E.: UMLDiff: an Algorithm for Object-Oriented Design Differencing. In: Proc. of ASE 2005, pp. 54–65 (2005)
30. Yoshimura, K., Narisawa, F., Hashimoto, K., Kikuno, T.: FAVE: Factor Analysis Based Approach for Detecting Product Line Variability from Change History. In: Proc. of MSR 2008, pp. 11–18 (2008)

Towards Understanding the Behavior of Classes Using Probabilistic Models of Program Inputs

Arbi Bouchoucha, Houari Sahraoui, and Pierre L'Ecuyer

DIRO, Université de Montréal, Canada
{bouchoar,sahraouh,lecuyer}@iro.umontreal.ca

Abstract. We propose an approach to characterize the behavior of classes using dynamic coupling distributions. To this end, we propose a general framework for modeling execution possibilities of a program by defining a probabilistic model over the inputs that drive the program. Because specifying inputs determines a particular execution, this model defines implicitly a probability distribution over the set of executions, and also over the coupling values calculated from them. Our approach is illustrated through two case studies representing two categories of programs. In the first case, the number of inputs is fixed (batch and command line programs) whereas, in the second case, the number of inputs is variable (interactive programs).

Keywords: Class role, dependency analysis, program behavior, Monte-Carlo simulation, probabilistic model.

1 Introduction

Program comprehension is an essential phase in software maintenance [7]. To implement new changes, software engineers have to acquire abstract knowledge on, among others, the program structure and the behavior, and the relationships among its elements [4]. This abstract knowledge helps relating a program implementation to conceptual knowledge about the application domain and, hence locates the elements affected by a change request. Understanding a complex program is similar to exploring a large city [1]. In both cases, having good maps (abstractions) facilitates considerably the comprehension. For cities, there is a good knowledge on what kind of useful information should be abstracted on maps such as streets, transportation indications, landmarks, etc. Landmarks (monuments, important buildings, train stations), for example, are used as references to quickly situate secondary elements. For software comprehension, the idea of landmarks was also used. Indeed in [11] and [13], key classes are identified to serve as starting points for program comprehension.

The identification of comprehension starting points is often based on coupling [11,13]. The rationale behind this decision is that elements that are tightly

---

[1] Leon Moonen, Building a Better Map: Wayfinding in Software Systems. Keynote talk, ICPC 2011.

V. Cortellessa and D. Varró (Eds.): FASE 2013, LNCS 7793, pp. 99–113, 2013.

coupled to other elements are likely to implement the most important concepts of a program. Coupling can be estimated from a static analysis of the source code, independently of any execution, *i.e.,* *static coupling.* However, this method could significantly over or under-estimate the coupling due to dynamic features such as polymorphism or dynamic class loading [1].

On the other hand, actual coupling between software elements could be captured at run time by a dynamic analysis, *i.e.,* considering what actually happens during the execution [2,12]. Thus, different executions of the same program usually lead to different values of the *dynamic coupling.* But then, from which execution(s) should the metric be computed? To circumvent the generalization issue, Arisholm et al. [2], pick an arbitrary set of executions and take the average of the coupling value over these executions. Similarly, Yacoub et al. [12] assign probabilities to a finite set of execution scenarios, compute the dynamic coupling for each scenario, and take the weighted average across scenarios as their final measure, where the weights are the probabilities. This represents the mathematical expectation of the metric under a probabilistic model where the number of possible realizations is finite. Such derivation methods certainly make sense if the set of chosen executions (and weights in the case of [12]) are representative of the variety of executions likely to be encountered when running the program. However, in practice, the number of possible executions is often extremely large, even infinite, and it may be difficult to directly assign a probability to each one. Moreover, perhaps more importantly, considering only a single value (or average) of coupling (static or dynamic) can hide a large amount of useful information on the variability of a class's behavior.

The purpose of this paper is to describe an approach for characterizing class behavior using dynamic coupling distributions. To this end, we propose a general framework to model execution possibilities by defining a probabilistic model over the inputs that drive the program. Because specifying the inputs determines a particular execution, this model defines implicitly a probability distribution over the set of executions, and also over the set of coupling values. In such a model, the distribution of the coupling values is in general too complicated to be closely approximated numerically, but it can be estimated via Monte Carlo simulation. Our approach is illustrated through two case studies representing two categories of programs. In the first case, the number of inputs is fixed (batch and command line programs) whereas, in the second case, the number of inputs is variable (interactive programs).

The remainder of this paper is organized as follows. In Section 2, we define how the probabilistic model is used to derive class coupling distributions over the executions. Then, Section 3 explains how a coupling distribution can be used to give insights of a class's behavior. In section 4, we illustrate our approach using two case studies corresponding to two categories of programs. Our approach is discussed and contrasted with the related work in Section 5. Finally, concluding remarks are given in Section 6.

2   Portraying Class Coupling

2.1   Approach Overview

When using deterministic algorithms, computer programs are driven by a set of external inputs that normally determine the entire execution sequence. We consider a computer program made up of several classes, say in Java for example, and a dynamic coupling metric at the class level whose value depends on the realizations of the input variables given to the program (see Figure 1). The total number of possibilities for these inputs (and then for the possible executions) is typically much too large to allow an explicit enumeration. Here we propose to define a probability distribution over the space of possible inputs. Once this distribution is determined, it can be used to generate representative sets of inputs. The coupling values corresponding to these inputs represent then the basis for the estimation of the coupling distribution of a class over the possible executions.

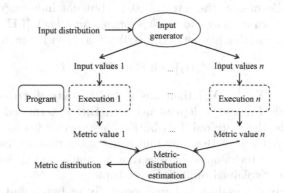

Fig. 1. Approach overview

2.2   Probabilistic Models for Input Data Generation

We consider two cases for how these input variables are defined or specified depending on the nature of programs:

(a) The number of inputs is fixed to d (a positive integer) and these inputs are represented by a random vector $\mathbf{X} = (X_1, \ldots, X_d)$. This case of inputs is found generally in batch and command-line programs where a set of parameters are specified for each execution.

(b) The number of inputs is variable (random) and the successive inputs can be seen as functions of the successive states of a Markov chain. This is the case of programs with interactions with a user or with the outside environment, where the probability distribution of the next input (and whether there is a next input or not) often depends on the values of the inputs that have already been given to the program so far.

Inputs Defined as a Random Vector. In the case of a random vector $\mathbf{X} = (X_1, \ldots, X_d) \in \mathbb{R}^d$, the input values can be given to the program before it starts its execution. In this model, we assume that $\mathbf{X}$ is a random vector with an arbitrary multivariate distribution over $\mathbb{R}^d$. This distribution could be discrete, continuous, or mixed, in the sense that for example some coordinates of $\mathbf{X}$ might have a normal or exponential distribution while others might take only integer values, or perhaps only binary values (0 and 1). The inputs, *i.e.*, coordinates of $\mathbf{X}$, are not assumed to be independent in general, but the situation where they are independent is a possibility; this is the simplest special case.

The multivariate random vector $\mathbf{X}$ has distribution F if for any $\mathbf{x} = (x_1, \ldots, x_d) \in \mathbb{R}^d$, we have $F(\mathbf{x}) = \mathbb{P}[\mathbf{X} \leq \mathbf{x}] = \mathbb{P}[X_1 \leq x_1, \ldots, X_d \leq x_d]$. The jth marginal distribution function is defined by $F_j(x_j) = \mathbb{P}[X_j \leq x_j]$. The random variables $X_1, \ldots, X_d$ are *independent* if and only if $F(X_1, \ldots, X_d) = F_1(x_1) \ldots F_d(x_d)$ for all $\mathbf{x} \in \mathbb{R}^d$. When $X_1, \ldots, X_d$ are not independent, a general way of specifying their joint (multivariate) distribution is via a copula [3].

A copula consists in specifying first a d-dimensional distribution whose marginals are uniform over the interval $(0, 1)$, but not independent in general. This distribution is called a *copula* (or *dependence function*). If $\mathbf{U} = (U_1, \ldots, U_d)$ denotes a random variable having this distribution, then for each j, we define

$$X_j = F_j^{-1}(U_j) = \inf\{x : F_j(x) \geq U_j\}.$$

The vector $\mathbf{X} = (X_1, \ldots, X_d)$ then has a multivariate distribution with the required marginals F_j, and a dependence structure determined by the choice of copula. That is, the marginal distributions are specified separately from the marginals. It is well known that any multivariate distribution can be specified in this way. Specific techniques for selecting a copula and generating random vectors from it are explained in [3,6], for example.

This case of input variables is found generally in batch and command-line programs where a set of parameters are specified for each execution. For example, when running *lpr* command in Linux, one should specify the printer name, the username, the number of copies, etc. When a parameter is not specified, *e.g.*, the printer name, this does not mean that one input is missing. It simply means that the default value will be used, here the default printer. Thus, the size of the input vector is always the same.

Inputs Modeled by a Markov Chain. The majority of programs nowadays do not have a fixed number of inputs, but the number of inputs (and their types) are themselves random variables. Consider for example, a program with a set of functions, each performed in a number of steps. Each step requires a certain number of parameters. The state of the execution (function and step) impacts the probability that a particular parameter is required, and if yes, the probability that this parameter takes a specific value. This is particularly true for programs that interact with a user or with the outside environment, where the probability distribution of the next input (and whether there is a next input or not) often depends on the values of the inputs that have already been given to the program so far. In this type of situation, the input process can be modeled naturally as a discrete-time Markov chain.

A naive way of specifying such a discrete-time Markov chain model would be to assume that $\{X_j, j \geq 0\}$ is a Markov chain over the set of real numbers (or a subset thereof), where X_j represents the jth input to the program. However, this is not realistic, because the next input X_{j+1} usually depends not only on X_j, but also on the values of the previous inputs. Therefore, the process $\{X_j, j \geq 0\}$ thus defined would not be a Markov chain.

A proper way to get around this problem is to model the input process by a Markov chain $\{S_j, j \geq 0\}$ whose state S_j at step j contains more information than just X_j. Such a Markov chain can be defined by a stochastic recurrence of the form $S_j = \gamma_j(S_{j-1}, X_j)$, for some transition functions γ_j, and the jth input X_j is assumed to have a probability distribution that depends on S_{j-1}, and to be independent of $X_0, \ldots, X_{j-1}$ conditional on S_{j-1}. This assumption ensures that $\{S_j, j \geq 0\}$ is a Markov chain, which means that whenever we know the state S_j, knowing also $S_0, \ldots, S_{j-1}$ brings no additional useful information for predicting the behavior of any X_ℓ or S_ℓ for $\ell > j$. We also assume that this Markov chain has a random stopping time τ defined as the first time when the chain hits a given set of states Δ: $\tau = \inf\{j \geq 0 : S_j \in \Delta\}$. This τ represents the (random) number of inputs that the program requires.

Another interesting example where Markov chains are used to model the inputs of a software is described in [14]. In this work, the interaction with a web site is defined as a set of mouse clicks on links corresponding to the URLs of Web-site pages. The probability that a particular page is accessed depends on the other pages already accessed, *i.e.*, previous inputs. The Markov-chain model is used to measure the navigability of Web sites.

2.3   Dynamic-Coupling Distribution Estimation

Case of Random Vector. A *dynamic metric* φ can be seen as a function that assigns a real number to any possible execution of the program. But since the realized execution depends only on the realization of $\mathbf{X}$, we can view the metric as a function of $\mathbf{X}$, and write $\varphi : \mathbb{R}^d \to \mathbb{R}$. Then, $Y = \varphi(\mathbf{X})$ is a real-valued random variable whose distribution depends on the distribution of $\mathbf{X}$, perhaps in a complicated way. Thus, the distribution of Y will not be known explicitly in general. However, we can use Monte Carlo simulation to estimate this distribution. It consists in generating n independent realizations of $\mathbf{X}$, say $\mathbf{X}_1, \ldots, \mathbf{X}_n$, and then computing the n corresponding realizations of Y, say $Y_1, \ldots, Y_n$. Then the empirical distribution of $Y_1, \ldots, Y_n$ is used to estimate the true distribution of Y. As a byproduct, it permits one to estimate certain summary characteristics of this distribution, such as the mean, the variance, etc., and to compute *confidence intervals* on these numbers [9].

For example, one can estimate $\mu = \mathbb{E}[Y]$, the mean of Y, by the sample average $\bar{Y}_n = \sum_{i=1}^n Y_i$. To assess the accuracy of this estimator, one can also compute a confidence interval on μ, which is a random interval of the form $[I_1, I_2]$ where I_1 and I_2 are two random borders defined so that

$\mathbb{P}[I_1 \leq \mu \leq I_2] \approx 1 - \alpha$ where $1 - \alpha$ is a preselected confidence level. For example, if we assume that $\bar{Y}_n$ has a normal distribution (which is practically never exactly true but can be a good approximation when n is large, thanks to the central limit theorem), then the confidence interval has the form

$$[\bar{Y}_n - z_{1-\alpha/2}S_n/\sqrt{n}, \ \bar{Y}_n + z_{1-\alpha/2}S_n/\sqrt{n}] \tag{1}$$

where S_n is the sample standard deviation of $Y_1, \ldots, Y_n$ and $z_{1-\alpha/2}$ satisfies $\mathbb{P}[Z \leq z_{1-\alpha/2}] = 1 - \alpha/2$, where Z is a standard normal random variable. Other techniques, such as bootstrap methods, for example, can be used when we think that the distribution of $\bar{Y}_n$ might not be close to normal. Confidence intervals on other quantities than the mean (for example, the variance of Y, or the correlation between two different metrics), can be computed in similar ways.

Of course, the whole empirical distribution itself always conveys more information for behavior understanding than the estimates of any of these statistics. For this reason, it is generally better in our opinion to study this distribution (for example in the form of a histogram) rather than (or in addition to) interprete, say, the average $\bar{Y}_n = (Y_1 + \cdots + Y_n)/n$ together with a confidence interval on the mathematical expectation $\mathbb{E}[Y]$.

Case of Markov Chain. A dynamic metric here is defined as a function φ which assigns a real number $Y = \varphi(S_0, S_1, \ldots, S_\tau, \tau) \in \mathbb{R}$ to each realization $(S_0, S_1, \ldots, S_\tau, \tau)$.

Again, if the Markov chain model is fully specified, we can simulate it and estimate the distribution of Y by the empirical distribution of n independent realizations $Y_1, \ldots, Y_n$, in the same way as in the random vector case.

2.4   Examples of Coupling Distributions

When considering dynamic coupling, different executions, corresponding to different inputs, could lead to different interactions between the considered class and the other elements of a program. Consequently, each execution results in a particular coupling value. After performing a relatively large sample of executions defined by the distribution of the inputs, those executions could be grouped according to their coupling values, which defines a distribution.

We conjecture that there is a causality chain between the input, the behavior, and the coupling value. Indeed, the input values may impact the execution control flow, *i.e.*, the class's behavior, which may lead to variations in the interactions between objects, and then in the class's coupling value. Note that variations in the interactions do not necessarily mean changes in the coupling value. The same value could be the result of different interaction sets. In the following paragraphs, we show examples of regular distributions that could be obtained. We discuss them in the basis of our conjecture. The relationship between the coupling values and the behavior will be discussed in Section 3.

Single-Bar Distribution ▃▐▌ This situation occurs when the class has the same coupling regardless of the inputs.

Exponential-like Distribution In this distribution, the lowest coupling value is obtained by the highest number of executions. Then the frequency of executions decreases as the coupling increases.

Normal-like Distribution This is another variation of the previous distributions. The distribution mode corresponds to a middle coupling value. The frequency of execution decreases gradually as the coupling value increases or decreases.

Multimodal Distribution Classes having this kind of distribution do not have a clear pattern for the frequency change with respect to the coupling change. When the coupling values have equal or close frequencies, the distribution takes the shape of a uniform distribution.

3 Understanding a Class's Behavior

3.1 Class Behavior

In the object-oriented programming paradigm, objects interact together in order to achieve different functionalities of a given program. Typically, the behavior of a program corresponds to the set of the implemented use cases. Each use case could have different scenarios depending on the inputs. Consider, for example, the use case of borrowing books in a library loan management system. The frequent and main scenario is to identify the reader, check his record, and register the loan. This scenario could be extended (*extend* relationship) by renewing the membership prior to the loan, for example, or truncated if the borrower exceeds the allowed number of books or if the concerned book cannot be borrowed (violation of use-case scenario *preconditions*).

These variations at the program level are reflected at the class level. As classes implement services that contribute to use cases. An alternative use-case scenario could require an additional service, do not use a service or use a variation of a service with respect to the main scenario. For example, when the loan is not registered, class *Book* will not decrease the number of available book copies. Therefore, a class could offer one or more services, each with possible variations. For a particular use case, the main scenario is the most frequently executed which in turn define a main and frequent contribution of a given class in this scenario. This contribution could vary according to the use case alternative scenarios.

3.2 Relating Coupling Distributions to Class Behavior

As mentioned earlier, we conjecture that there is a causality chain between the inputs, the class's behavior and the class's dynamic coupling. According to our probabilistic setting defined in Section 2, a set of representative executions is defined by the set of representative inputs. The execution sample produces a practical coupling distribution for each class of the program. The goal of our work is to use this distribution to understand the behavior of a class. Understanding a class's behavior in our setting means that we could identify the main behavior and its variations by looking at its coupling distribution. Relating the coupling distribution to the behavior is only valid if we accept the three following hypothesis:

H_1: *the same behavior results in the same coupling value and conversely*: A class that executes one or many services in different executions corresponding to the same use-case scenarios will produce the same, or very close, coupling values. Conversely, two equal or very close coupling values corresponding to two executions indicate that these executions are likely to trigger the same class behavior.

H_2: *an extended behavior generates more or equal coupling than the original one*: When an alternative scenario AS extends a main scenario MS, the coupling value corresponding to AS is at least equal to the one of MS. This means that (almost) all the interactions in MS remain in AS and that the extension could add new interactions.

H_3: *a truncated behavior generates less or equal coupling than the original one*: When an alternative scenario AS is executed because of a precondition violation of the main scenario, the coupling value corresponding to AS is at most equal to the one of MS. This could be explained by the fact that most of the behavior of MS is not performed, which may cancel many interactions.

The above-mentioned hypotheses could be assessed automatically for any studied system. It is possible to check if executions belonging to the same block, *i.e.*, having the same coupling value, trigger the same set of method calls [2]. It is also possible to evaluate the similarity between executions belonging to contiguous blocks, corresponding to two successive coupling values. In the following paragraphs, we propose intra and inter-block similarity measures to group executions by behavior based on coupling.

Intra-block similarity or internal similarity is measured by evaluating the diversity of method calls inside the block. Formally, for a block b of executions having a coupling value c_b, the internal similarity is defined as $IS(b) = c_b/n_b$, where n_b is the number of different method calls observed in all the executions of b. The ideal situation ($IS(b) = 1$) is that all the executions in b trigger the same set of method calls. In that case, $c_b = n_b$. The more the values are close to 1, the more we consider that executions reflect the same behavior. If we assume that executions belonging to the same block concern the same behavior, the next step is to identify if contiguous blocks have the same behavior, thus forming a behavior region, or if an important modification is observed. Modifications include transitions from a truncated scenario to the main scenario within the same use case, main-scenario extension, and use case change.

Inter-block similarity or external similarity allows to measure the difference in behavior between execution blocks. In a first step, it is important to identify methods calls that are relevant in an execution block to exclude marginal calls that represent non significant behavior variations. Relevant method calls are

---

[2] For the sake of simplicity, we consider in this section that coupling between classes is the total of different afferent and efferent method calls. The similarity measures of the following paragraphs could be easily adapted to other dynamic coupling measures.

those that appear in the majority of the executions of a block b. A method call a is said to be relevant for a block b if it appears in at least n percent of the executions in b. n is a threshold parameter, usually set to 50% (half of the block executions). Once the set $Rel(b)$ of relevant method calls are identified for each block b, the following step is to determine the behavior regions by comparing contiguous blocks recursively. The first block b_1 (the one with the lowest coupling value) is automatically included in the first region R_1. Then for each block $b_i, i > 1$, we evaluate its similarity with the region R_j containing the previous blocks. If the similarity is above a given threshold value, then b_i is assigned to the same region R_j, if not, it forms a new region R_{j+1}. External similarity is calculated as follows:

$$ES(R_j, b_i) = \frac{|Rel(R_j) \cap Rel(b_i)|}{|Rel(R_j) \cup Rel(b_i)|} \qquad (2)$$

where $Rel(R_j) = \bigcap_{b_k \in R_j} Rel(b_k)$.

When relating the coupling distributions to the behavior, the distribution examples given in Section 2.4, could be used as behavioral patterns. *Single-Bar* distribution defines an **Assembly-chain** pattern as the concerned class behaves in the same way regardless of the inputs. *Exponential-like* distribution is seen as a **Clerk** pattern. Like a clerk in an office, the class has one common behavior (main scenario of a use case), and this common behavior is gradually extended to deal with exceptional situations (alternative scenarios with extensions within the same use case). A third pattern **plumber** corresponds to the *Normal-like* distribution. Like for the *Clerk*, the common behavior is extended in some cases, but like for a plumber, some interventions do not require to perform this common behavior. This situation occurs when the main use-case scenario has preconditions that, for some executions, are not satisfied, which results in a truncated behavior, and then a lower coupling. Finally, we view a *Multimodal* distribution as a **Secretary** pattern. Classes having this kind of distribution are generally involved in different use cases. The choice of the behavior depends on the inputs, *e.g.*, utility classes. When the use cases have equal probabilities to be performed, the coupling distribution is uniform-like.

4   Illustrative Case Studies

4.1   General Setting and Implementation

To illustrate our approach, we present in this section the cases of two small Java programs: *Sudoku* (13 classes) and *Elevator* (eight classes) having inputs that are modeled by respectively a random vector and a Markov chain. For each program, we built a probabilistic input model according to the framework of Section 2. To simulate the inputs from the obtained input models, we have used the Java library *SSJ* [5], which stands for *Stochastic Simulation in Java*, and provides a wide range of facilities for Monte Carlo simulation in general. For each program, our simulation generated the input data for a sample of 1000 executions. For each execution, the inputs were given using a class *Robot* that simulates the interaction with the GUI, and a trace was produced using the tool *JTracert*[3]. These traces were then used to calculate the class coupling metrics. For the sake of generality, we considered a different coupling metric for each program, *IC_OM*(*c*) (*Import Coupling of a class c for Objects with distinct Methods*) for Sudoku and *IC_CM*(*c*) (*Import Coupling of a class c for Classes with distinct Methods*). The definitions of these dynamic metrics are given in [2]. *SSJ* was also used to produce the distribution histograms.

4.2 Case 1: Sudoku Grid Generator

System Description and Input Probabilistic Model. Sudoku grid generator has 10 inputs. Nine of them are positions in the grid (fixed spots) where the digits 1 to 9 should be placed. We assume a 9×9 grid with cells numbered from 1 (top-left) to 81 (bottom-right). The tenth input is the level of difficulty of the grid to be generated, in a scale from 1 to 5. Starting from the first nine inputs, the program generates a grid by filling the remaining 72 cells to produce a correct solution if one exists. If not, it displays a message indicating that no solution was found for this input. When a solution is found, the level of difficulty is used to determine the number of cells to hide when displaying the puzzle.

With respect to our framework, the input vector is $\mathbf{X} = (X_1, \ldots, X_{10})$ where $X_1, \ldots, X_9 \in \{1, 2, \ldots, 81\}$, with $X_i \neq X_j$ whenever $i \neq j$, and $X_{10} \in \{1, 2, \ldots, 5\}$. Given this space of inputs, the number of possible executions (or realizations of the input vector) is $N = 81 \times 80 \times \ldots \times 73 \times 5 \approx 4.73354887 \times 10^{17}$. In our model, we assume that each of those input vector realizations has the same probability $1/N$. This means that the positions of the 9 fixed digits are selected at random, uniformly and independently, without replacement (so they are all distinct), and that the level of difficulty is also selected at random, uniformly and independently of the other inputs. The distribution of the input vector is then $F(X_1, \ldots, X_{10}) = F_1(x_1) \ldots F_{10}(x_{10})$. All $F_1(x_1), \ldots, F_9(x_9)$ are considered as uniform. We can reasonably consider that the five levels of difficulty have also equal chances to be selected ($F_{10}(x_{10})$ is a uniform distribution).

Distributions and Interpretation. Table 1 summarizes the main findings related to the coupling distributions. The first observation is that for all classes of the Sudoku program, the similarity in behavior is very high between executions producing the same coupling value (average IS per class ranging from 82% to 100%). This indicates that our first hypothesis about the correlation between the coupling and the behavior is true in this case. Regarding the distributions, we found that the 13 classes are instances of the patterns described in Section 3. All exponential-like distributions include three regions, except for *GridConfiguration* with two regions. In all cases, the first, which contains the higher number of executions corresponds to the main scenario of a use case and the other regions highlight successive extensions. For example, the first region of the class *Solver*

---
[3] http://code.google.com/p/jtracert/

Table 1. Statistics about *Sudoku* program.

Class Name	IS(%)	Distribution	Regions
Solver	88.71	*Exponential-like*	$\{b_5, b_6, b_7\}$, $\{b_8, b_9, b_{11}\}$, $\{b_{12}, b_{13}, b_{14}\}$
Sudoku (main)	96.38	*Exponential-like*	$\{b_4, b_5\}$, $\{b_6, b_7, b_8\}$, $\{b_9, b_{10}\}$
Util	100	*Uniform-like*	$\{b_1\}$, $\{b_2\}$, $\{b_3\}$, $\{b_4\}$
Valid	90.66	*Normal-like*	$\{b_1, b_2\}$, $\{b_3, b_4, b_5, b_6\}$, $\{b_7, b_8\}$
GridGenerator	90.67	*Exponential-like*	$\{b_4\}$, $\{b_5, b_6, b_7\}$, $\{b_8, b_9, b_{11}\}$
GridFrame	100	*Single Bar*	$\{b_3\}$
GridConfiguration	85.20	*Exponential-like*	$\{b_4\}$, $\{b_5, b_6\}$
Grid	93.42	*Normal-like*	$\{b_1\}$, $\{b_2, b_3, b_4\}$, $\{b_5\}$
Case	87.25	*Uniform-like*	$\{b_1, b_2, b_3\}$
BoxPanel	100	*Single Bar*	$\{b_1\}$
ButtonPanel	82.66	*Exponential-like*	$\{b_2\}$, $\{b_3, b_4, b_5\}$
InitSquare	100	*Single Bar*	$\{b_3\}$
GridPanel	88.27	*Single Bar*	$\{b_3, b_4\}$

corresponds to the standard process of searching for a solution when the user initializes the grid and asks for a valid solution (see Figure 2-left). This behavior is very frequent because in most of the cases, a solution is easy to find. The second region corresponds to an extended behavior of the first one. Indeed, when a solution is difficult to find or may not exist, the solver uses another resolution strategy based on back-tracking, and then calls other methods, especially those of the class *Valid*. The third region that we identified for the *Solver* class, corresponds to a surprisingly less-frequent case where the solver checks if an existing solution is unique or not. This task requires that from the *Solver* class to use new interactions with classes *Sudoku*, *Grid* and *Valid*. The two normal-like distributions also have three regions with the first (lower values) indicating a truncated behavior due to precondition violations, the second (middle values) representing the common behavior, and the third (highest values) including common behavior extensions. The two uniform-like distributions were not similar in behavior. Whereas *Util* with four different coupling values, defines clearly four different services (regions) with almost equal frequencies, *Case*, with three coupling values includes only marginal variations of the same behavior which lead to a single region. Finally, single-bar distributions have a unique coupling value defining a unique behavior. The only case with two coupling values exhibits unbalanced frequencies but with similar behavior.

4.3   Case 2 : Elevator System

System Description and Input Probabilistic Model. The second program that we considered in this study is a simple elevator operating system. To run the program, the user has to give the number of elevators and the number of floors. Then it is possible to enter as many times as desired the events calling elevators from a particular floor to go up or down, and selecting the destination floors. The program ends when the user enters the event stop. Obviously, the

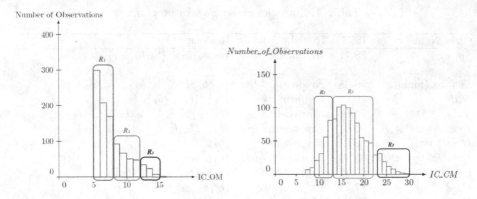

Fig. 2. Coupling distributions of classes *Solver* (left) and *ElevatorGroup* (right)

number of inputs cannot be fixed a priori. In that case, we model the program inputs by a Markov chain. We consider that there is an arbitrary number of subjects that use the elevators. Subject arrivals are random and mutually independent. Times between two successive arrivals are independent and identically distributed, and exponential with mean $1/\lambda$. In our simulation program, we took $\lambda = 1/2$. Each subject is modeled by a Markov chain that is triggered when he enters the building, and is stopped when he leaves it. The subjects' Markov chains are independent. A transition probability matrix is assigned to each subject. It defines the probabilities to travel between pairs of floors or to stay within the same floor. We also supposed that these Markov chains are homogenous, (i.e. the transition matrix doesn't change over time).

Distributions and Interpretation. Like for the first case, the average of internal similarities of all the classes are above 83% as shown in Table 2. Seven over the eight classes have average similarities of 93% or more. This confirms once again our intuition about the correlation between the coupling and the behavior uniformity. For the distributions, we observed some differences with the first case. One of them is a non regular distribution observed for the class *ArrivalSensor*. This distribution includes three blocks corresponding to three small coupling values, respectively 3 (for 20% of the executions), 4 (for 40%), and 5 (for 40%). This distribution could be considered, to some extent, as a single-bar one before the behavior in the three blocks is very similar. However, as we do not have a block that contains a clearly majority of executions, we classified it as "non regular". Another difference is that except for this marginal case, we did not observe single-bar distributions. This could be explained by the fact that the considered program is more complex than the one of Sudoku. This complexity introduces many variations in behavior.

The most frequent distribution is the exponential-like one, found for half of the classes. For example, class *Elevator* has three regions. The first region with the lower coupling values corresponds to the common elevator behavior with

Table 2. Statistics about *Elevator* program

Class Name	IS(%)	Distribution	Regions
ArrivalSensor	83.72	-	$\{b_3, b_4, b_5\}$
Elevator (main)	95.24	*Exponential-like*	$\{b_9, b_{10}, b_{11}, b_{12}\}$, $\{b_{13}, b_{14}, b_{15}, b_{16}, b_{17}\}$, $\{b_{18}, b_{19}, b_{21}, b_{23}, b_{24}\}$
ElevatorGroup	95.67	*Normal-like*	$\{b_9, b_{10}, b_{11}, b_{12}\}$, $\{b_{13}, b_{14}, b_{15}, b_{16}, b_{17}, b_{18}, b_{20}, b_{21}\}$, $\{b_{23}, b_{24}, b_{25}, b_{26}, b_{29}\}$
ElevatorControl	93.90	*Exponential-like*	$\{b_4, b_5, b_6, b_7\}$, $\{b_8, b_9, b_{10}, b_{11}, b_{12}, b_{13}, b_{14}\}$, $\{b_{15}, b_{16}\}$
ElevatorInterface	96.57	*Normal-like*	$\{b_{10}, b_{12}, b_{13}, b_{14}\}$, $\{b_{15}, b_{16}, b_{18}, b_{19}, b_{20}, b_{22}, b_{23}, b_{24}\}$, $\{b_{25}, b_{26}, b_{27}, b_{28}\}$
Floor	98.11	*Exponential-like*	$\{b_{12}, b_{13}, b_{14}\}$, $\{b_{15}, b_{16}, b_{17}, b_{19}, b_{20}\}$, $\{b_{21}, b_{23}, b_{25}, b_{27}\}$
FloorControl	96.24	*Uniform-like*	$\{b_6, b_8, b_{10}\}$ $\{b_{12}, b_{14}, b_{16}\}$, $\{b_{18}, b_{20}, b_{22}\}$, $\{b_{24}, b_{26}, b_{28}\}$
FloorInterface	92.99	*Exponential-like*	$\{b_2, b_3, b_4\}$, $\{b_5, b_6, b_7, b_8\}$, $\{b_9, b_{11}\}$

interactions mainly with *Floor* and *ArrivalSensor*. The coupling increases to deal with exceptional situations such as considering a new elevator call during the movement, and less frequently to manage a high level of calls, which requires to create a queue and to start a new thread to manage the behavior concurrency.

The three remaining distributions are normal-like (two classes) and uniform-like ones. To illustrate how two distributions could be impacted by the same variation in a use case, consider the distribution of class *ElevatorGroup* (normal-like) shown in Figure 2-right. We identified three regions and three blocks that were not included in any region. This is a variation of our algorithm that consists in not creating regions for single blocks that have low similarities with previous and following blocks together with a very low number of executions. The first region corresponds to a minimal behavior that results from the violation of preconditions during the creating of the elevators. Indeed, during the creation, *ElevatorGroup* checks if the number of elevators and the number of floors are within a certain range. Then, it checks if the number of elevators is consistent with the number of floors. The second region that we identified corresponds to the common behavior of assigning calls to elevators, etc. Finally, the third region corresponds to an exceptional situation related to one of the class *Elevator* in the previous paragraph. This situation concerns the management of busy periods with a high number of calls.

5   Related Work and Discussion

The work proposed in this paper crosscuts several research areas. Compared to contributions in dynamic coupling calculations, our approach allows to select a representative set of executions. Indeed, Arisholm et al. [2] pick an arbitrary set of executions and take the average of the metric value over these executions. Yacoub et al. [12] assign probabilities to a finite set of execution scenarios, compute the dynamic metric for each scenario, and take the weighted average across scenarios. Although assigning probabilities to executions is close to our approach, in practice, the number of possible executions is extremely large, which limits the applicability.

Our work defines probabilistic models for inputs that are used to generate representative samples of executions and then to better characterize the dynamic coupling. Stochastic simulation was used in software engineering, mainly to understand the development process (*e.g.*, [8]) or to characterize the evolution of a given program (*e.g.*, [10]). In both cases, the simulation is related to requirements and change request, but does not involve program inputs or class dependencies. The work of Zhou et al. [14] is maybe more or less closely related to our contribution. They propose a navigation model that abstracts the user Web surfing behavior as a Markov model. This model is used to quantify navigability. Modeling inputs as a Markov chain seems natural here because the inputs for Web sites are different from ones of classical software. Indeed, in this work, only mouse clicks on links are considered but not inputs using forms.

The work presented in this paper is an initial initiative to propose a framework for understanding the relationship between the coupling and the behavior of a class. Although the first findings are very encouraging, there are many open issues that need to be addressed. Firstly, in practice, it is difficult to define input distributions. When the program is in use, it is possible to record the inputs as the users provide them and after a certain period, estimate the distribution from the collected data. However, when the program is under development, *i.e.*, not released yet, these data are not available. Of course, one could decide theoretically that an input should have a particular distribution (say normal). Still, there is a need for estimating the distribution parameters (mean and variance in the case of normal distribution). Another problem concerns the nature of the input data. In our study, we considered inputs that take values in a finite set. In most of the programs, inputs could be strings with theoretically an infinite set of values such as person names, files, etc. The random generation of strings according to a particular distribution could be modeled easily. However, random generation of files, such as source code for compilers, is not an obvious task.

6   Conclusion

In this paper, we proposed a framework for modeling program inputs using a probabilistic setting. These models allow to derive class coupling metric distributions. We showed how these distributions could be used to understand the behavior of classes. We illustrated our approach with two small case studies. The first has a finite set of inputs, which are modeled by a random vector. In contrary, the second program has an infinite set of inputs that are modeled by a (homogenous) Markov chain. We observed in these cases that recurrent distribution patterns correspond to regular behavior schemes.

Our future work will be mainly dedicated to make our framework more effective. The issues to be addressed include scalability and support for input model definition. We additionally intend to assess more dynamic coupling metrics, so that to improve the generalizability of our approach.

References

1. Allier, S., Vaucher, S., Dufour, B., Sahraoui, H.A.: Deriving coupling metrics from call graphs. In: Int. Work. Conf. on Source Code Analysis and Manipulation, pp. 43–52 (2010)
2. Arisholm, E., Briand, L.C., Foyen, A.: Dynamic coupling measurement for object-oriented software. IEEE Trans. Softw. Eng. 30(8), 491–506 (2004)
3. Asmussen, S., Glynn, P.W.: Stochastic Simulation. Springer (2007)
4. Biggerstaff, T., Mitbander, B., Webster, D.: The concept assignment problem in program understanding. In: Int. Conf. on Software Engineering, pp. 482–498 (1993)
5. L'Ecuyer, P.: SSJ: A Java Library for Stochastic Simulation (2008), Software user's guide, available at http://www.iro.umontreal.ca/~lecuyer
6. Nelsen, R.B.: An Introduction to Copulas. Lecture Notes in Statistics, vol. 139. Springer (1999)
7. Rajlich, V., Wilde, N.: The role of concepts in program comprehension. In: 10th International Workshop on Program Comprehension, pp. 271–278 (2002)
8. Setamanit, S., Wakeland, W., Raffo, D.: Planning and improving global software development process using simulation. In: Int. Workshop on Global Software Development for the Practitioner (2006)
9. Shao, J.: Mathematical Statistics. Springer (1999)
10. Stopford, B., Counsell, S.: A framework for the simulation of structural software evolution. ACM Trans. Model. Comput. Simul. 18(4), 1–36 (2008)
11. Tahvildar, L., Kontogiannis, K.: Improving design quality using meta-pattern transformations: a metric-based approach. J. Softw. Maint. Evol. 16(4-5), 331–361 (2004)
12. Yacoub, S.M., Ammar, H.H., Robinson, T.: Dynamic metrics for object oriented designs. In: METRICS 1999, pp. 50–61 (1999)
13. Zaidman, A., Demeyer, S.: Automatic identification of key classes in a software system using webmining techniques. J. Softw. Maint. Evol. 20(6), 387–417 (2008)
14. Zhou, Y., Leung, H., Winoto, P.: Mnav: A markov model-based web site navigability measure. IEEE Trans. Softw. Eng. 33(12), 869–890 (2007)

Discovering Branching Conditions from Business Process Execution Logs

Massimiliano de Leoni[1], Marlon Dumas[2], and Luciano García-Bañuelos[2]

[1] Eindhoven University of Technology, Eindhoven, The Netherlands
[2] University of Tartu, Tartu, Estonia

Abstract. Process mining is a family of techniques to discover business process models and other knowledge of business processes from event logs. Existing process mining techniques are geared towards discovering models that capture the order of execution of tasks, but not the conditions under which tasks are executed – also called branching conditions. One existing process mining technique, namely ProM's Decision Miner, applies decision tree learning techniques to discover branching conditions composed of atoms of the form "v op c" where "v" is a variable, "op" is a comparison predicate and "c" is a constant. This paper puts forward a more general technique to discover branching conditions where the atoms are linear equations or inequalities involving multiple variables and arithmetic operators. The proposed technique combine invariant discovery techniques embodied in the Daikon system with decision tree learning techniques.

1 Introduction

The use of business process models to analyze and automate business operations is a widespread practice. Traditionally, business process models are obtained from interviews and workshops with domain experts and workers. Studies have shown however that models obtained in this way may deviate significantly from the way processes are actually conducted on a daily basis [1]. Workers tend to take shortcuts or workarounds in order to deal with special cases or to simplify their work. At the same time, contemporary enterprise systems maintain detailed records of transactions performed by workers, which can be exploited to discover models that more faithfully reflect the way processes are actually performed.

This observation has spawned a research area known as process mining [1], which is concerned with the automated discovery of process models and other knowledge of business processes from event logs. Several algorithms for automated process discovery have been developed, which strike different tradeoffs between accuracy and comprehensibility of the discovered models.

To illustrate the capabilities and limitations of these algorithms, we consider a process for handling loan applications (cf. Figure 1). This process starts when a loan application is made. First, the loan application details are entered into a system – in particular the amount and length of the loan which are hereby treated as variables of the process. Next, data about the applicant (e.g. age and

V. Cortellessa and D. Varró (Eds.): FASE 2013, LNCS 7793, pp. 114–129, 2013.

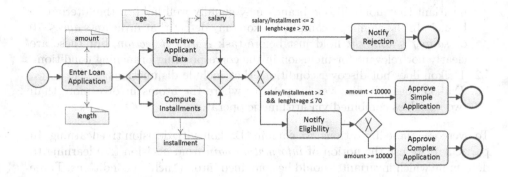

Fig. 1. Running example: loan application process model (in BPMN notation)

salary) are retrieved from the customer database. In parallel, the amount of each installment is calculated and stored as a variable. The request is eligible if the applicant's salary is more than twice the amount of the installment and they would finish paying installments by the age of 70. If the applicant is not eligible, the application is rejected. If eligible, the applicant is notified and their application is forwarded for approval. If the requested amount is less that 10000, a simple approval suffices; otherwise, a more complex approval is required.

The bulk of automated process discovery algorithms are focused on extracting control-flow relations between events or tasks in a process. In the working example, these algorithms would discover the sequence relations in the model, the parallel execution relations (the "+" gateways in Figure 1) and the conditional *branching points* where a choice is made between alternative branches (the "X" gateways in Figure 1). However, they do not discover the conditions attached to the outgoing branches of these branching points – also called *branching conditions*.

An attempt to address this limitation is the Decision Miner [2] embodied in the ProM toolset [1]. The Decision Miner applies decision tree learning to infer conditions composed of atoms of the form "v op c" where "v" is a variable, "op" is a comparison predicate and "c" is a constant. In the running example, the Decision Miner can discover the condition $amount \geq 10000$ (and its dual), but not the conditions attached to the leftmost branching point in the model.

This paper tackles the problem of discovering branching conditions where the atoms are equalities or inequalities involving arithmetic expressions on multiple variables. The starting point is the invariant detection technique embodied in the Daikon system [3]. A direct application of Daikon allows us to discover invariants that hold before (or after) a task is executed. The discovered invariants are of the form "v_1 op c" or "v_1 op v_2" where v_1 and v_2 are variables and c is a constant. By combining these invariants via conjunction, we can discover conditions that hold at the start of each branch. However, this approach has three limitations:

L1. Many of the invariants detected by Daikon are not suitable for inclusion in a branching condition. A branching condition should discriminate between the cases when one branch is taken and those when it is not taken, while an invariant that holds in one branch may equally well hold in the alternative branch. In the running example, Daikon may detect that invariants $age \leq 70$ or $salary \leq amount$ hold just before task *Notify Rejection*, but these are clearly not relevant for inclusion in the corresponding branching condition.

L2. Daikon does not discover conditions that include disjunctions.

L3. Daikon does not discover inequalities where the atoms involve more than two variables combined via arithmetic operators.

To overcome these limitations, we combine Daikon with decision tree learning. In particular, we use the notion of *information gain* from decision tree learning to determine which invariants should be combined into branching conditions. Three techniques of increasing degree of sophistication are proposed, which overcome each of the above three limitations in turn. The techniques have been validated on a set of test cases covering branching conditions with different structures.

The paper is structured as follows. Section 2 introduces ProM's Decision Miner and Daikon and discusses other related work. Section 3 presents the techniques for branching condition discovery while Section 4 documents their validation. Section 5 discusses some remaining limitations and directions for future work.

2   Background and Related Work

2.1   ProM Decision Miner

ProM's Decision Miner allows one to discover branching conditions for a given branching point in a process model. These conditions depend on the value of the variables of the process when the point is reached. Accordingly, the input of ProM's Decision Miner consists of an event log where each event contains: (i) a timestamp; (ii) an event type that allows to link the event to a task; and (iii) a set of ⟨variable, value⟩ pairs, representing the new values of variables modified by the event in question. The events in the log are grouped into traces, where each trace is a temporally-ordered sequence of events representing one execution of a process from start to end (also called a *case*). The mechanism used to group events in a log into traces is not relevant for this paper (see e.g. [1]).

ProM's Decision Miner assumes that a process model has been discovered from the event log prior to discovering the branching conditions. This process model can be obtained using one of the existing process discovery algorithms.

Given the event log, the discovered process model, and one of the branching points P in the model, ProM's Decision Miner first calculates, for each enablement of P in a trace (i.e. each traversal of P when replaying the trace against the model), the following: (i) the values of each variable in the process when P is enabled; and (ii) the identifier of the branch that was taken after the branching point was traversed (the *outcome*). A variable assignment and its associated outcome for a given enablement of P is called an observation instance. The set of observation instances of P is used to mine a decision tree. This decision tree is transformed into a disjunction of conjunctions of atomic expressions as follows: Each path from the root to a leaf labelled with outcome t_i becomes a conjunctive expression associated to branch t_i. The branching condition of a branch t_i is the disjunction of the conjunctive expressions derived from the paths leading to t_i.

ProM's original Decision Miner [2] cannot handle process models with cycles or with invisible ("skip") tasks. These limitations however are addressed in [4].

Since the internal nodes of a decision tree are labeled with expressions of the form variable-op-constant, the Decision Miner only discovers conditions consisting of atoms of this form. In the running example, the Decision Miner cannot discover the conditions associated with *Notify Rejection* and *Notify Eligibility*.

The Decision Miner assumes that the branches of a branching point are exclusive, i.e. exactly one of the branches is selected. Process modeling languages also support inclusive branching points where more than one branch can be taken in parallel. However, an inclusive branching point can be transformed into an exclusive branching point and one or more parallel gateways.

2.2 Invariant Discovery and Specification Mining

Daikon [5] is a dynamic analysis tool for inferring likely value-based invariants from a collection of execution traces. It operates by instantiating a set of invariant templates with the variables in the logs, and trying to match each instantiated template against the variable assignments recorded in the traces. It outputs a set of invariants with sufficient statistical support.

Daikon relies on code instrumentation tools that expose the value of variables at points of interest in a program. For example, Java bytecode can be instrumented so as to monitor actual parameters used in method calls. In this way, Daikon discovers method pre and postconditions, and derives object-level invariants.

Daikon comes with a large set of invariant templates, ranging from simple relational expressions on variable/value or variable/variable pairs (e.g., $x < y$) to sophisticated templates of linear relations over multiple variables (e.g., $x - 3 * y = 115$). Daikon usually discovers interesting invariants but it may also report irrelevant invariants. In our running example, for instance, Daikon may discover the invariant $length < salary$, assuming that both variables *length* and *salary* have integer values. To cope with this problem, Daikon uses static analysis of the target program source code to identify meaningful combinations of variables [6]. Such analysis may reveal, for instance, that variables *salary* and *installment* are used together in arithmetic expressions while variables *salary* and *length* are not. Daikon then avoids instantiating templates that combine variables *salary* and *length*, thus improving the relevance of the discovered invariants. In our setting, however, static analysis is not possible as no source code is available.

For the problem at hand, we can use Daikon to discover invariants for each task that follows a branching point in the target process model. These invariants could be put into conjunctive expressions, that would be then used as branching conditions. This approach has been explored in [7, 8]. However, Daikon may discover invariants that are not necessarily branching conditions. For example, $amount > 0$ holds for all activities in the process model in Figure 1. This atom may appear in all the branching conditions in the process model, even if it is not directly involved in the decision in question.

Several extensions of Daikon have been proposed. One of them [9] discovers object-level invariants including disjunctions (limitation L2 in Section 1). However, this extension requires the source code to be analyzed and in our problem setting no source code is available. Other related work includes alternative oracles for discovering potential invariants, such as the one proposed by [10], which produces higher-order polynomial invariants as opposed to only linear invariants as Daikon.

Daikon is an exemplar of a broader class of so-called specification mining techniques [11–13]. Specification mining is concerned with discovering temporal and data-dependent knowledge about a program or protocol. The discovered knowledge is represented, for example, as state machines. A distinctive feature of process mining compared to specification mining is that process mining is concerned with discovering concurrent behavior in addition to sequential behavior. Also, in process mining, no source code is assumed to be available.

3   From Invariants to Branching Conditions

This section proposes three techniques to address the limitations of Daikon highlighted in Section 1. Section 3.1 addresses L1. Section 3.2 extends the technique of Section 3.1 to address L2. Finally, Section 3.3 extends further to overcome L3. Section 3.4 discusses the case of N-ary branching points.

A binary branching point is denoted by a set $\{t_1, t_2\}$ where t_1 and t_2 are the first tasks of the two branches. For convenience, we associate each branching condition with the first task of the respective branch, i.e. with t_1 or t_2.

Daikon is trained on a set of observation instances relative to a task. Here, an observation instance is a function $i : V \to U$ that assigns a value $i(v)$ to each variable $v \in V$. Given a set $\mathcal{I}$ of observation instances, we abstract Daikon as a function DISCOVERINVARIANTSWITHDAIKON($\mathcal{I}$) that returns a conjunctive expression of atoms that are invariants with respect to instances in $\mathcal{I}$. Sometimes, Daikon is not able to discover invariants; in these cases, the special value $\bot$ is returned. Observation instances relative to a task are extracted from an event log as follows:

Definition 1 (Event Log). *Let T and V be a set of tasks and variables, respectively. Let U be the set of values that can be assigned to every variable $v \in V$. Let Φ be the set of all functions $V \nrightarrow U$ that define an assignment of values to a subset of variables in V. An **event log** $\mathcal{L}$ over T, V and U is a multiset of traces where each trace is a sequence of events of the form (t, ϕ), where $t \in T$ is a task and $\phi \in \Phi$ is an assignment of values to a subset of variables in V In other words, $\mathcal{L} \in \mathcal{B}((T \times \Phi)^*)$.*[1]

The observation instance relative to an execution of a task t in a given case (i.e. a process execution) consists of the values of the variables in the case prior to the execution of t. Algorithm 1 shows how observation instances are constructed from an event log. The output is a function I that associates each task $t \in T$ with

---

[1] $\mathcal{B}(X)$ the set of all multisets over X.

Algorithm 1. GENERATEOBSERVATIONINSTANCES

> **Data:** $\mathcal{L}$ – An event log over T and V
> **Result:** A function I that associated each task in T with a set of observation
>   instances

1 **Let** I be a function whose domain is T and $\forall t \in T.\ I(t) = \emptyset$.
2 **foreach** trace $\langle (t_1, \phi_1), \ldots, (t_n, \phi_n) \rangle \in \mathcal{L}$ **do**
3   **Let** M be a function whose domain is V and $\forall v \in V.\ M(v) = \bot$.
4   **for** $i \leftarrow 1$ **to** n **do**
5       $I(t_1) \leftarrow I(t_1) \cup M$
6   **foreach** variable v in the domain of ϕ_i **do** $M(v) \leftarrow \phi_i(v)$
7   **end**
8 **end**
9 **return** I

Algorithm 2. DISCOVERCONJUNTIVECONDITIONSWITHDAIKON (CD+IG)

> **Data:** $\mathcal{L}$ – An event log, P – A process model
> **Result:** A map that associates some transitions with the corresponding
>   branching conditions

1 $I \leftarrow$ GENERATEOBSERVATIONINSTANCES$(\mathcal{L})$
2 **foreach** $\{t_1, t_2\} \in$ BRANCHINGPOINTS(P) **do**
3    $C(t_1) \leftarrow$ DISCOVERINVARIANTSWITHDAIKON$(I(t_1))$
4    $C(t_2) \leftarrow$ DISCOVERINVARIANTSWITHDAIKON$(I(t_2))$
5    $C(t_1) \leftarrow$ BUILDCONJUNTIVEEXPR$(I(t_1), I(t_2), C(t_1))$
6    $C(t_2) \leftarrow$ BUILDCONJUNTIVEEXPR$(I(t_1), I(t_2), C(t_2))$
7   ADJUSTCONDITIONS$(I(t_1), I(t_2), C(t_1), C(t_2))$
8 **end**
9 **return** C

---

a set of observation instances relative to t. The algorithm is based on the principle
of replay. Each trace is associated with a function $M : V \rightarrow U$ that keeps the
assignment of values to variables. After an event is replayed, function M is
rewritten according to the event's value assignments. Initially, for each $v \in V$,
$M(v) = \bot$, where $\bot$ is a special value that identifies an undefined assignment.
Before replaying an event e for a certain task t, a new observation instance is
created and added to the set of instances for task t (line 5). Afterwards, e is
replayed and function M is rewritten accordingly (line 6).

For convenience, we will say that the observation instances of a branch are
the observation instances relative to the first task of that branch.

3.1   Discovery of Conjunctive Conditions

In order to construct the branching conditions from the invariants discovered
by Daikon, we leverage on the concept of *information gain*. In data mining, the
concept of information gain captures how well a given predicate distinguishes
between two or more possible outcomes (tasks in our case). In our context, the

---

Algorithm 3. BUILDCONJUNTIVEEXPR

Data: $\mathcal{I}_1, \mathcal{I}_2$ – Two sets of observation instances, P – A conjunctive expression
Result: A conjunction of a subset of the atoms in P that maximizes the
        information gain

1 **if** $P = \perp$ **then return** $\perp$
2 $S \leftarrow \{p_1, p_2, \ldots, p_n\}$ **s.t.** $P = p_1 \wedge p_2 \wedge \ldots \wedge p_n$
3 **Pick** $\overline{q} \in S$ **s.t.** $\forall q' \in S.\ IG(\mathcal{I}_1, \mathcal{I}_2, q') \leq IG(\mathcal{I}_1, \mathcal{I}_2, \overline{q})$
4 $\overline{P} \leftarrow \overline{q}$
5 $S \leftarrow S \setminus \{\overline{q}\}$
6 **while** $S \neq \emptyset$ **do**
7   **Pick** $\overline{q} \in S$ **s.t.** $\forall q' \in S.\ IG(\mathcal{I}_1, \mathcal{I}_2, \overline{P} \wedge q') \leq IG(\mathcal{I}_1, \mathcal{I}_2, \overline{P} \wedge \overline{q})$
8   **if** $IG(\mathcal{I}_1, \mathcal{I}_2, \overline{P} \wedge \overline{q}) > IG(\mathcal{I}_1, \mathcal{I}_2, \overline{P})$ **then** $\overline{P} \leftarrow \overline{P} \wedge \overline{q}\ \ S \leftarrow S \setminus \{\overline{q}\}$
9 **end**
10 **return** $\overline{P}$

---

information gain of a predicate P relative to a binary decision point leading
to tasks T1 and T2, is a measure of how well predicate P distinguishes the
observations instances where task T1 is executed from those where task T2 is
executed. A predicate that holds iff T1 is executed or a predicate that holds iff
T2 is executed has maximum information gain. A predicate that does not give
any gain (beyond random choice) when it comes to determining whether task
T1 or T2 is executed has zero information gain. Given a two sets of observation
instances leading to two tasks, the maximum possible value of the information
gain is called the *entropy*, as formally defined below.

Definition 2 (Entropy). *Let $\mathcal{I}'$ and $\mathcal{I}''$ be two sets of observation instances
that lead to the execution of to task t' and task t'', respectively. Moreover, let
$p(t)$ denote the probability of executing the task t. Then, the entropy of $\mathcal{I}'$ and
$\mathcal{I}''$ is defined as $H(\mathcal{I}', \mathcal{I}'') = -p(t') \cdot \log_2(p(t')) - p(t'') \cdot \log_2(p(t''))$. Since $p(t')$
can be expressed as $|\mathcal{I}'|/(|\mathcal{I}'| + |\mathcal{I}''|)$, we reformulate entropy as:*

$$H(\mathcal{I}', \mathcal{I}'') = -\left(\frac{|\mathcal{I}'|}{|\mathcal{I}'| + |\mathcal{I}''|} \cdot \log_2 \frac{|\mathcal{I}'|}{|\mathcal{I}'| + |\mathcal{I}''|} \right) - \left(\frac{|\mathcal{I}''|}{|\mathcal{I}'| + |\mathcal{I}''|} \cdot \log_2 \frac{|\mathcal{I}''|}{|\mathcal{I}'| + |\mathcal{I}''|} \right)$$

Entropy is 1 if sets $\mathcal{I}'$ and $\mathcal{I}''$ are of the same size. It becomes close to 0 if
the sets are of very different sizes. It is 0 if either $\mathcal{I}'$ or $\mathcal{I}''$ is empty (taking
$0 \log_2 0 = 0$). The intuition is that if we partition a set into a large subset
and a small one, this partition has little information, as the smaller set can be
encoded with few bits. Meanwhile, if we partition a set into equal-sized subsets,
more information is required to distinguish between the two subsets. Given two
disjoint sets of observation instances, our goal is to identify a predicate that
comes as close as possible to perfectly classifying instances between these two
sets and thus fully capturing the information in this partition of observation
instances. In other words, we seek a predicate that reduces as much as possible
the partition's entropy.

The information gain of a predicate P with respect to a set of instances is a measure that quantifies how much entropy is reduced by partitioning the set according to predicate P. A predicate that perfectly determines whether or not a given instance belongs to the set has an information gain equal to the entropy.

Definition 3 (Information Gain). *Let $\mathcal{I}'$ and $\mathcal{I}''$ be a set of observation instances for two tasks. The information gain of a predicate P with respect to $\mathcal{I}'$ and $\mathcal{I}''$ is defined as follows:*[2]

$$IG(\mathcal{I}',\mathcal{I}'',P) = H(\mathcal{I}',\mathcal{I}'') - \frac{(|\mathcal{I}'_P|+|\mathcal{I}''_P|)\cdot H(\mathcal{I}'_P,\mathcal{I}''_P)}{|\mathcal{I}'|+|\mathcal{I}''|} - \frac{(|\mathcal{I}'_{\neg P}|+|\mathcal{I}''_{\neg P}|)\cdot H(\mathcal{I}'_{\neg P},\mathcal{I}''_{\neg P})}{|\mathcal{I}'|+|\mathcal{I}''|}$$

Algorithm 2 describes the technique to discover conjunctive branching conditions. Initially, we generate the observation instances through Algorithm 1. Afterwards, the algorithm iterates on each branching point $\{t_1, t_2\}$. Conditions $C(t_1)$ and $C(t_2)$ are computed by Daikon using the observation instances relative to tasks $\{t_1, t_2\}$. Then, function BUILDCONJUNTIVEEXPR is called to build a conjunctive condition by combining the invariants discovered by Daikon in a conjunction that maximizes the IG relative to the outcomes of the branching point. The conditions are then adjusted to ensure that $C(t_1) = \neg C(t_2)$.

Algorithm 3 shows how function BUILD-CONJUNTIVEEXPR is implemented. In order to simplify the manipulation of conditions, we assume that the invariants discovered by Daikon are given as a conjunctive expression, i.e.

X_1	X_2	X_3
3	4	true
7	12	true
9	34	true
12	44	true

X_1	X_2	X_3
10	4	true
14	4	true
17	4	true
20	4	true

(a) t_1 (b) t_2

Fig. 2. Examples of observation instances relative to two tasks t_1 and t_2 of a binary branching point.

$P = p_1 \wedge p_2 \wedge \ldots \wedge p_n$. Let $S = \{p_1, p_2, \ldots, p_n\}$ be the set of atoms of P. If P is undefined (no invariant was discovered by Daikon) the algorithm returns $\bot$. Otherwise, the algorithm starts by picking the atom $\overline{q}$ with highest IG (line 6). This atom becomes the first conjunct in the result $\overline{P}$ (line 4). The algorithm continues by greedily adding a new atom $\overline{q}$ to the conjunctive expression $\overline{P}$ (line 9), provided that the conjunction $\overline{P} \wedge \overline{q}$ increases the IG. The loop stops when all the atoms in P have been considered. The resulting expression $\overline{P}$ is then returned (line 13).

Once the conditions are built for the two branches, they are adjusted so as to ensure that $C(t_1) = \neg C(t_2)$ (function ADJUSTCONDITIONS). The adjustment is performed as follows. If Daikon was unable to discover $C(t_1)$ (or $C(t_2)$), we set $C(t_1) = \neg C(t_2)$ (or vice versa). Otherwise, if the IG of $C(t_1)$ is higher (resp. lower) than that of $C(t_2)$, we set $C(t_2) = \neg C(t_1)$ (resp. $C(t_1) = \neg C(t_2)$).

As an example, let us suppose to have an event log and a process model with a branching point $\{t_1, t_2\}$. Using the event log as input, we apply Algorithm 1 to build the observation instances I', I'' relative to t_1 and t_2. Then, we employ Daikon with input I' and input I'', thus discovering invariant $C(t_1)$ and

---

[2] Given a set $\mathcal{I}$ of observation instances and a predicate P, $\mathcal{I}_P$ and $\mathcal{I}_{\neg P}$ denote the sub set of instances of $\mathcal{I}$ for which predicate P evaluates to true and to false, respectively.

Algorithm 4. DISCOVERDISJUNCTIVEEXPRESSIONWITHDAIKON (DD+IG)

Data: A – A set of alignments, P – Process Model
Result: A map that associates some transitions with the corresponding
branching conditions

1 $I \leftarrow$ GENERATEINSTANCETUPLE(A)
2 **foreach** $\{t_1, t_2\} \in$ BRANCHINGPOINTS(P) **do**
3       $C(t_1) \leftarrow false$
4       $C(t_2) \leftarrow false$
5       $DT \leftarrow$ BUILDDECISIONTREE($I(t_1), I(t_2)$)
6   **foreach** $(t, \overline{I}) \in$ ENUMERATEPARTITIONS(DT) **do**
7           $J \leftarrow$ DISCOVERINVARIANTSWITHDAIKON($\overline{I}$)
8           $J \leftarrow$ BUILDCONJUNTIVEEXPR($I(t_1), I(t_2), J$)
9           $C(t) \leftarrow C(t) \vee J$
10   **end**
11      $C(t_1) \leftarrow$ BUILDDISJUNTIVEEXPR($I(t_1), I(t_2), C(t_1)$)
12      $C(t_2) \leftarrow$ BUILDDISJUNTIVEEXPR($I(t_1), I(t_2), C(t_2)$)
13   ADJUSTCONDITIONS($I(t_1), I(t_2), C(t_1), C(t_2)$)
14 **end**
15 **return** C

$C(t_2)$ for t_1 and t_2, respectively. Daikon may discover the following invariants: $C(t_1)$ is $(x_1 < x_2 \wedge x_3 = true)$ and $C(t_2)$ is $(x_1 > 0 \wedge x_2 = 4 \wedge x_3 = true)$. Some atoms may be irrelevant as they do not discriminate the branch. E.g., to discover if any atom in $C(t_1)$ is irrelevant, we compute the IG of every atom: $IG(I', I'', (x_1 < x_2)) = 1$ and $IG(I', I'', (x_3 = true)) = 0$. We retain the atom with the highest IG, i.e. $x_1 < x_2$. Afterward, we pick $(x_3 = true)$; since $IG(I', I'', (x_1 < x_2 \wedge x_3 = true)) = IG(I', I'', (x_1 < x_2))$, we discard atom $(x_3 = true)$, so that $C(t_1)$ becomes the single atom $(x_1 < x_2)$. Similarly, atom $(x_3 = true)$ is discarded from $C(t_2)$: $C(t_2)$ is simplified as $(x_1 > 0 \wedge x_2 = 4)$. To finally obtain the branching conditions to associate with t_1 and t_2, we compute the IG of the simplified conditions $C(t_1)$ and $C(t_2)$: $IG(I', I'', C(t_1)) = 1$ and $IG(I', I'', C(t_2)) = 0.90$. Since the IG of $C(t_1)$ is higher, we set $C(t_2) = \neg C(t_1)$, i.e. $C(t_2)$ becomes $(x_1 \geq x_2)$.

3.2   Discovery of Disjunctive Conditions

Algorithm 4 (DD+IG) describes the technique for discovering disjunctive branching conditions. For each branching point $\{t_1, t_2\}$, we build a decision tree using the observation instances relative to tasks t_1 and t_2. In a decision tree, each path from the root to a leaf corresponds to an expression that is a conjunction of atoms of the form v op c. Such expressions are then used to partition the observation instances. In line 6, the invocation ENUMERATEPARTITIONS(DT) returns a set of pairs, one for each leaf node of the decision tree. In particular, if a pair $(t, \overline{I})$ is in the set, there exists a tree path to a leaf node associated with a classification attribute value t and $\overline{I}$ is the set of instances associated with that leaf. Note that there might be several leaves for each task t (t stands for $t1$ or $t2$). For each pair $(t, \overline{I})$, Daikon is used to discover the set of invariants J for partition $\overline{I}$. From J we build a conjunctive expression that maximizes the IG. The resulting conjunction is stored in $C(t)$. Once all partitions induced by the decision tree are analyzed, we proceed to combine the conjunctions into a disjunction. This is done by function BUILDDISJUNTIVEEXPR. The latter is similar to function BUILDCONJUNTIVEEXPR except that atoms (in this case conjunctions) are combined in disjunctions, looking at maximizing the IG. Finally, we adjust $C(t_1)$ and $C(t_2)$ to ensure $C(t_1) = \neg C(t_2)$.

3.3 Extensions for Arithmetic Operators

Daikon includes invariant templates to discover linear equalities with 2 or 3 variables and an optional constant. However, there are no equivalent templates for inequalities. In process models, inequalities are common and leaving these aside is a major restriction. For instance, the running example involves inequalities with 2 variables and a constant ($length + age \leq 70$ and $salary/installment \geq 2$).

To cope with this limitation, we propose to enrich the original log with so-called *latent variables*. A latent variable is defined as a variable derived by combining multiple variables in the original log by means of one arithmetic operator ($+$, $-$, $*$ or $/$). In the running example, an example of a latent variable is "salary_div_by_installment" = salary/installment.

We extend CD+IG and DD+IG with latent variables as follows. We identify the set of numerical variables and generate all combinations of N variables with one arithmetic operator (for each of the four arithmetic operators). Then, we augment the log by adding the latent variables and give it as input to Daikon. Daikon treats each latent variable as a regular variable. Thus, it discovers invariants involving one latent variable and one constant or one latent variable on one or both sides of an equality or inequality (e.g., $a + b \leq c * d$). The invariants thereby discovered are post-processed with either CD+IG and DD+IG. The extended techniques with latent variables are called CD+IG+LV and DD+IG+LV.

Importantly, invariants involving latent variables compete with invariants involving observed variables when CD+IG or DD+IG construct a branching condition out of the invariants returned by Daikon. Consider for example a situation where there are two numeric variables in the log ($x1$ and $x2$) and we seek to discover a branching condition $x1 \leq 8000 \wedge x2 \leq 8000$. Daikon naturally discovers invariant $x1 + x2 \leq 16000$ in addition to $x1 \leq 8000$ and $x2 \leq 8000$. Invariant $x1 + x2 \leq 16000$ may have a higher IG than each of the two other atoms taken separately. Thus, $x1 + x2 \leq 16000$ is integrated in the discovered condition and the other two invariants may then be left out if they do not increase the RIG. We observed this behavior when conducting preliminary tests. Accordingly, we adopt a two-step approach. In the case of CD+IG+LV, first, CD+IG (without latent variables) is run. If the result is not satisfactory (i.e., RIG below a threshold), CD+IG+LV is run again with all latent variables involving N terms (N is a tunable parameter). The same applies for DD+IG+LV.

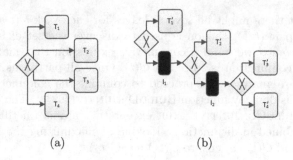

Fig. 3. N-ary to binary transformation

The complexity of CD+IG+LV and DD+IG+LV is combinatorial on N, since one latent variable is generated for each subset of size N of the variables in the log, and for each arithmetic operator. Thus these techniques are practical only for small values of N. Another limitation of CD+IG+LV and DD+IG+LV is that they only discover equalities or inequalities where each side involves a single type of arithmetic operator (only + or − or * or /). Introducing latent variables combining multiple types of arithmetic operators would lead to a higher combinatorial explosion when $N > 2$.

3.4   Extension to N-ary Branching Points

Hitherto, we have assumed that every branching point is binary. The technique can be extended to N-ary branching points as follows. Given an N-ary branching point, we rewrite this point into a number of of binary branching points by leaving one branch intact, collapsing the remaining $N-1$ branches into a separate branching point and so on recursively. For instance, the quaternary branching point in Figure 3(a) is rewritten into binary branching points in Figure 3(b). The transformed model has 2 new (black-filled) tasks (I_1 and I_2). These dummy (τ) tasks are introduced purely for the purpose of the branching condition discovery.

Any of the above techniques (CD+IG, DD+IG or their extensions with latent variables) can be applied to each binary branching point using the extended log. In the example, this allows us to discover the 6 conditions $C(t) - t \in \{T_1', T_2', T_3', T_4', I_1, I_2\}$. Having discovered the conditions for each binary branching point, the branching condition $C(T_i)$ of the ith branch of the N-ary branching point is then defined as the conjunction of $C(T_i')$ and each of the $C(I_j)$ where task I_j is on the path from the first binary branching point to T_i' in the rewritten model. In the example, this means that: $C(T_1) = C(T_1')$, $C(T_2) = C'(I_1) \wedge C(T_2')$, $C(T_3) = C'(I_1) \wedge C'(I_2) \wedge C(T_3')$ and $C(T_4) = C'(I_1) \wedge C'(I_2) \wedge C(T_4')$.

An N-ary branching point can be rewritten into binary ones in multiple ways depending on the order in which the N branches are refactored. Each rewriting leads to different branching conditions. Since we seek to maximize information gain, we perform the rewriting as follows. First we run CD+IG (or an extension) on each of the N original branches. We then select the branch for which the discovered condition has the highest Relative Information Gain (RIG). The RIG of a branching condition is the IG of the condition divided by the entropy of the observation instances of the branch in question and the union of the observation instances of all other branches. RIG is equal to 1 when the IG is equal to the entropy. This normalization of information gain relative to the entropy allows us to compare the gain of conditions in different branches (which may have different entropies). Having selected the branch with the highest RIG, we refactor this branch and apply the procedure recursively on the remaining branches.

4   Evaluation

The proposed techniques have been prototyped in Java using Daikon[3] for invariant detection and Weka[4] for decision tree learning. The prototype and the testbed presented below are available at http://sep.cs.ut.ee/Main/Branch Miner.

4.1   Testbed

We designed a battery of test cases covering different types of conditions. Daikon supports three primitive data types (integer, float and string) and sequences these primitive types. The testbed includes branching conditions with integers and strings. Strings are used to encode categorical (unordered) domains (i.e. enumerated types). Floats are not included in the testbed because Daikon handles integers and floats in the same way, and thus testing for both is redundant. We also left out sequences, because we consider they deserve a separate study.

The testbed includes conditions composed of atoms including variables with either categorical domain or numerical domain as follows. We defined 3 variables ($c1$, $c2$ and $c2p$) with categorical domains. Each domain includes 3 values: **C11**, **C12**. **C13** for $c1$ and **C21**, **C22**. **C23** for $c2$ and $c2p$. Since categorical domains are treated as unordered, we created atoms of the form variable-equals-constant and variable-equals-variable over the 3 variables. Thus two types of atoms were defined for categorical domains. We defined 4 variables ($x1$ to $x4$) over a numerical domain ($[1000, 15000]$)[5]. With these variables, we created atoms of the form variable-operator-variable and variable-operator-constant, where the operator can be $=$, $\leq$ and $\geq$. We did not produce atoms for operators $<$ and $>$ because these operators appear anyway in the negations of $\leq$ and $\geq$ and each test case includes a condition and its negation. Thus 3 types of atoms are defined over numerical variables. Test cases for $\geq$ and $=$ are omitted for the sake of brevity.

Given these atom types, we designed test cases covering 4 types of expressions: (i) single-atom; (ii) conjunctions of two atoms; (iii) disjunctions of two atoms; and (iv) disjunction of a conjunction and an atom. These test case design principles led us to 6 test cases for categorical domains and 15 for numerical domains

---

[3] http://groups.csail.mit.edu/pag/daikon/dist/
[4] http://www.cs.waikato.ac.nz/ml/weka/
[5] Daikon was configured to discover invariants of upper and lower bound for numerical variables in the range of their corresponding domain, the default being $[-1 \ldots 2]$.

of which only 5 are shown below for brevity. To test branching conditions with arithmetic operators, we introduced 2 additional variables ($x5$ and $x6$) and 3 additional cases (one single-atom, one disjunctive and one conjunctive) containing atoms with $\leq$, $>$ and $\geq$. The test cases are presented in Tables 1 and 2.

For each test case, we generated an event log of 200 execution traces via simulation using CPNTools[6]. The simulation model is a Coloured Petri net with three transitions. The first transition randomly assigns a value to each of the 9 variables ($c1$, $c2$, $c2p$, $x1$-$x6$) according to a uniform distribution. The other two transitions correspond to the branches of a branching point. One of these two transitions is labelled with the branching condition corresponding to the test case and the other with its negation. In the case of conditions $x_i = c$ and $x_i = x_j$ where x_i and x_j are numeric variables, we adjusted the random assignment so that these conditions hold in 50% of the cases. If we simply used a uniform distribution for these variables the probability of $x_i = c$ would be too low to generate enough traces that take the corresponding branch.

4.2   Results

Branching Conditions without Arithmetic Operators. Table 1 presents the original and the discovered conditions for the test cases without arithmetic operators. The table also shows the RIG (cf. Section 3.4) for each discovered condition. We observe that DD+IG discovered each of the original conditions in this category and the corresponding RIG is exactly one, indicating that the discovered conditions have perfect discriminative power. Meanwhile, CD+IG failed in case 11 with very low RIG, discovered alternative (equivalent) conditions in cases 3 and 6, and a similar (non-equivalent) condition in case 9. In these three latter cases, the original condition included a disjunction of atoms, which is equivalent to a conjunction of negations of the original atoms. This conjunction is discovered by the conjunctive approach with the caveat that the negated atoms involve the duals of the comparison operators of the original conditions. Thus, $c2 = c2p$ is discovered as $\neg(c2 \neq c2p)$ in case 6, while $c1 = \mathbf{C12}$ is discovered as $\neg(c1 \in \{\mathbf{C11},\mathbf{C13}\})$. For case 9, atom $x1 \leq 8000$ was discovered as $\neg(x1 \geq 9000)$ because Daikon does not discover invariants of the form "$x < C$" but instead it finds invariants with $\leq$. CD+IG failed in case 11 because both the original expression and its dual contain a disjunction.

Branching Conditions with Arithmetic Operators. Table 2 show the results of test cases for branching conditions with arithmetic operators. In all three cases, CD+IG+LV and DD+IG+LV succeeded to discover either the original condition, an alternative (equivalent) one or a similar (non-equivalent) one. In spite of having a RIG of 1.0, the solution to case 14 given by DD+IG+LV is unnecessarily elaborated, in addition to being non-equivalent to the original condition. It is clear that the presence of two disjoints comes from the

---

[6] http://cpntools.org

partitioning induced by the decision tree used in Algorithm 4. Not shown in the table is that CD+IG and DD+IG (without latent variables) failed in all these cases, as expected. They returned conditions with very low RIG.

Table 1. Test suite with no arithmetic operator

Case	Original	CD+IG	RIG	DD+IG	RIG
1	c1=**C12**	c1=**C12**	1.0	c1=**C12**	1.0
2	c1=**C12** ∧ c2=**C22**	c1=**C12** ∧ c2=**C22**	1.0	c1=**C12** ∧ c2=**C22**	1.0
3	c1=**C12** ∨ c2=**C22**	¬(c2 ∈ {**C23,C21**} ∧ c1 ∈ {**C11,C13**})	1.0	c2=**C22** ∨ c1=**C12**	1.0
4	c2=c2p	c2=c2p	1.0	c2=c2p	1.0
5	c2=c2p ∧ c1=**C12**	c2=c2p ∧ c1=**C12**	1.0	c1=**C12** ∧ c2=c2p	1.0
6	c2=c2p ∨ c1=**C12**	¬(c2≠c2p ∧ c1 ∈ {**C11,C13**})	1.0	c2=c2p ∨ c1=**C12**	1.0
7	x1≤8000	x1≤8000	1.0	x1≤8000	1.0
8	x1≤8000 ∧ x2≤8000	x2≤8000 ∧ x1≤8000	1.0	x2≤8000 ∧ x1≤8000	1.0
9	x1≤8000 ∨ x2≤8000	¬(x2≥9000 ∧ x1≥9000)	1.0	x2≤8000 ∨ x1≤8000	1.0
10	x1≤x2	x1≤x2	1.0	x1≤x2	1.0
11	x1≤8000 ∨ c2=**C22** ∧ x3≤x4	¬(**x1 ≥ 9000**)	**0.39**	x1≤8000 ∨ c2=**C22** ∧ x3≤x4	1.0

Table 2. Test suite with arithmetic operators

Case	Original	CD+IG+LV	RIG	DD+IG+LV	RIG
12	x1≤x2 ∧ x3+x4>15000	x1<x2 ∧ x3+x4≥16000	1.0	x1≤x2 ∧ x3+x4≥16000	1.0
13	x1≤x2 ∨ x3+x4>15000	¬(x1>x2 ∧ x3+x4≤15000)	1.0	¬(x1>x2 ∧ x3+x4≤15000)	1.0
14	x5*x6≥49	x5*x6≥49	1.0	x5*x6≥50 ∨ x5*x6 ∈ [49 . . . 56]	1.0

Execution Times. The experiments were conducted on a laptop, using a Java VM 1.7 on a 64 bit operating system. To gather the execution times, we ran every test case five times and took the average time of these runs. For the Conjunctive approach, the times had an average of 2 s, with 0.1 s of standard deviation, and a maximum of 2.18 s. For the Disjunctive approach, the average execution times was 11.2 s, with 0.8 s of standard deviation, and a maximum of 35.8 s.

Discussion. The results show that the proposed techniques have increased levels of precision (pecentage of correctly discovered conditions) but also decreasing performance. The results also show that the RIG of a discovered condition is a useful indicator of whether or not this condition has sufficient discriminative power. Thus, the techniques can be applied in a "trial-and-error" manner. Given a branching point, we can first apply CD+IG. If the RIG is less than a given threshold, we can apply DD+IG. If the resulting RIG is still low, we can introduce latent variables with the aim of maximizing the RIG of the discovered condition.

5   Conclusion

We have shown that a combination of invariant detection and decision tree learn-ing techniques allow us to discover a wide spectrum of branching conditions from business process execution logs, thereby allowing us to enhance the output of existing automated process discovery techniques. Specifically, we proposed three branching condition discovery techniques of increased level of complexity. The proposed techniques have been validated on synthetically-generated logs cover-ing branching conditions with varying structures. The test results show that the techniques discover non-trivial branching conditions in a few seconds (for the simpler technique) and in less than a minute for the more complex technique. In the future, we plan to apply the proposed techniques in practice on real-life event logs for example in the field of insurance where complex decisions are often involved when classifying claims, and similarly in the field of healthcare.

The approach to discover inequalities with more than two variables suffers from two key limitations. First, it is only possible to discover inequalities where each side has at most N variables (with N fixed) and where only one type of arithmetic operator appears in each side of the inequality. Second, the complexity of the approach increases combinatorially with N. Recent work [10] has put forward a technique to discover invariants consisting of equalities and inequalities among nonlinear polynomials. Adapting this technique for branching condition discovery is a direction for future work.

Acknowledgments. Work supported by EU's FP7 program (ACSI project).

References

1. van der Aalst, W.M.P.: Process Mining - Discovery, Conformance and Enhance-ment of Business Processes. Springer (2011)
2. Rozinat, A., van der Aalst, W.M.P.: Decision Mining in ProM. In: Dustdar, S., Fi-adeiro, J.L., Sheth, A.P. (eds.) BPM 2006. LNCS, vol. 4102, pp. 420–425. Springer, Heidelberg (2006)
3. Ernst, M.D., Perkins, J.H., Guo, P.J., McCamant, S., Pacheco, C., Tschantz, M.S., Xiao, C.: The Daikon system for dynamic detection of likely invariants. Science of Computer Programming 69, 35–45 (2007)
4. de Leoni, M., van der Aalst, W.M.P.: Discovery of data-aware process models. In: Proc. of the 28th ACM Symposium on Applied Computing (SAC 2013). ACM (2013)
5. Ernst, M.D., Cockrell, J., Griswold, W.G., Notkin, D.: Dynamically Discovering Likely Program Invariants to Support Program Evolution. IEEE Trans. Software Eng. 27, 99–123 (2001)
6. Guo, P.J., Perkins, J.H., McCamant, S., Ernst, M.D.: Dynamic inference of abstract types. In: Proc. of ISSTA 2006, pp. 255–265. ACM (2006)
7. Lorenzoli, D., Mariani, L., Pezzè, M.: Automatic generation of software behavioral models. In: Proc. of ICSE 2008, pp. 501–510. IEEE (2008)
8. Lo, D., Maoz, S.: Scenario-based and value-based specification mining: better to-gether. Autom. Softw. Eng. 19, 423–458 (2012)

9. Kuzmina, N., Paul, J., Gamboa, R., Caldwell, J.: Extending dynamic constraint detection with disjunctive constraints. In: Proc. of WODA 2008, pp. 57–63. ACM (2008)
10. Nguyen, T., Kapur, D., Weimer, W., Forrest, S.: Using dynamic analysis to discover polynomial and array invariants. In: Proc. of ICSE 2012, pp. 683–693. IEEE (2012)
11. Ammons, G., Bodík, R., Larus, J.R.: Mining specifications. In: Proc. of POLP 2002, pp. 4–16. ACM (2002)
12. Shoham, S., Yahav, E., Fink, S., Pistoia, M.: Static specification mining using automata-based abstractions. In: Proc. of ISSTA 2007, pp. 174–184. ACM (2007)
13. Lo, D., Khoo, S.C., Han, J., Liu, C. (eds.): Mining Software Specifications: Methodologies and applications. CRC Press (2011)

Exposing Behavioral Differences in Cross-Language API Mapping Relations

Hao Zhong[1], Suresh Thummalapenta[2], and Tao Xie[3]

[1] Laboratory for Internet Software Technologies, Institute of Software, CAS, Beijing, China
[2] IBM Research, Bangalore, India
[3] Department of Computer Science, North Carolina State University, Raleigh, USA
zhonghao@itechs.iscas.ac.cn, surthumm@in.ibm.com,
xie@csc.ncsu.edu

Abstract. Due to various considerations, software vendors often translate their applications from one programming language to another, either manually or with the support of translation tools. Both these scenarios require translation of many call sites of API elements (*i.e.*, classes, methods, and fields of API libraries). API mapping relations, either acquired by experienced programmers or already incorporated in translation tools, are much valuable in the translation process, since they describe mapping relations between source API elements and their equivalent target API elements. However, in an API mapping relation, a source API element and its target API elements may have behavioral differences, and such differences could lead to defects in the translated code. So far, to the best of our knowledge, there exists no previous study for exposing or understanding such differences. In this paper, we make the first attempt to expose and analyze behavioral differences in cross-language API mapping relations. From our result, we summarize eight findings and their implications that can improve effectiveness of translation tools, and also assist programmers in understanding the differences between mapped API elements of different languages during the translation process. Some exposed behavioral differences can indicate defects in translation tools, and four such new defects were confirmed by the developers of those tools.

1 Introduction

Since the inception of computer science, many programming languages (*e.g.*, COBOL, C#, and Java) have been introduced. To survive in competing markets and to address various business requirements, software companies or open source organizations often release variants of their applications in different languages. In total, as stated by Jones [12], nearly one third of the existing applications have versions in more than one language. There are three major factors for such phenomenon of having application variants in multiple languages. First, Application Programming Interface (API) libraries or engines are often released in more than one language to attract programmers in diverse backgrounds. Second, stand-alone applications are released in more than one language to acquire specific features of different programming languages. Finally, the market of mobile platforms is highly competitive, and different mobile platforms typically support different programming languages (*e.g.*, Andriod supports Java, iOS supports Objective C, and Windows Mobile supports C#). To survive in the competitive

V. Cortellessa and D. Varró (Eds.): FASE 2013, LNCS 7793, pp. 130–145, 2013.
© Springer-Verlag Berlin Heidelberg 2013

market, mobile application vendors tend to release variants of applications in different languages for multiple platforms.

State of the Art. To reduce development effort, a natural way to implement an application in a different language is to translate from an existing application. During the translation, programmers need to resolve many differences across two languages. Comparing with limited keywords and code structures, two languages typically have many API elements. As reported by El-Ramly *et al.* [7], it is critical to translate API elements correctly during the translation process. To translate API elements, programmers need to replace call sites of source API elements in one programming language systematically with their target API elements in another programming language, based on their known mapping relations. In practice, many programmers rely on their own understandings to translate API elements, but some experienced programmers also incorporate their understandings in translation tools. For example, programmers of db4o[1] developed a translation tool, call Sharpen, for translating db4o from Java to C#. To reduce the effort of translating API elements, they incorporated hundreds of API mapping relations inside Sharpen. Furthermore, to translate more API elements, researchers [27] proposed various approaches that mine API mapping relations automatically.

Given an entity E_1 (such as API classes, methods, and fields) in a language L_1, and another entity E_2 in another other language L_2, a mapping relation m is a triple $\langle E_1, E_2, f \rangle$ and describes that E_1 and E_2 have the same functionality f. API mapping relations are valuable to translate call sites of API elements, but they can introduce defects in the translated code silently. In an API mapping relation, E_1 and E_2 may have behavioral differences, and such differences can lead to defects. For a mapping relation m, a behavioral difference occurs, when translating between E_1 and E_2 leads to different output values or exceptions given the same input values and method sequences. For example, when translating Lucene.NET[2] from its Java version, a programmer, named Chrisopher Currens, expressed his concerns in an email:[3]

  "It could, also, hide bugs, since it's possible, however unlikely, something could port perfectly, but not behave the same way. A class that has many calls to string.Substring is a good example of this. If the name of the function is changed to the .Net version (.substring to .Substring), it would compile no problems, but they are very different."

The following code of Lucene.NET explains the behavioral difference.

```
Java code
01: protected String add_escapes(String str) {...
02:   String s = "0000" + Integer.toString(ch, 16);
03:   ret = s.substring(s.length() - 4, s.length()));
Translated C# code
04: protected internal String Add_escapes(String str){...
05:   String s = "0000" + System.Convert.ToString(ch, 16);
06:   ret = s.Substring(s.Length - 4, 4);
```

In this example, the second parameter of the substring(int,int) method in Line 03 denotes the end index of a return substring, whereas the second parameter of the Substring(int,int) method in Line 06 denotes the number of characters in a

---

[1] http://www.db4o.com

[2] https://cwiki.apache.org/LUCENENET/

[3] http://tinyurl.com/88xnf26

return substring. To resolve this difference, programmers of Lucene.NET changed the arguments accordingly during the translation. Due to a large number of API mapping relations, where some relations are quite complex [19], it is difficult for programmers to know all such behavioral differences of API mapping relations in advance. If programmers translate applications without realizing such behavioral differences, they can introduce defects in the translated code. If developers of translation tools are not aware of such behavioral differences, they may introduce defects in translation tools, and these defects could lead to further defects in the code translated by these tools.

Existing approaches [2, 3, 19, 21] cannot expose behavioral differences in cross-language API mapping relations effectively. For example, our previous work [19] compared API documents for behavioral differences when the APIs evolve, and cannot analyze behavioral differences for cross-language API mapping relations since their documents are fundamentally different. Srivastava *et al.* [21] compared API implementations for their behavioral differences, and their approach cannot analyze many API libraries whose code is not available. Bartolomei *et al.* [2, 3] list challenges to fix behavioral differences between Swing and SWT in the same programming language, but do not handle source code in different languages. To the best of our knowledge, many questions are still open. For example, are such behavioral differences pervasive? What types of behavioral differences are there? Which types of behavioral differences are more common than others? Are behavioral differences easy to be resolved?

Challenges. To answer the preceding questions, we need many API mapping relations for analysis, but it could take much effort for programmers to write them down manually. Instead, we choose to extract mapping relations that are already incorporated in translation tools. To achieve this goal, we have to overcome the following challenges.

Challenge 1. It is challenging to extract API mapping relations from translation tools, since developers of translation tools either use different formats for specifying API mapping relations, or hardcode API mapping relations in their tools' source code.

To address this challenge, instead of extracting API mapping relations directly from translation tools, we analyze translated results for extracting API mapping relations.

Challenge 2. Collected applications under translation may not cover some interesting API elements. In addition, it is difficult to align source API elements and their target API elements for complex mapping relations in collected applications.

To address the challenge, we synthesize the code under translation as test cases generated for all API elements of an API library. To generate test cases, we leverage two state-of-the-art techniques: random testing [17] and dynamic-symbolic-execution-based testing [9, 14, 24]. We generate test cases with simple code structures and minimum API elements, so that if a translated test case fails, it is easy to locate the behavioral difference of the API mapping relation in the failed test case.

Challenge 3. Translated code typically has compilation errors (*e.g.*, due to the API elements that do not fall into the scope of translatable API elements for the translation tool), so it is not feasible to expose behavioral differences via testing directly.

To address the challenge, we extract translatable API elements for a translation tool, and try to generate test cases that use only translatable API elements. For those generated test cases with compilation errors, we filter them out automatically.

Our Contribution. This paper makes the following major contributions:

- A tool chain, called TeMAPI, that detects behavioral differences among API mapping relations. With its support, we conduct the first empirical study on behavioral differences of mapped API elements between the J2SE and the .NET frameworks.
- Empirical results showing that behavioral differences are pervasive. We summarize exposed behavioral differences into eight findings, and discuss their implications that are valuable to vendors of translation tools for improving their tools, programmers who use these translation tools, and developers of API libraries for implementing more translatable APIs.
- Empirical results showing that some behavioral differences indicate defects in translation tools, and four defects were confirmed by the developers of translation tools.

Although we focus on cross-language API mapping relations in this paper, our process is general and can be applied to other software engineering problems where an API needs to be replaced with another API without changing the behavior of an application (*e.g.*, upgrading client code with the latest library [10], migrating to alternative APIs [16], or migrating to efficient APIs [13]).

2   Study Setup

Our process has three steps, and is not symmetry across the two languages under translation, since capabilities of translation tools are not symmetry and existing test-generation tools typically work for a single language rather than both languages under translation.

Step 1: Synthesizing and Analyzing Wrappers. For a translation tool that translates one language (L_1) to the other language (L_2), TeMAPI generates wrappers for API elements in L_1. In the synthesized code below, "|f.name|" denotes the name of a field f; "|m.name|" denotes the name of a method m; and "|no|" denotes the id of the synthesized wrapper method.

Static fields. TeMAPI synthesizes a getter for a public static field T f of a class C:

```
public T testGet|f.name||no|sfg(){ return C.f; }
```

If f is not a constant, TeMAPI synthesizes a setter wrapper as well for that field:

```
public void testSet|f.name||no|sfs(T p){ C.f = p; }
```

Static methods. Given a public static method Tr m(T1 p1,..., Tn pn) of a class C, TeMAPI synthesizes a wrapper method as follows:

```
public Tr test|m.name||no|sm(T1 p1,..., Tn pn){return C.m(p1,..., pn);}
```

When synthesizing wrapper methods for non-static fields or methods, TeMAPI takes constructors into considerations.

Non-static fields. Given a public non-static field T f of a class C, TeMAPI synthesizes a getter using each constructor C(C1 c1,..., Cn cn) of C as follows:

```
public T testGet|f.name||no|nfg(C1 c1,..., Cn cn){
   C obj = new C(c1,..., cn);
   return obj.f; }
```

If f is not a constant, TeMAPI synthesizes a setter wrapper as well for that field.

```
public void testSet|f.name||no|nfs(T p, C1 c1,...,Cn cn){
  C obj = new C(c1,..., cn);
  obj.f = p; }
```

Non-static methods. Given a public non-static method Tr m(T1 p1,...,Tn pn) of a class C, TeMAPI synthesizes a wrapper method using each constructor C(C1 c1, ..., Cn cn) of C as follows:

```
public Tr test|m.name||no|nm(T1 p1,...,Tn pn,C1 c1,...,Cn cn){
  C obj = new C(c1,..., cn);
  return obj.m(p1,..., pn); }
```

For example, for JLCA, TeMAPI synthesizes a wrapper method in Java for the Byte-ArrayInputStream.skip(long) method in Java as follows:

```
public long testskip24nm(byte c1[], long p1){
  ByteArrayInputStream obj = new ByteArrayInputStream(c1);
  return obj.skip(p1);}
```

TeMAPI groups all synthesized wrapper methods for one API class C to one synthesized class. After TeMAPI synthesizes wrapper methods, we use the translation tool under analysis to translate wrapper methods to the other language. For example, JLCA translates the preceding testskip24nm method into C# as follows:

```
public virtual long testskip24nm(sbyte[] c1, long p1){
  MemoryStream obj = new MemoryStream(SupportClass.ToByteArray(c1));
  MemoryStream temp_BufferedStream = obj;
  Int64 temp_Int64 = temp_BufferedStream.Position;
  temp_Int64=temp_BufferedStream.Seek(p1,System.IO.SeekOrigin.Current)-temp_Int64;
  return temp_Int64;}
```

TeMAPI extends existing compilers to find wrappers that are translated into the other language without compilation errors (referred to as *safe wrappers* in this paper). In particular, TeMAPI extends Visual Studio for C# code and Eclipse's Java compiler for Java code. From our experiences, translation tools are typically able to translate the simple code structures of synthesized wrappers, and all compilation errors are caused by untranslatable API elements in synthesized wrappers. TeMAPI compares safe wrappers with synthesized wrappers to extract the following two facts:

(1) The one-to-one mapping relations of API elements for the translation tool under analysis. For example, by comparing the first statements of the two testskip24nm methods in Java and in C#, TeMAPI extracts the mapping relation between the Byte-ArrayInputStream class in Java and the MemoryStream class in C# defined by JLCA, since the two methods declare two local variables with the same name, obj. Since translation tools typically do not modify names of variables, TeMAPI extracts such relations by using names. In Step 2, TeMAPI uses such relations to generate test cases in Java when leveraging Pex.

(2) The list of translatable API elements for the translation tool under analysis. For example, by comparing the first statements of the two testskip24nm methods in Java and in C#, TeMAPI adds the ByteArrayInputStream(InputStream) constructor

and the `skip(long)` method in Java to translatable API methods of JLCA, since their corresponding wrapper methods are translated without compilation errors. In Step 3, we use the list to limit the search scope of Randoop.

Step 2: Generating Test Cases with Pex. Pex [24] uses dynamic symbolic execution [9, 14] for generating test cases that exercise various paths in the code under test. Pex requires adding annotations (*e.g.*, [`TestClass()`]) to code under test for test generation. We use Pex to generate test cases for wrapper methods. In particular, for C#-to-Java translation tools, we use Pex to generate test cases in C# for synthesized wrapper methods in C# that are translated to Java without compilation errors, and for Java-to-C# translation tools, we use Pex to generate test cases in C# for translated wrapper methods in C# without compilation errors. When Pex generates test cases in C#, we set its parameters to allow it to exercise paths in API libraries.

TeMAPI uses the extracted mapping relations of API elements to translate generated test cases from C# into Java. Since test cases generated by Pex typically have limited API elements, extracted one-to-one mapping relations are adequate to translate test cases generated by Pex. Here, an alternative way is to use C#-to-Java translation tools to translate generated test cases. We do not choose this way, since we find that existing C#-to-Java translation tools cannot translate many API elements, and these tools do not support user-defined API mapping relations. Java and C# have different bounds for their literals. For example, the `long m0 = 2147483648` statement compiles well in C#, but it causes a compilation error: "The literal 2147483648 of type int is out of range". To resolve this difference, TeMAPI considers literals in C# as strings, and gets their values by corresponding API methods in Java.

To expose behavioral differences, TeMAPI uses two mechanisms for generating test oracles. First, TeMAPI inserts assert statements based on values of public fields or return values of public methods. For example, TeMAPI records that given an empty object, the `testappend175nm` wrapper method in C# returns a `StringBuilder` object whose `Capacity` is 16 and `Length` is 13, so TeMAPI derives a test case for the corresponding wrapper method in Java:

```
public void testappend175nm122(){
    Test_java_lang_StringBuffer obj = new Test_java_lang_StringBuffer();
    Object m0 = new Object();
    StringBuffer out = obj.testappend175nm(m0);
    Assert.assertEquals(16, out.capacity());
    Assert.assertEquals(13, out.length());}
```

This test case fails, since the `capacity()` method returns 34 and the `length()` method returns 24, so TeMAPI detects two behavioral differences. Here, TeMAPI ignores non-primitive or non-public fields of return objects, and thus may miss some behavioral differences that are not easy to be observed.

Second, TeMAPI uses expected assertions as test oracles. For example, when Pex explores a path, the method under exploration could throw exceptions. TeMAPI generates the following test case in Java based on inputs generated by Pex for one feasible path (in the C# wrapper method) that throws exceptions.

```
public void testskip24nm36(){
    try{
        Test_java_io_ByteArrayInputStream obj = new Test_java_io_ByteArrayInputStream();
```

```
long m0 = java.lang.Long.valueOf("2147483648").longValue();
byte[] c0 = new byte[0];
obj.testskip24nm(m0,c0);
Assert.assertTrue(false);
}catch(java.lang.Exception e){Assert.assertTrue(true);}}
```

This test case in Java fails, since given the preceding inputs, the skip(long) method in Java does not throw any exceptions, whereas the translated C# code does. Thus, TeMAPI detects a behavioral difference between the skip(long) method in Java and its translated C# code by JLCA.

Step 3: Generating Test Cases with Randoop. Randoop [17] randomly generates test cases based on already generated test cases in a feedback-directed manner. A wrapper method cannot help effectively generate method sequences in generated test cases, since it has fixed method sequences. To detect behavioral differences with method sequences of a translation tool, instead of generating test cases for wrapper methods, we use Randoop for API elements directly. Randoop generates test cases for arbitrary methods by default. To generate useful test cases for our purpose, we configure Randoop so that it generates method sequences only for the translatable API methods of the translation tool. Here, in Step 1, TeMAPI extracts translatable API methods of the translation tool with the support of synthesized wrappers.

Passing test cases are much useful to detect behavioral differences. If a passing test case fails after it is translated, it is easy to identify a behavioral difference, since the translated code should have the same behavior. If a translated failing test case fails, it is difficult to infer informative results, since the translation may and may not introduce more defects for causing the failure. Our preliminary study shows that Java-to-C# tools can translate many API elements. After TeMAPI removes all failing test cases, we use the translation tool under analysis to translate generated test cases from Java to C#. For example, TeMAPI generates a test case in Java as follows:

```
public void test413() throws Throwable {
  ByteArrayInputStream var2 = new ByteArrayInputStream(...);
  var2.close();
  int var5 = var2.available();
  assertTrue(var5 == 1);}
```

JLCA translates the generated test case from Java to C# as follows:

```
public void test413() throws Throwable{
  MemoryStream var2 = new MemoryStream(...);
  var2.close();
  long available = var2.Length - var2.Position;
  int var5 = (int) available;
  AssertTrue(var5 == 1);}
```

The preceding test case in Java passes, but the test case in C# fails. We thus detect a behavioral difference with method sequences.

In our tool chain, wrapper methods play an important role. First, some test generation tools need to instrument code under test. For example, Pex needs to add annotations to code under test. For those API libraries whose code is not available, our tool chain allows test generation tools to instrument wrapper methods for test generation. Second, by comparing translated wrappers with original wrappers, we implement a single technique to extract useful facts by comparing translated code, while different techniques

Table 1. Subject tools

Name	Version	Provider	Description
Java2CSharp	1.3.4	IBM (ILOG)	Java-to-C#
JLCA	3.0	Microsoft	Java-to-C#
Sharpen	1.4.6	db4o	Java-to-C#
Net2Java	1.0	NetBean	C#-to-Java
Converter	1.6	Tangible	C#-to-Java

are needed to extract such facts from different translation tools directly. Finally, wrapper methods expose a common interface for all the API elements, and thus help expose behavioral differences of API elements.

3 Empirical Results

In this section, we address the following research questions:

- Are behavioral differences pervasive in cross-language API mapping relations?
- What are the characteristics of behavioral differences concerning inputs and outputs?
- What are the characteristics of behavioral differences concerning method sequences?

In our study, we choose the translation tools in Table 1 as our subjects, since they are popular and many programmers recommend these tools in various forums. For Java-to-C# tools, TeMAPI synthesizes wrapper methods for J2SE 6.0[4], and ignores methods that include generics, since many translation tools cannot handle generics. For C#-to-Java tools, TeMAPI synthesizes wrapper methods for the .NET 4.0 framework clients[5], and ignores unsafe, delegate, and generic methods, and also the methods whose parameters are marked as out or ref. Java does not have these corresponding keywords, so existing translation tools typically do not translate the preceding methods. More details of our empirical results are available at http://sites.google.com/site/asergrp/projects/temapi.

Pervasiveness of Behavioral Differences. Table 2 shows the overall result. For Pex, column "Name" lists the names of translation tools, and column "Number" lists the number of generated test cases in Java. These number largely reflect how many API elements can be translated by corresponding tools. Columns "E-Tests" and "A-Tests" list the number of exception-causing and assertion-failing test cases, respectively. For the two columns, sub-columns "M" and "%" list the number and percentage of these test cases, respectively. For Randoop, column "Method" lists the number of translatable API methods; column "Java" lists the number of passing test cases in Java; and column "C#" lists the number of translated test cases in C# without compilation errors. Here, many test cases are translated with compilation errors for two factors, which are

---

[4] http://java.sun.com/javase/6/docs/api/
[5] http://msdn.microsoft.com/en-us/library/ff462634.aspx

Table 2. Overall testing result

Name	Number	Pex				Randoop				
		E-Tests		A-Tests		Method	Java	C#	A-Tests	
		M	%	M	%				M	%
Java2CSharp	15,458	5,248	34.0%	3,261	21.1%	1,996	15,385	2,971	2,151	72.4%
JLCA	33,034	8,901	26.9%	6,944	21.0%	7,060	16,630	1,067	295	27.6%
Sharpen	2,730	662	24.2%	451	16.5%	586	13,532	936	456	48.7%
Net2Java	352	40	11.4%	261	74.1%	n/a	n/a	n/a	n/a	n/a
Converter	762	302	39.6%	182	23.9%	n/a	n/a	n/a	n/a	n/a
Total	52,336	15,153	29.0%	11,099	21.2%	9,642	45,547	4,974	2,902	58.3%

not general or not related with API translation: (1) to prepare input values of translatable API methods, Randoop introduces API elements that are not translatable; (2) the number of compilation errors increases since Randoop produces many redundant code portions. We did not use Randoop to generate test cases for Net2Java and Converter, since the two tools translate too few API elements in C# to generate meaningful method sequences. In total, about half of the generated test cases fail, and the result shows that behavioral differences are pervasive in API mapping relations between Java and C#. The pervasive behavioral differences highlight the importance of our study.

Behavioral Differences Concerning Inputs and Outputs. TeMAPI leverages Pex to detect behavioral differences concerning inputs and outputs. As shown in Table 2, when leveraging Pex, more than 20,000 test cases failed. Given this large number of failures, we inspected 3,759 failing test cases selected as follows. For Net2Java and Converter, we inspected all the failing test cases, and for Java2CSharp, JLCA, and Sharpen, we inspected test cases of the java.lang package. We selected this package, since it is widely used in Java applications. Our findings are as follows:

Finding 1. 36.8% test cases show behavioral differences with respect to the handling of null inputs.

We found that many API methods in Java and their translated API methods in C# have behavioral differences when null values are passed as inputs. For example, JLCA translates the java.lang.Integer.parseInt(String,int) method in Java to the System.Convert.ToInt32(string,int) in C#. Given null and 10 as inputs, the method in Java throws NumberFormatException, but the method in C# returns 0. We notice that translation tools resolve some of these behavioral differences by providing custom functions. For example, java.lang.String.valueOf(Object) method in Java and the System.Object.ToString() in C# behave differently when a null value is passed as input. To resolve this difference, Sharpen translates the method in Java to its own implemented method in C#.

Implication 1. For implementers of API libraries, behaviors for null inputs are largely controversial. We suggest that implementers clearly define behaviors of null inputs. Our result shows that many such differences are left to programmers. When programmers translate API methods, they should handle null inputs carefully.

Finding 2. 22.3% test cases show differences among returned `string` values.

We found that two mapped methods typically return different `string` values. For example, each class in Java has a `toString()` method, and each class in C# has a `ToString()` method. Many translation tools map the two API methods, but the return values of the two methods are different in most cases. Besides the preceding two methods, many API classes declare methods such as `getName` or `getMessage`, and these methods also return `string` values that are quite different. Overall, we found that none of the five tools resolves this category of behavioral differences.

Implication 2. Although a method in Java and a method in C# have the same functionality, the two methods can return different `string` values. Programmers should be cautious while using these values, since they are typically different across languages.

Finding 3. 11.5% test cases show the behavioral differences of input domains.

We found that API methods in Java and their mapped API methods in C# can have different input domains. For example, the `java.lang.Double.shortValue()` method in Java accepts values that are larger than 32,767. JLCA translates the Java method to the `Convert.ToInt16(double)` method in C#. The C# method throws `OverflowException` when values are larger than 32,767 since it checks whether inputs are too large. As another example, the `java.lang.Boolean.parseBoolean (String)` method in Java does not check for illegal inputs, and returns `false` given an illegal input such as "test". Java2CSharp translates the method in Java to the `System.Boolean.Parse(String)` method in C#. The C# method throws `Format-Exception` given the same input since it checks for illegal inputs.

Implication 3. Programmers should be cautious while dealing with methods whose arguments are close to minimum or maximum values of respective data types, since the ranges of these values can be different between different languages. Cook and Dage [5] pointed out that an updated API method in a single programming language can also have different input domains. Adopting their approach may help deal with different input domains across languages.

Finding 4. 10.7% test cases show behavioral differences with respect to implementations.

We found that API libraries in different languages may have different implementations of the same functionalities. For example, we found that, unlike C#, Java considers "\" as an existing directory. Such differences can also indicate defects in translation tools. For example, Java2CSharp translates the `Character.isJavaIdentifierPart (char)` method in Java to the `ILOG.J2CsMapping.Util.Character.IsCSharp-IdentifierPart(char)` method in C#. Given an input "\0", the Java method returns `true`, but the C# method returns `false`. As another example, Java2CSharp translates the `java.lang.Integer.toHexString(int)` method in Java to the `ILOG.J2CsMap-ping.Util.IlNumber.ToString(int,16)` method in C#. Given -2147483648 as input, the method in Java returns "80000000", but the method in C# returns

"\080000000". Four behavioral differences including the preceding two were confirmed as defects by developers of Java2CSharp[6].

Implication 4. Implementers of API libraries can have different understandings on functionalities of specific methods. Some of such differences reflect different natures of different languages, and some other differences indicate defects in translation tools. Programmers should learn the natures of different programming languages (*e.g.*, different definitions of paths and files) to figure out such differences.

Finding 5. 7.9% test cases show behavioral differences with respect to handling of exceptions.

We found that some mapped API methods throw unmapped exceptions. For example, the `java.lang.StringBuffer.insert(int,char)` method in Java throws `ArrayIndexOutofBoundsException`, when indexes are out of bounds. Java2CSharp translates the method in Java to the `System.Text.StringBuilder.Insert(int, char)` method that throws `ArgumentOutOfRangeException` when indexes are out of bounds. Java2CSharp translates `ArrayIndexOutofBoundsException` in Java to `IndexOutOfRangeException` in C#. As Java and C# both allow unchecked exceptions, translated code can fail to catch corresponding exceptions.

Implication 5. Implementers of API libraries may design different exception handling mechanisms. This category of differences is quite challenging to be resolved for translation tools. When programmers translate `try-catch` statements, they should be aware of these differences. Otherwise, exception handling code may not be invoked in the translated version or may even become a dead code.

Finding 6. 2.9% test cases show the behavioral differences caused by constants.

We found that mapped constants may have different values. For example, the `java.lang.reflect.Modifier` class in Java has many constants to represent modifiers (*e.g.*, FINAL, PRIVATE, and PROTECTED). Java2CSharp translates these constants to the constants of the `ILOG.J2CsMapping.Reflect` class in C#. Between the two classes, constants such as VOLATILE and TRANSIENT are of different values. Sometimes different values reflect different settings of two languages. For example, translation tools often translate the `java.lang.Double.MAX_VALUE` field in Java to `System.Double.MaxValue` field in C#. The value of the former is 1.7976931348623157E+308, and the value of the latter is 1.79769313486232E+308.

Implication 6. Implementers of API libraries may store different values in constants, even if two constants have the same name. The different values sometimes reflect different settings such as different bounds of data types between two languages. Programmers should be aware of these differences while using constants.

The remaining 7.9% failing test cases are related to the API methods that return random values or values that depend on time. For example, the `java.util.Random.nextInt()` method returns random values, and the `java.util.Date.getTime()` method returns the number of milliseconds since Jan. 1st, 1970, 00:00:00 GMT. As another example, each Java class has a `hashCode()` method, and each C# class has also a `GetHashCode()` method. Translation tools often map the two methods. Since each

---

[6] http://tinyurl.com/3z45c5c

object has a unique hash code, the two methods of two receiver objects return different values. Since these exposed behavioral differences are false, they can be considered as false positives or limitations of our work.

Behavioral Differences Concerning Method Sequences. TeMAPI leverages Randoop to detect behavioral differences concerning method sequences. After browsing translated test cases, we notice that some translated test cases have compilation errors, even if these test cases use only translatable API elements.

Finding 7. API classes in Java and API classes in C# can have different inheritance hierarchies, and the difference can lead to compilation errors.

We found that API classes in Java can have different inheritance hierarchies with API classes in C#, and thus introduce compilation errors. For example, many compilation errors are introduced by type-cast statements, and one such example is as follows:

```
public void test87() throws Throwable{
    ...
    StringBufferInputStream var4 = ...;
    InputStreamReader var10 = new InputStreamReader((InputStream)var4, var8);}
```

Since the preceding two API classes in Java are related through inheritance, the test case has no compilation errors. JLCA translates the test case from Java to C# as follows:

```
public void test87() throws Throwable{
    ...
    StringReader var4 = ...;
    StreamReader var10 = new StreamReader((Stream)var4, var8);}
```

Since the two translated C# classes do not have the inheritance relation, the translated test case in C# has compilation errors.

Implication 7. A source API library and its target API library can design different inheritance hierarchies of classes. It is quite difficult for translation tools to resolve this category of behavioral differences. When programmers translate code, they should be aware of such differences. For example, when they translate cast statements, they should double check whether the target API elements have a similar inheritance hierarchy.

TeMAPI removed those translated test cases with compilation errors. Among remaining test cases, for each translation tool, we investigated only the first 100 failing test cases. The percentages are as follows:

Finding 8. 3.4% test cases fail for method sequences.

We found that random method sequences can violate specifications of API libraries. One category of such specification is described in our previous work [28]: closed resources should not be manipulated. Java sometimes allows programmers to violate such specifications although return values can be meaningless. Besides method sequences that are related to specifications, we found that field accessibility also leads to failures of test cases. For example, a generated test case in Java is as follows:

```
public void test423() throws Throwable{
    ...
    DateFormatSymbols var0 = new DateFormatSymbols();
    String[] var16 = new String[]...;
    var0.setShortMonths(var16);}
```

JLCA translates it to C# as follows:

```
public void test423() throws Throwable{
  ...
  DateTimeFormatInfo var0 = System.Globalization.DateTimeFormatInfo.CurrentInfo;
  String[] var16 = new String[]...;
  var0.AbbreviatedMonthNames = var16;}
```

In the translated test case, the last statement throws `InvalidOperationException` since a constant value is already assigned to `var0` in the previous line.

Implication 8. Legal method sequences can become illegal after translation, since the target language may be more strict to check method sequences, and other factors such as field accessibility can also cause behavioral differences. In most of such cases, programmers should deal with these differences themselves.

Remaining test cases failed for the following reasons: 45.0% for input domains, 34.0% for `string` values, 5.3% for different implementations, 4.0% for exception handling, 3.0% for `null` inputs, 2.0% for values of constants, and 0.3% for random values. The remaining 3.0% test cases fail, due to that translation tools translate API elements in Java to C# API elements that are not implemented yet. For example, Java2CSharp translates the `java.io.ObjectOutputStream` class in Java to the `ILOG.J2CsMapping.IO.IlObjectOutputStream` class in C# that is not yet implemented, and such translations lead to `NotImplementException`.

When generating test cases, Pex generates one test case for each feasible path, whereas Randoop uses a feedback-guided random strategy. As a result, the category distribution revealed by Pex more reflects the category distribution of unique behavioral differences than the category distribution revealed by Randoop, since each test case generated by Pex typically reflects a unique behavior.

Threats to Validity. The threats to internal validity include human factors for inspecting behavioral differences. To reduce these threats, we re-ran those failing test cases, and inspected those test cases carefully. This threat could be further reduced by involving more third-party members for inspecting the detected differences.

The threats to external validity of our evaluation include the representativeness of the subject translation tools, selected programming languages (Java and C#), and the selected package for inspection. In future work, this threat could be reduced by including more translation tools and inspecting test cases that are related to other packages. The threats to external validity of our evaluation also include unexplored behaviors of APIs. Taneja *et al.* [22] proposed an approach that generates test cases for database applications via mock objects. Thummalapenta *et al.* [23] proposed an approach that mines method sequences from real code for test generation. In future work, we plan to leverage their approaches and to integrate more testing tools (*e.g.*, JPF [25]), so that our work can detect more behavioral differences.

4   Discussion and Future Work

Improving Translation Tools and Detecting Related Defects. Our previous work [27] mines unknown mapping relations from existing projects with variants in different languages. In future work, we plan to extend our previous work [27] to resolve some detected behavioral differences. In addition, when programmers write code in an unfamiliar language, they may follow idioms of their familiar languages. This practice can lead to defects, since our findings show that differences between two programming languages can be subtle. In future work, we plan to propose approaches that leverage our findings to detect such defects as well.

Surveying Programmers with Language-Migration Experiences. When migrating legacy systems, many programmers choose to translate applications manually from scratch. Although they know many API mapping relations, they may not develop any translation tools, and our process cannot detect behavioral differences in their known mapping relations residing in their minds. In future work, we plan to conduct a survey to collect API mapping relations from those experienced programmers. In addition, we plan to conduct a survey to investigate whether these programmers are aware of behavioral differences exposed by us, and if they are, how they deal with such differences.

Analyzing Translation of More Programming Languages. To improve the potential impact of our work, we could analyze translation of more programming languages. Ravitch et al. [18] proposed an approach that generates bindings to expose low-level languages to high-level languages. In future work, we plan to adapt their wrappers, so that we can analyze translation of more programming languages, even if the two languages under analysis are fundamentally different.

5   Related Work

API Translation. API translation is an important aspect of language migration. (1) Language-to-language migration. Song and Tilevich [20] proposed an enhanced specification to improve source-to-source translation approaches. Zhong et al. [27] mined API mapping relations from existing applications in different languages to improve API translation. (2) Library update migration. Henkel and Diwan [10] proposed an approach that captures API refactoring actions to update client code with the latest APIs. Xing and Stroulia [26] proposed an approach that recognizes the changes of APIs by comparing the differences between two versions of libraries. Meng et al. [15] proposed an approach that mines API mapping relations from revision histories of API libraries. Balaban et al. [1] proposed an approach to migrate code when mapping relations of libraries are available. (3) Migrating from one API library to alternative libraries. Dig et al. [6] proposed *CONCURRENCER* that translates sequential API elements to concurrent API elements in Java. Nita and Notkin [16] proposed twinning to automate the process given that API mapping is specified. (4) Migrating to more efficient APIs. Kawrykow et al. [13] proposed an approach that compares client code with API implementation code, and thus allows programmers to choose more efficient APIs. Our work detects behavioral differences between mapped API elements, and the results can also help the preceding approaches translate applications resulting in fewer defects.

API Comparison. Shi et al. [19] compared API documents for behavioral differences when APIs evolve. Their approach is not suitable to compare API libraries in different languages, where API documents are typically fundamentally different. Hou and Yao [11] analyzed such behavioral differences for the intents behind API evolution.

Srivastava *et al.* [21] proposed an approach that compares API implementations for their behavioral differences, and cannot analyze the .NET frameworks whose code is not available. Bartolomei *et al.* [2, 3] reported their experiences on implementing wrappers between SWT and Swing. The preceding approaches compare APIs in a single language. Our work complements the preceding approaches by exposing behavioral differences of API elements in different languages.

Language Comparison. Researchers conducted various empirical comparisons on languages. Garcia *et al.* [8] presented a comparison study on six languages to reveal differences with respect to generics. Cabral and Marques [4] compared exception handling mechanisms between Java and .NET programs. To the best of our knowledge, no previous work systematically compares behavioral differences of API elements from different languages. Our work enables us to produce such a comparison study, complementing the preceding empirical comparisons.

6   Concluding Remarks

Behavioral differences among API elements of different languages are pervasive and could introduce defects in the translated code. Often, programmers are not aware of these differences either due to a large number of mapping relations or due to the fact that differences happen only for specific input values. In this paper, we presented the first empirical study that exposes behavioral differences among API elements between Java and C#. Our results can help improve existing translation tools and also assist programmers to better understand API behavioral differences between different languages.

Acknowledgments. Hao Zhong's work is supported by the National Natural Science Foundation of China No. 61100071. Tao Xie's work is supported in part by NSF grants CCF-0845272, CCF-0915400, CNF-0958235, CNS-1160603, and an NSA Science of Security Lablet Grant, as well as the National Science Foundation of China No. 61228203.

References

1. Balaban, I., Tip, F., Fuhrer, R.: Refactoring support for class library migration. In: Proc. 20th OOPSLA, pp. 265–279 (2005)
2. Bartolomei, T., Czarnecki, K., Lammel, R.: Swing to SWT and back: Patterns for API migration by wrapping. In: Proc. ICSM, pp. 1–10 (2010)
3. Bartolomei, T.T., Czarnecki, K., Lämmel, R., van der Storm, T.: Study of an API Migration for Two XML APIs. In: van den Brand, M., Gašević, D., Gray, J. (eds.) SLE 2009. LNCS, vol. 5969, pp. 42–61. Springer, Heidelberg (2010)
4. Cabral, B., Marques, P.: Exception Handling: A Field Study in Java and.NET. In: Ernst, E. (ed.) ECOOP 2007. LNCS, vol. 4609, pp. 151–175. Springer, Heidelberg (2007)
5. Cook, J., Dage, J.: Highly reliable upgrading of components. In: Proc. 21st ICSE, pp. 203–212 (1999)
6. Dig, D., Marrero, J., Ernst, M.: Refactoring sequential Java code for concurrency via concurrent libraries. In: Proc. 31st ICSE, pp. 397–407 (2009)

7. El-Ramly, M., Eltayeb, R., Alla, H.: An experiment in automatic conversion of legacy Java programs to C#. In: Proc. AICCSA, pp. 1037–1045 (2006)
8. Garcia, R., Jarvi, J., Lumsdaine, A., Siek, J.G., Willcock, J.: A comparative study of language support for generic programming. In: Proc. 18th OOPSLA, pp. 115–134 (2003)
9. Godefroid, P., Klarlund, N., Sen, K.: DART: Directed automated random testing. In: Proc. PLDI, pp. 213–223 (2005)
10. Henkel, J., Diwan, A.: CatchUp!: capturing and replaying refactorings to support API evolution. In: Proce. 27th ICSE, pp. 274–283 (2005)
11. Hou, D., Yao, X.: Exploring the intent behind API evolution: A case study. In: Proc. WCRE, pp. 131–140 (2011)
12. Jones, T.: Estimating software costs. McGraw-Hill, Inc., Hightstown (1998)
13. Kawrykow, D., Robillard, M.P.: Improving API usage through automatic detection of redundant code. In: Proc. ASE, pp. 111–122 (2009)
14. Koushik, S., Darko, M., Gul, A.: CUTE: a concolic unit testing engine for C. In: Proc. ESEC/FSE, pp. 263–272 (2005)
15. Meng, S., Wang, X., Zhang, L., Mei, H.: A history-based matching approach to identification of framework evolution. In: Proc. 34th ICSE, pp. 353–363 (2012)
16. Nita, M., Notkin, D.: Using twinning to adapt programs to alternative APIs. In: Proc. 32nd ICSE, pp. 205–214 (2010)
17. Pacheco, C., Lahiri, S., Ernst, M., Ball, T.: Feedback-directed random test generation. In: Proc. 29th ICSE, pp. 75–84 (2007)
18. Ravitch, T., Jackson, S., Aderhold, E., Liblit, B.: Automatic generation of library bindings using static analysis. In: Proc. PLDI, pp. 352–362 (2009)
19. Shi, L., Zhong, H., Xie, T., Li, M.: An Empirical Study on Evolution of API Documentation. In: Giannakopoulou, D., Orejas, F. (eds.) FASE 2011. LNCS, vol. 6603, pp. 416–431. Springer, Heidelberg (2011)
20. Song, M., Tilevich, E.: Enhancing source-level programming tools with an awareness of transparent program transformations. In: Proc. 24th OOPSLA, pp. 301–320 (2009)
21. Srivastava, V., Bond, M., McKinley, K., Shmatikov, V.: A security policy oracle: Detecting security holes using multiple API implementations. In: Proc. 32nd PLDI, pp. 343–354 (2011)
22. Taneja, K., Zhang, Y., Xie, T.: MODA: Automated test generation for database applications via mock objects. In: Proc. 26th ASE, pp. 289–292 (2010)
23. Thummalapenta, S., Xie, T., Tillmann, N., de Halleux, P., Schulte, W.: MSeqGen: Object-oriented unit-test generation via mining source code. In: Proc. ESEC/FSE, pp. 193–202 (2009)
24. Tillmann, N., de Halleux, J.: Pex–White Box Test Generation for .NET. In: Beckert, B., Hähnle, R. (eds.) TAP 2008. LNCS, vol. 4966, pp. 134–153. Springer, Heidelberg (2008)
25. Visser, W., Havelund, K., Brat, G., Park, S., Lerda, F.: Model checking programs. Automated Software Engineering 10(2), 203–232 (2003)
26. Xing, Z., Stroulia, E.: API-evolution support with Diff-CatchUp. IEEE Transactions on Software Engineering 33(12), 818–836 (2007)
27. Zhong, H., Thummalapenta, S., Xie, T., Zhang, L., Wang, Q.: Mining API mapping for language migration. In: Proc. 32nd ICSE, pp. 195–204 (2010)
28. Zhong, H., Zhang, L., Xie, T., Mei, H.: Inferring resource specifications from natural language API documentation. In: Proc. 24th ASE, pp. 307–318 (2009)

Explicit-State Software Model Checking
Based on CEGAR and Interpolation*

Dirk Beyer and Stefan Löwe

University of Passau, Germany

Abstract. Abstraction, counterexample-guided refinement, and interpolation are techniques that are essential to the success of predicate-based program analysis. These techniques have not yet been applied together to explicit-value program analysis. We present an approach that integrates abstraction and interpolation-based refinement into an explicit-value analysis, i.e., a program analysis that tracks explicit values for a specified set of variables (the precision). The algorithm uses an abstract reachability graph as central data structure and a path-sensitive dynamic approach for precision adjustment. We evaluate our algorithm on the benchmark set of the Competition on Software Verification 2012 (SV-COMP'12) to show that our new approach is highly competitive. We also show that combining our new approach with an auxiliary predicate analysis scores significantly higher than the SV-COMP'12 winner.

1 Introduction

Abstraction is one of the most important techniques to successfully verify industrial-scale program code, because the abstract model omits details about the concrete semantics of the program that are not necessary to prove or disprove the program's correctness. Counterexample-guided abstraction refinement (CEGAR) [13] is a technique that iteratively refines an abstract model using counterexamples. A counterexample is a witness of a property violation. In software verification, the counterexamples are error paths, i.e., paths through the program that violate the property. CEGAR starts with the most abstract model and checks if an error path can be found. If the analysis of the abstract model does not find an error path, the analysis terminates, reporting that no violation exists. If the analysis finds an error path, the path is checked for feasibility, i.e., if the path is executable according to the concrete program semantics. If the error path is feasible, the analysis terminates, reporting the violation of the property, together with the feasible error path as witness. If the error path is infeasible, the violation is due to a too coarse abstract model and the infeasible error path is used to automatically refine the current abstraction. Then the analysis proceeds. Several successful software verifiers are based on abstraction and CEGAR (e.g., [4, 6, 9, 14]). Craig interpolation is a technique from logics that yields for two contradicting formulas an interpolant that contains less information than the first formula, but still enough to contradict the second formula [15]. In software verification, interpolation can be used to extract information from infeasible error paths [19], where the resulting interpolants are used to refine

---

* An extended version of this article appeared as Tech. Report MIP-1205, University of Passau, 2012 [11].

V. Cortellessa and D. Varró (Eds.): FASE 2013, LNCS 7793, pp. 146–162, 2013.

```
1  extern int system_call();
2  int main(int x) {
3    int flag = 0, ticks = 0, result;
4    while(1) {
5      ticks = ticks + 1; result = system_call();
6      if(result == 0 || ticks > x) { break; }
7    }
8    if(flag > 0) { ERROR: return 1; }
9  }
```

Listing 1.1. Example to illustrate the effectiveness of CEGAR-based explicit-value analysis

the abstract model. Predicate abstraction is a successful abstraction technique for software model checking [16], because its symbolic state representation blends well with strongest post-conditions, and abstractions can be computed efficiently with solvers for satisfiability modulo theories (SMT) [3]. CEGAR and lazy refinement [20] together with interpolation [19] effectively refine abstract models in the predicate domain. The competition on software verification (SV-COMP'12 [5], Table 3) shows that these advancements had a strong impact on the success of participating tools (e.g., [6,9,23]).

Despite the success of abstraction, CEGAR, and interpolation in the field of predicate analysis, these techniques have not yet been combined and applied together to explicit-value analysis. We integrate these three techniques into an explicit-value analysis, a rather unsophisticated analysis that tracks for each program variable its current value explicitly (like constant propagation [1], but without join). First, we have to define the notion of abstraction for the explicit-value domain, and the precision of the analysis (i.e., the level of abstraction) by a set of program variables that the analysis has to track. Second, in order to automatically determine the necessary precision (i.e., a *small* set of program variables that *need* to be tracked) we use CEGAR iterations to discover finer precisions from infeasible error paths. Third, we define interpolation for the explicit-value domain and use this idea to construct an algorithm that efficiently extracts such a parsimonious precision that is sufficient to eliminate infeasible error paths.

Example. Consider the simple example program in Listing 1.1. This program contains a *while* loop in which a system call occurs. The loop exits if either the system call returns 0 or a previously specified number of iterations x was performed. Because the body of the function $system\_call$ is unknown, the value of $result$ is unknown. Also, the assumption $[ticks > x]$ cannot be evaluated to $true$, because x is unknown. This program is correct, i.e., the error location in line 10 is not reachable. However, a simple explicit-value model checker that always tracks every variable would unroll the loop, always discovering new states, as the expression $ticks = ticks + 1$ repeatedly assigns new values to variable $ticks$. Thus, due to extreme resource consumptions, the analysis would not terminate within practical time and memory limits, and is bound to give up on proving the safety property, eventually.

The new approach for explicit-value analysis that we propose can efficiently prove this program safe, because it tracks only those variables that are necessary to refute the infeasible error paths. In the first CEGAR iteration, the precision of the analysis is empty, i.e., no variable is tracked. Thus, the error location will be reached. Now, using our interpolation-inspired method to discover precisions from counterexample paths, the algorithm identifies that the variable $flag$ (more precisely, the constraint $flag = 0$) has to be tracked. The analysis is re-started after this refinement. Because $ticks$ is not in the precision (the variable is not tracked), the assignment $ticks = ticks + 1$ will not add new information. Hence, no new successors are added, and the analysis stops unrolling the loop. The assume operation $[flag > 0]$ is evaluated to *false*, thus, the error label is not reachable. Finally, the analysis terminates, proving the program correct.

In summary, the crucial effect of this approach is that only relevant variables are tracked in the analysis, while unimportant information is ignored. This greatly reduces the number of abstract states to be visited.

Contributions. We make the following contributions:

- We integrate the concepts of abstraction, CEGAR, and lazy abstraction refinement into explicit-value analysis.
- Inspired by Craig interpolation for predicate analysis, we define a novel interpolation-like approach for discovering relevant variables for the explicit-value domain. This refinement algorithm is completely self-contained, i.e., independent from external libraries such as SMT solvers.
- To further improve the effectiveness and efficiency of the analysis, we design a combination with a predicate analysis based on dynamic precision adjustment [8].
- We provide an open-source implementation of all our concepts and give evidence of the significant improvements by evaluating several approaches on benchmark verification tasks (C programs) from SV-COMP'12.

Related Work. The explicit-state model checker SPIN [21] can verify models of programs written in a language called Promela. For the verification of C programs, tools like MODEX can extract Promela models from C source code. This process requires to give a specification of the abstraction level (user-defined extraction rules), i.e., the information of what should be included in the Promela model. SPIN does not provide lazy-refinement-based CEGAR. JAVA PATHFINDER [18] is an explicit-state model checker for Java programs. There has been work [22] on integrating CEGAR into JAVA PATHFINDER, using an approach different from interpolation.

Dynamic precision adjustment [8] is an approach to fine-tune the precision of combined analyses on-the-fly, i.e., during the analysis run; the precision of one analysis can be increased based on a current situation in another analysis. For example, if an explicit-value analysis stores too many different values for a variable, then the dynamic precision adjustment can remove that variable from the precision of the explicit-value analysis and add a predicate about that variable to the precision of a predicate analysis. This means that the tracking of the variable is "moved" from the explicit to the symbolic domain. One configuration that we present later in Section 3 uses this approach.

The tool DAGGER [17] improves the verification of C programs by applying interpolation-based refinement to octagon and polyhedra domains. To avoid imprecision due to widening in the join-based data-flow analysis, DAGGER replaces the standard widen operator by a so called *interpolated-widen* operator, which increases the precision of the data-flow analysis and thus avoids false alarms. The algorithm VINTA [2] applies interpolation-based refinement to interval-like abstract domains. If the state exploration finds an error path, then VINTA performs a feasibility check using bounded model checking (BMC), and if the error path is infeasible, it computes interpolants. The interpolants are used to refine the invariants that the abstract domain operates on. VINTA requires an SMT solver for feasibility checks and interpolation.

More tools are mentioned in our evaluation section, where we compare (in terms of precision and efficiency) our verifier with verifiers of SV-COMP'12. There is, to the best of our knowledge, no work that integrates abstraction, CEGAR, lazy refinement, and interpolation into explicit-state model checking. We make those techniques available for the explicit-value domain.

2 Background

We use several existing concepts; this section reminds the reader of basic definitions.

Programs, Control-Flow Automata, States. We restrict the presentation to a simple imperative programming language, where all operations are either assignments or assume operations, and all variables range over integers [1]. The following definitions are taken from previous work [10]: A program is represented by a *control-flow automaton* (CFA). A CFA $A = (L, G)$ consists of a set L of program locations, which model the program counter, and a set $G \subseteq L \times Ops \times L$ of control-flow edges, which model the operations that are executed when control flows from one program location to another. The set of program variables that occur in operations from Ops is denoted by X. A *verification problem* $P = (A, l_0, l_e)$ consists of a CFA A, representing the program, an initial program location $l_0 \in L$, representing the program entry, and a target program location $l_e \in L$, which represents the error.

A *concrete data state* of a program is a variable assignment $cd : X \to \mathbb{Z}$, which assigns to each program variable an integer value. A *concrete state* of a program is a pair (l, cd), where $l \in L$ is a program location and cd is a concrete data state. The set of all concrete states of a program is denoted by $\mathcal{C}$, a subset $r \subseteq \mathcal{C}$ is called *region*. Each edge $g \in G$ defines a labeled transition relation $\stackrel{g}{\to} \subseteq \mathcal{C} \times \{g\} \times \mathcal{C}$. The complete transition relation $\to$ is the union over all control-flow edges: $\to = \bigcup_{g \in G} \stackrel{g}{\to}$. We write $c \stackrel{g}{\to} c'$ if $(c, g, c') \in \to$, and $c \to c'$ if there exists an edge g with $c \stackrel{g}{\to} c'$.

An *abstract data state* represents a region of concrete data states, formally defined as abstract variable assignment. An *abstract variable assignment* is a partial function $v : X \to \mathbb{Z} \cup \{\top, \bot\}$, which maps variables in the definition range of function v to integer values or $\top$ or $\bot$. The special value $\top$ is used to represent an unknown value, e.g., resulting from an uninitialized variable or an external function call, and the special value $\bot$ is used to represent no value, i.e., a contradicting variable assignment. We denote the *definition range* for a partial function f as $\text{def}(f) = \{x \mid \exists y : (x, y) \in f\}$, and the *restriction* of a partial function f to a new definition range Y as $f_{|Y} = f \cap (Y \times (\mathbb{Z} \cup \{\top, \bot\}))$. An abstract variable assignment v represents the region $[\![v]\!]$ of all concrete data states cd for which v is valid, formally:

---

[1] The framework CPACHECKER operates on C programs; non-recursive function calls are supported.

$[\![v]\!] = \{cd \mid \forall x \in \text{def}(v) : cd(x) = v(x) \text{ or } v(x) = \top\}$. An *abstract state* of a program is a pair (l, v), representing the following set of concrete states: $\{(l, cd) \mid cd \in [\![v]\!]\}$.

Configurable Program Analysis with Dynamic Precision Adjustment. We use the framework of configurable program analysis (CPA) [7], extended by the concept of dynamic precision adjustment [8]. Such a CPA supports adjusting the precision of an analysis during the exploration of the program's abstract state space. A *composite* CPA can control the precision of its component analyses during the verification process, i.e., it can make a component analysis more abstract, and thus more efficient, or it can make a component analysis more precise, and thus more expensive. A CPA $\mathbb{D} = (D, \Pi, \leadsto, \text{merge}, \text{stop}, \text{prec})$ consists of (1) an abstract domain D, (2) a set Π of precisions, (3) a transfer relation $\leadsto$, (4) a merge operator merge, (5) a termination check stop, and (6) a precision adjustment function prec. Based on these components and operators, we can formulate a flexible and customizable reachability algorithm, which is adapted from previous work [7, 12].

Explicit-Value Analysis as CPA. We now define a component CPA that tracks explicit values for program variables. In order to obtain a complete analysis, a composite CPA is constructed that consists of the component CPA for explicit values and another component CPA for tracking the program locations (CPA for location analysis, as previously described [8]). For the composite CPA, the general definitions of the abstract domain, the transfer relation, and the other operators are given in previous work [8]; the composition is done automatically by the framework implementation CPACHECKER.

The *CPA for explicit-value analysis*, which tracks integer values for the variables of a program explicitly, is defined as $\mathbb{C} = (D_{\mathbb{C}}, \Pi_{\mathbb{C}}, \leadsto_{\mathbb{C}}, \text{merge}_{\mathbb{C}}, \text{stop}_{\mathbb{C}}, \text{prec}_{\mathbb{C}})$ and consists of the following components [8]:

1. The abstract domain $D_{\mathbb{C}} = (C, \mathcal{V}, [\![\cdot]\!])$ contains the set C of concrete data states, and uses the semi-lattice $\mathcal{V} = (V, \top, \bot, \sqsubseteq, \sqcup)$, which consists of the set $V = (X \to \mathcal{Z})$ of abstract variable assignments, where $\mathcal{Z} = \mathbb{Z} \cup \{\top_{\mathcal{Z}}, \bot_{\mathcal{Z}}\}$ induces the flat lattice over the integer values (we write $\mathbb{Z}$ to denote the set of integer values). The top element $\top \in V$, with $\top(x) = \top_{\mathcal{Z}}$ for all $x \in X$, is the abstract variable assignment that holds no specific value for any variable, and the bottom element $\bot \in V$, with $\bot(x) = \bot_{\mathcal{Z}}$ for all $x \in X$, is the abstract variable assignment which models that there is no value assignment possible, i.e., a state that cannot be reached in an execution of the program. The partial order $\sqsubseteq \subseteq V \times V$ is defined as $v \sqsubseteq v'$ if for all $x \in X$, we have $v(x) = v'(x)$ or $v(x) = \bot_{\mathcal{Z}}$ or $v'(x) = \top_{\mathcal{Z}}$. The join $\sqcup : V \times V \to V$ yields the least upper bound for two variable assignments. The concretization function $[\![\cdot]\!] : V \to 2^C$ assigns to each abstract data state v its meaning, i.e., the set of concrete data states that it represents.

2. The set of precisions $\Pi_{\mathbb{C}} = 2^X$ is the set of subsets of program variables. A precision $\pi \in \Pi_{\mathbb{C}}$ specifies a set of variables to be tracked. For example, $\pi = \emptyset$ means that not a single program variable is tracked, and $\pi = X$ means that each and every program variable is tracked.

3. The transfer relation $\leadsto_C$ has the transfer $v \overset{g}{\leadsto} (v', \pi)$ if

(1) $g = (\cdot, \texttt{assume}(p), \cdot)$ and for all $x \in X$:

$$v'(x) = \begin{cases} \bot_Z & \text{if } (y, \bot_Z) \in v \text{ for some } y \in X \text{ or the predicate } p_{/v} \text{ is unsatisfiable} \\ c & \text{if } c \text{ is the only satisfying assignment of the predicate } p_{/v} \text{ for variable } x \\ \top_Z & \text{otherwise} \end{cases}$$

where $p_{/v}$ denotes the interpretation of p over variables from X for an abstract variable assignment v, that is, $p_{/v} = p \wedge \bigwedge_{x \in \text{def}(v), v(x) \in \mathbb{Z}} x = v(x) \wedge \neg \exists x \in \text{def}(v) : v(x) = \bot_Z$

or

(2) $g = (\cdot, \texttt{w} := exp, \cdot)$ and for all $x \in X : v'(x) = \begin{cases} exp_{/v} & \text{if } x = \texttt{w} \\ v(x) & \text{if } x \in \text{def}(v) \\ \top_Z & \text{otherwise} \end{cases}$

where $exp_{/v}$ denotes the interpretation of an expression exp over variables from X for an abstract value assignment v:

$$exp_{/v} = \begin{cases} \bot_Z & \text{if } (y, \bot_Z) \in v \text{ for some } y \in X \\ \top_Z & \text{if } (y, \top_Z) \in v \text{ or } y \notin \text{def}(v) \text{ for some } y \in X \text{ that occurs in } exp \\ c & \text{otherwise, where expression } exp \text{ evaluates to } c \text{ after replacing each} \\ & \text{occurrence of variable } x \text{ with } x \in \text{def}(v) \text{ by } v(x) \text{ in } exp \end{cases}$$

4. The merge does not combine states when control flow meets: $\text{merge}_C(v, v', \pi) = v'$.

5. The stop operator checks states individually: $\text{stop}_C(v, R, \pi) = (\exists v' \in R : v \sqsubseteq v')$.

6. The precision adjustment function computes a new abstract state with precision, based on the abstract state v and the precision π, by restricting the variable assignment v to those variables that appear in π, formally: $\text{prec}(v, \pi, R) = (v_{|\pi}, \pi)$.

The precision of the analysis controls which program variables are tracked in an abstract state. In other approaches, this information is hard-wired in either the abstract-domain elements or the algorithm itself. The concept of CPA supports different precisions for different abstract states. A simple analysis can start with an initial precision and propagate it to new abstract states, such that the overall analysis uses a globally uniform precision. It is also possible to specify a precision individually per program location, instead of using one global precision. Our refinement approach in the next section will be based on location-specific precisions.

Predicate Analysis as CPA. In a predicate analysis [16], the precision is defined as a set of predicates, and the abstract states track the strongest set of predicates that are fulfilled (cartesian predicate abstraction) or the strongest boolean combination of predicates that is fulfilled (boolean predicate abstraction). This means, the abstraction level of the abstract model is determined by predicates that are tracked in the analysis. Predicate analysis is also implemented as a CPA in the framework CPACHECKER, and a detailed description is available [10]. The precision is freely adjustable [8] also in the predicate analysis; we use this feature later in this article for composing a combined analysis.

Lazy Abstraction. The concept of lazy abstraction [20] proposes to refine the abstract states only where necessary along infeasible error paths in order to eliminate those paths. We implemented this using CPAs with dynamic precision adjustment, where the refinement procedure operates on location-specific precisions and the precision-adjustment operator always removes unnecessary information from abstract states.

Algorithm 1. CPA$(\mathbb{D}, R_0, W_0)$, adapted from [8]

Input: CPA $\mathbb{D} = (D, \Pi, \leadsto, \mathsf{merge}, \mathsf{stop}, \mathsf{prec})$,
      set $R_0 \subseteq (E \times \Pi)$ of abstract states with precision,
      subset $W_0 \subseteq R_0$ of frontier abstract states with precision,
      where E denotes the set of elements of the semi-lattice of D
Output: set of reachable abstract states with precision,
      subset of frontier abstract states with precision
Variables: sets reached and waitlist of elements of $E \times \Pi$
  reached $:= R_0$; waitlist $:= W_0$;
  while waitlist $\neq \emptyset$ **do**
    choose (e, π) from waitlist; remove (e, π) from waitlist;
    for each e' with $e \leadsto (e', \pi)$ **do**
      $(\hat{e}, \hat{\pi}) := \mathsf{prec}(e', \pi, \mathsf{reached})$;   // precision adjustment
      if isTargetState$(\hat{e})$ **then**
        return $\big(\mathsf{reached} \cup \{(\hat{e}, \hat{\pi})\}, \mathsf{waitlist} \cup \{(\hat{e}, \hat{\pi})\}\big)$;
      for each $(e'', \pi'') \in$ reached **do**
        $e_{new} := \mathsf{merge}(\hat{e}, e'', \hat{\pi})$;   // combine with existing abstract state
        if $e_{new} \neq e''$ **then**
          waitlist $:= \big(\mathsf{waitlist} \cup \{(e_{new}, \hat{\pi})\}\big) \setminus \{(e'', \pi'')\}$;
          reached $:= \big(\mathsf{reached} \cup \{(e_{new}, \hat{\pi})\}\big) \setminus \{(e'', \pi'')\}$;
      if $\neg$ stop$(\hat{e}, \{e \mid (e, \cdot) \in \mathsf{reached}\}, \hat{\pi})$ **then** // add new abstract state?
        waitlist $:=$ waitlist $\cup \{(\hat{e}, \hat{\pi})\}$;   reached $:=$ reached $\cup \{(\hat{e}, \hat{\pi})\}$
  return $(\mathsf{reached}, \emptyset)$;

Reachability Algorithm for CPA. Algorithm 1 keeps updating two sets of abstract states with precision: the set reached stores all abstract states with precision that are found to be reachable, and the set waitlist stores all abstract states with precision that are not yet processed, i.e., the frontier. The state exploration starts with choosing and removing an abstract state with precision from the waitlist, and the algorithm considers each abstract successor according to the transfer relation. Next, for the successor, the algorithm adjusts the precision of the successor using the precision adjustment function prec. If the successor is a target state (i.e., a violation of the property is found), then the algorithm terminates, returning the current sets reached and waitlist — possibly as input for a subsequent precision refinement, as shown below (cf. Alg. 2). Otherwise, using the given operator merge, the abstract successor state is combined with each existing abstract state from reached. If the operator merge results in a new abstract state with information added from the new successor (the old abstract state is subsumed) then the old abstract state with precision is replaced by the new abstract state with precision in the sets reached and waitlist. If after the merge step the resulting new abstract state with precision is covered by the set reached, then further exploration of this abstract state is stopped. Otherwise, the abstract state with its precision is added to the set reached and to the set waitlist. Finally, once the set waitlist is empty, the set reached is returned.

Counterexample-Guided Abstraction Refinement (CEGAR). CEGAR [13] is a technique for automatic stepwise refinement of an abstract model. CEGAR is based on three concepts: (1) a *precision*, which determines the current level of abstraction, (2) a *feasibility check*, deciding if an abstract error path is feasible, i.e., if there exists a

---

Algorithm 2. CEGAR($\mathbb{D}, e_0, \pi_0$)

Input: CPA with dynamic precision adjustment $\mathbb{D} = (D, \Pi, \rightsquigarrow, \text{merge}, \text{stop}, \text{prec})$,
       initial abstract state $e_0 \in E$ with precision $\pi_0 \in \Pi$,
       where E denotes the set of elements of the semi-lattice of D
Output: verification result *safe* or *unsafe*
Variables: set reached $\subseteq E \times \Pi$, set waitlist $\subseteq E \times \Pi$, error path $\sigma = \langle (op_1, l_1), ..., (op_n, l_n) \rangle$
   reached $:= \{(e_0, \pi_0)\}$; waitlist $:= \{(e_0, \pi_0)\}$; $\pi := \pi_0$;
   while *true* **do**
     (reached, waitlist) := CPA($\mathbb{D}$, reached, waitlist);
     if waitlist $= \emptyset$ **then**
       return *safe*
     else
       $\sigma :=$ extractErrorPath(reached);
       if isFeasible(σ) **then** // error path is feasible: report bug
         return *unsafe*
       else // error path is not feasible: refine and restart
         $\pi := \pi \cup$ Refine(σ);
         reached $:= (e_0, \pi)$; waitlist $:= (e_0, \pi)$;

---

corresponding concrete error path, and (3) a *refinement* procedure, which takes as input an infeasible error path and extracts a precision that suffices to instruct the exploration algorithm to not explore the same path again later. Algorithm 2 shows an outline of a generic and simple CEGAR algorithm. The algorithm starts checking a program using a coarse initial *precision* π_0. It uses Alg. 1 for computing the reachable abstract state space, returning the sets reached and waitlist. If the analysis has exhaustively checked all program states and did not reach the error, indicated by an empty set waitlist, then the algorithm terminates and reports that the program is safe. If the algorithm finds an error in the abstract state space, i.e., a counterexample for the given specification, then the exploration algorithm stops and returns the unfinished, incomplete sets reached and waitlist. Now the according abstract error path is extracted from the set reached using procedure extractErrorPath and analyzed for feasibility using the procedure isFeasible as *feasibility check*. If the abstract error path is feasible, meaning there exists a corresponding concrete error path, then this error path represents a violation of the specification and the algorithm terminates, reporting a bug. If the error path is infeasible, i.e., not corresponding to a concrete program path, then the precision was too coarse and needs to be refined. The algorithm extracts certain information from the error path in order to refine the precision based on that information using the procedure Refine for *refinement*, which returns a precision π that makes the analysis strong enough to refute the present infeasible error path in further state-space explorations. The current precision is extended using the precision returned by the refinement procedure and the analysis is restarted with this refined precision. Instead of restarting from the initial sets for reached and waitlist, we can also prune those parts of the abstract reachability graph (ARG) that need to be rediscovered with new precisions, and replace the precision of the leaf nodes in the ARG with the refined precision, and then restart the exploration on the pruned sets (cf. [11] for more details). Our contribution in the next section is to introduce new implementations for the feasibility check as well as for the refinement procedure.

Interpolation. For a pair of formulas φ^- and φ^+ such that $\varphi^- \wedge \varphi^+$ is unsatisfiable, a Craig interpolant ψ is a formula that fulfills the following requirements [15]: (1) the implication $\varphi^- \Rightarrow \psi$ holds, (2) the conjunction $\psi \wedge \varphi^+$ is unsatisfiable, and (3) ψ only contains symbols that occur in both φ^- and φ^+. Such a Craig interpolant is guaranteed to exist for many useful theories, e.g., the theory of linear arithmetic (implemented in SMT solvers). Interpolation-based CEGAR has been proven successful in the predicate domain. However, interpolants from the predicate domain, which consist of formulas, are not useful for the explicit domain. Hence, we need to develop a procedure to compute interpolants for the explicit domain, which we introduce in the following.

3   Refinement-Based Explicit-Value Analysis

The level of abstraction in our explicit-value analysis is determined by the precisions for abstract variable assignments over program variables. The CEGAR-based iterative refinement needs an extraction method to obtain the necessary precision from infeasible error paths. Our novel notion of interpolation for the explicit domain achieves this goal.

Explicit-Value Abstraction. We now introduce some necessary operations on abstract variable assignments, the semantics of operations and paths, and the precision for abstract variable assignments and programs, in order to be able to concisely discuss interpolation for abstract variable assignments and constraint sequences.

The operations *implication* and *conjunction* for abstract variable assignments are defined as follows: implication for v and v': $v \Rightarrow v'$ if $\mathrm{def}(v') \subseteq \mathrm{def}(v)$ and for each variable $x \in \mathrm{def}(v) \cap \mathrm{def}(v')$ we have $v(x) = v'(x)$ or $v(x) = \bot$ or $v'(x) = \top$; conjunction for v and v': for each variable $x \in \mathrm{def}(v) \cup \mathrm{def}(v')$ we have

$$(v \wedge v')(x) = \begin{cases} v(x) & \text{if } x \in \mathrm{def}(v) \text{ and } x \notin \mathrm{def}(v') \\ v'(x) & \text{if } x \notin \mathrm{def}(v) \text{ and } x \in \mathrm{def}(v') \\ v(x) & \text{if } v(x) = v'(x) \\ \bot & \text{if } \top \neq v(x) \neq v'(x) \neq \top \\ \top & \text{otherwise } (v(x) = \top \text{ or } v'(x) = \top) \end{cases}$$

Furthermore we define *contradiction* for an abstract variable assignment v: v is contradicting if there is a variable $x \in \mathrm{def}(v)$ such that $v(x) = \bot$ (which implies $[\![v]\!] = \emptyset$); and *renaming* for v: the abstract variable assignment $v^{x \mapsto y}$, with $y \notin \mathrm{def}(v)$, results from v by renaming variable x to y: $v^{x \mapsto y} = (v \setminus \{(x, v(x))\}) \cup \{(y, v(x))\}$.

The *semantics of an operation* $op \in Ops$ is defined by the strongest post-operator $\mathrm{SP}_{op}(\cdot)$ for abstract variable assignments: given an abstract variable assignment v, $\mathrm{SP}_{op}(v)$ represents the set of data states that are reachable from any of the states in the region represented by v after the execution of op. Formally, given a set X of program variables, an abstract variable assignment v, and an assignment operation $s := exp$, we have $\mathrm{SP}_{s:=exp}(v) = v_{|X \setminus \{s\}} \wedge v_{s:=exp}$ with $v_{s:=exp} = \{(s, exp_{/v})\}$, where $exp_{/v}$ denotes the interpretation of expression exp for the abstract variable assignment v (cf. definition of $exp_{/v}$ in Section 2). That is, the value of variable s is the result of the arithmetic evaluation of expression exp, or $\top$ if not all values in the expression are known, or $\bot$ if no value is possible (an abstract data state in which a variable is assigned to $\bot$ does not represent any concrete data state). Given an abstract variable assignment v and an assume operation $[p]$, we have $\mathrm{SP}_{[p]}(v) = v'$ with for all $x \in X$

we have $v'(x) = \bot$ if $(y, \bot) \in v$ for some variable $x \in X$ or the formula $p_{/v}$ is unsatisfiable, or $v'(x) = c$ if c is the only satisfying assignment of the formula $p_{/v}$ for variable x, or $v'(x) = \top$ in all other cases; the formula $p_{/v}$ is defined as in Section 2.

A *path* σ is a sequence $\langle (op_1, l_1), ..., (op_n, l_n) \rangle$ of pairs of an operation and a location. The path σ is called *program path* if for every i with $1 \le i \le n$ there exists a CFA edge $g = (l_{i-1}, op_i, l_i)$ and l_0 is the initial program location, i.e., σ represents a syntactic walk through the CFA. Every path $\sigma = \langle (op_1, l_1), ..., (op_n, l_n) \rangle$ defines a *constraint sequence* $\gamma_\sigma = \langle op_1, ..., op_n \rangle$. The *semantics of a program path* $\sigma = \langle (op_1, l_1), ..., (op_n, l_n) \rangle$ is defined as the successive application of the strongest post-operator to each operation of the corresponding constraint sequence γ_σ: $\mathsf{SP}_{\gamma_\sigma}(v) = \mathsf{SP}_{op_n}(...\mathsf{SP}_{op_i}(..\mathsf{SP}_{op_1}(v)..)...)$. The set of concrete program states that result from running σ is represented by the pair $(l_n, \mathsf{SP}_{\gamma_\sigma}(v_0))$, where $v_0 = \{\}$ is the initial abstract variable assignment that does not map any variable to a value. A program path σ is *feasible* if $\mathsf{SP}_{\gamma_\sigma}(v_0)$ is not contradicting, i.e., $\mathsf{SP}_{\gamma_\sigma}(v_0)(x) \ne \bot$ for all variables x in $\mathrm{def}(\mathsf{SP}_{\gamma_\sigma}(v_0))$. A concrete state (l_n, cd_n) is *reachable* from a region r, denoted by $(l_n, cd_n) \in Reach(r)$, if there exists a feasible program path $\sigma = \langle (op_1, l_1), ..., (op_n, l_n) \rangle$ with $(l_0, v_0) \in r$ and $cd_n \in [\![\mathsf{SP}_{\gamma_\sigma}(v_0)]\!]$. A location l is reachable if there exists a concrete state c such that (l, c) is reachable. A program is SAFE if l_e is not reachable.

The *precision for an abstract variable assignment* is a set π of variables. The *explicit-value abstraction* for an abstract variable assignment is an abstract variable assignment that is defined only on variables that are in the precision π. For example, the explicit-value abstraction for the variable assignment $v = \{x \mapsto 2, y \mapsto 5\}$ and the precision $\pi = \{x\}$ is the abstract variable assignment $v^\pi = \{x \mapsto 2\}$.

The *precision for a program* is a function $\Pi : L \to 2^X$, which assigns to each program location a precision for an abstract variable assignment, i.e., a set of variables for which the analysis is instructed to track values. A *lazy explicit-value abstraction* of a program uses different precisions for different abstract states on different program paths in the abstract reachability graph. The explicit-value abstraction for a variable assignment at location l is computed using the precision $\Pi(l)$.

CEGAR for Explicit-Value Model Checking. We now instantiate the three components of the CEGAR technique, i.e., precision, feasibility check, and refinement, for our explicit-value analysis. The precisions that our CEGAR instance uses are the above introduced precisions for a program (which assign to each program location a set of variables), and we start the CEGAR iteration with the empty precision, i.e., $\Pi_{init}(l) = \emptyset$ for each $l \in L$, such that no variable will be tracked.

The feasibility check for a path σ is performed by executing an explicit-value analysis of the path σ using the full precision $\Pi(l) = X$ for all locations l, i.e., all variables will be tracked. This is equivalent to computing $\mathsf{SP}_{\gamma_\sigma}(v_0)$ and check if the result is contradicting, i.e., if there is a variable for which the resulting abstract variable assignment is $\bot$. This feasibility check is extremely efficient, because the path is finite and the strongest post-operations for abstract variable assignments are simple arithmetic evaluations. If the feasibility check reaches the error location l_e, then this error can be reported. If the check does not reach the error location, because of a contradicting

---

Algorithm 3. Interpolate(γ^-, γ^+)

Input: two constraint sequences γ^- and γ^+, with $\gamma^- \wedge \gamma^+$ is contradicting
Output: a constraint sequence Γ, which is an interpolant for γ^- and γ^+
Variables: an abstract variable assignment v

$v := \mathsf{SP}_{\gamma^-}(\emptyset);$
for each $x \in \mathrm{def}(v)$ **do**
  if $\mathsf{SP}_{\gamma^+}(v_{|\mathrm{def}(v)\setminus\{x\}})$ is contradicting **then**
    $v := v_{|\mathrm{def}(v)\setminus\{x\}};$ // x is not relevant and should not occur in the interpolant
$\Gamma := \langle\rangle;$ // start assembling the interpolating constraint sequence
for each $x \in \mathrm{def}(v)$ **do**
  $\Gamma := \Gamma \wedge \langle[x = v(x)]\rangle;$ // construct an assume constraint for x
return Γ

---

abstract variable assignment, then a refinement is necessary because at least one constraint depends on a variable that was not yet tracked.

We define the last component of the CEGAR technique, the refinement, after we introduced the notion of interpolation for variable assignments and constraint sequences.

Interpolation for Variable Assignments. For each infeasible error path in the above mentioned refinement operation, we need to determine a precision that assigns to each program location on that path the set of program variables that the explicit-value analysis needs to track in order to eliminate that infeasible error path in future explorations. Therefore, we define an interpolant for abstract variable assignments.

An *interpolant* for a pair of abstract variable assignments v^- and v^+, such that $v^- \wedge v^+$ is contradicting, is an abstract variable assignment $\mathcal{V}$ that fulfills the following requirements: (1) the implication $v^- \Rightarrow \mathcal{V}$ holds, (2) the conjunction $\mathcal{V} \wedge v^+$ is contradicting, and (3) $\mathcal{V}$ only contains variables in its definition range which are in the definition ranges of both v^- and v^+ ($\mathrm{def}(\mathcal{V}) \subseteq \mathrm{def}(v^-) \cap \mathrm{def}(v^+)$).

Lemma. For a given pair (v^-, v^+) of abstract variable assignments, such that $v^- \wedge v^+$ is contradicting, an interpolant exists. Such an interpolant can be computed in time $O(m + n)$, where m and n are the sizes of v^- and v^+, respectively.

Proof. The variable assignment $v^-_{|\mathrm{def}(v^+)}$ is an interpolant for the pair (v^-, v^+).

The above-mentioned interpolant that simply results from restricting v^- to the definition range of v^+ (common definition range) is of course not the best interpolant. Interpolation for assignments is a first idea to approach the problem, but since we need to extract interpolants for paths, we next define interpolation for constraint sequences.

Interpolation for Constraint Sequences. A more expressive interpolation is achieved by considering constraint sequences. The *conjunction* $\gamma \wedge \gamma'$ of two constraint sequences $\gamma = \langle op_1, ..., op_n \rangle$ and $\gamma' = \langle op'_1, ..., op'_m \rangle$ is defined as their concatenation, i.e., $\gamma \wedge \gamma' = \langle op_1, ..., op_n, op'_1, ..., op'_m \rangle$, the *implication* of γ and γ' (denoted by $\gamma \Rightarrow \gamma'$) as $\mathsf{SP}_\gamma(v_0) \Rightarrow \mathsf{SP}_{\gamma'}(v_0)$, and γ is *contradicting* if $[\![\mathsf{SP}_\gamma(v_0)]\!] = \emptyset$, with $v_0 = \{\}$.

An *interpolant* for a pair of constraint sequences γ^- and γ^+, such that $\gamma^- \wedge \gamma^+$ is contradicting, is a constraint sequence Γ that fulfills the three requirements: (1) the implication $\gamma^- \Rightarrow \Gamma$ holds, (2) the conjunction $\Gamma \wedge \gamma^+$ is contradicting, and (3) Γ contains in its constraints only variables that occur in the constraints of both γ^- and γ^+.

Algorithm 4. Refine(σ)

Input: infeasible error path $\sigma = \langle (op_1, l_1), ..., (op_n, l_n) \rangle$
Output: precision Π
Variables: interpolating constraint sequence Γ

$\Gamma := \langle\rangle$; $\Pi(l) := \emptyset$, for all program locations l;
for $i := 1$ to $n - 1$ **do**
    $\gamma^+ := \langle op_{i+1}, ..., op_n \rangle$
    $\Gamma := $ Interpolate$(\Gamma \wedge op_i, \gamma^+)$ // inductive interpolation
    // extract variables from variable assignment that results from Γ
    $\Pi(l_i) := \{ x | (x, z) \in \mathsf{SP}_\Gamma(\emptyset) \text{ and } \bot \neq z \neq \top \}$
return Π

Lemma. For a given pair (γ^-, γ^+) of constraint sequences, such that $\gamma^- \wedge \gamma^+$ is contradicting, an interpolant exists. Such an interpolant is computable in time $O(m \cdot n)$, where m and n are the sizes of γ^- and γ^+, respectively.

Proof. Algorithm Interpolate (Alg. 3) returns an interpolant for two constraint sequences γ^- and γ^+. The algorithm starts with computing the strongest post-condition for γ^- and assigns the result to the abstract variable assignment v, which then may contain up to m variables. Per definition, the strongest post-condition for γ^+ of variable assignment v is contradicting. Next we try to eliminate each variable from v, by testing if removing it from v makes the strongest post-condition for γ^+ of v contradicting (each such test takes n SP steps). If it is contradicting, the variable can be removed. If not, the variable is necessary to prove the contradiction of the two constraint sequences, and thus, should occur in the interpolant. Note that this keeps only variables in v that occur in γ^+ as well. The rest of the algorithm constructs a constraint sequence from the variable assignment, in order to return an interpolating constraint sequence, which fulfills the three requirements of an interpolant. A naive implementation can compute such an interpolant in $O((m + n)^3)$.

Refinement Based on Explicit-Interpolation. The goal of our interpolation-based refinement for explicit-value analysis is to determine a location-specific precision that is strong enough to eliminate an infeasible error path in future explorations. This criterion is fulfilled by the property of interpolants. A second goal is to have a precision that is as weak as possible, by creating interpolants that have a definition range as small as possible, in order to be parsimonious in tracking variables and creating abstract states.

We apply the idea of interpolation for constraint sequences to assemble a precision-extraction algorithm: Algorithm Refine (Alg. 4) takes as input an infeasible program path, and returns a precision for a program. A further requirement is that the procedure computes *inductive* interpolants [6], i.e., each interpolant along the path contains enough information to prove the remaining path infeasible. This is needed in order to ensure that the interpolants at the different locations achieve the goal of providing a precision that eliminates the infeasible error path from further explorations. For every program location l_i along an infeasible error path σ, starting at l_0, we split the constraint sequence of the path into a constraint prefix γ^-, which consists of the constraints from the start location l_0 to l_i, and a constraint suffix γ^+, which consists of the path from the location l_i to l_e. For computing inductive interpolants, we replace the constraint prefix

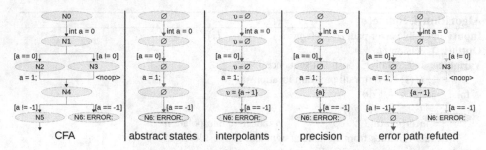

Fig. 1. Illustration of one refinement iteration; simple example CFA, infeasible error path with the abstract states annotated in the nodes (precision empty; nothing tracked), interpolants (i.e., variable assignments), precision extracted from interpolants, abstract states according to new precision after error path is refuted

by the conjunction of the last interpolant and the current constraint. The precision is extracted by computing the abstract variable assignment for the interpolating constraint sequence and assigning the relevant variables as precision for the current location l_i, i.e., the set of all variables that are necessary to be tracked in order to eliminate the error path from future exploration of the state space. This algorithm can be directly plugged-in as refinement routine of the CEGAR algorithm (cf. Alg. 2). Figure 1 illustrates the interpolation process on a simple example.

Auxiliary Predicate Analysis. As an optional further improvement, we implemented a combination with a predicate analysis (cf. [8]): If the explicit-value analysis finds an error path, this path is checked for feasibility in the predicate domain. If feasible, the result is *unsafe* and the error path is reported; if infeasible, the explicit-value domain is not expressive enough to analyze that program path (e.g., due to inequalities). We then ask the predicate analysis to refine its abstraction along that path, which yields a refined predicate precision that eliminates the error path but considering the facts along that path in the (more precise, and more expensive) predicate domain. We need to parsimoniously use this feature because the post-operations of the predicate analysis are much more expensive than the post-operations of the explicit-value analysis. In general, after a refinement step, either the explicit-value precision is refined (preferred) or the predicate precision is refined (only if explicit does not succeed). We also remove variables from the precision in the explicit-value domain if the number of different values on a path exceeds a certain threshold. A later refinement will then add predicates about such variables to the precision in the predicate domain. Note that this refinement-based, parallel composition of explicit-value and predicate analysis is strictly more powerful than a mere parallel product of the two analyses, because the explicit domain tracks exactly what it can efficiently analyze, while the predicate domain takes care of everything else.

4   Experiments

In order to demonstrate that our approach yields a significant improvement of verification efficiency and effectiveness, we implemented our algorithms and compared our new techniques to existing tools for software verification. We show that the application of abstraction, CEGAR, and interpolation to the explicit-value domain considerably improves the number of solved instances and the run time. Combinations of the new explicit-value analysis with a predicate-based analysis can further increase the number of solved instances. All experiments were performed using rules and hardware identical to SV-COMP'12 [5], restricting each verification task to the same run time and memory limits (900 s, 15 GB), such that our results are comparable to all results obtained there.

Compared Verification Approaches. For presentation, we restrict the comparison of our new approach to the SV-COMP'12 participants BLAST [6], SATABS [14], and the competition winner CPA-MEMO [23], all of which are based on predicate abstraction and CEGAR. Furthermore, to investigate performance differences in the same tool environment, we also compare with different configurations of CPACHECKER. BLAST won the category "DeviceDrivers64" in the SV-COMP'12, and got bronze in another category. SATABS got silver in the categories "SystemC" and "Concurrency", and bronze in another category. CPA-MEMO won the category "Overall", got silver in two more categories, and bronze in another category. We implemented our new concepts in CPACHECKER [9], a software-verification framework based on CPA. We compare with the existing explicit-value analysis (without abstraction, CEGAR, and interpolation) and with the existing predicate analysis [10]. We used the trunk version of CPACHECKER[2] in revision 6615.

Verification Tasks. For the evaluation of our approach, we use all SV-COMP'12 [3] verification tasks that do not involve concurrency properties (all categories except category "Concurrency"). All obtained experimental data as well as the tool implementation are available at http://www.sosy-lab.org/~dbeyer/cpa-explicit.

Quality Measures. We compare the verification results of all verification approaches based on three measures for verification quality: First, we take the run time, in seconds, of the verification runs to measure the *efficiency* of an approach. Obviously, the lower the run time, the better the tool. Second, we use the number of correctly solved instances of verification tasks to measure the *effectiveness* of an approach. The more instances a tool can solve, the more powerful the analysis is. Third, and most importantly, we use the scoring schema of the SV-COMP'12 as indicator for the quality of an approach. The scoring schema implements a community-agreed weighting schema, namely, that it is more difficult to prove a program correct compared to finding a bug and that a wrong answer should be penalized with double the scores that a correct answer would have achieved. For a full discussion of the official rules and benchmarks of the SV-COMP'12, we refer to the competition report [5]. Besides the data tables, we use plots of quantile functions [5] for visualizing the number of solved instances and the verification time. The quantile function for one approach contains all pairs (x, y) such that the maximum run time of the x fastest results is y. We use a logarithmic scale for the time range from 1 s to 1000 s and a linear scale for the time range between 0 s and 1 s.

Improvements of Explicit-Value Analysis. In the first evaluation, we compare two different configurations of the explicit-value analysis: CPA-EXPL refers to the existing implementation of a standard explicit-value analysis without abstraction and refinement, and CPA-EXPL$_{itp}$ refers to the new approach, which implements abstraction, CEGAR, and

---

[2] http://cpachecker.sosy-lab.org
[3] http://sv-comp.sosy-lab.org/2012

Table 1. Comparison with purely explicit, non-CEGAR approach

Category	CPA-EXPL			CPA-EXPL$_{itp}$		
	points	solved	time	points	solved	time
ControlFlowInt	124	81	8400	123	79	780
DeviceDrivers	53	37	63	53	37	69
DeviceDrivers64	5	5	660	33	19	200
HeapManipul	1	3	5.5	1	3	5.8
SystemC	34	26	1600	34	26	1500
Overall	217	152	11000	**244**	**164**	**2500**

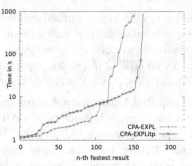

Fig. 2. Purely explicit analyses

Table 2. Comparison with predicate-based configurations

Category	CPA-PRED			CPA-EXPL$_{itp}$			CPA-EXPL-PRED			CPA-EXPL$_{itp}$-PRED		
	score	solved	time	score	solved	time	score	solved	time	score	solved	time
ControlFlowInt	103	70	2500	123	79	780	131	85	2600	141	91	830
DeviceDrivers	71	46	80	53	37	69	71	46	82	71	46	87
DeviceDrivers64	33	24	2700	33	19	200	10	11	1100	37	24	980
HeapManipul	8	6	12	1	3	5.8	6	5	11	8	6	12
SystemC	22	17	1900	34	26	1500	62	45	1500	61	44	3700
Overall	237	163	7100	244	164	**2500**	280	192	5300	**318**	**211**	5600

Table 3. Comparison with three existing tools

Category	BLAST			SATABS			CPA-MEMO			CPA-EXPL$_{itp}$-PRED		
	score	solved	time	score	solved	time	score	solved	time	score	solved	time
ControlFlowInt	71	51	9900	75	47	5400	140	91	3200	141	91	830
DeviceDrivers	72	51	30	71	43	140	51	46	93	71	46	87
DeviceDrivers64	55	33	1400	32	17	3200	49	33	500	37	24	980
HeapManipul	–	–	–	–	–	–	4	9	16	8	6	12
SystemC	33	23	4000	57	40	5000	36	30	450	61	44	3700
Overall	231	158	15000	235	147	14000	280	209	**4300**	**318**	**211**	5600

interpolation. Table 1 and Fig. 2 show that the new approach uses less time, solves more instances, and obtains more points in the SV-COMP'12 scoring schema.

Improvements of Combination with Predicate Analysis. In the second evaluation, we compare the refinement-based explicit analysis against a standard predicate analysis and to a combination of predicate analysis with CPA-EXPL and CPA-EXPL$_{itp}$, respectively: CPA-PRED refers to a standard predicate analysis that CPACHECKER offers (ABE-lf, [10]), CPA-EXPL-PRED refers to the combination of CPA-EXPL and CPA-PRED, and CPA-EXPL$_{itp}$-PRED refers to the combination of CPA-EXPL$_{itp}$ and CPA-PRED. Table 2 and Fig. 3 show that the new combination approach outperforms the approaches CPA-PRED and CPA-EXPL$_{itp}$ in terms of solved instances and score. The comparison with column CPA-EXPL-PRED is interesting because it shows that the combination of the two analyses is an improvement even without refinement in the explicit-value analysis, but switching on the refinement in both domains makes the new combination significantly more effective.

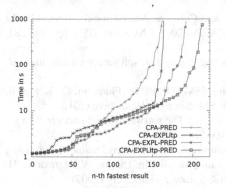 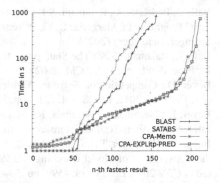

Fig. 3. Comparison with predicate-based configs   **Fig. 4.** Comparison with three existing tools

Comparison with State-of-the-Art Verifiers. In the third evaluation, we compare our new combination approach with three established tools: BLAST refers to the standard BLAST configuration that participated in the SV-COMP'12, SATABS also refers to the respective standard configuration, CPA-MEMO refers to a special predicate abstraction that is based on block-abstraction memoization, and CPA-EXPL$_{itp}$-PRED refers to our novel approach, which combines a predicate analysis (CPA-PRED) with the new explicit-value analysis that is based on abstraction, CEGAR, and interpolation (CPA-EXPL$_{itp}$). Table 3 and Fig. 4 show that the new approach outperforms BLAST and SATABS by consuming considerably less verification time, more solved instances, and a better score. Even compared to the SV-COMP'12 winner, CPA-MEMO, our new approach scores higher. It is interesting to observe that the difference in scores is much higher than the difference in solved instances: this means CPA-MEMO had many incorrect verification results, which in turn shows that our new combination is significantly more precise.

5   Conclusion

The surprising insight of this work is that it is possible to achieve —without using sophisticated SMT-solvers during the abstraction refinement— a performance and precision that can compete with the world's leading symbolic model checkers, which are based on SMT-based predicate abstraction. We achieved this by incorporating the ideas of abstraction, CEGAR, lazy abstraction refinement, and interpolation into a simple, standard explicit-value analysis. We further improved the performance and precision by combining our refinement-based explicit-value analysis with a predicate analysis, in order to benefit from the complementary advantages of the methods. The combination analysis dynamically adjusts the precision [8] for an optimal trade-off between the precision of the explicit analysis and the precision of the auxiliary predicate analysis. This combination out-performs state-of-the-art model checkers, witnessed by a thorough comparison on a standardized set of benchmarks.

References

1. Aho, A.V., Sethi, R., Ullman, J.D.: Compilers: Principles, Techniques, and Tools. Addison-Wesley (1986)
2. Albarghouthi, A., Gurfinkel, A., Chechik, M.: Craig Interpretation. In: Miné, A., Schmidt, D. (eds.) SAS 2012. LNCS, vol. 7460, pp. 300–316. Springer, Heidelberg (2012)

3. Ball, T., Podelski, A., Rajamani, S.K.: Boolean and Cartesian Abstraction for Model Checking C Programs. In: Margaria, T., Yi, W. (eds.) TACAS 2001. LNCS, vol. 2031, pp. 268–283. Springer, Heidelberg (2001)
4. Ball, T., Rajamani, S.K.: The Slam project: Debugging system software via static analysis. In: Proc. POPL, pp. 1–3. ACM (2002)
5. Beyer, D.: Competition on Software Verification (SV-COMP). In: Flanagan, C., König, B. (eds.) TACAS 2012. LNCS, vol. 7214, pp. 504–524. Springer, Heidelberg (2012)
6. Beyer, D., Henzinger, T.A., Jhala, R., Majumdar, R.: The software model checker BLAST. Int. J. Softw. Tools Technol. Transfer 9(5-6), 505–525 (2007)
7. Beyer, D., Henzinger, T.A., Théoduloz, G.: Configurable Software Verification: Concretizing the Convergence of Model Checking and Program Analysis. In: Damm, W., Hermanns, H. (eds.) CAV 2007. LNCS, vol. 4590, pp. 504–518. Springer, Heidelberg (2007)
8. Beyer, D., Henzinger, T.A., Théoduloz, G.: Program analysis with dynamic precision adjustment. In: Proc. ASE, pp. 29–38. IEEE (2008)
9. Beyer, D., Keremoglu, M.E.: CPACHECKER: A Tool for Configurable Software Verification. In: Gopalakrishnan, G., Qadeer, S. (eds.) CAV 2011. LNCS, vol. 6806, pp. 184–190. Springer, Heidelberg (2011)
10. Beyer, D., Keremoglu, M.E., Wendler, P.: Predicate abstraction with adjustable-block encoding. In: Proc. FMCAD, pp. 189–197. FMCAD (2010)
11. Beyer, D., Löwe, S.: Explicit-value analysis based on CEGAR and interpolation. Technical Report MIP-1205, University of Passau / ArXiv 1212.6542 (December 2012)
12. Beyer, D., Wendler, P.: Algorithms for software model checking: Predicate abstraction vs. IMPACT. In: Proc. FMCAD, pp. 106–113. FMCAD (2012)
13. Clarke, E.M., Grumberg, O., Jha, S., Lu, Y., Veith, H.: Counterexample-guided abstraction refinement for symbolic model checking. J. ACM 50(5), 752–794 (2003)
14. Clarke, E., Kröning, D., Sharygina, N., Yorav, K.: SATABS: SAT-Based Predicate Abstraction for ANSI-C. In: Halbwachs, N., Zuck, L.D. (eds.) TACAS 2005. LNCS, vol. 3440, pp. 570–574. Springer, Heidelberg (2005)
15. Craig, W.: Linear reasoning. A new form of the Herbrand-Gentzen theorem. J. Symb. Log. 22(3), 250–268 (1957)
16. Graf, S., Saïdi, H.: Construction of Abstract State Graphs with PVS. In: Grumberg, O. (ed.) CAV 1997. LNCS, vol. 1254, pp. 72–83. Springer, Heidelberg (1997)
17. Gulavani, B.S., Chakraborty, S., Nori, A.V., Rajamani, S.K.: Automatically Refining Abstract Interpretations. In: Ramakrishnan, C.R., Rehof, J. (eds.) TACAS 2008. LNCS, vol. 4963, pp. 443–458. Springer, Heidelberg (2008)
18. Havelund, K., Pressburger, T.: Model checking Java programs using JAVA PATHFINDER. Int. J. Softw. Tools Technol. Transfer 2(4), 366–381 (2000)
19. Henzinger, T.A., Jhala, R., Majumdar, R., McMillan, K.L.: Abstractions from proofs. In: Proc. POPL, pp. 232–244. ACM (2004)
20. Henzinger, T.A., Jhala, R., Majumdar, R., Sutre, G.: Lazy abstraction. In: Proc. POPL, pp. 58–70. ACM (2002)
21. Holzmann, G.J.: The SPIN model checker. IEEE Trans. Softw. Eng. 23(5), 279–295 (1997)
22. Păsăreanu, C.S., Dwyer, M.B., Visser, W.: Finding Feasible Counter-examples when Model Checking Abstracted Java Programs. In: Margaria, T., Yi, W. (eds.) TACAS 2001. LNCS, vol. 2031, pp. 284–298. Springer, Heidelberg (2001)
23. Wonisch, D.: Block Abstraction Memoization for CPACHECKER. In: Flanagan, C., König, B. (eds.) TACAS 2012. LNCS, vol. 7214, pp. 531–533. Springer, Heidelberg (2012)

Design Pattern-Based Extension of Class Hierarchies to Support Runtime Invariant Checks

John Lasseter and John Cipriano

Fairfield University, Fairfield CT 06824, USA
jlasseter@fairfield.edu, johnmikecip@gmail.com

Abstract. We present a technique for automatically weaving structural invariant checks into an existing collection of classes. Using variations on existing design patterns, we use a concise specification to generate from this collection a new set of classes that implement the interfaces of the originals, but with the addition of user-specified class invariant checks. Our work is notable in the scarcity of assumptions made. Unlike previous design pattern approaches to this problem, our technique requires no modification of the original source code, relies only on single inheritance, and does not require that the attributes used in the checks be publicly visible. We are able to instrument a wide variety of class hierarchies, including those with pure interfaces, abstract classes and classes with type parameters. We have implemented the construction as an Eclipse plug-in for Java development.

1 Introduction

Several, if not most, mainstream languages include features to support object-oriented programming, yet most of these (C++, C#, Java, Python, etc.) lack any native language support for the specification and runtime checking of class invariants. While it is usually easy enough to implement the invariant predicates themselves, manual addition imposes further requirements in order to implement the operational requirements of invariant checking and to handle the interplay of invariant specification and inheritance. Class invariants are further troublesome in that they involve direct access to an object's attributes. This makes manual addition particularly unappealing, as the available choices are invasive with respect to the original interface and implementation (to which we may not have access), compromise encapsulation, and are error-prone if done manually.

This paper presents a lightweight, non-invasive technique for automatically extending a collection of class definitions with a corresponding collection of structural invariant checks. The invariants are given as a stand- alone specification, which is woven together with the original source files to produce a new collection of drop- in replacement classes that are behaviorally indistinguishable from the originals in the absence of invariant- related faults but will expose such faults in a way that the original classes do not. Each replacement is defined to be a subclass (indeed, a *subtype* [1]) of the original class whose functionality it extends,

V. Cortellessa and D. Varró (Eds.): FASE 2013, LNCS 7793, pp. 163–178, 2013.
© Springer-Verlag Berlin Heidelberg 2013

and it can thus be substituted in any context in which the original occurs. The generation is itself completely automatic, and the incorporation into a test harness or other program is nearly seamless. We focus here on the Java language, a choice that complicates the overall strategy in some ways while simplifying it in others.

2   Background and Related Work

A *class invariant* is a conjunction of predicates defined on the values of an object's individual attributes and on the relationships between them. It characterizes an object's "legal" states, giving the predicates that must hold if the object is to represent an instance of that abstraction. Usually, a class invariant is given in conjunction with the *contracts* for each publicly-visible method of a class, *i.e.*, the preconditions that must hold on arguments to each method call and the consequent guarantees that are made as postconditions upon the method's return. Unlike the contracts, however, a class invariant is a property concerning only an object's *data values*, even (especially) when those values are not publicly visible. An invariant must hold at every point between the object's observable actions, *i.e.* upon creation of any object that is an instance of this class and both before and after every publicly-visible method call [2,3]. At other points, including non-visible method calls, it need not hold, and runtime checks are disabled in this case. Further, since runtime invariant checks can impose a non-trivial performance penalty on a system, in general, it is desirable to have a mechanism for leaving the checks in place during testing, while removing them from a final, production system. Finally, there is an important interplay between the subtype relation (which determines when one object can safely be substituted in a context calling for another [1]) and class invariants: if B is a subtype of A (as well as a subclass) then the invariant for B must include all of the constraints in A's invariant [2,3].

Some languages offer native support for invariant checking, but for Java and other languages that lack this, including such checks is challenging. A common approach is to make use of the language's assertion mechanism, by including assertions of the invariant at the end of each constructor body and at the beginning and end of the body of each public method [2]. If the language's assertions mechanism is used, disabling the checking functionality after testing is usually quite easy. However, this approach carries the disadvantage of requiring the class designer to code not only the predicates themselves but also an explicit handling of the inheritance requirements and the full execution model, discussed above. Both of these tasks must be implemented for each invariant definition, in each class.

To avoid the implementation burden of the assertions approach, we can use a tool that generates the invariant checks from either specialized annotations of the source code [4,5,6] or reserved method signatures [7,8,9]. Essentially, such tools offer language extensions to resemble native support for invariant definitions. In comparison to assertion-based approaches, they eliminate the requirement of implementing the execution model, a clear advantage. As with the assertions approach, annotation approaches are invasive, in that they require modification of the original source code. More substantially, the approach generally requires the use of a specialized, nonstandard compiler, whose development may not keep up with that of the language[1].

Instead, we can view the addition of runtime invariant checking across a class *hierarchy* as a kind of cross-cutting concern, *i.e.* code that is defined across several classes and hence resists encapsulation. Under this view, it is natural to approach this problem as one of aspect-oriented programming (AOP) [11], in which we can use a tool such as AspectJ [12] to define the checks separately as aspects. The entry and exit points of each method become the join points, the point cuts are inferred from a class's method signatures, and the invariant check itself becomes the advice [13,14]. Unlike annotation-based approaches, aspect weaving can be done without the need for a non-standard compiler, either through source code transformation or byte code instrumentation [15]. However, the AOP approach also presents several difficulties. For example, Balzer *et al.* note that mainstream tools such as AspectJ lack a mechanism to enforce the requirement that the definition of a class's invariant include the invariant of its parent class [16]. It is possible to write invariant checking "advice" so that it correctly calls the parent class's invariant check, but this must be done manually (*e.g.* [13]). A similar problem occurs in implementing the correct disabling of checks on non-public calls. Lastly, because aspects cannot in general be prevented from changing an object's state, the weaving of additional aspects may compose poorly with the aspect that provides the invariant check [17,16,18]. It is possible that another aspect could break the class invariant, and since interleaving of multiple aspects is difficult to control, it is possible the two aspects could interleave in such a way as to make the invariant failure go undetected.

The work closest in spirit to our own is the design pattern approach of Gibbs, Malloy, and Power ([19,20]. Targeting development in the C++ language, they present a choice of two patterns for weaving a separate specification of invariant checks into a class hierarchy, based on the well known *decorator* and *visitor* patterns [21]. However, the decorator approach involves a fairly substantial refactoring of the original source code. Moreover, the authors note that this technique interacts poorly with the need to structure invariant checks across a full class hierarchy. The refactoring in this case is complex, and it requires the use of multiple inheritance to relate the decorated classes appropriately, making it unsuitable for languages such as Java, which support only single inheritance. Their alternative is an application of the visitor pattern, in which the invariant checks are implemented as the *visit* methods in a single *Visitor* class. This pattern usually requires that the classes on the "data side" implement an *accept* method, which is used to dispatch the appropriate *visit* method, but in their use of it, only the top of the class hierarchy is modified to be a subclass of an "invariant facilitator", which handles all *accept* implementations. However, successful

---

[1] For example, JML has not seen active development since version 1.4 of the Java language [10].

implementation of the *visit* methods rests on the assumption that all fields are either publicly visible or have their values readily available through the existence of accessor ("getter") methods. Unless the language simply lacks a mechanism to hide this representation (*e.g.* Python), such exposure is unlikely to be the case, as it violates encapsulation, permitting uncontrolled manipulation of an object's parts, either directly or through aliasing [2].

The central thesis of our work is that, under assumptions common to Java and other statically-typed OO languages, these limitations—source code modification, multiple inheritance, and public accessibility of fields—are unnecessary for a design-pattern approach. The remainder of the present paper shows how to relax them.

3 Weaving Invariant Checking from Specifications

Our approach draws from the Gibbs/Malloy/Power design pattern efforts and from ideas in AOP in the treatment of invariant specifications as a cross-cutting concern. We begin with an assumption that the class invariants are given in a single specification file, separate from classes that they document. Each constraint is a boolean- valued Java expression, with the invariant taken to be the conjunction of these expressions. We assume (though do not hope to enforce) that these expressions are free of side effects, and that the invariant given for a child class does not contradict any predicates in inherited invariants. Otherwise, the particulars of the specification format are unimportant. The current version of our tool uses JSON [22], but any format for semi-structured data will do.

We focus on the Java programming language, which means that we assume a statically-typed, object-oriented language, with introspective reflection capabilities, support for type parameters in class definitions, single inheritance (though implementation of multiple interfaces is possible), and a uniform model of virtual method dispatch. We make some simplifications of the full problem. Specifically, we work only with synchronization- free, single-threaded, non-*final* class definitions, and we consider only instance methods of a class that admit overriding, *i.e.*, non-*static*, non-*final*[2] method definitions. We do not consider anonymous inner class constructs nor the *lambda expressions* planned for Java 8 [23]. Finally, we assume a class's field visibility grants at least access through inheritance (*i.e. protected* accessbility or higher). This last is made purely for the sake of simplifying the technical presentation, since, as discussed in section 5, introspection makes it easy to handle variables of any accessibility.

3.1 An Inheritance-Based Approach

As a first effort, we will try an approach that leverages the mechanism of inheritance and the redefinition of inherited method signatures through subtyping

---

[2] The *final* keyword has two uses in Java: to declare single-assignment, read-only variables and to prohibit extension of classes or overriding of methods. The latter form is equivalent to the *sealed* keyword in C#, and it is this usage we avoid here.

```
public class A'<T_A'> extends A<S_A'> {
  private int δ = 0;
  public A(τ_A x⃗) {
    super(x⃗);
    δ = δ + 1;
    φ₂();
  }
  public τ_{f_A} f_A(σ_{f_A} y⃗) {
    φ₁();   τ_{f_A} χ = super.f_A(y⃗);   φ₂();
    return χ;
  }
  private boolean inv() { return ρ_A; }
  private void φ₁() {
    if (δ == 0 && !inv())
      ⟨ handle invariant failure ⟩
    δ = δ + 1;
  }
  private void φ₂() {
    δ = δ - 1;
    if (δ == 0 && !inv())
      ⟨ handle invariant failure ⟩
  }
}
```

Fig. 1. Inheritance-based generation of invariant checks

polymorphism. The idea is to derive from a class and its invariant a subclass, in which we wrap the invariant in a new, non-public method (perhaps with additional error reporting features), similar to the "*repOK*" approach advocated by Liskov and Guttag [2]. To this new subclass, we also add methods ϕ_1 and ϕ_2 to handle the checking tasks at (respectively) method entry and exit points, and we use these to define constructors and overridden versions of every public method.

Let A be a class, with parametric type expression T_A defined on type parameters S_A, field declarations $\overrightarrow{\tau\,a}$, invariant ρ_A, constructor definition $A(\overrightarrow{\tau_A\,y})$ and public method $\tau_f\,f(\overrightarrow{\sigma_f\,z})$.

```
public class A<T_A> {
  τ a⃗;
  public A(τ_A x⃗) {  ...  }
  public τ_{f_A} f_A(σ_{f_A} y⃗) {  ...  }
}
```

We extend A with runtime checking of ρ_A by generating the subclass in Fig. 1, where $T_{A'}$ and $S_{A'}$ are identical to T_A and S_A (respectively), except perhaps for renaming of type parameters (*i.e.*, they are α-equivalent).

For each constructor in A', the body executes the "real" statements of the corresponding superclass constructor, followed by a check of ρ_A, whose execution is itself controlled by the ϕ_2 method. Likewise, the body of each public method f_A wraps a call to the superclass's version between checks of ρ_A, with execution controlled by the ϕ_1 and ϕ_2 methods. If f_A returns a value, then this value is captured in the overridden version in a "result" variable, χ. A method or constructor call is publicly-visible precisely when the call stack depth on a given A' object is 0, and this value is tracked by the additional integer-valued field δ. The ϕ_1 and ϕ_2 methods increment/decrement δ as appropriate, evaluating ρ_A only if $\delta = 0$.[3]

The inheritance-based approach suggests an easy mechanism for reusing code while adding the necessary invariant checks and capturing the distinction between publicly-visible and inner method calls. For the user, the burden consists of replacing constructor calls to A with the corresponding calls for A'. This may be an excessive requirement when A objects are used in production-level code, but in many settings where invariant checking is desirable, such constructor calls are limited to only a handful of sites. In the JUnit framework, for example, integration of A' objects into unit tests for A is likely quite simple, as object construction occurs mainly in the body of a single method, *setUp*.

Note the assumptions of uniform polymorphic dispatch and non-*final* declarations here. If a class cannot be extended (*e.g. String* and other objects in the *java.lang* package), then construction of a subclass that implements the invariant checks is obviously impossible. Similarly, a method whose dispatch is statically determined cannot be transparently overridden, and if declared *final*, it cannot be overridden at all. In many languages (notably, C# and C++) the default convention is *static* dispatch, with dynamic binding requiring an explicit *virtual* designation; in such cases, the inheritance construction is far less convenient and may be impossible without some refactoring of the original source code.

Unfortunately, our first attempt fails in two critical ways, which becomes apparent when we attempt to construct the invariant-checking extension across a hierarchy of class definitions. First of all, the inheritance hierarchy of a collection of objects requires a corresponding structure in the composition of invariant checks. This problem is very similar to the one encountered in the "decorator" approach of [20], but the multiple-inheritance solution given there is unavailable in a single-inheritance language such as Java. Consider a class B that is a subtype of A (written $B <: A$):

```
public class B<T_B> extends A<S_B>{
    τ⃗ b
    public B(τ_B y⃗) {  ...  }
    public τ_{g_B} g(σ_{g_B} z⃗) {  ...  }
}
```

Figure 2 depicts the problem[4]. The invariant for a B object, inv_B, must include the A invariant—*i.e.*, $inv_B = inv_A \wedge \rho_B$. However, a B' object cannot access the fields of its associated B object through inheritance and also reuse the functionality of the inv_A method. We might choose to have B' descend from A' instead,

---

[3] In the presence of concurrency, we would need a more sophisticated mechanism; keeping track of the call stack depth on an object for each thread, synchronizing all method calls on the object's monitor lock, and so on.

[4] There and throughout this paper, we write $[S/\tau]\,T$ to denote the substitution of type expression τ for the type parameter S in expression T, and use the shorthand $[S_1/\tau_1, S_2/\tau_2]\,T$ to denote the composition of type expressions $[S_1/\tau_1]\,[S_2/\tau_2]\,T$.

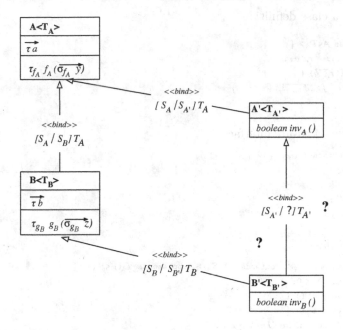

Fig. 2. Design flaw in the naive inheritance approach

but this only works if all fields in B are publicly accessible. As discussed above, this is unlikely to be the case.

The second, related failure is that inheritance does not facilitate a correct binding of the type parameters. Again, this is clear from Fig. 2. An instantiation of B supplies a type τ to the parameters S_B, which is used in turn to bind the parameters S_A with argument $[S_B/\tau, S_A/S_B]T_A$. When we instantiate B' instead, this same τ binds the parameters $S_{B'}$, with the resulting chain of arguments binding A's parameters S_A as $[S_{B'}/\tau, S_B/S_{B'}, S_A/S_B]T_A$. For correct use of the A' invariant check in this $B'\langle\tau\rangle$ object, we would need to bind the type parameter of A', $S_{A'}$, in the same way we do A's parameter, S_A; *i.e.* with argument $[S_{B'}/\tau, S_{A'}/S_{B'}, S_A/S_{A'}]T_A$, a binding that cannot be ensured, unless B' is a subclass of A'.

3.2   Exposing the Representation

Though unsuccessful on its own, we can use the inheritance approach of Section 3.1 as the basis for an auxiliary pattern, which we call an *exposure pattern*. The idea is to construct from the original hierarchy a corresponding set of classes that offers the interface of the original collection and in addition, a controlled exposure of each object's representation. The machinery for checking the invariants is factored into separate classes, as discussed in Section 3.3, below.

Consider a class definition

```
public class A<T_A> {
    τ₁ a₁;   ...   τ_k a_k;
    public A(τ_A y⃗) {  ...  }
    public τ_{f_A} f_A(σ_{f_A} z⃗) {  ...  }
}
```

We derive the *exposure* interface

```
public interface IA_E<T_{A''}> {
    τ₁ γ_{a₁}();
    ...
    τ_m γ_{a_m}();
}
```

and *exposed* class

```
public class A_E<T_{A'}>  extends  A<S_{A'}>  implements IA_E<S_{A'}> {
    private int δ = 0;
    private void φ₁() { ...}
    private void φ₂() { ...}
    protected boolean inv(InvV v) { ...}

    public  A_E(τ_A y⃗) {
        super(y⃗);   δ = δ + 1;   φ₂();
    }
    public  τ_{f_A} f_A(σ_{f_A} y⃗) {
        φ₁();   τ_{f_A} χ = super.f_A(y⃗);   φ₂();
        return χ;
    }

    public τ₁ γ_{a₁}(){ return a₁; }
    ...
    public τ_m γ_{a_m}(){ return a_m; }
}
```

where $T_{A'}$, $T_{A''}$ and $S_{A'}$, $S_{A''}$ are α-equivalent to T_A and S_A, as above. Note that the fields $a_1 \ldots a_m$ include all of the original $a_1 \ldots a_k$ and perhaps others, as discussed on page 171, below. The constructors and public methods in A_E are overridden in exactly the same manner as in the A' class of Section 3.1, and likewise the implementation of the $\phi_1()$ and $\phi_2()$ methods. The representation exposure happens through the $\gamma_{a_i}()$, a set of raw "getter" methods that expose each of the object's fields. In the presence of inheritance, the corresponding structure is realized not in the derived class but in the derived *interfaces*. Thus, for example,

```
public class B<T_B> extends A<S_B>{
    τ₁ b₁;   ...   τ_l b_l;
    public B(τ_B y⃗) {  ...  }
    public τ_{g_B} f(σ_{g_B} z⃗) {  ...  }
}
```

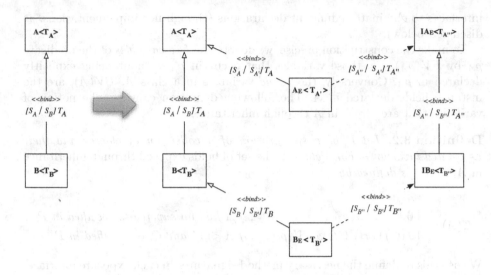

Fig. 3. Exposure pattern construction

gives rise to the interface and class definitions

```
public interface IB_E<T_B''> extends  IA_E<S_B''> {
   τ₁ γ_b₁ ();
   ...
   τ_n γ_bn ();
}

public class B_E<T_B'> extends B<S_B'> implements IB_E<S_B'> { ... }
```

The construction is illustrated in Fig. 3.

Correctness. Since the type expressions in a class definition are copied to its exposed class and interface (perhaps with α-renaming of the parameters), it is easy to see that

Proposition 3.1. *For any type expression τ, an instance of a class A has type $A\langle T(\tau)\rangle$ if and only if A_E and IA_E have types $A_E\langle T(\tau)\rangle$ and $IA_E\langle T(\tau)\rangle$, respectively.* □

The construction of the accessor methods is less obvious. While we construct $\gamma_{a_i}()$ for each of the fields $\{a_1, \ldots, a_k\}$, we may need to construct others, as well, in case the invariant ρ_A makes reference to any inherited fields for which we have not already constructed an interface. This can happen in the case of an incomplete specification of the class hierarchy and invariants. The simplest way to handle this is to include in the interface a $\gamma_{a_i}()$ for each declared field in the corresponding A classes and also for each variable that occurs without explicit declaration in the the predicate ρ_A. However, we can leverage the inheritance of interfaces to eliminate redundant declarations (though not implementations, as discussed below).

To make the construction precise, we denote the *free variables* of the predicate ρ_A by $FV(\rho_A)$, *i.e.* those variables that occur in ρ_A without being explicitly declared in ρ_A. Conversely, the *bound* variables in a class A, $BV(A)$, are the instance fields declared in A. The following definition captures the notion of variables that are "free" in A through inheritance:

Definition 3.2. *Let P be a specification of a collection of classes and their associated invariants. For a class A, the set of fields exposed through inheritance in A, $\mathcal{I}(A)$, is defined by*

$$\mathcal{I}(A) = \begin{cases} \emptyset & , \text{if } A \text{ has no superclass specified in } P \\ \mathcal{I}(C) \cup BV(C) \cup FV(\rho_C) & , \text{if } A <: C \text{ and } C \text{ is specified in } P \end{cases}$$

We use this to define the necessary method signatures in each exposure interface.

Definition 3.3. *Given class A and invariant ρ_A, the body of IA_E consists of the the signatures*

$$IA_E = \{\tau_{a_i}\gamma_{a_i}(); \mid a_i \in BV(A) \cup FV(\rho_A) \setminus \mathcal{I}(A)\}$$

where each τ_{a_i} is the declared type of a_i.

Definition 3.4. *For a field, τ_{a_i} a_i, either declared in or inherited by a class A, we say that a_i is successfully exposed for A if either*

- *there is an interface IA_E and subclass*
  `class A_E extends A implements IA_E`
  such that IA_E includes a method interface
  `τ γ_{a_i}();`
  and for every A_E object o, $o.\gamma_{a_i}() == o.a_i$
- *A is a subclass of C, and a_i is successfully exposed for C.*

Given A and ρ_A, the construction for IA_E in Definition 3.3 and the accompanying implementation A_E combine to give us the representation exposure we need for ρ_A. In particular,

Proposition 3.5. *If $x \in FV(\rho_A)$, then x is successfully exposed for A.* $\square$

Space Requirements. The primary difference between the exposure pattern construction and the inheritance-based effort of Section 3.1 lies in the construction of the exposure interfaces, whose inheritance structure is congruent to that of the original collection of classes. Like the earlier attempt, however, the collection of exposed *classes* does not share this same relation, and as a consequence, both approaches are subject to some unfortunate redundancy consequences. In particular, we cannot reuse code between distinct exposed classes, even when the classes they expose are related by inheritance. For example, if a class A contains fields a_1 and a_2 and public method $f()$ then the exposed class A_E must override $f()$, and it must include exposure methods γ_{a_1} and γ_{a_2}, according to the interface IA_E. If $B <: A$ contains fields b_1, b_2, and method $g()$, then it must override not only $g()$ but also $f()$, with the body of the overridden $f()$ identical to that in A_E. Likewise, it must implement not only the γ_{b_1} and γ_{b_2} methods from the IB_E interface, but also γ_{a_1} and γ_{a_2}.

Happily, all of this is easily automated, and it is reasonable to suppose the space overhead manageable. Note first that, with the exception of classes at the top of a specified hierarchy, the size of the interface generated for a class is proportional to the number of fields in that class. Recalling Definitions 3.2 and 3.3, we can see that this is so because

Proposition 3.6. *Let C be a class included in a specification P. For every class $A <: C$, $FV(\rho_A) \setminus \mathcal{I}(A) = BV(A)$.*

In other words, only for classes specified at the top of an inheritance hierarchy will we ever need to generate additional γ declarations in the corresponding interfaces. In all other cases, the accessor interfaces for inherited fields are inherited from the corresponding parent interfaces. Hence, the space required to extend a collection of classes depends only on the size of each class and the depth of the inheritance relationship in the collection. Specifically, if we assume a bound of n new field and method definitions on each class and an inheritance depth of h, then the overall space growth is given by

$$\sum_{i=1}^{h}\left(\sum_{j=1}^{i} n\right) = \left(\sum_{i=1}^{h} i\right) n = \left(\frac{h(h+1)}{2}\right) n \in \mathcal{O}(h^2 n)$$

It is difficult to give a general characterization of either n or h, but there is reason to suspect that both are manageable values in practice. McConnell recommends a limit of 7 new method definitions in a class [24]. Shatnawi's study [25] finds no significant threshold value for h. Classes in the JDK's *java.** and *javax.** libraries implement anywhere from less than 10 to over 100 new methods, while the largest depth of any inheritance tree is 8.

3.3   Adding the Invariant Checks

As in Gibbs/Malloy/Power [20], we implement the runtime invariant checks themselves through an application of the *visitor pattern* [21], in which the methods implementing the invariant checks are aggregated into a single class (the "visitor"), with the appropriate method called from within the class being checked (the "acceptor"). Unlike their approach, however, our exposure pattern allows us to do this without modification of any part of the original source files, not even at the top of the inheritance hierarchy.

Suppose we have a class $A{<}T_A{>}$, with invariant ρ_A. From these, we generate the exposed class $A_E{<}T_{A'}{>}$ and the exposure interface $IA_E{<}T_{A''}{>}$, as in Section

3.2. The specification of ρ_A and the access methods defined for IA_E are used to generate an invariant checking "visitor" class:

```
public class InvV {
  public <T_A_I>  void v_A(IA_E<S_A_I> obj) {
    τ_1 a_1  = obj.γ_1();
    ...
    τ_n a_n  = obj.γ_n();

    ⟨⟨ compute ρ_A and return the result ⟩⟩
  }
}
```

where T_{A_I} and S_{A_I} are equivalent to T_A and its parameters S_A, as above.

Runtime checking of ρ_A is invoked in the A_E methods through calls to that class's *inv* method, which serves as the "accept" method, handling dispatch of the appropriate invariant check:

```
public class A_E<S_A'> extends  A<S_A'>  implements IA_E<S_A'> {
  private int δ = 0;
  private void φ_1() { ...}
  private void φ_2() { ...}   // (as defined in Section 3.1)
  private boolean inv(InvV v) {
    v.v_A(this);
    return v.valid();
  }

  ...

}
```

Note that each $v_A()$ method in $InvV$ takes an argument of type IA_E and not A_E. This is necessary, because of the need to compose an invariant check with that of the object's superclass in each invariant method. For example, if we have $B <: A$, we define $v_B()$ as

```
public <T_B> void v_B(IB_E<S_B> obj) {
  v_A( (IA_E<S_B>) obj);
  ⟨⟨ compute ρ_B, as above ⟩⟩
}
```

Since A_E and B_E are not related by inheritance, it would not be possible to directly cast obj to its superclass's exposed version. Fortunately, the interface is all we need.

Finally, although we structure our solution here according to the traditional visitor pattern conventions, we do not really need the full generality of that pattern. In particular, it is unnecessary to support full double dispatch, as we only need one instance of $InvV$, and no $v_i()$ method will ever invoke a call back to the *inv*() method of an object (not even indirectly, since the ϕ_1 and ϕ_2 methods in a class prevent a call to *inv*() if one is already running). Our implementation of this approach as an Eclipse plugin instead drops the $InvV$ parameter from every *inv* method, relying instead on a single, static instance of the invariant visitor:

```
private boolean inv() {
  InvVv = InvV.getInstance();
  ...
}
```

4   Example: Unit Testing

Method contracts and class invariants are particularly useful in testing. In combination with test oracles, the use of runtime invariant and pre/post-conditions checks improves the exposure of faults as well as the diagnosability of faults when they are detected [26,27]. Our implementation as an Eclipse plug has proven useful in diagnosing invariant-related faults.

For example, a simple `List` interface provides an abstraction for the list data type. A standard way to implement this is with an underlying doubly-linked list, in which we keep a pair of "sentinel" head and tail nodes, with the "real" nodes in the list linked in between:

```
public abstract class AbstractList<T> implements List<T> {
  protected int size;
  ...
}

public class DLinkedList<T> extends AbstractList<T> implements List<T> {
  // inherited from AbstractList:  int size
  protected DNode<T> head, tail;  ...
}
```

Among other predicates, the invariant for *DLinkedList* requires that $\forall n \neq tail$, $n.next.prev = n$.

This was given as part of a project for the first author's data structures course, and among the student submissions received was this implementation of *remove()*, in which the *cur.prev* pointer is not correctly updated:

```
public boolean remove(T v) {
  DNode<T> cur = head.next;
  while (cur != tail) {
    if (cur.data.equals(v)) {
      DNode<T> prev = cur.prev;  cur = cur.next;  prev.next = cur;
      size--;
      return true;
    } else
      cur = cur.next;
  }
  return false;
}
```

A JUnit test suite failed to uncover this fault, passing this and the tests for 12 other methods:

```
public void testRemove() {
  ls.add("a"); ls.add("b"); ls.add("c"); ls.add("d"); ls.add("a"); ls.add("d");
  int sz = ls.size();
  assertTrue(ls.remove("a"));    assertTrue(ls.size() == sz - 1);
  sz = ls.size();
  assertTrue(!ls.remove("**"));    assertTrue(ls.size() == sz);
}
```

From the original source code and a specification of invariants our tool generates the classes and interfaces

```
public interface IExposedAbstractList<T> {
    int _getSize();
}
public interface IExposedDLinkedList<T> extends IExposedAbstractList<T> {
    DNode<T> _getHead();
    DNode<T> _getTail();
}

public abstract class ExposedAbstractList<T>
                   extends AbstractList<T> implements IExposedAbstractList<T> { ... }

public class ExposedDLinkedList<T>
                   extends DLinkedList<T> implements IExposedDLinkedList<T> { ... }

public class RepOKVisitor {
    ...
    public <T> void visit(IExposedAbstractList<T> _inst) { ... }
    public <T> void visit(IExposedDLinkedList<T> _inst) { ... }
    ...
}
```

Objects in a JUnit test suite are constructed in the *setUp()* method, and a simple modification was all that was needed to cause *testRemove()* to fail appropriately:

```
protected void setUp() {
//      ls = new DLinkedList<String>();
    ls = new ExposedDLinkedList<String>();
}
```

5   Conclusion and Future Work

The design pattern given here provides a fairly seamless approach for adding correct runtime invariant checking to a class hierarchy, through the construction of drop-in replacements that can be removed as easily as inserted. In addition to the core material presented here, there are a number of extensions possible.

For example, the presentation in this paper relies on the assumption above that all fields in a class are accessible through inheritance. Happily, this is an easy if tedious limitation to overcome. If instead the field is declared with only intra-object or intra-class access (*e.g.* Java's "`private`"), we can use the introspective capabilities of the language to manufacture a locally-visible *get* method. To access a `private` field x, for example, our implementation generates a γ_x that handles the unwieldy details of Java introspection:

```
private τ _getX() {
    Class klass = this.getClass();   Field field = null;
    while (field == null) {
        try {
            field = klass.getDeclaredField("x");   field.setAccessible(true);
        } catch (NoSuchFieldException e) {
            klass = klass.getSuperclass();
        }
    }
    τ x = null;
    try {
        x = (τ) field.get(this);
    } catch (IllegalAccessException e) {   e.printStackTrace();   throw new Error();   }
    return x;
}
```

Other extensions, such as the inclusion of anonymous inner classes, concurrency, or *final* classes/methods, remain as open challenges.

Finally, the work described here incorporates only the invariant checks, rather than full contracts, and it would clearly be useful to extend our design pattern to support this. While we conjecture that our technique is easily extendable to this purpose, the invariant checks present the most interesting problems, owing to their need for attribute access and hierarchical definition. Philosophically, ordinary unit testing already performs at least the behavioral components of contract checking, *i.e.* the checks of pre and post-conditions. What unit testing cannot do is determine whether the invariant continues to hold, as it is often impossible to access an object's fields. The difference lies in the fact that both pre and post conditions are inherently extensional specifications. They impose requirements on method arguments and return values, but on the object itself, all constraints are made upon the abstraction of the object, not the concrete implementation. That implementation— whose consistency with the abstraction is the core assertion of a class invariant—is by definition opaque to an object's user.

Acknowledgments. The ideas in this paper began with an assignment in the first author's Spring 2010 Software Construction class, and the students there provided valuable feedback. Our thanks also to Prof. Peter Boothe of Manhattan College, for help in analyzing the inheritance and method complexity of the JDK.

References

1. Liskov, B.H., Wing, J.M.: A behavioral notion of subtyping. ACM TOPLAS 16(6), 1811–1841 (1994)
2. Liskov, B., Guttag, J.: Program Development in Java: Abstraction, Specification, and Object-Oriented Design. Addison-Wesley (2001)
3. Meyer, B.: Object-Oriented Software Construction, 2nd edn. Prentice Hall (1997)
4. Flanagan, C., Leino, K.R.M., Lillibridge, M., Nelson, G., Saxe, J.B., Stata, R.: Extended static checking for Java. In: PLDI 2002, pp. 234–245. ACM Press (2002)
5. Leavens, G.T., Baker, A.L., Ruby, C.: Preliminary design of JML: A behavioral interface specification language for Java. ACM SIGSOFT Software Engineering Notes 31(3), 1–38 (2006)
6. Liu, H., Qin, L., Wang, J., Vemuri, N., Jia, X.: Static and dynamic contract verifiers for Java. In: Hamza, M.H. (ed.) SEA 2003, pp. 593–598. ACTA Press (2003)
7. Karaorman, M., Hölze, U., Bruno, J.: jContractor: A Java library to support design by contract. Technical Report TRCS98-31, University of California at Santa Barbara (1998)
8. Prasetya, W., Vos, T., Baars, A.: Trace-based reflexive testing of OO programs. Technical Report UU-CS-2007-037, Dept. of Information and Computing Sciences, Utrecht University (2007)
9. Prasetya, W., Vos, T., Baars, A.: Trace-based reflexive testing of OO programs with T2. In: STVV 2008, pp. 151–160. IEEE Press (2008)
10. Java Modeling Language (JML) Homepage, http://www.eecs.ucf.edu/~leavens/JML/

11. Kiczales, G., Lamping, J., Mendhekar, A., Maeda, C., Lopes, C.V., Loingtier, J.M., Irwin, J.: Aspect-Oriented Programming. In: Akşit, M., Matsuoka, S. (eds.) ECOOP 1997. LNCS, vol. 1241, pp. 220–242. Springer, Heidelberg (1997)
12. The AspectJ programming guide, http://www.eclipse.org/aspectj/doc/released/progguide/
13. Briand, L.C., Dzidek, W., Labiche, Y.: Instrumenting contracts with aspect-oriented programming to increase observability and support debugging. In: ICSM 2005. IEEE Press (2005)
14. Skotiniotis, T., Lorenz, D.H.: Cona: Aspects for contracts and contracts for aspects. In: Vlissides, J.M., Schmidt, D.C. (eds.) OOPSLA 2004 Companion, pp. 196–197. ACM Press (2004)
15. Czarnecki, K., Eisenecker, U.W.: Generative Programming: Methods, Tools, and Applications. Addison-Wesley (2000)
16. Balzer, S., Eugster, P.T., Meyer, B.: Can Aspects Implement Contracts? In: Guelfi, N., Savidis, A. (eds.) RISE 2005. LNCS, vol. 3943, pp. 145–157. Springer, Heidelberg (2006)
17. Agostinho, S., Moreira, A., Guerreiro, P.: Contracts for aspect-oriented design. In: SPLAT 2008. ACM Press, New York (2008)
18. Klaeren, H., Pulvermüller, E., Rashid, A., Speck, A.: Aspect Composition Applying the Design by Contract Principle. In: Butler, G., Jarzabek, S. (eds.) GCSE 2000. LNCS, vol. 2177, pp. 57–69. Springer, Heidelberg (2001)
19. Gibbs, T.H., Malloy, B.A., Power, J.F.: Automated validation of class invariants in C++ applications. In: ASE 2002, pp. 205–214. IEEE Pr. (September 2002)
20. Malloy, B.A., Power, J.F.: Exploiting design patterns to automate validation of class invariants. Software Testing, Verification and Reliability 16(2), 71–95 (2006)
21. Gamma, E., Helm, R., Johnson, R., Vlissides, J.: Design Patterns: Elements of Reusable Object-Oriented Software. Addison-Wesley (1995)
22. JSON Homepage, http://www.json.org/
23. Lambda expressions for the Java programming language, http://jcp.org/aboutJava/communityprocess/edr/jsr335/index2.html
24. McConnell, S.: Code Complete: A Practical Handbook of Software Construction. Microsoft Press (2004)
25. Shatnawi, R.: A quantitative investigation of the acceptable risk levels of object-oriented metrics in open-source systems. IEEE Transactions on Software Engineering 36(2), 216–225 (2010)
26. Briand, L.C., Dzidek, W., Labiche, Y.: Investigating the use of analysis contracts to improve the testability of object-oriented code. Software—Practice and Experience 33(7), 637–672 (2003)
27. Le Traon, Y., Baudry, B., Jézéquel, J.M.: Design by contract to improve software vigilance. IEEE Transactions on Software Engineering 32(6), 571–586 (2006)

Augmenting Sequence Enumeration with String-Rewriting for Requirements Analysis and Behavioral Specification

Lan Lin[1], Jesse H. Poore[2], Robert Eschbach[3],
Robert M. Hierons[4], and Christopher Robinson-Mallett[5]

[1] Department of Computer Science, Ball State University, Muncie, IN, USA
llin4@bsu.edu
[2] Department of Electrical Engineering and Computer Science,
University of Tennessee, Knoxville, TN, USA
poore@eecs.utk.edu
[3] ITK Engineering AG, Herxheim, Germany
robert.eschbach@itk-engineering.de
[4] School of Information Systems, Computing and Mathematics, Brunel University,
Uxbridge, Middlesex, UK
rob.hierons@brunel.ac.uk
[5] Berner & Mattner Systemtechnik GmbH, Berlin, Germany
christopher.robinson-mallett@berner-mattner.com

Abstract. Sequence enumeration is a method for deriving a system model based on informal requirements. Under sequence enumeration, stimulus (input) sequences are considered in a breadth-first manner, with the expected system response to each sequence given. Not all sequences of stimuli are considered since a sequence need not be extended if either it is illegal (it cannot be applied in practice) or it can be reduced to another sequence previously considered (the sequences take the system to the same state). Sequence enumeration is mostly a manual process, which leads to a model that can be used as the basis for automation. This paper describes a method, based on string-rewriting, that automates parts of sequence enumeration. This automation has the potential to reduce both the cost and time involved in sequence enumeration but also to reduce the scope for human error. In addition to outlining this method, we discuss our experiences in applying it to four case studies.

Keywords: software specification, sequence-based specification, sequence enumeration, string-rewriting, requirements engineering.

1 Introduction

Software development often starts with all sorts of functional *requirements*. They are generally written in a natural language, and contain ambiguities, omissions, inconsistencies, and errors. All these problems need to be resolved and the requirements need to be converted into a precise *specification* at an early stage

V. Cortellessa and D. Varró (Eds.): FASE 2013, LNCS 7793, pp. 179–193, 2013.
© Springer-Verlag Berlin Heidelberg 2013

in the development life cycle. The specification is important for later phases including code development, testing, as well as functional formal verification.

The *sequence-based specification* method [12,19–21] was developed for this purpose, providing a systematic way to convert imprecise and informal requirements into precise software specifications, through *sequence enumeration*. In this process, the developer or domain expert considers sequences of stimuli in a breadth-first manner, where sequences of a given length are examined in lexicographic order. For each such sequence, the developer gives the last output produced in response to the sequence. There are two situations in which a sequence need not be further extended: either it is illegal (it cannot be applied in practice) or it reaches a system state equivalent to one reached by a shorter or lexicographically earlier sequence. Sequence enumeration stops when no sequence needs to be extended and results in a table of sequences that defines a Mealy machine.

A significant benefit of sequence enumeration is that it results in a formal specification but without requiring the developer to use a formal notation. This specification can form the basis for other activities, such as automated (model-based) testing. The specification can also be automatically analyzed to determine whether it has certain expected, or desirable properties; this can result in requirements errors being found. The number of sequences considered is also equal to the number of transitions of the Mealy machine that represents the requirements and so the cost of sequence enumeration can be seen as being linear in terms of the complexity of the requirements. However, automation has the potential to allow sequence enumeration to scale further. This paper describes a method in which string-rewriting rules are used in order to automate the analysis of some sequences. This reduces the number of sequences that have to be considered, and thus can reduce both the cost of sequence enumeration and the potential for human error. We also explain how possible rules can be deduced from previous reductions; potentially these might be provided to the developer who can choose to accept or reject them. The overall approach has been implemented in our enumeration tool [18] and we describe the result of applying this tool to four case studies.

This work was motivated by the various observed patterns in analyzing enumerated sequences in field applications [2, 4, 10, 21]. With the new theory and accompanying tool support, more equivalence declarations can be handled automatically and consistently leading to fewer human errors. The result is an enhanced enumeration process. The method treats discrete systems, and systems modeled as discrete based on abstractions of events.

This paper is structured as follows. In Section 2 we describe sequence enumeration and a running example. Section 3 describes the proposed method that uses string-rewriting in sequence enumeration, while Section 4 outlines our experience in using this method with four case studies. Section 5 summarizes related work. Finally, Section 6 draws conclusions and discusses future work.

2   Developing a Behavioral Specification through Sequence Enumeration

Sequence-based specification [12, 19–21] uses a technique called sequence enumeration to discover the behavior of the software. The resulting specification can be converted to a state machine for implementation and testing.

To apply the method, one first identifies a *system boundary* that defines what is inside and outside the software-intensive system. This usually consists of a list of *interfaces* between the system and the *environment* of the software.

Throughout the paper we will use an automobile mirror electronic control unit (ECU) as a running example. The example was taken from [2] and modified to fit the page limit. The original requirements are collected in Table 1, with each sentence numbered (tagged) for easy reference.

Table 1. Requirements for the driver side car mirror ECU

Trace Tag	Requirement
1	There is a switch that toggles for adjustment of either the driver side or the passenger side mirror.
2	The driver side electronic control unit (ECU) initializes when the car key is in start position.
3	The driver side ECU processes inputs from position sensors and users.
4	The driver side ECU produces outputs to actuators and sends messages to other ECUs.
5	Control area network (CAN) bus used for communication among ECUs.
6	Signals for the passenger side mirror are put on the CAN bus and sent to the passenger side ECU.
7	Each mirror can be adjusted vertically and has extreme up and down positions.
8	Each mirror can be adjusted horizontally and has extreme inward and outward positions.
9	If requested movement cannot be made because the mirror is already in an extreme position, an error message is generated and sent via the CAN bus.

We identify a system boundary in Figure 1, and list the interfaces in Table 2 with traces to the tagged requirements. From the interfaces one further collects *stimuli* and *responses*. Stimuli refer to events (inputs, interrupts, invocations) in the environment that can affect system behavior. Responses refer to system behaviors observable in the environment. The stimuli and responses for the car mirror ECU are identified in Table 3 and Table 4.

We use S and R to denote the stimulus set and the response set, respectively. As the name "sequence enumeration" suggests, one explicitly enumerates all finite stimulus sequences from S^* (representing scenarios of use), first in increasing order of length, and within the same length lexicographically. We use λ

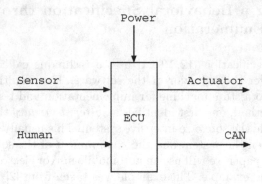

Fig. 1. A system boundary for the driver side car mirror ECU

Table 2. Interfaces for the driver side car mirror ECU

Interface	Description	Trace
Actuator	The actuators	4
CAN	The CAN bus	4, 5, 6
Human	The human users	3
Power	The power	2
Sensor	The position sensors	3

Table 3. Stimuli for the driver side car mirror ECU

Stimulus	Long Name	Description	Interface	Trace
MHI	Mirror horizontal inward	Horizontal inward movement of selected mirror	Human	8
MHO	Mirror horizontal outward	Horizontal outward movement of selected mirror	Human	8
MVD	Mirror vertical down	Vertical down movement of selected mirror	Human	7
MVU	Mirror vertical up	Vertical up movement of selected mirror	Human	7
PHEI	Position horizontal extreme inward	Horizontal position report of driver side mirror indicating the extreme inward position is reached	Sensor	8
PHEO	Position horizontal extreme outward	Horizontal position report of driver side mirror indicating the extreme outward position is reached	Sensor	8
PHNE	Position horizontal no extreme	Horizontal position report of driver side mirror indicating no extreme position is reached	Sensor	8
PVED	Position vertical extreme down	Vertical position report of driver side mirror indicating the extreme down position is reached	Sensor	7
PVEU	Position vertical extreme up	Vertical position report of driver side mirror indicating the extreme up position is reached	Sensor	7
PVNE	Position vertical no extreme	Vertical position report of driver side mirror indicating no extreme position is reached	Sensor	7
SM	Switch mirror	The switch toggled for selection of driver side or passenger side mirror	Human	1
START	Start	Car key in start position	Power	2

Table 4. Responses for the driver side car mirror ECU

Response	Long Name	Description	Interface	Trace
CERR	CAN mirror movement failure	Error message generated and put on CAN bus when mirror is already in extreme position and cannot make requested movement.	CAN	9
CMHI	CAN mirror horizontal inward	Message is generated and put on CAN bus for passenger side ECU for horizontal inward movement of passenger side mirror.	CAN	6, 8
CMHO	CAN mirror horizontal outward	Message is generated and put on CAN bus for passenger side ECU for horizontal outward movement of passenger side mirror.	CAN	6, 8
CMVD	CAN mirror vertical down	Message is generated and put on CAN bus for passenger side ECU for vertical down movement of passenger side mirror.	CAN	6, 7
CMVU	CAN mirror vertical up	Message is generated and put on CAN bus for passenger side ECU for vertical up movement of passenger side mirror.	CAN	6, 7
HI	Horizontal inward movement	Horizontal inward movement of driver side mirror	Actuator	8
HO	Horizontal outward movement	Horizontal outward movement of driver side mirror	Actuator	8
VD	Vertical down movement	Vertical down movement of driver side mirror	Actuator	7
VU	Vertical up movement	Vertical up movement of driver side mirror	Actuator	7

to denote the empty sequence. For our example, the stimuli are alphabetically ordered in Table 3. We concatenate stimuli to string prefixes with periods.

For each sequence one identifies a unique response based on the requirements. For instance, START.PHEI.MHO corresponds to: car key in start position, followed by a horizontal position report indicating that the driver side mirror has reached the extreme inward position, followed by a human command to move the driver side mirror outward. By Requirement 8, the software should produce response HO to make a horizontal outward movement.

When mapping stimulus sequences to responses, there are two special situations. In one case, a sequence generates no externally observable behavior, represented by *null* (denoted 0) in R. In the other case, a sequence is physically unrealizable (the sequence cannot happen in practice), hence we introduce another special response *illegal* (denoted ω) into R. Therefore, R always contains 0 and ω. A sequence is *illegal* when it maps to ω; otherwise, it is *legal*.

For each enumerated sequence v, one checks whether v takes the system to a situation encountered with a previous sequence u. This is the case if u and v, when further extended by any non-empty stimulus sequence w, will always generate the same response. For instance, START.MHI and START are two such sequences because we assume (by derived requirement D3 in Table 5; "derived" because there is no justification in the original requirements and hence we document and tag our assumption as a derived requirement) that any mirror adjustment command is ignored before receiving the position report. Two such sequences are *Mealy equivalent*, as they lead to the same state when the system is modeled as a Mealy machine [9]. Note that two Mealy equivalent sequences need not be mapped to the same response but their responses with respect to future extensions always agree. If a sequence is not Mealy equivalent to any previously enumerated sequence, it is *unreduced*; otherwise, it is *reduced* to the previously enumerated (Mealy equivalent) sequence that is itself unreduced.

Table 5. Derived requirements for the driver side car mirror ECU

Tag	Derived Requirement
D1	It is physically impossible for the ECU to experience an input without power.
D2	There is no externally observable response across the system boundary when ignition is turned on.
D3	Mirror adjustment commands ignored unless position signal has been received.
D4	No externally observable response when mirror position signal is received.
D5	No externally observable response when the mirror selection switch toggles.
D6	Re-powering on makes previous history irrelevant.
D7	When ignition is turned on, default mirror selection is on the driver side.
D8	When mirror selection switch goes to passenger side, any received or to-be-received driver side mirror position report will be ignored. Updated position signals are expected once switch goes back to the driver side.

One starts with the empty sequence. To get all sequences of length $n + 1$ (integer $n \geq 0$) one extends all sequences of length n by every stimulus in S, and considers the extensions in lexicographic order. This inherently combinatorial process can be controlled by two observations:

- If sequence u is reduced to a prior sequence v, there is no need to extend u, as the behaviors of the extensions are defined by the same extensions of v.
- If sequence u is illegal, there is no need to extend u by any stimulus, as all of the extensions must be illegal (i.e., physically unrealizable).

Therefore, only legal and unreduced (also called *extensible*) sequences of length n get extended by every stimulus for consideration at length $n + 1$. The process continues until all sequences of a certain length are either illegal or reduced to prior sequences. The enumeration becomes *complete*. This terminating length is discovered in enumeration, and varies from application to application.

Excerpts of an enumeration for the mirror controller is in Table 6 (for the complete enumeration table see [8]). Columns are for sequences, their responses, reductions, and traces to requirements. An unreduced sequence (highlighted) repeats itself in the "Equivalence" column. In constructing the enumeration, we found that supplemental information was needed for enumeration decisions regarding responses and equivalences. We include such information as "derived requirements" in Table 5. They are subject to validation by domain experts. This illustrates one benefit of sequence-based specification, that is, the identification of missing, inconsistent, and incorrect requirements through explicit enumeration.

Application of the method is facilitated with a prototype enumeration tool developed by the Software Quality Research Laboratory (SQRL) at the University

Table 6. Excerpts of an enumeration without applying string-rewriting

Sequence	Response	Equivalence	Trace
λ	0	λ	Method
MHI	ω	MHI	D1
...			
SM	ω	MHI	D1
START	0	START	2, D2
START.MHI	0	START	D3
START.MHO	0	START	D3
START.MVD	0	START	D3
START.MVU	0	START	D3
START.PHEI	0	START.PHEI	D4
...			
START.PVNE	0	START.PVNE	D4
START.SM	0	START.SM	D5
START.START	0	START	2, D2, D6
START.PHEI.MHI	CERR	START.PHEI	8, 9
START.PHEI.MHO	HO	START	8
START.PHEI.MVD	0	START.PHEI	D3
...			
START.PHNE.PVNE.PVNE	0	START.PHNE.PVNE	D4
START.PHNE.PVNE.SM	0	START.SM	D5, D7, D8
START.PHNE.PVNE.START	0	START	2, D2, D6

of Tennessee [18]. To produce a specification in the tool, one only needs to give
stimuli and responses short names to facilitate enumeration; no other notation
or syntax is required. The tool enforces enumeration rules by the recommended
workflow and maintains internal files (XML format) current with every action.
The mirror control example was produced using the tool.

3   Applying String-Rewriting to Sequence Enumeration

Deciding that two sequences are Mealy equivalent is not always easy. If one could
document any observed patterns (for instance, some pairs of inputs commute;
some are idempotent), and automatically apply these patterns when they are
seen again, it would reduce human effort and also enforce consistent decisions
throughout. We find that string-rewriting theory can be applied for this purpose.

3.1   Assumptions

By "enumeration" we refer to a, possibly partial, enumeration work product
following the process described in Section 2. It corresponds to a table mapping
stimulus sequences to responses, equivalent sequences, and traces. Sequences are
listed in increasing order of length, and within the same length lexicographically.

All rows are completely filled in. Table 6 shows excerpts of a complete enumeration table with 217 sequences. If the sequences have rows labeled 0 to 216, any subtable with the rows from 0 to i, $0 \le i \le 216$, is an enumeration.

We assume that we are always working with a *minimal* enumeration: no equivalence declarations have been missed. This is quite a strong assumption, but a starting point for our theoretical framework. We have also developed a theory that removes this assumption but it is outside of the scope of this paper.

3.2   Prefix Rewrite Rules

An enumeration is a possibly partial specification product. The reductions among enumerated sequences automatically define a set of *prefix rewrite rules*. If sequence u is reduced to prior sequence v, then u and v take the system to the same state from the initial state. For any $w \in S^*$, the state reached by uw is the same as that reached by vw. Hence we rewrite uw to the smaller sequence vw in length-lexicographic order representing the same state. We denote this prefix rewrite rule by $u \models v$, where $\models$ denotes the prefix-rewriting relation.

The first illegal sequence u, if there are any, also defines prefix rewrite rules. If we extend u by any stimulus $x \in S$, ux and u must take the system to the same state. We can rewrite any sequence that contains ux as a prefix to a shorter sequence by replacing ux with u. We have one such prefix rewrite rule for each stimulus x in S, denoted by $ux \models u$. To summarize, the following prefix rewrite rules are defined for an enumeration with stimulus set S:

- If sequence u reduces to a prior sequence v, then $u \models v$.
- If sequence u is the first illegal sequence, then $ux \models u$ for all x in S.   (1)

As an example, if we enumerate as in Table 6 and stop at Length 2, the following are defined: $x \models \text{MHI}$, where x is any stimulus except MHI; $\text{START}.v \models \text{START}$, where v is any stimulus in {MHI, MHO, MVD, MVU, START}; $\text{MHI}.x \models \text{MHI}$, where x is any stimulus in Table 3.

A *reduction system* has two parts, a set and a binary relation called the *reduction relation* on that set [3]. An enumeration with stimulus set S and prefix rewrite rules defined by (1) implies a reduction system: S^* is the set, and the reduction relation $\rightarrow$ on S^* is defined by $u \rightarrow v$ if and only if there exists $w \in S^*$ such that $u = lw$, $v = rw$ and $l \models r$ is a prefix rewrite rule. If no prefix rewrite rules apply to sequence u then u is said to be a *normal form* and we showed in [8] (all the conclusions that follow in this paragraph) that otherwise u prefix-rewrites to a Mealy equivalent sequence, and that rewriting continues until finally we get to a normal form. Rewriting is guaranteed to terminate, and a unique normal form is obtained for any stimulus sequence. With a completed enumeration, the normal form for every stimulus sequence is the smallest sequence in length-lexicographic order that takes the system to the same state. All sequences that rewrite to the same normal form sequence are Mealy equivalent.

3.3   String Rewrite Rules

A complete enumeration encodes a finite state automaton with Mealy outputs (a Mealy machine). Unreduced sequences represent system states and each row in the enumeration table defines the response and ending state for the transition with a particular stimulus and starting state. For instance, in Table 6 the sequence START.MHI is mapped to 0 and reduced to START. This indicates that from the state represented by unreduced sequence START, the outgoing arc triggered by MHI outputs 0 and loops back into the same state.

The process of deriving an incomplete enumeration could lead to *string rewrite rules* that reflect general structures of the state machine being identified. These could be exploited later to *infer* reductions. For example, one might decide that when two position reports in the same axis (horizontal/vertical) are received in a row, the more recent overrides the other. PHEI.PHNE ⊢ PHNE is such a rule with ⊢ denoting the string rewrite relation. In any sequence one may replace substring PHEI.PHNE (not necessarily as a prefix), with PHNE (hence a string rewrite rule). String rewrite rules can be generalized from already identified sequence reductions. We consider two situations:

- A single reduction suggests a string rewrite rule. Suppose sequence u reduces to the prior sequence v. If $u = w_1 l w_2$, and $v = w_1 r w_2$ for some $w_1, w_2 \in S^*$, then $l \vdash r$ is a potential string rewrite rule.
- Two reductions suggest a string rewrite rule. Suppose sequences u and v both reduce to prior sequence w (w is prior to both u and v) and $u = w_1 l w_2$, $v = w_1 r w_2$ for some $w_1, w_2 \in S^*$, then $l \vdash r$ is a potential string rewrite rule.

We require r be length-lexicographically smaller than l for any string rewrite rule $l \vdash r$, so that rewriting is always towards a smaller sequence in length-lexicographic order for deriving sequence reductions. Also for any u in S^*, ul and ur must be Mealy equivalent. To summarize, a string rewrite rule can be defined for an enumeration with stimulus set S as follows:

If the following hold:
- either sequence u reduces to sequence v, or sequences u and v reduce to the common prior sequence w. In both cases $u = w_1 l w_2$, and $v = w_1 r w_2$ for some $w_1, w_2 \in S^*$,
- r is length-lexicographically smaller than l,
- ul and ur are Mealy equivalent to each other for all u in S^*,

then $l \vdash r$. (2)

We have seen one rule, PHEI.PHNE ⊢ PHNE. Another is PHEI.MHI ⊢ PHEI identified when one reduces START.PHEI.MHI to START.PHEI.

An enumeration with string rewrite rules implies a reduction system: S^* is the set, and $\rightarrow$ on S^* is defined by $u \rightarrow v$ if and only if there exist $w_1, w_2 \in S^*$ such that $u = w_1 l w_2$, $v = w_1 r w_2$, and $l \vdash r$ is a string rewrite rule. We showed in [8] (all the conclusions that follow in this paragraph) that every stimulus sequence to which string rewrite rules apply string-rewrites to a Mealy equivalent sequence. Rewriting continues until a normal form is reached. Rewriting is guaranteed to terminate, but there may be more than one normal form for a sequence.

3.4   Combining Prefix String-Rewriting with String-Rewriting

When enumerating stimulus sequences we may have prefix rewrite rules defined by (1) and string rewrite rules defined by (2). We can combine these rules in a *mixed* reduction system as follows. Reduction relation $\rightarrow$ on S^* is defined by $u \rightarrow v$ if and only if one or both of the two conditions hold: there exists w and prefix rewrite rule $l \models r$ such that $u = lw$ and $v = rw$; or there exists $w_1, w_2 \in S^*$ and string rewrite rule $l \vdash r$ such that $u = w_1 l w_2$ and $v = w_1 r w_2$. If (prefix or string) rewrite rules apply to a sequence u then u rewrites to a Mealy equivalent sequence [8]. Rewriting continues until a normal form is derived. As with string-rewriting, rewriting is guaranteed to terminate, and more than one normal form might be obtained. For an incomplete enumeration, the next sequence to be enumerated in length-lexicographic order must have a unique normal form [8].

The reduction system can be used to predict the reduction of the next sequence to be enumerated based on the prefix and string rewrite rules. If the unique normal form is different than the sequence itself, it suggests a sequence reduction. If the sequence itself and the derived unique normal form are identical, the human specifier takes over and considers possible reduction. This suggests that we can develop enumerations and reduction systems concurrently through the process in Table 7, until a complete enumeration is constructed.

Table 7. Major steps of enumeration process with string-rewriting support

---

1: Let the enumeration with the stimulus set S contain only the empty sequence λ, mapped to 0 and unreduced. No rules are defined. The reduction system has an empty set as the reduction relation.

2: Repeat the steps below until the enumeration is complete.

3: Derive the (unique) normal form (say v) of the next sequence (say u) to be enumerated in length-lexicographic order in the current enumeration, using the current reduction system.

4: The human specifier defines the response (say r) of u.

5: If $v = u$, then the human specifier redefines v such that u is reduced to v by Mealy equivalence and the enumeration rules. If u cannot be reduced to any prior sequence, let u be unreduced.

6: Let the enumeration contain the sequence u. u is mapped to r and is either unreduced, or reduced to v by Step 5.

7: If the response mapping and the equivalence declaration for u define a prefix rewrite rule $l \models r$ by (1), then add to the reduction relation (ly, ry) for all $y \in S^*$.

8: If the human specifier identifies string rewrite rule $l \vdash r$ by (2) given the equivalence declaration of u, then add to the reduction relation (xly, xry) for all $x, y \in S^*$.

Suppose we apply the process to the mirror controller (for the complete enumeration see [8]). We continue discovering rewrite rules as we enumerate, extending a reduction system while we extend an enumeration. The rules accumulate until they determine another reduction, then string-rewriting is applied automatically. In this example over half of the reductions for the length-four sequences

(69 of 108) were through automatic string-rewriting. This accounts for almost a third of reductions (69/217) needed for a complete enumeration.

4   Case Studies

We implemented the theory in our specification tool [18], and used it to construct the car door mirror example. We observe that once the rewrite rules are discovered, they can be checked against the requirements to see if correct decisions have been made, and against each other to see if such decisions have been made consistently. Table 8 shows the rules grouped by rule structures and semantics.

Table 8. Grouping rewrite rules based on structures and semantics

I	S_6: PHEI.MHI ⊢ PHEI S_{16}: PHEO.MHO ⊢ PHEO
	S_{35}: PVED.MVD ⊢ PVED S_{48}: PVEU.MVU ⊢ PVEU
II	S_{10}: PHEI.PHEI ⊢ PHEI S_{11}: PHEI.PHEO ⊢ PHEO
	S_{12}: PHEI.PHNE ⊢ PHNE S_{19}: PHEO.PHEI ⊢ PHEI
	S_{20}: PHEO.PHEO ⊢ PHEO S_{21}: PHEO.PHNE ⊢ PHNE
	S_{28}: PHNE.PHEI ⊢ PHEI S_{29}: PHNE.PHEO ⊢ PHEO
	S_{30}: PHNE.PHNE ⊢ PHNE S_{40}: PVED.PVED ⊢ PVED
	S_{41}: PVED.PVEU ⊢ PVEU S_{42}: PVED.PVNE ⊢ PVNE
	S_{52}: PVEU.PVED ⊢ PVED S_{53}: PVEU.PVEU ⊢ PVEU
	S_{54}: PVEU.PVNE ⊢ PVNE S_{64}: PVNE.PVED ⊢ PVED
	S_{65}: PVNE.PVEU ⊢ PVEU S_{66}: PVNE.PVNE ⊢ PVNE
	$x.y \vdash y$, where $x, y \in$ {PHEI, PHEO, PHNE}
	$x.y \vdash y$, where $x, y \in$ {PVED, PVEU, PVNE}
III	S_{13}: PHEI.SM ⊢ SM S_{22}: PHEO.SM ⊢ SM
	S_{31}: PHNE.SM ⊢ SM S_{43}: PVED.SM ⊢ SM
	S_{55}: PVEU.SM ⊢ SM S_{67}: PVNE.SM ⊢ SM
	$x.$SM ⊢ SM, where $x \in$ {PHEI, PHEO, PHNE, PVED, PVEU, PVNE}
IV	S_{37}: PVED.PHEI ⊢ PHEI.PVED S_{38}: PVED.PHEO ⊢ PHEO.PVED
	S_{39}: PVED.PHNE ⊢ PHNE.PVED S_{49}: PVEU.PHEI ⊢ PHEI.PVEU
	S_{50}: PVEU.PHEO ⊢ PHEO.PVEU S_{51}: PVEU.PHNE ⊢ PHNE.PVEU
	S_{61}: PVNE.PHEI ⊢ PHEI.PVNE S_{62}: PVNE.PHEO ⊢ PHEO.PVNE
	S_{63}: PVNE.PHNE ⊢ PHNE.PVNE
	$x.y \vdash y.x$, where $x \in$ {PVED, PVEU, PVNE}, $y \in$ {PHEI, PHEO, PHNE}
V	S_{69}: SM.MHI ⊢ SM S_{70}: SM.MHO ⊢ SM
	S_{71}: SM.MVD ⊢ SM S_{72}: SM.MVU ⊢ SM
	SM.x ⊢ SM, where $x \in$ {MHI, MHO, MVD, MVU}

One might further identify patterns. For example, Group II shows a decision regarding receiving consecutive position reports in the same axis (horizontal or vertical). Only the latest report is important (this can be validated by domain experts). Since there are three reports for each axis, the number of such rules is $3 \times 3 \times 2 = 18$. The fact that Group II contains all the 18 rules demonstrates that this decision has been made consistently throughout the enumeration.

We can also augment our theory and discover more string rewrite rules by taking into consideration sequences that do not show up in the enumeration table, or sequences with specific patterns. Details are not discussed here due to the page limit (interested readers should see [8]). With these observations almost 90% of the length-four sequences and half of the total reductions would be derived automatically by string-rewriting. Table 9 shows the statistics.

Table 9. Percentages of automatic sequence reductions by applying rewriting

	With presented theory	With presented theory and observations
Length-four sequences only	$69/108 \approx 63.9\%$	$96/108 \approx 88.9\%$
All sequences in the enumeration	$69/217 \approx 31.8\%$	$103/217 \approx 47.5\%$

Table 10 shows for the car mirror ECU and each enumeration length: the number of sequences extended from the previous length, the number of sequences analyzed, as well as the potential number of sequences to be considered. For analyzed sequences we also record how many reductions are handled by string-rewriting and by humans. This shows the effectiveness of enumeration in controlling the combinatorial growth of the number of sequences to be examined.

Table 10. Sequences analyzed in the car mirror ECU enumeration

Length	Sequences Extended	Sequences Analyzed	Reductions by String-Rewriting	Reductions by Humans	Potential Sequences
0	0	1	0	1	1
1	1	12	0	12	12
2	1	12	0	12	144
3	7	84	7	77	1,728
4	9	108	96	12	20,736
total	18	217	103	114	22,621

We also applied the enumeration process to three published applications:

- *Satellite Operations Software (SOS)*: software component of a space vehicle that processes commands from the ground control system and supplies communications between an uplink ground site and a downlink ground site [21]
- *Mine Pump Controller Software (MPCS)*: control software of a mine pump that detects the water level, monitors carbon monoxide, methane and airflow levels, and operates the pump with assistance from human operators [11]
- *Weigh-In-Motion Data Acquisition Processor (WIMDAP)*: software for data acquisition used in a weigh-in-motion distributed system that acquires and processes data from load cells, performs real-time monitoring of the analog weight signal, and communicates asynchronously with the host computer [25]

We summarize the result in Table 11 (for the enumerations see [16,22,26]). The benefit of applying string-rewriting depends on the application and the skill of the analyst. For instance, the small number of automatic reduction derivations for the satellite operations software is because the state machine is essentially a chain with little branching. In any case the discovered rewrite rules help articulate unstated patterns or facts that are implicit in the requirements and provide additional criteria for validating specification decisions to requirements.

Table 11. Sequences analyzed in the three published applications

Application	SOS	MPCS	WIMDAP
Number of stimuli	23	10	14
Terminating enumeration length	9	5	4
Sequences extended	11	22	13
Sequences analyzed	254	265	219
Reductions by string-rewriting	17	47	58
Reductions by humans	237	218	161
Potential sequences	1,883,023,236,984	111,111	41,371

5 Related Work

Sequence-based specification emerged from the functional treatment of software described by Mills [13–15]. The development was most directly influenced by the *trace assertion method* of Parnas [1,17] and the algebraic treatment of regular expressions by Brzozowski [5]. One primary distinction of sequence-based specification is the constructive process used to discover a state machine model.

Rewriting systems were studied for *deterministic* versions of the trace assertion method [6,7,23,24]. The free choice of canonical traces in [23,24] (as representatives of equivalence classes), and a prefix-closed set of unreduced sequences by construction for any sequence-based specification manifest in the respective applications of rewriting.

In [23,24] a general trace rewriting relation is used and modified to address possibly non-terminating rewriting sequences. "Smart trace rewriting" was introduced to avoid unfruitful rewriting steps, resulting in a constrained prefix string-rewriting system that guarantees a unique normal form for every string.

Trace rewriting systems [6,7] algorithmically transform any word of a connected semiautomaton to its canonical form. It is shown that if one imposes prefix-continuity on the set of canonical words, the constructed prefix string-rewriting system is well-behaved. Prefix-continuous sets include prefix-closed sets as a special case. In a sequence-based specification the set of unreduced sequences is prefix-closed by construction.

Our work differs from the previous work in that rewriting techniques are applied to assist in the discovery of a state machine from requirements, and to augment the enumeration process with increased automation. We used unconditional forms of string-rewriting and prefix string-rewriting, and combined them in a mixed reduction system.

6   Conclusion

This paper described a method that used string-rewriting to automate parts of sequence enumeration. Two types of rewrite rules were outlined. Prefix rewrite rules are of the form $l \models r$ for sequences l and r. Such a rule says that l and r take the system to Mealy equivalent states when applied in the initial state. Thus, we can rewrite a sequence of the form $u = lw$ to $v = rw$. String rewrite rules generalised this by not requiring the rewriting to occur at the beginning of a sequence. Such a rule $l \vdash r$ allows one to rewrite a sequence of the form $u = w_1 l w_2$ to $v = w_1 r w_2$. Given a set of rewrite rules, it is possible to automatically determine whether a sequence u, being considered in sequence enumeration, rewrites to a sequence v previously considered. If this is the case then there is no need to extend u: we know that it reduces to v.

The prefix and string rewrite rules initially used will depend on domain knowledge. However, we also discussed heuristics that allow the developer to identify potential additional rules. Automation has the potential to both reduce the cost and time involved in sequence enumeration but also to reduce the scope for human error. In addition to outlining this method, we discussed four case studies. Our results are promising, although the degree to which application of these rewrite rules will expedite the enumeration process will vary with the application. The tool enforces the mathematics but hides the details. The proposed method also provides an opportunity for validation of specification decisions to requirements. This is valuable in offering a new insight or articulating an important fact about the requirements that was unstated.

Current research is focused on other practical matters relevant to the application and development of sequence-based specification. For instance, we expect a thorough treatment of abstractions and abstraction management to produce benefits. As application is usually facilitated by separation of inputs that do not interact (to reduce the size of the input alphabet in an enumeration), composition of sequence-based specifications is also of interest.

References

1. Bartussek, W., Parnas, D.L.: Using assertions about traces to write abstract specifications for software modules. In: Proceedings of the 2nd Conference of the European Cooperation on Informatics, Venice, Italy, pp. 211–236 (1978)
2. Bauer, T., Beletski, T., Boehr, F., Eschbach, R., Landmann, D., Poore, J.: From requirements to statistical testing of embedded systems. In: Proceedings of the 4th International Workshop on Software Engineering for Automotive Systems, Minneapolis, MN, pp. 3–9 (2007)
3. Book, R.V., Otto, F.: String-Rewriting Systems. Springer, Berlin (1993)
4. Broadfoot, G.H., Broadfoot, P.J.: Academia and industry meet: Some experiences of formal methods in practice. In: Proceedings of the 10th Asia-Pacific Software Engineering Conference, Chiang Mai, Thailand, pp. 49–59 (2003)
5. Brzozowski, J.: Derivatives of regular expressions. Journal of the ACM 11(4), 481–494 (1964)

6. Brzozowski, J., Jürgensen, H.: Theory of deterministic trace-assertion specifications. Technical report CS-2004-30, University of Waterloo (2004)
7. Brzozowski, J., Jürgensen, H.: Representation of semiautomata by canonical words and equivalences. International Journal of Foundations of Computer Science 16(5), 831–850 (2005)
8. Eschbach, R., Lin, L., Poore, J.H.: Applying string-rewriting to sequence-based specification. Technical report ut-cs-12-692, University of Tennessee, Knoxville (2012), http://web.eecs.utk.edu/~library/TechReports/2012/ut-cs-12-692. pdf
9. Gill, A.: Introduction to the Theory of Finite-State Machines. McGraw-Hill, New York (1962)
10. Hopcroft, P.J., Broadfoot, G.H.: Combining the box structure development method and CSP for software development. Electronic Notes in Theoretical Computer Science 128(6), 127–144 (2005)
11. Joseph, M. (ed.): Real-Time Systems: Specification, Verification and Analysis. Prentice Hall International, London (1996)
12. Lin, L., Prowell, S.J., Poore, J.H.: An axiom system for sequence-based specification. Theoretical Computer Science 411(2), 360–376 (2010)
13. Linger, R.C., Mills, H.D., Witt, B.I.: Structured Programming: Theory and Practice. Addison-Wesley, Boston (1979)
14. Mills, H.D.: Stepwise refinement and verification in box-structured systems. IEEE Computer 21(6), 23–36 (1988)
15. Mills, H.D.: The new math of computer programming. Communications of the ACM 18(1), 43–48 (1975)
16. MPCS: Mine pump controller software enumeration (2012), http://sqrl.eecs.utk.edu/btw/files/MPCS_sr.html
17. Parnas, D.L., Wang, Y.: The trace assertion method of module interface specification. Technical report 89-261, Queens University (1989)
18. Proto_Seq: ESP project (2012), http://sqrl.eecs.utk.edu/esp/index.html
19. Prowell, S.J., Poore, J.H.: Sequence-based software specification of deterministic systems. Software: Practice and Experience 28(3), 329–344 (1998)
20. Prowell, S.J., Poore, J.H.: Foundations of sequence-based software specification. IEEE Transactions on Software Engineering 29(5), 417–429 (2003)
21. Prowell, S.J., Trammell, C.J., Linger, R.C., Poore, J.H.: Cleanroom Software Engineering: Technology and Process. Addison-Wesley, Reading (1999)
22. SOS: Satellite operations software enumeration (2012), http://sqrl.eecs.utk.edu/btw/files/SOS_sr.html
23. Wang, Y., Parnas, D.L.: Simulating the behavior of software modules by trace rewriting. IEEE Transactions on Software Engineering 20(10), 750–759 (1994)
24. Wang, Y., Parnas, D.L.: Simulating the behavior of software modules by trace rewriting. In: Proceedings of the 15th International Conference on Software Engineering, Baltimore, MD, pp. 14–23 (1993)
25. Weigh-In-Motion: Weigh-In-Motion, Cube Management, and Marking User Manual, Oak Ridge National Laboratory, Oak Ridge, TN, Version 0.8.2. (2006)
26. WIMDAP: Weigh-in-motion data acquisition processor enumeration (2012), http://sqrl.eecs.utk.edu/btw/files/WIMDAP_sr.html

Scenario Realizability with Constraint Optimization*

Rouwaida Abdallah[1], Arnaud Gotlieb[2], Loïc Hélouët[3], and Claude Jard[4]

[1] ENS Cachan (antenne de Bretagne)
[2] SIMULA, Norway
[3] INRIA Rennes
[4] Université de Nantes
rouwaida.abdallah@irisa.fr, {arnaud.gotlieb,loic.helouet}@inria.fr,
claude.jard@univ-nantes.fr

Abstract. This work considers implementation of requirements expressed as High-level Message Sequence Charts (HMSCs). All HMSCs are not implementable, but a particular subclass called local HMSCs can be implemented using a simple projection operation. This paper proposes a new technique to transform an arbitrary HMSC specification into a local HMSC, hence allowing implementation. We show that this transformation can be automated as a constraint optimization problem. The impact of modifications brought to the original specification can be minimized w.r.t. a cost function. The approach was evaluated on a large number of randomly generated HMSCs. The results show an average runtime of a few seconds, which demonstrates applicability of the technique.

1 Introduction

In many system development methodologies, the user first specifies the system's use cases. Some specific instantiations of each use case are then aggregated and described using a formal language. In the context of distributed applications we consider, *high-level message sequence charts* (HMSCs) and their variants are very popular. They are standardized by the ITU [9], and a variant called *sequence diagrams* is part of the UML notation. HMSCs are particularly useful in early stages of development to describe interactions between processes (or objects).

In a later modeling step of the development, state diagrams (i.e. automata) prescribe a behavior for each of the processes. Finally, the processes are implemented as code in a specific programming language. **Parts of this design flow can be automated**. We consider here the automated transformation of HMSCs into the model of *communicating finite state machines* (CFSMs), which will serve as a skeleton for the development of future code. The produced CFSM model is called the implementation of the HMSC.

However, HMSCs are not always implementable. HMSCs are automata labelled by communication patterns involving several processes. When a choice

---

* Work supported by the ANR IMPRO(ANR-2010-BLAN-0317) of the French National Agency for Research.

V. Cortellessa and D. Varró (Eds.): FASE 2013, LNCS 7793, pp. 194–209, 2013.

between two patterns exists, all processes are assumed to behave according to the same pattern. However, in CFSM, processes are independent, and the global coordination of HMSCs might be lost in implementations when the HMSC is not *local*. A non-local HMSC contains a choice between two patterns in which the first events to be executed occur on distinct processes. Implementations of non-local HMSCs may exhibit more behaviors than the original specification, and can even deadlock. Non-local HMSCs can be considered as too incomplete or too abstract to be implemented. On the other hand, local HMSCs avoid the global coordination problem, and can always be implemented.

This paper proposes to extend the possibility of automated production of CFSMs by the use of a **localization procedure** that transforms any non-local HMSC into a local one. It guarantees that every choice in the transformed local HMSC has a *leader process*, which chooses one scenario and communicates its choice to the other processes. This can be achieved by adding new messages and processes in scenarios. Trivial but uninteresting solutions to the localization problem exist (force all processes to participate in all interactions, and choose the same leader for every choice). We are thus interested in finding solutions with the minimal number of added messages because they correspond to the less disturbing transformation of the specification. In our work, we propose to address the localization problem with a constraint optimization technique. We build a constraint model where variables represent leader processes or processes contributing to a scenario and constraints capture the localization properties of HMSCs. A cost function is then proposed to minimize the number of added messages. The experiments we ran on a large class of randomly generated HMSCs show that localization takes in general a few seconds on ordinary machines.

Several works address automatic synthesis from scenario models. We refer interested reader to [10] for a survey on synthesis algorithms. The question of whether an HMSC specification can be implemented by an equivalent CFSM was shown undecidable in general [2,11], so the key issue is to rely on implementable classes of HMSCs. Several CFSM implementation techniques have been proposed for local HMSCs [7,8,1], or regular HMSC [3]. A variant of HMSCs, where communication patterns label shared high-level actions of a network of automata is translated to Petri nets in [14]. Up to our knowledge, no algorithm was proposed so far to transform non-local specifications into local ones.

This paper is organized as follows: Section 2 gives the basic formal definitions on HMSCs. Section 3 defines localization of HMSCs. Section 4 proposes an encoding of localization as a constraint optimization problem, and shows the correctness of the approach. Section 5 evaluates the performance of our localization procedure with an experimentation, and comments the results. Section 6 concludes this work. For space reasons, proof of theorems are omitted, but can be found in a full version available at: http://hal.inria.fr/hal-00769656.

2   Basic Definitions

Message Sequence Charts (MSCs for short) describe the behavior of entities of a system called *instances*. It is frequently assumed that instances represent processes of a distributed system. MSCs have a graphical and textual notation, but are also equipped with a standardized semantics [13]. The language is composed of two kinds of diagrams. At the lowest level, basic MSCs (or bMSCs for short) describe interactions among instances. The communications are asynchronous. A second layer of formalism, namely High-level MSCs (HMSCs for short), is used to compose these basic diagrams. Roughly speaking, an HMSC is an automaton which transitions are labeled by bMSCs, or by references to other HMSCs. However, in the paper, we will consider without loss of generality that our specifications are given by only two layers of formalism: a set of bMSCs, and an HMSC with transitions labeled by these bMSCs.

Definition 1 (bMSCs). *A bMSC defined over a set of instances $\mathcal{P}$ is a tuple $M = (E, \leq, \lambda, \phi, \mu)$ where E is a finite set of events, $\phi : E \longrightarrow \mathcal{P}$ localizes each event on one instance. $\lambda : E \longrightarrow \Sigma$ is a labeling function that associates a type of action to each event. The label attached to a sending event is of the form $p!q(m)$ denoting a sending of message m from p to q. Similarly, the label attached to a reception is of the form $p?q(m)$ denoting a reception on p of a message m sent by q. Last, events labeled by $p(a)$ represent a local action a of process p. Labeling defines a partition of E into sets of sending events, reception events, and local actions, respectively denoted by E_S, E_R and E_L. $\mu : E_S \longrightarrow E_R$ is a bijection that maps sending events with a corresponding reception. If $\mu(e) = f$, then $\lambda(e) = p!q(m)$ for some p, q, m and $\lambda(f) = q?p(m)$. $\leq \subseteq E^2$ is a partial order relation called the causal order.*

It is required that events of the same instance are totally ordered: $\forall(e_1, e_2) \in E^2, \phi(e_1) = \phi(e_2) \Longrightarrow (e_1 \leq e_2) \vee (e_2 \leq e_1)$. For an instance p, let us call $\leq_p$ this total order. $\leq$ must also reflect the causality induced by the message exchanges, i.e. $\leq = (\bigcup_{p \in \mathcal{P}} \leq_p \cup \mu)^*$. The graphical representation of bMSCs defines instances as vertical lines. All events executed by an instance are ordered from top to bottom. Horizontal arrows represent messages from one instance to another. Figure 1-a) is an example of bMSC, with three instances A, B, C, exchanging two messages m_1, m_2. The events $e1$ and $e3$ are sending events, and the events $e2$ and $e4$ are the corresponding receptions.

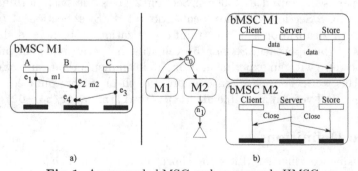

Fig. 1. An example bMSC and an example HMSC

For a bMSC M, we will denote by $min(M) = \{e \in E \mid \forall e' \in E, \ e' \leq e \Rightarrow e' = e\}$, the set of minimal events of M. Intuitively, each event in $min(M)$ can be the first event executed in M. An instance is called *minimal* if it carries a minimal event. A minimal instance (i.e. a process in $\phi(min(M))$) is an instance that can execute the first events in M. In other words, it can *decide* to start executing M rather than another scenario. A bMSC is *local* if it has a single minimal instance.

The semantics of a bMSC M is denoted by $Lin(M)$, and defined as the linearizations of M, that is sequences of actions that follow the causal ordering imposed by M. We refer interested readers to the full version for details. Basic MSCs only describe finite interactions. They have been extended with HMSCs to allow iteration, choices, and parallel composition. For simplicity, we restrict to HMSCs without parallel frames, and with only one hierarchical level. With these assumptions, HMSCs can be seen as automata labeled by bMSCs.

Definition 2 (HMSCs). *An HMSC is a graph $H = (I, N, \rightarrow, \mathcal{M}, n_0)$, where I is a finite set of instances, N is a finite set of nodes, $n_0 \in N$ is the initial node of H, $\mathcal{M}$ is a finite set of bMSCs, defined over disjoint set of events, and $\rightarrow \subseteq N \times \mathcal{M} \times N$ is the transition relation.*

In the rest of the paper, we consider without loss of generality that all nodes, except possibly the initial node and sink nodes, are choice nodes (i.e. have several successors by the transition relation). We will denote by $\mathcal{P}_i$ the set of active processes that interacts within a bMSC $M_i \in \mathcal{M}$. HMSCs also have a graphical representation: Nodes are represented by circles, references to bMSCs by boxes. The initial node of an HMSC is connected to a downward pointing triangle, and final nodes to an upward pointing triangle. The example of Figure 1-b) shows an example of HMSC, with two nodes n_0, n_1. Intuitively, this HMSC depicts a protocol in which three processes exchange data, before closing a session. This very simple HMSC allows for the definition of iterations: bMSC $M1$ can be repeated several times before the execution of bMSC $M2$. Note however that even if a bMSC $M1$ is seen before a bMSC $M2$ along a path of H, this does not mean that all events of $M1$ are executed before $M2$ starts. The semantics of an HMSC is defined using *sequential composition* of bMSCs.

We do not define formally sequential composition of bMSCs, and refer interested readers to the full version. Intuitively, composing sequentially two bMSCs M_1 and M_2 consists in drawing M_2 below M_1 to obtain a new bMSC. The sequential composition is denoted by $M_1 \circ M_2$. From this intuitive definition, we can immediately notice that if some events in $min(M_2)$ are located on processes that do not appear in M_1, then they are also minimal in $M_1 \circ M_2$. This raises two important remarks: first, executing $M_1 \circ M_2$ does not mean executing M_1 then M_2, but rather executing the bMSC obtained by concatenation of M_1 and M_2, and then minimal events in a concatenation $M_1 \circ \ldots M_k$ are not all located in M_1.

A *path* of H is a sequence of transitions $\rho = (n_1, M_1, n'_1) \ldots (n_k, M_1, n'_k)$ such that $n'_i = n_{i+1}$. A path is called *initial* if it starts from node n_0. Each path $\rho = (n_1, M_1, n'_1) \ldots (n_k, M_1, n'_k)$ defines a unique bMSC $M^\rho = M_1 \circ M_2 \cdots \circ M_k$. The semantics $\mathcal{L}(H)$ of a HMSC H is defined as the set of linearizations of all bMSCs M^ρ such that ρ is an initial path of H. With this semantics, HMSCs are very expressive. They are more expressive than finite state machines (they can describe non-regular behaviors, as shown by the example of Figure 1-b)).

The *implementation problem* consists in building a set of communicating machines $\mathcal{A} = \{A_1, \ldots A_k\}$ (one frequently uses as model the Communicating Finite State Machines (CFSM) proposed by [5]) such that $\mathcal{L}(\mathcal{A}) = \mathcal{L}(H)$. It is frequently assumed that these communicating machines are obtained by simple projection of the original HMSC on each instance. The *realizability problem* consists in deciding whether there exists an implementation $\mathcal{A}$ such that $\mathcal{L}(\mathcal{A}) = \mathcal{L}(H)$. Realizability was shown undecidable in general [2,11]. On the other hand, several papers have shown automatic and correct synthesis techniques for subclasses of HMSCs [7,8,3,1]. The largest known subclass is that of local HMSCs [4]. These results clearly show that automatic implementation can not apply in general to HMSC. However, non-local HMSCs can be considered as too abstract to be implemented, and need some refinement to be implementable. In the rest of the paper, we hence focus on a transformation mechanism that transforms an arbitrary HMSC into a local (and hence implementable) HMSC.

Let us consider the example of Figure 1-b). Node n_0 is a choice node, depicting a choice between two behaviors: either continue to send data (bMSC M_1), or close the data transmission (bMSC M_2). However, the deciding instance in M_1 is the *Client*, while the deciding instance in M_2 is the *Server*. At implementation time, this may result in a situation where *Client* decides to perform M_1 and *Server* decide concurrently to perform M_2, leading to a deadlock of the protocol. Such situation is called a non-local choice, and obviously causes implementation problems. It is then safer to implement HMSCs without non-local choices. At each choice, a single deciding instance chooses to perform one scenario, and all other non-deciding instances must conform to this choice.

Definition 3 (Local choice node). *Let $H = (I, N, \rightarrow, \mathcal{M}, n_0)$ be an HMSC. Let $c \in N$, c is a local choice if and only if for every pair of (non necessarily distinct) paths $\rho = (c, M_1, n_1)(n_1, M_2, n_2) \ldots (n_k, M_k, n_{k+1})$ and $\rho' = (c, M_1', n_1')(n_1', M_2', n_2') \ldots (n_q', M_k', n_{q+1}')$ there is a single minimal instance in M^ρ and in $M^{\rho'}$ (i.e. $\phi(min(M^\rho)) = \phi(min(M^{\rho'}))$ and $|\phi(min(M^\rho))| = 1$). H is called a local HMSC if all its nodes are local.*

Due to the semantics of concatenation, non-locality can not be checked on a pair of bMSCs leaving node c, but has to be checked for pairs of paths. Intuitively, locality of an HMSC H guarantees that every choice in H is controlled by a unique deciding instance. Checking whether an HMSC is local is decidable [8], and one can show that this question is in co-NP [1]. It was shown in [7] that for a local HMSC $H = (I, N, \rightarrow, \mathcal{M}, n_0)$, if for every $M_i \in \mathcal{M}$ we have $P_i = I$, then there exists a CFSM $\mathcal{A}$ such that $\mathcal{L}(\mathcal{A}) = \mathcal{L}(H)$. A solution was proposed to leverage this restriction in [1], and allow implementation of *any* local HMSC.

An immediate question that arises is: how to implement non-local HMSCs? In the rest of the paper, we propose a solution that transforms any non-local HMSC into a local one, hence allowing its implementation. This results in slight modifications of the original specification. We allow additional active instances and new messages in bMSCs, but do not change the structure of the HMSC. Consider the example of Figure 1-b). Replacing M_1 by the bMSC M_3 of Figure 2 solves the non-local choice problem. Similarly, replacing M_1 and M_2 respectively by M_4 and M_5 solves the the non-locality problem, but needs more messages.

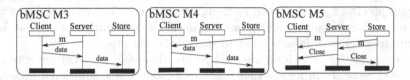

Fig. 2. Solutions for localization of HMSC in Figure 1-b)

This example raises several remarks. First, the proposed transformations are purely syntactic, and modifying the set of minimal instances does not always produce a meaningful specification. For this reason, the examples exhibit changes involving a single message type m. A meaning for additional message has to be chosen adequately by the designer once an HMSC is localized. The second remark is that there are several possibilities for localization. The first solution proposed adds one message in bMSC M_1 to obtain M_3. The second solution adds one message to M_1 and two to M_2, and one can notice that in M_5, the message between *Store* and *Client* is useless. Indeed, there exists an infinite number of transformations to localize an HMSC. This calls for the following solutions: we want to restrict to cheapest solutions (for instance solutions with a minimal number of added messages). As we will show later, once a deciding instance for a choice is fixed, one can compute the minimal number of messages needed to localize this choice. As a consequence, the solutions to a localization problem can be given in terms of choosing a deciding instances at each choice, and instances participating to bMSCs. Then, the localization can be easily tuned using different cost functions.

3   Localization of HMSCs

In this section, we show how to transform a non-local HMSC into a local one. This procedure called *localization* consists in choosing a single deciding instance for each bMSC M in the HMSC so that all choices become local, and then ensure that all other instances execute their minimal events only after the first event (the *choice*) of the deciding instance. This is done by adding messages, as in the examples of Fig. 2.

Definition 4. *Let M be a bMSC over a set of events E and processes P, with minimal events $e_1, \ldots, e_k$. A localized extension of M is a bMSC M' over a set of events $E' \supseteq E$ and over $P' \supseteq P$, such that there exists a minimal event $e_{min} \in E'$ and for every $e \leq f \in E$, we have $e \leq' f$. The unique minimal instance in a localized bMSC M is called the* leader *of M.*

Note that as there exists an infinite number of extensions for a bMSC M, choosing extensions that are as close as possible to the original model is desirable. The impact of localization can be simply measured as the number of added messages. A more generic approach is to associate a cost to communications between processes, and to choose extensions with minimal cost. This makes sense, as for instance the cost and delays for communications via satellite are higher than with ground networks. Similarly, the configuration of a system may prevent two processes p and q from exchanging messages. To avoid solutions with communications between p and q, one can design a cost function that associates a redhibitory (or even infinite) cost to such communications.

For a given bMSC M with k minimal events, there exists a localized extension over the same set of processes that contains exactly $k - 1$ additional messages. This localized extension is built when one picks up a deciding instance among the d the minimal instances of M, and create causal dependencies from the minimal event on instance d to all other minimal events with additional messages. Only $k - 1$ messages are necessary in this case, regardless to their respective ordering and place of insertion in the orginal bMSC. Another possibility is to pick up another non-minimal process among those of M that do not carry a minimal event as a leader, or even add a new process to M. In such cases, a localized extension can always be built with exactly k additional messages.

Localization of HMSCs is more complex than localization of bMSCs. For each non-local choice c, we have to ensure that *every branch* leaving c has the same leader. Hence, this is not a property purely local to bMSCs. As for bMSCs, we can define a notion of localized extension of a HMSC as follows:

Definition 5. Let $H = (I, N, \longrightarrow, \mathcal{M}, n_0)$ be an HMSC. $H' = (I, N, \longrightarrow', \mathcal{M}', n_0)$ is a localized extension of H iff there is a bijection $f : \mathcal{M} \to \mathcal{M}'$ such that $\forall M \in \mathcal{M}$, $f(M)$ is a localized extension of M, $\longrightarrow' = f(\longrightarrow)$, and H' is a local HMSC.

Localizing an HMSC H consists in finding $\mathcal{M}'$ and the bijection f. As mentionned above, as there exists a (potentially) infinite number of solutions, we consider the solutions with the smallest number of changes to the original model. We propose to address this problem with a cost function $\mathcal{F}$ that evaluates the cost of each possible transformation of H. The goal of our localization algorithm is thus to minimize $\mathcal{F}$. For the sake of simplicity in this paper, $\mathcal{F}$ counts the total number of messages and instances added in $\mathcal{M}'$. As localization transforms $\mathcal{M}$ into $\mathcal{M}'$, $\mathcal{F}$ is defined as a sum of individual costs of modifications. Formally,

$$\mathcal{F}(H, H') \triangleq \sum_{M \in \mathcal{M}} c_{M, f(M)}$$

where $c_{M,M'}$ is the individual cost to transform M into M'. When H is clear from the context, we will write $\mathcal{F}(H')$ instead of $\mathcal{F}(H, H')$. Let $M_i \in \mathcal{M}$ be a bMSC, $M_i' = f(M_i)$, I_{M_i}, $I_{M_i'}$ be the set of instances in M_i and M_i'. Let $k = |min(M_i)|$ be the number of minimal instances in M_i, l be the leader instance of M_i', and $x = |I_{M_i'}| - |I_{M_i}|$ be the number of new instances in M_i. We choose a constant $\theta \in [0, 1]$ and define the cost $c_{M_i, M_i'}$ for transforming M_i into M_i' as follows:

$$c_{M_i,M_i'} \triangleq \begin{cases} x * \theta + (k + x - 1) * (1 - \theta) & \text{if } l \in \phi(min(M_i)) \text{ or } l \notin I_{M_i} \\ x * \theta + (k + x) * (1 - \theta) & \text{otherwise} \end{cases}$$

Intuitively, $c_{M_i,M_i'}$ is the *barycenter* between the number of added messages, and the number of added instances, weighted by θ. We already know that the number of messages to add is at most $k - 1$ if we have k minimal instances. Adding x instances to M_i hence yields adding $(k + x - 1)$ messages if l is chosen among the minimal instances of M_i or among the new instances. Similarly, if the leader instance is chosen among instances that are not minimal w.r.t the causal ordering, one need to add $k + x$ messages to localize M_i. The value θ is chosen to penalize more the number of added processes or the number of added messages.

Let us illustrate the computation of $\mathcal{F}$ on an example. Let H_c be the HMSC on the right of Figure 3, and let H_c' be a localization of H_c. As mentionned above, $\mathcal{F}(H_c, H_c') = c_{M_1,M_1'} + c_{M_2,M_2'} + c_{M_3,M_3'}$. The leader of M_1' is C and, as $C \in min(M_1) = \{A, C\}$, then $c_{M_1'} = 1 - \theta$ (there is a single message added in M_1'). The leader of M_2' is also C, but C is not an instance of M_2, so $c_{M_2'} = \theta + (1 - \theta) = 1$ (there is a single message and a single instance added in M_2'). The leader of M_3' is again C. As C is an instance of M_3 but not a minimal instance we have $c_{M_3'} = 2 * (1 - \theta)$. As a result, $\mathcal{F}(H_c, H_c') = 1 - \theta + 1 + 2 * (1 - \theta) = 4 - 3 * \theta$. One can easily notice that H_c' is local. If we compare H_c with another localization H_c'', depicted at the right of Figure 3, we get that $c_{M_1,M_1''} = 2 - \theta$, $c_{M_2,M_2''} = 1$, $c_{M_3,M_3''} = 1 - \theta$ and finally, $\mathcal{F}(H_c, H_c'') = 4 - 2 * \theta$. Then $\mathcal{F}(H_c, H_c') \leq \mathcal{F}(H_c, H_c'')$ and thus, localization H_c' shoud be preferred to H_c''. This example shows that the cost funtion influences the choice of a particular localization solution.

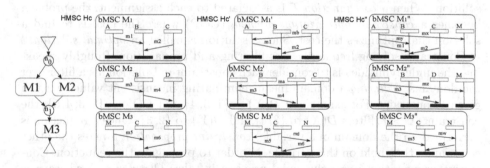

Fig. 3. localizing the HMSC Hc

The cost function $\mathcal{F}$ defined above that counts the number of new messages and processes in bMSCs is only an example, and other functions can be considered. For instance, a cost function can consider concurrency among events as an important property to preserve, and thus impose a penality everytime a pair of events e, e' is causally ordered in $f(M)$, but not in M.

Note also that several localization solutions can have the same cost. For instance, if $\mathcal{F}$ is used, the order in which messages are exchanged to obtain localized bMSCs is ignored. Considering that the cost function is influenced only by the number of added messages and added processes, we define $\mathcal{F}(H, \{(I_{M'}, l_{M'})\}_{M \in \mathcal{M}})$ as being the cost of a localization of H that satisfies $I_{M'} = I_{f(M)}$, where $f(M)$ has $l_{M'}$ as leader for every $M \in \mathcal{M}$. The localization problem can be formally defined as follows:

Definition 6. *Let $H = (I, N, \longrightarrow, \mathcal{M}, n_0)$ be a non-local HMSC, and $\mathcal{F}$ be a cost function. The* localization *problem for $H, \mathcal{F}$ consists in returning solutions $s_1, \ldots, s_k$, where each s_i is of the form $s_i = \{(I'_M, l'_M)\}_{M \in \mathcal{M}}$ such that $\mathcal{F}(H, \{(I_{M'}, l_{M'})\}_{M \in \mathcal{M}})$ is minimal, and where for each $M \in \mathcal{M}$, $I_{M'} \subseteq I$ is a set of instances appearing in $M' = f(M)$ and $l_{M'} \in I_{M'}$ is the leader of M'.*

4   Localization as a Constraint Optimization Problem

This section explains how a finite domain constraint optimization model is constructed from a given HMSC, to minimize the cost of the localization.

4.1   Constraint Solving over Finite Domains

A *constraint solving problem* is composed of a finite set of *variables* $X_1, \ldots, X_n$, where each variable X_i ranges over a finite *domain*, noted $D(X_i)$. An assignment of a variable is a choice of a value from its domain. A set of *constraints* $C_1, \ldots, C_m$ is defined over the variables and the goal in a constraint solving problem is to find *solutions*, i.e., assignments for all variables, that satisfy all constraints. A constraint solving problem is *satisfiable* if it allows at least one solution. When a *cost function* $\mathcal{F}$ is associated to each assignment, the problem becomes a *constraint optimization problem* (COP) where the goal is to find a solution that optimizes the cost. Such a solution is called an *optimal solution*.

Constraint solving frequently uses filtering and propagation. Roughly speaking, the underlying idea is to consider each constraint in isolation, as a filter over the domains. *Filtering* a domain means eliminating inconsistent values w.r.t. a given a constraint. For example, if $D(X) = \{1, 3, 4\}$ and $D(Y) = \{2, 3, 4, 5\}$, the constraint $X > Y$ filters $D(X)$ to $\{3, 4\}$ and $D(Y)$ to $\{2, 3\}$. Once a reduction is performed on the domain of a variable, *constraint propagation* awakes the other constraints that hold on this variable, in order to propagate the reduction. Constraint propagation is a polynomial process: it takes $O(n * m * d)$ where n is the number of variables, m is the number of constraints and d is the maximum number of possible values in the domains.

Constraint propagation and filtering alone do not guarantee satisfiability, and just prune the domains without trying to instantiate variables. For example, considering the constraint system shown above, the constraint $X > Y$ prunes the domains $D(X)$ to $\{3, 4\}$ and $D(Y)$ to $\{2, 3\}$ but $(3, 3)$ is not a solution of the constraint. The constraint system may even be unsatisfiable, while constraint propagation and filtering does not detect it (i.e., they ensure only *partial satisfiability*). Hence, an additional step called *labeling search* is needed to exhibit solutions. Labeling search consists in exploring the search space composed of the domains of uninstantiated variables. Interestingly, a labeling procedure can awake constraint propagation and filtering, allowing an early pruning of the search space. In the previous example, if X is labeled by 3 then the constraint $X > Y$ is awoken and automatically reduces the domain of Y to $\{2\}$. A labeling search procedure is *complete* when the whole search space is explored. Complete labeling search can eventually determine satisfiability (or unsatisfiability) of a constraint solving problem over finite domains. However, it is an exponential procedure in the worst case. This is not surprising as determining satisfiability of a constraint problem over finite domains is NP-hard [15].

During labeling search, when a solution s is found, the value $m = \mathcal{F}(s)$ of the cost function can be recorded, and backtracking can then be enforced by adding the constraint $\mathcal{F}(...) < m$ to the set of constraints (or $\mathcal{F}(...) \leq m$ if one wants to explore **all** optimal solutions). If another solution is found, then the cost function $\mathcal{F}$ will necessarily have a cost smaller than m. This procedure, called branch&bound [12], can be controlled by a timeout that interrupts the search when a given time threshold is reached. Of course, the current value of $\mathcal{F}$ in this case may not be a global minimum, but it is already an interesting value for the cost function, something that we call a *quasi-optimum*. For localization of HMSCs, selecting the local HMSC with the smallest cost is desirable but not always essential. On the other hand, mastering the time spent for localization is essential to scale to real-size problems.

4.2   From HMSC to COP

Variables. Localizing an HMSC H consists in selecting a set of participating instances and a minimal process for each bMSC appearing in H, such that every choice in the HMSC becomes a local choice. As this selection is not unique, we use constraint optimization techniques to provide characteristics of localized HMSCs with minimal cost. We propose to transform any HMSC into a constraint optimization problem, as follows: a couple of variables (X_i, Y_i) is associated to each bMSC $M_i \in \mathcal{M}$, where X_i represents the set of instances chosen for the bMSC $f(M_i)$, and Y_i represents the leader in $f(M_i)$. If I is the set of instances of H, every X_i takes its possible values in 2^I while Y_i takes a value in I.

Constraints. Our constraint model is composed of domain, equality and inclusion constraints. *Domain constraints*, noted DOM, are used to specify the domains of X_i and Y_i. Obviously, if a bMSC M_i is defined over a set of processes $\mathcal{P}_i$, we have $\mathcal{P}_i \subseteq X_i \subseteq I$. *Equality constraints*, noted EQU, enforce the locality property. For two bMSCs M_i, M_j such that there exists two transitions (n, M_i, n_1) and (n, M_j, n_2) in $\rightarrow$ originating from the same node n, $f(M_i)$ and $f(M_j)$ must have the same leader, i.e., $Y_i = Y_j$. We write $M_i \otimes M_j$, when such choice between M_i and M_j exists in H. Locality of HMSCs is also enforced by using *inclusion constraints*, noted $INCL$. Let $M_i, M_j \in \mathcal{M}$ be two bMSCs. We write $M_i \triangleright M_j$ when there exists a path $(n, M_i, n')(n', M_j, n'')$, i.e., when M_i is the predecessor of M_j in H. In such case, in any localization of H, the minimal instance of $f(M_j)$, represented by variable Y_j, must appear in the set of instances of $f(M_i)$, represented by variable X_i. In our constraint model, this is expressed by the constraint $Y_j \in X_i$. Similarly, the leader of a bMSC in the localized solution can only be one of its instances, so we have $Y_i \in X_i$ for every $M_i \in \mathcal{M}$.

It is worth noticing that the localization problem is always satisfiable, as there exists at least one trivial solution: select an instance in I as leader for all bMSCs, then add this instance if needed to every bMSC, and messages from this instance to all other instances. However, this trivial and uninteresting solution is not necessarily minimal w.r.t. the chosen cost function. We can now prove that our approach is *sound* and *complete* by considering the following definition:

Definition 7. *Let $H = (I, N, \rightarrow, \mathcal{M}, n_0)$ be an HMSC, the constraint optimization model associated to H is $CP_H = (\mathcal{X}, \mathcal{Y}, \mathcal{C})$ where $\mathcal{X} = \{X_1, \ldots, X_{|\mathcal{M}|}\}$ associates a variable to the set of instances appearing in each bMSC of $f(\mathcal{M})$, $\mathcal{Y} = \{Y_1, \ldots, Y_{|\mathcal{M}|}\}$ associates a variable to the leader selected for each bMSC of $f(\mathcal{M})$, and $\mathcal{C} = DOM \cup EQU \cup INCL$ is a set of constraints defined as follows:*

$$- DOM = \bigwedge_{i \in 1 \ldots |\mathcal{M}|} X_i \in 2^I \wedge \mathcal{P}_i \subseteq X_i \wedge Y_i \in I \ ;$$

$$- EQU = \bigwedge_{M_i, M_j | M_i \otimes M_j} Y_i = Y_j$$

$$- INCL = \bigwedge_{M_i, M_j | M_i \triangleright M_j} Y_j \in X_i \wedge \bigwedge_{i \in 1 \ldots |\mathcal{M}|} Y_i \in X_i$$

Then, solving the localization problem for an HMSC H amounts to find an optimal solution for CP_H, w.r.t. cost function $\mathcal{F}$. We have:

Theorem 1. *Computing solutions for a localization problem using an optimal solution search for the corresponding COP is a sound and complete algorithm.*

This result is not really surprising, as CP_H represents what is needed for an HMSC to become local. A proof of this theorem can be found in the full version of the paper.

5   Implementation and Experimental Results

To evaluate the approach proposed in the paper, we implemented a systematic transformation from HMSC descriptions to COPs and conducted an experimental analysis over a large number of randomly generated HMSCs. Our implementation contains three main components G, A and S and is described in Figure 4. G is a random HMSC generator, A is an analyzer that transforms a localization problem for a given HMSC into a COP, as described in the previous section. Finally S is a constraint optimization solver: we used the `clpfd` library of SIC-Stus Prolog [6]. The generator G takes an expected number of distinct HMSCs to generate (nbH), a number of bMSCs in each HMSC(nbB), and a number of active processes in each HMSC (nbP) as inputs. As output, it produces an xml file containing nbH randomly generated HMSCs.

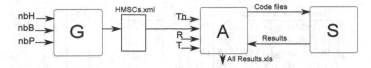

Fig. 4. The input and outputs of the generator, the analyser and the solver

The analyser A takes Th, the parameter θ of the cost function $\mathcal{F}$, a set of heuristics R, and a sequence of time-out values T, as inputs. These values can be considered as internal parameters for the constraint optimization solver: They allow us to evaluate different strategies. In the experiments, we considered several labeling heuristics to choose the variable and the value to enumerate first, e.g., *leftmost, first-fail, ffc, step* or *bisect*. *Leftmost* is a variable-choice heuristic that selects the first unassigned variable from a statically ordered list. *First-fail* is a dynamic variable-choice heuristic that selects first the variable with the current smallest domain. *Ffc* is an extension of *first-fail* that uses the number of constraints on a given variable as a tie-break when two variables have the same domain size. *Step* is choice-value heuristic that consists in traversing incrementally the variation domain of the current variable. Finally, *bisect* implements *domain splitting* which consists in dividing a domain into two subdomains and propagating the subdomain informations. For example, if x takes a value in an interval $[a, b]$, then *bisect* will propagate first $x \in [a, \frac{a+b}{2}]$, and then $x \in [\frac{a+b}{2}, b]$ upon backtracking. For each generated HMSC H and each heuristic $h_i \in R$, the analyser creates a prolog file that contains the corresponding COP. For efficiency reasons, a special attention has been paid to the encoding of variation domains and constraints. Subset domains were encoded using a binary representation and sets inclusion using efficient div/mod operations. The prolog file is then used as input of the solver. The sequence T represents the various instants at which the optimization process must temporarily stop, and returns the current value of the cost function. These values are quasi-optima, representing approximations of the global optimum. The combination between heuristics and time-out values is useful to compare different labeling strategies. Finally, the analyser A collects all the results returned by the solver with the time needed to provide a solution, and stores them for a systematic comparison.

The first step of the experiment consisted in a systematic evaluation of the performance of several heuristics to guide the solver. During this step, we considered several heuristics and time-outs. We do not report here all the results, but show only the results for one illustrative model. Figure 5 shows the time-aware minimization of the cost value with 12 different heuristics and time-outs between 1s and 14s for a chosen localization problem. Heuristics descriptions use the following syntax: *[b — u] / [left — ff — ffc] / [bisect — step] / [XYC — YXC — CXY — CYX]*, where b and u stand resp. for *bounded costs* and *unbounded costs*. The heuristic *bounded cost* evaluates a lower bound on the cost of a solution that can be reached from a given state. *Left, ff* and *ffc* stand for a variable-choice heuristic, *bisect* and *step* stand for value-choice heuristic, and XYC, etc. stand for the static order in which variables are fed to the solver. Bold

	heuristics \ runtime	1 s	2 s	3 s	4 s	5 s	6 s	7 s	12 s	13 s	14 s
0	u/left/step/XYC	23	23	22	22	22	22	19	19	19	19
1	u /left/step/YXC	19	**19**								
2	b/left/step/XYC	19	**19**								
3	b/left/step/YXC	**19**									
4	b/left/step/CYX	-	-	-	-	-	-	-	-	21	**19**
5	b/ff/step/XYC	22	19	19	19	19	**19**				
6	b/ff/step/YXC	30	19	19	19	19	**19**				
7	b/ff/step/CYX	30	19	19	19	19	**19**				
8	b/ffc/step/CYX	27	22	19	19	19	19	**19**			
9	b/left/bisect/XYC	**19**									
10	b/left/bisect/YXC	**19**									
11	b/left/bisect/CYX	-	-	-	-	21	**19**				

Fig. 5. Comparing heuristics with one representative example

values indicate *proved global minima*, non-bold values indicate *quasi-optima*, – indicates absence of result in the given time contract.

In Figure 5, heuristics 3,9,10 give the best results. The series of experiment that we run shows that heuristics with an estimation of cost, and a static ordering of variable evaluations have the best performance. Overall, the heuristics number 10 combining *bisect* (domain splitting), *left* (static variable ordering), and a cost evaluation exhibited the best results and was selected for the next steps of the experiment.

As next steps, we generated 11 groups of 100 random HMSCs, with 10 bMSCs, which is a reasonably large number, according to the existing literature on HMSCs. We then let the number of processes grow from 4 to 14. We also generated 12 groups of 100 HMSCs, containing exactly 8 processes, and let the number of bMSCs grow from 4 to 15. The goal of these series of experiments was to evaluate the influence of both the number of processes and the number of bMSCs on the

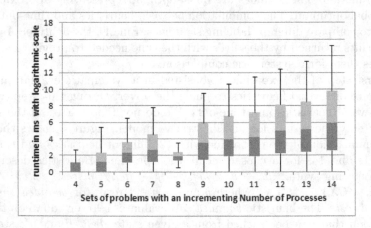

Fig. 6. The influence of the number of processes on the runtime execution

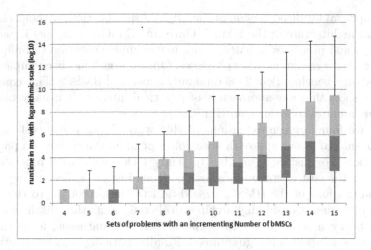

Fig. 7. The influence of the number of bMSCs on the runtime execution

runtime of our localization approach. We expected these parameters to influence the performance of localization, as increasing the number of bMSCs increases the number of variables, and increasing the number of processes increases the size of variables' domains. However, we have obtained solutions for all HMSCs, which allowed us to evaluate the impact of both parameters. The evaluation was performed on a machine equipped with INTEL $P9600$ core2 Duo at $2, 53$ Ghz, with $4Go$ of RAM. Results of both experiences are given in Figures 6 and 7, using box-and-whiskers plots to show the statistical distribution of datasets.

Both plots use logarithmic scales to tackle the big variance between runtime measurements. As expected, the plots show exponential curves but the runtime for each group remains quite low. For randomly generated HMSCs of reasonable size (such as the ones found in the literature), our experimental results show that localization using constraint optimization takes a few minutes in the worst cases, and an average duration of a few seconds. Actually, even for the largest cases (15 bMSCs with 14 processes), the runtime of our localization approach did not exceed 40 minutes. Although solving COPs over finite domains is NP-hard [15], as examples of existing HMSCs usually contain less than 15 bMSCs, our localization process appears to be of practical interest. Our results are encouraging, and show that the approach is fast enough to be used in practice. However, they have been obtained on random instances only, and thus further experiments on non-random instances are necessary to confirm this judgment.

6   Conclusion and Future Work

This paper has proposed a sound and complete method to transform arbitrary HMSCs into implementable ones. Our approach transforms an HMSC in a constraint optimization problem. The solution returned by a solver can be used to build an optimal localized version of the original specification, without changing the overall architecture of the HMSC. Once an HMSC is localized by addition of messages and processes in bMSCs, automatic implementation techniques can generate code for communicating processes. Our approach has been implemented and tested on a benchmark of 2300 randomly generated HMSCs. The experimental results show that our approach is of practical interest: it usually takes less than a few minutes to localize an HMSC.

There are four foreseen extensions of this work. First, other cost functions can be considered as our approach does not depend on the choice of a particular cost function. For instance, we plan to study localization with functions that accounts for the cost of communications between instances. Second, we plan to allow modifications of the HMSC, in addition to those brought to the bMSCs of the specification. Considering architectural constraints that disallow communications between some processes is another challenging issue, as in this case existence of a solution is not guaranteed. Finally, noticing that localization is a rather syntactic procedure, the question of designating a process as a leader or adding messages should also be addressed in more semantics terms.

Further work also includes the experimentation of our approach on industrial case studies, to evaluate its performance on non-random HMSCs. We have started a collaboration with a company that develops communicating systems and wants to generate test cases based on requirement design. Our approach will be useful to derive automatically test cases from HMSCs that were designed without any requirement on implementability.

References

1. Abdallah, R., Jard, C., Hélouët, L.: Distributed implementation of message sequence charts. Software and Systems Modeling (to appear, 2013)
2. Alur, R., Etessami, K., Yannakakis, M.: Realizability and Verification of MSC Graphs. In: Yu, Y., Spirakis, P.G., van Leeuwen, J. (eds.) ICALP 2001. LNCS, vol. 2076, pp. 797–808. Springer, Heidelberg (2001)
3. Baudru, N., Morin, R.: Synthesis of Safe Message-Passing Systems. In: Arvind, V., Prasad, S. (eds.) FSTTCS 2007. LNCS, vol. 4855, pp. 277–289. Springer, Heidelberg (2007)
4. Ben-Abdallah, H., Leue, S.: Syntactic Detection of Process divergence and Non-Local Choice in Message Sequence Charts. In: Brinksma, E. (ed.) TACAS 1997. LNCS, vol. 1217, pp. 259–274. Springer, Heidelberg (1997)
5. Brand, D., Zafiropoulo, P.: On communicating finite state machines. Technical Report 1053, IBM Zurich Research Lab. (1981)
6. Carlsson, M., Ottosson, G., Carlson, B.: An Open-Ended Finite Domain Constraint Solver. In: Hartel, P.H., Kuchen, H. (eds.) PLILP 1997. LNCS, vol. 1292, pp. 191–206. Springer, Heidelberg (1997)
7. Genest, B., Muscholl, A., Seidl, H., Zeitoun, M.: Infinite-state high-level MSCs: Model-checking and realizability. Journal on Comp. and System Sciences 72(4), 617–647 (2006)
8. Hélouët, L., Jard, C.: Conditions for synthesis of communicating automata from HMSCs. In: Proc. of FMICS 2000 (2000)

9. ITU-T. Message sequence charts (msc). In ITU standard Z.120 (1999)
10. Liang, H., Dingel, J., Diskin, Z.: A comparative survey of scenario-based to state-based model synthesis approaches. In: Proc. of SCESM 2006: the 2006 International Workshop on Scenarios and State Machines: Models, Algorithms, and Tools, pp. 5–12 (2006)
11. Lohrey, M.: Realizability of high-level message sequence charts: closing the gaps. Theoretical Computer Science 309(1-3), 529–554 (2003)
12. Marriott, K., Stuckey, P.J.: Programming with Constraints: An Introduction. MIT Press (1998)
13. Reniers, M., Mauw, S.: High-level Message Sequence Charts. In: SDL 1997: Time for Testing - SDL, MSC and Trends, Proc. of the 8th SDL Forum, pp. 291–306 (1997)
14. Roychoudhury, A., Thiagarajan, P.S.: Communicating transaction processes. In: ACSD 2003, pp. 157–166. IEEE Computer Society (2003)
15. Van Hentenryck, P., Saraswat, V.A., Deville, Y.: Design, implementation, and evaluation of the constraint language cc(fd). J. Log. Program. 37(1-3), 139–164 (1998)

ANDROMEDA: Accurate and Scalable Security Analysis of Web Applications

Omer Tripp[1], Marco Pistoia[2], Patrick Cousot[3],
Radhia Cousot[4], and Salvatore Guarnieri[5]

[1] Tel Aviv University and IBM Software Group, Israel
omert@il.ibm.com
[2] IBM Thomas J. Watson Research Center, USA
pistoia@us.ibm.com
[3] New York University, USA
pcousot@cs.nyu.edu
[4] École Normale Supérieure, France
radhia.cousot@ens.edu
[5] University of Washington and IBM Software Group, USA
sguarni@us.ibm.com

Abstract. Security auditing of industry-scale software systems mandates automation. Static taint analysis enables deep and exhaustive tracking of suspicious data flows for detection of potential leakage and integrity violations, such as cross-site scripting (XSS), SQL injection (SQLi) and log forging. Research in this area has taken two directions: program slicing and type systems. Both of these approaches suffer from a high rate of false findings, which limits the usability of analysis tools based on these techniques. Attempts to reduce the number of false findings have resulted in analyses that are either (i) unsound, suffering from the dual problem of false negatives, or (ii) too expensive due to their high precision, thereby failing to scale to real-world applications.

In this paper, we investigate a novel approach for enabling precise yet scalable static taint analysis. The key observation informing our approach is that taint analysis is a demand-driven problem, which enables lazy computation of vulnerable information flows, instead of eagerly computing a complete data-flow solution, which is the reason for the traditional dichotomy between scalability and precision. We have implemented our approach in ANDROMEDA, an analysis tool that computes data-flow propagations on demand, in an efficient and accurate manner, and additionally features incremental analysis capabilities. ANDROMEDA is currently in use in a commercial product. It supports applications written in Java, .NET and JavaScript. Our extensive evaluation of ANDROMEDA on a suite of 16 production-level benchmarks shows ANDROMEDA to achieve high accuracy and compare favorably to a state-of-the-art tool that trades soundness for precision.

Keywords: Security, Static Analysis, Taint Analysis, Information Flow, Integrity, Abstract Interpretation.

1 Introduction

Web-application security is an ever-growing concern. By design, Web applications feed on inputs whose source is untrusted, perform numerous security-sensitive operations

V. Cortellessa and D. Varró (Eds.): FASE 2013, LNCS 7793, pp. 210–225, 2013.
© Springer-Verlag Berlin Heidelberg 2013

(such as database accesses and transfers of Web content to remote machines), and expose data to potentially malicious observers. It is not surprising, then, that six out of the ten most critical Web-application vulnerabilities[1] are *information-flow violations*, which can break *integrity* (whereby untrusted inputs flow into security-sensitive computations) or *confidentiality* (whereby private information is revealed to public observers).

During the last decade, there has been intensive research on methods and algorithms for automatically detecting information-flow violations in Web applications. However, many of the published approaches are not readily applicable to industrial Web applications. Solutions based on type systems tend to be overly complex and conservative [34,20,27], and are therefore unlikely to enjoy broad adoption, whereas those based on program slicing are often unsound [33] or limited in scalability [14,28].

Our Approach. In this paper, we present ANDROMEDA, a sound and highly accurate static security scanner, which also scales to large code bases, being designed for commercial needs as part of a product offering, IBM Security AppScan Source.[2] ANDROMEDA performs a form of *abstract interpretation* [6] known as *taint analysis* [25]: It statically detects data flows wherein information returned by a "source" reaches the parameters of a "sink" without being properly endorsed by a "downgrader". Depending on whether the problem being solved is related to integrity or confidentiality, a *source* is a method that injects untrusted or secret input into a program, a *sink* is a method that performs a security-sensitive computation or exposes information to public observers, and a *downgrader* is a method that sanitizes untrusted data or declassifies confidential data, respectively. ANDROMEDA is equipped with a thorough configuration of triples of sources, sinks and downgraders for all known integrity and confidentiality problems, partitioned into *security rules*, such as XSS and SQLi.

The key idea behind ANDROMEDA is to track vulnerable information flows (emanating from sources) in a demand-driven manner, without eagerly building any complete representation of the subject application. ANDROMEDA builds a call-graph representation of the program based on intraprocedural type inference. Furthermore, when there is a need to compute an aliasing relationship, stemming from flow of vulnerable information into the heap, ANDROMEDA issues a granular aliasing query focused on the flow at hand, thereby obviating the need for whole-program pointer analysis. This enables (i) sound and efficient scanning of large applications, where typically only a small portion of the application requires modeling, and (ii) incremental-analysis capabilities, which allow to preserve valid parts of the old solution when rescanning the application following code changes. Both of these characteristics are enabled by the fact that ANDROMEDA does not need to build any form of whole-program representation.

In another view, ANDROMEDA can be thought of as an extended type system, where a fully automated context-sensitive, interprocedural, incremental inference engine automatically attaches security annotations to program locations and propagates them. ANDROMEDA enforces the following two properties:

1. The inference process is fully automated, and thus no complex, non-standard type system is forced on the developer.

---

[1] http://owasp.org.
[2] http://ibm.com/software/rational/products/appscan/source/.

2. The analysis is infinitely context sensitive (up to recursion), and consequently, it does not produce overly conservative results.

These properties lift the two most significant barriers that have so far prevented type systems from enjoying broad industrial adoption.

To our knowledge, ANDROMEDA is the first taint-analysis algorithm that performs demand-driven analysis from the bottom up, including representing the program's type hierarchy, call graph and data-flow propagation graph. This is the key to achieving both accuracy and scalability without sacrificing soundness. We are also not aware of any other security analysis featuring incremental scanning capabilities.

Contributions. This paper makes the following specific contributions:

– **Demand-driven taint analysis.** We present a demand-driven security analysis algorithm that is sound (even in the presence of multi threading), accurate and scalable. We describe the design of the entire analysis stack in support of this feature.
– **Incremental analysis.** ANDROMEDA enables efficient rescanning of the subject application following code changes. This is thanks to its ability to track vulnerable flows in a "local", on-demand fashion, which facilitates invalidation of only parts of the previous data-flow solution. We describe the data structures ANDROMEDA implements for efficient incremental analysis.
– **Framework and library support.** Beyond the core analysis, we describe novel extensions enabling effective modeling of framework and library code. These extensions are important for an analysis targeting real-world Web applications, which are built atop reusable frameworks.
– **Implementation and evaluation.** ANDROMEDA has been fully implemented. It supports Java, .NET and JavaScript programs, and is currently used in a commercial product. We present an extensive evaluation of ANDROMEDA, comparing it to a state-of-the-art security scanner [33] on a suite of 16 real-world Java benchmarks, which shows ANDROMEDA to be superior.

2   Motivation and Overview

To illustrate some of the unique features of ANDROMEDA, we use the `Aliasing5` benchmark from the Stanford SecuriBench Micro suite.[3] Designed for expository purposes, this example shows a Java Web application reading untrusted data from servlet parameters. Specifically, this example highlights the importance of tracking aliasing relationships between program variables and fields for sound security analysis, with `buf` flowing into two formal arguments of method `foo` (line 6).

The flow of the entire program is as follows: The `doGet` handler of the `Aliasing5` servlet first initializes a fresh `StringBuffer` object, `buf`, with the string `"abc"` (line 5). It then invokes method `foo`, such that its first two formal arguments (`buf` and `buf2`) are aliased. Next, `foo` assigns the content of an untrusted parameter, `"name"`, to variable `name`, in the source statement at line 10. This untrusted value subsequently

---

[3] `http://suif.stanford.edu/~livshits/work/securibench-micro`.

taints the buffer pointed-to by `buf` (line 11). Because of the aliasing relationship be-tween `buf` and `buf2`, the security-sensitive operation at line 13, which renders the content of `buf2` to the response HTML, becomes vulnerable.

```
1:   public class Aliasing5 extends HttpServlet {
2:     protected void doGet(HttpServletRequest req,
3:       HttpServletResponse resp)
4:       throws ServletException, IOException {
5:       StringBuffer buf = new StringBuffer("abc");
6:       foo(buf, buf, resp, req); }
7:     void foo(StringBuffer buf,
8:       StringBuffer buf2, ServletResponse resp,
9:       ServletRequest req) throws IOException {
10:      String name = req.getParameter("name");
11:      buf.append(name);
12:      PrintWriter writer = resp.getWriter();
13:      writer.println(buf2.toString()); /* BAD */ } }
```

Fig. 1. The `Aliasing5` Benchmark from the SecuriBench Micro Suite

To detect the vulnerability in this program, the security scanner must account for the aliasing between `buf` and `buf2` in `foo`. Existing approaches have all addressed this requirement by applying a preliminary whole-program pointer analysis, such as An-dersen's flow-insensitive analysis [1], to eagerly compute an aliasing solution before starting the security analysis [33]. Perfoming a global aliasing analysis places a sig-nificant limitation on the scalability of the client security analysis, which is mitigated (but not lifted) if the aliasing analysis is coarse (*i.e.*, context insensitive, flow insensi-tive, *etc*). In that case, however, the ensuing security analysis becomes imprecise, often yielding an excess of false reports due to spurious data flows.

ANDROMEDA, instead, performs on-demand alias resolution. It tracks symbolic rep-resentations of security facts, known as "access paths", and augments the set of tracked representations to account for aliases of tracked objects. Loosely speaking, an access path is a sequence of field identifiers, rooted at a local variable, such as `x.f.g`. This access path evaluates to the object o reached by dereferencing field `f` of the object pointed-to by `x`, and then dereferencing field `g` of o (or $\perp$ if no such object exists). (We provide a formal definition of an access path later, in Section 3.)

ANDROMEDA starts by modeling the effect of the source statement at line 10 as the seeding data-flow fact `name.*`. The `*` notation simply represents the fact that all ob-jects reachable through variable `name` are to be considered untrusted. Then, the flow at line 11 leads the analysis to track both `name.*` and `buf.content.*`. However, because there is a flow into the heap at line 11, the analysis further issues an on-demand interprocedural aliasing query, which establishes that `buf.content` is aliased with `buf2.content`. Therefore, the analysis additionally tracks `buf2.content.*`. This exposes the vulnerability at line 13, where the `toString` call renders `buf2.content` to the response HTML.

3 Core Taint Analysis

The ANDROMEDA algorithm takes as input a Web application, along with its set of supporting libraries, and validates it with respect to a specification in the form of a set of "security rules". A *security rule* is a triple $\langle Src, Dwn, Snk \rangle$, where Src, Dwn and Snk are patterns for matching sources, downgraders and sinks in the subject program, respectively. A pattern match is either a method call or a field dereference. A vulnerability is reported for flows extending between a source and a sink belonging to the same rule, without a downgrader from the rule's Dwn set mediating the flow.

The ANDROMEDA algorithm interleaves call-graph construction with tracking of vulnerable information flows. This is to avoid building eager whole-program representations. Both the call graph and the data-flow solution computed atop the call graph are expanded on demand, ensuring scalability while retaining a high degree of accuracy.

3.1 Type-Hierarchy and Call-Graph Construction

As mentioned earlier, ANDROMEDA refrains from building global program representations. Instead, it computes its supporting type hierarchy on demand. For this, AN-DROMEDA utilizes lazy data structures, which provide sophisticated mechanisms for caching and demand evaluation of type information at the granularity of individual methods and class fields.

Call-graph construction is also performed lazily. The call graph is built based on local reasoning, by resolving virtual calls according to an intra-procedural type-inference algorithm [3]. Call sites are not necessarily expanded eagerly (*i.e.*, before the data-flow analysis stage). Rather, an oracle is used to determine whether any given call site may lead to the discovery of source statements. Our oracle is sound, and is based on control-flow reachability between the calling method and source methods within the type-hierarchy graph [7].

3.2 Data-Flow Analysis

For a formal description of ANDROMEDA's data-flow analysis algorithm, we use a standard description of the program's state, based on the following domains:

$VarId$	Program variables	$Val = Loc \cup \{null\}$	Values
$FldId$	Field identifiers	$Env: VarId \to Val$	Environment
Loc	Unbounded set of objects	$Heap: Loc \times FldId \to Val$	Heap

A program state, $\sigma = \langle \mathbf{E}, \mathbf{H} \rangle \in States = Env \times Heap$, maintains the pointing from variables to their values, as well as from object fields to their values.

To describe the algorithm we use the following syntactic structures:

Statement	Meaning
x = new Object()	$[\![\mathtt{x} = \mathbf{new}\ \mathtt{Object}()]\!] \sigma = \sigma[\mathtt{x} \mapsto o \in Loc.\ o\ \text{is fresh}]$
x = y	$[\![\mathtt{x} = \mathtt{y}]\!] \sigma = \sigma[\mathbf{E}(\mathtt{x}) \mapsto \mathbf{E}(\mathtt{y})]$
x.f = y	$[\![\mathtt{x.f} = \mathtt{y}]\!] \sigma = \sigma[\mathbf{H}(\langle \mathbf{E}(\mathtt{x}), \mathtt{f} \rangle) \mapsto \mathbf{E}(\mathtt{y})]$
x = y.f	$[\![\mathtt{x} = \mathtt{y.f}]\!] \sigma = \sigma[\mathbf{E}(\mathtt{x}) \mapsto \mathbf{H}(\langle \mathbf{E}(\mathtt{y}), \mathtt{f} \rangle)]$

These are kept to a minimum to simplify the description of the analysis. Extending the core language to contain procedure calls is straightforward [5].

Instrumented Concrete Semantics. To track security facts, we instrument the concrete semantics to further maintain untrusted (or tainted) access paths. Informally, an access path is a symbolic representation of a heap location. For example, access path x.g denotes the heap location pointed-to by field g of the object pointed-to by variable x. Security analysis over access paths tracks the set of paths evaluating to untrusted values.

More formally, an *access path* is a (possibly empty) sequence of field identifiers rooted at a local variable; *i.e.*, an element in $VarId \times (FldId)^*$. The meaning of access path $x.f_1 \ldots f_n$ is the unique value $o \in Val$ reached by first dereferencing x using $\mathbf{E}$, and then following the references through $f_1 \ldots f_n$ in H, or $\perp$ if there are intermediate null dereferences in the path. This is defined inductively as follows:

$$[\![x.\epsilon]\!]\sigma = \begin{cases} \mathbf{E}(x) & x \in dom(\mathbf{E}) \\ \perp & \text{otherwise} \end{cases}$$

$$[\![x.f_1 \ldots f_n]\!]\sigma = \begin{cases} \mathbf{H}(\langle [\![x.f_1 \ldots f_{n-1}]\!], f_n \rangle) & [\![x.f_1 \ldots f_{n-1}]\!]\sigma \neq \perp, \\ & \langle [\![x.f_1 \ldots f_{n-1}]\!], f_n \rangle \in dom(\mathbf{H}) \\ \perp & \text{otherwise} \end{cases}$$

An instrumented concrete state is a triple, $\sigma = \langle \mathbf{E}, \mathbf{H}, \mathbf{T} \rangle$, where $\mathbf{T}$ is a set of *tainted access paths*. We assume a security specification, $\mathcal{S}$, which seeds the set $\mathbf{T}$ when evaluating certain assignment and field-read statements (according to the Src set of the provided security rules). The semantic rules for updating $\mathbf{T}$ appear in Figure 2.

$$\mathbf{T} \xrightarrow{x=new \ldots;} \mathbf{T}$$
$$\mathbf{T} \xrightarrow{x=y;} \mathbf{T} \cup \{x.f_1 \ldots f_n \colon y.f_1 \ldots f_n \in \mathbf{T}\}$$
$$\mathbf{T} \xrightarrow{x=y.f;} \mathbf{T} \cup \{x.f_1 \ldots f_n \colon y.f \ f_1 \ldots f_n \in \mathbf{T}\}$$
$$\mathbf{T} \xrightarrow{x.f=y;} \mathbf{T} \cup \{\mathbf{A}(x).f \ f_1 \ldots f_n \colon y.f_1 \ldots f_n \in \mathbf{T}\}$$

Fig. 2. Forward Data-flow Equations

$$\mathbf{A} \xrightarrow{x=new \ldots;} \mathbf{A}$$
$$\mathbf{A} \xrightarrow{x=y;} \mathbf{A} \cup \{y.f_1 \ldots f_n \colon x.f_1 \ldots f_n \in \mathbf{A}\}$$
$$\mathbf{A} \xrightarrow{x=y.f;} \mathbf{A} \cup \{y.f \ f_1 \ldots f_n \colon x.f_1 \ldots f_n \in \mathbf{A}\} \cup \{x.f_1 \ldots f_n \colon y.f \ f_1 \ldots f_n \in \mathbf{A}\}$$
$$\mathbf{A} \xrightarrow{x.f=y;} \mathbf{A} \cup \{y.f_1 \ldots f_n \colon x.f \ f_1 \ldots f_n \in \mathbf{A}\} \cup \{x.f \ f_1 \ldots f_n \colon y.f_1 \ldots f_n \in \mathbf{A}\}$$

Fig. 3. Backward Data-flow Equations

Access-path Widening. The key difficulty in using the symbolic access-path representation for static security analysis is that this representation of the heap, which is known as *storeless* [10], is unbounded. This problem manifests when dealing with recursive data

structures, such as linked lists. To deal with this problem, we apply widening by introducing a special symbol, $*$. An access path now has either the concrete form $x.f_1 \ldots f_n$,
or the widened form $x.f_1 \ldots f_n *$, where

$$[\![x.f_1 \ldots f_n *]\!]\sigma = \{o \colon \exists f_{n+1} \ldots f_k \in (FldId)^*. \, o = [\![x.f_1 \ldots f_n f_{n+1} \ldots f_k]\!]\sigma\}$$

That is, a widened access path potentially points to more than one object.

In this way, the analysis can track a bounded number of access paths in a sound
manner by restricting the length of an access path to some constant c, and allowing for
insertion of $*$ at the end of a path of length c instead of extending it when accounting
for the effect of a field-assignment statement.

On-demand Aliasing. As mentioned earlier, ANDROMEDA features the ability to
soundly track symbolic security facts. The key idea is to perform alias analysis on demand, when an untrusted value flows into an object field (*i.e.*, untrusted data flows into
the heap). We first illustrate this situation through a simple example, where we assume
that initially there is a single taint fact, $\mathbf{T} = \{z.g\}$, and the last statement—assigning a
value to o.sinkfld—is a sink, and as such must not be assigned an untrusted value:

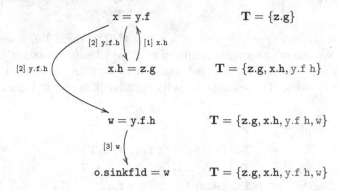

We highlight in red the access paths that would be missed by a forward data-flow
analysis without on-demand alias-analysis capabilities, such as the IFDS framework [24].
Such an analysis would ignore the assignment $x = y.f$ because it is not affected by $\mathbf{T}$,
thereby missing the aliasing relation between x.h and y.f.h at the point when it becomes
relevant, which is the following two statements: The first, x.h = z.g, contaminates x.h,
and thus also y.f.h, and the second dereferences y.f.h into w.

In constrast, ANDROMEDA is fully sound, as we prove in Theorem 1. ANDROMEDA
handles cases such as the above by performing on-demand alias analysis. Upon encoun-
tering the field-assignment statement x.h = z.g, ANDROMEDA traverses the control-
flow graph backwards seeking aliases of x.h. It then finds that y.f.h is an alias of x.h,
and propagates this additional security fact forward, which ensures that the security
vulnerability is discovered. The ANDROMEDA propagation steps are visualized above
using labeled edges, the label consisting of the step index (in square brackets) followed
by the learned taint fact.

Formally, ANDROMEDA computes a fixpoint solution for the equations in Figure 3
while traversing the control flow backwards from the statement performing the heap
update. The seeding value for $\mathbf{A}$ in our example is the singleton set $\{x\}$.

Theorem 1. *The* ANDROMEDA *data-flow analysis algorithm is sound. That is, in the fixpoint solution $\mathcal{F}$ computed by* ANDROMEDA *for program P with respect to specification S, for every control location c in the program and set A of access paths arising in $\mathcal{F}$ c, γ $A \supseteq A'$, where A' is the set of all concrete access paths that may arise in c in an execution of P.*

Proof (Sketch). First, we make the observation that our transformers (in Figure 2) are distributive (i.e., τ $X \cup Y \equiv \tau$ $X \cup \tau$ Y). This simplifies the proof by letting us consider singleton sets of access paths [24], making it clear that all the transformers not modifying the heap (i.e., all transformers except x.f=y*) are trivially sound. Finally, for field assignment, the backward equations (in Figure 3) guarantee that all aliases of* x *due to preceding statements (according to the control-flow order) are accounted for. The equations handle all possible cases, including forward and backward propagation due to field accesses, and thus result in a complete aliasing solution.*

3.3   Extensions: Library and Framework Modeling

Modern Web applications are often built atop one or more frameworks, such as Struts, Spring and JSF [29,35]. Frameworks typically invoke application code using reflective constructs, based on information provided in external configuration files, which complicates static analysis of Web applications.

To address this concern, ANDROMEDA is fully integrated with Framework For Frameworks (F4F), a recent solution augmenting taint-analysis engines with precise framework support [29]. F4F automatically generates Web Application Framework Language (WAFL) static-analysis artifacts, which can be integrated into a taint-analysis engine to ensure that the interaction of a Web application with the frameworks it uses is modeled soundly and accurately.

ANDROMEDA's integration with F4F exploits the fact that static analysis can operate on non-executable yet legal Java code. We transform the F4F output into synthetic code that soundly models data flows involving framework code. This choice has several advantages compared to direct modeling of frameworks within the ANDROMEDA engine, being (i) more lightweight (no need to directly generate Intermediate-Representation (IR) code), (ii) more portable and reusable (the synthetic Java code generated from the WAFL specification can be plugged into *any* existing analysis), as well as (iii) more intelligible to the developer (being presented with simple Java code instead of IR code).

Before statically analyzing an application, ANDROMEDA takes the WAFL output of F4F and transforms it as follows. Each call replacement has a synthetic method associated with it. This is the method that ANDROMEDA should consider in place of the one specified in the application source code. For every synthetic method, ANDROMEDA creates Java code corresponding to the instructions for that synthetic method that are specified in the output of F4F. In most cases, this can be done straightforwardly. However, there were several interesting problems that we had to address.

One case is simulating method invocations from synthetic methods. Such invocations are on uninitialized variables, which causes ANDROMEDA's intra-procedural type inference to ignore them. Solving this by initializing the variables is problematic: Some declared types are abstract, and some do not have a default constructor. Instead, AN-DROMEDA solves this problem by adding a level of indirection via a method call that returns null. Since the assignment to null is performed in a different procedure, AN-DROMEDA's type inference accepts the call as valid, with a result sufficient to model taint propagation faithfully.

Another problem arises when synthetic methods invoke default-scope or protected methods in a class of another package. Since these methods can only be invoked from classes in the same package, ANDROMEDA extends that package with an additional public synthetic class containing a public synthetic method that calls the default-scope or protected method, and returns its return value. Being public and in the same package as the restricted method, this synthetic method can be invoked without restrictions.

4 Incremental Security Analysis

A key feature of ANDROMEDA is its ability to update the scan report incrementally following code changes. For industry-scale Web applications, this feature is of crucial importance. Without it, long waiting times need be spent on reanalysis of the entire application following any code change, which complicates the integration of security scanning into the development lifecycle. Moreover, incremental scanning allows verification of fixes on the spot, which makes for a fluent and rapid remediation process.

The design of ANDROMEDA, emphasizing local and demand-driven representation of the subject program, is geared toward incremental scanning. We have implemented this feature such that neither the soundness nor the accuracy of the analysis are lost in rescanning, which leaves responsiveness as the main challenge. We address this concern by combining several optimizations and algorithms, which are described in the remainder of this section.

4.1 Change Impact Analysis

ANDROMEDA's ability to respond to code changes efficiently is founded on a change-impact analysis (CIA) algorithm spanning all the layers of data structures comprising ANDROMEDA, from the type hierarchy, through the call graph, and up to the propagation graph. Upon receiving a notification that a given compilation unit (CU) has changed, the CIA algorithm compares its new version to the previous one, which it caches exactly for this purpose. By the end of the comparison, CUs where differences were found are marked as either modified or deleted or added.

ANDROMEDA then localizes the changes to determine what the bottommost layer they affect is. For example, if a class is marked as modified due to a change made in one of its methods, then ANDROMEDA will reason only about that method in the ensuing stages of the update process. Moreover, if the method has changed in a way that affects neither the call sites it declares nor the (intraprocedural) type-inference solution computed for it, then there are no implications with respect to the call graph, and the notification can immediately flow to the highest layer of the hierarchy, which is the propagation graph. This focusing strategy translates into a major optimization, whereby lower layers of the hierarchy can often be skipped.

4.2   Efficient Data Structures

Since the type hierarchy and call graph of ANDROMEDA are built in a local fashion, using intra-procedural type inference (*cf.* Section 3.1), change notifications arriving at these data structures can be handled efficiently. For example, if the call graph is notified that method m has changed, then only the subgraph rooted at m needs to be modified. Furthermore, call sites in m where the type-inference solution for the receiver remains unchanged can safely be preserved throughout the update process. The challenge is with the propagation graph, which records transitive information flows.

Following a code change, certain parts of the propagation graph are invalidated, but detecting the obsolete data-flow edges is difficult without additional bookkeeping, because they are due to transitive flow of information. To this end, similarly to [26], we use a *support graph*, which is an auxiliary graph structure documenting how edges in the propagation graph, henceforth referred to as taint facts, were formed. Similarly to [24], we distinguish between two types of edges in the propagation graph: *path edges* and *summary edges*. Path edges correspond to normal intraprocedural flow, whereas summary edges bridge across call sites. This implies two types of edges in the support graph:

- Normal edges are of the form $tf_1 \rightarrow tf_2$, where tf_i denotes a taint fact.
- Summary edges are of the form $\langle tf_{1,1}, tf_{1,2} \rangle \rightarrow \langle tf_{2,1}, tf_{2,2} \rangle$, with the interpretation that summary edge $tf_{2,1} \rightarrow tf_{2,2}$ in the caller was learned based on edge $tf_{1,1} \rightarrow tf_{1,2}$ in the callee.

When the propagation graph is notified of a change in a particular method, it establishes the set I of taint facts that can immediately be discarded based on the change. It then consults the support graph, which computes the transitive closure of the facts in I. Corresponding edges are then removed from the propagation graph, and the fixpoint iteration process is renewed by updating the IR of every changed method, and then searching for new seeds and extending existing path edges.

5   Empirical Evaluation

In this section, we describe the experiments we conducted to measure ANDROMEDA's accuracy, performance and incremental capabilities.

5.1   Experimental Setup

ANDROMEDA is a client of the WALA framework.[4] It is written in Java and implemented as an Eclipse plugin. We have conducted two sets of experiments to evaluate ANDROMEDA:

1. **Standard Analysis.** We measure ANDROMEDA's performance and accuracy by applying it to a suite of 16 benchmarks, including applications appearing in [33] and [17], as well as several contemporary commercial applications. Benchmark

---

[4] http://wala.sf.net.

characteristics are provided at the leftmost columns of Figure 4. We compare AN-DROMEDA with Taint Analysis for Java (TAJ) [33] on 8 common benchmarks. TAJ, which is the most recent and advanced work on industrial taint analysis, is also a WALA client. The main difference is that TAJ utilizes whole-program pointer analysis, ensuring accuracy and scalability by enforcing *unsound* bounds. For scalability, TAJ uses a preset budget for call-graph and pointer-analysis construction. Similar bounds are used for accuracy (*e.g.*, filtering out witness flows beyond a given length).

2. **Incremental Scanning.** We measure average response time for reanalysis of two applications following several common code changes, such as deleting or adding a statement or a method.

We performed the experiments on a MacBook Pro laptop computer with a 2.66-GHz processor and 8 GB of RAM, running OS X V10.8 and Java Standard Edition Runtime Environment (JRE) V1.6.0_35 with 2.6GB of heap space.[5]

5.2   Standard Analysis

The results of the first experiment appear in Figure 4. To assess the accuracy of AN-DROMEDA, a security expert sampled at random 10 findings per benchmark, and classified them as either true positive (TP), false positive (FP) or unknown. A finding was classified as *unknown* if there was missing source code (*e.g.*, if the flow goes through library code), or the flow was valid but of low exploitability. The TAJ data comes from the original TAJ paper [33].

The experimental data gives a clear indication of ANDROMEDA's high accuracy. Compared to TAJ (on 8 of the benchmarks), ANDROMEDA finds substantially more issues, reporting 578 findings compared to a total of 280 findings reported by TAJ. Moreover, ANDROMEDA's findings are more accurate on 4 of the 5 benchmarks where accuracy data is available for TAJ, the only exception being Webgoat. The accuracy statistics are summarized in Figure 6. For performance, ANDROMEDA's average running time (on the common benchmarks) is 114 seconds, whereas the average scanning time of TAJ is 112 seconds, which is almost identical.

Our analysis of the findings suggests that the combination of soundness and framework modeling allows ANDROMEDA to find more application entrypoints, as well as follow data flows through more parts of the application, compared to TAJ. These account for ANDROMEDA's ability to find more quality findings than TAJ while retaining a better signal-to-noise ratio.

For the entire suite, ANDROMEDA's accuracy statistics show an average of 53% TPs, 11% FPs and 36% unknowns. ANDROMEDA's average running time is 298 seconds (AppA being an outlier). These numbers point to ANDROMEDA's high precision, which comes at the reasonable cost of 5 minutes on average per scan.

---

[5] The running times reported for TAJ are drawn from the original paper [33], where another execution environment, involving a Windows desktop machine, was used. Running-time comparisons should thus be considered with a grain of salt.

Benchmark	Characteristics			TAJ				ANDROMEDA			
	Version	Class Count	Line Count	Findings	Time (s)	TP	FP	Findings	Time (s)	TP	FP
AjaxChat	0.8.3	29	4147	-	-	-	-	14	30	70%	30%
AltoroJ	1.0	43	746	37	23	80%	20%	35	4	90%	10%
AppA	N/A	250	N/A	-	-	-	-	301	2555	20%	0%
Blojsom	3.1	254	19984	123	207	-	-	139	494	60%	30%
BlueBlog	1.0	38	650	12	6	50%	50%	13	16	100%	0%
Contineo	2.2.3	79	65744	-	-	-	-	228	573	90%	0%
Dlog	3.0-BETA-2	268	17229	6	221	-	-	30	51	60%	20%
Friki	2.1.1-58	35	2339	7	9	70%	20%	81	3	100%	0%
GestCV	1.0	124	107494	7	209	50%	50%	89	10	60%	10%
Ginp	1.0	73	387	49	28	-	-	122	62	40%	0%
JBoard	0.3	185	17500	-	-	-	-	74	330	10%	0%
JPetstore	2.5.6	116	25820	-	-	-	-	179	73	10%	0%
JugJobs	1.0	30	4815	-	-	-	-	39	32	60%	40%
Photov	2.1	239	210304	-	-	-	-	178	229	10%	0%
StrutsArticle	1.1	45	7897	-	-	-	-	25	35	10%	0%
Webgoat	5.1-20080213	192	17656	39	193	90%	10%	69	275	60%	40%

Fig. 4. Performance and Accuracy Results for TAJ and ANDROMEDA in Standard Scanning

Change Type	Response Time (s)			
	AltoroJ		Webgoat	
	Deletion	Addition	Deletion	Addition
Taint-propagator statement	2	2.2	1.9	2.2
Security sink	0.5	2	1.9	2.5
Security source	2.1	2.1	1.8	3.2
Irrelevant statement	1.9	2	2.5	2.8
Relevant method	2.2	1.9	1.8	2.7
Irrelevant method	2.2	1.7	1.7	1.7

	ANDROMEDA	TAJ
Average TPs	82%	68%
Average FPs	12%	30%
Average Unknowns	6%	2%

Fig. 6. Accuracy Statistics

Fig. 5. Response Times for Various Incremental Changes

5.3   Incremental Scanning

To measure ANDROMEDA's incremental features, we considered a set of common editing operations, including addition and deletion of statements and methods, which we classified according to the relevance of the statement or method to the solution computed by ANDROMEDA. A statement may either be a source, a sink, a taint propagator (participating in a vulnerable flow), or an operation lying oustide the ANDROMEDA data-flow solution. Similarly, a method may or may not participate in the solution.

We examined the effect of either adding or deleting a syntactic construct chosen from each of these 6 categories, which yielded 12 kinds of possible changes. For each change type, and each of the two benchmarks we used for this experiment, we applied the change 10 times. For each round, we chose a target at random from a pool of suitable candidates that we prepared in advance. The reported numbers are the average (in wall-clock seconds) across these 10 rounds.

The results of this evaluation are listed in Figure 5. Response times are largely within the range of 2-3 seconds per change, whereas the overall scanning time of Webgoat is 275 seconds. For AltoroJ, incremental scanning is less motivated, because analysis from scratch takes 4 seconds to complete. Still, the average response time for an incremental change in AltoroJ is 1.9 seconds, which is less than half of the time required for complete reanalysis. For Webgoat, a response is obtained after 2.2 seconds on average, which is less than 1% of the time needed for a fresh scan of this benchmark.

6 Related Work

There is a rich body of work on taint analysis. We here concentrate on static taint analysis, and refer the reader to [4,22] for a survey of dynamic taint-analysis techniques. An detailed overview of works on program slicing is given in [30] and references therein.

The notion of *tainted variables* became known with the Perl language. Typically, the data manipulated by a program can be tagged with security levels [9], which assume a poset structure. Under certain conditions, this poset is a lattice [8]. Given a program, the principle of *noninterference* dictates that low-security behavior of the program be not affected by any high-security data, unless that high-security data has been previously downgraded [12]. Taint analysis is an information-flow problem in which high data is the untrusted output of a source, low-security operations are those performed by sinks, and untrusted data is downgraded by sanitizers.

Volpano *et al.* [34] show a type-based algorithm that certifies implicit and explicit flows and also guarantees noninterference. Shankar *et al.* present a taint analysis for C using a constraint-based type-inference engine based on cqual [27]. Similarly to the propagation graph built by ANDROMEDA, a constraint graph is constructed for a cqual program, and paths from tainted nodes to untainted nodes are flagged.

Myers' Java Information Flow (Jif) [20] uses type-based static analysis to track information flow. Based on the Decentralized Label Model [21], Jif considers all memory as a channel of information, which requires that every variable, field, and parameter used in the program be statically labeled. Labels can either be declared or inferred. Ashcraft and Engler [2] also use taint analysis to detect software attacks due to tainted variables. Their approach provides user-defined sanity checks to untaint potentially tainted variables. Pistoia *et al.* [23] present a static analysis to detect tainted variables in privilege-asserting code in access-control systems based on stack inspection.

Snelting *et al.* [28] make the observation that Program Dependence Graphs (PDGs) and noninterference are related in that $dom(s_1) \not\rightarrow dom(s_2)$ implies $s_1 \notin backslice(s_2)$, where *backslice* is maps each statement s to its static backwards slice. Based on this observation, Hammer *et al.* [14] present an algorithm for verifying noninterference: For output statement s, $backslice(s)$ must contain only statements whose security label is lower than s. Though promising, this approach has not been shown to scale.

Livshits and Lam [17] analyze Java EE applications by tracking taint through heap-allocated objects. Their solution requires prior computation of Whaley and Lam's flow-insensitive, context-sensitive may-points-to analysis, based on Binary Decision Diagrams (BDDs) [38], which limits the scalability of the analysis [16]. The points-to relation is the same for the entire program ignoring control flow. By contrast, the PDG-based algorithm in [14] handles heap updates in a flow-sensitive manner, albeit at a much higher cost. Livshits and Lam's analysis requires programmer-supplied descriptors for sources, sinks and library methods dealing with taint carriers. Guarnieri *et al.* [13] present a taint analysis for JavaScript. Their work relies on Andersen's whole-program analysis [1]. While being sound, the analysis is not incremental, and has not been shown to scale to large programs.

Wassermann and Su extend Minamide's string-analysis algorithm [19] to syntactically isolate tainted substrings from untainted substrings in PHP applications. They label nonterminals in a context-free grammar with annotations reflecting taintedness and
untaintedness. Their expensive yet elegant mechanism is applied to detect both SQLi
[36] and XSS [37] vulnerabilities. Subsequent work by Tateishi *et al.* [32] enhances
taint-analysis precision through a string analysis that automatically detects and classifies downgraders in the application scope.

McCamant and Ernst [18] take a quantitative approach to information flow: Instead
of using taint analysis, they cast information-flow security to a network-flow-capacity
problem, and describe a dynamic technique for measuring the amount of secret data
that leaks to public observers.

ANDROMEDA's scalability stems from its demand-driven analysis strategy. Demand-
driven pointer analysis was originally introduced by Heintze and Tardieu [15]. Since
there have been several works on demand-driven points-to analysis via context-free-
language reachability [31,40,39]. For taint analysis, our empirical data suggests that
only a small fraction of a large program is expected to be influenced by source statements. Fuhrer *at al.* [11] take a demand-driven approach in replacing raw references
to generic library classes with parameterized references. At a high level, this analysis
resembles the alias analysis performed by ANDROMEDA, as constraints on type parameters are first propagated backwards to allocation sites and declarations, and from there
they are propagated forward.

7   Conclusion

We have presented ANDROMEDA, a security-analysis algorithm featuring local, demand-
driven tracking of vulnerable information flows. Thanks to this design choice, AN-
DROMEDA scales to large codes while being highly accurate, and additionally features
incremental scanning capabilities. ANDROMEDA is part of a commercial product. Our
experimental evaluation of ANDROMEDA, comparing it to a state-of-the-art scanner that
sacrifices soundness for accuracy, shows ANDROMEDA to be favorable.

References

1. Andersen, L.O.: Program Analysis and Specialization for the C Programming Language.
   PhD thesis, University of Copenhagen, Copenhagen, Denmark (May 1994)
2. Ashcraft, K., Engler, D.: Using Programmer-Written Compiler Extensions to Catch Security
   Holes. In: S&P (2002)
3. Bacon, D.F., Sweeney, P.F.: Fast static analysis of c++ virtual function calls. In: OOPSLA,
   pp. 324–341 (1996)
4. Chang, W., Streiff, B., Lin, C.: Efficient and Extensible Security Enforcement Using Dynamic Data Flow Analysis. In: CCS (2008)
5. Cheng, B., Hwu, W.W.: Modular interprocedural pointer analysis using access paths: design,
   implementation, and evaluation. In: Proceedings of the ACM SIGPLAN 2000 Conference
   on Programming Language Design and Implementation, pp. 57–69 (2000)
6. Cousot, P., Cousot, R.: Abstract Interpretation: A Unified Lattice Model for Static Analysis
   of Programs by Construction or Approximation of Fixpoints. In: POPL, pp. 238–252 (1977)

7. Dean, J., Grove, D., Chambers, C.: Optimization of Object-Oriented Programs Using Static Class Hierarchy Analysis. In: Olthoff, W. (ed.) ECOOP 1995. LNCS, vol. 952, pp. 77–101. Springer, Heidelberg (1995)
8. Denning, D.E.: A Lattice Model of Secure Information Flow. CACM 19(5) (1976)
9. Denning, D.E., Denning, P.J.: Certification of Programs for Secure Information Flow. CACM 20(7) (1977)
10. Deutsch, A.: A Storeless Model of Aliasing and Its Abstractions Using Finite Representations of Right-regular Equivalence Relations. In: ICCL (1992)
11. Fuhrer, R., Tip, F., Kieżun, A., Dolby, J., Keller, M.: Efficiently Refactoring Java Applications to Use Generic Libraries. In: Gao, X.-X. (ed.) ECOOP 2005. LNCS, vol. 3586, pp. 71–96. Springer, Heidelberg (2005)
12. Goguen, J.A., Meseguer, J.: Security Policies and Security Models. In: S&P (1982)
13. Guarnieri, S., Pistoia, M., Tripp, O., Dolby, J., Teilhet, S.: Saving the World Wide Web from Vulnerable JavaScript. In: ISSTA (2011)
14. Hammer, C., Krinke, J., Snelting, G.: Information Flow Control for Java Based on Path Conditions in Dependence Graphs. In: S&P (2006)
15. Heintze, N., Tardieu, O.: Demand-Driven Pointer Analysis. In: PLDI (2001)
16. Lhoták, O., Hendren, L.J.: Context-Sensitive Points-to Analysis: Is It Worth It. In: CC (2006)
17. Livshits, V.B., Lam, M.S.: Finding Security Vulnerabilities in Java Applications with Static Analysis. In: USENIX Security (2005)
18. McCamant, S., Ernst, M.D.: Quantitative Information Flow as Network Flow Capacity. In: PLDI (2008)
19. Minamide, Y.: Static Approximation of Dynamically Generated Web Pages. In: WWW (2005)
20. Myers, A.C.: JFlow: Practical Mostly-static Information Flow Control. In: POPL (1999)
21. Myers, A.C., Liskov, B.: A Decentralized Model for Information Flow Control. In: SOSP (1997)
22. Newsome, J., Song, D.: Dynamic Taint Analysis for Automatic Detection, Analysis, and Signature Generation of Exploits on Commodity Software. In: NDSS (2005)
23. Pistoia, M., Flynn, R.J., Koved, L., Sreedhar, V.C.: Interprocedural Analysis for Privileged Code Placement and Tainted Variable Detection. In: Gao, X.-X. (ed.) ECOOP 2005. LNCS, vol. 3586, pp. 362–386. Springer, Heidelberg (2005)
24. Reps, T., Horwitz, S., Sagiv, M.: Precise Interprocedural Dataflow Analysis via Graph Reachability. In: POPL (1995)
25. Sabelfeld, A., Myers, A.C.: Language-based Information-flow Security. IEEE Journal on Selected Areas in Communications 21, 5–19 (2003)
26. Saha, D.: Incremental Evaluation of Tabled Logic Programs. PhD thesis, State University of New York at Stony Brook, Stony Brook, NY, USA (2006)
27. Shankar, U., Talwar, K., Foster, J.S., Wagner, D.: Detecting Format String Vulnerabilities with Type Qualifiers. In: USENIX Security (2001)
28. Snelting, G., Robschink, T., Krinke, J.: Efficent Path Conditions in Dependence Graphs for Software Safety Analysis. TOSEM, 15(4) (2006)
29. Sridharan, M., Artzi, S., Pistoia, M., Guarnieri, S., Tripp, O., Berg, R.: F4F: Taint Analysis of Framework-based Web Applications. In: OOPSLA (2011)
30. Sridharan, M., Fink, S.J., Bodík, R.: Thin Slicing. In: PLDI (2007)
31. Sridharan, M., Bodík, R.: Refinement-based Context-sensitive Points-to Analysis for Java. In: ACM SIGPLAN Conference on Programming Language Design and Implementation (PLDI 2006), Ottawa, ON, Canada, pp. 387–400 (June 2006)
32. Tateishi, T., Pistoia, M., Tripp, O.: Path- and Index-sensitive String Analysis Based on Monadic Second-order Logic. In: ISSTA (2011)

33. Tripp, O., Pistoia, M., Fink, S.J., Sridharan, M., Weisman, O.: TAJ: Effective Taint Analysis of Web Applications. In: PLDI (2009)
34. Volpano, D., Irvine, C., Smith, G.: A Sound Type System for Secure Flow Analysis. JCS 4(2-3) (1996)
35. Vosloo, I., Kourie, D.G.: Server-centric web frameworks: An overview. ACM Comput. Surv. 40(2), 4:1–4:33 (2008)
36. Wassermann, G., Su, Z.: Sound and Precise Analysis of Web Applications for Injection Vulnerabilities. In: PLDI (2007)
37. Wassermann, G., Su, Z.: Static Detection of Cross-site Scripting Vulnerabilities. In: ICSE 2008 (2008)
38. Whaley, J., Lam, M.S.: Cloning Based Context-Sensitive Pointer Alias Analysis Using Binary Decision Diagrams. In: PLDI (2004)
39. Yan, D., Xu, G., Rountev, A.: Demand-driven context-sensitive alias analysis for java. In: Proceedings of the 2011 International Symposium on Software Testing and Analysis, pp. 155–165 (2011)
40. Zheng, X., Rugina, R.: Demand-driven alias analysis for c. In: Proceedings of the 35th Annual ACM SIGPLAN-SIGACT Symposium on Principles of Programming Languages, pp. 197–208 (2008)

VerChor: A Framework for Verifying Choreographies

Matthias Güdemann[1], Pascal Poizat[2], Gwen Salaün[1], and Alexandre Dumont[1]

[1] Inria, Grenoble INP, France
[2] LIP6 UMR 7606 CNRS – Université Paris Ouest, Nanterre, France

1 Introduction

Nowadays, modern applications are often constructed by reusing and assembling distributed and collaborating entities, *e.g.*, software components, Web services, or Software as a Service in cloud computing environments. In order to facilitate the integration of independently developed components (*i.e.*, peers) that may reside in different organizations, it is necessary to provide a global contract to which the peers participating in a service composition should adhere. Such a contract is called *choreography*, and specifies interactions among a set of services from a global point of view. This contract is the reference for the further development steps (service selection, code generation, maintenance, reconfiguration, etc.). The specification and formal analysis of this contract is therefore crucial and must be handled carefully by the designer to avoid an erroneous design, which would be very costly if discovered lately in the development process. Unfortunately, only limited effort, *e.g.* [3,6,1], has been spent to develop formal verification tools, which can automatically detect issues such as deadlocks or erroneous behaviours in the choreography specification.

In this paper, we propose a modular framework for performing automatically a number of crucial verification tasks on choreography specifications. Our framework accepts as input the following interaction-based choreography description languages: (i) XML-based languages (WS-CDL), (ii) graphical notations (BPMN 2.0 choreographies), and (iii) formal description models (Chor, conversation protocols). In order to favour extensibility and reusability of our framework, we

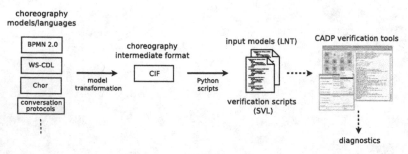

propose an intermediate format (CIF) for representing choreography description languages. This intermediate format allows to accept several existing languages

V. Cortellessa and D. Varró (Eds.): FASE 2013, LNCS 7793, pp. 226–230, 2013.
© Springer-Verlag Berlin Heidelberg 2013

as input. It can also serve as an expressive standalone specification language for choreographies and can be easily extended with new choreography constructs. Another advantage is that it makes possible to use jointly several formal verification tools and techniques as back-end, provided that a connection to those tools exist. We have already developed a connection to the CADP verification toolbox [2] via a translation to the LNT process algebra, one of the CADP input specification languages. This enables the automated verification of some key choreography analysis tasks (repairability, realizability, conformance, etc.). Our framework is extensible with other front-end and back-end connections to, respectively, other choreography languages and formal verification tools.

2   Verification

This section presents some key properties, which are of utmost importance when designing choreography-based distributed system. They can be verified automatically in our framework using model and equivalence checking techniques.

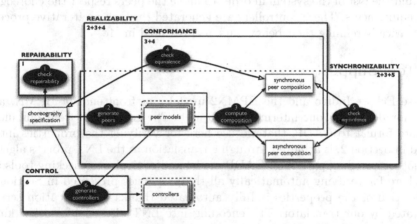

Repairability. A choreography is not repairable when at some point in its behaviour there is a non-deterministic choice between interactions involving different sending peers. Such a design is erroneous because there is no way to make the corresponding distributed implementation respect the choreography requirements. Detecting automatically (non-)repairable choreographies is difficult, because there are situations where such a non-deterministic choice actually corresponds to the initial part of an interleaving of several interactions, and in that case, the choreography is repairable.

Synchronizability. Synchronizability analyzes a set of peers and checks that all interaction sequences in the asynchronous system are also possible in the synchronous one. This property is necessary for ensuring the realizability and conformance of possibly infinite systems (choreographies with loops). A recent result [1] that we reuse here proves that checking synchronizability is decidable and proposes a decision procedure for verifying this property.

Realizability. This property checks whether the distributed version of the system behaves exactly as specified in the choreography. This is crucial in a top-down development process, where peers are obtained via projection [6] from the choreography, in order to ensure that the implementation perfectly matches the global specification. In our framework, we can check equivalence-based notions of realizability, as those used in [1,5,6].

Conformance. In a bottom-up development process, peers are being reused and integrated into a new composition. The choreography serves as a contract that the implementation under construction must respect. From a verification point of view, it can be checked exactly as realizability, except that projection is not necessary. Conformance checking takes as input a choreography and a set of peers, whereas realizability checking only requires a choreography specification.

Control for Enforcing Realizability. If a choreography is not realizable (or conformant *wrt.* a set of peers) yet repairable, we can enforce the distributed system to respect the (synchronizability and) realizability of a choreography by generating distributed controllers. They act locally by interacting with their peer and the rest of the system in order to make the peers respect the choreography requirements. These controllers are generated through an iterative process, automatically refining their behaviours, as presented in [4].

3   Tool Support

We use Eclipse Indigo and the BPMN2 modeler as front-end for BPMN, and XML for describing our intermediate format. The connection from our intermediate format to CADP, that we use here for verifying the properties introduced in Section 2, is achieved through a translation to the LNT process algebra (see [5] for encoding patterns). CADP model and equivalence checking tools are used here for verifying automatically all the properties presented in Section 2. Verification of the properties is fully automated thanks to verification scripts generated by our translator. The encoding into LNT also enables other kinds of formal analysis with CADP, such as deadlock search, simulation, or checking temporal properties written in MCL using the Evaluator 4.0 model checker.

Experiments. We show experimental results on some examples of our database, which contains more than 200 choreographies (many of them are real-world examples found in the literature). It is worth observing that translation time (from the input languages to CIF and LNT) is negligible even for huge examples. For each experiment, the table gives the number of peers (P), interactions (Inter.), and selection operators (Sel.). Then, we give the size of the corresponding LTS and the size of the largest intermediate state space for generating the asynchronous version of the distributed system (number of states and transitions), and the overall time for checking whether the choreography is repairable (R_p), generating all LTSs (synchronous and asynchronous versions of the distributed system), and verifying synchronizability (S_c) and realizability (R).

We can see that BPMN choreographies can result in huge LTSs (see example 7), because BPMN parallel operators are expanded in all the possible

Ex.	Lang.	|P|	|Inter.|	|Sel.|	$\|S\|/\|T\|$	Async. parallel compo. $\|S\|/\|T\|$	Time	Verif. R_p | S_c | R
1	Chor	3	10	1	21 / 29	127 / 200	48s	√ | √ | √
2	BPMN	6	19	1	580 / 1,828	4,054 / 12,814	1m43s	√ | √ | √
3	BPMN	6	19	1	18 / 20	750 / 3,298	1m40s	√ | √ | √
4	BPMN	6	19	1	580 / 1,842	16,129 / 51,317	1m45s	√ | √ | √
5	CP	7	11	1	11 / 11	158,741 / 853,559	5m47s	√ | × | ×
6	BPMN	12	25	4	577 / 2,499	$\sim\!1^*10^6$ / $\sim\!7^*10^6$	8m43s	√ | √ | √
7	BPMN	15	31	5	65,556 / 573,479	$\sim\!2^*10^6$ / $\sim\!18^*10^6$	1h34m	√ | × | ×

interleaved behaviours when the corresponding LTS is generated. We note that the overall time for generating LTSs for choreography and both distributed systems (synchronous and asynchronous) as well as for verifying properties R_p, S_c, and R is reasonable for medium-size choreographies, see for instance examples 2, 3, 4, 6 in the table. It is most costly to check realizable examples because it deserves an exhaustive exploration of all cases, whereas if the choreography is not realizable, the analysis stops when a violation is found. The two causes of explosion are the number of peers (*e.g.*, 15 peers in example 7) and the degree of parallelism, that is the number of branches and interactions executed in concurrent branches of the choreography. If the choreography is not realizable, we generate local controllers which synchronize together in order to enforce the distributed system to respect the order of messages as specified in the global contract. For instance, example 5 presents several ordering issues if peers are generated using projection. In that case, our process requires 6 iterations to construct these controllers, meaning that 6 additional synchronization messages are necessary to make the system realizable. It takes about 20 minutes for this example to successfully check synchronizability/realizability using equivalence checking and exploit the resulting counterexample to refine controllers, until completion of the process.

Acknowledgements. This work is supported by the Personal Information Management through Internet (PIMI) ANR project.

References

1. Basu, S., Bultan, T., Ouederni, M.: Deciding Choreography Realizability. In: Proc. of POPL 2012 (2012)
2. Garavel, H., Lang, F., Mateescu, R., Serwe, W.: CADP 2010: A Toolbox for the Construction and Analysis of Distributed Processes. In: Abdulla, P.A., Leino, K.R.M. (eds.) TACAS 2011. LNCS, vol. 6605, pp. 372–387. Springer, Heidelberg (2011)
3. Foster, H., Uchitel, S., Magee, J., Kramer, J.: LTSA-WS: A Tool for Model-based Verification of Web Service Compositions and Choreography. In: Proc. of ICSE 2006 (2006)
4. Güdemann, M., Salaün, G., Ouederni, M.: Counterexample Guided Synthesis of Monitors for Realizability Enforcement. In: Chakraborty, S., Mukund, M. (eds.) ATVA 2012. LNCS, vol. 7561, pp. 238–253. Springer, Heidelberg (2012)

5. Poizat, P., Salaün, G.: Checking the Realizability of BPMN 2.0 Choreographies. In: Proc. of SAC 2012 (2012)
6. Salaün, G., Bultan, T., Roohi, N.: Realizability of Choreographies Using Process Algebra Encodings. IEEE T. Services Computing 5(3) (2012)

Javanni: A Verifier for JavaScript

Martin Nordio[1], Cristiano Calcagno[2], and Carlo Alberto Furia[1]

[1] Chair of Software Engineering, ETH Zurich, Switzerland
{firstname.lastname}@inf.ethz.ch
[2] ETH Zurich, Imperial College London and Monoidics Ltd.
ccris@doc.ic.ac.uk

Abstract. JavaScript ranks among the most popular programming languages for the web, yet its highly dynamic type system and occasionally unintuitive semantics make programming particularly error-prone. This paper presents Javanni, a verifier for JavaScript programs that can statically detect many common programming errors. Javanni checks the absence of standard type-related errors (such as accessing undefined fields) without requiring user-written annotations, and it can also verify full functional-correctness specifications. Several experiments with JavaScript applications reported in the paper demonstrate that Javanni is flexibly usable on programs with non-trivial specifications. Javanni is available online within the CloudStudio web integrated environment.

1 Introduction

Originally developed by Netscape as a scripting language for lightweight web programming, JavaScript has rapidly become one of the most widely used programming languages[1] for the web. Its popularity has greatly exceeded its primary target—client-side web programming for nonprofessionals—and the language is now routinely used to develop large applications, such as Google Docs and Google Maps, and even some critical software such as on-line banking. Unfortunately, the original language design includes a number of quirks[2] which, combined with a highly dynamic and weakly-typed type system that mixes heterogeneous programming paradigms, make JavaScript programming particularly error-prone. Simple errors such as accessing undefined fields, invoking undefined functions, or calling functions with the wrong number of actual parameters are workaday in JavaScript programming. Even if programming frameworks exist (such as the Google Web Toolkit) that automatically translate from a higher-level language, a large part of JavaScript applications are still written by hand, with consequent risks in terms of reliability and security.

This paper describes Javanni, a static verifier for JavaScript programs that can detect many of these frustrating errors. Javanni translates JavaScript programs into Boogie [4], and then uses the Boogie verifier to check correctness properties on the translated program. Javanni is completely automatic, does not require user-written annotations, and can detect common type-related errors including: (1) invocation of undefined functions; (2) writing of undeclared variables; (3) reading of undefined values (e.g. undeclared or

---

[1] http://www.tiobe.com
[2] https://www.destroyallsoftware.com/talks/wat

V. Cortellessa and D. Varró (Eds.): FASE 2013, LNCS 7793, pp. 231–234, 2013.
© Springer-Verlag Berlin Heidelberg 2013

uninitialized variables or fields); (4) incorrect number of actual parameters in function calls.

The focus of most related approaches to JavaScript verification [1,3] is restricted to standard type analysis. In contrast, Javanni supports full functional correctness properties; to our knowledge, this kind of support is available only in another quite recent work based on separation logic [2].

In the translation to Boogie, Javanni automatically introduces a specification of correct typing behavior in the form of pre- and postconditions of functions; on top of these, users may add custom assertions to the input programs and verify arbitrary functional properties of their JavaScript applications. The specification generated automatically by Javanni frames good programming practices, such as some discipline in field declaration and initialization, and hence Javanni may report false positive; in most cases, however, the reported errors are at least indicative of poor programming practices. The translation also applies *method inlining* and *loop unrolling* to improve verification accuracy without requiring extra annotations.

Javanni is a component of the CloudStudio [5] web-based multi-language integrated development environment, available online at http://cloudstudio.ethz.ch/. Section 3 presents a set of JavaScript programs that have been verified using Javanni, against both the automatically generated specification and more complex functional properties. Javanni is implemented in Java using the Rhino JavaScript framework. For a demo video, see http://www.youtube.com/watch?v=K8yboTQZ9p0.

2   Verifying JavaScript

For each JavaScript input program J, Javanni creates a Boogie file B_J containing an encoding of the source J annotated with assertions that formalize correctness properties. The translation also introduces some specification functions and axioms, used to enforce the semantics of the original JavaScript source in the Boogie language. This section succinctly illustrates the main features of the translation.

Type boxing and unboxing. To accommodate JavaScript's dynamically-typed variables within Boogie's static type system, Javanni includes *boxing* and *unboxing* functions in the translation. JavaScript variables (and fields) get a generic reference type **ref** in Boogie. Whenever we need to use some variable x according to its actual dynamic type (e.g., **int** or **bool**), we unbox it: $unbox(x)$ in Boogie returns the value attached to x. Boxing works conversely; e.g., $box(42)$ returns a reference attached to the integer 42. Additional axioms declare the behavior of arithmetic and Boolean operations with respect to boxing and unboxing primitive (e.g., $unbox(box(i)+box(j))=i+j$).

Object creation. JavaScript supports field initialization with the **prototype** keyword: C.**prototype**.$a = v$ sets field a of class C to value v whenever an instance of C is created. Javanni introduces *initializer* predicates to encode the semantics of field initialization in Boogie. Javanni defines a predicate $init . C(this: \textbf{ref}, h: Heap)$ for each class C that holds for references $this$ attached to objects whose fields satisfy the initializations (in a given model h of the heap). For example, a class $Student$ initialized with $Student$.**prototype**.$age = 18$ determines a predicate initializer with body $init . Student(this, h) \{ h[this, age] = 18 \}$. Initializers also keep track of which member functions are defined. For each function f member of C, $init$. $C(this$, $h)$ specifies that $h[$ $this$, $func\$f] \neq undef$, where $func\$f$ is a fictitious field of C added to represent f in Boogie. Creations of an object o of class C become two assumptions in Boogie: **assume** $allocated[o$, $h]$ (reference o is not undefined or **null**) and **assume** $init$. $C(o$, $h)$ (the initializations hold); Boogie's **assume** statements are used as postulated facts in the reasoning.

Type correctness assertions. Javanni automatically generates Boogie assertion statements that encode the type correctness of invocations and readings of functions, variables, and fields. If Boogie can discharge all the **assert** statements, there are no type errors of these kinds. For example, every field access of the form x . a determines two assertions in Boogie: the target is defined (**assert** $allocated[x$, $h]$); and the field is defined (**assert** $Heap[x,a] \neq undef$). More complex assertions encode type conformance and correctness of function invocations.

Contracts. To verify full functional correctness properties in JavaScript programs, Javanni supports preconditions, postconditions, and assume and assert instructions a la Boogie. While JavaScript does not natively support assertions, Javanni recognizes method calls with the special names $requires$ (preconditions), $ensures$ (postconditions), and $assume$ and $assert$. These methods directly translate to the corresponding **requires**, **ensures**, **assume** and **assert** instructions in Boogie.

Inlining and loop unrolling. Boogie is a *modular* verifier: it reasons about function invocations using only the pre- and postconditions of the callees. This means that if function *foo* calls *bar* but the latter has no postcondition, Boogie will be oblivious of the effects of *bar* when reasoning about *foo*. To reduce the amount of user-written annotations required to reason modularly in Boogie, Javanni features *inlining*: replace a call to *bar* within *foo* with a copy of *bar*'s code, so that its effects within *foo* can be evaluated directly. A similar feature is *loop unrolling*, useful to reason inductively about loops without loop invariants. Unrolling replaces a loop by a sequence (of finite length) of conditional executions of its body; the depth of the unrolling can be set by users to find the best trade-off between scalability and annotation burden.

3   Case Study

Table 1 lists a set of examples verified using Javanni. For each example, it shows the length (in LOC) of the JavaScript source, the length of the specification added manually, the length of the Boogie source generated by Javanni without and with inlining and loop unrolling, and the time taken to check the Boogie program (on a Windows 7 machine with a 3.1 GHz dual core Intel Pentium processor and 4GB of RAM). The examples are available at http://se.inf.ethz.ch/people/nordio/javanni/.

Programs 1–2 only include standard type correctness properties generated automatically by Javanni. Program 1 is a collection of small JavaScript applets from http://www.jsworkshop.com; program 2 is one single larger application, a poker game, from the same source. Programs 3–6 are JavaScript implementations of object-oriented standard examples also used in previous work of ours [7,6], each equipped with functional specifications (pre- and postcondition) for each method. In this case, verification also required intermediate assertions, but these were much fewer than in [7,6]

Table 1. JavaScript programs automatically verified with Javanni

NAME	LOC JS	LOC SPEC	LOC BOOGIE	LOC INLINED	TIME [S]	FEATURE
1. JS workshop	237	0	2448	3400	3.3	Type Correctness
2. Poker game	320	0	1139	12240	11.0	Type Correctness
3. Cell / Recell	130	21	580	1372	0.6	Functional
4. Counter	42	6	325	431	0.5	Functional
5. Expression	79	2	381	595	0.5	Functional
6. Sequence	102	3	440	1216	0.6	Functional
Total	**910**	**32**	**5313**	**19254**	**16.5**	

thanks to Javanni's inlining and unrolling. Programs 3–4 use object-oriented features to model: cells that store integer values (3); and a counter (4). Program 5 features non-negative integer expression objects which can be evaluated. Program 6 models integer sequences including monotone, strict, arithmetic, and Fibonacci sequences.

4 Conclusions

This paper presented the essential features of Javanni, a verifier for JavaScript programs. Javanni works by automatically transforming JavaScript programs into the Boogie verification language; it then uses the Boogie verifier to determine if the original JavaScript program is correct. Verifying standard type correctness properties does not require special annotations; functional properties, on the other hand, are also supported and specified by means of standard pre- and postconditions, which define the expected behavior of methods. To improve verification accuracy without requiring extra annotations, Javanni's translation applies *method inlining* and *loop unrolling*. The case study suggests that these techniques can be instrumental in reducing the annotation burden required to automatically verify programs in practice.

Acknowledgments. This work was partially supported by the Swiss SNF (proj. ASII 200021-134976); and by the Gebert-Ruf Stiftung through CloudStudio's funding.

References

1. Anderson, C., Giannini, P., Drossopoulou, S.: Towards Type Inference for JavaScript. In: Gao, X.-X. (ed.) ECOOP 2005. LNCS, vol. 3586, pp. 428–452. Springer, Heidelberg (2005)
2. Gardner, P., Maffeis, S., Smith, G.D.: Towards a program logic for javascript. In: POPL, pp. 31–44 (2012)
3. Jensen, S.H., Møller, A., Thiemann, P.: Type Analysis for JavaScript. In: Palsberg, J., Su, Z. (eds.) SAS 2009. LNCS, vol. 5673, pp. 238–255. Springer, Heidelberg (2009)
4. Leino, K.R.M.: This is Boogie 2. Technical report, Microsoft Research (2008)
5. Nordio, M., et al.: Collaborative software development on the web, arXiv:1105.0768v3 (2011)
6. Tschannen, J., Furia, C.A., Nordio, M., Meyer, B.: Usable Verification of Object-Oriented Programs by Combining Static and Dynamic Techniques. In: Barthe, G., Pardo, A., Schneider, G. (eds.) SEFM 2011. LNCS, vol. 7041, pp. 382–398. Springer, Heidelberg (2011)
7. Tschannen, J., Furia, C.A., Nordio, M., Meyer, B.: Verifying Eiffel programs with Boogie. In: BOOGIE Workshop (2011), http://arxiv.org/abs/1106.4700

Model-Based Implementation
of Parallel Real-Time Systems

Ahlem Triki[3], Jacques Combaz[2], Saddek Bensalem[3], and Joseph Sifakis[1,2]

[1] EPFL, Lausanne, Switzerland
joseph.sifakis@epfl.ch
[2] Verimag/CNRS, Gières, France
{jacques.combaz,joseph.sifakis}@imag.fr
[3] Verimag/Grenoble University, Gières, France
{ahlem.triki,saddek.bensalem}@imag.fr

Abstract. One of the main challenges in the design of real-time systems is how to derive correct and efficient implementations from platform-independent specifications.

We present a general implementation method in which the application is represented by an *abstract* model consisting of a set of interacting components. The abstract model executes sequentially components interactions atomically and instantaneously. We transform abstract models into *physical* models representing their execution on a platform. Physical models take into account execution times of interactions and allow their parallel execution. They are obtained by breaking atomicity of interactions using a notion of partial state. We provide safety conditions guaranteeing that the semantics of abstract models is preserved by physical models. These provide bases for implementing a parallel execution engine coordinating the execution of the components. The implementation has been validated on a real robotic application. Benchmarks show net improvement of its performance compared to a sequential implementation.

1 Introduction

Model-based design allows deriving correct implementations from formal specifications of the application. It involves successive transformations from *abstract* models, i.e. platform-independent representations of the application software, to concrete system models taking into account platform properties such as hardware architecture constraints and execution times.

A model-based design flow for real-time systems seeks satisfaction of two types of properties. *Correctness*, that is preservation of the essential properties of the application software. This is usually established under the assumption that the available resources are sufficient for running the application. *Efficiency*, that is the available resources such as memory, time, and energy are used in an optimized manner. A key issue in this context is the efficient use of the parallelism offered by the platform, e.g. by multi-core architectures.

V. Cortellessa and D. Varró (Eds.): FASE 2013, LNCS 7793, pp. 235–249, 2013.
© Springer-Verlag Berlin Heidelberg 2013

Existing model-based implementation techniques use specific programming models. Synchronous programs can be considered as a network of strongly synchronized components. Their execution is a sequence of non-interruptible steps that define a logical notion of time. In a step each component performs a quantum of computation. An implementation is correct if the worst-case execution times (WCET) for steps are less than the requested response time for the system. For asynchronous real-time programs e.g. Ada programs, there is no notion of execution step. Components are driven by events. Fixed priority scheduling policies are used for sharing resources between components. Scheduling theory allows to estimate system response times for known periods and time budgets.

Recent implementation techniques consider more general programming models [1–3]. The proposed approaches rely on a notion of logical execution time (LET) which corresponds to the difference between the release time and the due time of an action, defined in the program using an abstract notion of time. To cope with uncertainty of the underlying platform, a program behaves as if its actions consume exactly their LET: even if they start after their release time and complete before their due time, their effect is visible exactly at these times. This is achieved by reading for each action its input exactly at its release time and its output exactly at its due time. Time-safety is violated if an action takes more than its LET to execute.

We present a general implementation method for real-time systems based on an abstract timed model. In this model, the application software is a set of components whose behavior is defined by timed automata [4]. As shown in [5], using timed automata allows more general timing constraints than LET used in [1–3], such as lower bounds, upper bounds, and time non-determinism. Components can synchronize their actions and communicate through (multiparty) *interactions*. In addition to interactions, we also consider *priorities* which are partial order relations between interactions. Priorities are essential for building correct real-time systems. They allow direct expression of real-time scheduling policies used for meeting the timing constraints of the application. Very often these policies also enforce determinism, which is necessary to have reproducible execution. The operational semantics of the abstract model assumes a sequential, atomic and instantaneous execution of the interactions. Following the approach in [5] *physical* models can be automatically built from the abstract model. A physical model represents the execution of the corresponding abstract model on a given platform. It takes into account (non zero) execution times of actions by breaking the atomicity of their execution. In this paper, we show how to build physical models allowing parallel execution of interaction by extending the approach presented in [6] for untimed models. In such physical models, interactions can be executed even from partial states, that is, even if one or more components are still executing. We prove that the semantics of abstract models is preserved by physical models when considering additional conditions characterizing safe execution. We explain how to compute these conditions using approximations of the reachable states of the system. The correctness of the physical models requires also that the platform is sufficiently fast for running the application.

We define an execution engine that implements the operational semantics of physical models. When a component completes its computation, it sends to the engine its current state. The engine uses a scheduler that can execute component interactions based on the partial knowledge of the state of the system. From an initial state of the system, it proceeds as follows.

1. Compute the set of interactions enabled by the non-executing components, i.e. the ones whose state is known. Some of the enabled interactions may be unsafe to execute as they are potentially in conflict with other interactions that may be enabled when the execution of busy components completes.
2. Among the enabled interactions, determine the subset of enabled interactions that are safe to execute. Safe interactions preserve the semantics of the application software. If all components have completed, the state of the system is fully known and all the enabled interactions are safe.
3. If the set of safe interactions is empty, wait for more components to complete their execution and go to 1. Otherwise, select a safe interaction according to a real-time scheduling policy (e.g. Earliest Deadline First) and execute it.

The rest of the paper is structured as follows. Section 2 explains how to build physical models and discusses the problem of their correctness. Section 3 defines the implementation method in terms of an execution engine. It also provides experimental results for a robotic case study showing the interest of the approach. The last section concludes the paper.

2 Modeling Parallel Real-Time Systems

2.1 Preliminaries

We consider discrete-time models, that is, time is represented using the set of non-negative integers denoted by $\mathbb{N}$. We assume that time progress is measured by *clocks*. Clocks are non-negative integer variables increasing synchronously. A clock can be reset (i.e. set to 0) independently of other clocks. Given a set of clocks X, a *valuation* $v : X \to \mathbb{N}$ is a function associating with each clock x its value $v(x)$. Given a subset of clocks $X' \subseteq X$ and a clock value $l \in \mathbb{N}$, we denote by $v[X' \mapsto l]$ the valuation that coincides with v for all clocks $x \in X \setminus X'$, and that associates l to all clocks $x \in X'$. It is defined by:

$$v[X' \mapsto l](x) = \begin{cases} l \text{ if } x \in X' \\ v(x) \text{ otherwise.} \end{cases}$$

Guards are used to specify when actions are enabled. We consider simple constraints on clocks X which are atomic formulas of the form $x \sim k$, where $x \in X$, $k \in \mathbb{N}$, and $\sim$ is a comparison operator such that $\sim \in \{\leq, \geq\}$. They are used to build general constraints defined by the following grammar:

$$c := \mathsf{true} \mid \mathsf{false} \mid x \leq k \mid x \geq k \mid c \wedge c \mid c \vee c \mid \neg c.$$

We simplify $\neg(x \leq k)$ into $x \geq k + 1$, and $\neg(x \geq k)$ into $x \leq k - 1$ This allows putting any constraint c into the following disjunctive form: $c = c_1 \vee c_2 \vee \ldots \vee c_n$

such that expressions c_i are conjunctions of simple constraints. The evaluation of a clock constraint c for a valuation v of clocks X denoted by $c(v)$, is obtained by replacing each clock x by its value $v(x)$.

A *guard* g is a clock constraint c with an *urgency type* $\tau \in \{$ l, d, e $\}$, denoted by $g = [c]^\tau$. Urgency types are used to specify the need for an action to progress when it is enabled (i.e. when its clock constraint is true) [7]. *Lazy* actions (i.e. non-urgent) are denoted by l, *delayable* actions (i.e. urgent just before they become disabled) are denoted by d, and *eager* actions (i.e. urgent whenever they are enabled) are denoted by e.

The predicate urg[g] that characterizes the valuations of clocks for which the guard $g = [c]^\tau$ is *urgent* is defined by:

$$\text{urg}[g](v) \iff \begin{cases} \text{false} & \text{if } g \text{ is lazy, i.e. if } \tau = \text{l} \\ c(v) \wedge \neg c(v+1) & \text{if } g \text{ is delayable, i.e. if } \tau = \text{d} \\ c(v) & \text{if } g \text{ is eager, i.e. if } \tau = \text{e.} \end{cases}$$

We denote by G(X) the set of guards over a set of clocks X.

Given guards $g_1 = [c_1]^{\tau_1}$ and $g_2 = [c_2]^{\tau_2}$, the conjunction of g_1 and g_2 is denoted by $g_1 \wedge g_2$ and is defined by $g_1 \wedge g_2 = [c_1 \wedge c_2]^{\max \tau_1, \tau_2}$, considering that urgency types are ordered as follows: l $<$ d $<$ e. Henceforth, given a guard $g = [c]^\tau$ and a valuation v, we also write $g(v)$ for the expression $c(v)$.

2.2   Abstract Models

Definition 1 (abstract model). *An* abstract model *is a timed automaton $M = (A, Q, X, \longrightarrow)$ such that:*

- *A is a finite set of (observable) actions. In addition to actions A, we consider internal action β. We denote by A^β the set of actions $A \cup \{\beta\}$*
- *Q is a finite set of control locations*
- *X is a finite set of clocks*
- *$\longrightarrow \subseteq Q \times (A^\beta \times G(X) \times 2^X) \times Q$ is a finite set of labeled transitions. A transition is a tuple (q, a, g, r, q') where a is an action executed by the transition, g is a guard over X and r is a subset of clocks that are reset by the transition. We write $q \xrightarrow{a,g,r} q'$ for $(q, a, g, r, q') \in \longrightarrow$.*

An abstract model describes the platform-independent behavior of the system. Timing constraints, that is, guards of transitions, take into account only user requirements (e.g. deadlines, periodicity, etc.). The semantics assumes timeless execution of actions.

Definition 2 (abstract model semantics). *An abstract model $M = (A, Q, X, \longrightarrow)$ defines a transition system TS. States of TS are pairs (q, v), where q is a control location of M and v is a valuation of the clocks X.*

- *Actions. We have $(q, v) \xrightarrow{a} (q', v[r \mapsto 0])$ if $q \xrightarrow{a,g,r} q'$ in M and $g(v)$ is true.*
- *Time steps. For a waiting time $\delta \in \mathbb{N}$, $\delta > 0$, we have $(q, v) \xrightarrow{\delta} (q, v + \delta)$ if for all transitions $q \xrightarrow{a,g,r} q'$ of M and for all $\delta' \in [0, \delta[$, $\neg\text{urg}[g](v + \delta')$.*

In an abstract model, time can progress only if no transition is urgent. Urgency corresponds to priorities induced by the timing constraints: urgent transitions have priority over time progress. We denote by $\mathsf{wait}(q, v)$ the *maximal waiting time* allowed at (q, v). Notice that it satisfies $\mathsf{wait}(q, v + \delta) = \mathsf{wait}(q, v) - \delta$ for all $\delta \in [0, \mathsf{wait}(q, v)]$, and is formally defined as follows:

$$\mathsf{wait}(q, v) = \min \left(\left\{ \delta \geq 0 \;\middle|\; \bigvee_{q \xrightarrow{a_i, g_i, r_i} q_i} \mathsf{urg}[g_i](v + \delta)^{\cdot} \right\} \cup \{ +\infty \} \right).$$

Given an abstract model $M = (\mathsf{A}, \mathsf{Q}, \mathsf{X}, \longrightarrow)$, a finite (resp. an infinite) *execution sequence* of M from an *initial* state (q_0, v_0) is a maximal sequence of observable actions and time-steps $(q_i, v_i) \overset{\sigma_i}{\rightsquigarrow} (q_{i+1}, v_{i+1})$, $\sigma_i \in \mathsf{A} \cup \mathbb{N}$ and $i \in \{ 0, 1, 2, \ldots, n \}$ (resp. $i \in \mathbb{N}$), such that $\rightsquigarrow$ is the transitive closure of $\longrightarrow$ for β-transitions, that is, $(q_i, v_i) \overset{\sigma_i}{\rightsquigarrow} (q_{i+1}, v_{i+1})$ if $(q_i, v_i) \overset{\beta}{\longrightarrow}{}^* (q_i', v_i') \overset{\sigma_i}{\longrightarrow} (q_i'', v_i'') \overset{\beta}{\longrightarrow}{}^* (q_{i+1}, v_{i+1})$.

Example 1. Consider an abstract model $M = (\mathsf{A}, \mathsf{Q}, \{x\}, \longrightarrow)$ with two actions $\mathsf{A} = \{sync_1, p\}$, two states $\mathsf{Q} = \{q^1, q^2\}$, a single clock x, and two transitions $\longrightarrow = \{ (q^1, sync_1, \emptyset, \{x\}, q^2), (q^2, p, [10 \leq x \leq 20]^d, \emptyset, q^1) \}$ (see Figure 1). It can be easily shown that the execution sequences of M from the initial state $(q^2, 0)$ are infinite repetitions of the sequence $(q^2, 0) \overset{\delta_1}{\longrightarrow} (q^2, \delta_1) \overset{p}{\longrightarrow} (q^1, \delta_1) \overset{\delta_2}{\longrightarrow} (q^1, \delta_1 + \delta_2) \overset{sync_1}{\longrightarrow} (q^2, 0)$, where $10 \leq \delta_1 \leq 20$.

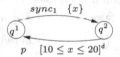

$$sync_1 \quad \{x\}$$
$$q^1 \qquad q^2$$
$$p \quad [10 \leq x \leq 20]^d$$

Fig. 1. Example of abstract model

Definition 3 (composition of abstract models). *Let $M_i = (\mathsf{A}_i, \mathsf{Q}_i, \mathsf{X}_i, \longrightarrow_i)$, $1 \leq i \leq n$, be a set of abstract models. We assume that their sets of actions and clocks are disjoint, i.e. for all $i \neq j$ we have $\mathsf{A}_i \cap \mathsf{A}_j = \emptyset$ and $\mathsf{X}_i \cap \mathsf{X}_j = \emptyset$. A set of interactions γ is a subset of 2^{A}, where $\mathsf{A} = \bigcup_{i=1}^n \mathsf{A}_i$, such that any interaction $a \in \gamma$ contains at most one action of each component M_i, that is, $a = \{ a_i \mid i \in I \}$ where $a_i \in \mathsf{A}_i$ and $I \subseteq \{ 1, 2, \ldots, n \}$. The composition of the abstract models M_i, $1 \leq i \leq n$, by using a set of interactions γ, denoted by $\gamma(M_1, \ldots, M_n)$, is the composite abstract model $M = (\gamma, \mathsf{Q}, \mathsf{X}, \longrightarrow_\gamma)$ such that $\mathsf{Q} = \mathsf{Q}_1 \times \mathsf{Q}_2 \times \ldots \times \mathsf{Q}_n$, $\mathsf{X} = \bigcup_{i=1}^n \mathsf{X}_i$, and $\longrightarrow_\gamma$ is defined by the rules:*

$$\frac{a = \{a_i\}_{i \in I} \in \gamma \qquad g = \bigwedge_{i \in I} g_i \qquad r = \bigcup_{i \in I} r_i \qquad \forall i \in I . \; q_i \overset{a_i, g_i, r_i}{\longrightarrow}_i q_i' \qquad \forall i \notin I . \; q_i' = q_i}{(q_1, \ldots, q_n) \overset{a, g, r}{\longrightarrow}_\gamma (q_1', \ldots, q_n')}$$

$$\frac{\exists i \in \{1, \ldots, n\} \;.\; q_i \overset{\beta, g_i, r_i}{\longrightarrow}_i q_i' \qquad \forall j \neq i \;.\; q_j' = q_j}{(q_1, \ldots, q_n) \overset{\beta, g_i, r_i}{\longrightarrow}_\gamma (q_1', \ldots, q_n')}$$

A composition $M = \gamma(M_1, \ldots, M_n)$ of abstract models M_i, $1 \leq i \leq n$, can execute two type of transitions: interactions $a = \{a_i\}_{i \in I} \in \gamma$ which corresponds to synchronizations of actions a_i of models M_i, $i \in I$, and internal actions β of the models M_i. An interaction $a = \{a_i\}_{i \in I} \in \gamma$ is enabled from a state of M if all actions a_i are enabled.

In a composite model $M = \gamma(M_1, \ldots, M_n)$, many interactions can be enabled at the same time introducing a degree of non-determinism in the behavior of M. In order to restrict non-determinism, we introduce priorities that specify which interaction should be executed among the enabled ones. A priority on $M = \gamma(M_1, \ldots, M_n)$ is a relation $\pi \subseteq \gamma \times Q \times \gamma$ such that for all q the relation $\pi_q = \{ (a, a') \mid (a, q, a') \in \pi \}$ is a partial order. We write $a\pi_q a'$ for $(a, q, a') \in \pi$ to express the fact that a has weaker priority than a' at state q. That is, if both a and a' are enabled at state q, only the action a' can be executed. Thus, priority $a\pi_q a'$ is applied only when the conjunction of the guards of a and a' is true. Let $q \overset{a, g, r}{\longrightarrow}_\gamma q'$ and $q \overset{a', g', r'}{\longrightarrow}_\gamma q''$ be transitions of M such that $g = [c]^\tau$ and $g' = [c']^{\tau'}$. Applying priority $a\pi_q a'$ boils down to transforming the guard g of a into the guard $g_\pi = [c \wedge \neg c']^\tau$ and leaving the guard g' of a' unchanged.

Henceforth, we denote by $\text{en}_q(a)$ the predicate characterizing the valuations of clocks for which an interaction a is enabled at state q. It is defined by:

$$\text{en}_q(a) = \begin{cases} \text{false} & \text{if } \nexists(q, a, g, r, q') \in \longrightarrow_\gamma \\ \displaystyle\bigvee_{(q, a, [c]^\tau, r, q') \in \longrightarrow_\gamma} c & \text{otherwise.} \end{cases}$$

Definition 4 (priority). *Given a composite model $M = (\gamma, Q, X, \longrightarrow_\gamma)$, the application of a priority π to M defines a new model $\pi M = (\gamma, Q, X, \longrightarrow_\pi)$ such that $\longrightarrow_\pi$ is defined by the rule:*

$$\frac{q \overset{a, g, r}{\longrightarrow}_\gamma q' \qquad g = [c]^\tau \qquad g_\pi = \Big[c \wedge \neg \bigvee_{a\pi_q a'} \text{en}_q(a')\Big]^\tau}{q \overset{a, g_\pi, r}{\longrightarrow}_\pi q'}$$

Example 2. Consider an abstract model $M = \pi\gamma(M_1, M_2, M_3)$ such that:

- abstract models M_1, M_2, and M_3 are provided by Figure 2,
- interactions $\gamma = \{a_1, a_2, a_3\}$ are defined by $a_1 = \{sync_1, sync_2, sync_3\}$, $a_2 = \{p, q\}$ and $a_3 = \{r, s\}$,
- priority π is such that $a_2\pi_q a_3$ for any control location q of M.

From the initial state $(q_1^1, q_2^1, q_3^1, 0)$, it can be easily shown that the execution sequences of M have the following form: $((q_1^1, q_2^1, q_3^1), 0) \overset{a_1}{\longrightarrow} ((q_1^2, q_2^2, q_3^2), 0) \overset{5}{\longrightarrow} ((q_1^2, q_2^2, q_3^2), 5) \overset{a_3}{\longrightarrow} ((q_1^2, q_2^3, q_3^1), 5) \overset{\delta_2}{\longrightarrow} ((q_1^2, q_2^3, q_3^1), 5 + \delta_2) \overset{a_2}{\longrightarrow} ((q_1^1, q_2^1, q_3^1), 5 + \delta_2) \overset{a_1}{\longrightarrow} ((q_1^2, q_2^2, q_3^2), 0)$, where $5 \leq \delta_2 \leq 15$. Notice that control location err cannot be reached in M_2 due to the application of priority $a_2\pi_q a_3$ for $q = (q_1^2, q_2^2, q_3^2)$.

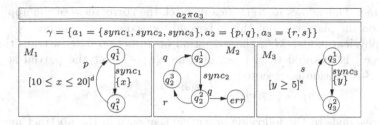

Fig. 2. Example of composition of abstract models with priorities

2.3 Building Physical Models

Abstract models are platform-agnostic representations of applications in which action execution is atomic and instantaneous. Physical models represent the behavior of the application software running on a platform. They take into account the fact that action execution may take non-zero time. To this purpose we break atomicity of actions and introduce execution times. The transition of an action a of an abstract model is replaced by a sequence of two consecutive transitions of the corresponding physical model (see Figure 3). The first transition marks the beginning of the execution of action a, and the second transition marks its completion. These transitions are separated by a *partial* state denoted by $\perp$. The execution time of the action corresponds to the waiting time at state $\perp$.

$$q \xrightarrow{a \quad g \quad r} q' \xrightarrow{\perp t} \qquad q \xrightarrow{a \quad g \quad r} \perp_t \dashrightarrow^{\beta} q'$$

Transition   Corresponding sequence of

$t = (q, a, g, r, q')$ in M.   transitions in $M^\perp$.

Fig. 3. Transformation of transitions of the abstract model

Definition 5 (physical model). *Let $M = (A, Q, X, \longrightarrow)$ be an abstract model. We define the associated physical model as the timed automaton $M^\perp = (A, Q \cup Q^\perp, X, \longrightarrow_\perp)$ such that:*

- *$Q^\perp$ is the set of* partial *states such that there is one partial state for each transition of M, that is, $Q^\perp = \{ \perp_t \mid t \in \longrightarrow \}$*
- *$\longrightarrow_\perp$ is defined by the rule:*

$$\frac{q \xrightarrow{a,g,r} q' \qquad t = (q, a, g, r, q')}{q \xrightarrow{a,g,r}_\perp \perp_t \qquad \perp_t \xrightarrow{\beta,[\text{true}]^l,\emptyset}_\perp q'}$$

In the physical model $M^\perp$, we assume arbitrary execution times for actions, ranging from 0 to $+\infty$, which is modeled by the guard [true]l for β-transitions. Notice that $M^\perp$ can be further constrained if bounds of the execution times of actions are known. For instance, if we know an estimate $WCET(a)$ of the worst-case execution time [8] of an action a, the associated timing constraint is $[x_a \leq WCET(a)]^d$ instead of [true]l, where x_a is a clock that is reset whenever

a is started. This allows us to statically check the correctness of the application running on the platform, but this is beyond the scope of this paper.

In a physical model $M^\perp$, the execution of an action a by a transition $t = (q, a, g, r, q')$ is followed by a lapse of time $\delta(a) \in \mathbb{N}$ at the partial state $\perp_t$, before a β-transition is executed:

$$(q, v) \overset{a}{\rightsquigarrow} (\perp_t, v[r \mapsto 0]) \overset{\delta(a)}{\rightsquigarrow} (q', v[r \mapsto 0] + \delta(a)). \tag{1}$$

This corresponds to the following execution sequence in the abstract model M, if such a sequence is feasible:

$$(q, v) \overset{a}{\rightsquigarrow} (q', v[r \mapsto 0]) \overset{\delta(a)}{\rightsquigarrow} (q', v[r \mapsto 0] + \delta(a)). \tag{2}$$

Notice that the time step $\delta(a)$ of $M^\perp$ in (1) may not be a time step of M in (2) if $\delta(a) > \mathsf{wait}(q', v[r \mapsto 0])$, meaning that the physical model violates timing constraints defined in the corresponding abstract model. In this case, we say that the considered execution sequence is not *time-safe*. We compare execution sequences of abstract and physical models based on the usual notion of *weak simulation* [9]. It can be shown that if all execution sequences of $M^\perp$ are time-safe, then $M^\perp$ is weakly simulated by M, considering that a state of the form $(\perp_t, v)$ of $M^\perp$, $t = (q, a, g, r, q')$, is simulated by the state (q', v) of M.

A correct implementation must execute only time-safe sequences. Time-safety violations occur in a physical model when the execution time of an action is larger than what is allowed by the timing constraints of the corresponding abstract model. Correct implementations are obtained for platforms that are sufficiently fast for executing the application without violating time-safety. In this case, the physical model preserves the semantics of the abstract model as shown in [5]. When this cannot be ensured for a given platform, we propose to detect time-safety violations at run-time and to stop the system in order to prevent the application from incorrect executions.

Composition. In Definition 5, physical models $M^\perp$ represent the behavior of a single abstract model M running on a platform. In [5] the physical model of a composition $M = \pi\gamma(M_1, \ldots, M_n)$ of abstract models M_i is $M^\perp$. That is, each execution of an interaction $a = \{a_i\}_{i \in I} \in \gamma$ is split into two transitions executed sequentially, one for the beginning of the execution of a, and the other one for its completion. The time elapsed between the execution of these transitions corresponds to the execution time of a. Notice that during this time all the components $M_1, \ldots, M_n$ are waiting for the completion of interaction a, even the ones that are not participating to a (i.e. components M_i, $i \notin I$), that is, in $M^\perp$ interactions are executed sequentially. We propose a different definition for physical models that can execute interactions in parallel.

Given a composition $\pi\gamma(M_1, \ldots, M_n)$ of abstract models M_i, $1 \leq i \leq n$, the physical model $M^\| = \pi\gamma(M_1^\perp, \ldots, M_n^\perp)$ is computed in two steps.

1. For each component M_i we compute its corresponding physical model $M_i^\perp$ representing the execution of M_i on a dedicated execution platform.
2. The physical model $M^\|$ is obtained by composing physical models $M_i^\perp$, $1 \leq i \leq n$, with respect to interactions γ and priority π.

In the physical model $M^{\parallel}$, the execution of an interaction $a = \{a_i\}_{i \in I}$ of the abstract model M can be decomposed as follows. First, the beginning of the execution of a is represented by a single transition in $M^{\parallel}$, as in $M^{\perp}$. Second, each component $M_i^{\perp}$ completes by executing its internal β-transition. In contrast to $M^{\perp}$ in which the completion of a corresponds to a single β-transition, in $M^{\parallel}$ components complete asynchronously and independently. This allows to start new interactions even if one or more components are still executing.

Example 3. Consider the abstract model $M = \pi\gamma(M_1, M_2, M_3)$ of Example 2. Figure 4 shows the corresponding physical model $M^{\parallel} = \pi\gamma(M_1^{\perp}, M_2^{\perp}, M_3^{\perp})$. Consider that execution times for actions $sync_1$, $sync_2$, and $sync_3$, are respectively 4, 7, and 12. Consider also that the execution time is 5 for actions p, q, r, and s.

It can be easily shown that $M^{\parallel}$ admits the single execution sequence: $((q_1^1, q_2^1, q_3^1), 0) \xrightarrow{a_1} ((\perp_{t_1^{12}}, \perp_{t_2^{12}}, \perp_{t_3^{12}}), 0) \xrightarrow{4} ((q_2^1, \perp_{t_1^{12}}, \perp_{t_3^{12}}), 4) \xrightarrow{3} ((q_1^2, q_2^2, \perp_{t_3^{12}}), 7) \xrightarrow{a_2} ((\perp_{t_1^{21}}, \perp_{t_2^{2e}}, \perp_{t_3^{12}}), 7) \xrightarrow{5} ((q_1^1, err, q_3^1), 12)$. Notice that this execution sequence leads to a state that is not reachable in M due to priority $a_2 \pi_q a_3$. Since a_3 is disabled at partial state $(q_1^2, q_2^2, \perp_{t_3^{12}})$, the priority cannot apply to a_2 which is executed. That is, the physical model $M^{\parallel}$ is not correctly implementing the semantics of the abstract model M.

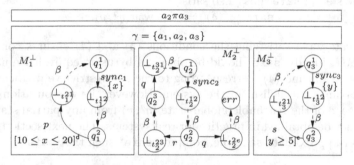

Fig. 4. Physical model of Example 2

Correctness. Consider a composition $M^{\parallel} = \pi\gamma(M_1^{\perp}, \ldots, M_n^{\perp})$ of physical models $M_i^{\perp} = (A_i, Q_i \cup Q_i^{\perp}, X_i, \longrightarrow_i), i \in \{1, \ldots, n\}$ and the corresponding abstract model $M = \pi\gamma(M_1, \ldots, M_n)$. Given a state (q, v) of $M^{\parallel}$, $q = (q_1, \ldots, q_n)$, a component M_i is *busy* at (q, v) if it is in a partial state $q_i \in Q_i^{\perp}$. Otherwise, M_i is said to be *ready*. We say that a state (q, v) is *partial* if at least one component is busy, otherwise (q, v) is said to be *global*.

As shown in Example 3, the physical model $M^{\parallel}$ may violate the semantics of M due to incorrect execution from partial states. From global states, the transitions executed in M and $M^{\parallel}$ are the same. We consider that $M^{\parallel}$ is correct if it can be weakly simulated by M, considering that partial states (q, v) of $M^{\parallel}$ are related through the simulation relation to global states (q^g, v) of M, such that q^g is the control location reached from q after all busy components complete. Notice that the uniqueness of q^g comes from the fact that the execution of β-transitions is deterministic and confluent [6].

Consider the execution of an interaction a in $M^{\|} = \pi\gamma(M_1^{\perp}, \ldots, M_n^{\perp})$ from the partial state (q, v), and the corresponding global state (q^g, v) in M. As explained in [6], if a is enabled at (q, v), it is also enabled at (q^g, v). However, in order to respect the semantics of the abstract model M, a should be disabled due to priority π if there exists an interaction b enabled at state (q^g, v) such that $a\pi_{q^g}b$. The priority π is defined only on global states q^g. Thus, a should be blocked if enabledness of interaction b cannot be decided at (q, v). Notice also that the application of priority $a\pi_{q^g}b$ depends on the global state q^g.

Similarly, a time step δ enabled in $M^{\|}$ at partial state (q, v) can be disallowed in M at the corresponding global state (q^g, v) if $\delta > \mathsf{wait}(q^g, v)$, i.e. if an interaction a involving busy components is urgent at state $(q^g, v + \delta')$ s.t. $\delta' < \delta$.

To prevent $M^{\|}$ from incorrect execution, we define the predicate $\mathsf{safe}_{(q,v)}(\sigma)$ characterizing the states from which execution of an interaction $\sigma \in \gamma$ or of a time step $\sigma \in \mathbb{N}$ will not violate global state semantics. Clearly, for global states (q, v) we have $\mathsf{safe}_{(q,v)}(\sigma) = \mathsf{true}$ (i.e. the behavior of $M^{\|}$ is already safe for global states). For an interaction a, a partial state (q, v) and its corresponding global state (q^g, v), the predicate safe must satisfy:

$$\mathsf{safe}_{(q,v)}(a) \implies \nexists b \in \gamma \,.\, a\pi_{q^g}b \wedge (q^g, v) \xrightarrow{b} (q', v'). \tag{3}$$

For a time step δ, safe must also satisfy:
$$\mathsf{safe}_{(q,v)}(\delta) \implies \delta \leq \mathsf{wait}(q^g, v). \tag{4}$$

Any predicate safe satisfying the conditions (3) and (4) ensures correct execution in $M^{\|}$. Ideally, safe should be obtained by using equivalence instead of implication in (3) and (4), corresponding to the less restrictive predicate allowing the maximal parallelism in the system. However, its computation requires the knowledge of the reachable global state (q^g, v) from any partial state (q, v), which cannot be obtained in practice for real systems. The next section explains how to over-approximate safe, i.e. compute safe^* such that $\mathsf{safe}^* \implies \mathsf{safe}$.

3   Parallel Real-Time Implementation

We use concepts presented in the previous section to implement a parallel real-time execution engine for BIP programs. The BIP—Behavior / Interaction / Priority—framework [10] is intended for the design and analysis of complex, heterogeneous embedded applications. BIP is a highly expressive, component-based framework with rigorous semantics. It allows the construction of complex, hierarchically structured models from atomic components characterized by their behavior and their interfaces (communication ports). Such components are abstract models extended with variables. Transitions are labeled by ports, boolean guards on variables, and timing constraints that may involve expressions on variables. Transition execution may assign new values to variables, computed by user-defined functions (in C). Atomic components are composed by layered application of interactions and priorities. Interactions express synchronization constraints and define the transfer of data between the interacting components. Priorities are used to filter amongst possible interactions and to steer system evolution so as to meet performance requirements e.g., to express scheduling policies. Priorities define partial orders between interactions that can change dynamically. They are provided as sets of rules including boolean guards on components variables.

3.1   Computing Timing Constraints of Interactions

The execution engine which is responsible for the coordination between components, computes enabled interactions on-line. To decide which interactions are enabled at a given state, it expresses their guards based on a single global clock t. This clock measures the absolute time elapsed since the system has been started and is never reset. It is used to express timing constraints on local clocks of components in the following manner. It uses a valuation $w : X \to N$ in order to store the absolute time $w(x)$ of the last reset of a clock x with respect to the clock t. The valuation v of the clocks X can be computed from the current value of t and w by using the equality $v = t - w$. Henceforth, states (q, v) are represented as tuples (q, w, t), where $w : X \to N$ is a clock valuation giving the most recent reset times and $t \in N$ is the value of the current (absolute) time.

Given a state $s = (q, w, t)$, the engine computes guards $g = [c^\tau]$ of interactions a as follows. It rewrites simple constraints $x \sim k$, $\sim \in \{\leq, \geq\}$, involved in c using the global time t and reset times w, i.e. $x \sim k \equiv t \sim k + w(x)$. This allows reducing any conjunction of simple constraints into an interval constraint $l \leq t \leq u$. By using the disjunctive form defined in Section 2.1 we can put c in the following form:

$$c = \bigvee_{i=1}^{n} l_i \leq t \leq u_i, \tag{5}$$

such that $u_i + 1 < l_i$ for all $i \in \{1, \ldots, n-1\}$. We associate to a its *next activation* time $\mathsf{next}_s(a)$ which is the next value of the global time for which a is enabled, and its *next urgency* time $\mathsf{deadline}_s(a)$ which is the next value of the global time for which a is urgent. They are computed from (5) as follows:

$$\mathsf{next}_s(a) = \min_{1 \leq i \leq n} \mathsf{next}_s([l_i \leq t \leq u_i]^\tau)$$
$$\mathsf{deadline}_s(a) = \min_{1 \leq i \leq n} \mathsf{deadline}_s([l_i \leq t \leq u_i]^\tau),$$

such that for $g_i = [l_i \leq t \leq u_i]^\tau$, $\mathsf{next}_s(g_i)$ and $\mathsf{deadline}_s(g_i)$ are defined by:

$$\mathsf{next}_s(g_i) = \begin{cases} \mathbf{max} \ \{ \ t, l_i \ \} & \text{if } t \leq u_i \\ +\infty & \text{otherwise,} \end{cases} \qquad \mathsf{deadline}_s(g_i) = \begin{cases} u_i & \text{if } t \leq u_i \ \wedge \ \tau = \mathsf{d} \\ l_i & \text{if } t < l_i \ \wedge \ \tau = \mathsf{e} \\ t & \text{if } t \in [l_i, u_i] \ \wedge \ \tau = \mathsf{e} \\ +\infty & \text{otherwise.} \end{cases}$$

We denote by γ_q the set of interactions enabled at control location q. The function wait defined in Section 2.2 satisfies $t + \mathsf{wait}(s) = \min_{a \in \gamma_q} \mathsf{deadline}_s(a)$.

3.2   Execution Engine Algorithm

The execution engine behaves as a controller for the application (see Figure 5). It detects time-safety violation during the execution and allows execution of safe interactions only, based on the predicate `safe` of Section 2.3. As explained in Section 2.3, given the current control location q the evaluation of `safe` depends on the guards of interactions enabled at global control location q^g reachable from q. It also depends on the priority π_{q^g} that applies at q^g. This requires knowing what will be the validated guards after the completion of the busy components. This is not possible in general, since they may depend on the values of the variables of the busy components. Hence, when necessary they are over-approximated in the following way. Clock constraints $x \sim k$ are approximated to true whenever k cannot be evaluated statically (e.g. if k is an expression involving non-constant variables). Boolean guards are also approximated to true if they involve expressions that cannot be evaluated statically. For given state $s = (q, w, t)$, the execution engine computes the next interaction to be executed as follows.

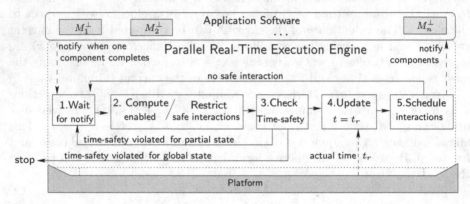

Fig. 5. Architecture of parallel real-time engine

1. It waits for notification from components finishing their execution. Components send their enabled ports (transitions), on which they are willing to interact, with their guards.
2. Based on the received notifications, it computes the set of interactions γ_q enabled at q. Notice that they involve only ready components. They correspond to the application of the operational semantics of interactions γ.
   It restricts guards of enabled interactions to enable only safe execution. This is achieved by applying the operational semantics of priority π, using the approximated guards for the priority rules and for the interactions involving busy components, which guarantees equation (3) of Section 2.3.
3. It checks if time-safety is violated, i.e. if $t_r > \text{deadline}_s(a)$ for an interaction a, where t_r is the current value of the actual time. Notice that for interactions involving busy components, to guarantee equation (4) of Section 2.3 we compute deadline_s based on approximated guards and considering delayable guards as eager.
   If time-safety is violated for some enabled interaction $a \in \gamma_q$ the execution is stopped[1]. If time-safety is violated for an interaction involving busy com-

---

[1] Actually, instead of stopping the application any recovery policy can be considered when time-safety is violated.

ponents, the engine goes to 1 to wait for the completion of more components in order to determine whether time-safety is actually violated or not.

4. It updates the global time t with the actual time t_r, i.e. $t := t_r$.

5. It chooses an enabled interaction a among the safe ones, that is, such that $\text{next}_s(a) < +\infty$ and $\text{next}_s(a) \leq \min_{a' \in \gamma} \text{deadline}_s(a')$. The choice of a can be based on a given real-time scheduling policy (e.g. EDF). The chosen interaction a is executed as soon as possible, i.e. at the global time $\text{next}_s(a)$. If no such interaction exists, either s is a global state and there is a deadlock, or s is a partial state and the engine goes to 1.

3.3 Use Case: A Robotic Application

We made experiments on the marXbot platform [11], a miniature mobile robot composed of 3 main modules. The base module providing rough-terrain mobility thanks to treels (combination of tracks and wheels). It embeds also 16 infrared proximity sensors for detection of obstacles. The rotating distance scanner module including 4 infrared long range sensors is used to build 2D map of its environment. And finally, the module of the main processor which is an ARM11 running Linux-based operating system and communicating through CAN bus with 10 micro-controllers (dsPIC33) managing sensors and actuators.

We consider an experimental setup for an obstacle avoidance scenario. Initially, the robot moves straight and turns whenever it detects an obstacle. We used BIP to implement the application, which is composed of (see Figure 6):

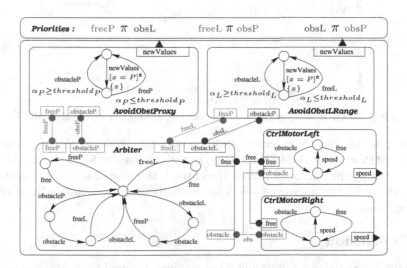

Fig. 6. The obstacle avoidance application

– Components *AvoidObstProxy* and *AvoidObstLRang* responsible for reading the values of the proximity and long range sensors. If one of these components detects the presence of an obstacle, it transmits its direction to component

Arbiter through interaction *obs*. Otherwise, it sends message *free* indicating the absence of obstacle.

- From messages received from *AvoidObstProxy* and *AvoidObstLRang*, *Arbiter* computes the new direction of the robot, which is sent to components *CtrlMotorLeft* and *CtrlMototRight* which are the controllers of the motors
- *CtrlMotorLeft* and *CtrlMototRight* determine the speed to apply to the left and right treels, based on the direction received from *Arbiter*.

To avoid collisions, we give priority to obstacles detected by *AvoidObstProxy* over the ones detected by *AvoidObstLRang*, which is implemented by rule *obsL* π *obsP*. We also give priority to presence of obstacles over than their absence, corresponding to rules *freeP* π *obsL* and *freeL* π *obsP*.

Using BIP, we generated C++ code for the main processor. We compared the application running with the parallel engine proposed in Section 3, with the same application running with the sequential engine of [5]. Its performance is measured by varying the period used for reading sensors in *AvoidObstProxy* and *AvoidObstLRang*. For each tested period, we ran the application 5 times under similar conditions. As shown in Figure 7, with the sequential engine the minimal period for a correct operation of the robot is 130 ms. For smaller periods time-safety may be violated which stops the application. The minimal period with the parallel engine is 60 ms, which drastically improved the reactivity of the robot.

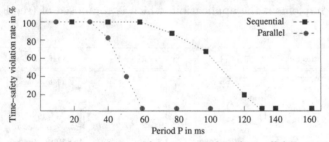

Fig. 7. Time-safety violations for sequential and parallel executions

The parallel engine executes each component using a thread, allowing *AvoidObstProxy* and *AvoidObstLRang* to wait in parallel for new values of the sensors sent by the microcontrollers. In contrast, the sequential engine treats the interaction with the microcontrollers sequentially leading to the addition of the waiting times.

4 Conclusion

We have presented an implementation method for real-time applications. It is based on a general abstract timed model, a platform-independent representation in which the application is a set of components subject to timing constraints, multi-party interactions, and priorities. Abstract models assume sequential, atomic and instantaneous execution of interactions between the components. We formally defined physical models describing the execution of abstract models on a given platform. They take into account (non zero) execution times of interactions, and allow their parallel execution by breaking their atomicity.

In real-time systems, priorities are essential for the expression of scheduling policies and resource management. We show that special care should be taken to preserve global state semantics when executing interactions subject to priorities in parallel. Global state semantics assumes a perfect knowledge of the system state. In parallel execution, the execution engine has only a partial knowledge of the system's state. We provide a condition for safe parallel execution of enabled interactions. The condition guarantees that despite partial state knowledge, if an interaction is enabled at a partial state then it will remain enabled in the global state reached after all the executing components have completed their execution. We have implemented a parallel execution engine that correctly schedules the execution of interactions based on an approximation of the safety condition. The approach has been validated on a real robotic application for which we generated C++ code. We provided benchmarks for this application showing net improvement of performance with respect to a sequential implementation.

References

1. Ghosal, A., Henzinger, T.A., Kirsch, C.M., Sanvido, M.A.A.: Event-Driven Programming with Logical Execution Times. In: Alur, R., Pappas, G.J. (eds.) HSCC 2004. LNCS, vol. 2993, pp. 357–371. Springer, Heidelberg (2004)
2. Henzinger, T.A., Horowitz, B., Kirsch, C.M.: Giotto: a time-triggered language for embedded programming. Proc. of the IEEE 91(1), 84–99 (2003)
3. Aussaguès, C., David, V.: A method and a technique to model and ensure timeliness in safety critical real-time systems. In: ICECCS, pp. 2–12. IEEE Computer Society (1998)
4. Alur, R., Dill, D.L.: A theory of timed automata. Theor. Comput. Sci. 126(2), 183–235 (1994)
5. Abdellatif, T., Combaz, J., Sifakis, J.: Model-based implementation of real-time applications. In: Carloni, L.P., Tripakis, S. (eds.) EMSOFT, pp. 229–238. ACM (2010)
6. Basu, A., Bidinger, P., Bozga, M., Sifakis, J.: Distributed Semantics and Implementation for Systems with Interaction and Priority. In: Suzuki, K., Higashino, T., Yasumoto, K., El-Fakih, K. (eds.) FORTE 2008. LNCS, vol. 5048, pp. 116–133. Springer, Heidelberg (2008)
7. Bornot, S., Gößler, G., Sifakis, J.: On the Construction of Live Timed Systems. In: Graf, S. (ed.) TACAS 2000. LNCS, vol. 1785, pp. 109–126. Springer, Heidelberg (2000)
8. Wilhelm, R., Altmeyer, S., Burguière, C., Grund, D., Herter, J., Reineke, J., Wachter, B., Wilhelm, S.: Static Timing Analysis for Hard Real-Time Systems. In: Barthe, G., Hermenegildo, M. (eds.) VMCAI 2010. LNCS, vol. 5944, pp. 3–22. Springer, Heidelberg (2010)
9. Milner, R.: Communication and concurrency. PHI Series in computer science. Prentice Hall (1989)
10. Basu, A., Bozga, M., Sifakis, J.: Modeling heterogeneous real-time components in BIP. In: SEFM, pp. 3–12. IEEE Computer Society (2006)
11. Magnenat, S.: Software integration in mobile robotics, a scienc to scale up machine intelligence. PhD thesis (2010)

A Grey-Box Approach for Automated GUI-Model Generation of Mobile Applications

Wei Yang[1,2,*], Mukul R. Prasad[1], and Tao Xie[2,**]

[1] Software Systems Innovation Group, Fujitsu Labs. of America, Sunnyvale, CA
mukul.prasad@us.fujitsu.com
[2] Department of Computer Science, North Carolina State University, Raleigh, NC
wei.yang@ncsu.edu, xie@csc.ncsu.edu

Abstract. As the mobile platform continues to pervade all aspects of human activity, and mobile applications, or mobile apps for short, on this platform tend to be faulty just like other types of software, there is a growing need for automated testing techniques for mobile apps. Model-based testing is a popular and important testing approach that operates on a model of an app's behavior. However, such a model is often not available or of insufficient quality. To address this issue, we present a novel grey-box approach for automatically extracting a model of a given mobile app. In our approach, static analysis extracts the set of events supported by the Graphical User Interface (GUI) of the app. Then dynamic crawling reverse-engineers a model of the app, by systematically exercising these events on the running app. We also present a tool implementing this approach for the Android platform. Our empirical evaluation of this tool on several Android apps demonstrates that it can efficiently extract compact yet reasonably comprehensive models of high quality for such apps.

1   Introduction

The mobile platform is projected to overtake the desktop platform as the global Internet platform of choice in the very near future [1]. There has been a decisive shift to mobile devices in numerous application areas such as email, social networking, entertainment, and e-commerce [1, 2]. This trend has prompted an explosive growth in the number and variety of mobile apps being developed. As of June 2012, Android's Google Play had over 600,000 apps that had been downloaded more than 10 billion times in total [3]! Users typically have a choice between several apps with similar functionality. Thus developers are required to develop high quality apps in order to be competitive. On the other hand, mobile apps are usually developed in relatively small-scale projects, which may not be able to support extensive and expensive manual testing. Thus, it is particularly important to develop automated testing tools for mobile apps.

---

* This author was an intern at Fujitsu Labs. of America for the duration of this work.
** This author was supported in part by NSF grants CCF-0845272, CCF-0915400, CNF-0958235, CNS-1160603, and an NSA Science of Security Lablet Grant.

V. Cortellessa and D. Varró (Eds.): FASE 2013, LNCS 7793, pp. 250–265, 2013.

For the purpose of this research, we use Android apps as a representative of mobile apps in general. Most tools and frameworks [4–8] currently available for testing Android apps are simply aids for (manual) test-case authoring, deployment, debugging, and visualization. There are no effective industrial products for automated test-case *generation* per se. Recognizing this inadequacy, researchers have very recently begun to develop such techniques [9–13]. This paper attempts to build on this fairly nascent body of research.

Mobile apps are a subset of the more general class of event-driven applications and specifically event-driven Graphical User Interface (GUI) applications. However, they have the following characteristics that make them suitable for specific automated testing techniques.

- **Small size.** Mobile apps are typically much smaller and simpler than desktop applications, both in terms of the physical footprint as well as behavior. Desktop applications can be large, feature-rich, and computationally intensive. However, a significant fraction of mobile apps are designed as "micro-apps" to solve small and specific tasks [14]. Furthermore, the size of mobile apps is constrained by the limited processing, storage, and display resources of the mobile device. The small size of mobile apps enables automatic testing techniques to be feasible and applicable to real-world apps.
- **Event-centric.** Mobile devices have evolved to be small-screen devices without a keyboard. Since typing is onerous on such devices, mobile apps are designed around a rich set of user gestures as input events. Thus, on the one hand, the role of typed data is somewhat diminished in mobile apps in contrast to desktop applications. On the other hand, the richer set of user gestures in mobile apps needs to be incorporated into any testing process.
- **Simple & Intuitive GUI.** Users of desktop GUI applications might be expected to refer to documentation or tutorials to fully comprehend how to use the applications. In contrast, mobile apps are expected to have a simple and intuitive user interface where most, if not all, usage scenarios of an app should be evident to average users, from the GUI.

Model-based testing [15] is a popular and important type of testing that uses a model of the application under test as a basis for constructing test cases. Automated model-generation techniques that dynamically analyze the GUI of the application have been previously developed for desktop GUI applications [16] and for AJAX web applications [17]. However, the limited degree of automation of these tools and the incompleteness of the resulting models have posed barriers for their industrial adoption. Such limitations can be attributed, in part, to the nature of their target application domains. For example, the GUIs of feature-rich desktop applications or web applications can have a large, potentially unlimited, number of states. Thus, techniques such as Crawljax [17] either bound their exploration or require user-specified state abstractions to extract a finite model. Techniques such as GUITAR [16], on the other hand, resort to more imprecise event-based models. By contrast, as observed above, mobile apps have substantially smaller and simpler GUIs. This characteristic raises the possibility of more complete and automated GUI state-space exploration in mobile apps.

Second, automated crawling techniques typically require knowledge of the set of GUI widgets supporting actions (e.g, clicks) and precisely what actions are supported on each such widget. For web applications, much of this information is represented in client-side JavaScript code, which is notoriously difficult to analyze. Thus, this information needs to be manually specified. For desktop GUI applications, this analysis is not that important since user actions are mostly simple mouse clicks. However, as noted above, supporting a rich array of user gestures is an integral part of mobile-app design. Further, as we demonstrate in this work, mobile app development frameworks are quite amenable to automatic analysis and extraction of this information. The objective of this work is to build a novel, customized and more efficacious automated GUI-model generator for mobile apps, particularly Andriod apps, by exploiting these observations.

Our approach uses static analysis of the app source code to extract the actions supported by the GUI of the app. This information is typically not available to a purely black-box analysis and is far more expensive to extract through a dynamic white-box approach [9]. Next, we use dynamic crawling to build a model of the app by systematically exercising the extracted events on the live app. We concur with the view of previous work [16, 17] that a dynamic analysis is far simpler and more precise than static analysis for analyzing GUIs. However, we exploit the smaller, simpler, and highly event-centric interface of mobile apps to build a more efficient and automated crawler.

Specifically, this paper makes the following main contributions:

- A dynamic, grey-box GUI reverse-engineering approach for mobile apps, which we identify as a specialized type of event-driven GUI apps.
- A novel static analysis to support the dynamic GUI crawling.
- A tool implementing this grey-box approach of automated model extraction for Android apps.
- An evaluation of this tool on several real-world Android apps for demonstrating its efficacy at generating high-quality GUI models.

2   Background and Problem Definition

Model-based testing [15] is an approach for software testing orchestrated around a model of the application under test. The model is typically an abstract representation of the application behavior and may be constructed either manually [18] or using automatic techniques [16]. This model is used to construct a suite of test cases to test the application. Various techniques of model-based testing have been proposed in the literature [19, 20].

One of the crucial steps in model-based testing is the creation of the model itself. When performed manually, it is usually a laborious and error-prone process. There is a body of work [11, 16, 17] that tries to partially or completely automate the process of extracting models from GUI applications. The general approach is to automatically and systematically interact with the GUI of the live, running application, in an attempt to extract and record a model of the usage scenarios supported by it. GUI applications are a subset of general event-driven applications and include types of applications such as web applications and desktop GUI applications as well as mobile apps.

As discussed in Section 1, mobile apps have special characteristics that distinguish them from other types of event-driven applications. This paper addresses the problem of automated GUI-model generation for mobile apps.

Problem Definition. Given a mobile app, efficiently generate a high-quality model representing the valid input event sequences accepted by the app, where quality is measured by the following criteria:

1. *Coverage. Every reachable program statement of the app should be executed by running at least one of the event sequences included in the model.*
2. *Precision. The model should not include invalid events, i.e., events that are not supported by widgets on a given screen.*
3. *Compactness. The size of the model, in relation to the number of event sequences that it represents, should be as small as possible.*

Note that the above problem definition uses statement coverage as the coverage criterion. However, the approach presented here would be equally applicable to any other suitable code coverage criteria.

3   Related Work

Automated Model Extraction. Our work falls under the broad category of automated model-generation techniques. The GUITAR [16] tool by Memon et al. is one of the earliest and most prominent representatives of this category. GUITAR reverse-engineers a model of a GUI application directly from the executing GUI. A recent extension of the tool, Android-GUITAR [21] supports Android apps. GUITAR uses formalisms of GUI forests and event-flow graphs to represent the structure and execution behavior of the GUI, respectively. However, the event-flow graph representation typically includes many false event sequences, which may need to be weeded out later.

The Crawljax [17] tool by Mesbah et al. is an automatic model extractor targeted to AJAX web applications. In contrast to GUITAR, it uses a state-machine representation to capture the model because of the stateful nature of AJAX user-interfaces. However, AJAX applications present particularly challenging targets for automatic model extraction because of their large (sometimes unbounded) state space. Therefore, in practice, manually specified state abstractions are required to extract a model with high coverage but manageable size. WebMate [22] is another, more recent, model extractor for web applications. The ICRAWLER [13] tool by Joorbachi et al. is a reverse-engineering tool for iOS mobile apps and such tool also uses a state-machine model. The emphasis there is on dealing with the idiosyncrasies of the iOS platform. All of the above tools have no means of deducing actionable GUI elements and supported actions on each screen. This information typically needs to be supplied to the tools. Some tools, such as Android-GUITAR, exercise only the default *tap* action on widgets.

However, doing so provides less than optimal coverage of the behavior. Our proposed approach is unique in that it uses an efficient static analysis to automate and solve this aspect of model discovery for the Android platform.

Automated Testing of Mobile Apps. Hu and Neamtiu [23] propose an approach that exercises the app under pseudo-random event sequences produced by the Android *Monkey* tool and analyzes the log files of this execution for certain kinds of faults. The AndroidRipper [11] tool also performs stress testing of an Android app but by systematically crawling its GUI. These approaches can sometimes reveal unexpected and interesting faults. However, their objective is to stress-test the app rather than to create a reusable model for use in future testing, as in our case. Takala et al. [18] present a case study of applying model-based testing for testing Android apps. The M[agi]C [10] tool is used to generate test cases for apps using a combination of model-based testing and combinatorial testing. Previous approaches [10, 18] work off a GUI model of the app and such model could potentially be generated using our proposed approach. More recently, Anand et al. [9] have applied concolic execution to generate feasible event sequences for Android apps. However, the computation-intensive nature of symbolic analysis coupled with an explosion in the sheer number of event sequences being enumerated limits their approach to fairly short event sequences. Our approach, by contrast, can efficiently exercise fairly deep event sequences. Mirzaei et al. [12] use static analysis to deduce the set of feasible event sequences and represent them using a context-free grammar (CFG). The deduced event sequences are then analyzed through symbolic execution. Their proposed static analysis is conceptually a generalization of our proposed action-inference analysis. However, the lack of algorithmic details and limited evaluation there makes a direct comparison with our approach difficult.

4   A Motivating Example

We use an Android app called *SimpleTipper* as an example to illustrate our approach. SimpleTipper is a simplified version of the open-source app, TippyTipper (http://code.google.com/p/tippytipper/), used to calculate the tip amount for a meal. Figure 1 illustrates its functionality. It consists of five screens. On the opening (*Input*) screen, the user enters the meal bill amount through a numeric keypad. The DEL button erases one digit. The CLEAR button or a longClick on DEL clears the textfield. Clicking the Calculate button takes the user to the second (*Result*) screen, which shows the total cost including the calculated tip. The third screen is the *Menu* screen. It is opened by clicking the Menu button on either the *Input* or the *Result* screen. The About option on the menu leads to the fourth screen, *About*, with information about the app. The Settings option on the menu directs the user to the fifth screen, *Settings* with two setting options. Checking either of them on or off influences the tip calculation.

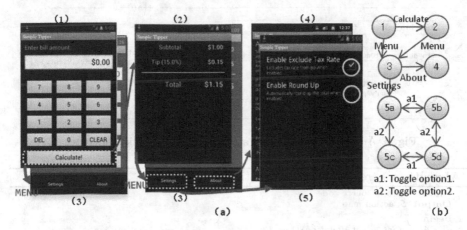

Fig. 1. Overview of SimpleTipper(a) and its state graph(b)

5 Proposed Approach

We propose a grey-box approach for automatically extracting a model of a given mobile app. First, we use static analysis of the app's source code to extract the set of user actions supported by each widget in the GUI. Next, a dynamic crawler is used to reverse-engineer a model of the app, by systematically exercising extracted actions on the live app. Our model has been designed to provide sufficient state abstraction for compactness, without unduly compromising its precision. The following sections describe these elements of our approach.

5.1 Action Inference Using Static Analysis

As explained earlier, supporting a wide array of user gestures is an integral aspect of mobile app design. A model representing only the default *click* action would miss a significant portion of the app's behavior. For example, in Figure 1(a), the longClick behavior of the DEL button on screen (1) would be omitted. Further, the Settings and About screens of the app cannot be accessed without the Menu button. These states constitute much of the app's state space, as shown in Figure 1(b). On the other hand, simply firing all possible actions on each widget would bring in invalid actions into the model and lower its precision. Thus, knowledge of the precise set of GUI actions is essential to generating a high-quality model.

Our approach uses static analysis to infer these actions. We make the observation that in the Android framework a user action is defined by either (a) registering an appropriate event listener for it or, (b) by inheriting the event-handling method of an Android-framework component. We term the former as *registered action* and the latter *inherited action*. For both these categories, identifying an action involves three basic steps: (1) identify the place where an action is instantiated or registered; (2) locate the component on which the action would

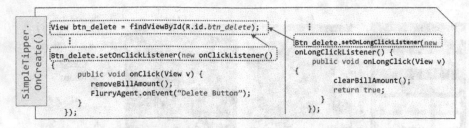

Fig. 2. An illustration of using static analysis for action inference

---

Algorithm 1. registeredactiondetection

Input : $\mathcal{A}$: app source code
Output: $\mathcal{E}$: action map

```
1  begin
2      ActionSet ← getAllActions()
3      EntryPoints ← getAllEntryPoints()
4      foreach P ∈ EntryPoints do
5          CG ← makeCallGraph(A, P)
6          foreach X ∈ ActionSet do
7              L ← getEventRegMethod(X)
8              PNodeSet ← getParentNode(CG, L) // Get all L's callers
9              foreach PNode ∈ PNodeSet do
10                 s ← findCallTo(PNode, L)
11                 v ← getCallingObject(s)
12                 i ← backLocate(v, A)
13                 ID ← getParameter(i)
14                 E.add(ID, X)
15             end
16         end
17     end
18 end
```

---

be fired; (3) extract an identifier of the component that the crawler can later use to recognize the corresponding object and fire the action.

Algorithm 1 presents the analysis to detect registered actions. It essentially iterates over all program-entry points (*EntryPoints*) and all actions (*ActionSet*) supported by the mobile framework (Lines 6-16). For each entry point $\mathcal{P}$ and action $\mathcal{X}$, it extracts the call graph of the app (Line 5) and locates a set of statements *PNodeSet* (Line 8) containing instances of a valid event-listener registering statement $\mathcal{L}$ for action $\mathcal{X}$. Finally, for each statement *PNode* in *PNodeSet* it performs a backward slice on *PNode* to locate an initialization statement of the widget on which the instance of $\mathcal{L}$ was called (Lines 10-12). The backward slice is used to get an identifier *ID* of the component (Line 13) that is registered in the action map $\mathcal{E}$ with the action $\mathcal{X}$. Figure 2 shows a code snippet where the developer defines click as well as longClick actions on the button DEL shown on screen (1) in Figure 1(a). To identify components on which to fire *longClick*, we first use the call graph to find the methods where *setOnLongClickListener* is called. It happens to be called in method *onCreate* of activity *SimpleTipper*. Then we locate the statement calling *setOnLongClickListener* in *onCreate* and get object *btn_delete* that the listener is registered to. Finally we backslice to get the initialization statement of *btn_delete*, get its ID btn_delete, and add

---

Algorithm 2. inheritedActionDetection

Input : $\mathcal{A}$: app source code
Output: $\mathcal{E}$: action map

```
1  begin
2      ActionSet ← getAllActions()
3      CH ← getClassHierarchy(A)
4      Klass ← getUserClass(CH) // Get user defined classes
5      foreach Class ∈ Klass do
6          foreach X ∈ ActionSet do
7              L ← getActionHandlMethod(X)
8              M ← getDeclaredMethod(Class, L)
9              if L ∈ M then
10                 ID ← getNameOrID(L, M)
11                 E.add(ID, X)
12             end
13         end
14     end
15 end
```

---

the ID-action pair to the action mapping used by the crawler. Thus, when the crawler encounters a screen with component btn_delete, it fires a longClick on it.

Algorithm 2 describes the inherited action detection. We first get class hierarchy CH of the whole app (Line 3). Then, we use app's namespace to filter non-user-defined classes (Line 4). For each of the user-defined classes, if the class overrides the action handling method $\mathcal{L}$ (Line 8), we regard the action $\mathcal{X}$ as valid, then we extract the Activity name or registered ID of the class (Line 10), and add the ID-action pair in the action mapping (Line 11).

5.2 Model Definition

We model the GUI behavior of an Android app as a finite-state machine. As noted by others [16, 17], GUI apps in general could have a large, potentially infinite number of UI states. However, our aim is to exploit the simple and intuitive GUI design of mobile apps to derive a compact yet high-quality model.

The model design is inspired by the UI-design principles espoused by the Android team. The Android User Experience Team [4] suggests that developers should "make places in the app look distinct" to give users confidence that they know their way around the app. In other words, different screens of the app should and typically do have stark *structural* differences not just minor stylistic ones. In addition, we would like to capture and reflect important differences such as a button being enabled or disabled. Such differences are reflected in the attributes of GUI components that support user actions. Finally, to keep the model compact, we ignore differences in the UI state resulting from different data values input by the user.

We use these principles to define a UI state, which we term as a *visual observable state*. Our model is a finite-state machine over these states with the user actions constituting the transitions between these states. The structure of a GUI screen in Android is represented by a tree of different GUI components, called a *hierarchy tree*. Further, we classify GUI components as *executable components* and *display components*. The former support user actions (which are detected by our static analysis) while the latter are just for display purposes. Thus, a visual observable state in our model is composed of the hierarchy tree of the UI screen, as well as a vector of attribute values of each of the executable components. The chosen attributes are ones that result in an observable change to the GUI component but excluding ones bearing user-supplied text values or values derived from them. It is fairly easy to manually identify the relevant attributes for each type of UI component, once, for all apps.

Figure 1(b) shows the state model of SimpleTipper. Each of screens (1) and (2) correspond to a unique state. Note that different values of the bill amount, input by the user in screen (1) do not give rise to different states. Further the pop-up dialog box launched by hitting the Menu button corresponds to state (3), irrespective of whether it is launched from states (1) or (2). For screen (5), the Settings screen, the two checkboxes are executable components. Their state changes give rise to the four different states 5a-5d for the app.

5.3   Crawling Algorithm

The objective of the crawling algorithm is to exhaustively explore all the app's states by firing *open actions, i.e.,* actions that have previously not been exercised by the crawler, on each observed state. The crawling process ends if the model has no *open states, i.e.,* states that have open actions to be fired. This process can potentially be done through a simple depth-first search (DFS) on the UI states. However, the key challenge here is the backtracking step, *i.e.,* undoing the most recent action done by DFS, on reaching a previously seen state. Crawljax [17] solves this issue, in the case of web applications, by re-loading the initial state and replaying all but the last action leading up to the current state. This strategy is possible in our case too, but can be fairly expensive, as shown in our evaluation. We refer to this strategy as standard DFS in the sequel.

Algorithm 3. crawlapp

> **Input** : $\mathcal{A}$: app under test, $\mathcal{E}$: action map
> **Output**: $\mathcal{M}$: crawled model

```
1 begin
2       M ← ∅; s ← getOpeningScreen(A)
3       while s ≠ null do
4             s ← forwardCrawlFromState(s, A, M, E) // forward crawl from s
5             s ← backtrack(s, A)
6             if isInitialState(s) then s ← findNewOpenState(s, M, A)
7       end
8 end
```

Mobile platforms, such as Android, provide a Back button to undo actions. But this button is designed for app navigation and is context-sensitive. Thus, it is not a reliable mechanism for backtracking to precisely the previous state. For example, on state 5d of Figure 1, pressing the Back button will not lead us back to previous state 5b or 5c, not even to the previous screen (3), but to the screen (1) or (2) from where it was reached. Thus, the Back button need not take the navigation back to the immediately preceding state but to any of its ancestors. Hitting `Back` a finite number of times will eventually take the app to the initial screen. Our crawler uses a modified depth-first search, which tries to crawl only "forward" as much as possible using the `Back` button to backtrack when needed.

Algorithm 3 describes this strategy. It repeats a sequence of three steps till it can make no further progress at which point it terminates. The first step is a forward-crawling step implemented by function *forwardCrawlFromState()* (Line 4). In this step the algorithm recursively visits states with open actions. It fires an open action and continues crawling till it reaches a state with no open actions. At this point function *backtrack()* (Line 5) is called to backtrack from the current state till another open state is found or one of the initial states of the crawl model is reached. In the former case forward crawling is resumed from this open state. In the latter case the function *findNewOpenState()* (Line 6) is used to find and crawl to a new open state and forward crawling is continued from there.

Algorithm 4. forwardCrawlFromState

Input : s_c: state to crawl forward from, $\mathcal{A}$: app under test
         $\mathcal{M}$: crawled model being generated, $\mathcal{E}$: action map
Output: s: current state at the end of crawling

```
1  begin
2  │  s_x ← s_c
3  │  while s_x ≠ null do
4  │  │  s ← s_x
5  │  │  if isNewState(s) then
6  │  │  │  initActions(s, E, A)
7  │  │  │  addToModel(s, M)
8  │  │  end
9  │  │  e ← getNextOpenAction(s)
10 │  │  if e = null then s_x ← null
11 │  │  else
12 │  │  │  s_x ← execute(s, e, A)
13 │  │  │  updateOpenActions(s, e)
14 │  │  │  addToModel(s, e, s_x, M)
15 │  │  end
16 │  end
17 │  return s
18 end
```

Algorithm 4 implements the function *forwardCrawlFromsState()* for forward crawling from a given state s_c. It iterates Lines 4-15 on the current state s, obtaining an open action e on s (*getNextOpenAction()*, Line 9) and executing it, to potentially reach another open state (function *execute()* on Line 12). The set of open actions of s is accordingly updated by function *updateOpenActions()* (Line 13) to reflect the changes. Further, the executed transition $s \xrightarrow{e} s_x$ is added to the model $\mathcal{M}$ by function *addToModel()* on Line 14. As an illustration, to completely crawl the sub-graph formed by states 5a-5d in Figure 1(b), the standard DFS would need to backtrack several times whereas our algorithm would cover it in a single forward crawl through the sequence Menu $\mapsto$ Settings $\to$ a1 $\to$ a2 $\mapsto$ a1 $\to$ a2 $\to$ a2 $\to$ a1 $\to$ a2 $\to$ a1 , by continuing to fire open actions.

6 Tool Implementation

We have implemented our reverse-engineering approach in a tool called ORBIT. It is composed the action detector and the dynamic crawler. Figure 3 shows an overview of ORBIT.

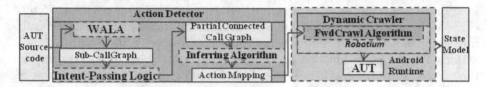

Fig. 3. Overview of the ORBIT tool

Action Detector. The action detector is implemented using the *WALA* static-analysis framework [24]. Android apps are event-driven and therefore organized as a set of event-handler callback methods. Thus, static analysis of just the app code gives a set of partial, disconnected sub call-graphs. The remaining behavior resides in the Android SDK, which we do not explicitly analyze. However, our tool incorporates an *intent-passing logic* module, created based on our knowldege of the Android SDK. For a given app, this module automatically builds a mapping of intent-sending methods and intent filters by analyzing the app's source code and manifest file. This mapping essentially connects the sub call graphs into a *partial connected call graph*. It is partial because for some intent-passing mechanisms like intent broadcasting whose behavior is affected by the runtime state of the Android system, we are unable to infer this information statically. Then we apply the action-inference algorithm described in Section 5.1 on the partial connected call graph to generate the *action mapping*.

Dynamic Crawler. Our crawler is built on top of the Robotium [5] Android test framework and implements the algorithms explained in Section 5.3. Although the crawler gets the list of actions from the Action Detector, it implements special handling for certain components such as *dynamically-created GUI components* and *system-generated GUI components* that are not statically declared.

Dynamically-created GUI components typically appear in Android containers like *ListView*, as a list of dynamically-created child components. Each child has the identical behavior, defined by the container. In such cases, the crawler represents the container as one of the two abstract states: an empty list and a non-empty list. Further, it randomly chooses *only one* of the child components to crawl further, by firing actions defined in the container.

System-generated GUI components typically have system-defined IDs and predefined actions. For example, the system-generated *context menu* is a ListView object, with ID *select_dialog_listview* and different menu options as child components, each with different behaviors. The crawler identifies such components at runtime and systematically crawls each child, rather than treating it as a generic container.

7   Evaluation

To assess the efficacy of our automated model extraction, we conducted a study addressing the following research questions:

RQ1: Is the proposed GUI crawling algorithm more efficient than a standard depth-first state-traversal algorithm?

RQ2: Are the widget and screen actions inferred by static analysis effective in enhancing the behavior covered by the generated model?

RQ3: Can our tool generate a higher-quality model, more efficiently, compared to other state-of-the-art techniques?

Subjects. For our study, we use eight open-source Android apps that have also been used by other work on automated testing of mobile apps [10, 11, 21]. They are mostly small to medium-sized apps spanning a variety of application categories and are listed in Table 1.

Results. To address the three research questions, we carry out a corresponding experiment for each of the questions on all subjects. Among the subjects, *Notepad* can be started with multiple notes (Notepad2) or no note (Notepad0), which will substantially change the initial state of the crawling. To eliminate bias, we carry out every experiment on Notepad for both scenarios.

To address R1, we record the time spent, the coverage as well as the counts of forward actions (any actions other than back) and back actions exercised during both DFS traversing and our crawling (FwdCrawl) in Table 2. As shown in the Table, although both DFS and FwdCrawl can cover most of an app's behavior, DFS takes 70% more time to traverse all 9 subjects together.

The second experiment is to run our traversal algorithm with click actions only instead of inferred actions. To address R2, we record the coverage and counts

Table 1. Test subjects used in the evaluation

Subject	#LOCs	#Activities	Category	Purpose
TippyTipper	2238	5	Tool	Dining tip calculator
OpenManager	1595	6	Business	File manager for Android
Notepad	332	3	Productivity	Note creation and management
TomDroid	3711	3	Business	Online note reading
Aarddict	4518	4	Books & Reference	Aard Dictionary for Android
HelloAUT	234	1	Entertainment	Shape drawing & coloring
ContactManager	497	2	Productivity	Contacts manager
ToDoManager	323	2	Productivity	Task-list creation and management

Table 2. Comparison of standard DFS-based crawling vs. proposed forward crawling

Subject	FwdCrawl				DFS			
	Time(sec)	Coverage(%)	#Fwd	#Back	Time(sec)	Coverage (%)	#Fwd	#Back
TippyTipper	198	78	61	15	512	82	134	52
OpenManager	480	63	92	18	822	56	209	29
Notepad2	102	82	25	4	147	83	39	12
Notepad0	80	78	18	2	75	71	15	2
TomDroid	340	70	78	23	459	58	61	8
AardDict	173	65	15	2	397	60	20	8
HelloAUT	156	86	46	0	278	85	61	0
ContactManager	125	91	20	1	137	92	22	2
ToDoManager	178	75	60	2	294	74	84	4

Table 3. Comparison of Crawling with and without Action Inference

Subject	#clicks		#longClicks		#menu		#States		Coverage(%)	
	C	C+I	C	C+I	C	C+I	C	C+I	C	C+I
TippyTipper	21	55	–	2	–	4	3	9	47	78
OpenManager	50	67	–	19	–	4	10	20	39	63
Notepad2	2	13	–	3	–	9	2	7	39	82
Notepad0	0	8	–	1	–	9	0	7	14	78
TomDroid	3	52	–	0	–	26	2	9	36	70
AardDict	4	15	–	0	–	7	3	7	43	64
HelloAUT	15	34	–	0	–	12	4	8	53	86
ContactManager	20	20	–	0	–	0	5	5	92	92
ToDoManager	60	60	–	0	–	0	7	7	76	76

of *clicks*, *longClicks*, and *menu*, the three most common actions fired during crawling. The results show that non-click actions constitute only 22% of the total actions but firing these actions during crawling increases the coverage by 34% on average. The low proportion of these actions also supports the argument made in Section 5 that blindly firing all supported actions will produce a large number of invalid edges in our model. Table 3 also shows that our crawling produces fairly compact models with a few states.

We also compare ORBIT with other existing Android GUI ripping tools to address R3. In Table 4, we compare ORBIT with *Android GUITAR* [21], *Android GUI Ripper* [11] and Android's *Monkey* tool. As Android GUI Ripper takes substantially long time to run, we use the runs of its generated test cases to do the comparison. The time of each run was recorded from the start of the AUT (App Under Testing) to the generation of coverage report. The time along with coverage shows that our crawler is 32%-75% faster while constructing a 5%-140% more complete model than Android GUITAR and Android GUI Ripper.

Table 4. Comparison of ORBIT with other tools

Subject	Monkey		Android GUITAR		Android GUI Ripper		ORBIT	
	Time(sec)	Cov.(%)	Time(sec)	Cov.(%)	Time(sec)	Cov.(%)	Time(sec)	Cov.(%)
TippyTipper	83	41	322	47	-	-	198	78
OpenManager	90	29	-	-	-	-	480	63
Notepad2	127	60	-	-	-	-	102	82
Notepad0	122	59	-	-	-	-	80	78
TomDroid	69	46	-	-	529	40	340	70
AardDict	124	51	-	-	694	27	173	65
HelloAUT	98	71	117	51	-	-	79	98
ContactManager	90	53	247	61	-	-	125	91
ToDoManager	115	71	194	71	-	-	121	75

For illustration purposes, we also compare our tool against the Android Monkey tool. Monkey fires a pseudo-randomly-generated action sequence, of a specified length, on the app. For our subjects, we found that the maximum coverage achieved by Monkey tended to saturate at around 1200 events. For our experiment, we ran Monkey 10 times with a 1500 event count on each app, and report the median of the coverage achieved in these 10 runs in Table 4. Indeed, for the given event count, Monkey is much faster than ORBIT but achieves substantially lower coverage. This result underscores the benefit of the systematic crawling performed by ORBIT.

8   Discussion

Crawling algorithm. Our crawling algorithm is faster than DFS for every subject except *Notepad0*. By examining the execution log, we found that our algorithm had traversed two more states than DFS, accounting for the difference. Such result is due to the randomness in the choice of the next action to explore and to the side effects of execution. When crawling by DFS, the crawler happened to click the *delete note* button first before clicking the *open note* button. Since there are no notes left after deletion, the crawler cannot visit the edit note screen. Our crawling happened to click the edit button before delete, so we are able to traverse the editing screen. The randomness can be mitigated by carrying out multiple runs. We also plan to consider controlling the order of event sequences as part of future work.

Selection of subjects. Our evaluation is based on subjects drawn from existing related tools, and we try to avoid bias by including all subjects used to evaluate Android GUITAR and GUI Ripper in previous work. However, we do see a preference in the choice of subjects made by these tools. Both of the tools seemed to select subjects with few non-click actions. For GUI Ripper, both the subjects do not have longClick actions, although we did find a later version of TomDroid that has longClicks. For GUITAR, because GUITAR does not support non-click actions, two of its subjects, ContactManager and ToDoManager, do not support non-click actions at all. In general, Android apps have a wide variety of actions, and we apply our methodology against on apps with multiple actions and those with only one or two kinds of actions. The both results show that our methodology is effective on both of the cases.

ORBIT vs Android GUITAR. As Android GUITAR can fire only click actions, it seems unfair to use our results with action inference for comparison. If we compare our click-only runs with GUITAR, we observe that for most of the subjects, Android GUITAR's coverage rate in Table 4 is comparable to our click-only coverage in Table 3. So we infer that our advantage in model completeness is largely attributable to the action-detection technique. Another difference between the two tools is that GUITAR was initially created for desktop applications and its event-flow model typically contains many invalid paths, while ORBIT is designed specifically for mobile apps, and uses a more precise state-based model, which would also integrate well with other state-based testing techniques.

Manual effort. The only manual work in our approach is to manually select attributes of executable components to compose the visual observable states for the GUI. This effort is a one-time effort for a mobile platform. As we have already performed this exercise for Android apps, additional effort will be required only when applying our technique on other mobile platforms to make minor adjustments or revisions for Android.

9 Conclusion

In this paper, we have proposed an approach for automatically reverse-engineering GUI models of mobile apps. We described our tool called ORBIT that implements our approach for Android, and presented the results of our empirical evaluation of this tool on several Android apps. The results showed that for these apps, ORBIT efficiently extracted high-quality models fully automatically.

References

1. comScore Inc.: State of the Internet: Q1 (2012),
   http://www.comscore.com/Insights/Presentations_and_Whitepapers/2012/
   State_of_US_Internet_in_Q1_2012
2. netimperative: Twitter's mobile ad revenue overtakes desktop PCs (2012),
   http://www.digitalstrategyconsulting.com/netimperative/news/2012/06/
   twitters_mobile_ad_revenue_ove.php
3. engadget.com: Google Play hits 600,000 apps, 20 billion total installs (2012),
   http://www.engadget.com/2012/06/27/google-play-hits-600000-apps/
4. Android Developers Site, http://developer.Android.com/
5. Google Project Hosting: Robotium, http://code.google.com/p/robotium/
6. Pivotal Labs: Robolectric, http://pivotal.github.com/robolectric/
7. Bitbar: Testdroid, http://testdroid.com/
8. Contus: Mobile App Testing, http://mobileappstesting.contussupport.com/
9. Anand, S., Naik, M., Harrold, M.J., Yang, H.: Automated concolic testing of smartphone apps. In: Proc. 20th ACM SIGSOFT International Symposium on the Foundations of Software Engineering, FSE 2012, pp. 59:1–59:11 (2012)
10. Nguyen, C.D., Marchetto, A., Tonella, P.: Combining model-based and combinatorial testing for effective test case generation. In: Proc. International Symposium on Software Testing and Analysis, ISSTA 2010, pp. 100–110 (2012)
11. Amalfitano, D., Fasolino, A.R., Tramontana, P., De Carmine, S., Memon, A.M.: Using GUI ripping for automated testing of Android applications. In: Proc. 27th IEEE/ACM International Conference on Automated Software Engineering, ASE 2012, pp. 258–261 (2012)
12. Mirzaei, N., Malek, S., Păsăreanu, C.S., Esfahani, N., Mahmood, R.: Testing Android apps through symbolic execution. SIGSOFT Softw. Eng. Notes 37, 1–5 (2012)
13. Joorabchi, M.E., Mesbah, A.: Reverse engineering iOS mobile applications. In: Proc. 19th Working Conference on Reverse Engineering, WCRE 2012, pp. 177–186 (2012)
14. Syer, M.D., Adams, B., Zou, Y., Hassan, A.E.: Exploring the development of microapps: A case study on the Blackberry and Android platforms. In: Proc. IEEE 11th International Working Conference on Source Code Analysis and Manipulation, SCAM 2011, pp. 55–64 (2011)
15. Pezzè, M., Young, M.: Software testing and analysis - process, principles and techniques. Wiley (2007)
16. Memon, A., Banerjee, I., Nagarajan, A.: GUI ripping: Reverse engineering of graphical user interfaces for testing. In: Proc. 10th Working Conference on Reverse Engineering, WCRE 2003, pp. 260–269 (2003)
17. Mesbah, A., van Deursen, A., Lenselink, S.: Crawling AJAX-based Web applications through dynamic analysis of user interface state changes. ACM Trans. Web 6(1), 3:1–3:30 (2012)

18. Takala, T., Katara, M., Harty, J.: Experiences of system-level model-based GUI testing of an Android application. In: Proc. 4th IEEE International Conference on Software Testing, Verification and Validation, ICST 2011, pp. 377–386 (2011)
19. Dias Neto, A.C., Subramanyan, R., Vieira, M., Travassos, G.H.: A survey on model-based testing approaches: a systematic review. In: Proc. 1st ACM International Workshop on Empirical Assessment of Software Engineering Languages and Technologies, WEASELTech 2007, pp. 31–36 (2007)
20. Shafique, M., Labiche, Y.: A systematic review of model based testing tool support. Technical Report SCE-10-04, Carleton University, Canada (2010)
21. Sourceforge: Android GUITAR, http://sourceforge.net/apps/mediawiki/guitar/index.php?title=Android_GUITAR
22. Dallmeier, V., Burger, M., Orth, T., Zeller, A.: WebMate: a tool for testing Web 2.0 applications. In: Proc. Workshop on JavaScript Tools, JSTools 2012, pp. 11–15 (2012)
23. Hu, C., Neamtiu, I.: Automating GUI testing for Android applications. In: Proc. 6th International Workshop on Automation of Software Test, AST 2011, pp. 77–83 (2011)
24. Sourceforge: WALA, http://wala.sourceforge.net/wiki/index.php

A Mechanized Model for CAN Protocols

Francesco Bongiovanni[1] and Ludovic Henrio[2]

[1] Joseph Fourier University and LIG Labs, Grenoble
[2] INRIA-I3S-CNRS, University of Nice Sophia Antipolis

Abstract. Formal reasoning on Peer-to-Peer (P2P) systems is an intimidating task. This paper focuses on broadcast algorithms for Content Addressable Network (CAN). Since these algorithms run on top of complex P2P systems, finding the right level of abstraction in order to prove their functional correctness is difficult. This paper presents a mechanized model for both CAN and broadcast protocols over those networks. We demonstrate that our approach is practical by identifying sufficient conditions for a protocol to be correct and efficient. We also prove the existence of a protocol verifying those properties.

Keywords: Structured P2P, CAN, broadcast algorithm, theorem proving.

1 Introduction

Structured Overlay Networks (SONs) are a class of P2P systems that emerged in the last decade to provide an abstraction of a lookup service over a large number of distributed nodes. These technologies are widespread and can be found at the heart of companies such as Amazon, Facebook and Twitter [4,9].

Distributed applications operate now at a very large scale, and interactions between computers are no longer limited to *one-to-one* communications. Broadcast communication primitives simplify the application development by avoiding to explicitly write code for dissemination. In the context of a P2P system, communication primitives can be designed to take advantage of the logical topology to communicate efficiently. More important, such generic primitives can be proved to be correct, which increases the confidence the programmer and the user have in the system. In this article we are particularly interested in a broadcast algorithm running on top of the Content Addressable Network (CAN) [14] in which the broadcasted message is received *exactly once* by each node; we say that such a broadcast algorithm is *efficient*. Previous works such as M-CAN [15] and Meghdoot [6] also attempt to leverage CAN in order to build an efficient dissemination infrastructure that can be used by distributed applications.

However, there is no free lunch. Building high-assurance distributed applications which are *correct* remains a very difficult challenge but various methods have emerged over the years to tackle it [1,2,5,11,19]. Theorem proving seems to be among the best method to prove generic properties on distributed systems of *arbitrary size*; in particular verification techniques based on model-checking are,

V. Cortellessa and D. Varró (Eds.): FASE 2013, LNCS 7793, pp. 266–281, 2013.
© Springer-Verlag Berlin Heidelberg 2013

in general, limited to systems of a predefined size and suffer from combinatorial explosion. This article promotes the use of theorem proving in the safe design of distributed systems, more particularly concerning the CAN overlay network.

We present here a mechanized model of CAN that will help the design of communication primitives and the formal proof of their properties. We use this model to define the characteristics and the properties of broadcast primitives. Our first contribution is thus a set of abstractions, properties, and theorems regarding the topological and the communication aspects of CAN. We formalize the *CAN network*, the *messages* over such a network, and a notion of *connectivity*: a zone is connected if any two nodes of this zone can communicate, possibly indirectly. Some of these proven abstractions can be reused with resembling topologies such as the Delaunay triangulation protocol (DT protocol) [10] and the Voronoi-based Overlay Network (VON) [8], widely used in online games. Our second contribution is to use our framework to characterize broadcast protocols and *prove the existence of an efficient broadcast* protocol by presenting a naive yet efficient *correct-by-construction* protocol and which directly leverage the topology of the structure; we do not build and maintain an extra layer on top of CAN (such as a broadcast tree) but rather make use of locally available information. Knowledge of the entire network is necessary for proving intermediary lemmas, but we show that such a knowledge is not used by the protocol itself.

We are interested in the proofs of *functional correctness* of broadcast algorithms for CAN, and of the fact that there is a protocol for which each node receives a message exactly once. We present selected Isabelle/HOL definitions and theorems to give an overview on how to reason about such algorithms and prove their properties. Our model is general and flexible enough to study CAN networks, as it provides the formalization of basic building blocks composing it. However, we are not interested in formalizing the full CAN protocol but rather on the minimal set of abstractions needed to reason about communication protocols for CANs. Overall, not only this paper proves that it is possible to design an efficient broadcast protocol for CAN but also that we can formally prove its correctness and efficiency. Compared to a realistic P2P network, we do not consider node churn in this study. Also we assume that reliability of point-to-point communication is an orthogonal concern that should be studied independently.

In §2, we present the CAN overlay network, the existing broadcast primitives for CAN, and the objectives of this paper. In §3 we present a mechanized model of CAN along with the proven abstractions making up the model. Broadcast algorithms are presented in §4. Finally we compare our study to other related work in §5.

2 Background and Motivation

A CAN [14] is a structured P2P network based on a d-dimensional Cartesian coordinate space, labelled $\mathcal{D}$. This space is dynamically partitioned among all nodes in the system such that each node is responsible for storing data, in the form of *(key, value)* pairs, in a sub-zone of $\mathcal{D}$. Each node is responsible for a zone, and the set of zones is disjoint and covers the whole space. To store (k, v)-pairs, the key k is deterministically mapped onto a point in $\mathcal{D}$, using consistent hash functions, and the value v is stored by the node responsible for the zone containing this point. The search for the value corresponding to a key k is achieved by applying the same hash function on k in order to find the node responsible for storing the value. The routing process starts at the query originator and traverses iteratively its neighbors (a node only knows its adjacent neighbors), until the zone responsible for the key to store/retrieve is reached.

To limit the load on the network, we want to minimize the number of messages necessary to perform a broadcast. We first define precisely the hypotheses on the network topology to know exactly on which kind of networks our algorithms are valid. There are several ways to construct a broadcast algorithm depending on the structure of the CAN:

- The appendix of the seminal paper [14] suggests to build a construction tree, where a node is child of another if it joined this other node. This construction tree can be used to perform an efficient broadcast but the root of the tree would be overloaded. The main drawback of this approach is that keeping the tree structure when nodes leave leads to strong constraints (only a leaf node can take the place of a leaving node) and may require huge data transfers.
- In M-CAN [15] and Meghdoot [6], a CAN is defined as a structure where each node is responsible for an hyperrectangle: when a node leaves the network, its neighbour(s) can, for example, extend their own zone with the zone left by the leaving node. The only structure that can be exploited by a broadcast protocol is the graph of neighbors. Maintaining a spanning tree on such a structure with nodes joining and/or leaving the network is far from trivial.
- A CAN can be defined as a structure where each node is responsible for an area with no particular shape. This structure fits with the protocol described in [14] (Sec. 2.3): when a node leaves the network, its neighbour becomes responsible for its area. This is the most general case (it encompasses the two previous ones), and the one used here. Even in this unconstrained setting, we prove that an efficient broadcast algorithm exists.

Thus, we represent the network as a graph and provide an efficient algorithm on such a graph; computing a minimum spanning tree on this potentially evolving graph without global knowledge of the graph seems impossible. However, in a CAN, geometrical information can be exploited to avoid any two nodes from sending the same information to the same node. In this paper, our objective is to rely on a notion: "is a set of points connected?" which can be computed locally and to prove that, from this notion, we can design an efficient broadcast algorithm. The algorithm we propose here does not tolerate changes in the network during the broadcast, but it does support changes in the network between two broadcasts. Considering the case where a peer joins or leaves the CAN, i.e. node churn, is left for future work.

Figure 1 shows an efficient broadcast as ensured by M-CAN [15], the protocol sends messages first vertically (to a single neighbor above or below) and then horizontally, avoiding duplicates by sending only to the node that touches the

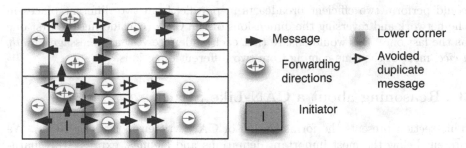

Fig. 1. M-CAN: Efficient flooding in 2 dimensional CAN

lower corner. Unfortunately, this algorithm does not eliminate all duplicates if the dimension is greater than two. In a publish/subscribe context, Meghdoot [6], built atop CAN, also proposes a mechanism to avoid duplicates but requires the broadcast to originate from one corner of the zone to be covered. We underline here that no broadcast algorithm atop CAN has been actually formally specified.

Using an interactive theorem prover such as Isabelle/HOL [13] and its higher-order logic provides us the expressiveness needed to formalize distributed algorithms and reason about them. A higher order logic naturally supports the formalization of the data structures of the algorithms; it also provides the reasoning tools to prove properties on those algorithms and structures. The expressiveness of Isabelle's logic allows us to reason about an abstraction of the system we design, meaning that we can abstract away some details of the CAN overlay and focus on the aspects ensuring the properties of the broadcast algorithm.

Our motivation is to put forward abstractions for proving correctness properties of distributed algorithms on top of CAN, and to promote the development of distributed algorithms *proven correct*. CAN is a difficult setting for proofs, because the structure entails a geometrical structure, which is more difficult to handle in Isabelle than inductive structures. We abstract away most of the geometrical notions, and rely on the notion of connection between nodes, expressed as a neighbor relation. We focus on two properties of broadcast protocols:

– **Efficiency:** a node receives only one message during a broadcast.
– **Coverage:** all the nodes receive the message (correctness property).

We write our specification in such a way that an external reader familiar with basic logic and mathematics can understand it. Indeed, our purpose is to make our results accessible and convincing for the community of distributed systems, including people not familiar with formal methods.

Efficiency vs. Robustness. One can easily argue that duplicating messages can actually increase the robustness of the broadcast in case of communication failures. However, the redundancy provided by a non-efficient broadcast algorithm is not satisfactory. Indeed with an inefficient algorithm, as shown in Figure 1, some nodes receive the message once, while other can receive it more than twice. Relying on an efficient algorithm is a better starting point in order to design robust algorithms in a smarter way. For example, to increase robustness, one could perform two efficient broadcasts in parallel from two different places in the network and reversing the dimensions of the CAN (considering the first one as the last one); this would ensure that each node receives each message *exactly twice*, most of the time coming from two different directions.

3   Reasoning about a CAN-Like Structure

This section presents the formalization of CAN written in Isabelle/HOL[1]. We present below the most important definitions and lemmas, expressed in mathematical style; some notions will be defined informally but most of the details are omitted; instead we prefer to give some insights regarding the principles of the formalization. For manipulating structures we use the following notations: ! accesses an element of a list; # adds an element at the beginning of the list; @ appends two lists; *fst* and *snd* access the elements of a pair.

A first crucial question when formalizing a complex structure like a CAN is which level of abstraction should be used, and which notions of Isabelle/HOL should represent basic notions of CAN networks. We chose to represent a CAN by a set of nodes, a zone for each node, and a neighboring relationship, stating whether any two nodes are neighbors. More precisely, a *CAN* is a set of integers identifying the different nodes. A function *CZ* matches each node to a *Zone*; a *zone* is simply a set of points, where each point is represented by a tuple of integers: *CZ N* is the zone under the responsibility of the node N. Also we require that the set of nodes is finite and the set of their zones partitions the whole space into disjoint zones covering the whole space. Each node is responsible for a zone that never changes and is called the zone of a node; note that our broadcast algorithm will also rely on some zones, i.e. sets of points.

Definition 1 (CAN). *The set of valid CANs is defined as follows:*

$CAN \equiv \{(Nodes, CZ, Neighbours).Nodes \in \mathcal{P}(\mathbb{N}) \wedge CZ \in \mathbb{N} \rightarrow Zone \wedge Neighbours \in \mathcal{P}(\mathbb{N} \times \mathbb{N})$
$\wedge \ symbNodes \ is \ finite \wedge Neighbours \ is \ finite$
$\wedge \ \forall x, y. \ (x, y) \in Neighbours \Rightarrow (y, x) \in Neighbours \wedge \forall x. \ (x, x) \notin Neighbours$
$\wedge \ \forall tup. \ \exists N \in Nodes. \ tup \in CZ(N)$
$\wedge \ \forall N, N' \in Nodes. \ CZ(N) \neq \varnothing \wedge N \neq N' \Rightarrow \neg(CZ(N) \ intersects \ CZ(N')) \ \}$

We also define three auxiliary functions *Nodes*, *Zones*, and *Neighbour* returning each part of a *CAN*. We adopt a formalization more general and flexible than the strict CAN protocol, more precisely:

- As discussed in Section 2, each node is responsible for a zone of any shape, whereas in most CANs, each node should always be responsible for a single hyperrectangle. We believe that this formalization is better adapted to model a dynamic CAN with nodes joining/leaving the network.
- *We do not relate zones with the concept of neighbor.* This alleviates us from geometric reasoning: we mainly rely on two relationships: "is a node neighbor of another?" and "do two zones intersect?" This allows us to reason at a topological level rather than a geometrical level.

---

[1] see: www-sop.inria.fr/oasis/personnel/Ludovic.Henrio/misc.

We thus define a predicate Z *intersects* Z' that checks whether a zone Z intersects a zone Z': it is true if Z and Z' have at least one point (tuple) in common. In the following, we say that *"a node intersects a zone Z"* if the zone of the node intersects Z. Then we define *NodesInZone* C Z, the set of nodes whose zones intersect the zone Z:

$$NodesInZone\ C\ Z = \{N \in Nodes(C).\ Zones(C,N)\ intersects\ Z\}$$

We define the size of a zone *ZoneSize* C Z as the number of nodes it contains. Then we define the connectivity of a CAN zone. This notion is close to the geometrical notion of path connectivity but dedicated to the CAN networks. The idea is that a zone is connected if a message can go between any two nodes in the zone passing only through nodes intersecting the zone. In the context of a broadcast algorithm, we will know that in such a zone the broadcast is possible; this notion will also give us a criteria that we have to follow when dividing the area to be covered into smaller zones. We state that a zone is connected if between any two nodes intersecting the zone, there is a path of nodes intersecting the zone where two consecutive nodes of the path are neighbors.

Definition 2 (Connected).

Connected C Z $\Leftrightarrow$ $\forall N, N' \in NodesInZone\ C\ Z.$
$\quad\quad \exists NL$ *a list of distinct nodes starting by N and finishing by N'.*
$\quad\quad \forall i < length(NL) - 1.\ NL!i \in NodesInZone\ C\ Z \wedge Neighbour(C, NL!i, NL!(i+1))$

Lemmas. To reason about CAN structures, we define several generic lemmas related to topology. These lemmas ease the reasoning on connectivity, intersection and nodes. Some typical lemmas prove generic properties on connectivity or intersection on the union or the intersection of zones. These small lemmas will reveal particularly useful for proving the properties of broadcast protocols.

Lemma 1, for instance, states that the union of two connected zones is connected if two nodes of the two zones are neighbors.

Lemma 1 (Connected-union).

$$\frac{Connected\ C\ Z \quad Connected\ C\ Z' \quad N \in NodesInZone\ C\ Z \quad N' \in NodesInZone\ C\ Z' \quad Neighbour(C, N, N')}{Connected\ C\ Z \cup Z'}$$

We also prove a symmetric lemma, allowing us to find neighboring nodes in two zones, provided those two zones and their union are connected (and the union contains at least two nodes).

Reasoning by Induction on a Zone. We also provide induction principles that allow one to prove a property related to a zone by induction on the size of the zone. A trivial induction lemma expresses directly induction on the number of nodes in the zone on which the property is verified. More interestingly, one can prove a property by adding one by one the nodes belonging to the zone of interest; this allows some form of structural induction on a CAN zone.

Theorem 1 (induct-node-zone2).

$$\frac{P(\varnothing) \qquad \forall Z.\, P(Z) \Rightarrow \forall N{\in}Nodes(C).N{\notin}NodesInZone\ C\ Z \Rightarrow \forall Z'.\, NodesInZone\ C\ Z' = \{N\} \Rightarrow P(Z{\cup}Z')}{P(Z)}$$

This theorem states that, if (1) we prove that a property P is true for an empty zone, and (2) we prove that if P is true for a zone then it is true for a zone intersecting one more node; then the property is true for all zones. The proof of this induction principle mainly relies on the fact that the set of all nodes of the CAN C must cover the entire space.

Messages and Message Paths. Once the network is defined, we define messages and paths followed by messages. As we will use messages to perform a broadcast towards a zone, a message is made of four parts: an identifier for the message m (which could represent also its payload), a source node x, a destination node y, and the zone Z to which it must be transmitted. We also define an abbreviation $<m|x,y,Z>$ for defining a *Message*. *Message-source*, *Message-dest*, and *Message-zone* are functions accessing the last three fields.

We believe it is important to provide tools to reason about the path followed by a message. Indeed, communication inside CAN heavily relies on the notion of paths. For this, we define a path as a set of consecutive messages, and provide tools to reason inductively on those path.

Definition 3 (valid-path). *valid-path is a predicate that checks whether the message path ML is valid, i.e. each message is sent from the destination of the previous message.*

$$valid\text{-}path\ msgs\ ML \Leftrightarrow ML \neq [] \wedge distinct(ML) \wedge \forall i < length(ML).\ ML!i \in msgs)$$
$$\forall i < length(ML) - 1.\ Message\text{-}dest(ML!i) = Message\text{-}source(ML!(i+1))$$

For a path to be valid, we additionally require that no two messages are the same; indeed, we will only consider paths of messages among a finite set *msgs* and we would like to consider only paths of finite length, this allows us to reason about the longest path in a zone. We provide various lemmas for building (valid) paths and reasoning about them.

4 Broadcast Algorithms over a CAN

Defining a broadcast in a natural way using Isabelle/HOL is not trivial; here we decide to put an emphasis on the way messages are processed. Our formalization is centered around the specification of messages which are the *consequences* of a given message and on the specification of the *set of messages* used to broadcast the original message. Then we define the way messages are broadcasted by an inductive definition, where messages are "processed" one message after the other sequentially. In our formalization, *Broadcasts* are triple made of a *CAN*, a message set, and an initiator node constrained by several well-formedness rules.

Definition 4 (Broadcast).

$$Broadcast \equiv \big\{(C, msgs, init).\ init \in Nodes(C)$$
$$\wedge\ \forall m,x,y,Z,m',Z'.\ <m|x,y,Z>{\in}msgs \wedge <m'|x,y,Z'>{\in}msgs \Rightarrow (m{=}m' \wedge Z{=}Z')$$
$$\wedge\ \forall <m|s,d,Z>{\in}msgs.\big(s \in Nodes(C) \wedge d \in Nodes(C) \wedge Neighbour(C,s,d) \wedge$$
$$\big(s{=}init \vee \exists ML.(valid\text{-}path\ msgs\ ML \wedge destination(ML){=}s \wedge source(ML){=}init)\big)\big)\big\}$$

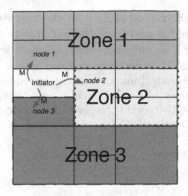

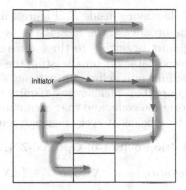

Fig. 2. Zone node list (ZNL) definition   **Fig. 3.** Naive efficient broadcast

The constraints expressed in the definition state that: (1) There is a single message between any 2 nodes. (2) The initiator is a node of the CAN. (3) All messages are exchanged between neighbor nodes of the CAN, and thus the broadcast pattern respects the CAN protocol. (4) All messages must be sent by a node that has been reached by a list of messages *MsgL* originating from the initiator. The existence of such a valid path ensures that a broadcast only relies on messages transmitted from nodes to nodes, and no message is spontaneously created (except for the initiator of course). Note that it is not sufficient to require that each message source is the destination of another message, because that would allow loops of messages not passing by the initiator. We denote $<C,M,n>$ a *Broadcast*, and define functions *BC-CAN*, *BC-msgs*, and *BC-init* to access its fields. We can then define a predicate checking whether a broadcast covers the whole CAN, i.e., whether each node of the CAN is either the initiator or the destination of a message:

Definition 5 (Coverage).

$Coverage\ (C, msgs, init) \Leftrightarrow \forall N \in Nodes(C).N = init \vee \exists m, s, Z.\ <m|s, N, Z> \in msgs$

We decided to rely on the notion of zone to be covered to define a broadcast algorithm because this seems quite adapted to the structure of the CAN. This zone to be covered can have two purposes depending on the algorithm. First it allows the specification of broadcast protocols where only the nodes in a given zone have to receive the message. Also, since we are interested in an efficient algorithm that minimizes the number of messages necessary to broadcast the information, it seems reasonable to split efficiently the zone to be covered in order to avoid sending a message to the same node twice. A broadcast algorithm can be entirely characterized by a function that, given a node N receiving a message and the zone Z to be covered by the message, returns a list of pairs (*Zone, Node*), that we call ZNL (*Zone-Node list*). Each pair (Z_i, N_i) of the ZNL consists of Z_i, a sub-zone of Z, and N_i a neighbour of N belonging to Z_i: the message is forwarded to N_i that is now responsible for covering Z_i. The zone Z_i must be connected (as defined above) otherwise it would be impossible to cover it while staying inside Z_i. Figure 4 illustrates the notion of ZNL for the first step of the broadcast: the message to be broadcasted is sent from the initiator to its neigbhors belonging to three different zones to be covered, which in turn, will be responsible for broadcasting the message to the zone they received.

Definition 6 defines an *optimal ZNL*, which underpins an efficient broadcast. To guarantee efficiency, we require that the zones of the list form a partition of the original zone, and that each node belong to the zone it receives. A broadcast will be efficient if every message generates an optimal ZNL.

Definition 6 (Set-of-Optimal-ZNL).

$$Set\text{-}of\text{-}Optimal\text{-}ZNL\ C\ N\ Z \equiv \{ZNL. \bigcup_{i<length(ZNL)} fst(ZNL!i) = Z$$
$$\wedge\ (\forall i < length(ZNL).\ Neighbour(C, N, snd(ZNL!i))\ \wedge\ Connected\ C\ fst(ZNL!i)$$
$$\wedge\ snd(ZNL!i) \in NodesInZone\ C\ fst(ZNL!i)$$
$$\wedge\ \forall j < length(ZNL).(j \neq i \Rightarrow\ snd(ZNL!i) \neq snd(ZNL!j) \wedge$$
$$NoNodeInBothZones\ fst(ZNL!i)\ fst(ZNL!j)))\}$$

Definition 7 specifies the set of messages of a broadcast algorithm based on *ZNLmap*, which is a function that, given a node and zone, returns an optimal ZNL. The set of messages of the broadcast is defined by induction rules expressing how messages are processed. The inductive definition is of the form *ZNL-BC-msgs C Mid init znlmap msgs ML* where *C* is the CAN network, *Mid* is the message identifier, *init* is the initiator node, and *znlmap* is the *ZNLmap* used by this instance of the algorithm.

Definition 7 (ZNL-BC-msgs).

$$ZNL\text{-}BC\text{-}msgs\ C\ Mid\ init\ znlmap\ \varnothing\ [< Mid|init, init, Entire\text{-}Space\backslash Zones(C, init) >]$$

$$\frac{ZNL\text{-}BC\text{-}msgs\ C\ Mid\ init\ znlmap\ msgs\ < Mid'|s, d, Z > \#ML}{ML' = map\ (\lambda ZN.\ < Mid'|d, snd(ZN), fst(ZN)\backslash Zones(C, snd(ZN)) >)\ (znlmap(Z, d))}{ZNL\text{-}BC\text{-}msgs\ C\ Mid\ init\ znlmap\ (msgs \cup \{< Mid'|s, d, Z >\})\ ML@ML'}$$

The inductive definition works as follows: it takes one by one messages in *ML*, called the list of *messages to be treated*, processes them and put them in the *set of treated messages, msgs*. Processing a message consists in using the function *znlmap* to compute the consequences of this message: for each couple (Z_i, N_i) returned by $(znlmap(Z, d))$, a new message with destination N_i and zone Z_i minus the zone of N_i which we just covered is created and put in the new *ML* list. The original message that has been processed is then put in *msgs*. The rules of Definition 7 are applied iteratively treating one message after the other. At the end, *ML*, the list of messages to be treated is empty, and *msgs*, the set of treated messages contains the list of messages of the broadcast.

Relying on a *znlmap* function is important here because it ensures that the broadcast algorithm is built without the knowledge of the messages already sent by the protocol. This ensures that only the knowledge of the current node and the zone to be covered is used to decide which message to send. We will see in the definition of the efficient broadcast how the *znlmap* function can be modified to take into account local information (i.e., neighbors and their zones).

Some design choices have been made in the way messages are actually processed in our formalization. Messages are treated sequentially, but this of course does not correspond to the parallelism that occur in a real system. However this classical simplification has no consequence on the properties of interest here. More important is the fact that the messages to be treated (*ML*) are represented as a list, this total ordering is artificial and one could improve the representation by defining an equivalence relation allowing reordering of messages. However, the list is a good structure to reason inductively on the messages and to allow rules to be applied iteratively. Concerning treated messages (*msgs*), as we do not perform any further computation on them, a list was not necessary and we considered them to be a set; a multiset is not necessary because it is easy to prevent the same message to be sent twice between the same nodes.

We prove that the set of messages generated by an optimal ZNL constitutes a valid broadcast that covers the entire network:

Theorem 2 (ZNL-BC).

$$\frac{ZNL\text{-}BC\text{-}msgs\ C\ Mid\ init\ znlmap\ Finalmsg\ []\quad init \in Nodes(C)}{\forall (Z,N) \in History(C,init,Finalmsg,[]).znlmap(Z,N) \in (Set\text{-}of\text{-}Valid\text{-}ZNL\ C\ N\ Z)}$$
$$\frac{}{(C,Finalmsg,init) \in Broadcast}$$

Theorem 3 (coverage-ZNL).

$$\frac{ZNL\text{-}BC\text{-}msgs\ C\ Mid\ init\ znlmap\ Finalmsg\ []\quad N,init \in Nodes(C)}{\forall (Z,N) \in History(C,init,Finalmsg,[]).znlmap(Z,N) \in (Set\text{-}of\text{-}Valid\text{-}ZNL\ C\ N\ Z)}$$
$$\frac{}{\exists s,Z.\ <Mid|s,N,Z> \in Finalmsg}$$

In these two theorems, we consider the last step of induction, when the list of messages to be treated is empty ([]). Also, we require that for each zone and node of *History*, *znlmap* verifies *set-of-Optimal-ZNL*. *History*(...) is the set of pairs (zone, destination node) that influenced the previous treatment of messages, and will influence the processing of the next message if there is one. In other words, it is the set of pairs (zone,destination node) for the set of treated messages (*msgs*), and the next message to be treated (head of *ML*), plus the couple (initiator node, entire space). We also proved additional lemmas ensuring correctness and easing further proofs, e.g. that the message content is unchanged during the process.

The theorems presented above are not sufficient to prove that the final step of the induction (where no more message is to be treated) is reachable. That is why we proved that ensuring $\forall Z\ N.\ znlmap(Z,N) \in Set\text{-}of\text{-}Optimal\text{-}ZNL\ C\ N\ Z$ is sufficient to ensure progress from each step. However, this is still not sufficient to ensure reachability of the final step while we do not ensure that the broadcast process is finite. Also, the approach presented above requires to compute, from the beginning, the function *znlmap*, which is unrealistic. Below, we prove the existence of an efficient broadcast, built step by step, which ensures reachability of the final step.

An Efficient Broadcast Algorithm A simple but efficient algorithm can be designed by constructing ZNLs as follows: suppose a node N receives a message with a given zone Z to cover, where $Z \cup CAN\text{-}Zones(C,N)$ is connected. We split this zone into several zones Z_i, where each zone is connected, no zone touches another ($i \neq j \Rightarrow Z_i \cup Z_j$ is not connected), and each zone contains a node N_i neighbour of

N. We first prove that such a decomposition necessarily exists (Lemma 2). The decomposition is optimal if the same node does not belong to two zones, which is true because, for any two zones, $Z_i \cup Z_j$ is not connected. We can thus prove that under the conditions mentioned above ($Z \cup CAN\text{-}Zones(C, N)$ is connected), an optimal decomposition exists (Lemma 3).

Lemma 2 (Zone-decomposition).

$\exists zl. \bigcup_{i<length(zl)} zl!i = Z \wedge \forall i < length(zl). \, Connected \; C \; zl!i \wedge \forall i, j < length(zl).i \neq j \Rightarrow \neg Connected \; C \; zl!i \cup zl!j$

Lemma 3 (OptimalZNL-existence).

$$\frac{N \in Nodes(C) \qquad Connected \; C \; (Z \cup Zones(C, N)) \qquad N \notin NodesInZone \; C \; Z}{\exists ZNL. \, ZNL \in Set\text{-}of\text{-}Optimal\text{-}ZNL \; C \; N \; Z}$$

Then, we forward the message to each of the neighbour N_i, delegating to it the zone Z_i minus the zone of N_i; note that this new zone verifies the hypothesis above, and thus the decomposition mechanism can be applied recursively until each node receives the message. The drawback of the decomposition lemma is that it seems to require the knowledge of C. More precisely we need to know C to decide whether a zone Z is connected or not. In a real CAN, geometrical connectedness is sufficient to ensure network connectedness, and thus connectedness can be computed without knowing the exact network topology. Consequently, in a real CAN, the decomposition can be computed locally at the node that needs to forward the information.

Remember that, to reason about the whole algorithm, we parametrized *ZNL-BC* by the *znlmap*, supposed to be known originally, not computed at each step. To prove that our algorithm works, we need to compute the optimal *znlmap* at each step with local information. This issue can be resolved in two steps. First, we show that the messages of the broadcast are only sensitive to the values of *znlmap* for the history $History(\dots)$. Second, we show that, provided the history is optimal, we can treat one more message and provide an extended *znlmap* that is still optimal for the new history. Additionally, we prove side conditions on the set of messages treated and to be treated so that, e.g., we can prove that the algorithm terminates.

Theorem 4 (Progress-ZNL).

$$\frac{ZNL\text{-}BC\text{-}msgs \; C \; Mid \; init \; znlmap \; msgs \; MList \qquad init \in Nodes(C)}{MList \neq [] \qquad \forall (Z, N) \in History(C, init, msgs, MList).znlmap(Z, N) \in (Set\text{-}of\text{-}Valid\text{-}ZNL \; C \; N \; Z)}$$

$\exists Mlist', znlmap'. \, msgs \cup set(Mlist) \subseteq msgs \cup \{MList!0\} \cup set(MList') \wedge$
$\qquad (Message\text{-}zone(MList!0)) = \varnothing \; \vee$
$\bigcup_{i<length(MList')} NodesInZone \; C \; Message\text{-}zone(MList'!i) \subset \bigcup_{i<length(MList)} NodesInZone \; C \; Message\text{-}zone(MList!i)) \wedge$
$\forall (Z, N) \in History(C, init, msgs \cup \{MList'!0\}, MList').znlmap(Z, N) \in (Set\text{-}of\text{-}Valid\text{-}ZNL \; C \; N \; Z)$

The consequences of those last steps are twofold. First, they allow us to build the znlmap at each step by finding, each time we treat a message, the new zone-node-list corresponding to the new message. Also, the specification above ensures that our algorithm terminates: it can always progress (because of the optimality of the ZNL) and we exhibited a well-founded order along which the set of messages to be treated decreases: at each step, the size of the zone to be covered by all the messages to be treated decreases strictly (i.e. the number of nodes intersecting it), or it stays the same and the number of messages to be treated decreases strictly.

Finally, we prove the two following theorems stating that the same node is not reached twice. More precisely, at each step, if a node received a message (it is the destination of a message treated or to be treated) then it is not the destination of another message, and it is not in a zone to be covered. Several intermediate lemmas guarantee the fact that zones to be covered are well-separated and finally, we prove that, at the last step of the broadcast protocol, no two nodes receive the message. Overall, we have proved that there is a broadcast protocol that do not send twice the message to the same node.

Theorem 5 (Efficiency-final-step).

$$\frac{ZNL\text{-}BC\text{-}msgs\ C\ Mid\ init\ znlmap\ Finalmsg\ []\quad init \in Nodes(C)\quad M, M' \in Finalmsg}{Message\text{-}dest(M) \neq Message\text{-}dest(M')}$$
$$M \neq M'\quad \forall (Z, N) \in History(C, init, Finalmsg, []).znlmap(Z, N) \in (Set\text{-}of\text{-}Valid\text{-}ZNL\ C\ N\ Z)$$

Theorem 6 (Efficiency-existence).

$$\frac{init \in Nodes(C)}{\exists Finalmsg, znlmap.\ ZNL\text{-}BC\text{-}msgs\ C\ Mid\ init\ znlmap\ Finalmsg\ []}$$
$$\land\ \forall M, M' \in Finalmsg.\ (M \neq M' \Rightarrow Message\text{-}dest(M) \neq Message\text{-}dest(M'))$$

All the steps shown above ensure that the *znlmap* function can be built iteratively from local information, and that no knowledge of the message history is necessary to build it. Concerning locality, we rely on the local decidability of the predicate "*Connected C Z*", which can be evaluated without the knowledge of the whole network in the case of a real CAN thanks to geometrical considerations. Relying only on local knowledge is crucial for a P2P algorithm but we cannot prove it formally here. To solve this issue the solution would be to prove that the Lemma 3 is true in a n dimensional space without knowledge of the whole network; such a proof would require the geometrical formalization of a CAN which is out of the scope of this study.

Concluding Remarks. It is important for us to have a formalism for expressing the CAN broadcast that is easy to understand. Although the specification we showed here is inductive and thus not in a classical form for a broadcast algorithm, we think it is clear enough to be convincing, and that it is easy to implement the program corresponding to our definitions. This way of expressing a broadcast algorithm is not as natural as one would expect because a form of event-based formulation of the algorithm "when a message M is received, send messages M1, M2, and M3" would be more adapted. However, such an event-like formulation is not well supported in Isabelle/HOL, even if we could try to provide new abbreviations for expressing message transmission more easily. In fact, the definition of *ZNL-BC* distinguishes the messages for which the consequence have already been computed from the others, which is crucial in our proofs, changing this definition to a more implicit set-oriented one would make the proofs even more complex or unfeasible.

In our proofs, we rely on a single axiom that states that the entire space is connected, which is a necessary prerequisite that we are not able to prove since we do not relate neighborhood with any geometrical notion.

The current specification and proofs consist of almost 5000 lines of Isabelle, for more than 150 lemmas and theorems. The length of the proofs is however not uniform: simple properties on the network or the connectivity could take a couple of lines, whether advanced properties on connectivity, and most of the properties of the broadcast algorithm require dealing with a lot of cases, or rely on complex inductions, they necessitate several hundreds of lines.

5   Related Work

A fair amount of work has been done on the verification of distributed systems. This section presents representative works that use theorem provers for reasoning on distributed algorithms, or discuss the formalization of DHT protocols.

Chou [18] proposes a reasoning infrastructure using HOL to formalize and verify distributed algorithms and validates his approach on a propagation of information with feedback algorithm. In the same line of direction, the work done by Qiao Haiyan [7] reports experiences in verifying distributed algorithms in constructive type theory using the Agda/Alfa proof assistant and provides a methodology mixing testing and verification of distributed algorithms. Ridge, in his work [17], takes an *operational approach* to distributed systems verification. His goal is to demonstrate, through a combination of symbolic evaluation and invariant checking, that the verification of distributed system is feasible down to the executable code level. His work relies on previous notable efforts, such as a rigorous approach to describe network protocols [16], a formal model of the OCaml programming language, and an operational verification of OCaml code. Charron-Bost and Merz [3] formally verified a modified version of the Paxos consensus algorithm using Isabelle/HOL. They modeled the consensus algorithm using the Heard-Of model (HO), a round-based computational model for fault-tolerant distributed systems. Their abstractions and proven properties as well as the formalization of the HO model can be used to study a large class of distributed algorithms; however the formalization does not embed any topological aspects of the underlying topology. Contrary to "classical" distributed algorithms such as consensus, distributed algorithms running on top of structured P2P systems, can not abstract away the underlying infrastructure, particularly if the algorithm relies on it. A formalization of an efficient broadcast algorithm on top of CAN has to rely on the needed abstractions and proofs regarding the topological aspects of CAN in order to prove the efficiency of the algorithm. The closest works on distributed algorithms for P2P systems are Meghdoot [6] and M-CAN [15] which are broadcast/multicast algorithms atop CAN which claim partial efficiency in terms of number of exchanged messages; they were briefly described in Section 2. Unfortunately no formalization nor any proofs were presented in these works. On the contrary, our objective is to use formal methods to prove with high confidence the correctness and efficiency of dissemination protocols.

Borgström et al. [2] were interested in the verification of DHT protocols. They formalized and verified a variant of Chord in static settings (i.e. no churn) using

CCS, a process algebra. In a subsequent work, Bakshi et al. [1] used π-calculus to prove the correctness properties of Chord in the pure-join model of the protocol. Zave, in her work [19] proved the Chord protocol in its two models: the *pure-join* and *full*, using the Alloy analyzer. By providing a rigorous correctness proof of the pure-join model and that the full model of the protocol she proved that the original Chord protocol is indeed not correct.

Pastry was also the subject of a recent verification effort [11], which focus was to ensure the correctness of Pastry's algorithms. The *join* and *lookup* protocols were specified using TLA^+ and the properties verified using the TLC model checker and the TLAPS proof assistant. Compared to the model-checking in general, theorem proving requires the help of the programmer to prove properties that are valid on an arbitrary number of processes. We focused in this paper on the pure use of Isabelle/HOL because most of our reasoning were about topology and induction, but we do not exclude the use of a proof assistant in conjunction with SMT solvers [12] in the future to ease reasoning, or reason more deeply about liveness properties for example.

6 Conclusion

To the best of our knowledge, we are the first ones to formalize an abstraction of the CAN overlay network using a theorem prover, and provide a framework to reason about those networks. This formalization efforts should increase the understanding of distributed algorithms for structured P2P networks, and the confidence one has in their correctness. We define formally all the constructs necessary to specify and prove properties of a broadcast algorithm on top of CAN. This paper presented the most important notions and support lemmas we designed in order to provide a convenient level of abstraction for reasoning on communication algorithms while abstracting away the geometrical concerns. The structured network represented is more general than a CAN: in a CAN, zones are necessarily hyperrectangles, whereas ours could be any tuple set. We prefer relying on a less restrictive definition of the structure to see which properties of our algorithm are verified in those conditions and also to lay down the groundwork for future challenges such as node churn. Later, requirements on the structure can be added to prove further properties, e.g. an algorithm may only be efficient if the zones are hyperrectangles. Difficult parts of the formalization concern reasoning by induction on a set that is finite but not inductively defined. To ease this kind of reasoning when dealing with zones, we developed an induction principle based on the number of nodes inside a zone (theorem *induct-node-zone-2*, Section 3). The reasoning relies on the topology of the network, defined by a neighbor relation, and related lemmas deal with the notion of *connected* zone, i.e. a node where any two nodes can (indirectly) communicate. We used this framework to describe a class of broadcast algorithms that relies on the notion of "zone to be covered". *We proved that there exists an algorithm that covers the whole network without sending twice a message to the same node.* This development also shows the capabilities of our framework.

In the future, we plan to formalize an algorithm that sends more messages in parallel than the one we exhibited here. Also, a next logical step would be to see how we can take *churns*, i.e. nodes joining/leaving the network, into consideration in our formalization since P2P systems exhibit dynamic behaviors and we can not overlook this feature.

References

1. Bakhshi, R., Gurov, D.: Verification of peer-to-peer algorithms: A case study. Electronic Notes in Theoretical Computer Science 181, 35–47 (2007)
2. Borgström, J., Nestmann, U., Onana, L., Gurov, D.: Verifying a Structured Peer-to-Peer Overlay Network: The Static Case. In: Priami, C., Quaglia, P. (eds.) GC 2004. LNCS, vol. 3267, pp. 250–265. Springer, Heidelberg (2005)
3. Charron-Bost, B., Merz, S.: Formal verification of a consensus algorithm in the heard-of model. Int. J. Software and Informatics 3(2-3) (2009)
4. DeCandia, G., Hastorun, D., Jampani, M., Kakulapati, G., Lakshman, A., Pilchin, A., Sivasubramanian, S., Vosshall, P., Vogels, W.: Dynamo: amazon's highly available key-value store. In: SOSP, pp. 205–220. ACM (2007)
5. Guo, H., Wu, M., Zhou, L., Hu, G., Yang, J., Zhang, L.: Practical software model checking via dynamic interface reduction. In: SOSP, pp. 265–278. ACM (2011)
6. Gupta, A., Sahin, O.D., Agrawal, D.P., El Abbadi, A.: Meghdoot: Content-Based Publish/Subscribe over P2P Networks. In: Jacobsen, H.-A. (ed.) Middleware 2004. LNCS, vol. 3231, pp. 254–273. Springer, Heidelberg (2004)
7. Haiyan, Q.: Testing and Proving Distributed Algorithms in Constructive Type Theory. In: Gurevich, Y., Meyer, B. (eds.) TAP 2007. LNCS, vol. 4454, pp. 79–94. Springer, Heidelberg (2007)
8. Hu, S.Y., Chen, J.F., Chen, T.H.: VON: a scalable peer-to-peer network for virtual environments. IEEE Network 20(4), 22–31 (2006)
9. Lakshman, A., Malik, P.: Cassandra: a decentralized structured storage system. SIGOPS Oper. Syst. Rev. 44(2), 35–40 (2010)
10. Liebeherr, J., Nahas, M., Si, W.: Application-layer multicasting with delaunay triangulation overlays. IEEE Journal on Selected Areas in Communications 20(8), 1472–1488 (2002)
11. Lu, T., Merz, S., Weidenbach, C.: Towards Verification of the Pastry Protocol Using TLA$^+$. In: Bruni, R., Dingel, J. (eds.) FORTE 2011 and FMOODS 2011. LNCS, vol. 6722, pp. 244–258. Springer, Heidelberg (2011)
12. Merz, S., Vanzetto, H.: Automatic Verification of TLA+ Proof Obligations with SMT Solvers. In: Bjørner, N., Voronkov, A. (eds.) LPAR-18 . LNCS, vol. 7180, pp. 289–303. Springer, Heidelberg (2012)
13. Nipkow, T., Paulson, L.C., Wenzel, M.T. (eds.):Isabelle/HOL: a proof assistant for higher-order logic. LNCS, vol. 2283. Springer, Heidelberg (2002)
14. Ratnasamy, S., Francis, P., Handley, M., Karp, R., Shenker, S.: A Scalable Content-Addressable Network. In: SIGCOMM, pp. 161–172. ACM (2001)
15. Ratnasamy, S., Handley, M., Karp, R.M., Shenker, S.: Application-Level Multicast Using Content-Addressable Networks. In: Crowcroft, J., Hofmann, M. (eds.) NGC 2001. LNCS, vol. 2233, pp. 14–29. Springer, Heidelberg (2001)
16. Ridge, T., Norrish, M., Sewell, P.: A Rigorous Approach to Networking: TCP, from Implementation to Protocol to Service. In: Cuellar, J., Sere, K. (eds.) FM 2008. LNCS, vol. 5014, pp. 294–309. Springer, Heidelberg (2008)

17. Ridge, T.: Verifying distributed systems: the operational approach. In: POPL, Savannah, GA, USA, p. 429 (2009)
18. Chou, C.T.: Mechanical verification of distributed algorithms in higher-order logic. The Computer Journal 38(2), 152 (1995)
19. Zave, P.: Using lightweight modeling to understand chord. Computer Communication Review 42(2), 49–57 (2012)

Enforcing QVT-R with mu-Calculus and Games

Julian Bradfield and Perdita Stevens

School of Informatics
University of Edinburgh

Abstract. QVT-R is the standard Object Management Group bidirectional transformation language. In previous work, we gave a precise game-theoretic semantics for the checkonly semantics of QVT-R transformations, including the recursive invocation of relations which is allowed and used, but not defined, by the QVT standard. In this paper, we take up the problem of enforce semantics, where the standard attempts formality, but at crucial points lapses into English. We show that our previous semantics can be extended to enforce mode, giving a precise semantics taking the standard into account.

1 Introduction

QVT-R is the OMG standard *bidirectional* model transformation language [8]. It is bidirectional in the sense that, rather than simply permitting one model to be built from others, it permits changes to be propagated in any direction, something which seems to be essential in much real-world model-driven development. The same transformation can be read as specifying the circumstances under which models are consistent (checkonly mode) or as specifying exactly how one model should be modified so as to restore consistency that has been lost (enforce mode). This dual use of the same transformation text is beneficial in engineering terms; separate texts for checkonly and enforce transformations would be a maintenance nightmare. In earlier work [3,12] we gave formal semantics for QVT-R in checkonly mode, including transformations in which a relation may recursively invoke itself; this feature is used even in the example in [8], and presents interesting complications which we tackled using the modal mu calculus. A thorough understanding of checkonly mode is prerequisite to understanding enforce mode, because of the requirement (hippocraticness) that running a transformation in enforce mode should not modify models which are already consistent.

In this paper, we go on to give a formal semantics for QVT-R in enforce mode. Unlike previous work, we do not restrict to the case where the target model is created afresh from the source model; we work with the general case in which there is an existing target model which must be taken into account when producing a new version. This, the typical case of bidirectional transformation arising in model-driven development, is more complex – even when the transformation is not recursive – because there will usually be many different target models that are consistent with the given source model, and the preexisting target model influences which one is produced.

As an illustrative example, consider the following transformation (given in ModelMorf's QVT-R syntax), which operates on models that have two kinds of model elements MEtop and MEchild. Both kinds have names; MEtop elements can also have children which are of type MEchild. We represent such models in the obvious way as forests, and notate them using the names of elements, e.g. $\{N \to \{child1, child2, child2\}\}$ represents a model containing one element of type MEtop with name "N", having three children of type MEchild whose names are "child1", "child2", "child2". Notice that there is nothing to prevent two model elements having the same name (no key declaration, for example).

```
transformation NonTopEnforce (m1 : TwoLayerMM1 ; m2 : TwoLayerMM2) {
top relation R {
  n : String;
  firstchild : TwoLayerMM1::MEchild;
  secondchild : TwoLayerMM2::MEchild;
  enforce domain m1 me1:MEtop {name = n, child = firstchild};
  enforce domain m2 me2:MEtop {name = n, child = secondchild};
  where { S(firstchild,secondchild); }}

relation S {
  n : String;
  enforce domain m1 me1:MEchild {name = n};
  enforce domain m2 me2:MEchild {name = n};}}
```

Models are consistent according to this transformation provided that two directional checks succeed. For every MEtop element me1 in m1, there must be an MEtop element me2 of the same name in m2, such that the name of every child of me1 occurs as the name of a child of me2. The check in the m2 direction is symmetric.

Running this transformation in checkonly mode in ModelMorf, consulting [8], yields no surprises. Running it in enforce mode lets us illustrate semantic choices that [8] has made and some odd behaviour of ModelMorf. Let m1 be $\{N \to \{child1, child2, child3\}\}$ throughout. If m2 is identical, of course it is not modified (except that ModelMorf, for some reason, rewrites all the xmi:ids): check-before-enforce ensures that, since the models are already consistent, no change is made. Next, let m2 be the empty model, and enforce so that a new m2 is created from m1. ModelMorf produces $\{N \to \{child1\}, \{N \to \{child2\}, \{N \to \{child3\}\}$ (not the copy of m1 that some might intuitively expect). This is consistent with (our reading of) [8]; it arises because each valid binding to variables in R is checked independently. Thus for each binding to me1, (n and firstchild for which no matching binding is found, new objects are created for me2 and secondchild and the child property of me2 is set to secondchild.

Next consider $m2 = \{N \to \{child1, child2, cuckoo\}\}$. Interpreting this as the name of the third child being wrong, we would intuitively expect the least change modification to be made, i.e. for the name "cuckoo" to be changed to "child3". By the same argument as above, however, we see that ModelMorf is in accord with [8] in actually returning $\{N \to \{child1, child2\}, \{N \to \{child3\}\}\}$. Rather than modify an existing child, a whole new binding is created to be the match. Here we have the first obvious use of the delete phase: the `child` named "cuckoo" has been removed. Why is this? We may argue: because if it had been left alone – if ModelMorf had returned $\{N \to \{child1, child2, cuckoo\}, \{N \to \{child3\}\}\}$ – the resulting version of `m2` would not have been consistent with `m1` *when checked in the direction of* `m1`. Even though any run of ModelMorf has a direction (in contrast to [8] in which a transformation being evaluated in checkonly mode involves checks in all directions, as explained in detail in [12]), ModelMorf does ensure that the result of an enforce transformation passes the checkonly transformation in all directions, not just in the same direction as the enforce.

Finally, however, consider `m2` $= \{N \to \{child1, child2, child2\}\}$. In this case, the checkonly transformation run in the direction of `m1` will already succeed; the only problem is when running the checkonly transformation in the direction of `m2`, as there is no valid match for valid binding of `me1` to the unique `MEtop` and `firstchild` to the `MEchild` with `name` "child3". We would expect $\{N \to \{child1, child2, child2\}, \{N \to \{child3\}\}\}$ as the result of enforcement. In fact, however, ModelMorf unnecessarily deletes one of the "child2" `MEchilds`, giving exactly the same result as in the "cuckoo" case. As we shall discuss, the interpretation of element deletion in [8] is problematic and so it is not very surprising that ModelMorf sometimes gives odd results. We discuss this further in section 4.3.

We will return to these examples after presenting our semantics.

2   Related Work

The first crucial feature of QVT-R enforce mode with which this paper is concerned is its true bidirectional nature. That is, the model which is computed as the result of a QVT-R transformation in enforce mode depends on two (or in general, more) models: the "source" model(s) and the existing "target" model. The second feature we emphasise is the possibility of recursion, in which one relation may invoke another, or even itself, on different or the same arguments. Both of these features are important to practical usability of QVT-R, as we argued more fully in [3] for recursion and in [11] for bidirectionality.

Most previous work on model transformations, and to our knowledge all previous work on QVT-R enforce mode, does not address either of these features. Rather, it formalises only the special case in which the original target model is empty, so that the QVT-R transformation simply produces the target model from the source model (we will call this "unidirectional QVT-R"); and it assumes that the *when-where* graph, the "call graph" of QVT-R relations, is acyclic ("acyclic QVT-R").

Triple graph grammars [10] do have this property of modifying an existing target model in the light of a source model. This works, roughly, by jointly parsing the input graph models, making use of (or constructing) a *correspondence graph* that connects them, so that a hypothetical source model consistent with the current target model, together with a sequence of rules that would lead from the hypothetical to the current source model, is known. Then this sequence of rules is applied to the current target model to give the result target model. By placing careful restrictions, it is possible to ensure that the process succeeds and gives a uniquely defined result [7]. Greenyer and Kindler [6] gave a translation from QVT Core to Triple Graph Grammars (TGGs), and informally discuss trying to extend the approach to QVT-R, although they do not provide a semantics for QVT-R. Unfortunately, as discussed at length in [12], the claim in [8] that QVT-R can be translated in a semantics-preserving way to QVT Core is not sustainable (QVT Core is insufficiently expressive), so this approach does not lead to a semantics for QVT-R. The same problem may apply to [4] which a semantics for QVT-R enforce mode (with both unidirectional and acyclic restrictions) using coloured petri nets; it states that it is consistent with [8]'s incorrect translation to QVT Core. Another paper in this tradition is [14] which discusses using CPN theory as implemented in a model transformation framework called TROPIC to provide debugging facilities for QVT-R transformations. Again, the paper addresses only the unidirectional use of QVT-R.

Romeikat and others [9] translated QVT-R transformations, restricted to the acyclic case, to QVT Operational. The focus is on unidirectional use of QVT-R. The bidirectional case is discussed briefly, but not in detail; it seems to be considered only where all model elements are identified by key expressions. A different approach is to give semantics to QVT-R using algebraic specification, as exemplified by [1], which describes the MOMENT-QVT tool. This work, too, addressed only the unidirectional use of QVT-R. Recursive relation invocations are not discussed and do not seem to be allowed for.

The two extant tools addressing QVT-R are Medini and ModelMorf. As discussed in [12], Medini deliberately departs from [8]. ModelMorf is thus the most reliable (although not infallible) implementation and the one we compare our semantics with.

3   Preliminaries

3.1   QVT-R

A transformation T is defined over a finite set of (usually two) *metamodels* (types for the input models) and, when executed in enforce mode, can be thought of as a function from tuples of models, each conforming to the appropriate metamodel, to an updated model (or failure). In any execution there is a *direction*, that is, a distinguished model which is being checked/enforced. The argument models are also known as *domains* and we will be discussing transformation execution in the direction of the kth domain. That is, the kth argument model is being checked/enforced against the others. See [12] for further discussion; here we assume some familiarity with QVT-R.

We use the notions of variables, values, typing, bindings and expressions. In QVT-R these matters are prescribed, building on the MOF metamodelling discipline and OCL. The available types are the metaclasses from any of the metamodels, together with a set of base types (defined in OCL) such as booleans, strings and integers, and collections. Values are instances of these. The expression language is an extension of OCL over the metamodels. QVT-R is a typed language, with some type inference expected.

In this paper, as in the previous work, we do not depend on QVT-R's particular choices in these matters, but provide a framework applicable to any similar language. We assume given sets Var of typed variables, Val of values and $Expr$ of typed expressions over variables. We write $fv(e)$ for the set of free variables in $e \in Expr$. $Constraint$ is the subset of $Expr$ consisting of expressions of type Boolean. A (partial) set of $bindings$ B for a set $V \subseteq Var$ of variables will be a (partial) function $B : V \rightharpoonup Val$ satisfying the typing discipline. We write $B' \succeq B$ when $dom(B') \supseteq dom(B)$ and B' and B agree on $dom(B)$. We assume given an evaluation partial function $eval : Expr \times Binding \rightharpoonup Val$ defined on any (e, b) where $fv(e) \subseteq dom(b)$. Like [8] we will assume all transformations we consider are statically well-typed.

A transformation T is structured as a finite set of $relations$ $R_1 \ldots R_n$, one or more of which are designated as top relations. A QVT-R relation is not (just) a mathematical relation – it consists of: a unique name; for each domain a typed $domain$ $variable$ and a $pattern$; and optional $when$ and $where$ clauses. We allow $when$ or $where$ clauses to contain arbitrary boolean combinations of $relation$ $invocations$ and boolean constraints (from $Constraint$). A relation invocation consists of the name of a relation together with an ordered list of argument expressions. Evaluating these expressions yields values for the domain variables of the invoked relation. We write $rel(T)$ for the set of names of relations in T and $top(T) \subseteq rel(T)$ for the names of relations designated top. A pattern is a set of typed variables together with a constraint ("domain-local constraint") over these variables and the domain variable. A variable may occur in more than one pattern, provided that its type is the same in all.

The set of all variables used (in QVT-R declarations can be implicit) in a relation R will be denoted $vars(R)$. The subset of $vars(R)$ mentioned in the $when$ clause of R is denoted $whenvars(R)$. The subset mentioned in the domains other than the kth domain is denoted $nonkvars(R)$. The set containing the domain variables is denoted $domainvars(R)$. These subsets of $vars(R)$ may overlap.

3.2   Game/mu-Calculus Semantics for QVT-R

In [3], we gave our semantics both in terms of a game and in terms of a modal mu-calculus formula, the two presentations being equivalent. Although the game version is easier to understand, the logical version is more concise and easier to adapt; so for reasons of space, we here give details only in the logical form.

The meta-logic for our semantics is modal mu-calculus. We refer to [3] for a fuller explanation of the logic and its relation to the game. Here we recap briefly the key points. The structures for the logic are transition systems – i.e. edge-labelled graphs – and formulae are true or false at states (nodes) in the systems. The formula $[a]\phi$ is true at s iff ϕ is true at every state reached from s by a single a-transition ('a-successor'); $\langle a \rangle \phi$ is true iff ϕ is true at some a-successor. The greatest and least fixpoints $\nu Z.\phi(Z)$ and $\mu Z.\phi(Z)$ are formally co-inductive and inductive definitions, but are best understood as allowing the specification of looping behaviour – infinite loops for greatest fixpoints, and finite (but unbounded) loops for least fixpoints. Establishing a formula corresponds to constructing a winning strategy in the game for Verifier where she chooses at $\vee$ and $\langle\rangle$, and Refuter chooses at $\wedge$ and $[]$. See [2] for a detailed explanation of the relation between modal mu-calculus, parity automata, and parity games.

Our semantics translates a QVT-R checkonly transformation instance into a modal mu calculus model-checking instance. Again, we refer to [3] for a full explanation. The key points are that we build a transition system encoding all the non-logical information about the models and the transformation, and we build a formula encoding the purely logical aspects.

Apart from a distinguished initial node, nodes of the transition system we construct each consist of a pair (R, B) where $R \in rel(T)$ and $B : vars(R) \rightharpoonup Val$ is a set of (well-typed, as always) bindings. In order to be able to handle cases where the same relation may be invoked more than once in the *when* or *where* clause of another relation, we begin by labelling each relation invocation in the static transformation text with a natural number, so that an invocation $R(e_1, \ldots, e_n)$ is replaced by $R^i(e_1, \ldots, e_n)$ for an i unique within the transformation; invoking the relation at invocation i will be modelled by a transition labelled invoke$_i$. Figure 1 defines the LTS formally. Note that the direction parameter k affects the meaning of *nonkvars*.

The boolean flag is needed to handle negation, and in particular the negation implicit in *when* clauses. When the flag is *true*, the players have their usual roles; when the flag is *false*, they swap turns, so that Verifier handles [] and so on.

The mu calculus formula does not represent the domain variables, the patterns or the arguments to the relation invocations: all that information is represented in the transition system, and the invoke$_i$ transitions and modalities connect the LTS and formula appropriately. Figure 1 defines the translation process formally.

Note that *tr2* is used to translate *when* and *where* clauses, building an environment that maps relations to mu variables in the process. Relation invocations are translated using the environment if the relation has been seen before, and otherwise, using a new fixpoint.

As discussed in [3], the possibility of recursive relation invocations in *when* clauses leads to potential undefined results. We adopt the well-formedness requirement defined and justified in [3], that there must be an even number of negations and *whens* between two invocations of a relation.

4   Enforcement

The description of enforcement semantics in [8], as with its description of checkonly semantics, does not address how to treat relations that are called in the *when* and *where* clauses of other relations. The "formal" semantics in Annex B uses a predicate logic formula, although it is actually understood as an imperative program. The only way to interpret this, is that relation invocations other than at top level are treated as pure predicates. Consequently, object creation

Input: Transformation T defined over metamodels M_i, models $m_i : M_i$, direction k.
Output: Labelled transition system $lts(T, m_i, k) = (Initial, A, S, \longrightarrow)$
Nodes:
$S = \{Initial\} \cup \{(R, B) : R \in rel(T), B : vars(R) \rightharpoonup Val\}$
Labels:
$A = \{\text{challenge}, \text{response}, \text{ext1}, \text{ext2}\} \cup \{\text{invoke}_i : i \in \mathbb{N}\}$
Transitions:

Initial $\xrightarrow{\text{challenge}}$ (R, B) if $R \in top(T)$ and $dom(B) = whenvars(R) \cup$
$\qquad\qquad\qquad\qquad nonkvars(R)$

$(R, B) \xrightarrow{\text{response}}$ (R, B') if $dom(B) = whenvars(R) \cup nonkvars(R)$ and $B' \succeq B$
$\qquad\qquad\qquad\qquad$ and $dom(B') = vars(R)$

$(R, B) \xrightarrow{\text{ext1}}$ (R, B') if $dom(B) = domainvars(R)$ and $B' \succeq B$
$\qquad\qquad\qquad\qquad$ and $dom(B') = domainvars(R) \cup whenvars(R) \cup$
$\qquad\qquad\qquad\qquad nonkvars(R)$

$(R, B) \xrightarrow{\text{ext2}}$ (R, B') if $dom(B) = domainvars(R) \cup whenvars(R) \cup$
$\qquad\qquad\qquad\qquad nonkvars(R)$ and $B' \succeq B$ and $dom(B') = vars(R)$

$(R, B) \xrightarrow{\text{invoke}_j}$ (S, B') if S is invoked at the invocation labelled j in the
$\qquad\qquad\qquad\qquad$ where clause of R with arguments e_i, $dom(B) =$
$\qquad\qquad\qquad\qquad vars(R)$ and $dom(B') = domainvars(S)$ with $\forall i \in$
$\qquad\qquad\qquad\qquad domainvars(S).B' : v_i \mapsto eval(e_i, B)$

$(R, B) \xrightarrow{\text{invoke}_j}$ (S, B') if S is invoked at the invocation labelled j in the
$\qquad\qquad\qquad\qquad$ when clause of R, with arguments e_i, $dom(B) \supseteq$
$\qquad\qquad\qquad\qquad whenvars(R)$ and $dom(B') = domainvars(S)$ with
$\qquad\qquad\qquad\qquad \forall i \in domainvars(S).B' : v_i \mapsto eval(e_i, B)$

LTS definition

Input: Transformation T. **Output:** $tr(T)$ given by:

$$tr(T) = \bigwedge_{R_i \in top(T)} tr1(R_i)$$

$$tr1(R_i) = [\text{challenge}] (\langle \text{response} \rangle (tr2_\emptyset(where(R_i), true) \vee$$
$$tr2_\emptyset(when(R_i), false))$$

$$tr2_E(\phi, true) = \phi$$
$$tr2_E(\phi, false) = \neg\phi$$
$$tr2_E(e \text{ and } e', true) = tr2_E(e, true) \wedge tr2_E(e', true)$$
$$tr2_E(e \text{ and } e', false) = tr2_E(e, false) \vee tr2_E(e', false)$$
$$tr2_E(e \text{ or } e', true) = tr2_E(e, true) \vee tr2_E(e', true)$$
$$tr2_E(e \text{ or } e', false) = tr2_E(e, false) \wedge tr2_E(e', false)$$
$$tr2_E(\text{not } e, b) = tr2_E(e, \neg b)$$
$$tr2_E(R^i(e_1 \ldots e_n), true) = \langle \text{invoke}_i \rangle E[R] \qquad\qquad \text{if } R \in \text{dom}E$$
$$tr2_E(R^i(e_1 \ldots e_n), true) = \langle \text{invoke}_i \rangle \nu X. ([\text{ext1}] \qquad\qquad \text{otherwise}$$
$$(\langle \text{ext2} \rangle tr2_{E[R \mapsto X]}(where(R), true) \vee$$
$$tr2_{E[R \mapsto X]}(when(R), false))$$
$$tr2_E(R^i(e_1 \ldots e_n), false) = [\text{invoke}_i] (\neg E[R]) \qquad\qquad \text{if } R \in \text{dom}E$$
$$tr2_E(R^i(e_1 \ldots e_n), false) = [\text{invoke}_i] \mu X. (\langle \text{ext1} \rangle \qquad\qquad \text{otherwise}$$
$$([\text{ext2}] tr2_{E[R \mapsto \neg X]}(where(R), false) \wedge$$
$$tr2_{E[R \mapsto \neg X]}(when(R), true))$$

Mu calculus formula definition

Fig. 1. Definition of the checkonly translation

or update happens only in top level relation calls. As we saw in the introduction, this leads to the creation of many new objects in top level bindings, where a smaller change could be achieved by recursively enforcing the lower level relation. In this paper we present only semantics following the approach of [8].

The [8, Annex B] enforcement specification breaks into two steps: first, create (or modify) any objects in the target required to satisfy the transformation; secondly, delete certain objects in the target not required to exist by the transformation. We use the same phases.

4.1 Extending the QVT Game/Logic for Enforcement

Determining that two models are consistent, in our semantics, amounts to finding a winning strategy for Verifier, or alternatively establishing the truth of a formula expressed in mu-calculus. To play an enforcement game, we need to give Verifier additional moves: if she is unable to win the checkonly game at a certain point, she has the option to change the model and try again. In mu-calculus terms, this amounts to adding disjunctions at appropriate places in the formula, with formulae involving a model-changing transition.

The model-changing is encoded thus: the states of the transition system in Fig. 1 are extended to be of the form $(Initial, M)$ or (R, B, M) so that they carry the (entire) target model M as part of the state, and the transitions defined there leave it untouched. For technical reasons, the models M also include a 'modification record' for each model element, saying whether a given property has been changed.

4.2 The Object Creation/Update Phase

The first extension to our previous semantics is to force the re-start of checking/enforcement after a model update. While Annex B does not discuss this, it is obvious that after a model update, all top relations may need to be checked again. (Of course a tool might optimise.) Therefore we wrap the entire top level formula in a least fixpoint, so that the first line of Fig. 1 'formula definition' is changed to

$$tr(T) = \mu W. \bigwedge_{R_i \in top(T)} tr1(R_i)$$

where the variable W will appear later in the translation, and the fixpoint has to be minimal because for enforcement to succeed, only a finite number of updates can be done.

Per Annex B, object creation (or update) occurs if, after source and *when* bindings are chosen, there is no binding to the target variables that satisfies the domain pattern. In our game, this occurs at the point following a challenge transition taken by Refuter. If Verifier is unable to choose bindings that let her win, or to win by challenging the *when* clause, she has the possibility to update the model, so line 2 of Fig. 1 'formula definition' becomes

$tr1(R_i) = [\text{challenge}] (\langle \text{response} \rangle (tr2_\emptyset(where(R_i), true))$

$$\lor \; tr2_\emptyset(when(R_i), \mathit{false})$$
$$\lor \; \langle \mathrm{update} \rangle W)$$

and the update transitions are defined by

$$(R, B, M) \overset{\mathrm{update}}{\longrightarrow} (\mathrm{Initial}, M') \quad \text{if } (*)$$

where the side-condition property (*) must capture when changing the model to M' is legal. (*) depends on whether the kth domain variable, say me:ME, is already in $dom(B)$ (which will be the case if $me \in whenvars(R)$), and whether a key constraint is specified for ME. If $me \notin dom(B)$ and ME has no key constraint, then M' is a model formed from M by creating a new object, say o, of type ME, with properties set according to the kth domain pattern of R with bindings from B.

However, the domain pattern does not (usually) specify all properties of o and, for enforcement to succeed, properties that are not specified may nevertheless matter, as they may have to take values which will cause a *where* clause to succeed – note that the actual point in the transformation at which the values of these properties of o matter could be arbitrarily many invocations away from R. [8] does not specify how such properties are to be set, but a useful tool must find correct values as often as possible (not "if they exist", because it is clear that the problem in general is noncomputable, given a constraint language as powerful as OCL). In our semantics, we model an update transition for *every* legal choice of the properties. A choice is legal if it obeys the metamodel and domain pattern (including domain-local constraints). Note that our transition system already contained infinite branching because of the potentially infinite choices for bindings; we will shortly discuss how a transformation engine could ensure determinacy by searching systematically for a winning strategy (and thus always finding the same one, even if there are many).

If a new object o cannot be created because me was already bound (say to o') in B, then (*) must permit no update transition unless there is a key specification for ME, because only then will it be legal to modify properties of o'.

Now consider the case where there is a key specification for ME such that the bindings in B determine an object (say o') in M (regardless of whether this is because B includes a binding of me to o' itself, or because it includes bindings for key properties that determine o'). Then (*) is adjusted to make M' the result of modifying properties of o', that have not already been marked 'modified' to a different value, in any way which is valid according to the metamodel, domain pattern, and domain local constraint as before, and setting the modification flag on the object's modified properties. (The reason for the modification flag is that enforcement is required to fail if an object is modified in inconsistent ways.)

Corresponding moves are added to the game presentation, allowing Verifier a move modifying the target model if she cannot win by either providing bindings from the current model or challenging the when clause. (Details are elided as, although simple, they do become long-winded: if Verifier tries to choose an update move when in fact she could have won by one of the other move types –

that is, if she makes an unnecessary change to the model – we need to let Refuter win by demonstrating that her update was unnecessary. This corresponds to the inverting of Boolean flags in the short circuit evaluation version of the mu formula below.)

A logical formula has no order of evaluation built in, whereas the imperative interpretation of Annex B does. It is possible to impose an order of evaluation externally upon the model-checker; it is also possible to modify the formula to simulate it. This makes no difference to whether our enforcement formula succeeds, but it does affect the model that results from evaluating whether enforcement succeeds. If our formula is to do updates only when needed, we can simulate short-circuit evaluation by modifying the new formula thus:

$$tr1(R_i) = [\text{challenge}] (((\langle \text{response} \rangle (tr2_\emptyset(where(R_i), true)))$$
$$\lor tr2_\emptyset(when(R_i), false)$$
$$\lor (([\text{response}] \; tr2_\emptyset(where(R_i), false))$$
$$\land tr2_\emptyset(when(R_i), true) \land \langle \text{update} \rangle W))$$

so that Verifier can only successfully choose the update branch if the other branches fail. (Here we use [3, Lemma 1].)

There is one issue that is best dealt with by the evaluation/model-checking procedure, rather than in the formula or game. There is, in general, nothing to stop Verifier from making unnecessary updates, by choosing an update transition that does not in fact satisfy the *where* clause; she will then re-start, and update again. With sufficient additional book-keeping in the model and formula, this could be avoided; however, it is simpler to invoke the notions of 'canonical tableau' or 'optimal progress measures' from the theory of mu-calculus model-checking, so that the model-checker constructs the strategy with the smallest number of updates. (So-called bottom-up model-checkers do this automatically; top-down model-checkers do not. See [2].)

At this point, our semantics matches that of Annex B after the create phase. Showing that the formula is true amounts to constructing a winning strategy for Verifier in the game, and the constructed model is extracted by examining the update transitions in the winning strategy (or, in practice, by examining the trace of updates taken during construction).

Enforcement may involve creating and choosing properties for many new objects. It is also possible that an object created by one update may be used (e.g. with modification) by a subsequent update. It is therefore possible in general that the constructed model depends on the order of transition choices in modalities, which in turn depends on the order in which source bindings are checked – in our terms, on the order in which Refuter makes choices when challenging. While this is also the case in Annex B, it is desirable that an enforcement algorithm should be deterministic, which requires fixing the order of all choices. It is not feasible or sensible to encode this into the logic; rather it is appropriately done by specifying how the mu-calculus model-checking algorithm proceeds, or equivalently how the construction of a winning strategy proceeds. While all real model-checkers make such choices, they do not normally expose them; if the result of enforcement is to be unique, the choices must be explicit. For example, we might specify that formulae are checked left to right, and that when choosing a transition, the possible transitions are ordered according to their internal representations and the lowest in the order is taken.

4.3   The Deletion Phase

Here we need to be cautious because a literal reading of [8] (sections 7.10.2 and Annex B) gives behaviour that is clearly undesirable and contradicts Model-Morf's behaviour. [8] specifies that certain elements of the target model, that constitute valid bindings of domain k variables, are deleted if they are not 're-quired to exist' by the relation. For example, if model m1 contains an E1type with name 'foo', and m2 contains no E2type called 'foo', then enforcing the relation

```
top relation Zap {
  n : String;
  domain m1 e1:E1type { name=n };
  domain m2 e2:E2type { name=n };
  when { n = 'foo'; } }
```

on m2 would, in addition to creating a new E2type called 'foo', delete all E2type elements in the old m2, because they are not required to exist by the relation. It is hard to believe that this is the desired result, and indeed ModelMorf does not do this (it sensibly creates a new 'foo' E2type, leaving other E2types alone).

To see what is probably intended, consider the same relation without the *when* clause, which ought to embody a more stringent consistency check:

```
top relation Matchname {
  n : String;
  domain m1 e1:E1type { name=n };
  domain m2 e2:E2type { name=n };}
```

Bidirectionally, this says every E1type element in one domain has a (not necessarily unique) matching-named element in the other. Suppose we enforce on m2, and there is an element e called 'foo' in m2 with no match in m1. We expect it to be deleted. [8] will delete it because it is 'not required'. However, the real reason for deleting is surely that it fails the relation *in the direction* m1; it is not that e is not required, it is that its *absence* is required for Matchname to check in the m1 direction (as we are not allowed to create an element in m1).

Deciding that we should delete objects whose absence is required, we can implement the deletion phase more easily: for each checked (source) domain j (e.g. m1 above), we set up the transition system and formula for checking in the direction of the jth domain, and then modify the formula exactly as before, but replacing update by delete, and add transitions

$$(R, B, M) \xrightarrow{\text{delete}} (\text{Initial}, M') \quad \text{if } (**)$$

where property (**) is: M' is the model formed from M by deleting the object bound in B to the top level domain variable of the kth domain (which is now a source domain for the checkonly formula). In the typical case of two domains, we only need run the delete step once; where there are $k > 2$ checked domains and we are enforcing on the kth, we must run the deletion step for each of the domains $j = 1, \ldots, k - 1$.

If this formula evaluates to true, the resulting model is read off from the winning strategy as before.

4.4 Putting It together

Enforcement now amounts to first evaluating the creation formula; if it is true, read off the model and evaluate the deletion formula. If that is true, read off the model. If either stage fails, then enforcement fails, either because there is no way to restore consistency, or because the simple-minded update strategy is not powerful enough to do so.

There is one further check needed: the resulting model must be checked (in checkonly mode) *ab initio*, as it is possible that inconsistency in the transformation arises from the combination of creation and deletion – for example, an object might be required to exist by checking in direction k, but required not to exist by checking in the direction k'.

This procedure *can* be coded up to produce a single giant transition system and formula, but the process is not enlightening, and does not simplify correctness.

5 Example

Consider the example NonTopEnforce with m1 $= \{N \to \{child1, child2, child3\}\}$, from Section 1, enforcing against an empty model m2. We demonstrate a "best" winning strategy (canonical tableau) for Verifier: as discussed this avoids unnessary updates. Refuter will challenge in R by binding $\{n \mapsto \text{'N'}, firstchild \mapsto c1\}$ where c1 is one of the three children, say the one with name 'child1'. (In mu calculus terms, we pass through [*challenge*] and along a challenge transition to a game position with this binding.) Verifier will be unable to find matching bindings and there is no *when* clause so she will update the model. (In mu calculus terms, the first two disjuncts of the short-circuiting formula are false so model checking proceeds to the ⟨*update*⟩ disjunct.) There are no key expressions and me2 is not bound, so Verifier creates a new MEtop element and sets its properties according to the domain pattern: that is, its name will be 'N'. She must also create a MEchild element to bind to secondchild but is not constrained as to its properties: all of the infinitely many choices are legal game moves and correspond to infinitely many update transitions each to a different modified model. Playing a best strategy, however, she creates an MEchild with name 'child1'. Play now restarts at the initial position with the modified model. If Refuter were to make the same challenge this time, he would lose because

Verifier now has bindings with which to match. If, instead, he challenges with one of the other children, say with binding $\{n \mapsto \text{'N'}, firstchild \mapsto c2\}$ where $c2$'s name is 'child2', exactly the same thing will happen. Although Verifier could this time choose matching bindings, she could not *win* by doing so (in mu calculus terms, although $\langle response \rangle tt$ is true, $\langle response \rangle (tr2_\emptyset(where(R_i), true))$ is false) and so she will choose to create a new MEtop element, again with name 'N', and a new MEchild to be the value of its child property and to bind to secondchild. Repeating once more we find that the result of the create phase of the game (playing with a best strategy so that no junk has been created) is $\{N \rightarrow \{child1\}, \{N \rightarrow \{child2\}, \{N \rightarrow \{child3\}\}$. (In mu calculus terms we have unwound the fixpoint W three times, once for each update; no fewer unwindings would lead to success.) The checkonly game in direction m1 is won by Verifier already so no deletions are required.

6   Properties of Transformations

In [11] we formalised properties that, we argued, should hold of bidirectional transformations; other work in this direction includes [5,13]. Now that we have formal semantics for QVT-R in both checkonly and enforce mode, it makes sense to ask whether it has properties of interest. Recall that a bidirectional transformation $R : M \leftrightarrow N$ can be modelled by a triple $R \subseteq M \times N$ (slight abuse of notation), $\overrightarrow{R} : M \times N \rightarrow N$, $\overleftarrow{R} : M \times N \rightarrow M$. In QVT-R, $R(m,n)$ should be true iff R returns true when run in checkonly mode (either direction) on models m and n, while $\overrightarrow{R}(m,n)$ returns n' if R run in enforce mode with source m and target n, i.e. in the direction of n, modifies n to n'. Because enforcement is not guaranteed to succeed in our setting (whether because of inconsistency or uncomputability), we must modify the framework to make $\overrightarrow{R}$ and $\overleftarrow{R}$ partial functions, which may return $\perp$.

Relatively uncontroversial properties are (partial) *correctness* and *hippocraticness*. We prove that these both hold of every well-defined QVT-R transformation, interpreted according to our checkonly and enforce semantics.

Theorem 1. *Given our semantics, QVT-R is (partially) correct: that is, for any well-defined transformation R and models m and n, if $\overrightarrow{R}(m,n) \neq \perp$, then $R(m, \overrightarrow{R}(m,n))$, and dually.*

Proof. By construction, our enforcement semantics ensures that any transformation execution finishes with a full checkonly evaluation, and fails if this is not satisfied.

Theorem 2. *Given our semantics, QVT-R is hippocratic: that is, for any well-defined transformation R and models m and n, $R(m,n) \Rightarrow \overrightarrow{R}(m,n) = n$ and dually.*

Proof. Our enforcement semantics is the evaluation of a formula which (via the simulation of short-circuit evaluation) only proceeds into a branch containing model-changing transitions if the models do not already satisfy the checkonly formula (proved correct in [3]).

Undoability, the third property discussed in [11], is more problematic. As is now well-understood, although theoretically desirable because it gives good algebraic properties, it is in practice too strong. It is straightforward to construct an example in which both our semantics and ModelMorf fail undoability: deleting, and then recreating, a piece of information on one side results in the loss of anything on the other side that was "stuck" to the deleted and recreated information. Thus we cannot expect QVT-R transformations to be undoable.

7   Conclusions and Future Work

By giving formal semantics to QVT-R enforce mode, we have clarified issues, particularly with object deletion, in the standard, and we have brought this hard problem into the much studied and well understood domain of model-checking. Our semantics relies on model-checking algorithms that can compute the canonical tableau or best winning strategy; in the case of finite models, this is routine, and in the case of infinite models there is an extensive body of work on algorithms for well-behaved families of infinite models. Our semantics, like our earlier checkonly semantics [3], has two equivalent formulations. We translate an enforce problem into a modified mu calculus model checking problem – the model checking process computes the changes needed to a model, and these changes are then verified by model checking. This presentation is convenient for proofs, because it enables us to exploit properties of mu calculus. The alternative, equivalent formulation, in terms of simple two-player games, is more convenient for direct use.

We hope that our semantics work may help to inform designers of future bidirectional languages. One lesson, we suggest, is that while the syntax of QVT-R is appealing in the intuitiveness of individual relations, the way in which QVT-R connects relations is probably not optimal.

In future, aiming to define a QVT-R-like language with semantics that better support MDD, we will consider semantic variations, including those (such as the bisimulation-like game [12], and reducing the special treatment of top relations [3]) that we considered in previous work on checkonly but for space reasons have not explored here. Variations specific to enforce mode include specifying deterministic update transitions, making use of information gathered in previous steps of the evaluation. More fundamentally we will explore allowing updates in recursive relation invocations, corresponding to on-the-fly enforcement of lower level relations. The present semantics, like [8], ensures that each change to the target model, considered locally, is necessary, and also that the minimum number of distinct updates is done. However, as we have seen, updates can be larger than necessary. Understanding what precise senses of minimal change are desirable, achievable and supportable by tools is a challenging and interesting problem.

Acknowledgements. We thank the referees for their constructive suggestions, including some that could not be addressed in this version for space reasons. The first author is partly supported by UK EPSRC grant EP/G012962/1 'Solving Parity Games and Mu-Calculi'.

References

1. Boronat, A., Carsí, J.Á., Ramos, I.: Algebraic Specification of a Model Transformation Engine. In: Baresi, L., Heckel, R. (eds.) FASE 2006. LNCS, vol. 3922, pp. 262–277. Springer, Heidelberg (2006)
2. Bradfield, J.C., Stirling, C.: Modal mu-calculi. In: Blackburn, P., van Benthem, J., Wolter, F. (eds.) Handbook of Modal Logic, vol. 3, pp. 721–756. Elsevier (2007)
3. Bradfield, J., Stevens, P.: Recursive Checkonly QVT-R Transformations with General *when* and *where* Clauses via the Modal Mu Calculus. In: de Lara, J., Zisman, A. (eds.) FASE 2012. LNCS, vol. 7212, pp. 194–208. Springer, Heidelberg (2012)
4. de Lara, J., Guerra, E.: Formal Support for QVT-Relations with Coloured Petri Nets. In: Schürr, A., Selic, B. (eds.) MODELS 2009. LNCS, vol. 5795, pp. 256–270. Springer, Heidelberg (2009)
5. Diskin, Z.: Algebraic Models for Bidirectional Model Synchronization. In: Czarnecki, K., Ober, I., Bruel, J.-M., Uhl, A., Völter, M. (eds.) MODELS 2008. LNCS, vol. 5301, pp. 21–36. Springer, Heidelberg (2008)
6. Greenyer, J., Kindler, E.: Comparing relational model transformation technologies: implementing query/view/transformation with triple graph grammars. Software and System Modeling 9(1), 21–46 (2010)
7. Hermann, F., Ehrig, H., Orejas, F., Czarnecki, K., Diskin, Z., Xiong, Y.: Correctness of Model Synchronization Based on Triple Graph Grammars. In: Whittle, J., Clark, T., Kühne, T. (eds.) MODELS 2011. LNCS, vol. 6981, pp. 668–682. Springer, Heidelberg (2011)
8. OMG. MOF2.0 query/view/transformation (QVT) version 1.1. OMG document formal/2009-12-05 (2009), http://www.omg.org
9. Romeikat, R., Roser, S., Müllender, P., Bauer, B.: Translation of QVT Relations into QVT Operational Mappings. In: Vallecillo, A., Gray, J., Pierantonio, A. (eds.) ICMT 2008. LNCS, vol. 5063, pp. 137–151. Springer, Heidelberg (2008)
10. Schürr, A., Klar, F.: 15 Years of Triple Graph Grammars. In: Ehrig, H., Heckel, R., Rozenberg, G., Taentzer, G. (eds.) ICGT 2008. LNCS, vol. 5214, pp. 411–425. Springer, Heidelberg (2008)
11. Stevens, P.: Bidirectional model transformations in QVT: Semantic issues and open questions. Journal of Software and Systems Modeling (SoSyM) 9(1), 7–20 (2010)
12. Stevens, P.: A simple game-theoretic approach to checkonly QVT Relations. Journal of Software and Systems Modeling, SoSyM (2011); Published online March 16, 2011
13. Stevens, P.: Observations relating to the equivalences induced on model sets by bidirectional transformations. EC-EASST, 049 (2012)
14. Wimmer, M., Kusel, A., Schoenboeck, J., Kappel, G., Retschitzegger, W., Schwinger, W.: Reviving QVT Relations: Model-Based Debugging Using Colored Petri Nets. In: Schürr, A., Selic, B. (eds.) MODELS 2009. LNCS, vol. 5795, pp. 727–732. Springer, Heidelberg (2009)

Implementing QVT-R Bidirectional Model Transformations Using Alloy

Nuno Macedo and Alcino Cunha

HASLAB — High Assurance Software Laboratory
INESC TEC & Universidade do Minho, Braga, Portugal
{nfmmacedo,alcino}@di.uminho.pt

Abstract. QVT Relations (QVT-R) is the standard language proposed by the OMG to specify bidirectional model transformations. Unfortunately, in part due to ambiguities and omissions in the original semantics, acceptance and development of effective tool support has been slow. Recently, the checking semantics of QVT-R has been clarified and formalized. In this paper we propose a QVT-R tool that complies to such semantics. Unlike any other existing tool, it also supports meta-models enriched with OCL constraints (thus avoiding returning ill-formed models), and proposes an alternative enforcement semantics that works according to the simple and predictable "principle of least change". The implementation is based on an embedding of both QVT-R transformations and UML class diagrams (annotated with OCL) in Alloy, a lightweight formal specification language with support for automatic model finding via SAT solving.

1 Introduction

Model-Driven Engineering (MDE) is an approach to software development that focuses on models as the primary development artifact. In MDE different models may capture different views of the same system (typically different models are used to specify structural and dynamic issues) or may be used at different levels of abstraction (code is obtained by refining platform-independent models to platform-specific ones). All these (possibly overlapping) models should be kept somehow consistent, and changes to one model should be propagated to all the others in a consistent manner. Ideally, specifications of transformations between models should be *bidirectional*, in the sense that a single artifact denotes transformations that can be used in both directions. Moreover, these transformations cannot just map a source to a target model and vice-versa: if some source information is discarded by the transformation, to propagate an update in the target back to a new consistent source access to the original source model is also required, so that discarded information can be recovered.

To support the MDE approach the Object Management Group (OMG) has launched the Model-Driven Architecture (MDA) initiative, which prescribed the usage of UML [16] and OCL [17] for the specification of (object oriented) models and constraints over them. To specify transformations between models, the OMG

V. Cortellessa and D. Varró (Eds.): FASE 2013, LNCS 7793, pp. 297–311, 2013.
© Springer-Verlag Berlin Heidelberg 2013

proposed the Query/View/Transformation (QVT) standard [15]. While QVT provides three different languages for the specification of transformations, the most relevant to MDE is the *QVT Relations* (QVT-R) language, that allows the specification of a bidirectional transformation by defining a single declarative consistency relation between two (or more) meta-models. Given this specification the transformation can be run in two modes: *checkonly*, to test if two models are consistent according to the specified relation; or *enforce*, that given two models and an execution direction (picking one of them as the target) updates the target model in order to recover consistency. The standard prescribes a "check-before-enforce" semantics, that is, enforce mode cannot modify the target if the models happen to be already consistent according to checking semantics.

Effective tool support for QVT-R has been slow to emerge, which hinders the universal adoption of this standard. In part, this is due to the incomplete and ambiguous semantics defined in [15]. While the checking semantics has recently been clarified and formalized [19,3,9], the enforcement semantics still remains largely obscure and even incompatible with other OMG standards. Namely, it completely ignores possible OCL constraints over the meta-models, thus allowing updates that can lead to ill-formed target models. Likewise, none of the existing QVT-R model transformation tools supports such constraints, which makes them unusable in most realistic scenarios. Unfortunately, there are other problems that affect them. Some do not even comply to the standard syntax and support only a "QVT-like" language (including not providing both running modes as required by the standard). Others support only a subset of QVT-R that is not expressive enough to support truly non-bijective bidirectional transformations (for example, ignoring the original target model in the enforce mode). Some purposely disregard QVT-R intended semantics (including checking semantics) and implementing a new (still unclear and ambiguous) one. In most cases it is not clear if the supported checking semantics is equivalent to the one formalized in [19,3,9]. And finally, none clarify the problems and ambiguities in the standard concerning enforcement semantics, and none presents a simple enough alternative for this mode that makes its behavior predictable to the user.

In this paper, we propose a QVT-R bidirectional model transformation tool that addresses all these issues. Both the meta-models and transformation specifications may be annotated with OCL, and it supports a large subset of the standard QVT-R language, including execution of both modes independently as prescribed. The main restriction is that recursion must be non-circular (or well-founded), which is satisfied in most of the interesting case-studies. The checking semantics closely follows the one specified in the standard, being equivalent to the one formalized in [19,3,9]. Finally, instead of the ambiguous (and OCL incompatible) enforcement semantics proposed in the standard, our tool follows the clear and predictable *principle of least change* [13], and restores consistency by simply returning target models that are at a minimal distance from the original. In particular, the"check-before-enforce" policy required by QVT-R is trivially satisfied by this semantics. Our tool supports two different mechanisms to measure the distance between two models: the *graph edit distance* (GED) [21], that just counts insertions and deletions of nodes and edges in the graph that corresponds to a model; and a variation where the user is allowed to parameterize which operations should count as valid edits, by attaching them to the meta-model and specifying their pre- and post-conditions in OCL.

To achieve this, we propose an embedding of both QVT-R transformations and UML class diagrams (annotated with OCL) in Alloy [11], a lightweight formal specification language with support for automatic model finding via SAT solving. Alloy is based on relational logic, which has been shown to be very effective to validate and verify object-oriented models. Its relation with the MDA has also been explored before. In particular, tools to translate UML class diagrams annotated with OCL to Alloy have been proposed [1,6], on top of which we build our embedding. The proposed tool already proved effective in debugging existing transformations, namely helping us unveiling several errors in the well-known object-relational mapping that illustrates the QVT-R specification [15].

Section 2 introduces the QVT-R language, describes the standard checking semantics, presents some of the problems with the enforcement semantics, and proposes and formalizes a simpler alternative based one the *principle of least change*. Section 3 presents our embedding of UML class diagrams (annotated with OCL) and QVT-R transformations in Alloy. Finally, Section 4 analyzes some related work, while Section 5 draws conclusions and points to future work.

2   QVT Relations

In this section we introduce the basic concepts and the semantics of the QVT-R language. A more detailed presentation can be found in the standard [15].

2.1   Basic Concepts

A QVT-R specification consists of a *transformation* T between a set of models that states under which conditions they are considered consistent. For the remainder of this paper, we will restrict ourselves to transformations between two meta-models for simplicity purposes, although most concepts could be generalized to n-directional transformations. From T, QVT-R requires the inference of three artifacts: a relation $T \subseteq M \times N$ that tests if two models $m \in M$ and $n \in N$ are consistent and transformations $\overrightarrow{T} : M \times N \to N$ and $\overleftarrow{T} : M \times N \to M$ that propagate changes on a *source* model to a *target* model, restoring consistency between the two. Transformations can be executed in two modes: *checkonly* mode, where the models are simply checked for consistency, denoted as $T\,(m, n)$; and *enforce* mode, where $\overrightarrow{T}$ or $\overleftarrow{T}$ is applied to inconsistent models in order to restore consistency, depending on which of the two models should be updated. Note that both transformations take as extra argument the original model: if we originally had consistent models $m \in M$ and $n \in N$, and m is updated to m', $\overrightarrow{T}$ takes as input both m' and n to produce the new consistent n'. This way we are able to retrieve from n information discarded in the transformation. This formalization of QVT-R is inspired by the concept of *maintainer* [13], and was first proposed

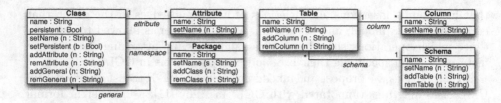

Fig. 1. Class diagrams of the UML and RDBMS meta-models

in [18]. Naturally, when the transformations propagate an update the result is expected to be consistent. Formally, we say that the transformation is *correct* if:

$$\forall\, m \in M, n \in N : \boldsymbol{T}\,(m, \overrightarrow{\boldsymbol{T}}\,(m, n)) \wedge \boldsymbol{T}\,(\overleftarrow{\boldsymbol{T}}\,(m, n), n)$$

The transformations are also required to follow the "check-before-enforce" policy (also known as *hippocraticness* [18]), that can be formalized as follows:

$$\forall\, m \in M, n \in N : \boldsymbol{T}\,(m, n) \Rightarrow \overrightarrow{\boldsymbol{T}}\,(m, n) = n \wedge \overleftarrow{\boldsymbol{T}}\,(m, n) = m$$

A QVT-R transformation is defined by a set of *relations*. A relation consists of a *domain pattern* for each meta-model of the transformation, that defines which objects of the model it relates by pattern matching. It also may include *when* and *where* constraints, that act as a kind of pre- and post-conditions for the relation application, respectively. These constraints may contain arbitrary OCL expressions. The abstract syntax of a relation is the following:

```
[top] relation R { [variable declarations]
          domain M a : A { π_M }
          domain N b : B { π_N }
          [when { ψ }] [where { φ }] }
```

In relation R, the domain pattern for meta-model M consists of a *domain variable a* and a template π_M for its properties, which candidate objects of type A must match. Likewise for the domain pattern π_N for meta-model N. To simplify the presentation, the above syntax restricts relations to have exactly one domain variable per meta-model. In a pattern template, an equality denotes an inclusion test if the multiplicity of the property is different from one. Templates can be complemented with arbitrary OCL constraints. Relations can optionally be marked as top, in which case they must hold for all objects of the specified class. Otherwise, they are only required to hold for particular objects when invoked in a where clause.

As an example, we will define a simplified version of the classic object-relational mapping transformation that illustrates the QVT-R specification [15]. Although simplified, this version still exhibits some of the problems of the original version, which we will describe in the next section. Figure 1 depicts a simplified version of the object and relational meta-models, including possible edit operations. Figure 2 defines a transformation Uml2Rdbms, whose goal

```
transformation Uml2Rdbms              // AttributeToColumn
  (uml:UML,rdbms:RDBMS) {             relation A2C {
  // PackageToSchema                    domain UML c:Class {};
  top relation P2S {                    domain RDBMS t:Table {};
    n:String;                           where { PA2C(c,t);
    domain UML p:Package {                      SA2C(c,t); } }
      name=n };                       // PrimitiveAttributeToColumn
    domain RDBMS s:Schema {           relation PA2C {
      name=n }; }                       n:String;
  // ClassToTable                       domain UML c:Class {
  top relation C2T {                      attribute=a:Attribute {
    n:String;                               name=n } };
    domain UML c:Class {                domain RDBMS t:Table {
      persistent=true,                    column=cl:Column {
      namespace=p:Package,                  name=n } }; }
      name=n };                       // SuperAttributeToColumn
    domain RDBMS t:Table {            relation SA2C {
      schema=s:Schema,                  domain UML c:Class {
      name=n };                           general=g:Class {}};
    when { P2S(p,s); }                  domain RDBMS t:Table {};
    where { A2C(c,t); } }              where { A2C(g,t); } } }
```

Fig. 2. Simplified version of the Uml2Rdbms QVT-R transformation

is to map every persistent class in a package to a table in a scheme with the same name. Each table should contain a column for each attribute (including inherited ones) of the corresponding class. A constraint of the UML meta-model that cannot be captured by class diagrams, neither QVT-R key constraints, is the requirement that the association general should be acyclic. One must resort to OCL to express it, for example by adding the invariant context Class inv: not self.closure(general)->includes(self).

There are two top relations: P2S that maps each package to a schema with the same name, and C2T that maps each class to a table with the same name. To ensure that classes are only mapped to tables if they belong to related packages and schemas, the relation C2T invokes P2S (with concrete domain variables) in the when clause. For a concrete class c and table t, C2T also calls relation A2C in the where clause, that will be responsible to map the attributes of c to columns of t. A2C directly calls PA2C, that translates the attributes directly declared in c to columns on table t, and SA2C, that recursively calls A2C on the generals of c, so that inherited attributes are also translated to columns of t.

2.2 Checking Semantics

QVT-R's checking semantics assesses if two models are consistent according to the specified transformation. Although the consistency test is by itself important, it is also an essential feature in enforce mode since it must "check-before-enforce".

The semantics of a relation differs whether it is invoked at the top-level or with concrete domain variables. The specified top-level semantics is directional. As such, from each relation R two consistency relations $R_\blacktriangleright : M \times N$ and $R_\blacktriangleleft : M \times N$ must be derived, to check if $m : M$ is R-consistent with $n : N$ and if $n : N$ is R-consistent with $m : M$, respectively. The former can be formalized as follows:

$$R_\blacktriangleright (m : M, n : N) \equiv \forall\, xs \mid \psi_\triangleright \wedge \pi_M \Rightarrow (\exists\, ys \mid \pi_N \wedge \phi_\triangleright)$$
$$\textbf{where } xs = \mathsf{fv}(\psi \wedge \pi_M) \,\cup\, \{a : A\}, ys = (\mathsf{fv}(\pi_N \wedge \phi) \,\cup\, \{b : B\}) - xs$$

Here $\mathsf{fv}(e)$ retrieves the set of free variables from the expression e, so xs denotes the set of variables used in the **when** constraint and the source pattern, while ys is the set of variables used exclusively in the **where** constraint and in the target pattern. Given a formula ψ, $\psi_\triangleright$ denotes the same formula with all relation invocations replaced by the respective directional version. This semantics is rather straightforward: essentially, for every element $a : A$ that satisfies the **when** condition and matches the M domain pattern, there must exist an element $b : B$ that satisfies the **where** condition and matches the N domain pattern. The semantics in the opposite direction is dual. Two models are consistent according to a QVT-R transformation T if they are consistent for all top relations in both directions. Assuming that Top_T is the set of all top level relations we have:

$$\boldsymbol{T} (m : M, n : N) \equiv \forall\, R : \mathsf{Top}_T \mid R_\blacktriangleright (m, n) \wedge R_\blacktriangleleft (m, n)$$

The QVT-R standard [15] defines rather precisely the top-level semantics, but is omissive about the semantics of relations invoked with concrete domain variables. Recent works on the formalization of QVT-R check semantics [19,3,9] clarify that it is essentially the same as the top-level – still directional, but defined over specific meta-model classes by fixing the domain variables. As such, from each relation R with domain variables of type A and B, two consistency relations $R_\triangleright : A \times B$ and $R_\triangleleft : A \times B$ are inferred, to check if two concrete objects a and b are consistent:

$$R_\triangleright (a : A, b : B) \equiv \forall\, xs \mid \psi_\triangleright \wedge \pi_M \Rightarrow (\exists\, ys \mid \pi_N \wedge \phi_\triangleright)$$
$$\textbf{where } xs = \mathsf{fv}(\psi \wedge \pi_M), ys = \mathsf{fv}(\pi_N \wedge \phi) - xs$$

Although it may be tempting (and probably more intuitive) to define $R_\blacktriangleright$ in terms of $R_\triangleright$, that is $R_\blacktriangleright (m, n) \equiv \forall\, a : A \mid \exists\, b : B \mid R_\triangleright (a, b)$, this definition is not semantically equivalent to the one presented above, as already discussed in [3]. For instance, consider the semantics (in the direction of UML) of relation PA2C from the Uml2Rdbms transformation:

PA2C$_\blacktriangleleft$ $(m : \mathtt{UML}, n : \mathtt{RDBMS}) \equiv$
    $\forall\, t : \mathtt{Table}, cl : \mathtt{Column}, n : \mathtt{String} \mid cl \in t.\mathsf{column} \wedge cl.\mathsf{name} = n \Rightarrow$
        $\exists\, c : \mathtt{Class}, a : \mathtt{Attribute} \mid a \in c.\mathsf{attribute} \wedge a.\mathsf{name} = n$
PA2C$_\triangleleft$ $(c : \mathtt{Class}, t : \mathtt{Table}) \equiv$
    $\forall\, cl : \mathtt{Column}, n : \mathtt{String} \mid cl \in t.\mathsf{column} \wedge cl.\mathsf{name} = n \Rightarrow$
        $\exists\, a : \mathtt{Attribute} \mid a \in c.\mathsf{attribute} \wedge a.\mathsf{name} = n$

Consider a simple UML model where a Class a with an Attribute x extends a Class b with an Attribute y. Consider also a RDBMS with a Table a with Columns x and y. While PA2C$_\blacktriangleleft$ holds for this pair of instances, PA2C$_\triangleleft$ returns false for every pair of Class and Table.

Due to this asymmetry and the directionality of the semantics, the behavior of QVT-R transformations may not be the expected one. In particular, Uml2Rdbms as defined in the standard does not have a bidirectional semantics, in the sense that the only pairs of consistent and valid finite models are ones where all classes are non-persistent and there are no tables. To see why this happens, consider the relations A2C and SA2C when checked in the direction of Class. These relations call each other recursively, and their non top-level semantics is:

$$A2C_\triangleleft \ (c: \texttt{Class}, t: \texttt{Table}) \equiv PA2C_\triangleleft \ (c, t) \wedge SA2C_\triangleleft \ (c, t)$$
$$SA2C_\triangleleft \ (c: \texttt{Class}, t: \texttt{Table}) \equiv \exists \, g: \texttt{Class} \mid g \in c.\texttt{general} \wedge A2C_\triangleleft \ (g, t)$$

Assuming the transformation takes into account the OCL constraint requiring general to be acyclic, A2C$_\triangleleft$ (c, t) never holds in a finite model, since c will be required to have an infinite ascending chain of generals. This is due to the under-restrictive SA2C domain pattern in the RDBMS side (empty in this case), that requires every Table to have a matching Class with a general, which, due to recursion, is also required to have a general, and so on. This is but one of the problems that occur in the original specification of this transformation, and is another example of the ambiguities that prevail in the QVT standard [15]: while it requires consistency to be checked in both directions, the case-study used to illustrate it was clearly not developed with bidirectionality in mind. Note that checking consistency only in the direction of RDBMS does not suffice, since, for example, it will not prevent spurious tables to appear in the target schema.

Concerning recursion we can distinguish two situations: one is well-founded recursion, where the call graph of the transformation contains a loop, but in any evaluation it is traversed only finitely many times; another is cyclic (or infinite) recursion, where such a loop may actually be traversed infinitely many times (e.g., when a relation directly or indirectly calls itself with the same arguments). The semantics of well-founded recursion is not problematic, but the standard is omissive about what should happen when infinite recursion occurs. A possible interpretation is that it should not be allowed, although in general it is undecidable to detect it. Similarly to some QVT-R formalizations [19,9], the embedding presented in this paper is not well-defined when infinite recursion occurs.

Recently, a formal semantics of QVT-R was proposed [3] that is well-defined even in presence of infinite recursion, by resorting to the modal mu calculus. To see why taking OCL constraints into account is fundamental, a transformation conforming to this semantics, but that ignores the requirement that general is acyclic, would consider a (ill-formed) UML model with a single persistent Class a that generalizes itself consistent with a RDBMS model with a Table a.

To prevent the above described problem in the Uml2Rdbms transformation, one could tag columns with the path to the particular general they originated from, and then refine the RDBMS domain pattern to prevent problematic recursive calls.

A simpler alternative is to resort to the transitive closure operation (recently added to OCL [17]), and just map at once all declared or inherited attributes of a given class to columns of the respective table. In this new version of Uml2Rdbms (that will be considered in the remainder of the paper), A2C, PA2C and SA2C are replaced just by the following alternative definition of A2C:

```
relation A2C { cn:String; a:Attribute; g:Class;
  domain UML c:Class {} { (c->closure(general)->includes(g) or g=c) and
                          g.attributes->includes(a) and a.name=cn };
  domain RDBMS t:Table { column=cl:Column { name=cn } }; }
```

The OCL constraint in the UML domain pattern acts as a pre-condition when applying the transformation in the direction of RDBMS, and as a post-condition in the other direction. As such, it could not be specified in the when clause, since it would act as (an undesired) pre-condition for both scenarios.

2.3   Enforcement Semantics

Unlike the checking semantics, and as far as we know, no attempt has been made to completely formalize the enforcement semantics described in the standard [15]. Although it has many ambiguities and omissions, due to the reasons presented next, we believe that the intended semantics for this mode is quite undesirable. Instead, we propose an alternative that is easy to formalize, more flexible, and more predictable to the end-user.

In the QVT-R standard, update propagation is required to be deterministic. This is a desirable property, since it makes its behavior more predictable. However, to ensure determinism, every transformation is required to follow very stringent syntactic rules that reduce update translation to a trivial imperative procedure. Namely, it should be possible to order all constraints in a relation (except for the target domain pattern), such that the value of every free variable is fixed by a previous constraint. Although not clarified in the standard, this means that relations that are invoked in when and where constraints are either invoked with previously bound variables, or are required to also be deterministic, even if the intention was to only make update propagation deterministic. For example, in transformation Uml2Rdbms, update propagation in the direction of RDBMS will only be deterministic for relation C2T if at most one s is consistent with p according to relation P2S (note that s is still free in the when clause). In this particular example that happens to be true, but in general such determinism is undesirable since it forces relations to be one-to-one mappings, limiting the expressiveness of the language. Moreover, it defeats the purpose of a declarative transformation language, since one is forced to think in terms of imperative execution and write more verbose transformations. For example, our simpler version of A2C using transitive closure would not be allowed, since the value of g is not known a priori when enforcing consistency in the direction of UML.

Another problem is the predictability of update propagation. Being deterministic is just part of the story – it should be clear to the user why some particular element was chosen to be updated instead of another. The only mechanism proposed by QVT-R to control updatability are *keys*. For example, we could add the command **key** Table (name, schema); to our running example to assert that tables are uniquely identified by the pair of properties name and schema. If an update is required on a table to restore consistency (for example, when an attribute is added to a class), such key is used to find a matching table. When found, an update is performed, otherwise a new table is created. This works well when all domains involved in relations have natural keys, which again points to have only one-to-one mappings, but fails if such keys do not exist. In those cases, the standard prescribes that update propagation should always be made by means of creation of new elements, even if sometimes a simple update to an existing element would suffice. Since creation requires defaults for mandatory (multiplicity one) properties, this would result in models with little resemblance with the original (which would basically be discarded).

Our alternative enforcement semantics is based on the *principle of least change*, first proposed in the context of *maintainers* [13], and that enforces predictability by requiring updates to be as small as possible. QVT-R "check-before-enforce" policy is just a particular case of this more general principle. Let $\Delta_M : M \times M \to \mathbb{N}$ be an operation that computes the update distance between elements of M. Then, the principle of least change states that the models returned by the transformations $\overrightarrow{T}$ and $\overleftarrow{T}$ are just the consistent models closest to the original. Formally, we have:

$$\forall\, m \in M, n, n' \in N : \boldsymbol{T}\,(m, n') \Rightarrow \Delta_N\,(\overrightarrow{\boldsymbol{T}}\,(m, n), n) \leqslant \Delta_N\,(n', n)$$
$$\forall\, m, n' \in M, n \in N : \boldsymbol{T}\,(m', n) \Rightarrow \Delta_M\,(\overleftarrow{\boldsymbol{T}}\,(m, n), m) \leqslant \Delta_M\,(m', m)$$

Assuming that the distance is only null when the model is unchanged (i.e., $\Delta\,(n, n') = 0 \equiv n = n'$), it is trivial to show that these properties reduce to hippocraticness when the models m and n are already consistent. Note, that this principle by itself does not ensure determinism, although it reduces substantially the set of possible results. If among the returned models the user further wishes to favor a particular subset, keys or OCL constraints can be added to the metamodel to guide the transformation engine. In the next section we will describe the implementation of the proposed semantics. We will also propose two different techniques to measure update distance between models. In one of them, the user is allowed to parameterize which operations should count as valid edits, thus providing an extra mechanism to achieve determinism if the user so desires.

3   Embedding QVT-R in Alloy

In this section we present our embedding of QVT-R in Alloy [11]. Due to space limitations some knowledge of Alloy will be assumed, although we believe most definitions will be clear from context.

3.1   UML Class Diagrams Annotated with OCL

The models upon which our transformations are defined consist of UML class diagrams annotated with OCL constraints. Some translations have been proposed to embed such models in Alloy, namely [1,6]. We will base our embedding on the translation proposed in [6], since, unlike other proposals, it covers an expressive OCL subset that includes closure and operation specification via pre- and pos-conditions. Here, we will just briefly present this translation.

Classes and associations (including attributes) can be directly translated to signatures and relations in Alloy. Likewise for the inheritance relationship, that Alloy also supports. Since Alloy instances are built from immutable atoms, we resort to the well-known *local state idiom* [11] to capture updates to a given model. This means that a special signature will be introduced to represent each meta-model, whose atoms will denote different models (or evolutions of a given model). To each relation (representing an association or an attribute) an extra column of this type is added, to allow its value to change in different models. We also extend the translation proposed in [6] to allow classes to have different elements in different models: for each class a special binary relation with the same name will capture the objects of that class that belong to each model. Boolean attributes are encoded similarly: a binary relation captures which objects have the attribute set to `true` in each model. For example, the `Class` class of our `UML` meta-model is translated to the following signature declaration.

```
sig Class { class : set UML, attribute : Attribute -> UML,
            general : Class -> UML, namespace : Package -> UML,
            name : String -> UML, persistent : set UML }
```

The binary relation `class` captures the `Class` objects that exist in each `UML` model. The remaining relations model the respective `Class` associations and attributes. With the relational composition operator we can access the values of these relations for a given `UML` model `m`. For example, `general.m` is a relation that maps each `Class` to its `general` in model `m`, and `persistent.m` is the set of `Classes` that have the attribute `persistent` set to `true` in that model.

Constraints must also be generated to ensure the correct multiplicities, and that relations only relate elements in the same model (inclusion dependencies). For example, fact **all** `m:UML` | `namespace.m` **in** `class.m` -> **one** `package.m` is generated to capture the cardinality constraints of association `namespace`, and to force it, for each `UML` model `m`, to be a subset of the cartesian product between `class.m` and `package.m` (respectively, the sets of `Classes` and `Packages` of model `m`). OCL invariants are also automatically translated to Alloy facts, resulting in universal quantifications over the given type. For example, the OCL invariant stating that `general` is acyclic is translated to Alloy as **all** `m:UML, self:class.m` | `self` **not in** `self.^(general.m)`, where `^(general.m)` is the transitive closure of relation `general` projected over `m`.

3.2 QVT-R Transformations

For each relation R we declare two Alloy predicates to specify $R_{\triangleright}$ and $R_{\triangleleft}$. Besides the respective domains elements, these are also parameterized by the models they are being applied to. Since in Alloy predicates cannot call each other recursively, predicates $R_{\triangleright}$ and $R_{\triangleleft}$ are defined in terms of auxiliary relations specified by comprehension. Top relations $R_{\blacktriangleright}$ and $R_{\blacktriangleleft}$ are also specified by predicates, which are only parameterized by the models. The definition of all these predicates follows closely the formalization of Section 2.2. For example, C2T$_▶$ is specified as follows:

```
pred When_C2T_RDBMS [m:UML, n:RDBMS, p:Package, s:Schema] {
  P2S_RDBMS[m,n,p,s] }
pred Pattern_C2T_UML [m:UML, c:Class, n:String, p:Package] {
  n in c.name.m && c in persistent.m && p in c.namespace.m }
...
pred Top_C2T_RDBMS [m:UML,n:RDBMS] {
 all c:class.m, n:String, p:package.m, s:schema.n |
 When_C2T_RDBMS[m,n,p,s] && Pattern_C2T_UML[m,c,n,p] =>
 some t:table.n |
   Pattern_C2T_RDBMS[n,t,n,s] && Where_A2C_RDBMS[m,n,c,t] }
```

Predicates are used to specify the when and where clauses, and the domain patterns of each relation. Note that predicate P2S_RDBMS is the predicate specifying P2S$_▷$. Note also how, in the specification of C2T$_▶$, quantifications are restricted to range over the respective models.

The checking semantics of the transformation is a predicate that checks all top relations in both directions. In our running example we have:

```
pred Uml2Rdbms [m:UML,n:RDBMS]{ Top_P2S_RDBMS[m,n] && Top_P2S_UML[m,n]
                  && Top_C2T_RDBMS[m,n] && Top_C2T_UML[m,n] }
```

Regarding enforcement semantics, as described in Section 2.3, we implement the principle of least change, which requires the measurement of the update distance between two models. We propose two different mechanisms for measuring such distance. The first one is the *graph edit distance* (GED) [21], which counts the distance between two graphs as the number of node and edge insertions and deletions needed to obtain one from the other. Note that an Alloy instance is isomorphic to a labelled graph whose nodes are the atoms, and whose edges are tuples in relations. With this mechanism, Δ_{UML} can be computed as follows:

```
fun Delta_UML [m,m':UML] : Int {
  (#((class.m - class.m') + (class.m' - class.m))).plus[
  (#((name.m - name.m') + (name.m' - name.m))).plus[...]] }
```

Assuming m' represents an updated version of m, this function sums up, for every signature and relation, the size of their symmetric difference in both models. To avoid Alloy's standard wrap around semantics for integers, model finding is executed with option Forbid Overflow [14].

This simple definition for distance assumes a fixed repertoire of edit operations which may not be desirable. In particular, there is no control over the "cost" of complex operations. For example, changing the name of a class will have a cost of 2, since it requires deleting the current name edge and inserting a new one, while adding a new attribute to a class will cost 3, since it requires creating a new attribute, setting its name, and adding it to the class. One may wish both these operations to be atomic edits and have the same unitary cost. Also, one may wish to allow only particular edits in order to control non-determinism.

As such, we propose an alternative measure, where the user is allowed to specify in the meta-model which edit operations that are allowed for each class. We require them to be specified using pre- and post-conditions defined in (a subset of) OCL, to be automatically converted to Alloy using the translation procedure defined in [6]. Essentially, each operation will originate an Alloy predicate that checks if it holds between given pre- and post-models. For example, Figure 1 defines the interface of possible edit operations for our running example.

Given the specifications of operations, we constrain models to form an ordering, where each step corresponds to the application of an edit operation.

```
open util/ordering[UML]
pred setName [p:Package, n:String, m,m':UML] { ... }
pred addClass [p:Package, n:String, m,m':UML] { ... }
...
fact { all m:UML, m':m.next | {
            some p:package.m, n:String | setName[p,n,m,m'] or
            some p:package.m, n:String | addClass[p,n,m,m'] or ... } }
```

In this case, Δ_{UML} will be the number of models (intermediate steps) required to achieve a consistent target, which, as we will see next, will be determined by the scope of the signature denoting the respective meta-model.

3.3   Executing the Semantics

Executing the transformation in checkonly mode is fairly simple: we just need to check the consistency predicate for a pair of concrete models. To represent a concrete model, we use singleton signatures to denote specific objects and facts to fix the interpretation of relations. For example, a UML model M with two classes A and B with no attributes in a single package P, where A is persistent and extends the non-persistent B, can be specified as follows:

```
one sig M extends UML {}
one sig P extends Package {}
one sig A,B extends Class {}
fact { class.M = A + B && package.M = P && namespace.M = A->P + B->P &&
       general.M = A->B && no attribute.M && persistent.M = A && ... }
```

To check if UML model M is consistent with RDBMS model N the command **check** { Uml2Rdbms[M,N] } is issued, with the scope of each signature being set to the number of elements of the respective class in each of the two models. Regarding enforce mode with GED minimization, in order to determine a new UML model M' consistent with RDBMS model N, with original model M, the command **run** { Uml2Rdbms[M',N] && Delta_UML[M,M']=Δ } is issued with increasing values Δ (starting at 0). In this case, the scope of each signature is set to the number of elements of the respective class plus Δ, to allow complete freedom in the choice of edit operations. The calculation and increment of both Δ and the scope is performed automatically by our tool. To execute the enforce mode with user-specified edit operations the command **run** { Uml2Rdbms[M',N] && M=first && M'=last } is issued with increasing scopes Δ (plus one) for signature UML. The original and target models are constrained to be the first and last in the model ordering, respectively. Determining the scope for the remaining signatures is not straightforward in this case, since edits can be arbitrary operations. For the moment we are using a rough approximation, that assumes creation of new objects to be specified via existential quantification: for every increment of Δ, the scope of a signature is increased by the maximum number of such quantifications over all edit operations.

The user is required to specify an upper-bound for Δ that limits the search for consistent targets. If several consistent models are found at the minimum distance our tool warns the user and allows him to see the different alternatives. If the user then desires to reduce such non-determinism, he can, for example, add extra OCL constraints to the meta-model or narrow the set of allowed edit operations to target a specific class of models.

4   Related Work

Regarding tools support for QVT-R transformations, Medini and ModelMorf are the main existing functional tools. Medini [10] is an Eclipse plugin for a subset of the QVT-R language. Although popular, its (unknown) semantics admittedly disregards the semantics from the QVT standard (it does not have a checkonly mode for instance). ModelMorf [20] allegedly follows the QVT standard closely (although once again the concrete semantics are unknown), since its development team was involved in the specification of the standard. However, the development of the tool seems to have stopped. None of these tools has support for OCL constraints on the meta models. Other prototype tools have been proposed but once again the implemented semantics are not completely clear. Moment-QVT [2] is an Eclipse plug-in for the execution of QVT-R transformations by resorting to the Maude rewriting system; [12] proposes the embedding of QVT-R in Colored Petri Nets; [8] discusses the possible implementation of QVT-R transformations in TGGs. All these tools support only unidirectional transformations, in the sense that they ignore the original target model. As such, they are not able to retrieve information not present in the source, leading to the generation of completely new models every time the transformation is applied. Once again, none supports OCL constraints on the meta-model.

A technique that follows an approach similar to ours is the JTL tool [5], although it does not support QVT-R, but rather a restricted QVT-like language. Like ours, JTL generates models by resorting to a solver (the DLV solver), which is able to retrieve some information from the original target. However, it is not clear how the solver chooses which information to retrieve or how the new model is generated. It also forces the totality of the transformation, returning inconsistent models in case there is no consistent one.

Regarding the validation of QVT-R transformations two approaches have been proposed that also rely on solvers. In [7] the authors use Alloy to verify the correctness of QVT-R specifications, in order to guarantee the well-formedness of the output and avoid run-time errors. In [4] OCL invariants of the shape "forall-there-exist" are inferred from QVT-R transformations (much like the checking semantics), that allow the validation of QVT-R specifications under a set of properties. It supports OCL constraints in the meta-model and recursive calls are translated to recursive OCL specifications. However, both these approaches are not focused on enforce mode and its semantics, and do not analyze the behavior of the transformation for concrete input models. Using our embedding we can do so, and also support the validation of similar properties, like checking if a transformation is injective or that all consistent models are well-formed.

5   Conclusions and Future Work

This paper proposed a QVT-R bidirectional model transformation tool, supporting both the standard checking semantics and a clear and precise enforcement semantics based on the principle of least change. It also supports meta-models annotated with OCL constraints and specification of allowed edit operations, which allows its applicability to non-trivial domains and provides a fine-grained control over non-determinism. The implementation is based on an embedding in Alloy, taking advantage of its model finding abilities. Although we only described the support for bidirectional transformations, our embedding can trivially be generalized to the multi-directional scenario, where updates on multiple models are propagated to a designated target, another feature not currently offered by any existing QVT-R tool.

Being solver-based, the main drawback of the proposed tool is performance. Improving it is the main goal of our future work: we intend to explore incremental solving techniques to speed-up the execution of successive commands with increasing scope, and to define mechanisms to infer which parts of target model can be fixed *a priori* in order to speed-up solving. However, even in its present status the tool is already fully functional and can be used to perform transformations of medium-sized models. In particular, it already proved effective in debugging existing transformations, namely helping us unveiling several errors in the well-known object-relational mapping that illustrates QVT-R specification.

Acknowledgements. The authors would also like to thank the anonymous reviewers for the valuable comments and suggestions. This work is funded by ERDF - European Regional Development Fund through the COMPETE Programme (operational programme for competitiveness) and by national funds through the FCT - Fundação para a Ciência e a Tecnologia (Portuguese Foundation for Science and Technology) within project FCOMP-01-0124-FEDER-020532. The first author is also sponsored by FCT grant SFRH/BD/69585/2010.

References

1. Anastasakis, K., Bordbar, B., Georg, G., Ray, I.: On challenges of model transformation from UML to Alloy. Software and Systems Modeling 9, 69–86 (2010)

2. Boronat, A., Carsí, J.Á., Ramos, I.: Algebraic Specification of a Model Transformation Engine. In: Baresi, L., Heckel, R. (eds.) FASE 2006. LNCS, vol. 3922, pp. 262–277. Springer, Heidelberg (2006)
3. Bradfield, J., Stevens, P.: Recursive Checkonly QVT-R Transformations with General *when* and *where* Clauses via the Modal Mu Calculus. In: de Lara, J., Zisman, A. (eds.) FASE 2012. LNCS, vol. 7212, pp. 194–208. Springer, Heidelberg (2012)
4. Cabot, J., Clarisó, R., Guerra, E., de Lara, J.: Verification and validation of declarative model-to-model transformations through invariants. Journal of Systems and Software 83(2), 283–302 (2012)
5. Cicchetti, A., Di Ruscio, D., Eramo, R., Pierantonio, A.: JTL: A Bidirectional and Change Propagating Transformation Language. In: Malloy, B., Staab, S., van den Brand, M. (eds.) SLE 2010. LNCS, vol. 6563, pp. 183–202. Springer, Heidelberg (2011)
6. Cunha, A., Garis, A., Riesco, D.: Translating between Alloy specifications and UML class diagrams annotated with OCL (2012), http://www.di.uminho.pt/~mac/Publications/AlloyMDA.pdf
7. Garcia, M.: Formalization of QVT-Relations: OCL-based static semantics and Alloy-based validation. In: MDSD Today 2008. pp. 21–30. Shaker Verlag (2008)
8. Greenyer, J., Kindler, E.: Comparing relational model transformation technologies: implementing Query/View/Transformation with Triple Graph Grammars. Software and System Modeling 9(1), 21–46 (2010)
9. Guerra, E., de Lara, J.: An algebraic semantics for QVT-relations check-only transformations. Fundam. Inform. 114(1), 73–101 (2012)
10. ikv++ technologies ag: medini QVT, http://projects.ikv.de/qvt/
11. Jackson, D.: Software Abstractions: Logic, Language, and Analysis, revised edn. MIT Press, London (2012)
12. de Lara, J., Guerra, E.: Formal Support for QVT-Relations with Coloured Petri Nets. In: Schürr, A., Selic, B. (eds.) MODELS 2009. LNCS, vol. 5795, pp. 256–270. Springer, Heidelberg (2009)
13. Meertens, L.: Designing constraint maintainers for user interaction (1998), manuscript available at http://www.kestrel.edu/home/people/meertens
14. Milicevic, A., Jackson, D.: Preventing Arithmetic Overflows in Alloy. In: Derrick, J., Fitzgerald, J., Gnesi, S., Khurshid, S., Leuschel, M., Reeves, S., Riccobene, E. (eds.) ABZ 2012. LNCS, vol. 7316, pp. 108–121. Springer, Heidelberg (2012)
15. OMG: MOF 2.0 Query/View/Transformation specification (QVT), version 1.1 (January 2011), http://www.omg.org/spec/QVT/1.1/
16. OMG: OMG Unified Modeling Language (UML), version 2.4.1 (August 2011), http://www.omg.org/spec/UML/2.4.1/
17. OMG: OMG Object Constraint Language (OCL), version 2.3.1 (January 2012), http://www.omg.org/spec/OCL/2.3.1/
18. Stevens, P.: Bidirectional model transformations in QVT: semantic issues and open questions. Software and System Modeling 9(1), 7–20 (2010)
19. Stevens, P.: A simple game-theoretic approach to checkonly QVT relations. Software and System Modeling (2011), http://dx.doi.org/10.1007/s10270-011-0198-8
20. Tata Research Development and Design Centre: ModelMorf, http://www.tcs-trddc.com/trddc_website/ModelMorf/ModelMorf.html
21. Voigt, K.: Structural Graph-based Metamodel Matching. Ph.D. thesis, University of Desden (2011)

Abstraction and Training of Stochastic Graph Transformation Systems

Mayur Bapodra and Reiko Heckel

Department of Computer Science, University of Leicester, UK
{mb294,reiko}@mcs.le.ac.uk

Abstract. Simulation of stochastic graph transformation systems (SGTS) allows us to analyse the model's behaviour. However, complexity of models limits our capability for analysis. In this paper, we aim to simplify models by abstraction while preserving relevant trends in their global behaviour. Based on a hierarchical graph model inspired by membrane systems, structural abstraction is achieved by "zooming out" of membranes, hiding their internal state. We use Bayesian networks representing dependencies on stochastic (input) parameters, as well as causal relationships between rules, for parameter learning and inference. We demonstrate and evaluate this process via two case studies, immunological response to a viral attack and reconfiguration in P2P networks.

Keywords: stochastic graph transformation, abstraction, Bayesian networks, membrane systems.

1 Introduction

Graph transformation systems (GTS) are a rule-based approach to modelling processes of structural change. Rules capture *local* behaviour in terms of preconditions and effects of atomic operations. In stochastic graph transformation systems (SGTS), each rule is assigned a probability distribution dictating the delay in its application, once enabled [10]. Such stochastic models allow us to observe emergent, *global* behaviour through simulation. For example, in a model of a peer-to-peer (P2P) network, we may specify operations of peers joining and leaving the network, making connections, etc. while being interested in a global property such as the probability of the overall network to be connected. Similarly for a study of viral attack and immunological response on cell tissue, the probability of tissue recovery or death will be of interest. This requires a detailed model of reactions such as virus multiplication, immune reaction, cell death and regeneration.

In any realistic scenario, such models will be large and complex. Detailed state representations lead to large state spaces with a high rate of low-level change and a large set of rules, creating scalability issues for analysis. Raising the level of abstraction, a model can be reduced to improve scalability, but for the price of potentially distorting analysis results. Related to the level of representation is the choice of delay distributions for rules. For example in an abstract version of

V. Cortellessa and D. Varró (Eds.): FASE 2013, LNCS 7793, pp. 312–326, 2013.

the immunological response model, a rule for a cell to be damaged beyond repair specifies an operation that takes several steps in the concrete version. The delay of the abstract rule should therefore correspond to the combined delays of the steps required at the concrete level.

In this paper, we address the interconnected problems of structural abstraction and the choice of delay distributions and their parameters. Structural abstraction is based on a hierarchical graph model inspired by membrane systems [20], where details of the lower level of the hierarchy can be hidden. As a result, the model becomes smaller in terms of the number of rules, the number of graph elements in each graph, and therefore the number of matches per rule. This increases the scalability of stochastic simulation, i.e., larger populations can be simulated over longer periods of simulated time.

The abstraction problem arises when comparing model with reality as well as between models at different levels of detail. We focus on the latter, which is easier to experiment with using stochastic simulation. Referring to the concrete and abstract models as $SGTS_1$ and $SGTS_2$, resp., the approach is based on three key ideas: Structural abstraction at the type level induces instance level projections of graphs and rules allowing us to relate concrete and abstract states and operations. Dynamic, quantitative analysis of conflicts and dependencies between operations allows us to discover cases where rules in $SGTS_2$ fail to reproduce the causal relationships between rules $SGTS_1$, or vice versa, potentially leading to the need to refine the abstract model. A Bayesian Network (BN) [21], constructed as a result of the dependency analysis of $SGTS_2$, allows us to infer stochastic parameters by training. In particular, training aims to match the throughputs (number of applications / time) of the rules of the two models. Our hypothesis is that by matching behaviour at this local level, we preserve the trends (if not absolute values) in the global properties of the models.

This leads to the following process, with steps being iterated as required.

1. Derive $SGTS_2$ as projection of $SGTS_1$ to a sub-type graph TG_2 of TG_1.
2. Simulating $SGTS_1$, perform dynamic dependency analysis over $SGTS_2$.
3. Define a Bayesian network representing the dependencies of $SGTS_2$.
4. Use parameter sweep of simulations of $SGTS_2$ to create training data for the BN. This process is known as *learning* in a BN.
5. Enter throughput data of $SGTS_1$ as evidence into the network and infer the stochastic parameters of $SGTS_2$ needed to replicate $SGTS_1$'s throughputs. This process is known as *inference* in a BN.
6. Test the parameters by running stochastic simulations of $SGTS_2$.

We demonstrate and evaluate this process via two case studies based on models of a P2P network and immunological response introduced in Sect. 3, full details of which are given in [4] and [3] respectively. Background on SGTS and BN is given in Sects. 2 and 4, resp. Sect. 4 also introduces the derivation of a BN from a SGTS and describes stochastic parameter training. Sect. 5 evaluates the results of the case studies, and Sect. 7 concludes the paper.

2   Stochastic Graph Transformation

A *typed graph transformation system* $\mathcal{G} = (TG, P, \pi)$ consists of a *type graph TG*, defining node/edge types and attributes, a set of *rule names* P and a function π defining for each name $p \in P$ a *rule* $\pi(p) = L \to R$ consisting of TG-typed graphs L, R whose intersection $L \cap R$ is called the interface of the rule. The left-hand side L represents the precondition and the right-hand side R the postcondition of the rule, whose applications transform *instance graphs*, also typed over TG. Rules can be equipped with negative application conditions (NACs) specifying forbidden context. Formally, the *application* $G \overset{p,m}{\Longrightarrow} H$ of rule p at a *match* m : $L \to G$ subject to NACs, is defined by the single-pushout (SPO) approach [16].

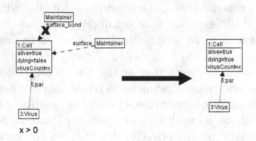

Fig. 1. Rule R2 for viral attack on last maintainer of a living cell (concrete model)

An example rule is shown in Fig. 1. It models the reaction in which a virus destroys the last maintainer in a cell (as indicated by the NAC), changing its status to dying. Fig. 2 shows the type graph for the viral attack model, defining a hierarchy of tissues, cells and organelles. Rules like those of Fig. 1 are defined over this type graph.

A *stochastic graph transformation system* $\mathcal{SG} = (TG, P, \pi, F)$ consists of a graph transformation system $\mathcal{G} = (TG, P, \pi)$ and a function $F : P \to [0,1]^{\mathbb{R}_+}$ associating to each rule name in P a probability distribution function $F(p)$: $\mathbb{R}_+ \to [0,1]$. Generalised SGTS, based on semi-Markov processes, allow the specification of arbitrary distributions of delays as opposed to just exponential distributions [14]. Exponential distributions model processes which depend on occurrences of random events, such as the collision between virus and *immuno* in a cell. They are characterised by a rate, i.e., the inverse of the average delay between two such events, if enabled. For operations with defined start and end points, such as the death of a cell once all maintainers are removed by viruses, normal (or lognormal) distributions are appropriate, given by mean and variance. Once started, there is an expected waiting time for the process to finish.

Given a start graph G_0, the behaviour of $\mathcal{SG}$ can be explored by simulation. For this purpose, the simulation tool GraSS [24] has been developed. The simulation works as follows. For a graph G, *events* $E(G)$ are pairs (p, m) of a rule p and an enabling match m. States (G, t, w) of the simulation are given by the current graph G, the simulation time t, and the *schedule* $w : E(G) \to \mathbb{R}_+$ mapping events to their scheduled times. Initially, the current graph is the start graph $G = G_0$, the time is set to $t = 0$ and the scheduled time $w(p, m) = RN_{F(p)}$ for each enabled event (p, m) is selected randomly based on p's probability distribution. Then, for each simulation step

1. the first event $e = (p, m)$ is identified and rule p applied at match m to the current graph G producing the new current graph H via $G \overset{p,m}{\Longrightarrow} H$.
2. the simulation time is advanced to $t = w(e)$
3. the new schedule w', based on an updated set of enabled events $E(H)$, is defined by removing from the schedule all events in $E(G) \setminus E(H)$ and adding new events $(p', m') \in E(H) \setminus E(G)$ with time $w'(p', m') = RN_{F(p')}$ selected randomly based on p''s distribution.

The result is a *(simulation) run* $s = (G_0, t_0) \overset{p_1, m_1}{\Longrightarrow} \cdots \overset{p_n, m_n}{\Longrightarrow} (G_n, t_n)$, i.e., a transformation sequence where graphs labelled by time stamps $t_0, \ldots, t_n \in \mathbb{R}_+$ with $t_i < t_{i+1}$ for all $i \in \{0, \ldots, n-1\}$.

Graph transformation rules describe immunological response at a cellular level, as well as auxiliary operations such as virus replication, cell death and regeneration. Stochastic simulation allows us to determine the probability of tissue death once invaded by a set number of viruses. The average time taken for a tissue to come to either eliminate the viruses or suffering death can also be extracted. These are examples of global properties, as opposed to more local ones such as the throughput, i.e., the number of applications over time, of particular rules of the system.

3   Structural Abstraction

Since stochastic simulation is resource intensive, we aim to simplify hierarchical models, such as the one discussed above, by hiding details at the lowest level of the hierarchy. Formally, an abstraction relation $f : S\mathcal{G}_1 \to S\mathcal{G}_2$ between the concrete SGTS $S\mathcal{G}_1 = (TG_1, P_1, \pi_1, F_1)$ and the abstract SGTS $S\mathcal{G}_2 = (TG_2, P_2, \pi_2, F_2)$ is given by an inclusion of the type graphs $TG_2 \subseteq TG_1$ and a surjective mapping $f : P_1 \to P_2$ of rule names that is compatible with the projection of rules of $S\mathcal{G}_1$ to TG_2.

Fig. 2 shows the abstract type graph, forgetting about the contents of cells but retaining viruses, which can also exist in the tissue between cells. Attributes *alive*, *dying*, *virusCount* provide a boolean or numerical representation of information that is held in graphical form in the concrete model, but lost in the abstract one. These *aggregating attributes* are redundant in the concrete model, as expressed by invariants such as *The number of Virus nodes connected to a Cell node by par edges equals the value of the virusCount attribute of that Cell node.* Such invariants can be expressed in OCL or using a graphical constraint and either tested during the simulation or verified statically.

For an instance graph G of TG_1 such as in the top right of Fig. 2, $G|_{TG_2}$ denotes its projection to the abstract type graph via a pullback, as shown in the

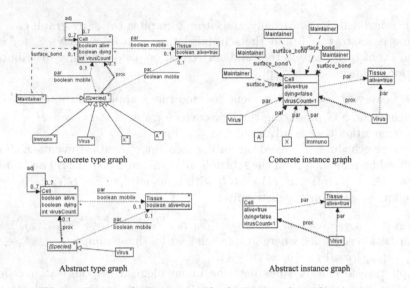

Fig. 2. Type and instance graphs for immunological response

Fig. 3. Rule A_IR2 for viral attack on last maintainer of a living cell (abstract model)

bottom right. The contents of cells are hidden in the abstraction. In a similar way, rules in the concrete model are projected to the abstract type graph to create the set of abstract rules. The result is shown in Fig. 3 for the rule in Fig. 1, where the aggregating attributes retain aspects of the structural details (e.g., dying). Formally, for all $p \in P_1$, $\pi_2(f(p)) = \pi_1(p)|_{TG}$, i.e., the rule associated to concrete p equals that of abstract $f(p)$ upon projection to the abstract type graph [11]. If a concrete rule does not have any effect on cells or aggregating attributes (i.e., elements typed in TG_2), but is only concerned with manipulating elements lost in the abstraction (i.e., those typed in $TG_1 \setminus TG_2$), the result of the projection is a rule with no effect at all. We call such rules *idle*. Applications of idle rules as part of a sequence can be skipped because they do not change the graph. Thus, the abstract system may have less (non-idle) rules and abstract sequences may be shorter than their concrete counterparts. While idle rules can be disregarded, NACs in non-idle rules either have to be preserved entirely (no negative elements are lost under projection) or completely removed (at least one negative element is lost) by the projection [2].

Figure 3 shows the result of projecting the rule depicted in Figure 1, the virus destroying the last maintainer of a *Cell*, onto the abstract type graph. In this case, the rule is not idle and the single NAC is lost entirely. Abstraction leads to a smaller set of rules, and a smaller number of graph elements for each rule application and graph, making simulation less resource-intensive (see Section 5). The full set of concrete and abstract rules can be found at [3].

Given a transformation sequence $s_1 = (G_0 \overset{p_1,m_1}{\Longrightarrow} \cdots \overset{p_n,m_n}{\Longrightarrow} G_n)$ in $\mathcal{SG}_1$, there exists a corresponding sequence $f * (s_1) = (G_0|_{TG_2} \overset{f(p_1),m_1|_{TG_2}}{\Longrightarrow} \cdots \overset{f(p_n),m_n|_{TG_2}}{\Longrightarrow} G_n|_{TG_2})$ in $\mathcal{SG}_2$. That means, under the assumptions above, mapping $f* : \mathcal{G}_1^* \to \mathcal{G}_2^*$ provides us with an abstraction not just of states and operations, but also of transformation sequences: Behaviour is preserved under abstraction [11].

We continue deriving the abstract model by defining its rules' probability distributions. After determining the type of distribution to be used, we create a Baysian network based on the causal relationships between rules, from which the distributions are inferred.

4   From SGTS to Bayesian Networks

In general, abstract rules may follow different types of distributions than their concrete counterparts. In particular, a rule representing an entire sequence of concrete steps could be normally distributed even if each concrete rule has an exponential distribution. Simulating the concrete model, we can detect matches for abstract rules and so measure the delays between the enabling and application of the rule. Plotting this data allows us to decide the shape of the distribution.

Having determined the types of the distributions, we use Bayesian networks to derive their parameters. The structure of the network is defined by the conflicts and dependencies of abstract rules. We say that rule p *enables* p' if there exists a sequence $G \overset{p,m}{\Longrightarrow} X \overset{p',m'}{\Longrightarrow} H$ such that the match m' for p' in X cannot be extended to G, i.e., the second step is dependent on the first. This is the case if p creates elements required for p''s application, or deletes elements that violate a negative application condition of p'. Dually, given $H \overset{p,m}{\Longleftarrow} G \overset{p',m'}{\Longrightarrow} H'$, rule p *disables* p' if the match m' for p' is not preserved in H, i.e., the application of p is in conflict with the subsequent application of p'. This happens if p deletes elements needed for p''s application or creates elements violating p''s NAC.

While conflicts and dependencies can be analysed statically, like with many static methods this often results in an over approximation of the actual dependencies and conflicts occurring in simulation runs. A dynamic approach can take into account reachability, i.e., only report cases where the steps concerned are reachable from the start state. It can also provide statistics on *how many* matches for p' are generated or destroyed on average per application of p, thus allowing us to judge the significance of a dependency or conflict.

Since we are not able to simulate the abstract system before defining its stochastic parameters, we execute the concrete model and use our abstraction function $f : \mathcal{SG}_1^* \to \mathcal{SG}_2^*$ to derive abstract runs to record what we call *diagonal conflicts and dependencies* between concrete and abstract rules: According to our notion of abstraction, abstract rules $f(p)$ arise from concrete ones p that are not idle under projection to the abstract type graph TG_2. At the same time, each abstract rule, being typed over $TG_2 \subseteq TG_1$, is also implicitly typed over

TG_1. Therefore, it is possible to check for conflicts and dependencies between concrete and abstract steps while simulating the concrete system. Since overlaps of concrete and abstract rules can only be based on elements that are preserved in the abstraction, a dependency between a concrete rule p non-idle under projection and an abstract rule $f(p')$ is also a dependency between the abstract counterpart $f(p)$ and $f(p')$, and vice versa. The same is true for conflict. That means, diagonal conflicts and dependencies can be used in place of abstract ones.

The result of the analysis is recorded in the *dynamic incidence matrix* $DIM : P \times P_2 \to \mathbb{R}$ where $P \subseteq P_1$ is the subset of concrete rules with non-idle projections. For each rule $p \in P$ the matrix describes the average change in the number of matches for rules in P_1 caused by p's application. The runtime conflicts and dependencies recorded here provide the information needed to derive the structure of the BN.

A BN is an acyclic graph $G_B = (V, E, src, tg, \lambda)$. V is a set of vertices such that each $v \in V$ represents a variable (discrete or continuous). E is a set of directed edges such that each $e \in E$ has a source and target vertex $src(e)$ and $tg(e)$ in V, respectively. The function $\lambda : V \to [0,1]^{\mathbb{R}+}$ assigns to each vertex a probability distribution such that for all $v \in V$, $\lambda(v) = Q(v|V_{in}(v))$ where $V_{in}(v)$ is the set of nodes with edges towards v. Q represents a probability distribution for the value of v given the values of all variables on which v is conditionally dependent. The foundations of BNs in Bayes' Theorem are discussed in [12].

We use the BN's vertices to represent parameters of abstract rules' probability distributions as well as average rule throughputs. For exponential distributions, this parameter is the rate. For lognormal distributions, we represent the mean only. The variance is inherited from corresponding rules in the concrete model and confirmed via plotting the distributions of delays for abstract rules measured in concrete simulations. We therefore have a BN consisting of two distinct sets of nodes: input nodes representing stochastic parameters and output nodes representing the average throughput for each rule. For each rule an edge connects its parameter and throughput node, modelling the dependency of the throughput on the rule's distribution. In addition, conflicts and dependencies are represented as edges between throughput nodes. Because of the way data is propagated through the network by the training algorithm, the direction of edges between throughput nodes is irrelevant. We can therefore avoid cyclic networks, even if dependency and conflict relations are cyclic, by choosing a total order on rule names to direct edges in the network from "smaller" to "larger" names.

Definition 1 (BN of SGTS). *Assume $SG = (TG, P, \pi, F)$ with arbitrary total order $<$ on P. The BN representing SG is a graph $B = (V, E, src, tg, \lambda)$ with functions*

- *$f_{in} : P \to V$ assigning to each rule a vertex representing its stochastic parameter (rate or mean for exponentially or lognormal distributions, respectively);*
- *$f_{out} : P \to V$ assigning to each rule a vertex representing its throughput;*

such that

- *for every $p \in P$, there is exactly one edge in B from $f_{out}(p)$ to $f_{in}(p)$;*

 – for all $p_1, p_2 \in P$ such that p_1 disables or enables p_2, there is exactly one
  edge in B between their respective output nodes, from $f_{out}(p_1)$ to $f_{out}(p_2)$ if
  $p_1 < p_2$, or from $f_{out}(p_2)$ to $f_{out}(p_1)$ if $p_2 < p_1$.

To generate the *DIM*, while running the stochastic simulation of the concrete
model we trace matches for abstract rules, their creation and destruction by concrete rule applications. The matrix records the *average* change in the number of
matches over the entire simulation time. The results are given in Table 1, with a
negative number indicating a net conflict between two rules (more matches being
destroyed than created), and a positive entry a net dependency. The resulting
BN is shown in Fig. 4.

Table 1. Dynamic incidence matrix for abstract rules over concrete model (aggregate
of diagonal conflicts and dependencies)

Abstract rule	Applied Concrete Rule								
	VC	IR	VA2	CD	TD	CR	VT	VM	SM
A_VC	0	-0.408	-1.0	0	0	0	0.44	0.943	0
A_IR	0	-0.408	-1.0	0	0	0	0.44	0.943	0
A_VA2	0	-0.408	-1.0	0	0	0	0.44	0.943	0
A_CD	0	0	1.0	-1.0	0	0	0	0	0
A_TD	0	0	0	0.0347	-1.0	0	0	0	0
A_CR	0	0	0	0.544	0	-1.45	0	0	0
A_VT	0	0	3.8	-1.83	0	0.0744	-0.642	0	0
A_VM	0	0	-0.0548	0	0	0.0208	0	-1.0	0.00755
A_SM	0	0	0	5.82	-78.8	0	0	-4.70	-0.00708

 While the structure of the net is fixed by the dependencies and conflicts, the
net itself is not complete without a probability distribution λ at each node.
Tools, such as Bayes Server [1], are able to learn these distributions if sufficient
training data is available for every variable. The data must be varied enough
so that the network can learn the effect of changes in values of one variable on
another. Each row of training data includes stochastic parameters and resulting
throughputs for all abstract rules, as measured by a batch of simulations.

 The purpose of training is to match the throughputs measured for the abstract
model with those of the concrete one. Once the probability distributions are
learnt for every abstract variable in the network, we enter the known throughputs from the concrete model as evidence, i.e., fixing the values of the nodes
representing outputs. The probability distributions at the remaining unknown
variables, the stochastic parameters, will be perturbed as a result of this evidence, giving us their most likely values given the required throughput. This
process is iterated, starting with a broad sweep of abstract stochastic parameters and refining their choices successively to sample the vicinity of parameters
derived in the previous iteration. Thus, subsequent rounds of learning more and
more precisely replicate the throughputs of the concrete model by the abstract
one.

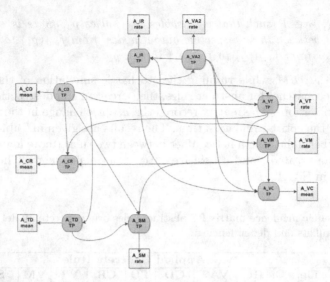

Fig. 4. BN representing dependencies and conflicts in the abstract model

In order to decide when to stop the process, we have to assess how closely concrete and abstract throughputs are matched with a given set of parameters. This is done by simulating the abstract model, measuring its throughputs, and calculating the distance between these and the concrete model's by the formula below as the product of the differences between average throughputs for each rule. If $\overline{y_c(p)}$ and $\overline{y_a(f(p))}$ are the average throughputs for non-idle concrete rule p and its abstract counterpart, respectively:

$$M = \prod_{p \in P} \overline{\frac{\overline{y_c(p)} - \overline{y_a(f(p))}}{\overline{y_c(p)}}}$$

A value closer to zero indicates a better match between concrete and abstract throughputs. However, M also gives an intuitive judgement of distance. For example, for a set of 9 abstract rules as with our case study, a value of M at 10^{-9} indicates that on average the throughput for each rule is within 10% of that measured in the concrete model.

5   Evaluation

The BN in Fig. 4 was implemented in Bayes Server. A sample tissue consisting of 18 cells with 5 initial viruses was created as a start graph for simulation, using 12271 different sets of stochastic parameters with 50 simulation runs of each. The global behaviour variables measured were *total percentage of tissue deaths* (as opposed to complete virus eliminations), and *average simulated time* to complete tissue death or virus elimination. Once learning and inference were completed, in each iteration the extracted stochastic parameters were used to run 6 stochastic simulation batches on the abstract model, each of 100 runs, to measure its throughputs and determine the distance with the concrete model. The abstract immunological response model underwent 3 iterations of parameter training before termination criteria were met. The resulting average throughputs of each iteration along with the associated distances M are shown in Table 2. The minimum value of M achieved was 2.71×10^{-8} for the second iteration.

Table 2. Throughputs (TP) in concrete and abstract immunological response models

	Concrete Model	Abstract Model Iteration 1	Abstract Model Iteration 2	Abstract Model Iteration 3
A_IR TP average	1.041	0.750	0.763	0.809
A_VA2 TP average	0.333	0.406	0.371	0.381
A_VM TP average	0.333	0.415	0.407	0.408
A_VC TP average	0.996	0.748	0.720	0.776
A_VT TP average	1.066	0.798	0.771	0.819
A_SM TP average	20.443	21.743	20.313	21.005
A_CD TP average	0.333	0.406	0.371	0.381
A_CR TP average	0.125	0.101	0.097	0.105
A_TD TP average	0.012	0.017	0.015	0.015
Distance Measure, M		1.15×10^{-6}	2.71×10^{-8}	7.60×10^{-8}

The throughputs show a good congruence between concrete and abstract model. Perturbation of any of the parameters in the abstract model increases the distance measure M, indicating that training was successful in finding a minimum distance of local behaviours. With the second iteration as the final parameter set for the abstract model, the global behaviours deviate significantly. For example, the average percentage of tissue death in the abstract model (Iteration 2) was measured as 42.7%, as opposed to 30.2% in the concrete model. This is not unexpected since not all rules in the concrete model are also present as abstract rules. Hence, the distributions of abstract rules have to account for delays of rules lost in the abstraction. For example, the reaction rule in Fig. 1 depends on rules, hidden in the abstract view, of creating the *immunos* from A resources, an auxiliary species in each cell. The delay of the immunological response reaction rule has to encompass this preliminary process. At the same time, immune reaction is in conflict with, for example, the multiplication of viruses. Increasing the delay will therefore change the balance of the corresponding race condition, thus limiting the ability of delay to compensate for rules missing in the abstract model.

It should be pointed out that the model could easily be trained to replicate global rather than local behaviour, but this would limit its use significantly, making it too specific on the particular property of interest. Alternatively, to ensure a closer match of the functional behaviour, aggregating attributes could be introduced to *Cell* as counters for all of the remaining types that are hidden. However, bringing the abstract model closer to the concrete one would of course counter our original objective of simplifying the model.

While global properties are not reproduced with their absolute values, trends and dependencies are preserved. Fig. 5 shows the result of a sensitivity analysis where we alter the delay of the Cell Regeneration rule to monitor its effect on the percentage of tissue death occurring before simulation time reaches 200 arbitrary units. We alter the mean parameter of the lognormal distributions proportionately. The graph shows a similar trend in both models, with an increase in tissue death, subject to fluctuations due to variance in simulation runs, followed by a decline as cell regeneration slows down. While the maxima do not agree, they occur at approximately similar points. This shows that while global properties may not be deduced from simulations of an abstract model, we can still infer patterns and trends of global behaviour. This in itself is a useful insight into a model.

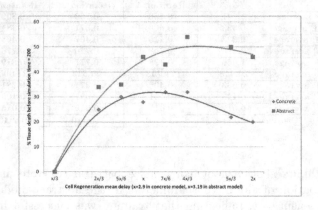

Fig. 5. Sensitivity of % Tissue Death on Cell Regeneration (concrete vs abstract)

Running a simulation of 100 runs on a 64bit Intel Core i5 2.53GHz CPU with 6GB of memory, using the 32bit Eclipse plug-in version of the software resulted in a 72% saving in runtime for the abstract model over the concrete one.

To evaluate the results on another example, a second case study was created, based on the model of a P2P VoIP network. Full details are given in [4], but the objective was for concrete and abstract models to be functionally bisimilar [13], no rules become idle upon abstraction and conflicts and dependencies are preserved and reflected. All distributions are exponential. However, the models still differ in their stochastic behaviour, due to different numbers of matches for corresponding rules at both levels caused by the projection. Parameter training took 3 iterations, the best results being produced during the second iteration at a distance M of 2.94×10^{-10}. The global behaviour matches more closely than in the immune response model: Percentage of disconnected super peer pairs is 11.4 in the concrete model vs. 12.8 in the abstract one, and that of connected clients only varies between 60.4 and 60.3.

Fig. 6 shows the dependency of the percentage of disconnected super pairs on the rate of the CreateShortcut rule, which creates redundant links to reduce the probability of loss of connectivity. Just as in the immune response case, there is

Table 3. Throughputs (TP) measured in concrete and abstract VoIP models

	Concrete Model	Abstract Model Iteration 1	Abstract Model Iteration 2	Abstract Model Iteration 3
A_NC TP average	1.230	1.080	1.197	1.198
A_LC TP average	1.250	1.154	1.251	1.228
A_NS TP average	0.902	0.897	0.821	0.874
A_PC TP average	0.016	0.020	0.030	0.024
A_TL TP average	0.729	0.763	0.796	0.782
A_TS TP average	0.909	0.907	0.841	0.888
A_TU TP average	0.472	0.285	0.358	0.379
A_CS TP average	0.623	0.963	0.780	0.876
Distance Measure, M		3.93×10^{-9}	2.94×10^{-10}	1.10×10^{-9}

a very good match of the trends in both models, even if absolute values are not exactly replicated throughout. Again, there is a significant gain in performance on abstraction, with a 66% reduction in runtime for 20 simulation runs.

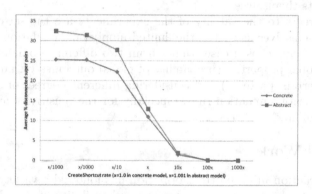

Fig. 6. Sensitivity of % Disconnected Super Pairs on CreateShortcut rate (concrete vs abstract)

Summarising, we were able to show that

- abstraction by projection, with aggregating attributes replacing some of the graphical structure lost, provides a simple and effective way of reducing the complexity of the model, increasing scalability;
- our approach to parameter training using Bayesian networks, defined on the basis of dynamic dependency and conflict analysis, allows us to find a good match of the local behaviours of concrete and abstract models as given by the throughputs of corresponding rules;
- absolute values of global properties are only replicated closely where the models are functionally (but not stochastically) bisimilar;
- trends in global properties, as expressed by their sensitivity with respect to the parameters of essential rules, are reproduced faithfully even if models are not bisimilar;

Before turning to related work, let us discuss possible threats to the validity of the evaluation. During training, variances of lognormal distributions for abstract rules are inherited from the corresponding concrete rules. For the Bayesian network, these variances are therefore not variables, but constants. Mean and rate parameters are inferred so as to replicate the concrete model's throughputs as closely as possible, given these variances. Fixing the variances obviously limits the flexibility of training and thus leads to larger deviations of abstract from concrete throughputs. However, while being one reason for not matching throughputs perfectly, this limitation of training does not affect the validity of the experiments, which are aimed at showing the match of global properties or trends.

The quality of the fit between concrete and abstract throughputs also depends on the distance measure used to control the iteration of training and simulation. The measure M introduced in Sect. 4 has been chosen for its ability to cope with smaller datasets, and its linear variation, over more elaborate notions such as Student's t-test and Mahalanobis distance [8]. Again, this choice could affect the quality of the match between concrete and abstract throughputs, but not the experiments themselves.

Obvious threats to the validity of the experiments are the selection of the experiments themselves as well as the limited number of simulation runs. As to the former, we have chosen case studies from two different domains, focussing on different global properties (probability of global outcomes vs. number of occurrences of certain patterns) and considering different degrees of abstraction. A larger number of simulation runs, especially for the sensitivity analysis, was beyond the available resources.

6   Related Work

Work on abstraction in graph transformation has followed a variety of motivations. In [19], it is a means to improve comprehensibility of complex GTS by hiding and retrieving substructures as required. To enable analysis of models, many approaches aim at reducing the state space or behaviour representation. [5] uses *neighbourhood abstraction* to group graph elements via an equivalence relation up to some radius defining a node's neighbourhood. This allows the level of precision to be adjusted if the current abstraction does not allow the verification of properties. [25] uses a similar approach, but abstracted nodes are characterised by satisfaction of temporal logic formulae representing some behavioural property of the concrete system. In [22], based on shape graphs introduced in [23], nodes are grouped by structural similarity with multiplicities to capture concrete representations of an abstract *shape*. Several states are therefore combined into a single structure. In counterexample-guided abstraction refinement based on unfoldings [15], the behaviour of a GTS is represented by a Petri graph representing an approximated unfolding. In all approaches, abstraction works at the level of the state space or unfolding, or requires a different notion of GTS at the abstract level. Our approach is based on abstraction of standard typed GTS. We simplify type graph, start graph and rules, but the graph transformation approach is unchanged. Analogous to the use of aggregating attributes to increase precision, many approaches provide means to fine-tune the level of abstraction to the properties of interest. In our case these are based on preserving or reflecting essential conflicts and dependencies, rather than reachability.

While this work focuses on a non-deterministic, discrete, stochastic approach to modelling reactions, [7] is a similarly rule-based technique that aims to formulate a reduced, *deterministic* system of differential equations (ODEs) for a reaction system. This is achieved by framing the dynamics in terms of functionally distinct patterns known as fragments (rather than traditionally disjoint species), followed by methods derived from abstract interpretation to further reduce the number of ODEs. Also from a continuous, deterministic paradigm, [6] derives a *refinement* from a more abstract representation of a reaction system, both by replacing reactants with subtypes, or by adding possible reactivity. The resulting system preserves numerical properties (analogous to global trends in our work) without having to perform expensive model-fitting for each subsequent refinement.

With an aim related to our training of stochastic parameters, [17] presents an algorithm known as PEGG (Parameter Estimation for Graph Grammars) which can extract parameters for rules in context-free graph grammars from sequences of graphs resulting from the application of rules. This is useful for modelling based on observations of a system that is executable but with unknown parameters, where parameter estimation aims to determine these parameters. While conceptually close, the limitation to context-free graph grammars means that the approach is not applicable to general graph transformation systems.

7   Conclusion

We have demonstrated a methodology for abstraction of GTS and training their stochastic parameters. Evaluating the approach in two case studies we found that, while absolute values of global properties are not always preserved, the abstract model replicates faithfully trends and dependencies of the concrete one. In future work we plan to explore the relation between the number of matches of concrete and abstract rules and their stochastic parameters as well as the possibility of scaling systems by enlarging or reducing their start graphs.

References

1. Bayes server, intelligent systems specialists, http://www.bayesserver.com/ (retrieved December 9, 2012)
2. Arijo, N., Heckel, R.: View-based modelling and state-space generation for graph transformation systems. ECEASST 47 (2012)
3. Bapodra, M., Heckel, R.: Case study - hypothetical immunological response rules (December 2012), http://www.cs.le.ac.uk/people/mb294/docs/CaseStudyRules_v3.pdf
4. Bapodra, M., Heckel, R.: Case study - VoIP rules (October 2012), http://www.cs.le.ac.uk/people/mb294/docs/VoIPCaseStudyRules.pdf
5. Bauer, J., Boneva, I., Kurbán, M., Rensink, A.: A modal-logic based graph abstraction. Graph Transformations, 321–335 (2008)

6. Iancu, B., Czeizler, E., Czeizler, E., Petre, I.: Quantitative refinement of reaction models. To appear: International Journal of Unconventional Computing
7. Danos, V., Feret, J., Fontana, W., Harmer, R., Krivine, J.: Abstracting the differential semantics of rule-based models: exact and automated model reduction. In: 2010 25th Annual IEEE Symposium on Logic in Computer Science (LICS), pp. 362–381. IEEE (2010)
8. De Maesschalck, R., Jouan-Rimbaud, D., Massart, D.: The Mahalanobis distance. Chemometrics and Intelligent Laboratory Systems 50(1), 1–18 (2000)
9. Drewes, F., Hoffmann, B., Plump, D.: Hierarchical graph transformation. In: Foundations of Software Science and Computation Structures, pp. 98–113. Springer (2000)
10. Heckel, R., Lajios, G., Menge, S.: Stochastic graph transformation systems. Fundamenta Informaticae 74(1), 63–84 (2006)
11. Heckel, R., Corradini, A., Ehrig, H., Löwe, M.: Horizontal and vertical structuring of typed graph transformation systems. Mathematical Structures in Computer Science 6(6), 613–648 (1996)
12. Heckerman, D., et al.: A tutorial on learning with Bayesian networks. Nato Asi Series D Behavioural And Social Sciences 89, 301–354 (1998)
13. Joyal, A., Nielson, M., Winskel, G.: Bisimulation and open maps. In: Proceedings of Eighth Annual IEEE Symposium on Logic in Computer Science, LICS 1993, pp. 418–427. IEEE (1996)
14. Khan, A., Torrini, P., Heckel, R.: Model-based simulation of VoIP network reconfigurations using graph transformation systems. Electronic Communications of the EASST 16 (2009)
15. König, B., Kozioura, V.: Counterexample-Guided Abstraction Refinement for the Analysis of Graph Transformation Systems. In: Hermanns, H., Palsberg, J. (eds.) TACAS 2006. LNCS, vol. 3920, pp. 197–211. Springer, Heidelberg (2006)
16. Löwe, M.: Algebraic approach to single-pushout graph transformation. Theor. Comput. Sci. 109, 181–224 (1993)
17. Oates, T., Doshi, S., Huang, F.: Estimating Maximum Likelihood Parameters for Stochastic Context-Free Graph Grammars. In: Horváth, T., Yamamoto, A. (eds.) ILP 2003. LNCS (LNAI), vol. 2835, pp. 281–298. Springer, Heidelberg (2003)
18. Palacz, W.: Algebraic hierarchical graph transformation. Journal of Computer and System Sciences 68(3), 497–520 (2004)
19. Parisi-Presicce, F., Piersanti, G.: Multilevel graph grammars. In: Graph-Theoretic Concepts in Computer Science, pp. 51–64. Springer (1995)
20. Păun, G.: Introduction to membrane computing. Applications of Membrane Computing, 1–42 (2006)
21. Pourret, O., Nam, P., Naïm, P., Marcot, B., et al.: Bayesian networks: a practical guide to applications, vol. 73. Wiley (2008)
22. Rensink, A., Distefano, D.: Abstract graph transformation. Electronic Notes in Theoretical Computer Science 157(1), 39–59 (2006)
23. Sagiv, M., Reps, T., Wilhelm, R.: Solving shape-analysis problems in languages with destructive updating. ACM Transactions on Programming Languages and Systems (TOPLAS) 20(1), 1–50 (1998)
24. Torrini, P., Heckel, R., Ráth, I.: Stochastic simulation of graph transformation systems. Fundamental Approaches to Software Engineering, 154–157 (2010)
25. Yamamoto, M., Tanabe, Y., Takahashi, K., Hagiya, M.: Abstraction of Graph Transformation Systems by Temporal Logic and Its Verification. In: Meyer, B., Woodcock, J. (eds.) VSTTE 2005. LNCS, vol. 4171, pp. 518–527. Springer, Heidelberg (2008)

Discovering Math APIs by Mining Unit Tests

Anirudh Santhiar, Omesh Pandita*, and Aditya Kanade

Department of Computer Science and Automation, Indian Institute of Science
{anirudh_s,pandita.omesh,kanade}@csa.iisc.ernet.in

Abstract. In today's API-rich world, programmer productivity depends heavily on the programmer's ability to discover the required APIs. In this paper, we present a technique and tool, called MATHFINDER, to discover APIs for mathematical computations by mining unit tests of API methods. Given a math expression, MATHFINDER synthesizes pseudo-code to compute the expression by mapping its subexpressions to API method calls. For each subexpression, MATHFINDER searches for a method such that there is a mapping between method inputs and variables of the subexpression. The subexpression, when evaluated on the test inputs of the method under this mapping, should produce results that match the method output on a large number of tests. We implemented MATH-FINDER as an Eclipse plugin for discovery of third-party Java APIs and performed a user study to evaluate its effectiveness. In the study, the use of MATHFINDER resulted in a 2x improvement in programmer productivity. In 96% of the subexpressions queried for in the study, MATH-FINDER retrieved the desired API methods as the top-most result. The top-most pseudo-code snippet to implement the entire expression was correct in 93% of the cases. Since the number of methods and unit tests to mine could be large in practice, we also implement MATHFINDER in a MapReduce framework and evaluate its scalability and response time.

1 Introduction

In today's API-rich world, programmer productivity depends heavily on the programmer's ability to discover the required APIs and to learn to use them quickly and correctly. Significant research efforts are therefore targeted at aiding programmers in API discovery. A programmer can search for APIs using a wide spectrum of techniques. They range from keywords [15, 3], types [16, 24], tests [11, 13], and code snippets [17], to formal specifications [29] or combinations of the above [21]. These approaches try to address the problem of API discovery in a general programming context and may face challenges in terms of precision of results or require programmers to invest too much effort in formulating the query (e.g., require a first-order logic specification).

In this paper, we address the problem of API discovery for mathematical computations. Mathematical computations are at the heart of numerous application domains such as statistics, machine learning, image processing, engineering or

---

* Now at Microsoft India.

V. Cortellessa and D. Varró (Eds.): FASE 2013, LNCS 7793, pp. 327–342, 2013.

scientific computations, and financial applications. Compared to general programming tasks, mathematical computations can be specified more easily and rigorously, using mathematical notation with well-defined semantics. Many interpreted languages like Matlab, Octave, R, and Scilab, are available for prototyping mathematical computations. It is a common practice to include prototype code to formalize math algorithms (e.g., in [25, 4]). The language interpreter gives a precise *executable semantics* to mathematical computations. Unfortunately, interpreted languages are not always suitable for integration into larger software systems of which the mathematical computations are a component. This is because of commercial and technical issues involving performance overheads, portability, and maintainability. In such cases, the programmer implements the mathematical computations in a general-purpose language.

General-purpose programming languages usually support only basic math operations. For example, `Java.lang.Math` supports elementary functions for exponentiation, logarithm, square root, and trigonometry. Advanced math domains are supported by third-party libraries. Availability of a number of competing libraries, their API sizes, and varying support for primitive operations make it difficult for programmers to select appropriate libraries. We present an approach for discovering math APIs to compute a given (set of) math expression(s). A programmer can pose expressions from the algorithm she wants to implement as queries. For example, suppose she asks for API methods to compute v = v ./ normf(v) (where v is a matrix of doubles). Here, normf stands for the Frobenius norm, and ./ is matrix-scalar division.

Our technique, called MATHFINDER, returns pseudo-code to compute the expression by mapping subexpressions to method calls of individual libraries. For example, MATHFINDER identifies a method `double DoubleMatrix.norm2()` from a third party library as suitable for computing the subexpression normf(v). It identifies that v should be mapped to `this` and the result is available in the return value of the method call. MATHFINDER uses this mapping between variables in the subexpression and method parameters to emit an appropriate method call. In the synthesized pseudo-code, it declares an object v of type `DoubleMatrix`. This object corresponds to the variable v used in the expression. MATHFINDER emits `double T1 = v.norm2()` in the pseudo-code to implement normf(v). Here T1 is a temporary variable. MATHFINDER also discovers if a method is likely to modify the input parameters (i.e. it discovers likely side-effects of methods). In this example, `norm2()` does not modify the receiver.

Discovering APIs and the information about setting up of parameters and determining side-effects automatically is a challenging problem. Formal specifications of semantics of methods may help us solve this problem. Specification languages like JML [12] are designed for annotating Java code with specifications. However, their use is not widespread yet. On the other hand, it is easy to get an under-approximate *operational specification* of a method in the form of *unit tests*. Unit testing is well-adopted in practice, supported by tools like JUnit[1]. We therefore use (the set of input/output objects in) unit tests as a

---

[1] `junit.org`

description of method semantics. While we chose Java as the target programming language, our technique can work with other languages.

The key insight in MATHFINDER is to use an interpreter for a math language (such as Scilab[2]) to evaluate subexpressions on unit tests of library methods. The result of the interpretation on inputs of a test can be compared to the output of the test. Our *hypothesis* is that if a subexpression results in the same value as the output of a method on a large number of tests, the method can be used for computing the subexpression. The subexpression cannot directly be evaluated on data from unit tests because the math types used in the expression are independent from the datatypes used in library APIs. We therefore require the library developer to provide code to convert library datatypes to types of the math interpreter. Thus, any library developer can hook her library into MATH-FINDER. In our running example, the library developer provides code to map objects of the type `DoubleMatrix` to double matrices used by the math interpreter. Writing code to convert library objects to data values of the interpreter is a one time task and was fairly straight-forward in our case.

Given an expression, MATHFINDER extracts subexpressions from it. Given a subexpression and a method, MATHFINDER computes the set of all candidate mappings between variables of the subexpression and method parameters, called *actuals-to-formals mappings*. The mappings should respect the correspondence between library datatypes and math types provided by the library developer. MATHFINDER then searches for a mapping that maximizes the number of unit tests on which the subexpression gives results equivalent to the method outputs. For example, there is only one possible actuals-to-formals map, (v, this), between the subexpression normf(v) and the method norm2(). We use the library developer's code to assign values contained in `this` to v. Then, normf(v) evaluates to a value equal to the return value of `norm2()` on every test of `norm2()` in a test-suite with 10 tests. Alongside, MATHFINDER also infers likely *side-effects* of a method call by comparing the input-output values of method parameters.

Our approach falls in the category of specification-driven API discovery [29, 21]. Unlike logical specifications used as queries in these approaches, the queries to MATHFINDER are executable and succinct. On the library developer's front, the specifications are easy to obtain − just the unit tests and a programmatic mapping from library datatypes to the math types. In contrast, in test-driven API discovery approaches [20, 8, 11, 21, 13], the programmer query is itself in the form of unit tests specific to a library. The unit tests are evaluated on library methods. Thus, the programmer has to know about library datatypes and invest time in writing unit tests. In our approach, the programmer query is independent of library datatypes (it uses mathematical types of the interpreted language). The same query applies to all libraries that are hooked into MATHFINDER. Other approaches cited above target API discovery for general programming tasks, whereas, we present a more specific approach for mathematical computations.

We have implemented MATHFINDER as an Eclipse plugin for discovering third-party Java APIs. We performed a user study to evaluate whether

---

[2] `scilab.org`

MATHFINDER improves programmer productivity, when compared to standard practices such as the use of Javadoc, Eclipse code completion, and keyword-driven web or code search. All participants were permitted to use any of these techniques. On the same programming tasks, the participants who used MATHFINDER were twice as fast on average as those who did not use MATHFINDER.

MATHFINDERS's results were quite precise across multiple libraries. The API method retrieved as the top-most result against a subexpression query was correct 96% of the time. The top-most pseudo-code snippet to implement the entire expression was correct in 93% of the cases. During the course of evaluating MATHFINDER, we found discrepancies between MATHFINDER's output and the Javadoc of JBlas library. While MATHFINDER indicated no side-effect on some methods, their Javadoc explicitly states that they perform computations "in-place"[3]. We studied the method implementations and found that the documentation was indeed inaccurate and the methods had no side-effects.

Our technique is inherently data-parallel. Since the test suite collection can be quite large in practice, we also implemented it in the Hadoop[4]MapReduce framework. It scaled to a large collection of unit tests consisting of over 200K tests and returned results in average 80.5s on an 8-core machine. These results are cached for real-time retrieval using the plugin.

We present an overview of MATHFINDER in the next section. We discuss the technique in Sections 3–4 and evaluate it in Section 5. We survey related approaches in Section 6. We sketch future directions and conclude in Section 7.

2   Overview

```
1 % input: matrix W of doubles, and
2 % double scalars d, v_error
3 pagerank(W, d, v_error)
4    N = size(W, 2);
5    v = rand(N, 1);
6    v = v./normf(v);
7    last_v = ones(N, 1)*INF;
8    M_hat = d*W + (1−d)/N*ones(N, N);
9    cur = normf(v−last_v);
10   while( cur > v_error)
11       last_v = v;
12       v = M_hat*v;
13       v = v./normf(v);
14       cur = normf(v−last_v);
15   end
```

Fig. 1. Scilab code for PageRank (adapted from Wikipedia)

In this section, we illustrate the MATHFINDER technique with an example. Consider the Scilab code in Fig. 1 for the PageRank algorithm [18], a ranking algorithm used by Google.

Even this reasonably small algorithm requires 9 matrix operators that are not supported by the standard Java library. The exact meaning of these operators is not critical for the present discussion. Selecting a third-party library that supports all of them is a tedious and time-consuming task. The four open-source Java libraries that we surveyed, namely, Colt, EJML, Jama,

---

[3] jblas.org/javadoc/index.html, e.g., the add method.
[4] hadoop.apache.org

and JBlas[5] contain over 400 methods in the classes implementing double matrices. Of these, only JBlas (containing over 250 methods for matrix operations) supports all the required operators. The programmer must identify that JBlas is the right library. Further, the programmer must select appropriate methods and learn how to set up method parameters, and about side-effects of method calls, if any.

The programmer can use MATHFINDER to query for APIs to implement each expression in the algorithm. MATHFINDER gives an aggregate score to the libraries indicating how many of the required subexpressions can be implemented using methods from each library. The programmer can then easily identify JBlas as the only *functionally complete* library to implement PageRank.

Suppose the programmer wants to find out how to implement the assignment in line 6, v = v ./ normf(v) (discussed earlier in Section 1). In this paper, we use the math types *double* standing for double scalars, and *double M*, for double matrices. The variable v is given the type *double M* in the query

$$\text{double } M \text{ v}; \text{ v = v ./ normf(v)};$$

The expression form "LHS = RHS" indicates that the programmer wants methods to implement the RHS, and the types of the result and the LHS should be the same. Though many interpreted math languages perform dynamic type inferencing, we need type declarations to make the query unambiguous because operators used in these languages can be polymorphic. For example, ./ denotes both matrix-scalar division and element-wise division of matrices. For each library, its developer provides a mapping between math types and classes used in her library (like in Table 1), and code for converting values from the library's objects to values of the math type. This helps us translate type signatures and data between library types and math types. Thus, the queries themselves are independent of the target libraries.

Table 1. Library classes for the math type *double M*

Library	Class
Colt	DenseDoubleMatrix2D
EJML	DenseMatrix64F
Jama	DoubleMatrix
JBlas	Matrix

MATHFINDER then parses the math expression and decomposes it into subexpressions (similar to three-address code generation in compilers [1]). The subexpressions have a single operator on the RHS by default. v = v ./ normf(v) is decomposed as

$$\text{double T1}; \text{ double } M \text{ v}; \text{ T1 = normf(v)}; \text{ v = v ./ T1};$$

Operator precedence enforces the sequential ordering of computation and temporary variables like T1 are used to explicate data flow. Since the types of the operators are fixed by the chosen interpreted language, the types of the temporaries can be inferred. Here, MATHFINDER infers that T1 is a *double*. Our technique also permits the programmer to guide the search at a granularity other

---

[5] respectively, acs.lbl.gov/software/colt/, code.google.com/p/efficient-java-matrix-library/, math.nist.gov/javanumerics/jama/, jblas.org

Table 2. Results obtained against the subexpression T1 = normf(v)

Method	Actuals-to-formals Map	Score
double Algebra.normF(DoubleMatrix2D)	(v, arg1), (T1, return)	1.0
static double NormOps.normF(D1Matrix64F)	(v, arg1), (T1, return)	1.0
static double NormOps.fastNormF(D1Matrix64F)	(v, arg1), (T1, return)	1.0
double Matrix.normF()	(v, this), (T1, return)	1.0
double DoubleMatrix.norm2()	(v, this), (T1, return)	1.0
static double NormOps.fastElementP(D1Matrix64F,double)	(v, arg1), (T1, return)	0.3

than individual operators in order to find a single API method to implement a larger subexpression, or even the entire expression.

MATHFINDER now picks each subexpression and mines unit tests of library methods to find the methods to implement it, along with the map from subexpression variables to the formal parameters of the method. The method parameters must range over library datatypes (or their supertypes) corresponding to the math types of the subexpression variables. The results obtained against the subexpression T1 = normf(v) are shown in Table 2. In the actuals-to-formals maps in Table 2, arg1 stands for the first argument. MATHFINDER can also search for methods inherited from a superclass of a class identified by the library developer as implementing a math type. In this example, methods over DoubleMatrix2D and D1Matrix64F of the Colt and EJML libraries are also discovered. These are, respectively, supertypes of DenseDoubleMatrix2D and DenseMatrix64F identified in Table 1.

Recall our hypothesis that the relevance of a method to implement a subexpression is proportional to how often its unit tests match the subexpression on interpretation. We assign scores to methods based on this observation and rank them in decreasing order of their scores. As an example of a low-ranked method, we show the NormOps.fastElementP method of EJML in Table 2. It computes the p-norm and coincides with normf only on those tests that initialize its second parameter to 2. Its score (0.3) is much lower than the score of the methods that compute normf exclusively.

MATHFINDER then uses the results mined against each subexpression to issue a pseudo-code snippet. The snippet takes a set of input objects, returns an output object, and performs the computation queried for. The input objects correspond to variables from the RHS of the query and the output object, to the LHS variable. By convention, objects are given the same name as the variables they correspond to. A sequence of API method calls, with a call corresponding to every operator used in the query, is used to generate the output object. In this sequence, if the return value of a method is passed as an argument to another, then their library types should be compatible, and the output object is the return value of the last method. MATHFINDER suggests this snippet from JBlas

```
DoubleMatrix v; double T1; T1 = v.norm2(); v = v.div(T1);
```

where div is discovered to implement v = v ./ T1.

MATHFINDER can thus automate the process of API discovery and comprehension to a large extent. The programmer will still have to verify the validity of the results and translate the pseudo-code to Java code by introducing object instantiations as necessary. The programmer can use snippets from different libraries for different (sub)expressions in her algorithm, provided she writes code to convert between datatypes of the different libraries.

3   Problem Statement

In this section, we define the problem of math API discovery formally. Consider a query Q which is decomposed into sub-queries. A sub-query has type-declarations of variables, followed by a subexpression $x = e$, such that there is exactly one operator in e. We denote a sub-query by q. Given q, our objective is to find methods that can be used to implement e. Let m be a method such that there is a non-empty set $\Lambda(q, m)$ of actuals-to-formals maps, based on the type mapping given by the library developer.

Let $\lambda \in \Lambda(q, m)$ be an actuals-to-formals map . It maps variables in e to input parameters of m and maps the variable x to an output variable of m (either the return value or a parameter modified by side-effect). Let a unit test σ of m map m's input/output variables to Java objects. Let f be a function from Java objects to data values of the interpreter. The library developer programatically encodes f. Given a unit test σ of a method m and an actuals-to-formals map λ, for a subexpression $x = e$, σ' gives the values of variables occurring in $x = e$. For a variable y,

$$\sigma'(y) = f(\sigma(y')), \text{ where } y' = \lambda(y).$$

The mapping σ' can be extended to expressions in a natural way. For example, $\sigma'(\text{normf}(\text{v})) = \text{normf}(\sigma'(\text{v}))$, where the interpreter computes normf. The subexpression $x = e$ *evaluates* to true on a unit test σ, under an actuals-to-formals map λ, if $\sigma'(x) = \sigma'(e)$. A sub-query evaluates to true on a unit test if its subexpression does. Let N be the total number of unit tests of m, and k the number of tests on which q evaluates to true, under a particular actuals-to-formals map λ. The problem is then to find an actuals-to-formals map λ^* that maximizes k/N. We call λ^* the *maximizing actuals-to-formals map* (MAFM) and the corresponding value of k/N, the *maximal test frequency* (MTF).

Ranking API Methods against Sub-query q. The MTF quantifies the *relevance* of the method. Since the same number of unit tests may not be available for every method, the *confidence* in a retrieved method does not depend on its MTF alone. For example, if two methods match a query on all their tests, but one has only 1 test while the other has 10, intuitively, the confidence in the latter is higher. We therefore normalize the number of tests per method using a constant c, by scaling the MTF by the minimum of N/c and 1. We consider a method with side-effects more difficult to use than one without, and impose a *side-effect penalty*, *sep*, on it. We set *sep* to a small positive constant for methods with side-effects and to 0 otherwise. We assign scores to methods according to:

$$\text{Score}(q, m) \triangleq \min(\tfrac{N}{c}, 1) \cdot \tfrac{k}{N} \cdot \tfrac{1}{1+sep}$$

We then rank (sort) the methods in the decreasing order of their scores (e.g. see Table 2).

Generating Pseudo-code for Expressions. In general, a math expression may have many operators, with multiple candidate methods available to implement each. Consider a query Q and a set of candidate methods $\{m_1, \ldots, m_n\}$ to implement it. These are obtained by decomposing the query into sub-queries $\{q_1, \ldots, q_n\}$, and matching them as outlined earlier. The decomposition is type-correct (by construction) in the math language; however, a pseudo-code snippet to implement it must respect the type-constraints imposed by the map between library types and math types as well.

The problem is then to filter the set of all possible candidate-method sets to only those that are type-consistent, and then generate pseudo-code snippets. This can be done with an exhaustive search over the ranked lists of methods retrieved against the sub-queries. The snippets are ranked by taking the average of the scores of the methods:

$$\text{Score}(Q, \{m_1, \ldots, m_n\}) \triangleq \tfrac{1}{n} \cdot \sum_{i=1}^{n} \text{Score}(q_i, m_i)$$

4   Unit Test Mining

In this section, we present an algorithm to compute scores of API methods against a (sub)expression containing a single operator on the RHS.

Sequential Algorithm. We first present a sequential algorithm for mining unit tests (See Fig. 2).

Input: Query $q \equiv x = e$, unit tests of method m
Output: The MAFM and MTF for m
1: $\Sigma \leftarrow$ set of unit tests of m
2: **for each** $\sigma \in \Sigma$ **do**
3:     Look for side-effects in σ
4:     **for each** $\lambda \in \Lambda(q, m)$ **do**
5:         Let σ' be obtained from σ, f and λ
6:         **if** $\sigma'(x) = \sigma'(e)$ **then**
7:             $\text{Count}(\lambda) \leftarrow \text{Count}(\lambda) + 1$
8:         **end if**
9:     **end for**
10: **end for**
11: Let λ^* be such that $\text{Count}(\lambda^*)$ is maximum
12: $\text{MTF} \leftarrow \text{Count}(\lambda^*)/|\Sigma|$

Fig. 2. Sequential Mining Algorithm

As input, the algorithm takes the query q, with query expression $x = e$, and a method m (together with its unit tests). Its goal is to compute the number of unit tests that match q under every actuals-to-formals map of m. For each unit test of m (line 2), the algorithm iterates over the space of actuals-to-formals maps $\Lambda(q, m)$, and constructs a map σ' from query variables to values (in terms of the interpreter data-types, line 5). If under a particular actuals-to-formals map, the query evaluates to true (line 6) we increment a counter (the counter is initially set to 0). Finally, the algorithm returns the maximal actuals-to-formals map λ^* and the maximum test frequency. This algorithm also detects

side-effects; it identifies side-effects on each method parameter (line 3) by equat-
ing the input/output values of the parameter. If there exists a test where they do
not match, it sets *sep* to a small positive constant (not shown in Fig. 2).

MapReduce Version. We can easily parallelize our mining algorithm. In particular, the innermost loop (over λ, line 4) can be executed over different unit
tests in parallel. We exploit this data-parallelism to obtain a scalable MapReduce
version of the mining algorithm.

In the MapReduce programming model [5], the input data to a *mapper* is a set
of key-value pairs. The mapper's computation is applied to each key-value pair
independently. It can thus be distributed over multiple nodes. After processing
a key-value pair, the mapper can emit an arbitrary number of intermediate key-
value pairs. These pairs represent partial results. The framework then performs a
distributed group-by operation on the intermediate key, and accumulates all the
values associated with it in a list. The *reducer* gets as its input the intermediate
keys and the corresponding lists. It typically goes over the list of values associated
with a key to compute a final result (aggregate). In a MapReduce framework,
the user only has to provide implementations of the mapper and the reducer;
the framework handles distribution, fault-tolerance, scheduling etc.

Our MapReduce algorithm is supported by a distributed index of unit tests.
We omit details of the index organization in the interest of space. Unit tests are
read from the index as the mapper's input. The mapper evaluates the subexpression on a test under every actuals-to-formals map, emitting an intermediate
key-value pair $\langle \lambda, true \rangle$ or $\langle \lambda, false \rangle$ for each. This partial result says whether
the subexpression evaluated to true or false under a particular λ. After the run-
time performs a distributed group-by operation, a key-value pair arriving at a
reducer contains an actuals-to-formals map λ (key) and a list of booleans (value).
Every entry in this list was generated by evaluating λ on some unit test. Values of k and N are calculated for a particular λ by iterating over this list. λ^*
(the maximizing actuals-to-formals map) is the key that maximizes k/N over all
key-value pairs. In our implementation, we lift this algorithm to work on indices
containing unit tests of multiple methods from across libraries.

5   Implementation and Evaluation

Implementation. We implemented the MapReduce version of the mining algorithm in the Apache `Hadoop` framework, with Scilab as the interpreter. We
ran the mining algorithm on a unit test index containing unit tests from our
target libraries, that we wrote using JUnit. We used `Serialysis`[6] to serialize
input/output values from the unit tests, and provided hooks in our framework
for specifying the mapping between library and math types. As an optimization,
we cached the top k methods retrieved against every operator in the interpreted
language in an *operator index*, which is a Java HashMap, serialized to disk.

---

[6] `weblogs.java.net/blog/emcmanus/serialysis.zip`

We implemented MATHFINDER as an Eclipse plugin that interfaces Eclipse with the API discovery and snippet-generation engines. In Eclipse, the MATHFINDER view offers a search bar to type math expressions in. We parse, type-check and decompose expressions into subexpressions using the Antlr3[7] framework. Subexpressions are answered in real-time by looking up the operator index.

User Study. We conducted a user study to measure whether MATHFINDER improves programmer productivity on mathematical programming tasks when compared to reading Javadoc, using Eclipse code-completion, and keyword-driven web or code search. To measure this, we picked a set of four mathematical programming tasks (see Table 3 for a summary) that required third-party libraries to complete. Only the first task could be implemented using any target library, while the others required a careful evaluation of the APIs to find a functionally complete target library. We presented the algorithms to the participants as method stubs in Eclipse.

We deemed participants to have completed a task when their program passed all our unit tests. The main barrier to implementation was the lack of direct Java support, rather than algorithmic subtleties.

Table 3. Summary of the tasks used in the user study

Task	Algorithm Name	Description
1	Conjugate Gradient	Linear Equation Solving
2	Chebyshev	Polynomial Interpolation
3	PageRank	Webpage Ranking
4	Rayleigh Iteration	Eigenvalue Computation

We chose small tasks, expecting the participants to finish them within two hours. There were 16 unique operators across the tasks, and 5 to 8 queries in each task whose implementation required method composition. The target libraries were Colt, EJML, Jama and JBlas.

Our participants were 5 industry professionals and 3 graduate students not affiliated to our research group. Two participants attempted every task, one without MATHFINDER and one with MATHFINDER. Those in the *control group* were allowed to use Javadoc, Eclipse code completion, and web or code search engines; in addition, those in the *experimental group* were allowed to use MATHFINDER. We gave the participants handouts describing the operators used in the tasks, and a mapping between library types and math types (similar to Table 1).

Timing Results. Table 4 shows the timing results of the user study. All times are in minutes. MATHFINDER users finished 1.96 times as fast as the control-group participants on average. Though the study is not large enough to measure the difference with statistical significance, these results suggest that MATHFINDER helps improve productivity.

Control group participants reported that they found selecting an API that best

Table 4. Task completion times

Task	Control group	Experimental group(speed-up)
1	95m	51m(1.86x)
2	93m	64m(1.45x)
3	97m	39m(2.49x)
4	75m	30m(2.50x)

---

[7] antlr.org

supported their task difficult, often requiring a search over Javadoc pages of multiple libraries. We expected participants to pick keywords out of operator descriptions in the handout (e.g., "matrix multiplication") and use Google or code search engines, but surprisingly, only one participant did so. This may be due to the difficulty of analyzing a number of independent search results, pertaining to individual operators in the task. Almost all control group users relied on Eclipse code completion. This proved unhelpful at times, given the sheer number of methods in some relevant API classes, similar names, and because the required functionality was spread across multiple classes. For example, there are at least 16 methods in the `CommonOps` class of `EJML` with a prefix "mult", and all have something to do with matrix multiplication. `JBlas` has 19 such methods in the `DoubleMatrix` class. Although we did not provide type-based API discovery tools [16, 24] to aid participants, we believe that these would not have altered the outcome significantly. Type-based queries can result in many spurious results for math APIs because a large number of methods operate over the same types. For example, the JBlas library has over 60 methods that take two `DoubleMatrix` objects as input and return a `DoubleMatrix` object. Searching by method signatures cannot distinguish, say, matrix addition from matrix multiplication.

MATHFINDER users, on the other hand, were able to formulate queries directly from the tasks, and all of them reported that the tool was easy to use. With the tool, they were able to quickly gauge the extent of library support for their task across libraries, and zero-in on the right library. The queries returned precise results, and usually, the participants did not have to look beyond the top ranked snippet. They copied the suggested snippets into the workspace and completed them, consulting the Javadocs only to find appropriate constructors. This experience leads us to believe that MATHFINDER will deliver larger productivity gains with more complex tasks and diverse API requirements.

Precision and Recall We evaluate the precision of our approach on both API discovery and synthesis of pseudo-code snippets. To evaluate precision of API discovery, we picked the set of unique operators from across the tasks; there were 16. Of these, Colt supports 7, EJML 13, Jama 13 and JBlas 14. For unsupported operators, MATHFINDER returns empty results, since it picks only results with a score above a threshold (0.75). The precision on operators supported by individual libraries is given in Table 5. The precision is high (96% on average), despite the fact that these libraries use different class definitions, calling conventions, etc. Also, MATHFINDER retrieved all relevant methods from all libraries (recall 1), with two exceptions. One was the eyes operator, used to generate identity matrices. The corresponding JBlas method eyes was not retrieved. This

Table 5. Precision of API Discovery

Library	$\dfrac{\text{\#correct@rank-1}}{\text{\#supported-operators}}$
Colt	6/ 7(86%)
EJML	13/13(100%)
Jama	13/13(100%)
JBlas	13/14(93%)
Total	45/47(96%)

method takes only one argument (equal to both the number of rows and columns), whereas the eyes operator in Scilab takes two integer arguments (rows and columns) separately. A relaxed type matching may help us identify methods like eyes that take fewer parameters than the subexpression variables. The other exception was the transpose operator. MATHFINDER mapped it to an incorrect method of Colt. Later, we were able to attribute it to having missed a special case in mapping library datatypes to interpreter datatypes. This implementation issue was easy to fix, but we only report results prior to the fix.

There were 24 expressions in total in all the tasks. The operators used in these expressions were not supported by every library. Therefore, to measure the precision of pseudo-code snippet synthesis on a library, we only considered expressions that could be implemented fully using it. With this restriction, Colt supports 6 expressions, EJML 17, Jama 15, and JBlas 17. For the expressions that could be implemented, we evaluated, for each library, whether the top-most code snippet MATHFINDER returned was correct. The results are given in Table 6. The precision across libraries is 93% on average. Our technique is able

Table 6. Precision of synthesized pseudo-code snippets

Library	$\dfrac{\#\text{correct-snippet}}{\#\text{expressions}}$
Colt	2/ 6(33%)
EJML	17/17(100%)
Jama	15/15(100%)
JBlas	16/16(100%)
Total	50/54(93%)

to mine operator to method maps as well as maps from actuals to formals accurately, which in turn means that the synthesized pseudo-code snippets are precise. Colt's precision was low because 4/6 expressions used transpose (which was mapped to an incorrect method).

Threats to Validity Threats to *internal validity* include *selection bias* where the control and experimental groups may not be equivalent at the beginning of the study, and *testing bias* where pre-test activities may affect post-test outcomes. To prevent selection bias, we conducted a survey before the study and paired programmers with similar levels of Java expertise. We then assigned them the same task, but chose their group (control or experimental) randomly. To mitigate testing bias, we gave the experimental group participants a 20 minute presentation on the tool instead of a hands-on tutorial. Threats to *external validity* arise because our results may not generalize to other groups of programmers and programming tasks. To ensure a level playing field, we made sure none of our participants had prior exposure to the target APIs. But this meant that we had to leave out expert users of the target APIs. Therefore, the study does not assess the benefits of MATHFINDER to domain experts and whether selecting another candidate library is as difficult for them as for programmers with no experience with any of the libraries. As target APIs, we picked popular open-source third-party libraries which we believe are representative. However, further studies are needed to validate the findings for other APIs in the math domain.

Scalability and Response Time. Our retrieval target collection had 406 methods: 41 methods from Colt, 70 from EJML, 45 from Jama, and 250 from JBlas.

We obtain the time for API discovery using 10, 200 and 500 tests/method against queries involving operators used in the tasks. With 10 tests/method, the experiments were performed on a desktop running Ubuntu 10.04 with an Intel i5 CPU (3.20GHz, 4GB RAM). We used a single mapper and reducer to run the MapReduce implementation of the mining algorithm. With 200 and 500 tests/method, the experiments were carried out on a machine running CentOS 5.3, with 8 Xeon quad-core processors (2.66GHz, 16GB RAM). The machine could run up to 7 mappers and 2 reducers. For computing scores, we set the side-effect-penalty to 0.2. The processing time per query was 3.7s on average with 10 tests/method (desktop), 56.7s with 200 tests/method and 80.5s with 500 tests/method (multi-core processor). The precision of results did not vary significantly with 200 or 500 tests/method, suggesting that for the domain we considered, our technique is able to achieve high precision with only a few tests/method. The study shows that our implementation scales to an index with over 200K test records.

Limitations. Our ranking function does not take into account performance or efficiency of API implementations. It does not rank an API method that is a specialization of the math operator lower. We cannot discover compositions of API methods to implement a single operator. Our approach, in its current form, cannot discover APIs that take function objects as parameters, e.g., one of our target libraries, Colt, has a set of functions available through a function `assign` which takes function objects as input. The equality between query and method outcomes is relaxed, in that, double precision numbers computed by the interpreter and by an API method are said to be equal if they are within $\epsilon = .001$ of each other. The incompleteness or errors in data (unit tests) can affect precision of results. This is true of any data mining approach.

6   Related Work

In text search, the popularity of web search engines shows that keyword-driven queries are used extensively. In programming, the main utility of web search engines seems to be to retrieve library documentation. Commercial code search engines (e.g. Codase, Google code search, Koders, Krugle, etc.)[8] retrieve declarations and reference examples given library and method names. These approaches are difficult to use if the programmer does not know the suitable libraries or methods to begin with. Some research tools like Assieme [9], Codifier [2], and Sourcerer [14] can perform syntactic search using richer program structure. The MATHFINDER approach is purely *semantic* and does not use keywords or program structure for search.

Several approaches [22, 28, 16, 24] use types for API discovery. These approaches discover API call sequences to go from an input type to an output type by mining API declarations and in some cases, client source code. A dynamic analysis approach, MatchMaker [27], discovers API sequences by mining program traces. In our experience, the objects set up using math APIs are easy

---

[8] respectively, `codease.com`, `code.google.com/hosting`, `koders.com`, `krugle.org`

to initialize and do not require a sequence of calls to set up state before they may be used. Since types alone may not be enough for accurate API discovery, some techniques combine them with structural contexts including comments, field/method names, inheritance relations, and method-parameter, return-type, and subtype relations [26, 10, 23, 6]. Types are also combined with keywords in Keyword Programming [15] and SNIFF [3]. Apart from APIs, type-based code completion approaches such as InSynth [7] and the work of Perelman et al. [19] also search over variables in the typing context.

The main limitations of type-driven approaches include (i) the assumption that the programmer has (partial) knowledge of the types and (ii) the lack of precise semantic information in the queries. In MATHFINDER, the programmer formulates queries over mathematical types (of the interpreted language used) and not over library types. Thus, the same query is enough to discover APIs across multiple libraries. Our queries are math expressions over interpreted operators and can accurately identify methods for the operators in the query expression.

Prime [17] queries are partial programs, from which it mines partial temporal specifications and matches them against an index of temporal specifications built from example code from the web. We have already compared our work, in Section 1, with more closely related approaches like specification-driven [29, 21] and test-driven [20, 8, 11, 21, 13] techniques for API discovery.

7   Conclusions and Future Work

This paper presents a novel technique to search for math APIs. A programmer submits a math expression directly as a query to MATHFINDER which returns pseudo-code for computing it by composing library methods. The approach combines executable semantics of math expressions with unit tests of methods to mine a mapping from expression variables to method parameters and detects likely side-effects of methods. We show that the approach improves programmer productivity, gives precise results, and scales to large datasets.

The availability of rigorous specifications make mathematical computations an attractive choice for automated code synthesis. The existence of mature libraries makes the synthesis problem in this domain more about API discovery than algorithm discovery. Our work is a step toward API-driven synthesis.

Some methods may take more parameters than the corresponding math operator. Mining initializations to these parameters from unit tests is an interesting future direction. We also plan to explore more general queries involving predicates. API migration is a potential application of our unit test mining approach. The semantics of APIs to be migrated can be specified in math notation, to obtain matching APIs from other libraries using MATHFINDER.

Acknowledgements. We thank the volunteers of the user study, and the members of the Software Engineering and Analysis Lab for their help during the user study. We also thank the anonymous reviewers for their valuable feedback.

References

1. Aho, A.V., Lam, M., Sethi, R., Ullman, J.D.: Compilers: Principles, Techniques, and Tools. Prentice-Hall (2006)
2. Begel, A.: Codifier: a programmer-centric search user interface. In: Workshop on Human-Computer Interaction and Information Retrieval (2007)
3. Chatterjee, S., Juvekar, S., Sen, K.: SNIFF: A Search Engine for Java Using Free-Form Queries. In: Chechik, M., Wirsing, M. (eds.) FASE 2009. LNCS, vol. 5503, pp. 385–400. Springer, Heidelberg (2009)
4. Datta, B.N.: Numerical Methods for Linear Control Systems. Elsevier Inc. (2004)
5. Dean, J., Ghemawat, S.: MapReduce: Simplified data processing on large clusters. In: OSDI, pp. 137–150 (2004)
6. Duala-Ekoko, E., Robillard, M.P.: Using Structure-Based Recommendations to Facilitate Discoverability in APIs. In: Mezini, M. (ed.) ECOOP 2011. LNCS, vol. 6813, pp. 79–104. Springer, Heidelberg (2011)
7. Gvero, T., Kuncak, V., Piskac, R.: Interactive Synthesis of Code Snippets. In: Gopalakrishnan, G., Qadeer, S. (eds.) CAV 2011. LNCS, vol. 6806, pp. 418–423. Springer, Heidelberg (2011)
8. Hall, R.J.: Generalized behavior-based retrieval. In: ICSE, pp. 371–380 (1993)
9. Hoffmann, R., Fogarty, J., Weld, D.S.: Assieme: finding and leveraging implicit references in a web search interface for programmers. In: UIST, pp. 13–22 (2007)
10. Holmes, R., Murphy, G.C.: Using structural context to recommend source code examples. In: ICSE, pp. 117–125 (2005)
11. Hummel, O., Janjic, W., Atkinson, C.: Code Conjurer: Pulling reusable software out of thin air. IEEE Software 25(5), 45–52 (2008)
12. Leavens, G.T., Baker, A.L., Ruby, C.: JML: A notation for detailed design. In: Behavioral Specifications of Businesses and Systems, pp. 175–188 (1999)
13. Lemos, O.A.L., Bajracharya, S., Ossher, J., Masiero, P.C., Lopes, C.: A test-driven approach to code search and its application to the reuse of auxiliary functionality. Inf. Softw. Technol. 53(4), 294–306 (2011)
14. Linstead, E., Bajracharya, S.K., Ngo, T.C., Rigor, P., Lopes, C.V., Baldi, P.: Sourcerer: mining and searching internet-scale software repositories. Data Min. Knowl. Discov. 18(2), 300–336 (2009)
15. Little, G., Miller, R.C.: Keyword programming in Java. In: ASE, pp. 84–93 (2007)
16. Mandelin, D., Xu, L., Bodík, R., Kimelman, D.: Jungloid mining: helping to navigate the API jungle. In: PLDI, pp. 48–61 (2005)
17. Mishne, A., Shoham, S., Yahav, E.: Typestate-based semantic code search over partial programs. In: OOPSLA, pp. 997–1016 (2012)
18. Page, L., Brin, S., Motwani, R., Winograd, T.: The PageRank citation ranking: Bringing order to the web. Technical Report 1999-66, Stanford InfoLab (1999)
19. Perelman, D., Gulwani, S., Ball, T., Grossman, D.: Type-directed completion of partial expressions. In: PLDI, pp. 275–286 (2012)
20. Podgurski, A., Pierce, L.: Behavior sampling: a technique for automated retrieval of reusable components. In: ICSE, pp. 349–361 (1992)
21. Reiss, S.P.: Semantics-based code search. In: ICSE, pp. 243–253 (2009)
22. Rittri, M.: Retrieving Library Identifiers via Equational Matching of Types. In: Stickel, M.E. (ed.) CADE 1990. LNCS, vol. 449, pp. 603–617. Springer, Heidelberg (1990)
23. Sahavechaphan, N., Claypool, K.: XSnippet: mining for sample code. In: OOPSLA, pp. 413–430 (2006)

24. Thummalapenta, S., Xie, T.: Parseweb: a programmer assistant for reusing open source code on the web. In: ASE, pp. 204–213 (2007)
25. Vesanto, J., Himberg, J., Alhoniemi, E., Parhankangas, J.: Self-Organizing Map in Matlab: the SOM toolbox. In: Proc. of the Matlab DSP Conf., pp. 35–40 (2000)
26. Ye, Y., Fischer, G.: Supporting reuse by delivering task-relevant and personalized information. In: ICSE, pp. 513–523 (2002)
27. Yessenov, K., Xu, Z., Solar-Lezama, A.: Data-driven synthesis for object-oriented frameworks. In: OOPSLA, pp. 65–82 (2011)
28. Zaremski, A.M., Wing, J.M.: Signature matching: a key to reuse. In: FSE, pp. 182–190 (1993)
29. Zaremski, A.M., Wing, J.M.: Specification matching of software components. ACM Trans. Softw. Eng. Methodol. 6(4), 333–369 (1997)

POGen: A Test Code Generator Based on Template Variable Coverage in Gray-Box Integration Testing for Web Applications

Kazunori Sakamoto[1], Kaizu Tomohiro[2], Daigo Hamura[2], Hironori Washizaki[1], and Yoshiaki Fukazawa[1]

[1] Waseda University
Tokyo, Japan
kazuu@ruri.waseda.jp, {washizaki,fukazawa}@waseda.jp
[2] Google Japan Inc.
Tokyo, Japan
{tkaizu,daigoh}@google.com

Abstract. Web applications are complex; they consist of many subsystems and run on various browsers and platforms. This makes it difficult to conduct adequate integration testing to detect faults in the connections between subsystems or in the specific environments. Therefore, establishing an efficient integration testing method with the proper test adequacy criteria and tools is an important issue.

In this paper, we propose a new test coverage called template variable coverage. We also propose a novel technique for generating skeleton test code that includes accessor methods and improves the template variable coverage criterion, using a tool that we developed called POGen. Our experiments show that template variable coverage correlates highly with the capability to detect faults, and that POGen can reduce testing costs.

Keywords: software testing, web application, test coverage, test code generation, template engine.

1   Introduction

The importance of web applications has grown immensely with the popularization of the Internet. Web applications are based on the client-server model, and require collaboration among client and server programs. This indicates that web applications consist of various subsystems such as web servers, authentication servers and database servers. Moreover, client programs run on various browsers and platforms. Some faults might occur in the connections between the subsystems or in the specific environments [1]. Therefore, an efficient and comprehensive testing method is required to eliminate these faults.

Software testing methods can be roughly classified by their level and technique. There are four levels of testing during the development process: unit testing, which verifies the functionality of a specific section of the code; integration testing, which verifies the interfaces between components; system testing,

V. Cortellessa and D. Varró (Eds.): FASE 2013, LNCS 7793, pp. 343–358, 2013.

which verifies that the entire software meets its requirements; and acceptance testing, which verifies that the requirements are met from the user's perspective. For simplicity, we consider any testing except unit testing as integration testing in this paper. Testing methods can also be classified into three techniques: white-box testing (a.k.a. structure based testing), which utilizes knowledge of how the code is implemented; black-box testing (a.k.a. specification based testing), which tests the functionality of the code without any knowledge of how the code is implemented; and gray-box testing, which utilizes partial knowledge of the internal data structures and algorithms.

Testing frameworks such as JUnit automate the testing process by writing test code. Test code constitutes an executable program including test cases. A test case consists of a test scenario, which invokes functions of the production code, and a test oracle, which determines whether the program works as expected by observing the program state as the test scenario is executed.

Template engines are typically introduced during web application development as part of the web framework, such as Struts and Ruby on Rails. There are two types of template engines: those that run on the server side, such as ejs [2] and JSF [3], and those that run on the client side, such as Closure Templates [4]. A template engine generates an HTML document by embedding string representations of variables or expressions referring to the states of executable programs into the HTML template. Therefore, web applications must be able to handle both the static content of the HTML document and the dynamic content that changes as the program is executed. Finding faults related to the static content is relatively easy, whereas finding faults related to the dynamic content is difficult because whether the faults are exposed or not depends on the execution path.

In this paper, we propose a new test coverage criterion called template variable coverage. Template variable coverage focuses on the variables and expressions for embedding in HTML templates (hereafter referred to as template variables), which are important for testing a web application's functionality related to the dynamic content of an HTML document. To improve the template variable coverage criterion, we also propose a gray-box integration testing method using a tool that we developed called POGen. POGen generates skeleton test code with accessor methods for template variables by analyzing HTML templates.

The contributions of this paper are as follows:

- Template variable coverage, a new criterion of test adequacy to verify the dynamic content corresponding to the execution results of web applications,
- POGen, a novel test code generator for improving template variable coverage criterion,
- An evaluation of the correlation between template variable coverage and the capability to detect faults and
- An evaluation of POGen with respect to its ability to reduce writing and maintenance costs.

POGen is released as open source software on http://code.google.com/p/pageobjectgenerator/.

2 Motivating Example

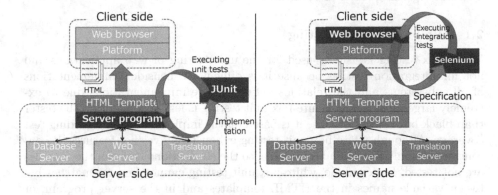

Fig. 1. White-box unit testing (left) and black-box integration testing (right) for a sample web application

List 1.1. An HTML template of the input page using Closure Templates

```
1   {template .addition}
2     <form action="result">
3       <input type="text" name="left"> + <input type="text" name="right">
4       <input type="submit" name="calc" value="Calculate">
5     </form>
6   {/template}
```

List 1.2. An HTML template of the result page using Closure Templates

```
1   {template .result}
2     <p>{$left}+{$right}=<div>{$answer}</div></p>
3     <ul>{call .items}{param list: $histories /}{/call}</ul>
4   {/template}
5   {template .items}
6     {foreach $item in $list} <li>{$item}</li> {/foreach}
7   {/template}
```

In this section, we present an example to demonstrate our technique. We shall consider a web application for a simple calculator supporting addition. The calculator has two additional features for translating string representations of numbers such as "fourteen" and for recording and showing past inputs. Figure 1 shows the architecture of the web application. The web application consists of three servers: a web server for handling web pages with a template engine, a translation server for handling number strings and a database server for managing the input history.

The web application consists of two web pages: an input page for inputting numbers to add and a result page for showing the result of the calculation. Lists 1.1 and 1.2 show the HTML templates of the input and result pages using Closure Templates. The result page shows the translated numbers, the addition result and the history of the given numbers and results. We discuss three testing methods regarding this web application.

2.1   White-Box Unit Testing

White-box testing is usually used for the unit testing of web applications and not for integration testing because it is difficult to consider implementations of all subsystems and the relations between these implementations due to extremely large subsystems. White-box unit testing is less dependent on the tester than black-box testing because it is based on the implementation, including test coverage. Although white-box unit testing exhaustively verifies features, it concentrates on only one module at a time, so the connections between the modules are not tested. For example, white-box unit testing cannot find mismatches between variable names in the HTML templates and in the server program, or the invocation of an inappropriate function from the server program. Therefore, faults that can be found with white-box unit testing are limited.

2.2   Black-Box Integration Testing

Black-box testing is usually used for the integration testing of web applications as opposed to white-box testing. Black-box testing only requires the testers to know what the web application is supposed to do, and the testers can easily try to manipulate the web application on a web browser. Black-box integration testing can be done at a low cost, and can find faults between connections of modules on the real environment. However, it is hard to exhaustively verify the dynamic content of the HTML document because the testers have no information on how the application is implemented. Black-box integration testing also depends heavily on the tester. For example, a tester of our sample web application may only concentrate on the answer value and not test the left and right values to verify the calculation feature. As another example, a tester may leave out the translation feature. Therefore, black-box integration testing may overlook faults due to its dependency on the tester and the lack of test adequacy criteria.

2.3   Gray-Box Integration Testing

To find faults that can be overlooked by both white-box unit testing and black-box integration testing, we propose a gray-box integration testing method for verifying web applications. This method makes use of information gathered from the HTML templates and the application's specifications.

List 1.2 contains four template variables: {$left}, {$right}, {$answer} and {$item}. Note that $histories and $list are not template variables because they are not inserted into the HTML document replacing them with their values during execution. The template variables indicate the dynamic content of the HTML document corresponding to the outputs from the server program of the web application, and they can be used to verify the connections between subsystems. For example, faults in the addition feature are exposed through {$answer}, while those in the translation feature are exposed through {$left}, {$right} and {$answer}, and those in the history feature are exposed through {$item}. Therefore, gray-box integration testing allows testers to find faults efficiently and exhaustively by exposing the dynamic content of the HTML document marked by template variables.

3   Template Variable Coverage

Template engines replace template variables with the string representations of the template variables' values. We can extract the dynamic content of an HTML document by analyzing HTML templates; template variables are marked by special notations, such as {$answer} in List 1.2. Note that we make no distinction between variables and expressions in template variables.

We propose a new coverage criterion called template variable coverage which indicates test adequacy with respect to the dynamic content of the HTML document. Template variable coverage allows testers to conduct exhaustive gray-box integration testing. Moreover, it provides a quantitative measure for assessing the quality of a set of test cases.

Definition 1. Let C_{tmp} be the template variable coverage, V_{all} the number of all template variables, and V_{test} the number of template variables which are referred by test cases during testing. C_{tmp} is defined by formula (1). Note that $V_{all} \supseteq V_{test}$ and $0 \leq C_{tmp} \leq 1$ hold.

$$C_{tmp} = \frac{V_{test}}{V_{all}} \qquad (1)$$

List 1.3. A test case with JUnit and Selenium for verifying the addition feature

```
1  WebDriver driver = new ChromeDriver();
2  // some code to initialize the driver
3  driver.findElementByName("left").sendKeys("1");
4  driver.findElementByName("right").sendKeys("two");
5  driver.findElementByName("calc").submit();
6  assertEquals("3", findElement(By.cssSelector("p > div")).getText());
```

List 1.3 shows a conventional test case to verify the addition feature of the web application. This test case only refers to one template variable, {$answer}, out of the four template variables: {$left}, {$right}, {$answer} and {$item}. Thus, the template variable coverage for this test case is 25%. It is 75% if a test case refers to {$left}, {$right} and {$answer}.

Assumption 1. Template variable coverage is a test adequacy criterion that indicates how exhaustively the test cases observe outputs from web applications. We therefore assume that template variable coverage correlates positively with the test quality, or the capability to find faults with the set of test cases.

4   POGen: Test Code Generator to Improve the Coverage

We propose a novel technique to generate skeleton test code for improving the template variable coverage criterion using POGen. POGen supports gray-box integration testing based not only on the specifications of the web application but also on the HTML templates.

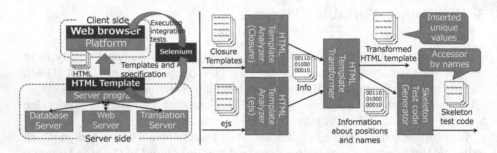

Fig. 2. Gray-box integration testing for the sample web application (left) and the architecture of POGen (right)

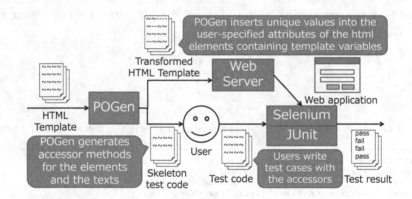

Fig. 3. Illustration of the role of POGen in gray-box integration testing

The left side of Figure 2 shows the relation between the sample web application and gray-box integration testing based on the HTML template. To help conduct gray-box integration testing, we developed a tool called POGen for analyzing HTML templates and generating skeleton test code with Selenium and JUnit. POGen extracts template variables which indicates the dynamic content and the operable HTML elements such as `<a>`, `<link>`, `<input>`, `<textarea>`, `<select>` and `<button>` elements. POGen also generates skeleton test code designed with the PageObject design pattern [5], which has high maintainability and contains accessor methods for the template variables and the operable HTML elements. POGen thus reduces the writing and maintenance costs.

The right side of Figure 2 shows the architecture of POGen. POGen consists of three components: the HTML template analyzer, the HTML template transformer and the test code generator. POGen generates accessor methods for HTML elements containing template variables and operable HTML elements. To increase maintainability, the methods depend not on the HTML structure but on the names of template variables and operable HTML elements. POGen transforms HTML templates for exposing HTML elements containing template variables and operable HTML elements for test purposes only.

Figure 3 shows the process of gray-box integration testing with POGen.

1. Testers feed the HTML template files to be tested into POGen.
2. POGen analyzes and transforms the HTML templates by inserting unique values into the specified attributes of the HTML elements containing template variables and the operable HTML elements.
3. POGen generates skeleton test code with accessor methods for the HTML elements by referring to the inserted attribute values.
4. Testers enhance the generated skeleton test code and write test cases.
5. The transformed HTML templates are deployed on the web server.
6. Gray-box integration testing is conducted by running the test cases.

4.1   HTML Template Analyzer

The POGen HTML template analyzer extracts the HTML elements by finding, naming and then analyzing the template variables and operable HTML elements. After these three steps, which are described below, the HTML template analyzer passes the positions of the template variables and the operable HTML elements into the HTML template transformer.

The HTML template analyzer first finds the template variables and the operable HTML elements by parsing the HTML template, and records positions. For the HTML template in List 1.1, the analyzer will find three operable elements of `<input>`. For the HTML template in List 1.2, the analyzer will find four template variables: {$left}, {$right}, {$answer}, and {$item}.

In the next step, the analyzer determines the names of the extracted template variables and the extracted operable HTML elements to generate accessor methods. The analyzer names the template variables with the texts of the template variables removing the head and tail sign characters and replacing the other sign characters with underscore characters '_'. The analyzer also names the operable HTML by concatenating the types of the HTML elements with the id attribute values, name attribute values or the texts. For the HTML template in List 1.1, the analyzer will name the first operable elements "INPUT_left". For the HTML template in List 1.2, the analyzer will name {$left} "left".

In the analyzing step, the analyzer determines if the extracted HTML elements appear in loop statements, such as for and foreach statements. Depending on whether the template variables are repeated or not, POGen generates accessor methods returning a list of HTML elements or a single HTML element, respectively. In List 1.2, {$item} is a repeated template variable.

POGen currently supports Closure Templates, ejs, erb and JSF. We can easily extend POGen by adding parsers for other template engines.

4.2   HTML Template Transformer

The HTML template transformer inserts unique values for user-specified attributes, such as id and class, into HTML elements containing template variables. This allows the generated accessor methods to depend on the names determined by the analyzer and not on the structure of the HTML document. If the targeted HTML element already contains a value for the specified attribute, then the transformer uses the existing value, either as is for attributes like id that only accept a single value, or by inserting another unique value into the existing value for attributes like class that accept space-separated values. Users can choose any attribute to be inserted by POGen to avoid changing a web application's behavior. In addition, the transformer inserts special HTML comments into the HTML template so that accessor methods can acquire text representations of the template variables.

List 1.4. An HTML template transformed by the POGen to generate accessor methods

```
1   {template .addition}
2     <!-- POGen,left,{$left} --><!-- POGen,right,{$right} -->
3     <p class="_pogen_1">{$left}+{$right}=
4       <!-- POGen,answer,{$answer} --><div class="_pogen_2">
5       {$answer}</div></p>
6     <ul>{call .items}{param list: $histories /}{/call}</ul> {/template}
7   {template .items}
8     {foreach $item in $list}
9       <!-- POGen:item:{$item} --><li class="item _pogen_3">{$item}</li>
10    {/foreach}
11  {/template}
```

The HTML template in List 1.2 with values of class attributes and HTML comments inserted by the transformer is shown in List 1.4. POGen backs up the original HTML templates before they are transformed.

4.3   Test Code Generator

The test code generator generates skeleton test code containing accessor methods for the extracted HTML elements. The test code is designed by the PageObjects design pattern with JUnit and Selenium. The names of the accessor methods consist of the texts, the types of the HTML elements and the attribute values. The accessor methods can be invoked using only the names determined by the analyzer. This makes the test code independent of the HTML structure.

The PageObjects design pattern modularizes test code in terms of page classes, allowing testers to write test cases as if writing in a natural language by treating page classes and their methods. The page class contains methods corresponding to features provided to the user by the web page, such as login and addition features, as well as fields indicating HTML elements and accessor methods for acquiring information on the page. The modularization improves the maintainability of test code by reducing the amount of necessary code modifications resulting from frequent updates to web applications. Web application updates commonly result in changes to the structure of HTML documents, which necessitates modifications in the operations of DOM trees in the methods of page classes. However, changes in web page features and information are rarely required. Therefore, modifications to test cases are rarely required.

For each web page, POGen generates page classes that have two accessor methods for each HTML element containing template variables. One accessor method returns the object indicating the HTML element. This method allows testers to write various operations for the HTML element by providing methods for simulating user manipulations from Selenium. The other accessor method returns the string representation of the template variable. POGen also generates an accessor method for each operable HTML element because the operable HTML elements are frequently referred in test code.

POGen requires users to enhance the generated skeleton test code by writing feature methods such as **login** and **add** methods. Users can write test cases after enhancing the page classes. The generated test code is distinguished from the user-written code by the comments GENERATED CODE START and GENERATED CODE END. When updating the test code to support changes in the web applications, only the generated test code is changed by POGen.

List 1.5. Skeleton test code generated by POGen for the result page template given in List 1.2 for the sample web application

```
1   public class ResultPage extends AbstractPage {
2     /* ------------------- GENERATED CODE START -------------------- */
3     @FindBy(className = "_pogen_1") private WebElement _left, _right;
4     @FindBy(className = "_pogen_2") private WebElement _answer;
5     @FindBy(className = "_pogen_3") private WebElement _item;
6     public WebElement getElementOfLeft () {/*abbrev.*/}
7     public WebElement getElementOfRight () {/*abbrev.*/}
8     public WebElement getElementOfAnswer () {/*abbrev.*/}
9     public List<WebElement> getElementsOfItem () {/*abbrev.*/}
10    public String getTextOfLeft () {/*abbrev.*/}
11    public String getTextOfRight () {/*abbrev.*/}
12    public String getTextOfAnswer () {/*abbrev.*/}
13    public List<String> getTextsOfItem() {/*abbrev.*/}
14    /* ------------------- GENERATED CODE END -------------------- */
15  }
```

List 1.5 shows the skeleton test code generated by POGen for the HTML template in List 1.4. The getElementOfLeft method returns the WebElement object indicating the <p> element containing {$left} by using the class attribute value _pogen_1. The WebElement object provides various operations such as sendKeys, which simulates keyboard inputs, and click, which simulates mouse clicks. The getTextOfLeft method returns the String object of {$left} by parsing the HTML comment (e.g. <!-- POGen,left,{$left} -->) inserted by POGen. The generated accessor methods are surrounded by GENERATED CODE

START and GENERATED CODE END so that these methods will be updated according to the changes made in the web applications.

List 1.6. Enhanced skeleton test code generated by POGen for the input page template given in List 1.1 for the sample web application

```
1  public class InputPage {
2    /* -------------------- GENERATED CODE START -------------------- */
3    // Abbreviate generated skeleton test code
4    /* -------------------- GENERATED CODE END -------------------- */
5    public ResultPage add(String left, String right) {
6      getElementOfINPUT_left().sendKeys(left);
7      getElementOfINPUT_right().sendKeys(right);
8      getElementOfINPUT_calc().submit();
9      return new ResultPage(driver);
10   }
11 }
```

List 1.7. A JUnit test case using the skeleton test code generated by POGen

```
1  public class ResultPageTest {
2    @Test public void add1And2() {
3      WebDriver driver = new ChromeDriver();
4      // some code to initialize the driver
5      ResultPage resultPage = new InputPage(driver).add(1, "two");
6      assertEquals(resultPage.getTextOfAnswer (), "3");
7    }
8  }
```

List 1.6 shows sample test code enhanced by testers to write test cases. List 1.7 shows a test case based on the generated test code in Lists 1.5 and 1.6. This add1And2 test case asks the web application to add "1" and "two". Then it determines whether the text representation of the template variable {$answer} equals the expected value of three. In summary, POGen reduces the writing and maintenance costs of test code by introducing the PageObjects design pattern, and by generating skeleton test code that contains accessor methods.

5   Evaluation

To assess the effectiveness of template variable coverage and POGen, we conducted a set of experiments and compared the results against conventional methods. Specifically, we investigated the following research questions:

- RQ1: Is template variable coverage correlated with a test's capability to detect faults?
- RQ2: How can our approach improve a test's capability to find faults?
- RQ3: How can our approach facilitate writing test code?
- RQ4: How can our approach facilitate maintaining test code?

Table 1. The subject web application for Experiment 1

Name	Pages	Test cases	LLOC of production code	LLOC of test code	Killed mutants	All mutants
booking	11	16	2282	634	58	248

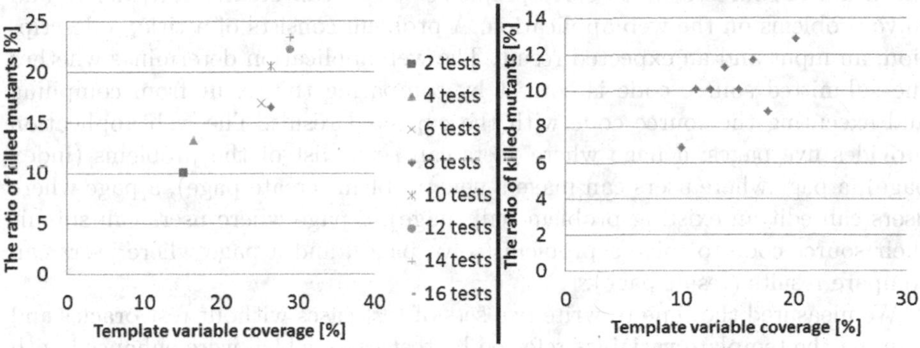

Fig. 4. The graphs which illustrates the correlation with the template variable coverage and the killed mutants for the subject web application with the different number of the test cases (left) and with the same number of the two test cases (right)

5.1 Experiment 1

To verify Assumption 1 and investigate RQ1, we measured template variable coverage and the number of killed mutants generated by SimpleJester for the subject web applications. Note that the mutation testing tools such as SimpleJester embed faults called mutants, and then measure the detected faults called killed mutants by executing the test with targeted test code. The subject web application was the Seam Framework example called booking (https://github.com/seam/examples). Table 1 shows its name, the number of pages and test cases, the logical lines of code (LLOC) of production code and test code, and the number of killed mutants and all of the mutants. To measure the correlation with the template variable coverage and the number of the killed mutants, we randomly reduced test cases.

Figure 1 shows two graphs, whose vertical axis represents the ratio of the killed mutants over all of the mutants, whose horizontal axis represents the template variable coverage and whose labels represent the number of the remaining test cases. Whereas the graph on the left side shows the correlation with the different number of the test cases, the graph on the right side shows the correlation with the same number of the two test cases. As the figure shows, the template coverage correlates highly with the killed mutants, or the capability to detect faults independently of the number of test cases. Therefore, we confirm *Assumption 1* is approved in this example.

5.2   Experiment 2

To investigate RQ2 and RQ3, we conducted an empirical experiment on an open source web application (`https://github.com/TakenokoChocoHolic/almond-choco`), such as that found on TopCoder, which provides online compiling and execution of source code to solve problems. Users can create, edit, delete and solve problems on the web application. A problem consists of a title, a description, an input and an expected result. The web application determines whether the submitted source code is correct by comparing the result from compiling and executing the source code with the expected result. The web application provides five pages: a page where users can see a list of the problems (index page), a page where users can make a new problem (create page), a page where users can edit an existing problem (edit page), a page where users can submit their source code to solve a problem (solve page), and a page where users can compare results (result page).

We measured the time to write two sets of test cases without test oracles and counted the template variables referred by test cases which were enhanced with test oracles within 20 minutes. We tested three bachelor's and three master's degree students studying computer science (S1, S2 c and S6).

Table 2. The results of times to write test cases except for test oracles and the number of template variables referred in test cases which are enhanced with test oracles within 20 minutes

A set of test cases	S1	S2	S3	S4	S5	S6	Average
Test cases 1	13 mins	10 mins	14 mins	-	-	-	12.3 mins
with POGen	9 vars	8 vars	7 vars	-	-	-	8 vars
Test cases 1	-	-	-	29 mins	52 mins	34 mins	38.3 mins
without POGen	-	-	-	4 vars	3 vars	5 vars	4 vars
Test cases 2	-	-	-	7 mins	13 mins	15 mins	8.3 mins
with POGen	-	-	-	5 vars	6 vars	8 vars	6.3 vars
Test cases 2	14 mins	36 mins	59 mins	-	-	-	36.3 mins
without POGen	4 vars	4 vars	3 vars	-	-	-	3.6 vars

This experiment consists of two steps: writing test cases without test oracles and writing test oracles to enhance written test cases within 20 minutes with or without POGen. In the first step, the examinees wrote two sets of test cases with the test specification written in natural language. The test cases 1 represent a set of three test cases: updating a problem, solving a problem correctly and wrongly with Python. The test cases 2 also represent a set of three test cases: creating a problem, deleting a problem and solving a problem correctly with Ruby. S1, S2 and S3 wrote the test cases 1 with POGen and then wrote the test cases 2 without POGen. On the other hand, S4, S5 and S6 wrote test cases 1 without POGen and then wrote the test cases 2 with POGen. In the next step, they wrote test oracles for each own test cases within 20 minutes in the same flow.

Table 2 shows the result of this experiment. As the table shows, POGen reduced the writing time of the test cases by approximately 66%. Moreover, the template variables referred by the enhanced test cases with POGen are more than ones without POGen. POGen helps testers to write test code which observes more template variables to detect more faults. Therefore, POGen can reduce costs of writing test code and improve the template variable coverages.

5.3   Experiment 3

Table 3. The LLOC values of skeleton test code generated by POGen, actually used test code in manually written test code and manually written test code for the web application in Experiment 2

	Index	Create	Edit	Solve	Result	Test cases	Sum
Actually used	82	47	88	44	43	0	304
(Generated by POGen)	(164)	(54)	(164)	(65)	(49)	(0)	(496)
Manually written	12	7	13	6	0	105	143

Table 3 shows LLOC values for the whole POGen-generated skeleton test code, for the actually used section of the generated skeleton test code and for a manually written test code for the web application in Experiment 2. There are six LLOC values for page classes and test cases using page classes and the sum in Table 3. The test code contains six test cases for creating problems, editing problems, submitting a source code with Python and Ruby correctly and submitting a source code with Python wrongly.

As the table shows, POGen reduced the writing cost of test cases by generating page classes with accessor methods for HTML elements containing template variables and for operable HTML elements. Through POGen, the testers were able to access HTML elements using only the names of the template variables or the operable HTML elements, without any knowledge of the XPath or CSS selector. POGen successfully reduced the LLOC by about 68% in this experiment.

5.4   Experiment 4

To evaluate the reduction of maintenance cost and investigate RQ4, we changed the design of the web application in Experiment 3 to modify the DOM structure. POGen makes manual changes to the test code unnecessary because the accessor methods depend on the names of template variables and not on the structure of the HTML document.

List 1.8. HTML templates of the result page with ejs before and after changing the design of the web application

```
1  <!-- Before changing the HTML template of the result page -->
2  <div><%= result %></div><br />
3  actual = [<span><%= out %></span>]<br />
4  expect = [<span><%= ex %></span>]
5  <!-- After changing the HTML template of the result page-->
6  <p> Your answer is <b><%= result %></b>!  </p>
7  <p> Your program's ouput is [<span><%= out %></span>].  </p>
8  <p> Then, our expected ouput is [<span><%= out %></span>].  </p>
```

List 1.8 shows the HTML template of the result page with ejs before (top) and after (bottom) changing the design of the web application. The generated skeleton test code provided the accessor methods with the same signatures. For example, the `getTextOfResult` method returned the string representation of the template variable result both before and after the change. If the names of the template variables are changed, then the test code must be changed manually due to changes in the names of the generated accessor methods. As we investigated web applications in a company, template variable name changes, however, occurred much less than structural changes to HTML documents. Roest et al. also [6] claim XPath for selecting DOM elements causes fragile tests. Therefore, POGen reduce maintainance costs by improving maintainability of test code.

6 Limitations

Dependency on template engines: Our technique cannot elucidate the dynamic components which are created using web frameworks or DOM API without template engines. However, many web frameworks such as Struts and Ruby on Rails have template engines, and developers typically use template engines.

Regeneration of accessor methods for template variables: When a template variable occurs more than once in an HTML template, POGen names the corresponding accessor methods differently with sequential numbers. Therefore, the names of accessor methods are changed when the same template variables are added into or removed from the HTML template, and the test code must be changed manually.

Assessing input values for testing: Template variable coverage cannot assess input values themselves. For example, template variable coverage does not change when the value "2" is used instead of "two" for {$right}. However, this limitation are common in structural test coverage criteria.

7 Related Works

Staats et al. [7] claim that one should not only refer to the test coverage but also to the test oracles when discussing test quality. Schuler et al. [8] propose a new coverage criterion called checked statement coverage, which enhances existing statement coverage for white-box testing in terms of test oracle quality.

Template variable coverage also considers both test coverage and test oracles, and therefore, our technique can enhance test quality for web applications.

Kodaka et al. [9] provide a tool for determining if the dynamic text generated by JSP is equal to the text expected by users. In contrast, POGen generates accessor methods for both HTML elements and texts containing template variables. Thus, our technique can test web applications with greater flexibly.

Mesbah et al. [10] propose a new technique for testing web applications with invariants and their crawler which supports AJAX user interfaces. Roest et al. also [6] propose a new technique for extracting patterns for invariants from dynamic contents such as tables and lists. Whereas their approaches generates invariants, which are independent on test scenarios, our approach generates accessors for template variables, which are dependent on test scenarios.

There are many researches of model based testing for web applications and GUI applications such as [11], [12] and [13]. Their approach only generate test scenarios without test oracles and cannot treat the web pages which do not appear in models. POGen, on the other hand, helps testers to write test code including test oracles. Thus, our technique can work well with conventional methods and conduct test web applications flexibly and reasonably.

8 Summary and Future Works

In this paper, we elucidated the problems in existing testing methods through motivating examples. We proposed a novel coverage criterion called template variable coverage, as well as a novel technique to improve the template variable coverage with a tool called POGen. POGen generates skeleton test code, which includes accessor methods for the dynamic components of web applications, by analyzing HTML templates. Moreover, we evaluated the effectiveness of the template variable coverage and POGen in empirical experiments.

In the future, we will evaluate our approach and template variable coverage for real-world web applications with the mutation testing tools specific to web applications. We will also propose a new set of coverage criteria based on existing coverage criteria, which will target branches in HTML templates and production code on the server side to evaluate test quality from various viewpoints.

References

1. Choudhary, S.R., Prasad, M.R., Orso, A.: CrossCheck: Combining Crawling and Differencing to Better Detect Cross-browser Incompatibilities in Web Applications. In: Proceedings of the 2012 IEEE Fifth International Conference on Software Testing, Verification and Validation (ICST 2012), pp. 171–180 (2012)
2. Jupiter Consulting: EJS - JavaScript Templates, http://embeddedjs.com/.
3. Oracle: JavaServer Faces, http://www.oracle.com/technetwork/java/javaee/javaserverfaces-139869.html
4. Google: Closure Tools – Google Developers, https://developers.google.com/closure/templates/

5. Simon Stewart PageObjects,
   http://code.google.com/p/selenium/wiki/PageObjects
6. Roest, D., Mesbah, A., van Deursen, A.: Regression Testing Ajax Applications: Coping with Dynamism. In: Proceedings of the Third International Conference on Software Testing, Verification and Validation, pp. 127–136 (2010)
7. Staats, M., Whalen, M.W., Heimdahl, M.P.E.: Programs, tests, and oracles: the foundations of testing revisited. In: Proceedings of the 33rd International Conference on Software Engineering (ICSE 2011), pp. 391–400 (2011)
8. Schuler, D., Zeller, A.: Assessing Oracle Quality with Checked Coverage. In: Proceedings of the 2011 Fourth IEEE International Conference on Software Testing, Verification and Validation (ICST 2011), pp. 90–99 (2011)
9. Kodaka, T., Uehara, T., Katayama, A., Yamamoto, R.: Automated testing for Web applications using Aspect-oriented technology. IPSJ SIG Notes 2007(33), 97–104 (2007)
10. Mesbah, A., van Deursen, A.: Invariant-based automatic testing of AJAX user interfaces. In: Proceedings of the 31st International Conference on Software Engineering (ICSE 2009), pp. 210–220 (2009)
11. Andrews, A.A., Offutt, J., Alexander, R.T.: Testing Web applications by modeling with FSMs. In: Software and System Modeling, pp. 326–345 (2005)
12. Sprenkle, S., Cobb, C., Pollock, L.: Leveraging User-Privilege Classification to Customize Usage-based Statistical Models of Web Applications. In: Proceedings of the 2012 IEEE Fifth International Conference on Software Testing, Verification and Validation (ICST 2012), pp. 161–170 (2012)
13. Mariani, L.: AutoBlackTest: Automatic Black-Box Testing of Interactive Applications. In: Proceedings of the 2012 IEEE Fifth International Conference on Software Testing, Verification and Validation (ICST 2012), pp. 81–90 (2012)

Testing with Inputs and Outputs in CSP

Ana Cavalcanti[1] and Robert M. Hierons[2]

[1] University of York, UK
[2] Brunel University, UK

Abstract. This paper addresses refinement and testing based on CSP models, when we distinguish input and output events. From a testing perspective, there is an asymmetry: the tester (or the environment) controls the inputs, and the system under test controls the outputs. The standard models and refinement relations of CSP are, therefore, not entirely suitable for testing. Here, we adapt the CSP stable-failures model, resulting in the notion of input-output failures refinement. We compare that with the **ioco** relation often used in testing.Finally, we adapt the CSP testing theory, and show that some tests become unnecessary.

1   Introduction

As a process algebra, CSP [20] is a well established notation, with robust semantics and tools; it has been in use for more than twenty years. The availability of a powerful model checker has ensured the acceptance of CSP both in academia and industry. In the public domain, we have reports on applications in hardware and e-commerce [1,10]. In addition, CSP has been combined with data modelling languages to cope with state-rich reactive systems [8,16,22,7,18].

Admittedly, model-based testing is not a traditional area of application for CSP. It remains the case, however, that when a CSP model is available, the possibility of using it for testing is attractive, especially in industry. In fact, a testing theory is available for CSP [4], and more recently, the use of CSP as part of testing techniques has been explored by a variety of researchers [15,21,5].

A difficulty, however, is the fact that CSP models do not distinguish between input and output events: they are all synchronisations. In testing, though, there is an asymmetry: the system under test (SUT) controls outputs, while the tester controls inputs. In this paper, we follow a suggestion in [19] to define a stable-failures model parameterised by sets $\mathcal{I}$ and $\mathcal{O}$ of input and output events. We call it the input-output failures model, and define input-output failures refinement.

The stable-failures model is a suitable starting point for our work because, as usual in testing, we assume that both models and systems are divergence free. In models, divergence is regarded as a mistake, and when testing an SUT, a divergence cannot be distinguished from a deadlock. On the other hand, we cater for nondeterminism in the model and in the SUT; for that, we consider failures and failures refinement, since the traces model does not capture nondeterminism.

In the software testing community, there has been much interest in input-output labelled transition systems (IOLTSs) [2], and it is typically assumed that

V. Cortellessa and D. Varró (Eds.): FASE 2013, LNCS 7793, pp. 359–374, 2013.

it is possible to observe quiescence, a state in which all enabled events are inputs and it is not possible to take an internal transition. Most approaches use the **ioco** implementation relation [23]; observations are traces that include inputs, outputs, and quiescence, the only type of refusal that can be observed.

For CSP, we define that, in the presence of inputs and outputs, a state is stable if it is not divergent, that is, stable according to the standard model, and no output is enabled. These are quiescent states, but we can observe the inputs that are enabled: models need not be input enabled. This means that a stable state in CSP is not necessarily a quiescent state in the sense adopted in IOLTS: in the standard stable-failures model, there is no notion of input, and here we do not enforce input-enabledness. We show that **ioco** and input-output failures refinement are incomparable: there are processes P and Q such that P conforms to Q under **ioco** but not under input-output failures refinement, and vice-versa. For input-enabled processes, however, **ioco** is stronger.

Other lines of work are related to ours in that they investigated refusals for inputs [11,3,2]. These, however, allow refusals to be observed in states from which an output is possible. The traditional explanation regarding the observation of a refusal set R is that, if the tester offers only events of R, we observe a refusal if the composition of the tester and the SUT deadlocks. Usually a tester does not block outputs from the SUT and so the composition of the SUT and the tester cannot deadlock if an output is available. As a result, we do not consider a state to be stable if an output is possible (since the SUT can change state) and so do not allow the observation of refusals in such states.

The testing theory of CSP identifies (typically infinite) test sets that are sufficient and necessary to establish (traces or failures) refinement with respect to a given CSP specification. To take advantage of knowledge about inputs and outputs, here we adapt that theory for input-output failures refinement.

In summary, we make the following contributions. First, we define input-output failures, and show how they can be calculated. The existing failures model of CSP does not cater for inputs and outputs. We also define input-output failures refinement and prove that it is incomparable with **ioco**. This relates our results to the extensive body of work on testing based on IOLTS. To obtain a refinement relation that is stronger than **ioco**, we need to use the refusal-testing model of CSP; we are exploring this issue in our current work. Finally, we adapt the CSP testing theory to input-output failures refinement, and show that some tests in the exhaustive test set for failures refinement become unnecessary.

Next, we present CSP and IOLTS. In Section 3, we present the new CSP model that considers inputs and outputs, and its refinement notion. Section 4 discusses the relationship between input-output failures refinement and **ioco**. Testing is addressed in Section 5. We conclude in Section 6.

2   Preliminaries

This section presents the notations and concepts that we use in this paper.

2.1   CSP and Its Stable-Failures Model

In CSP, the set Σ includes all events of interest. In addition, a special event $\checkmark$ is used to indicate termination, and is included in the set $\Sigma^{\checkmark} = \Sigma \cup \{\checkmark\}$. Inputs and outputs are not distinguished in Σ, and none of the CSP models caters for this distinction in controllability. We address this issue in Section 3.

The process $STOP$ represents a deadlock: a process that is not prepared to engage in any synchronisation; its only trace is the empty sequence $\langle\rangle$ of events. $SKIP$, on the other hand, terminates without engaging in any event: its traces are $\langle\rangle$ and $\langle\checkmark\rangle$. A prefixing $c \rightarrow P$ is ready to engage in a communication c, and then behave like the process P. A communication may be a simple event on which the process is prepared to synchronise, an input, or an output.

An external choice $P \square Q$ offers the environment the possibility of choosing P or Q by synchronising on one of the events that they offer initially. For instance, $out.1 \rightarrow SKIP \square out.2 \rightarrow STOP$ offers the choice to synchronise on $out.1$ (and then terminate) or $out.2$ (and deadlock). If an event is available from both P and Q, then the choice is internal: made by the process. In general $P \sqcap Q$ is the process that makes itself an internal choice to behave as P or Q.

An input communication is like $in?x$, for instance, in which a value is read through a channel in and assigned to the variable x. Also, an output $out!e$ communicates the value of the expression e through the channel out. In CSP, however, these are just modelling conventions that use events whose names are composed of a channel name and a value. For example, if the type of the channel in is T, then $in?x \rightarrow STOP$ is an abbreviation for an iterated external choice $\square\, v : T \bullet in.v \rightarrow STOP$, where the environment is offered a choice to synchronise on any of the events $in.v$, where v is a value in T. Additionally, the output $out!1$ is just an abbreviation for the synchronisation $out.1$.

Parallelism can be described by the operator $P \,[\![\, X \,]\!]\, Q$, where P and Q are executed in parallel, synchronising on the events in the set X. For instance, in $(in?x \rightarrow out!x \rightarrow SKIP) \,[\![\, \{\!|in|\!\} \,]\!]\, (in!3 \rightarrow STOP)$, the processes synchronise on $in.3$, then $in?x \rightarrow out!x \rightarrow SKIP$ independently offers to synchronise on $out.3$, and terminates. Since $in!3 \rightarrow STOP$ deadlocks, the whole process deadlocks. The set $\{\!|in|\!\}$ contains all events $in.v$, where v is a value of the type of in.

The events on which the parallel processes synchronise are visible to the environment. To make them internal, we have the hiding operator: $P \setminus X$ is the process that behaves like P, except that occurrences of events in X are hidden.

If R is a renaming relation, that associates (old) event names to new names, the process $P[\![R]\!]$ is that obtained by renaming the events in P according to R. If an event e is related to two (or more) events in R, then every occurrence of e in P gives rise to an external choice in $P[\![R]\!]$ based on the new events.

Stable failures. This semantic model of CSP characterises a process P by its set $traces(P)$ of traces and $failures(P)$ of stable failures. The latter are pairs (s, X), where s is a trace of P, after which P does not diverge, but may deadlock if only the events in the refusal set X are offered. This model distinguishes external and internal choices (which define the same sets of traces) and can be used to reason about liveness properties (which are related to absence of deadlock).

Failures refinement $P \sqsubseteq_F Q$ of a process P by a process Q is defined as $traces(Q) \subseteq traces(P) \wedge failures(Q) \subseteq failures(P)$. So, the refined process Q can only engage in sequences of synchronisations (traces) that are possible for P, and can only deadlock when P can. Traces refinement $P \sqsubseteq_T Q$ requires only traces inclusion. It is not difficult to show that failures refinement can also be characterised as the conjunction of traces refinement and **conf**, a conformance relation used by the testing community [4]. It is defined as follows.

$$Q \text{ conf } P \cong \forall t : traces(P) \cap traces(Q) \bullet Ref(Q, t) \subseteq Ref(P, t)$$
$$\text{where } Ref(P, t) \cong \{ X \mid (t, X) \in failures(P) \}$$

This is concerned only with traces allowed by both P and Q, but requires that after those, Q can deadlock only if P can.

2.2   CSP Testing Theory

A testing theory identifies testability hypotheses, notions of test and test experiment, the verdict of an experiment, and an exhaustive test set.

First of all, to reason formally about testing it is necessary to discuss formal models and thus to assume that the SUT behaves like an unknown model described using a given formalism. This is often called the *minimum hypothesis* [9]. The formalism is usually the language used for specifications. Both in [4] and here, it is assumed that the SUT behaves like an unknown CSP process.

Secondly, nondeterminism in the SUT can cause problems since whether a test leads to a failure being observed or not might depend on how nondeterminism is resolved. The standard testability hypothesis used to overcome this is that there is some known k such that the application of a test T a total of k times is guaranteed to lead to all possible responses of the SUT to T. The implications of this for testing from CSP specifications have been discussed [4].

An exhaustive test set is a (potentially infinite) set of tests that are necessary and sufficient to establish conformance with respect to a given relation [9]. The CSP testing theory identifies exhaustive test sets for traces refinement and **conf**.

Given a (specification) process P, for traces refinement, the CSP testing theory considers tests for pairs (s, a) such that s is a trace of P, but $s \frown \langle a \rangle$ is not. Given such a pair (s, a) we obtain $T_T(s, a)$ defined as follows [4].

$$T_T(\langle\rangle, a) = T_T(\langle\checkmark\rangle, a) = pass \to a \to fail \to STOP$$
$$T_T(\langle b \rangle \frown s, a) = inc \to b \to T_T(s, a)$$

We use verdict events *inc*, *pass*, and *fail*; the last of these events observed before a deadlock indicates the outcome of the test. If the trace s cannot be followed, we have an *inconclusive* verdict. If s is executed, then we have a *pass*, but if after that the forbidden event a occurs, then we have a *failure*.

Execution $Execution_Q^P(T)$ of a test T for an SUT Q is described by the process $(Q \, [\![\, \alpha P \,]\!] \, T) \backslash \alpha P$. In words, the processes Q and T are executed in parallel, synchronising on the set of events αP used in the specification, which are hidden. The set $\alpha P \subseteq \Sigma$ contains all events that P might use; its definition is a modelling decision. If the events of αP were visible, that is, not hidden, then the environment could potentially interfere with the test execution. By hiding them, we specify that they happen as soon as possible, that is, as soon as available in Q. The verdict events establish the outcome of the test execution.

Example 1. For the specification $Rep = in?x \rightarrow out!x \rightarrow Rep$, and for the empty trace, and forbidden continuation $out.0$, we have $pass \rightarrow out.0 \rightarrow fail \rightarrow STOP$ as a test for traces refinement. Similar tests arise for all output events $out.x$. With the trace $\langle in.0 \rangle$, we choose the value 0 to provide as input and have a test $inc \rightarrow in.0 \rightarrow pass \rightarrow out.1 \rightarrow fail \rightarrow STOP$.   □

Example 2. A very simple traffic light controller that can be terminated at any point using an event end can be specified as follows.

$$Lights = red \rightarrow (amber \rightarrow (green \rightarrow Lights \,\Box\, end \rightarrow SKIP) \,\Box\, end \rightarrow SKIP)$$
$$\Box$$
$$end \rightarrow SKIP$$

Some of its tests for traces refinement are $pass \rightarrow amber \rightarrow fail \rightarrow STOP$ and $inc \rightarrow red \rightarrow inc \rightarrow amber \rightarrow inc \rightarrow green \rightarrow pass \rightarrow green \rightarrow fail \rightarrow STOP$. □

Using T_T, we obtain the following exhaustive test for traces refinement [4].

$$Exhaust_T(P) = \{ T_T(s, a) \mid s \in traces(P) \land a \notin initials(P/s) \}$$

The process P/s characterises the behaviour of P after engaging in the trace s, and $initials(P)$ gives the set of events initially available for interaction with P.

As defined above, Q **conf** P requires checking that after a trace of both P and Q, the refusals of Q are refusals of P as well. For that, we check that after a trace of P, Q cannot refuse all events in a minimal acceptance set A of P. An acceptance set A is such that (s, A) is not a failure of P; it is minimal if it has no acceptance set as a proper subset. Formally, testing for **conf** is performed by proposing to Q the traces s in $traces(P)$, and then an external choice over the events a in a minimal acceptance set of P. For a trace s and a (minimal) acceptance set A, the test process $T_F(s, A)$ is defined as follows.

$$T_F(\langle \rangle, A) = fail \rightarrow (\Box\, a \in A \bullet a \rightarrow pass \rightarrow STOP)$$
$$T_F(\langle a \rangle \frown s, A) = inc \rightarrow a \rightarrow T_F(s, A)$$

As for traces-refinement tests, the last event before a deadlock gives the verdict.

The exhaustive test set for conformance to P is shown below; it contains all $T_F(s, A)$ formed from traces $s \in traces(P)$, and minimal acceptance sets A [4].

$$Exhaust_{conf}(P) = \{ T_F(s, A) \mid s \in traces(P) \land A \in \mathcal{A}_s \}$$

The set $\mathcal{A}_s = min_{\subseteq}(\{ A \mid (s, A) \notin failures(P) \})$ contains the minimal acceptances after s. As already indicated, for failures refinement, the exhaustive test set is $Exhaust_T(P) \cup Exhaust_{conf}(P)$, covering traces refinement and **conf**.

2.3 Input-Output Labelled Transition Systems

An input-output labelled transition system (IOLTS) is a labelled transition system in which we distinguish between inputs and outputs. IOLTSs have received much attention in the software testing literature, due to the asymmetry between input and outputs in testing. Formally, IOLTSs can be defined as follows.

Definition 1. *An input-output labelled transition system is defined by a tuple* $P = (\mathcal{P}, \mathcal{I}, \mathcal{O}, \mathcal{T}, p_{in})$ *in which* $\mathcal{P}$ *is a countable set of states,* $p_{in} \in \mathcal{P}$ *is the initial state,* $\mathcal{I}$ *is a countable set of inputs,* $\mathcal{O}$ *is a countable set of outputs, and* $\mathcal{T} \subseteq \mathcal{P} \times (\mathcal{I} \cup \mathcal{O} \cup \{\tau\}) \times \mathcal{P}$*, where* τ *represents an internal action, is the transition relation. The sets* $\mathcal{I}$ *and* $\mathcal{O}$ *are required to be disjoint and* $\tau \notin \mathcal{I} \cup \mathcal{O}$*. A transition* (p, a, p') *means that from* p *it is possible to move to* p' *with action* $a \in \mathcal{I} \cup \mathcal{O} \cup \{\tau\}$*. A state* $p \in \mathcal{P}$ *is quiescent if all transitions from* p *are labelled with inputs. We represent quiescence by* δ *and extend* $\mathcal{T}$ *by adding the transition* (p, δ, p) *for each quiescent* p*, calling the resulting relation* $\mathcal{T}_\delta$*. Further, P is input enabled if for all* $p \in \mathcal{P}$ *and* $?i \in \mathcal{I}$ *there is some* $p' \in \mathcal{P}$ *such that* $(p, ?i, p') \in \mathcal{T}$*.*

A sequence $s = a_1, \ldots, a_n \in (\mathcal{I} \cup \mathcal{O} \cup \{\delta\})^*$ of actions is a trace of P if there exists a sequence $(p_1, a_1, p_2), (p_3, a_2, p_4), \ldots, (p_n, a_n, p_{n+1})$ of transitions in $\mathcal{T}_\delta$ such that P can move from p_{in} to p_1 through a sequence of internal transitions (those with action τ) and for all $1' \le i \le n$ it is possible to move from p_{2i} to p_{2i+1} through internal transitions. Given an IOLTS P, we let $tr^{\mathbf{io}}(P)$ denote the set of traces of P. Roughly speaking, an IOLTS action corresponds to a CSP event, except that δ is not a CSP event, and $\checkmark$ is not an action in IOLTSs.

3 Failures with Inputs and Outputs

The traces of a process P are not affected by the controllability of the events. Therefore, the distinction between inputs and outputs does not affect the trace model of CSP. Controllability, however, affects the notion of failures.

We define the input-output stable failures $IOfailures^{(\mathcal{I}, \mathcal{O})}(P)$ of a process in a context where the disjoint sets $\mathcal{I}$ and $\mathcal{O}$ of events identify the inputs and the outputs. Synchronisation events, which do require agreement from the environment, are regarded as inputs. Stability here is characterised by the unavailability of outputs (as well as internal events). A process that is ready to output is not in a stable state because we assume that outputs are under the sole control of the process: they do not require synchronisation, and therefore cannot be refused by the environment. A process that can output can, therefore, choose to output and evolve to a new state before considering any interaction with the environment.

It is our assumption that the SUT need not be input enabled, but we implicitly require the environment to be input enabled, since it cannot block outputs from the SUT. It is clear that many systems are not input enabled since, for example, they provide interfaces where certain fields or buttons may not be available depending on the state. (Such an SUT might be regarded as input enabled if we consider inputs at the level of events such as mouse clicks, but this level of abstraction is rarely suitable for modelling.) Such an SUT normally does not provide the user with the option to refuse outputs, since it controls the user interface: to block outputs the user has to close down the interface, a process that may send an input to the SUT in any case.

Our definition of $IOfailures^{(\mathcal{I},\mathcal{O})}(P)$ in terms of the set $failures(P)$ of failures of P is as follows. (This definition is similar to that of a hiding $P \setminus \mathcal{O}$, but the output events are not removed from the trace.)

Definition 2. $IOfailures^{(\mathcal{I},\mathcal{O})}(P) = \{ (s, X) \mid (s, X \cup \mathcal{O}) \in failures(P) \}$

As already said, the stable states are those in which the output events are not available: those in which P can refuse all of them. They are characterised by a failure $(s, X \cup \mathcal{O})$. For each of them, we keep in $IOfailures^{(\mathcal{I},\mathcal{O})}(P)$ the failure (s, X). Since refusals are downward closed, (s, X) is also a failure of P. By considering just the failures for which $(s, X \cup \mathcal{O}) \in failures(P)$, we keep in $IOfailures^{(\mathcal{I},\mathcal{O})}(P)$ just the failures of P in its stable states. For every process P and disjoint sets $\mathcal{I}$ and $\mathcal{O}$, the pair $(traces(P), IOfailures^{(\mathcal{I},\mathcal{O})}(P))$ satisfies all the healthiness conditions of the stable-failures model [20]. Proof of this and all other results presented here can be found in an extended version of this paper [6].

Example 3. We present the input-output failures of the process $E3$ below, in the context indicated in its definition; the events corresponding to communications over the channels inA and inB are inputs, and those over $outA$ and $outB$ are outputs. We have inputs in choice and an input in choice with an output.

$$E3 = \left(inA?x \to STOP \,\square\, inB?x \to \left(\begin{array}{l} inA?x \to outA!1 \to STOP \\ \square \\ outB!1 \to outA!1 \to STOP \end{array} \right) \right)$$

For conciseness, we omit below the parameter $(\{\!| inA, inB |\!\}, \{\!| outA, outB |\!\})$ of $IOfailures$. Also, if the value x communicated in an event $c.x$ does not matter, we write $c?x$ in failures. For example, $(\langle inA?x \rangle, \{\!| inA, inB, outA, outB, \checkmark |\!\})$ represents a set of failures: one for each of the possible values of x in $inA.x$.

$$\begin{aligned} IOfailures(E3) = \{ &(\langle\rangle, \{\!| outA, outB, \checkmark |\!\}), \ldots \\ &(\langle inA?x \rangle, \{\!| inA, inB, outA, outB, \checkmark |\!\}), \ldots, \\ &(\langle inB?x, inA?x, outA.1 \rangle, \{\!| inA, inB, outA, outB, \checkmark |\!\}), \ldots, \\ &(\langle inB?x, outB.1, outA.1 \rangle, \{\!| inA, inB, outA, outB, \checkmark |\!\}), \ldots \} \end{aligned}$$

In the above description, we omit the failures that are obviously included due to downward closure of refusals. For instance, the empty trace $\langle\rangle$ is paired with all subsets of $\{\!| outA, outB, \checkmark |\!\}$ in $IOfailures(E3)$. We observe, however, that there are no failures for traces $\langle inB?x \rangle$ or for traces $\langle inB?x, inA?x \rangle$ and $\langle inB?x, outB.1 \rangle$, for any values of x. This is because, after each of them, an output is available. So, the states after these traces are not stable.   □

Example 4. For outputs in choice, we have the example below.

$$E4 = out!0 \to inA?x \to STOP \,\square\, out!1 \to inB?x \to STOP$$

$$IOfailures(E4) = \{ (\langle out.0 \rangle, \{ out, inB, \checkmark \}), \ldots, (\langle out.1 \rangle, \{ out, inA, \checkmark \}), \ldots,$$
$$(\langle out.0, inA?x \rangle, \{ out, inA, inB, \checkmark \}), \ldots,$$
$$(\langle out.1, inB?x \rangle, \{ out, inB, inB, \checkmark \}), \ldots \}$$

There are no failures for $\langle \rangle$, since outputs are immediately available.   □

Input-output failures cannot distinguish between internal and external choice of outputs. In the example above, for instance, the failures would not change if we had an internal choice. This reflects the fact that, in reality, the environment cannot interfere with outputs. As shown by the next example, however, input-output failures can distinguish internal and external choice in other situations.

Example 5. We have a nondeterministic choice between an input and an output.

$$E5 = inp?x \rightarrow STOP \sqcap out!1 \rightarrow STOP$$

Corresponding to the possibility of the (internal) choice of $inp?x \rightarrow STOP$, we have failures for $\langle \rangle$. They indicate that an input cannot be refused in this case.

$$IOfailures(E5) = \{ (\langle \rangle, \{ out, \checkmark \}), \ldots,$$
$$(\langle inp?x \rangle, \{ inp, out, \checkmark \}), \ldots, (\langle out.1, \rangle, \{ inp, out, \checkmark \}), \ldots \}$$

If we were to use an external choice in $E5$, then its initial state would be unstable, as $out.1$ would be possible, and there would be no failure for $\langle \rangle$.   □

Calculating input-output failures. As illustrated, not all traces are included in an input-output failure. This is also the case in the standard stable-failures model, where missing traces are those that lead to a divergent state. Here, missing traces lead to a state where either divergence or an output is possible.

Using Definition 2, we can calculate characterisations of input-output failures for the various CSP processes. A summary is provided in Table 1; proof of all these results is provided in [6]. To allow us to consider $IOfailures^{(\mathcal{I},\mathcal{O})}(P)$ as characterising a semantics for CSP processes P with inputs and outputs, we need to define some well formedness rules. First, as already indicated, the sets $\mathcal{I}$ and $\mathcal{O}$ of inputs and outputs must form a partition of Σ.

Second, in a parallelism $P \llbracket X \rrbracket Q$, the processes P and Q must have the same inputs and outputs $\mathcal{I}$ and $\mathcal{O}$, and X can only contain inputs ($X \subseteq \mathcal{I}$). If X contains an output, unstable states of P and Q in which outputs are available may become deadlocked, and so stable, if P and Q cannot agree on the output. This is a strong restriction, but we observe that it is necessary only for the compositional calculation of input-output failures (and consequently for the use of $IOfailures^{(\mathcal{I},\mathcal{O})}(P)$ as a semantic function). It is always possible to use Definition 2 to calculate input-output failures directly.

Third, for renaming, we require that the controllability of events is not changed: renamed inputs are still inputs, and similarly, renamed outputs are still outputs. In this way, given the sets $\mathcal{I}$ and $\mathcal{O}$ of inputs and outputs of $P\llbracket R \rrbracket$, we characterise its input-output failures in terms of those for P when its input and outputs are the relational images of $\mathcal{I}$ and $\mathcal{O}$ under R^{-1}, the inverse of R.

Table 1. $IOfailures^{(\mathcal{I},\mathcal{O})}(P)$ semantics

Process P	$IOfailures^{(\mathcal{I},\mathcal{O})}(P)$
$STOP$	$\{(\langle\rangle, X) \mid X \subseteq \Sigma^{\checkmark}\}$
$SKIP$	$\{(\langle\rangle, X) \mid X \subseteq \Sigma\} \cup \{(\langle\checkmark\rangle, X) \mid X \subseteq \Sigma^{\checkmark}\}$
$a \to P$	$\{(\langle\rangle, X) \mid a \notin \mathcal{O} \wedge a \notin X\} \cup \{(\langle a\rangle \frown s, X) \mid (s, X) \in IOfailures^{(\mathcal{I},\mathcal{O})}(P)\}$
$P \sqcap Q$	$IOfailures^{(\mathcal{I},\mathcal{O})}(P) \cup IOfailures^{(\mathcal{I},\mathcal{O})}(Q)$
$P \square Q$	$\{(\langle\rangle, X) \mid (\langle\rangle, X) \in IOfailures^{(\mathcal{I},\mathcal{O})}(P) \cap IOfailures^{(\mathcal{I},\mathcal{O})}(Q)\} \cup$
	$\{(s, X) \mid (s, X) \in IOfailures^{(\mathcal{I},\mathcal{O})}(P) \cup IOfailures^{(\mathcal{I},\mathcal{O})}(Q) \wedge s \neq \langle\rangle\} \cup$
	$\{(\langle\rangle, X) \mid X \subseteq \Sigma \wedge \langle\checkmark\rangle \in traces(P) \cup traces(Q)\}$
$P \llbracket X \rrbracket Q$	$\{(u, R) \mid \exists\, Y, Z \bullet$
	$\quad Y \cup Z \cup \mathcal{O} = R \cup \mathcal{O} \wedge (Y \setminus (X \cup \{\checkmark\})) \cup \mathcal{O} = (Z \setminus (X \cup \{\checkmark\})) \cup \mathcal{O} \wedge$
	$\quad \exists\, s, t \bullet (s, Y) \in IOfailures^{(\mathcal{I},\mathcal{O})}(P) \wedge (t, Z) \in IOfailures^{(\mathcal{I},\mathcal{O})}(Q) \wedge$
	$\quad u \in s \llbracket X \rrbracket t\}$
$P \setminus X$	$\{(s \setminus X, Y) \mid (s, Y \cup X) \in IOfailures^{(\mathcal{I},\mathcal{O})}(P)\}$
$P; Q$	$\{(s, X) \mid s \in \Sigma^* \wedge (s, X \cup \mathcal{O} \cup \{\checkmark\}) \in IOfailures^{(\mathcal{I},\mathcal{O})}(P)\} \cup$
	$\{(t \frown u, X) \mid t \frown \langle\checkmark\rangle \in traces(P) \wedge (u, X) \in IOfailures^{(\mathcal{I},\mathcal{O})}(Q)\}$
$P\llbracket R \rrbracket$	$\{(s', X) \mid \exists\, s\ R\ s' \wedge (s, R^{-1}(X)) \in IOfailures^{(R^{-1}(\mathcal{I}), R^{-1}(\mathcal{O}))}(P)\}$

The input-output failures of $STOP$ and $SKIP$ are the same as their standard failures. For $a \to P$, the characterisation is slightly different. Before a takes place, it cannot be refused, but this is a stable state only if a is not an output. So, we only include failures for $\langle\rangle$ if a is not an output. For internal and external choices, parallelism, hiding and sequence, input-output failures can be calculated in much the same way as standard failures. In the definition of $IOfailures^{(\mathcal{I},\mathcal{O})}(P\llbracket R \rrbracket)$, we write $R^{-1}(X)$ for the relational image of the set X under R.

Input-output failures refinement. Having introduced a new notion of failure, we can now introduce the corresponding definition of refinement.

Definition 3 (Input-output Failures Refinement).

$$P \sqsubseteq_{IOF}^{(\mathcal{I},\mathcal{O})} Q \mathrel{\widehat{=}} traces(Q) \subseteq traces(P) \wedge$$
$$IOfailures^{(\mathcal{I},\mathcal{O})}(Q) \subseteq IOfailures^{(\mathcal{I},\mathcal{O})}(P)$$

This is a straightforward adaptation of the notion of failures refinement.

Chaos is the bottom of this relation (as well as of the standard failures-refinement relation). This is the process that can nondeterministically choose to deadlock, accept or reject any of the inputs, and produce any of the outputs. Its set of failures includes all possible failures, and consequently, so does its set of input-output failures: $(s, X \cup \mathcal{O}) \in failures(Chaos)$ for every s and X. Like in the standard model, the top of the refinement relation is **div**, the process that diverges immediately. Its set of (input-output) failures is empty, independently of which events are inputs and which are outputs. Recursion is handled as in the standard failures model: as the least fixed point with respect to $\subseteq$.

Reduction of nondeterminism and possible deadlocks is a way of achieving input-output failures refinement. For example, we can refine the process $E5$ in Example 5 to either $inp?x \rightarrow STOP$ or $out!1 \rightarrow STOP$. We have the following.

Lemma 1. $P \sqcap Q \sqsubseteq_{IOF}^{(\mathcal{I},\mathcal{O})} P$ and $P \sqcap Q \sqsubseteq_{IOF}^{(\mathcal{I},\mathcal{O})} P \square Q$

This follows directly from the definitions; all proofs omitted here are in [6].

4   Input-Output Failures Refinement and ioco

As already mentioned, much of the work on testing is based on labelled-transition systems, and to cater for inputs and outputs, IOLTSs have been widely explored. In this context, the implementation relation **ioco** [23] is normally adopted. In the context of CSP, on the other hand, the conformance relation is refinement, and in the previous section we introduced input-output failures refinement ($\sqsubseteq_{IOF}^{(\mathcal{I},\mathcal{O})}$). In this section, we explore the relationship between **ioco** and $\sqsubseteq_{IOF}^{(\mathcal{I},\mathcal{O})}$.

First of all, we provide a definition of **ioco**. We use two functions: given a state q and a trace $s \in (\Sigma \cup \{\delta\})^*$, q **after** s is the set of states reachable from q using s. Furthermore, we have that $\mathbf{out}(q)$ is the set of $a \in (\mathcal{O} \cup \{\delta\})$ such that, from q, the next observable event could be a. This definition extends to sets of states in the usual way: for a set $\mathcal{P}'$ of states we have that $\mathbf{out}(\mathcal{P}') = \cup_{q \in \mathcal{P}'} \mathbf{out}(q)$.

Definition 4. *If Q is input enabled, we say that Q conforms to P under **ioco**, written Q **ioco** P, if $\mathbf{out}(Q$ **after** $s) \subseteq \mathbf{out}(P$ **after** $s)$, for every $s \in tr^{\mathbf{io}}(P)$.*

As a simplifying assumption **ioco** requires implementations to be input enabled, which is natural for some domains of application. This avoids, for example, accepting an implementation that can initially either deadlock or behave like P as a valid implementation of P (a feature, for instance, of the CSP traces model).

Input-enabled processes cannot have (reachable) termination states. This indicates that **ioco** does not distinguish termination from deadlock, but that is not all. Conformance under **ioco** does not guarantee refinement.

Theorem 1. *There are Q and P such that Q **ioco** P, but not $P \sqsubseteq_{IOF}^{(\mathcal{I},\mathcal{O})} Q$.*

The observation of input-output failures can provide additional observational power, when compared to traces that include quiescence. For example, it is possible to distinguish internal and external choice of inputs. So, it is no surprise that Q **ioco** P does not imply that $P \sqsubseteq_{IOF}^{(\mathcal{I},\mathcal{O})} Q$. Proofs of the above theorem and of all other theorems in the sequel can be found in [6].

On the other hand, under **ioco** it is possible to observe the failure to produce output (quiescence) before the end of a trace, while under input-output failures refinements we only observe refusal sets at the end of a trace.

Theorem 2. *There are Q and P such that $P \sqsubseteq_{IOF}^{(\mathcal{I},\mathcal{O})} Q$, but not Q **ioco** P.*

We observe that the above results are not specific to input-output failures.

In summary, $\sqsubseteq_{IOF}^{(\mathcal{I},\mathcal{O})}$ and **ioco** are generally incomparable. On the other hand, if we consider only input-enabled processes then **ioco** is strictly stronger.

Theorem 3. *If Q and P are input enabled and Q **ioco** P, then $P \sqsubseteq_{IOF}^{(\mathcal{I},\mathcal{O})} Q$. It is possible, however, that $P \sqsubseteq_{IOF}^{(\mathcal{I},\mathcal{O})} Q$, but not Q **ioco** P.*

These results do not reflect on the value of one or the other conformance relation. In the context of CSP, refinement, rather than **ioco** is the natural notion of conformance, and input-enabledness is not an adopted assumption, although it is possible to define input-enabled processes in CSP.

5   Testing

This section explores testing; we adapt the work developed for stable failures refinement [4] described in Section 2. As already said, the notion of a trace is not affected by the distinction between inputs and outputs. We can therefore reuse the previous approach for testing for traces refinement. Additionally, like in [4], we define the relation **conf**$^{\mathcal{O}}$ that models the requirements, under $\sqsubseteq_{IOF}^{(\mathcal{I},\mathcal{O})}$, on the input-output failures. As expected, it is similar to **conf**.

$$Q \text{ \textbf{conf}}^{\mathcal{O}} P \cong \forall t : traces(P) \cap traces(Q) \bullet Ref^{\mathcal{O}}(Q,t) \subseteq Ref^{\mathcal{O}}(P,t)$$
$$\text{where } Ref^{\mathcal{O}}(P,t) \cong \{X \mid (t,X) \in IOfailures^{(\mathcal{I},\mathcal{O})}(P)\}$$

The following shows the relevance of **conf**$^{\mathcal{O}}$.

Lemma 2. $P \sqsubseteq_{IOF}^{(\mathcal{I},\mathcal{O})} Q \Leftrightarrow traces(Q) \subseteq traces(P) \wedge Q \text{ \textbf{conf}}^{\mathcal{O}} P$

The proof is similar to that in [4] for $\sqsubseteq_T$ and **conf**, and is in [6].

Since $Exhaust_T(P)$ is exhaustive with respect to traces refinement, it is sufficient to show how an exhaustive test can be produced for **conf**$^{\mathcal{O}}$. Like for **conf**, by definition, to check Q **conf**$^{\mathcal{O}}$ P it is sufficient to check the refusal sets in states reached by traces in $traces(P) \cap traces(Q)$. Since Q is not known, we introduce tests to check the refusal sets after traces of P.

We use an approach similar to that of [4], which is formalised in the definition of T_F as presented in Section 2.2. At the end of a trace of P, we give a verdict *fail*, but propose a choice of events which, if accepted by Q, lead to a *pass* verdict. In the case of **conf**$^{\mathcal{O}}$, however, we observe that if a trace leads to a state of P that is unstable because it may produce an output, then a potentially non-conformant implementation might deadlock, produce an unexpected output, or move to another stable state before producing an output. Deadlock is not allowed, and our tests for **conf**$^{\mathcal{O}}$ check that. Unexpected outputs are checked by the tests for traces refinement. Finally, moving to another stable state may or may not be allowed (due to the presence of nondeterminism), and whether the inputs then required are allowed or not is also checked by traces refinement. We, therefore, do not need as many tests for **conf**$^{\mathcal{O}}$ as we needed for **conf**.

Example 6. Consider the following example in which there is an internal choice between an input and two possible outputs.

$$E8 = inp?x \to STOP \sqcap (out!1 \to STOP \square out!2 \to STOP)$$

Under stable failures the maximal refusal sets after $\langle \rangle$ are $\{out.1, out.2, \checkmark\}$ and $\{inp, \checkmark\}$, and so the minimal acceptances $\mathcal{A}_{\langle \rangle}$ contains all sets that contain $out.1$ and one input and all sets that contain $out.2$ and one input. For each of these, we have one test for **conf**. On the other hand, in the initial internal choice, only the choice of $inp?x$ corresponds to a stable state and in this state only outputs are refused. In this case, as formalised below, the minimal acceptances is the set of sets that contain only one input. So, we have fewer tests for **conf**$^{\mathcal{O}}$.   □

Formally, like for $Exhaust_{conf}$, we consider pairs $(s, A) \notin IOfailures^{(\mathcal{I}, \mathcal{O})}(P)$. We, however, restrict ourselves to $A \subseteq \mathcal{I}$. This is justified by the following lemma.

Lemma 3. *For every P with output events $\mathcal{O}$, set of events Y such that $Y \subseteq \mathcal{O}$, and $(s, X) \in IOfailures^{(\mathcal{I}, \mathcal{O})}(P)$, we have $(s, X \cup Y) \in IOfailures^{(\mathcal{I}, \mathcal{O})}(P)$.*

The proof of this lemma is in [6]. Due to its converse $(s, A \cup Y) \notin IOfailures^{(\mathcal{I}, \mathcal{O})}(P)$ implies $(s, A) \notin IOfailures^{(\mathcal{I}, \mathcal{O})}(P)$. Therefore, since for the construction of tests we are interested in minimal acceptances, it is enough to consider $A \subseteq \mathcal{I}$. We check that such an A is not a refusal set of a *stable state* of Q reached by s.

We check this by using a test based on s followed by an external choice of the events in $A \cup \mathcal{O}$. The set $\mathcal{O}$ is included to ensure that we get verdict *fail* only through the observation of a refusal of A in a stable state of Q, in which outputs are not available. If the test deadlocks, then this means that (s, A) is in $IOfailures^{(\mathcal{I}, \mathcal{O})}(Q)$ and so we return verdict *fail*. If an event from $A \cup \mathcal{O}$ occurs after s then we return verdict *pass*. In fact, if an output is produced, the state reached by s was not stable, and an *inc* verdict would also be appropriate, but this distinction is not necessary: what we want to ensure is that a deadlock is not possible. Finally, if s is not followed, then the verdict is *inc*. This leads to the test $T_F(s, A \cup \mathcal{O})$, using the previously defined function T_F.

In conclusion, we obtain the following test set for input-output failures.

$$Exhaust_{conf}^{\mathcal{O}}(P) = \{T_F(s, A \cup \mathcal{O}) \mid s \in traces(P) \wedge A \in A_s^{\mathcal{O}}(P)\}$$
$$A_s^{\mathcal{O}}(P) = min\{A \subseteq \mathcal{I} \mid (s, A) \notin IOfailures^{(\mathcal{I}, \mathcal{O})}(P)\}$$

This test is exhaustive for **conf**$^{\mathcal{O}}$.

Example 7. We consider $E8$ again. In $IOfailures^{(\mathcal{I}, \mathcal{O})}(E8)$, the failures with trace $\langle \rangle$ have subsets of $\{out.1, out.2, \checkmark\}$ as refusals, and so $A_{\langle \rangle}^{\mathcal{O}}(E8)$ is the set of sets that contain only one input as already said. For each of these, we have one test that also accepts all outputs. For example, $T_F(\langle \rangle, \{inp.1\} \cup \mathcal{O})$.   □

Theorem 4. *For Q and P such that $traces(Q) \subseteq traces(P)$, Q **conf**$^{\mathcal{O}}$ P if, and only, if there is no $T_F(s, A \cup \mathcal{O}) \in Exhaust_{conf}^{\mathcal{O}}(P)$ such that Q fails $T_F(s, A \cup \mathcal{O})$.*

It might appear that $Exhaust^{\mathcal{O}}_{conf}(P)$ does not check refusals after traces s that cannot take P to a stable state. This is not the case: since s cannot reach a stable state of P, for all $A \subseteq \mathcal{I}$ we have $(s, A) \notin IOfailures^{(\mathcal{I},\mathcal{O})}(P)$ and so $A^{\mathcal{O}}_s(P) = min\{A \subseteq \mathcal{I} \mid (s, A) \notin \varnothing\} = min\{A \subseteq \mathcal{I}\}$. Thus, $A^{\mathcal{O}}_s(P) = \{\varnothing\}$. As required, the SUT Q fails the corresponding test $T_F(s, \mathcal{O})$ if s can reach a stable state of Q, in which case $Ref(Q, s)$ is non-empty despite $Ref(P, s)$ being empty. The other special case is where s can reach a deadlock or terminating state of P, in which case $\{A \subseteq \mathcal{I} \mid (s, A) \notin IOfailures^{(\mathcal{I},\mathcal{O})}(P)\}$ is empty and so $A^{\mathcal{O}}_s(P)$ is empty. We therefore obtain no tests for input-output failures with s; this is what we expect since all refusal sets are allowed after s.

We now consider how $Exhaust^{\mathcal{O}}_{conf}(P)$ relates to the set $Exhaust_{conf}(P)$ for testing for stable-failures refinement [4]. In the case of $E8$, we have already noted that there are twice as many tests in $Exhaust_{conf}(E8)$. The traffic light example is more extreme since under input-output failures the only stable states are terminating states. Thus, $Exhaust^{\mathcal{O}}_{conf}(Lights) = \{T_F(\langle\rangle, \mathcal{O}), T_F(\langle red\rangle, \mathcal{O}), T_F(\langle red, amber\rangle, \mathcal{O}), \ldots\}$: these tests check that the SUT cannot deadlock or terminate without first receiving end. In contrast, $Exhaust_{conf}(Lights)$ would also include tests such as $T_F(\langle red\rangle, \{end\})$ and $T_F(\langle red\rangle, \{amber\})$, which check that after red the process cannot refuse $amber$ and also cannot refuse end. The following shows how the sets $A_s(P)$ and $A^{\mathcal{O}}_s(P)$ relate, the proof being in [6].

Lemma 4. *If* $(s, A) \in A^{\mathcal{O}}_s(P)$ *then there exists* $Y \subseteq \mathcal{O}$ *where* $(s, A \cup Y) \in A_s(P)$.

Thus, for every test produced for input-output failures refinement there is a corresponding test produced for stable failures refinement. This shows that $Exhaust^{\mathcal{O}}_{conf}(P)$ contains no more tests than $Exhaust_{conf}(P)$. As we have seen with $E6$ and $Lights$, $Exhaust^{\mathcal{O}}_{conf}(P)$ can contain fewer tests.

6 Conclusions

This paper has explored a model, a refinement relation, and a testing theory for CSP where we distinguish between inputs and outputs. This distinction is important for testing since the tester (that is, the environment) controls inputs and the SUT controls outputs. It is normal to assume that the environment does not block outputs and, as a result, the composition of a tester and the SUT can only deadlock if the SUT is in a stable state where outputs are not available. We have thus defined a notion of failures, called input-output stable failures, which distinguish between inputs and outputs and only allow refusals to be observed in stable states where no outputs are enabled. We have defined the notion of input-output failures, showed how these can be calculated for (well-formed) CSP processes and defined a corresponding notion of refinement. We have also showed how this relates to **ioco** and adapted the CSP testing approach of [4].

Refusals in the presence of inputs have been studied in [11,3,2]. The key difference between these previous approaches and ours is that they allowed refusals to be observed in states where outputs are enabled. One possible justification for this approach is the symmetry between the SUT and the tester, neither of which need to be input enabled; such a tester can block outputs and so can observe refusals in states where outputs are enabled. What we suggest is that there are systems that are not input enabled but whose environment is input-enabled. It seems likely that there will be classes of system for which we can observe refusals in states in which outputs are enabled, and so we can use implementation relations previously defined for IOLTSs, but also classes of systems for which these previous approaches are not suitable. For example, synchronous devices constitute environments that are not input enabled, on the other hand, as previously discussed, systems that write to the screen (or to any asynchronous device) and basically control its interface have an environment that is input enabled.

In occam, a programming language based on CSP [14], for instance, inputs are distinguished from outputs. (This is, of course, necessarily the case in a programming language.) In that context, there are restrictions on the use of outputs. It is not possible, for instance, to have two outputs offered in an external choice, since in this case, we have a nondeterminism as to the choice of output communication that is going to be carried out. In abstract models, on the other hand, such nondeterminism is not a problem.

In [15], the lack of inputs and outputs in CSP is handled by defining a notion of test execution that takes this issue into account. The direction of the events is used to determine how to carry out the tests and determine a verdict. All this is formally defined, but soundness cannot be justified in the framework of CSP.

There are several lines of future work. Recent work has extended **ioco** to the case where there are distributed observations, leading to the **dioco** implementation relation [12]. Like **ioco**, the **dioco** implementation relation is only defined for input-enabled implementations. In addition, most of the work in this area has assumed that specifications are also input-enabled and the generalisations to the case where the specification need not be input-enabled are rather complex [12]. Observing refusal of inputs might help simplify treatment of an input not being enabled, but only in quiescent states; this could lead to simpler and more general implementation relations for distributed systems.

We have observed that input-output failures refinement does not imply conformance under **ioco** because **ioco** allows partial observation of refusals before the end of a trace. The $\mathcal{RT}$ model for CSP allows the observation of a sequence of events and refusal sets, and so it should be possible to adapt it to the case where we distinguish between inputs and outputs as well, and in this case produce a refinement relation strictly stronger than **ioco**.

The testing theory of *Circus* [17], an algebra that combines Z [24] and CSP, is similar to that of CSP. It is based on symbolic tests, and already takes advantage of the conventions of CSP to represent inputs and outputs more compactly. To leverage the results here to that context, though, we need an input-output failures model in the UTP [13], the semantic framework of *Circus*.

References

1. Barrett, G.: Model checking in practice: The T9000 Virtual Channel Processor. IEEE TSE 21(2), 69–78 (1995)

2. Bourdonov, I.B., Kossatchev, A., Kuliamin, V.V.: Formal conformance testing of systems with refused inputs and forbidden actions. ENTCS 164(4), 83–96 (2006)
3. Briones, L.B., Brinksma, E.: Testing Real-Time Multi Input-Output Systems. In: Lau, K.-K., Banach, R. (eds.) ICFEM 2005. LNCS, vol. 3785, pp. 264–279. Springer, Heidelberg (2005)
4. Cavalcanti, A.L.C., Gaudel, M.-C.: Testing for Refinement in CSP. In: Butler, M., Hinchey, M.G., Larrondo-Petrie, M.M. (eds.) ICFEM 2007. LNCS, vol. 4789, pp. 151–170. Springer, Heidelberg (2007)
5. Cavalcanti, A., Gaudel, M.-C., Hierons, R.M.: Conformance Relations for Distributed Testing Based on CSP. In: Wolff, B., Zaïdi, F. (eds.) ICTSS 2011. LNCS, vol. 7019, pp. 48–63. Springer, Heidelberg (2011)
6. Cavalcanti, A.L.C., Hierons, R.M.: Testing with inputs and outputs in CSP - Extended version. Technical report (2012), http://www-users.cs.york.ac.uk/~alcc/CH12.pdf
7. Cavalcanti, A.L.C., Sampaio, A.C.A., Woodcock, J.C.P.: A Refinement Strategy for Circus. Formal Aspects of Computing 15(2-3), 146–181 (2003)
8. Fischer, C.: How to Combine Z with a Process Algebra. In: Bowen, J.P., Fett, A., Hinchey, M.G. (eds.) ZUM 1998. LNCS, vol. 1493, pp. 5–25. Springer, Heidelberg (1998)
9. Gaudel, M.-C.: Testing can be formal, too. In: Mosses, P.D., Nielsen, M. (eds.) CAAP 1995, FASE 1995, and TAPSOFT 1995. LNCS, vol. 915, pp. 82–96. Springer, Heidelberg (1995)
10. Hall, A., Chapman, R.: Correctness by construction: Developing a commercial secure system. IEEE Software 19(1), 18–25 (2002)
11. Heerink, L., Tretmans, J.: Refusal Testing for Classes of Transition Systems with Inputs and Outputs. In: FORTE/PSTV, IFIP Conference Proceedings, vol. 107, pp. 23–38. Chapman & Hall (1997)
12. Hierons, R.M., Merayo, M.G., Núñez, M.: Implementation relations and test generation for systems with distributed interfaces. Distributed Computing 25(1), 35–62 (2012)
13. Hoare, C.A.R., He, J.: Unifying Theories of Programming. Prentice-Hall (1998)
14. Jones, G.: Programming in occam 2. Prentice-Hall (1988)
15. Kahsai, T., Roggenbach, M., Schlingloff, B.-H.: Specification-based testing for refinement. In: SEFM, pp. 237–246. IEEE Computer Society (2007)
16. Mahony, B.P., Dong, J.S.: Blending Object-Z and Timed CSP: An Introduction to TCOZ. In: ICSE 1998, pp. 95–104. IEEE Computer Society Press (1998)
17. Oliveira, M.V.M., Cavalcanti, A.L.C., Woodcock, J.C.P.: A UTP Semantics for Circus. Formal Aspects of Computing 21(1-2), 3–32 (2009)
18. Roggenbach, M.: CSP-CASL: a new integration of process algebra and algebraic specification. Theoretical Computer Science 354(1), 42–71 (2006)
19. Roscoe, A.W.: The Theory and Practice of Concurrency. Prentice-Hall (1998)
20. Roscoe, A.W.: Understanding Concurrent Systems. In: Texts in Computer Science. Springer (2011)
21. Sampaio, A., Nogueira, S., Mota, A.: Compositional Verification of Input-Output Conformance via CSP Refinement Checking. In: Breitman, K., Cavalcanti, A. (eds.) ICFEM 2009. LNCS, vol. 5885, pp. 20–48. Springer, Heidelberg (2009)
22. Schneider, S., Treharne, H.: Communicating B Machines. In: Bert, D., Bowen, J.P., Henson, M. C., Robinson, K. (eds.) ZB 2002. LNCS, vol. 2272, pp. 416–435. Springer, Heidelberg (2002)

23. Tretmans, J.: Test Generation with Inputs, Outputs, and Quiescence. In: Margaria, T., Steffen, B. (eds.) TACAS 1996. LNCS, vol. 1055, pp. 127–146. Springer, Heidelberg (1996)
24. Woodcock, J.C.P., Davies, J.: Using Z–Specification, Refinement, and Proof. Prentice-Hall (1996)

Author Index